REMOTE BRITAIN

Landscape, People and Books

DAVID ST JOHN THOMAS

REMOTE BRITAIN

Landscape, People and Books

F

FRANCES LINCOLN LIMITED
PUBLISHERS

To Sheila: wife, travelling companion
and critic (see page 194)

Frances Lincoln Limited
4 Torriano Mews
Torriano Avenue
London NW5 2RZ

Remote Britain

A catalogue record for this book is available from the British Library

ISBN: 9780711230545

Printed in China

1 3 5 7 9 8 6 4 2

CONTENTS

Except when first introduced, the author's *Journey Through Britain: Landscape, People and Books,* uniform with this new work, is referred to simply as *Journey.* The paperback edition, which sold out, is being reissued in paperback to coincide with the publication of this work.

· I ·

INTRODUCTION

The Land of Common Sense

Remote Britain is a delight, and my passion for it will soon be obvious. It includes some of the world's best cliff scenery, and most of Britain's mountains. In contrast with harsh earlier times, it is home to an unusually happy though still thin population with, I believe, a better value system than in the country as a whole. For one thing it is still the land of common sense, though full of paradoxes.

The first paradox is that almost everywhere in remote areas people are happier and better off when communications improve. Easier access is responsible for many populations rebuilding. Only in a few places is it now declining. But, welcome though they generally are, might the stream of incomers so increase that it destroys the very values that attract them? New building is evident even on most islands, and some roads which one used to almost guarantee having to oneself are now busy and serve strings of new homes.

The second is that in many areas the landscape has suffered with the decline of the aristocracy. The first lines of the now unacceptable and unsung verse of 'All things bright and beautiful' rang particularly true in Scotland: 'The rich man in his castle, The poor man at his gate.' Today there is a very noticeable difference in what is happening between coastal areas and in upland areas and the Glens. Incomers, or 'white settlers', are more attracted by islands and seaside areas, than the very remote island ones where the aristocracy have also loosened their grip.

Sporting estates have been hit by the egalitarian movement that most of us accept as desirable though not liking some of the consequences. It has only been the nouveau riche created by the property and investment boom, spanning the end of the last millennium and start of this, that has prevented decline devastating more of what we have come to see as the natural, though in fact highly artificial, upland and glen sporting environments. This is a subject I go into in the chapter 'Through the Glens'.

Another paradox is that, while in the past farmers were subsidised for over-production, economics then forced so much livestock off the land that huge tracts began to be overgrown by bracken and other coarse vegetation – added to which currently the chief subsidy paid to farmers is for set-aside, fields where weeds grow rampant. Very recently, and after most of this book had been written, have many farm crops (though not milk) again become more profitable.

Nothing more demonstrates the violent pendulums of 'policy' than what has happened to sheep even during the period this book has taken shape. When we made our first journey, sheep were almost as much treasured as in the cruel days of the Highland Clearances, when humans were displaced to make way for the more profitable four-legged beasts. Soon, however farmers were complaining about poor prices and, starting with small crofters who had kept only a handful, sheep steadily disappeared. Now you can travel many miles in any part of Remote Britain without seeing a single flock... and yet, at the time of writing, there is an outcry about the high price of food.

Who will take care of the countryside if farming massively retreats? It is a question inevitably raised on my journeying. Cause and effect are rarely fully understood let alone foreseen. What city dwellers, finding it harder to camp beside rivers, because the grass has grown longer, and complaining about the price of meat, would connect both to sheep? Look forward to coming across more such paradoxes in later chapters. It should however be stressed this is not a political or preaching book. My aim is to share my love of Remote Britain, which means getting into the minds of its people, their hopes and fears. Remote Britain has much to teach us.

What is 'Remote?'

What, anyway, does one mean by remote. The word certainly conveys different things to different people. If it were not for the fact that it is the gateway to hundreds of square miles of much greater remoteness, the holiday town of Pitlochry, with its theatre now 'winterised' for all-year productions, might be seen as isolated. However, when some companies charge extra delivery charge because of the postcode, locals huff and puff. Remote? Ridiculous. Compared with many places, it's dead central.

In our home town, the little resort of Nairn, on the Moray Firth sixteen miles east of Inverness, we count ourselves lucky to be near an airport and mainline railway, and to live in an oasis of civilisation with much wilder, less populated lands north, south, east and west. However, when friends tell us they'll pop in to see us while visiting Edinburgh, they are horrified to hear that it takes us longer to reach the Scottish capital than it does to get to London from Torquay. 'Why on earth do you live there?' I've been asked accusingly. A company specialising in herringbone brick-laid drives advertised it undertakes surveys without obligation anywhere on the mainland, but my enquiry was answered with: 'We don't do Islands.' Perhaps they thought the sea began at Perth. Much the same things happen in parts of Cornwall, West Wales and Lincolnshire.

At the other extreme, there are those who say that virtually nowhere in Britain is remote in the way that the Falklands or Antarctica are. Others assume that my title implies I cover only outliers such as the Isles of Scilly and the Shetlands. Then, again, to some remoteness simply implies being off the beaten track, or perhaps a long way from a road. In America it was once claimed that on that basis, somewhere in the middle of a huge freight marshalling yard near Chicago was the remotest. It was certainly the hardest point for any ordinary person to reach by car or on foot. In Britain, I asked the Ordnance Survey which was the most remote spot that could be reached by road. Though not claiming infallibility, they kindly answered:

> We think that probably the most remote spot is Kinloch Hourn at grid reference 195060, 807060 though the last bit is a private road. Nearby there is a jetty onto Loch Beag (194590, 806890) which can be reached by a small public road (though these could also be reached by boat via the Sound of Sleat and Loch Hourn).
>
> Other suggestions are:
>
> Near Coire an Fhearna at 270980, 817890 (a private road extends it to 265580, 813170);
>
> The west end of Loch Beannacharain at grid reference 221870, 851950;
>
> The road along Glen Cassley at 238910, 916720;
>
> The west end of Loch Arkaig at grid reference 198740, 791580;
>
> The east end of Loch Affric at grid reference 220090, 823370.

One way or another, remoteness stirs passions. Estate agents paradoxically mark down the price of houses for being too close to a busy road, airport, or pub and also for being too cut off, out of things. While there are millions who couldn't possibly live away from a centre of population, and shudder when they're driven somewhere truly out of the way, a growing minority are desperate to escape from urban living.

A Scottish solicitor, William Henry, is renowned for taking holidays in especially remote outposts of humanity (some of them now abandoned) from St Kilda ('a real privilege to go ashore in Village Bay where people used to live and hold their "Parliament" to plan the day's activities, and to see the stupendous cliffs and marvellous light – but you soon realise just why civilian life ceased to be possible') to Tristan da Cunha ('where most people went back to the island way of life after they'd temporarily come to Britain following the famous volcanic eruption').

'What it comes down to,' he says, 'is the fascination of how people survive in out-of-the-way places: the combination of physical effort, community spirit and perhaps a touch of idealism. Perhaps I'm guilty myself of an idealised view, yet there's something to be learnt from such places.' I caught him on the point of moving from fairly remote Kirkcudbright, where he's spent all his life, following his father in the firm he is just leaving, to move to a large Edinburgh practice, where he will specialise in agricultural affairs, in the Scottish tradition, the firm describing itself as Solicitors and Asset Managers. 'Though the clients will come in from the country, I'm not sure how easily I'll adjust to city living.'

Perhaps we all need our own degree of remoteness? While first thoughts might naturally be geographical, these days the yardstick might be better measured in journey times from the big centres, for high speed railways and motorways cheat. For example, an hour's journey covers more miles going north and west than east and south of London. Journey lengths arbitrarily control degrees of remoteness even on peninsulas and islands.

According to some, it all depends on value systems, cities and their commuter suburbs versus country, remote or not. And so one can go on. Another kind of remoteness is psychological, for example where outsiders feel unwelcome and ill at ease, the locals sticking closely together as in the Welsh Valleys, packed with houses and nowadays with take-aways rather than mines, but still amazingly self-contained with continuing rivalry between parallel valleys separated by a narrow high ridge. Yes, I even visit Merthyr Tydfil.

Then again, if calmness is psychological, one can point to all kind of peaceful enclaves. In London the waterside calm of Little Venice is an obvious example. Ask London taxi drivers to take you to the most remote place within ten miles and, after initial surprise and maybe discussion with another cabbie, you'll get a variety of suggestions: some quiet enclaves, even a church just off Fleet Street, to furthest possible places yielding a good fare. Said one driver: 'Remote in London? If you don't know anyone, they tell me, it's the loneliest place anywhere. Americans say they can't afford even to buy a decent meal, and anyway none of the waiters speak proper English like we do.' I quote more London cabbies in my last chapter.

Essex has oases, too, including Saffron Walden, typical of places which are not in the least geographically remote but have somehow managed to keep themselves distinctive, out of the mainstream of contemporary bustle. Stansted Airport is only a few miles away but, because of their routing, few planes can be heard. Essex also has coastal remoteness especially in Foulness. (See chapter XXXVII.) Another example is Much Wenlock in Shropshire, a delightful old-fashioned oasis close to new-town Telford. Much Wenlock was in *Journey*.

Another definition of remoteness might be where one feels happy, liberated. Or, said several people on our travels where people might have lived in Biblical days. As I was writing this, our regional daily chimed in with a story headed: 'Jesus would "want to live in the Highlands".' It analysed a poll ahead of a National Christian Resources Exhibition. Over half the respondents said he would adopt a rural lifestyle; only 7 per cent opted for an inner city tower block. 'Scotland occupied two of the top five spots where the public think he would settle in the UK. The Highlands were the favourite.'

Remoteness a State of Mind

'You know what,' somebody said to me on Dorset's Isle of Purbeck. 'Remoteness is a state of mind'. To which my son Gareth, who happened to be with me, added that remoteness is where people – especially men – find it easier to satisfy connectivity. He was commenting on the large number of bird and wildlife watchers, walkers and photographers, who were gaining deep satisfaction simultaneously from being somewhere special and from their hobby. Mainly alone, and seeming to enjoy their individuality in fabulous surroundings, they were nonetheless only too anxious to explain who they were, their hopes and fears and plan for the day. Though strictly speaking a peninsula, the Isle of Purbeck is included in my South Coast Islands.

There is yet another aspect of remoteness: where people work as opposed to live. Those who most thoroughly experience a feeling of being utterly cut off have undoubtedly always been our deep-sea fishermen, which is my main justification for including Grimsby, though out on a limb and attracting few visitors, it also qualifies in some other ways. On land (or rock) lighthouses, still seen as beacons of hope even in the sat. nav. age, were once the most isolated places where people worked. At one time, too, large numbers of Britons settled in far remoter places in the Empire than could ever be found in Britain. Cheekily, in a book on England, I also include in Episodes 2 a brief account of a visit to the Falklands to which (West Falkland at that) a former member of staff moved with her husband 'for a more natural way of life'.

Remoteness – welcomed or feared – is undoubtedly a personal thing, and my selection of places visited for this book, though influenced by all the factors quoted, was inevitably my own. It has given the opportunity to revisit some familiar haunts in a new light, and to explore others I have long wanted to see but lacked the opportunity. So I have been to many islands, from the very north of Shetland to the Isles of Scilly, to peninsulas where there is geographical curiosity and colour if not utter remoteness, to less-visited coastlines and Wolds of Yorkshire and Lincolnshire.

National Parks, Scotland and the South West naturally figure prominently, the next two chapters which might be seen as part of an extended introduction being especially Cornish, Welsh and Scottish influenced. As should be the case in all good travel books, there is a mixture of the obvious and the unexpected.

The Other *Journey*

Though it should be stressed that this is a self-contained new work, the content has to a small extent been influenced by what was included in my *Journey Through Britain: Landscape, People and Books.* For the benefit of readers who have that title or who might buy it in a further paperback edition planned to appear shortly after this current work's launch, I have included some references to it. To avoid tedious repetition, it is hereafter called just *Journey*. There is very little duplication between the two titles.

In passing, *Journey* sold well and seems to have given much pleasure, one reader saying he had enjoyed it so much that he was saving the end to read as a treat on Christmas Day. Almost exactly the same number of letters came from men and women, but the shorter letters of a general thanks nature came from women, who referred especially to places they had known earlier in life, while virtually all the hobby-orientated ones were from men. For this purpose, however, I have not counted walking as a hobby but part of a general appreciation of the countryside. Every letter has been welcome. There is certainly a great fellowship celebrating our nation's uniqueness, especially the great contrasts of landscape and lifestyle in so small a country.

The Anatomy of Remote Britain

Draw a line from the River Exe in Devon to the mouth of the Tweed in Northumberland and Britain is fairly neatly divided into upland and lowland. To the west and north, the uplands include large areas over a thousand feet above sea level, and their lower-lying parts are usually hilly. Poor thin soils combined with high rainfall discourages arable farming. While milk may come from the uplands, most of the home-grown crops we eat are from flatter south and east where soil is fertile even on much of its modest hills. They rarely exceed five or six hundred feet above sea level.

It is no surprise that most of Remote Britain is in the uplands, and that people there tend to be poorer but also more independent and to take action themselves when outsiders fail. A random example (there will be many more) when, following a RNLI reorganisation, North Yorkshire's Runswick Bay lifeboat was withdrawn, the villagers raised money for their own *Spirit of Runswick*.

In every way the landscape is more dominant in the highland part of Britain. It is where country and cliff lovers take their holidays, where naturalists and archaeologists are disproportionately attracted because man has been less overwhelming in his development. We'll never fully know what archaeological treasures lie under London, but have a much better idea of early life in the Orkneys and Shetland. And though there are big cities in the 'uplands', nearly all of them have geography and climate forcibly stamped on them and enjoy great countryside including a National Park on their doorstep.

No division is perfect. There are undoubtedly many highly independent types in parts of East Anglia and Lincolnshire, and it's harder to feel more remote than on the Fens. And while lowland Britain boasts few cliffs, the high unstable ones along the Jurassic Coast near Lyme Regis get disproportionately in the news. In one respect, however, that puts them the right side of the border, for it is not where the sea is roughest as along the Atlantic that much land is being lost, but along the coasts of lowland Britain, because of their less stable soils and rocks. We again discover places at which coastal erosion is an annual threat rarely out of the news and causing real distress. While the population of lowland Britain increases faster, its physical size has been in steady decline for centuries.

Well advised or not, increasingly officials determine whether land should be sacrificed to the sea. The environmental group, Natural England, caused a particular outcry in Norfolk. It is said that because of rising sea levels, the present defences between Eccles on Sea and Winterton-on-Sea are unsustainable, and that a new sea wall should be built sacrificing about 25 square miles. They include half a dozen villages and five fresh water lakes. North Norfolk's Liberal Democrat MP would see a sizeable part of his constituency disappear, yet hadn't been told of the proposal before an announcement was made. No local consultations had taken place, so the outcry was predictable.

There is no doubt that more land on the east coast will be lost, but who is to say what should be spent on delaying tactics? Mr Charlie England came into the news when the Environmental Minister, ruling on an enquiry, gave him the right to defend his house on the eroding cliff at Easton Bavents, north of Southwold in Suffolk. Mr England was appealing against a ruling by Natural England that, since the cliffs had special scientific interest, nature should be allowed to take its own course and he had been stopped from using his own money to defend his home.

The minister's ruling will encourage others along the North Sea whose only hope is to spend their own money in playing Canute. For older people, whose property has become unsaleable, all that can be hoped for is to delay the inevitable for the rest of their lives. Delaying tactics or buying time seems more useful against the context of the great push of our time to reduce global warming when we all know that, over the millennia, our lands have been shaped by infinitely greater climate extremes than anything now on the horizon.

In a fair society, compensation might automatically be given to those who have lost their homes and been unable to insure them even at higher rates for many years. A fall-back government insurance scheme with above-average but affordable premiums might anyway not actually prove very costly. It won't happen.

Though these examples are from Remote Britain within the lowland part of the country, they typify how people in remote areas have to fight for their rights and how, when government fails, their common sense drives a determination, not merely to make the best of things, but to flourish. In remote areas people have time for each other. Neighbours are real. Less and less, alas, is that true of overcrowded places.

Too Many, Too Few People?

A recent report glumly suggests that England's population will increase by a third during the next half century. The present average population per square mile will thus go up from 1,010 to 1,349, making us the most crowded major European nation. In only twenty years, London's 'crowd' is expected to be 13,910 per square mile. Think of what large blocks of lightly-developed land does to the average.

Nearly everyone agrees that much of the South East is already horribly over developed, but the policies of successive governments have not prevented it happening, and now seem more intent on allowing building on green belts than to stop it in future.

Though London's parks are remarkably successful, most people will have to travel further to get into real countryside, fresh air and less-polluted night skies. Remote Britain will inevitably have a greater role to play. Yet there are danger signals, here. As already hinted, too many may ultimately be attracted to kill the very remoteness that attracted them. Those wanting to get out of the rat race, economic fugitives, former residents attracted back by improved communications, all contribute to populations rebuilding where for generations the cry has been about too few people to support viable communities. Another reason is commuting: especially around their edges, all our National Parks are constantly under threat from more people living further from where they work. Currently Inverness is said to be Britain's fastest-growing city, though many more 'go native' as the local expression has it for living in the country while working in the town. Surrounding villages are increasingly just dormitories without their own shops and community life.

It is not only the sheer number of people, but their detailed distribution that matters. The building lobby, and especially superstores, naturally favour cheaper-to-develop green-field sites, while huge central areas wait regeneration. Yet let us not be despondent. Even if Skye became over-populated, its sheer ruggedness is pretty resilient. And much has also changed for the better. Glasgow may still be a city with problems, but is one of many to make good use of its river front after decades of neglect. Fish again swim further up many less-polluted rivers.

And one thing I especially enjoy about Remote Britain is seeing how well newcomers usually integrate. There'd be many fewer thriving societies, and much less known about local history, without them. Only in one area did we see the local culture overwhelmed by misplaced suburbia. That, surprisingly, is on (and especially around the edges of) the Fens, where large, well-manicured gardens that would seem more at home in the Stockbroker Belt have totally changed the scene.

Perhaps the government-funded Natural England welcomes them as it was reported to have favoured a plan to build more homes in South East England because that means more gardens. As farming becomes more 'efficient', it is gardens that are the increasing resort of song thrushes, skylarks and butterflies. Around two million gardens, an astonishing number compared to other nations, with their mixture of trees, bushes, decorative plants, lawns and vegetables, have a combined area almost as big as England's largest National Park. For millions of people, their garden is a surviving speck of remoteness, the only place where many come in regular touch with nature.

Everywhere one finds distinctive local industries hurt by standardisation, a subject I can scarcely avoid even in what might be seen as a trilogy of introductions. If you are impatient to get travelling, go to chapter IV, but hopefully return to complete the trilogy. And everywhere the great saviour yet common enemy is tourism. I gave vent to my feelings about Theme Park Britain in *Journey*, and for this title will restrain myself, yet is it not deplorable that as a nation possibly our greatest remaining commercial skill is showing ourselves off? Alas, it is frequently in a pretty standardised, commercialised and superficial way.

Fully to enter into the spirit of Remote Britain, you must be prepared to slow down, not so much to 'do' this and that as just 'to be'. The great individuality of place is the theme of my third chapter. Though it has spiritual overtones, anyone can attempt to accept the message of both Britain's most southerly and most northerly Bishops I cite. Just be.

Above all, respect the great individuality of place, enjoying local values, scenery and wildlife, and don't kill the golden egg by contributing to making everywhere the same. Slowing down and just 'being' is a wonderful start.

Hot News

It is no accident that regional newspapers and broadcasts are more popular in Remote Britain than in crowded areas. In mainstream England, even cities close together may have rivalry but usually little in common. In the South West, not merely does the news, with high coastal and moorland input, tend to be more interesting in itself, but people across the entire region have much in common. *The Western Morning News* and the BBC's TV Spotlight South West are among the best of their genres, the counterparts in the Highlands and Islands also commanding well above average loyalty.

To make the point about the news being interesting, different from what you'd expect in middle England, here is a miscellany based on recent cuttings from the Highlands and Islands edition of *The Press & Journal*. In one way or another, most take us back to the land.

The first beaver has been born in the Highlands for 400 years. Though the Scottish Executive prevented their reintroduction, they may have spread from Scandinavia. In Sweden, wetlands have been said to have become eighty times more productive in terms of biomass since their reintroduction. The Highland-based author and conservationist, Sir John Lister-Kaye, says that the beavers, adding to Scotland's inadequate wetlands by building their dams, help other species such as ospreys. (The well-being and seemingly constant attack on our local ospreys and their nests, is frequently in the news and widely commented upon in everyday conversation.)

A 4,000-year old water-heater (or 'Bronze Age sauna') is expertly to be rebuilt away from the sea threatening it in the Shetland island of Bressay. Also in the Shetlands, peat beds are being reopened, the long work of digging, drying and transporting for domestic use having again become worthwhile because of the rising cost of 'convenience' fuels.

For the first time, there is a full history of Cape Wrath, written by the driver of the mini-bus that takes visitors across the remote area (alas used extensively by the military) on the private isolated road from foot ferry to the lighthouse on the mighty headland. *A Light in the Wilderness,* by David Hird, is published by the Loch Croispol Bookshop in nearby Durness.

The Morvern Community Development Company, co-ordinating things on a west coast peninsula, now has a professional manager. With a £300,000 grant to be spread over ten years from the owners of the controversial Glensanda coastal quarry, the aim is to ensure that compensating improvements are made elsewhere in the remote peninsula.

Also in Morvern, at Loch Teacuis, one of the world's rarest coral-like structures has been discovered growing healthily. This is only the fourth known colony, one other also being in Scotland, two in Ireland and one in Italy. Tubeworms build the structure off the seabed, tubes twisting round each other, branching into coral-like structures, in places merging to form reef-like forms. They provide space and food for many other marine organisms. Each tube houses a single worm that emerges to feed on passing plankton.

On Staffa, crafty puffins have learnt to wait for visitors to land to give protection so that they can fly into their burrows without attacks from seagulls. Over 400 pairs of puffins nest on the basalt island made famous by Mendelssohn; often marauding seagulls cause loss but, when people are around, the puffins realise they are safe.

Allan Jones, who runs Gairloch's community car scheme (volunteers give vital lifts to those who cannot drive themselves) has won an award to visit remote areas of Australia to exchange experiences.

Scottish bank notes are legal tender, but occasionally rejected in England. (Declining one, a London taxi driver once told me he 'didn't believe in them'.) Even the Prime Minister, though a Scot, says he cannot force Sassenachs to accept them.

Practicalities Including Hotels

A few practical points to round off. I am still best known as the founder and for thirty years chairman of the Devon publisher David & Charles, which is one reason why books (especially of local interest) and their authors are one of my ingredients. On the sale of David & Charles, I moved to Nairn, on the Moray Firth on the edge of the Highlands, preferring as explained Britain's extremities to its more-populated areas. Most journeys therefore begin from Nairn, though only a couple of the movements from one part of the country to another are described in detail. My wife, of whom more in a moment, and I have a second home in Bath, where as readers of *Journey* might recall, Little Car is based. She claims to have been transmogrified into Little Car 2, also a Micra.

Hotels are another familiar ingredient, since we have had to spend much time in them, expectations of being spoilt or just well looked after frequently being fulfilled though sometimes definitely not. While we still find the AA's *Hotel Guide* helpful with its percentage rating system, increased commerciality has driven it up market, some hotel groups as well as many ordinary market town individual hotels no longer finding it worthwhile paying the increased charge for inclusion. Under Condé Nast, our other favourite, *Johansen's Hotel Guide* has also gone up market with subscribers expected to pay for a separate volume on small hotels. In future most of us will no doubt select as well as reserve our hotels online. Frequently it is cheaper to do so, though websites vary vastly in quality and the value of users' comments is limited by the inclusion of professional complainers who would never be content and, at the other extreme, 'planted' reviews by associates and friends.

A common complaint: good plain British fare has become increasingly rare. Many chefs unnecessarily complicate things, and we find that multiple rosettes can be as much a warning as a recommendation. Turning to bedrooms, sadly we find ourselves increasingly preferring the happy-standard rooms of the better group hotels to the highly-individual ones of what are becoming known as boutique hotels. While the overall impression of the latter is usually pleasing (and very photographable), so often there is something inconvenient: pretty curtains that don't drawn smoothly, a lack of space for luggage, a telephone or light switch hard to reach, a window stuck open or too much furniture causing a 'pinch point'. Above all, many bathrooms are designed for impression and are horridly inconvenient: inadequate shelving already cluttered, temperamental plumbing, short or badly-positioned mirrors that many cannot conveniently use, baths without grab handles needed by older visitors.

Fawlty Towers lives on in many guises, some owners positively antagonistic. As in all walks of life, it is caring, training and constant overseeing that counts. Yet some hoteliers, newcomers to the business included, succeed with efficient reception, porters who are not on permanent disappearance, and all staff with a smile. What a difference it makes.

Some readers of *Journey* tell me they have followed in our footsteps around parts of Britain, staying at some of the same hotels. However, partly driven by financial incentives, hotel ownership is changing more rapidly than ever while, since it was not possible to bring our normal home life to a halt for months on end, our journeys have had to be taken over a period of several years. With rare indicated exceptions, hotels, people, everything are described as we found them. 'We' nearly always includes my supportive wife Sheila, whose own knowledge of Britain has increased in leaps and bounds but whose domestic life has been frequently disrupted. She has always eased the complicated task of planning, researching and digesting not to mention the preparations of complex itineraries and constant packing.

Again, warm thanks go to all who made the journeys so interesting and have answered numerous queries. Anne and Lorna in the office again helped with some research, typing and index-making. Once more my charity, The David St John Thomas Charitable Trust, benefits from a small royalty on all sales.

Incidentally my son Gareth quoted earlier is publisher of *Journey*, and of this title, in Australia and New Zealand. In both these lands you can experience more remoteness than is possible in Britain. As I have already hinted, what makes remoteness so fascinating here is the huge range of geology, landscape, wild and human life, along with architectural and other inheritances, packed into so small an area. We are terribly overcrowded in such a small country, yet have huge areas of sparse population, where villages and hamlets occasionally still wither, along with some of the world's finest moorland and cliff scenery. It is the variety and the juxtaposition that makes it all so fascinating.

So join me in the different kinds of remote Britain, starting in chapter IV with a happy return to the west of Cornwall and a leisurely visit to the Isles of Scilly, followed many chapters later by a detailed study of the Western Isles. The latter is probably the most different part of our own country, and the least visited, certainly for its size. Requiring only one ferry crossing, the drive from north to south stretches 120 miles, further than between London and Norwich. Even when you say that, few people – accustomed to the much smaller scale used to show the islands in road atlases – really take it in. Repeat, 120 miles. But, then, who remembers that Scotland, with just 10 per cent of our population, is 40 per cent of Britain's land area? Or that just 1 per cent are spread across the 16 per cent that comprises the Highlands and Islands? We are indeed a land of contrast. Enjoy them with me. And to quote from Gerard Manley Hopkins:

> What would the world be, once bereft
> Of wet and of wilderness? Let them be left,
> O let them be left, wilderness and wet;
> Long live the weeds and the wilderness yet.

· II ·

REMOTE BRITAIN AT WORK

The Holistic Life

Once the majority of men in remote areas were in full-time work, the largest single number on the land. Today there are substantial Scottish glens where those in full-time local employment can almost be counted on the fingers of a single hand: a couple of tenant farmers, and maybe three or four gamekeepers.

The list of jobs that have been lost is endless. Corn and other small mills, breweries, foundries, factories and quarries, shops and schools, churches and medical practices have all fallen victim to the grinding of the wheels of centralisation. Scarcity and quotas of fish have seriously hurt many coastal areas. Changes in social patterns mean that few women now go into service and full-time gardeners are a rarity.

For those who, perhaps having retired from the Armed Forces, decided they wanted to work for themselves, probably the largest number managed a Post Office, with or without shop. Post Office closures rob many of a job. If the PO counter is removed and fewer people enter the premises, the closure of the village's remaining small trader is often inevitable, causing not only less work but social hardship. In some villages the loss has been mitigated by the establishment of community centres including a shop, but that generally only works in especially remote areas where people are most forced to pull together.

So, now that the revolution is almost complete, it is welcome to the land where work is enjoyed even if incomes have to be scrambled together and the taxman is seldom on top. Life is led very differently in Remote Britain and this applies especially to how livings are earned.

You'll find few workaholics on the islands and remote mainland extremities, yet productivity is often greater. There is usually no journey to work. Office politics are minimal, meetings only held when really needed and most training done on the job. As mentioned later, staff turnover is lower in small teams reporting directly to the owners. However, many people work for themselves, a variety of paid-for tasks, many seasonal, often being mixed with voluntary work and hobby activities – keeping a few livestock, growing fruit and vegetables, offering bed-and-breakfast or afternoon tea, repairing clocks, teaching music or coaching youngsters. That may not produce much wealth but, avoiding boredom, it yields an holistic lifestyle.

Fulfilling the dream of getting out of the rat race usually pays off. Life is happier with little demarcation between 'work' and the rest of life. Stress levels are lower and perhaps above all there's more time for neighbours.

In much of the 19th and 20th centuries, economic necessity drove down populations in most of Britain's extremities. Though memories and loyalties remained strong, when sea passages took weeks it wasn't practical for emigrants ever to see their homeland again. In more recent times, those forced to move to a city, or even to far-flung places overseas to pursue a career, frequently return for their golden years – just one of a number of reasons why many populations are starting to rebuild.

A great boost has been given by better communications, especially the telephone and the Internet. Nowhere is this more apparent than in Skye, where many earning their living online mingle with traditional crofters. The decline of industry and highly centralised offices is a world-wide phenomenon I recently saw described as an 'historical re-integration of our productive and social spheres'. Many more are again working from home, as farmers, blacksmiths, village shopkeepers and others traditionally have done.

When people are free to choose where they live, with lower house prices, great scenery and lack of congestion, it is remoter areas that often benefit disproportionately. It is perhaps natural that Skye's romantic setting and relative accessibility should appeal especially to graphic and web-site designers, who fit naturally with the longer-established painters and jewellery makers. Those working on computers often themselves paint or make things, adding to the plethora of notices such as 'Paintings for Sale' or 'Pottery'. It is somewhat similar wherever we go in Remote Britain: most incomers, joyous they had had the courage to make the move, stressing it doesn't matter where they are these computer-based days and that they spread working hours for general convenience. Supper, a walk and then a short online session before bed is a natural routine in the land of long summer daylight.

On Bodmin Moor, we found someone perhaps in his late sixties, who moved from the Midlands a decade or so ago, beavering away at his computer, a dog beside him, programming for a Home Counties company looking after the affairs of a group of sixty garages owned by Ford. 'I might as well be in the Sahara... apart from this,' he says pointing to a huge view including a glimpse of the Camel Estuary.

'We've taken deep root; people are really nice,' he added, and wasn't the only older person to make the point that not only did he have no need to see his bosses but prefers not to. 'They might think I was getting on a bit.' There's another thing: work and pleasure mixed holistically means that 'retirement' isn't a fixed event and can often be gradual, according to circumstances.

Miscellany of Jobs

That applies especially to those with more than one string to their work bow. Skye web-site designers, painting or making things is just one pairing. Offering bed-and-breakfast, renting holiday homes, serving afternoon tea, part-time teaching or coaching or relief taxi driving might go along with a voluntary session for a charity in the nearest town or 'helping out' for pay in a shop or café, which for some, who otherwise work on their own, brings useful social contact. On one island, our taxi driver had copies of her books for sale to her captive audience.

Even the famous have a portfolio of ways of earning a living. The explorer, Robin Hanbury-Tenison, not only writes books, broadcasts, lectures and farms, but with his wife, has time to run a bed-and-breakfast and two holiday homes – and still gives time to charitable work. We'll meet him later on Bodmin Moor.

We do it ourselves with a curious mix of paid-for and voluntary activities. At this point in writing, I was told that an arable farmer with a sizeable cow herd, extensive woodland, sawmill and joinery, had arrived to take down our eucalyptus tree which, fed by sewage out of a drain (rune in Scotland) which has already twice been blocked, has become so tall as to threaten our holiday cottage.

'What are you doing?' asks Fraser White, who farms in the deep countryside near Nairn on the Moray Firth.

'Writing on how people earn their living in remote areas – how generally there's a healthier lifestyle and greater common sense.'

'Of course there is. We have to *think out* our livings, and have to stay fit and be safety conscious because we can't afford to be off. That's the difference between town and country. Townies can take sickies; we can't, we know it, and we stay well.' His two grown-up sons are part of the tree-felling team.

Jewellery

Jewellery making seems to have become a Remote Britain speciality. Peace and quiet and grand scenery stimulate the imagination, the Scottish islands producing especially fine work. Though I feature particular firms in the Western Islands and in Shetland, perhaps best known for its fine gold and silver jewellery is Orkney, where Sheila Fleet's designs are particularly popular. Though not unique to Remote Britain, you'll find pendants, rings and earrings being designed and made along with paintings for sale much more frequently per head of the sparse population. Sales are helped by the natural desire of creative people to support each other. Shops sell more than their own wares – locally-made soap along with jewellery, for example, while hotels showcase local products and, at least in one case, even costume jewellery made by a waitress.

Knitting and lacework and weaving is a theme on many remote islands including several of the Shetlands, where it has always been almost exclusively a woman's thing to earn 'pocket money' – especially treasured before there were employment opportunities in the nearest village or town, or any means of travel other than walking. We will find out some of the details on our visit to the islands... including the fact that it is largely older women who keep up the tradition. Young ones with cars prefer to mix with other people in offices or shops. Spinning wool and weaving heavy cloth for Harris Tweeds, once largely an individual, home-based activity, is something we come across in the Western Isles, including Harris itself. That is one of numerous Scottish islands (and indeed parts of the Highlands) where men eked out a thin living with a combination of equally uncertain fishing and crofting. Anything women earned often saved the day as opposed to being pocket money.

Men and women sold their time to anyone who would give them work, collecting seaweed, giving early tourists boat rides, and in more recent times part-time taxi driving, bed-and-breakfasting, and anything else that would bring in a few bob. Road construction has often proved a temporary boon. Where time isn't sold it might be lent especially between crofters, as indeed still happens among farmers everywhere at harvest time today. The State pension is especially valued here among the younger retired who still work. It represents many more hours work than in the prosperous south east.

Many ways of keeping oneself busy and earning cash are hobby orientated. Altogether a much smaller proportion of people are locked into doing what they don't like, 'working out' time till the pension starts. Contentment as well as common sense are met more frequently, but it's against the background of lower expectations. Generally speaking, the more remote, the lower the average earnings.

Perhaps the greatest entrepreneurs of all are those holding a variety of appointments on the least-populated islands. Gigha and the small Orkney island of Papa Westray provided us with examples of one man doing seven or eight things before his retirement. They met the ferry, drove a taxi, were postman, garage attendant, shop assistant, and so on – and the trustee of nearly every islander's private affairs. Tying up the ferry and visiting ships, and manning the airstrip's 'fire engine' by coupling it up to a Land Rover shortly before the landing of an occasional plane on the turf, still goes with driving the school bus and other occupations, including artistic ones, among which authorship and self and commercial publishing has increased rapidly in recent years. We will meet examples on our travels. Many of the books are on local history, while museums of local interest employ many paid, and still more volunteers. We find examples even in Britain's northern extremity on the island of Unst.

Though starvation may be a thing of the past, hardship, making do and real poverty are not. The scene is not acceptable to many bright kids who move out, making it harder for those who remain. The lack of young companionship has indeed made it a struggle to retain Polish catering staff in, for example, the Western Isles' Uists.

Women generally find it easier to find jobs than men who have suffered disproportionately from the decline in employment opportunities on national rates of pay. Where they exist at all, rural railways employ far fewer people. Once the staff at a village station, though paid almost as well as their counterparts in heavily-populated Britain, had a relatively cushy life, with long gaps between trains for hobbies and even jobbing gardening or servicing bicycles. Teachers and doctors are now among the few still paid as much as southern colleagues in generally poorer remote areas though, as elsewhere, plumbers are among those commanding a premium. In many areas incomers have put a strain on local builders and sub-contractors.

Another reason why male employment is generally scarcer is that, time and time again, it has been the few large enterprises that have collapsed, leaving many struggling to find other work, often a long way from home. The Western Isles provide several examples, and we will come across others. Especially the military's sudden withdrawal hurts men more than women: we see how grievous this has been in the most northerly island of Unst.

In recent years the fabrication of oil rigs has brought only short-lived riches to several places in the North of Scotland. Between them, the two closed yards within a few miles of each other on the Moray and Cromarty Firths employed 4,000 when I moved to the area in 1990. Now only the merest maintenance staff are given work. The collapse of a fish farming syndicate leaves scores suddenly without a job. Highland & Islands Enterprise has been slow to learn the social as well as economic lesson of putting too many eggs in too few baskets. Though it's now a score of years since it happened, closure of the Invergordon aluminium smelter left a trail of social hardship, broken marriages and unruly children across a swathe of Ross & Cromarty and parts of Inverness-shire that exists to this day.

In the very remote areas things are naturally different. While teachers and parsons generally move infrequently in Remote Britain, at the extremes of remoteness, attracting people at all is often difficult. Thus in isolated Fair Isle, stuck out in the Atlantic half way between Orkney and Shetland, finding a teacher is a recurring problem, while the National Trust had to advertise one of its cottages in a major publicity campaign to find a tenant. We meet the American hat maker who was chosen. The same need to advertise has happened at other islands with tiny populations. Canna is an example where, sensibly, applicants are asked to submit a 'marketing plan' for their economic survival.

In the Isles of Scilly, also stuck out in the Atlantic, the problem is the opposite. There is such a demand for homes for new residents and holiday lets that property is well nigh unaffordable on any normal salary.

If I had to award a prize for the most entrepreneurial island group, the two chief contenders would be at opposite ends of the country: the Orkneys and Scillies. The Orkneys may lack trees but have fine pastures and, long before the term 'value added' entered the business lingo, they specialised in quality cheese, while fishing has been made more profitable by the famous Orkney Herring sold in small tubs with various sauces. Orkney chairs, spacious, upright with a high canopy-like back, are still home made. The Orkneys have their own distinctive knitwear too. With two World Heritage archaeological sites, Orkney's up-market tourism flourishes, and many roadside notices encourage splashing out on something original including the jewellery already mentioned, paintings, knitwear and chairs.

The Isles of Scilly and Cornish Enterprise

The Isles of Scilly might be called the Fortunate Islands, but paying the bills (scarce housing and all prices inflated by high transport costs) is a real challenge for many especially those wanting to set up home for the first time. It has been the Bishop of Truro, Bishop Bill Ind, who has helped draw attention to the problems, even of attracting a vicar and headmaster. His visits to the islands in the TV series *An Island Parish*, have mobilised opinion and officialdom.

Partly thanks to his inspiration, a new spirit of enterprise has helped establish a variety of new businesses, from brewing and ice cream making to a renewed local fishing (a godsend to the surprisingly numerous high-class hotels and restaurants) and making stained glass windows and high-class fabrics, the latter to give hotels and holiday homes a distinctive touch. The wave of enthusiasm has even resulted in the launch of Britain's smallest radio station, Radio Scilly, strengthening the already strong sense of belonging.

It shows what can be achieved with sparkle and determination. We have indeed seen such regeneration applied to certain sectors elsewhere, but not across so broad a front involving different islands as in the Isles of Scilly. Much has happened even in the months since our visit on the first journey for this book.

It is said that down every lane in mainland Cornwall you will find notices offering goods or services. Bed-and-Breakfast, Fresh Eggs, Potatoes, Paintings or Art, Bait (for fishing), Urchins, Rhubarb, Pottery, Electrical Repairs, Decorating, Honey, Daffodils, Jade, Home-made Jewellery, Sculptures, Internet Tuition, Fresh Crabs: the list is endless, naturally adjusting with the season. Many flowers, eggs and vegetables are left on gateside tables with honesty boxes.

Neglected by industry, and with even china clay and fishing in decline, wage rates are low, though house prices certainly aren't. Traditionally the Cornish mined and fished. In modern times the mining or fishing is into visitors' wallets. Certainly I find myself digging into mine more often than elsewhere, especially for car parking, some of which is private and pricey.

'Tourism is a kind of farming,' it was once explained to me. 'In theory it's dependant on outside circumstances, including the weather and natural supply and demand. In practice it is largely what you make of it: exploit scarcity, let visitors feel you're their friend. Only between ourselves do we grumble about things. The public face has to be a smile.' With this tradition, it has been easy for natives and incomers alike to stretch the concept to anything they can produce or do or make for reward. Anyway, don't most visitors enjoy their gullibility?

As in the rest of Remote Britain, incomes are frequently made up of numerous bits and pieces, but here there's a special emphasis on doing things in your own way at your own pace. If there's been a good season, the bed-and-breakfast signs come down earlier than if the going has been tough. The Cornish are not over greedy. Beyond decent survival, lifestyles and independence are the things most prized. Ingenuity is always on hand should it be needed, which it certainly is in dealing with the 'unjust' taxman. With income arising in so many ways, no doubt many would anyway find it genuinely difficult to produce a totally accurate tax return, though I suspect that Cornwall's gross domestic product is seriously understated. 'And why not? What have they done for us?'

Cornwall is also a county in which a surprising number of unexpected businesses suddenly take root and develop into worthwhile enterprises. For instance, in the chapter on Bodmin Moor we meet a successful book publisher. There are several others dotted around the county, some serious commercial concerns, hobby driven but still turning in a profit. The Twelvehead Press, mainly devoted to transport, is an example. Alison Hodges of Penzance put the well-established firm named after her on hold when an overseas employment opportunity arose but picked it up again on her return, and is producing outstanding titles mainly on West Cornwall. Bookselling, wholesaling (Tormark), mail-order servicing and printing, which scarcely used to exist at all, have each thrown up irregular but useful growth. As in the rest of Remote Britain, there was quick acceptance of the Internet.

The rise of the Lost Gardens of Helligan and the Eden Project (both profiled in *Journey)* has undoubtedly increased organised tours, which include other popular gardens, especially in the west. Group hotels are still rare but many individually or at least West Country-run ones have come up in the world. How different the scene is from the 1950s when one of my journalism and broadcasting jobs was to report the then mass down-market holiday scene. In so many ways, nearly all expressing individuality, Cornwall has found its feet. There's a real clan-feeling, too, businesses supporting each other. It's not Buy British but Buy Cornish. Brownie points are lost by incomers even going outside their own town for building services.

Having discovered Fowey Fish's mail-order service on previous travels, we occasionally use it, since the best of Scotland's catches immediately leaves the country and our local choice is poor. Orders arrive perfect, chilled, in twenty two hours. Once they asked if I would like a bottle of Camel Valley Brut to serve at a dinner party I'd mentioned. 'It's really brilliant. Oh, not sure if we have any left, let me check... just one chilled bottle.' It never was unchilled for we soon enjoyed it at home. We then ordered a case direct from the winery and tease many guests who, with repeated guesses, fail to identify its origin, until 'It couldn't be English; It's too good?' I tell them they're half right. It's Cornish, not English. The Scots appreciate that.

Wine and Cheese

Though there are now many successful English winemakers, Camel Valley is exceptional. Two years running its Sparkling Brut has been chosen as a best wine by *Money Week*, whose Matthew Jokes says: 'in the under twenty-quid stakes I'd rather drink Camel Valley Brut than any other wine on the planet.'

Camel Valley's founder, Bob Lindo, told me that such notices really do help. 'It takes a long time to establish a brand, but if you've the right product it can be done.'

When we visit the vinery on a south-facing slope in the Camel Valley, our guide is his son, Sam: 'Dad wondered what to do when he came out of the RAF as a pilot. He looked at sheep farms here and in Shetland. Camel Valley won, but our neighbours told us we'd bought the worst farm for miles.

Now I think the neighbours admire us; we've certainly been accepted. There are 16 acres of vines on the slope, dropping from 150 metres down to just a few metres above sea level at the river.'

'Dad' is away on a world tour of wineries to see what can be gleaned to add to their already enviable expertise. Sam explains: 'The enemy is oxygen. Techniques to improve control are improving all over. We want an element of fruit in the wine and have a modernist approach and aren't blinkered by what people tell us about traditional ways. It is try and learn... but takes a long time to judge and know. One thing we do know is that we're right not to use cheap corks from Portugal. Our grape varieties are not however experimental new ones, and we feel others will come to regret planting them.'

Because of the proximity to the sea, frost isn't a serious risk, but rainfall at blossom time washed out one year's crop. 'By the time replacement blossoms opened, there wasn't enough season left.'

He adds: 'I was thirteen when the first grapes were planted, and sixteen when we first picked. We're creating history, and it would be nice to have descendants here in a hundred year's time. Meanwhile it's been good to grow up in Cornwall. We feel Cornish and sales to local restaurants and shops are good. One restaurant in London stocks us, as do Fortnum & Mason, and occasionally Waitrose, but we're a niche business and want to keep it that way.' There are three faces to the business: growing (they still have to buy in some grapes), making and selling.

This morning we are by no means the only ones spending real money in their stylish retail outlet. Camel Valley Sparkling Brut accounts for half the output, other varieties include Pinot Noir.

These days Cornwall serves more of its own bill of fare in restaurants and hotels than do those in Scotland and Wales. Breakfast options at one hotel include Camel Valley Sparkling Brut along with Cornish kippers, Pennytinny Porker sausages, and a local 'Citrus Sensation' marmalade.

Lunches frequently feature crab salads and sandwiches, some of which are as gorgeously generous as they are delicious. Dinners often offer Cornish dishes for all three courses, including crab or lobster bisque, a variety of fish whose like we never see in Scotland, while ice creams are nearly always locally made and cheese boards may exclusively feature Cornish cheeses. The latter offer a rich variety of taste – once you know your way around them. The problem is that many staff, especially from Eastern Europe, cannot pronounce leave alone explain them.

The most iconic Cornish cheese is Yarg, a full-flavoured soft cheese easily distinguishable by the dried nettle leaves wrapping it. What a wonderful way to get free publicity: at the beginning of each season, finding it newsworthy, television helps in the appeal for more nettle pickers. What confused us, however, was the name versus the place of the Yarg makers. Lynher Dairies actually in the Lynher Valley in east Cornwall, were once involved, and the name – perhaps confusingly – has been retained even though all production is at Ponsanooth, near Falmouth, where the owners are Catherine and Ben Mead. Our appointment with Catherine Mead was conveniently changed to follow our visit to the Bishop of Truro nearby. Back to Yarg in a moment.

Cheese *is* still produced in the Lynher Valley, by the Cornish Cheese Company, who spotted a gap in the market for young blue cheese that could compete with imported cheeses and UK rivals such as Dorset Blue. Production started in 2001.

The unique taste and character? Vegetarian rennet and special starter cultures are added to the milk to make the cheeses, which are dry salted by hand before being left to mature for 12-14 weeks. The blueing occurs with a little help from nature and by piercing the cheese each week with stainless steel rods, allowing in air which helps the blue mould to spread throughout. So successful has the unique blue cheese been that making other kinds has been abandoned to concentrate on it. It is available from specialist outlets throughout the UK.

Though it begins differently, the story of Cornish Yarg has a similar ending. It was first made in the Lynher Valley by the Gray family until, in 1984, they sold the recipe and rights to the Horrells, who also farmed on the edge of Bodmin Moor. The business was growing rapidly when the Horrells met the Meads who were interested in farm diversification. For a time the families successfully divided but co-ordinated specialisations: an unusual tale of two married couples working harmoniously from well-separated farms. It was after the Horrells retired in 2006, selling their farm, that production was concentrated at Ponsanooth – skilfully expanded with Objective One European Union money then available in high-unemployment Cornwall.

'We've never really looked back,' Catherine Mead tells me at the end of a busy day when the last of about thirty workers are leaving and two of the three sons call in for a lift home after school. 'These days we process about two million gallons of milk to make just over 200 tons of cheese, distributed nationally with a weekly despatch to America. It may be niche, but it is the kind of business Cornwall needs... and milk production on its own isn't what it used to be.

But there's more to it than that. To meet the demand, we expanded earlier, but further growth isn't now an option. Keeping a happy atmosphere is priority. We always remember that employees don't leave companies. They leave managers. So personal contact with good labour relations and self-sustaining quality are our best course. We're a new product using raw milk, our pastures aren't over treated with fertilisers, our cows stay out year round, more cows less yield, less stress, longer life with ten or eleven lactations.'

Triumphantly, she concludes: 'We buck every trend,' a sentiment so often heard in Remote Britain where people running small and medium-sized businesses think things out for themselves, unsullied by the mind set and often expensive ways of doing things in over-populated areas. Here staff are treasured as individuals. Yet you'll find Yarg in Tesco and Sainsbury as well as Waitrose and in 'our heartland' of specialist shops – or you can purchase it direct by mail from the farm. It is a highly distinctive product, as soft as the Cornish climate, the nettles wrapping it contributing to the ripening and flavour.

'There's an eight week nettle-picking season. We must use local people; it would be far too dangerous to depend on last-minute Polish labour. We freeze the nettles which makes them easier to handle. They give a high-impact, visual touch and help form a natural mould in the ripening process. They are put on the cheese by our band of "nettlers". The natural flavour we end up with is unique.'

Though they concentrate very much on Yarg – there's a Wild Garlic Yarg variation with garlic leaves replacing nettles – they also make Stithians, an individual farmhouse cheese served by British Airways and the herb-flavoured Cornish Garland. That doesn't stop her extolling the virtues of other Cornish cheeses, while experience is occasionally exchanged with the makers of Cornish Blue. If it's a slightly involved story, therein lies its Cornishness. Learning from mistakes, bucking the system and opportunistically burrowing into a niche market are the hallmarks of Remote Britain.

Footnote. This chapter had just been written when *John Southern* from Dobwalls, near Liskeard, phoned to confirm that the Forest Railway, two interlinked 15-

inch hilly circuits using huge 'miniature' locomotives, had closed and been dismantled. Once one of Cornwall's main tourist attractions – in 37 years it carried seven million passengers – even by the time *Journey* was written (pages 196-7) it had been hit by the county's declining visitor numbers. But what killed it was 'the deadly bed-fellows of Health & Safety and Insurance'.

John explains: 'Most of the time it was great fun; not very profitable, but you get your reward from "thank yous" and kisses and we had plenty of them. We gave lots of pleasure. Then it ceased to be fun. Just one example: Health & Safety determined the tracks should be fenced in. The system had been designed to let people see from the trains and to photograph the trains without interruption. Fencing it in spoilt it. If you're not making money or having fun, it's time to get out, so we did.'

Even running my publishing house of David & Charles had ceased to be the fun it once was before I sold it because of this and that regulation and inspection. The over-regulated UK is killing entrepreneurship. If you can't enjoy it, the only other motive for running a business is making money, which is exactly what most now concentrate on doing with short-term perspectives, though ultimately not in their own, leave alone the nation's, best interest. Remote Britain bucks the trend when it can, but many of today's small to medium-sized businesses succeed because they are cherished and despite today's kill-joy government policies.

· III ·

THE GREAT INDIVIDUALITY OF PLACE

The Old Testament and Tess

In spare time during the last two weeks my emotion's have been in overdrive as I alternated rereading Thomas Hardy's *Tess of the D'Urbervilles* with studying a spiritual book containing numerous references to the Old Testament.

How can one stop oneself from sympathising, if not falling in love with Tess, buffeted by cruel circumstances in a harsh landscape so vividly drawn as to become one of the principal characters in its own right? *Tess* is an extremely skilful, not to mention powerful, piece of writing. In passing, my first reading of it at the end of the 1940s, listening to the radio serialisation in the 1950s, and seeing the more recent television version, left such strong memories that the rereading immediately reveals how radio and television handled it, and particularly how TV introduced a number of non-Hardy scenes, an action-packed one emphasising the piquancy of timing. As we will see in a moment, that is revealing.

During my reading, my main feeling, was how strong is the likeness between much of the Old Testament and *Tess*. It could indeed be a quiz question: what does the Bible have in common with Victorian novels, the Old Testament with Thomas Hardy? Other, that is, than an outdated value system and theology. Again in passing, among the many rich seams in *Tess,* is the demonstration of how the old ultra-strict faith was under strain as the countryside itself was rapidly changing. The answer I'd be looking for would be: the importance of place.

In both books, where people came from, spent their lives and died, and especially where important events happened, were of profound importance. It remained so in Dickens, throughout the Victorian era, and possibly to World War One. In both the Bible and Hardy, places are real (if renamed in *Tess*) and often symbolic. The Bible's desert is replaced by Hardy's harsh empty upland. Perhaps both the Bible and *Tess* could be seen as symbolic. Hardy delves into many deep issues. A man, but not a woman, could dismiss a premarital sexual experience as irrelevant. Being a younger member of a former great family carried a huge burden. Where would the Church be and how would parsons earn their living if ecclesiastical rules were not totally obeyed? What forces was education of the poor unleashing?

So how is it that place has been relegated in importance by space and, more recently, especially by time? In today's fiction, it matters less where things happened than when, not what part of a community we belong to but how quickly we get on.

That's where television comes in. Always stressing action and tension, it has obviously helped promote the priority of time. But there are a lot of other reasons why we have lost the deep sense of 'being', belonging in our very own place. One is undoubtedly that people move around far more, and a huge number anyway don't live anywhere really individual or particularly memorable. In many suburbs they are inevitably more concerned with their own speck of earth's space than being part of a unique and vibrant local community.

To many commuters, the journey to work and back is simply space to force their way through. Another hammer blow to the sense of belonging has been the centralisation of services. Closures of local Post Offices, schools and hospitals have torn the soul out of many communities, the actions of different authorities being largely uncoordinated so that the knock-on damage is gratuitously greater than it need be. A Post Office is far more likely to die in a village without a school, for example. Market consumerism pays little heed to place: apart from engendering greed, it is all about scale and timing, but it is again at a cost, especially to children daily transported to another environment, and to the sick (especially the terminally ill) forced away from familiar surroundings and faces.

To take a local example, like most small towns, Nairn once largely controlled its own affairs. Well within living memory, if a culvert were blocked, you phoned the council office. The Town Clerk personally answered and told the engineer, who hated a waiting list and took quick action. Now we are governed by the Highland Regional Council whose far-flung members can vote on issues affecting us in opposition to our handful of local councillors. Quick response isn't possible with divided bureaucracy. When a flood threatened our back door and we needed sandbags, I was transferred from department to uninterested department until I was back where I started. Seemingly it was nobody's responsibility, though the sandbags did arrive – three days later.

Another thing: you may have noticed that when older people lose themselves in recounting memories of the old days, it is usually of places with their own individual ways and oddities. I've many personal memories but few of them are about the Essex suburb where I had the misfortune to spend my first seven years – and those I do have aren't about the road in which we lived or our neighbours but rare trips to somewhere with more character.

The reason that since boyhood I've avoided living in the core of Britain, is that I felt a need to belong somewhere specific and am old-fashioned enough to cherish my place. As West Country people put it, I need 'to belong to be'. So when the time came to sell my business in Devon, I moved to the North of Scotland. The extremities are more individual than the middle.

It is the extremities that this book mainly celebrates, though the whole work, as *Journey* before it, could be said to be a tribute to the role of place. People constantly ask me what is my favourite place, to which I answer 'Where I am'. It is not a trick answer for, though I desperately need an inspirational home base, I live fully and am frequently over-joyed by the individuality of each place of distinction we visit. I am not alone in that, yet another reason why place has been relegated is that, even on holiday, most people now move around restlessly, only scratching the surface – as do those on some organised tours hopping between a handful of easy-to-park-at 'must see' attractions.

When the annual holiday meant a fortnight in the same place each year, usually more colourful than where people actually lived, its character could be soaked up and experienced deeply. Many indeed were so delighted that they decided it was the place to which they would move as soon as they retired, or perhaps establish a holiday home, however primitive. That now seldom happens though, when deciding to opt out of the rat race, more people consciously do sample likely locations where they feel they could put down roots. Though rapid sampling sounds dangerous, the right place usually speaks for them and, as we see later, most are happy with their choice. For me, indeed Nairn was love at first sight, though I was only there accidentally. Yes, places do speak.

Throughout the history of civilisation, many artists and especially musicians have been inspired and renewed by leisurely holiday stays, especially perhaps in Italy. And our own dramatically varying landscapes continue to inspire writers, these days more unusually non-fiction ones, some of whose local offerings are considered in later chapters. I never cease to wonder at how much there is to learn about a small area and have devoted a chapter to the lower Wye Valley as the result of reading a fine new volume in the New Naturalist series. The book goes into incredible detail – the lichens growing on the walls of Tintern Abbey, for example – without ever trivialising them. We'll meet the author – and his book-writing wife.

Bishop of Truro

I was developing these and other thoughts when it occurred to me that a useful person to meet for this book might be the Bishop of Truro, the Rt Rev Bill Ind, since retired. His television appearances, first in a *Seaside Parish* (Boscastle) and then *An Island Parish* (the Isles of Scilly), demonstrated a great and practical empathy for place. So I'm in the Bishop's Palace, not in the shadow of the modern cathedral but at Lis Escop, near the King Harry Ferry and the National Trusts' Trelissick Gardens. Built in 1967, with a glorious view of the River Fal, it is on lease from the National Trust. The setting is wonderfully peaceful in colourful mature grounds of trees and flowering shrubs, with a vegetable garden.

The gardener pops in for a cup of tea. We discuss the merits and behaviour of various plants that thrive in this almost, but not totally, frost-free spot. Then the Bishop's wife, followed by Meg the brown Burmese, apologises for the fact that the dentist in Truro is running late. Time to take in more detail such as a programme of the Devoran Spring Flower Show and the many awards the Bishop has won – and details of Feock Home & Garden Club. And to think more about what I'm coming to regard as the sanctity of place.

When Bishop Bill arrives at amazing speed he relaxes and is open to what I've in mind. 'Ah, place, very profound: localism, the other side of globalisation that everyone talks about.' He certainly knows about remote and individual places for, already passed normal retirement age, he has been a Bishop since he was 44. First he was Suffragan Bishop of Grantham, where his responsibility included a large part of the Fens. Soon he's telling me of three especially remote villages I should visit – 'Nobody ever goes to them' – on our forthcoming trip to Cambridgeshire and Lincolnshire.

It was in 1997 that, out of the blue, he received a letter inviting him to become Bishop of Truro – among the first batch of appointments made by the new Labour government. So he's led clergy and laity in remote and under-privileged areas for most of his working life.

His love of Cornwall comes across strongly and his actions to defend it have been so consistent that it would be easy to think of him as a Cornishman. He isn't, but is going to miss 'the only English county that wasn't a shire' in his retirement in Wiltshire. Cornwall first made an impact when the family took a week's holiday in Tintagel in 1968. With a delightful sense of the ridiculous but with no time for nonsense officialdom, he's been a popular choice. He must also have made an impact on the Fens for, when I tell a Reader in one of the places he says I should visit, that I'm calling on his recommendation, the instant reaction is: 'Whatever you want I'll do it.' We'll meet David Beeton in Tydd St Mary 'where the only English pope was once vicar' in chapter XXIX. So, the Bishop says, closing his eyes, leaning back, hands behind his head: 'Places such as where we are right now are very important. People want to get married here.' Cogitating for a moment, he explains: 'Personally I'm not interested in church politics or the corridors of power and I'm delighted to be a long way from London. Cornwall has a sense of being its own place, a decent style of life where you don't so often hear "you can't do that" and can just get on with it. It's very level in the soul strata. I don't bother with rubbish but do my own thing. I'd only been here a fortnight when I went to Pendeen for a Moody and Sankey evening. You are who you are here, not what London thinks you should be.

Cornwall *is* its own place and I passionately defend it. I've become more and more militant about it even in the House of Lords. With its Celtic spirituality, its very different early history, a Prayer Book Rebellion (1549) even before mining and John Wesley, and its rain (where else do people treat it so seriously that a newspaper runs a free umbrella offer?), it really is different. There are busy places in Cornwall, but a lot of remote ones too, on Bodmin Moor especially. When you drive back after dark, you don't see any lights to the north of the A30 between Okehampton and Launceston. There are some pretty isolated places along and just inland from the north coast up to and around Bude. I've met people who have never been to Truro, leave alone London. Cornishness survives: there's even a GCSE course on the Cornish language, now spoken by 4,000 people.

But, as in Lincolnshire, also on the edge, there are still a lot of poor people. Wage rates are low. Things became more apparent when the government agreed to separate Devon and Cornwall in terms of economic life. Against a median economy score of 100, Cornwall scores 54. Cornwall's not been really understood or well treated, yet there's a deeper sense of being, of the mingling of past and present. If they are not as well paid, people are generally happier. Yes, it's about belonging, it's a great place even though more jobs are essential and there's a huge gap between rich and poor.'

When I point out that indigenous Cornish people have recently become outnumbered by incomers, he adds that, like him, newcomers quickly come under the spell and are often the stoutest defenders of Cornwall. But: 'Nowhere is so little understood. Londoners don't even realise how far away we are. Someone said to me that he knew the West Country but cited Tewkesbury which is more than twice as far from Penzance as it is from London.'

Now to the Most Northerly Bishop

Shortly before the retirement of Bishop Bill, the country's most southerly Bishop, our own extreme northerly Diocese (Moray, Ross & Caithness) had just appointed a young new one: Bishop Mark Strange. In a chance meeting, I discovered his views on the spirituality of 'thin' spaces were just as strong. I shouldn't have been surprised, for anyone receptive to God who has to travel round the beautiful Highlands cannot fail to be moved. 'The sheer breathtaking beauty is sometimes so overwhelming it's physically painful,' he says.

In common with so many others, he has always drawn special inspiration from Iona: 'A beautiful island set in a sea with a very special light, a thin place where Heaven comes close and it is hard not to be moved by the long history of how over the centuries so many Christians have found it anchoring.

Another place which is also very special to me is the abandoned Monastery of St Maelrubha [c642-c722] near Applecross. The feeling of sharing the great view right out to Skye that must first have so impressed the saint is quite overwhelming.' Maelrubha, apostle of the Picts, came from Ireland, evangelised Skye and, in addition to his monastery at lonely Applecross, built a chapel on an island in Loch Maree where his spring was said to have great healing powers.

As in the Diocese of Truro, the Bishop is not based near the Cathedral, but out in the country – at a place called Arpafeelie on the Black Isle with a tiny Episcopal church close by. 'It's set on an ordinary hillside, yet it's very individual. The church has three hundred years of prayerful history, the very stones put in place by the founders of what became the last Gaelic speaking Episcopal Church. It was closed for a time, but has gained new life, partly because the Black Isle is more accessible now there's a bridge.'

Previously Rector of Elgin, Bishop Mark says they loved their walled garden there, 'but we were always conscious of what was going on around us. Now we have a field next to us, and it is consciousness of a very different type. Actually there's a rabbit running across as I speak. It was great seeing the field ploughed – I don't need to consult the lectionary to see when Rogation Sunday is – and we're spending our time immersed in the seasons. Barley is coming on there now. I hope we'll see it harvested and that it goes into a good drink.

So even this is a very special spot where God's creation is about making you slow down. The whole family's delighted; for the first time in years, spontaneously we found ourselves kicking a ball.

Retreats have always helped me slow down but, in a place you can really identify with, it's much easier as an ordinary everyday thing. I tell people in our remote parishes how lucky they are. As so many more folk have become separated from nature, there's a greater realisation that we need to find time to connect with it. Find somewhere apart to take a walk, I say. Just be.'

At which point, on a bright though chilly June morning, white waves breaking over the deep-blue sea bringing back some of the sand it stole in an earlier gale, that's just what I'm going to do. 'I shan't think in formal words,' I say.

'Words aren't necessary for being,' he replies. 'Sort yourself out, commune, enjoy the past and the present but be prepared for change, for without that none of us thrive.' Which was his message at a special service to confirm five youngsters and one older person, after which I had the chance encounter with him. His sermon's message: Without change, the church will die.

On my walk I meet city southerners here to refresh their spirits. You can almost see them unwinding, enjoying the trivial things of life which are so vital yet easy to ignore in the pressure 'to get on'.

Theology of Place

Down in Cornwall, beside the Fal, Bishop Bill had recommended a newish book, *A Christian Theology of Place,* by John Inge. With long lines in small print, it is not easy reading and, for my taste, relies too heavily on numerous quotes from others without always properly digesting them. It does however make important points – and some of the quotations are very worthwhile. This one about being rooted comes from America's Simon Weil's *The Need for Roots.*

> To be rooted is perhaps the most important need of the human soul. It is one of the hardest to define. A human being has roots by virtue of his real, active, and natural participation in the life of a community, which preserves in living shape certain particular treasures of the past and certain particular expectations of the future. This participation is a natural one, in the sense that it is naturally brought about by place, conditions of birth, profession, and social surroundings. Every human being needs to have multiple roots. It is necessary for him to draw well-nigh the whole of his moral, intellectual, and spiritual life by way of the environment of which he forms a natural part.

John Inge emphasises that place in the Old Testament is primarily a category of faith: 'God, people, and place are all important.' In the New Testament, place is often sacramental, Jerusalem especially, sacked in AD70 after which Christianity was steadily taken over by the

Gentiles and opposed by many of the Jews who had first come under its influence. Place has always had a key role in the history of Christianity: Paul's conversion on the road to Damascus, for instance. It was also of vital importance to John Wesley whose extensive *Journals* have almost as much to say about the character of different localities as do the accounts of Celia Fiennes and Daniel Defoe of their travels. Though we have just heard how Cornish people are still different, they are no longer quite the race-apart as when Wesley turned them from drunken mobs into law-abiding tea drinkers, described in *Journey*. Linked with tourism, place still promotes pilgrimages to shrines or early UK Christian sites, the latter especially in Scotland including Iona, and the North of England's Lindisfarne or Holy Island.

Was it the Western intellectual tradition that degraded place, eclipsing it by an emphasis first upon space and second upon time? John Inge suggests so. Its defeat, he says, has been relatively recent in history, 'reaching a dehumanisation in the 20th century'. He adds that theologians have yet to give sufficient attention to place because they remain 'wedded to the norms of modernity'.

Pilgrimage

Another new title recommended by Bishop Bill is *Divine Landscapes: A pilgrimage through Britain's sacred places,* by Ronald Blythe, a novelist who writes the weekly *Church Times* back-page countryside *Word from Wormingford.* Since he lives in East Anglia and the paperback is published by the Canterbury Press in Norwich, an East Anglian bias is to be expected, though the introduction sets a wide perspective:

> We in this country live in an ancient gazetteer of prayer and worship... Britain's natural contours are drawn all over with religious symbols and references, most of them Christian, though many from earlier faiths. There is hardly a field or hill, let alone a village or town, which cannot be read in religious terms. Architecture and plants, weather and views, creatures and stones, seasons and roads, rivers and soils, gardens and forests, skies and shores, 'all that is', as Julian of Norwich summed it up, are doubly immersed in the sacred and in the scientific. In an old country where everything from a hut to the kingdom itself was once placed under divine protection, a complex underlying 'holy land' is only to be expected.

Among many interesting points Ronald Blythe makes is that the priest can never belong to his parish as much as those already well anchored in it. The same goes for teachers and doctors. Most of the book is devoted to a series of walks, with many asides, bringing in the usual gallery of saints, mystiques and writers. Norwich naturally has one of the geographically-based chapters which take us through a trawl of familiar spiritual sites though often with unusual reflections.

The longest chapter, over fifty pages, called 'How to make a pilgrimage without leaving home', is about John Bunyan's allegorical countryside. Bunyan's feat, he says, was to correlate the long walk Jesus made through Palestine with a walk made through life by a typical 17th century Englishman.

'He inaugurated a whole new love and understanding of Christ, where they could step with him: '*The Pilgrim's Progress* had sanctified an English county in a manner which no other book has done before or since.' At which point let me inject that, though Ronald Blythe pays scant attention to Remote Britain, much of the historical action is set in places that then would have been far more remote than they are today. Sadly, for me that is one of the book's unstated conclusions.

The other unusual chapter is about 'the Black Map', which startlingly reminds us that atrocities once happened as much in Britain as elsewhere, 'for around London and within a terrible arc of investigation from Lynn to Oxford... six hundred profoundly believing Christian people were slaughtered by the state during the reigns of the half-sisters Queen Mary and Queen Elizabeth.' He continues:

> Men and women, boys and girls, weavers, farmworkers, aristocrats, an archbishop and newly ordained young priests, the semi-literate and great scholars, artists and poets, all suffered the most atrocious deaths which the law allowed, burnt for heresy under Mary if they stuck to the 'new' religion, hanged, drawn and quartered under Elizabeth for treason if they propagated the 'old'.

Again the thought strikes me that then, in those terrible days, nearly everywhere would have felt as remote if not more so than my selection of Remote Britain is today. Now the South East is 'civilised', but at what a price. Does progress inevitably mean stamping out individuality?

The Evils of Centralism

While place will always have a special role, most would agree that the sheer scale and centralisation of today's institutions, if really justified, has had to be paid for expensively. We hark back to geography: layouts we can instantly comprehend, to continuity between past and present, and to individualism. While ever complicating our lives, we long for the simple – the lives close to nature that would have been led in the old abandoned homes we still see in poorer country areas.

But now the sounds of population fail,

No cheerful murmurs fluctuate in the gale,
No busy steps the grass-grown footway tread,
But all the bloomy flush of life is fled.

They are perhaps the obvious few lines to cite from Goldsmith's *The Deserted Village,* yet it is in the poem's long verses telling us of how people wooed, whitewashed their cottages, grew their crops, saved to pay off debts, and so on, which evoke what was really lost.

I never pass a deserted Scottish house or cottage, with only the rhubarb surviving in the garden among the many crops that up to perhaps a generation ago once fed hungry mouths, without wondering what experiences went with living in that place: what night-time wildlife might have been heard, what sunrises and sunsets impressed, what smells and rainbows stirred the senses. But more than that, I sadly cogitate how those moving, or forcibly moved out, coped with their new environment, and whether or not the loss was irreplaceable. And, especially on sombre days, I wonder just where we may die. I recall the joy the view of the mouth of the Teign's estuary, the triangular red sandstone Ness headland, and the Shaldon Ferry plying to and fro, gave my mother's mother in her final weeks. To spend life's last days with only walls to look at must be especially hard for those of us who celebrate the individuality of place. As if to emphasis their artificiality, hotels increasingly display art that is ultra-impressionistic, sometimes only brashly-coloured space. Above all I am saddened by memories of my mother, on her death bed in a hospital in Leamington Spa, as far from the sea as it is possible to get. 'I'd so like to see the sea just once more,' she said, adding that she wouldn't even have a chance to breathe the air outside again.

The desperate need for the respect of place is perhaps best revealed where people are shunted around like chattels as in slum clearances and the demolition of many tower blocks. Wherever there is a sudden inflow of newcomers, such as in the 'overspill' area in the east of Northampton, where in some school classes as few as one in ten pupils were raised locally, uncenteredness and distress abound. Family break ups and above-average crime follow. Even if moved to luxurious new buildings, people flail without roots and established friendships.

London's East End and Glasgow's Gorbals were real places with deep traditions, while it took decades for a sense of belonging to build in Milton Keynes and Glasgow's new-town Cumbernauld. Though happily most people now realise that the community spirit in Nottingham's Victoria was far easier killed than rekindled in 'nicer' development, planners still dream unrealistically. It takes decades for new or greatly expanded towns to become real places.

Locally, the example of the consequences of attracting hundreds to work in the new Invergordon aluminium smelter only to see it collapse was cited in the previous chapter. Now there's the threat of a new town between Inverness and Nairn, described by one councillor as the most imaginative piece of work the planners have yet achieved. Local feeling has not been properly consulted; indeed quite false claims are being made of public acceptance, while the artist's drawing of the finished 'community' is ridiculously out of keeping with likely reality. With such bulldozing planning push, another social disaster may be inevitable. Even if some lessons from the past are learnt, the official mindset cannot apply them to different situations and the greed for expansion reigns.

Elsewhere in remote Scotland, often it is the ever-changing military families, especially in outposts such as Benbecula, who fail to integrate and enjoy the fellowship of the place. How can the children of incomers staying only two or three years be expected to integrate with kids steeped in Gaelic ways?

Individualism and respect for place naturally survive better in remote than central Britain, and readers attracted to this book will undoubtedly have a special appreciation of our rich traditional heritage beyond the obvious castles, churches and other historic buildings – though much of the joy in visiting them is actually in the individualism of place surrounding them. As we will find in later chapters, thousands have now happily moved out of the rat race to discover somewhere they can really call home. Roots take time to put down. They grow surprisingly quickly in Cornwall and some Scottish islands, but take longer in West Wales where the neighbours may converse with each other in Welsh, leaving incomers feeling left out.

Happily in many places, incomers are soon part of their local communities and fierce defenders of them. There's much more to their lives than work and the journey to it, meals at a posh restaurant and a cruise or other 'holiday of a lifetime' without really getting to know anywhere. Life enacted on the stage of the place where people belong is more fulfilling and less dependent on TV, though it has to be regretted that many in Scotland, with its reputation for heavy drinking and its terrible health record, are blind to the beauty around them and lack curiosity. Only a small minority of mainland Scots have ever been to Skye.

'Back to Localism'

'It's back to localism' one incomer in a remote area of North Devon tells me. 'I know where every road and lane leads, I notice the milk tanker and school bus – almost as much as, years ago before I was forced to move to London, my life was largely timed around the comings and goings of branch-line trains. There's rhythm to it. The seasons have again become important. Unconsciously I keep tabs on what all the neighbours are up to and can't help caring about them. London friends think I must be lonely out here, but it's the reverse.'

Wherever we live we have to contend with the effects of centralisation of services but, helped by local-action groups, Remote Britain is often capable of beating Authority. So Nairn cottage hospital is being rebuilt rather than closed. Once it was feared that all railways north of Perth would be chopped; unimaginable though it was half a century ago, we actually have an improved train service all the way to Thurso and Wick. And while we no longer have counties in Scotland, the use of the old names, continues with welcoming notices on the borders.

As the following chapters tell, the independence of Place is vigorously defended. Localism thrives, with better public halls, cultural, practical and sporting organisations in profusion, a pride in telling visitors about the area's special characteristics, and a confidence that it is here to stay. It needs more people such as Bishop Bill to inspire and lead, but let us not be downhearted. Celebrate Remote Britain's great individuality of Place and all it stands for.

· IV ·

BRYHER AND TRESCO

Early Promise

The sun shines as we wait at Bath for the 9.01am train to Penzance. There is a Travelling Chef on board, and soon we have two English breakfasts sizzling away and occupying the entire table between us. It may be foolish, but I just love meals on the move; it undoubtedly was silly, for we didn't even need one between us. But it sets a happy mood as we are bound for the Isles of Scilly. Don't look them up under Scilly Isles for that is not how they are usually known.

There is sheer delight in the journey across the Somerset Levels and, in Devon running along the Exe, along the Sea Wall at Dawlish, and beside the Teign before catching a glimpse of Haytor and climbing the Dartmoor foothills. The journey's highlight is crossing Brunel's 1859 masterpiece over the Tamar and then seeing it fullside-on after a sharp turn. Down through the spine of Cornwall, with a panorama of decaying mine stacks, the white heaps of the waste of the later china clay industry, ancient almshouses and villages, and Truro Cathedral looked down upon from a high viaduct. As Cornwall narrows there are glimpses of both coasts. Finally we run alongside Mount's Bay cradling St Michael's Mount before reaching the ugly but instantly-recognisable terminus at Penzance. Joy, with the crisp, early spring sunshine announcing that the best of the year will soon be upon us.

We had been in Penzance in late autumn, only just escaping from Cornwall before an untimely early blizzard trapped hundreds of motorists on the main A30 across Bodmin Moor. Thanks to the card of the Penzance Taxi Company still in my wallet and a call on the mobile phone, we find our favourite driver waiting at the buffer stop. 'Well, my handsome, if you like it so much down here, why don't you move like I did. What [addressing Sheila] do you think, my lover?'

We check into a hotel just beyond Marazion. Now a snooze? 'No, it's such a lovely afternoon... let's see if we can make it to the Mount.' No sooner have we reached the road than a bus obligingly picks us up...

a double decker whose passenger complement we increase to five for the short hop down to Marazion. It is good to be walking across the causeway in just our own company; the last twice I headed over 500 people brought from London by special trains my company organised. It was notably warmer now in March than on those summer afternoons. Though most of the Mount, including the much-photographed castle home of the St Levan family perched atop, is closed, a café encourages a few early visitors to take their tea into the sunshine. Nature's natural colours vividly enhanced, the whole scene looks like those posters summer visitors suspiciously believe are down to their artists' imagination. If you could reliably buy such an experience as this, what wouldn't it cost?

Contentedly stepping over the gaps gouged out by winter storms, we retrace our steps back over the causeway, following and followed by large families of overseas visitors as happy as any there will be this year. Prepared for a long trudge back to the hotel, our smiles widen as another double decker hoves into sight, the driver charging only half of what we had paid to descend.

To bed relaxed as though we have already spent a week on holiday. Tomorrow to an enchanted island!

Wasted Day?

'There'll be a long delay, my handsome, but they'll make you comfortable.' People are milling round in crisis mood and the taxi driver has difficulty parking anywhere near the Heliport doorway. It is obvious why. St Michael's Mount that had stood out so crystal clear yesterday, along with most of Penzance and the surrounding hills, has disappeared in thick fog.

'Don't know when we'll start flying,' says the check-in man. 'We'll make an announcement in half an hour.' They are words we hear repeatedly at forty five rather than thirty minute intervals over the next hours. We are told that St Mary's on the Scillies is clear, 'and let's hope we'll soon see St Michael's Mount'. Soon we indeed do, but then the Scillies are again enveloped in fog. Once our starting and finishing points are clear. 'But there's no diversionary airport out of fog, and we need one.'

Spirits rise as a helicopter is pushed out from its hangar and sponged down like a prize car. Within an hour it is pushed back inside. That is after we have read *The Western Morning News*, on which I began my career as a reporter. We catch the chef just before he goes off duty. Never was a basic toasted sandwich more welcome. Not that we are exactly bored for, this being Cornwall, everyone is interested in everyone else's business. We have talked to many passengers who have come and then gone – not onto a helicopter, but back into mainland life. Many who pop over to the Scillies on business will try again tomorrow. Others attempting to leave urgent parcels are told that, even if flying does start, there's a backlog of cargo.

'Perhaps we should have risked the boat,' says Sheila.

'There is no boat,' replies a new-found friend, adding, 'In winter they lay her up and pay the staff for doing nothing. But don't be sorry for us: moving to the Scillies was the best thing we've ever done.'

Another announcement: 'We still hope to fly and will let you know the position in half an hour.' That is the moment the idea for this book is born. Did I head this section 'Wasted Day?' In one sense, yes, of course. But no day is ever wasted. There is time to gaze, think, dream, touch the productive unconscious. *Journey*, my last travel book, has sold well and is now also in paperback, and *For the Love of a Cat* is nearly finished. What next? Another British travel book, perhaps, but with what excuse? Ah, why not *Remote Britain*? We have been talking about collecting more islands. Though *Journey* also favoured the nation's periphery, it hadn't delved deep into the real extremities. Even the Scillies, though mentioned, hadn't been visited afresh. Not only the idea for my next book, but at the next announcement I realise that we have 'earned' £150 from our insurance company for being delayed by over twelve hours.

'Ladies and gentlemen, I'm sorry to say we still can't fly, and now must give up for today.' So a quick call to the Cornish Range at Mousehole, on Penzance's other side, where in November we had enjoyed a distinguished fish dinner and had noticed it was a Restaurant with Rooms and to the Penzance Taxi Company to take us there.

Four months later and living at the other end of Britain, we sit at the same table choosing precisely the same dishes: crab cake with a luscious fresh taste, and perfect Dover sole. There are other attractive options, but when we next return it will be for the same again. What better recommendation?

The address is Chapel Street. Penzance's Chapel Street is one of my favourite; I once did a television item about its great variety of historic buildings, ranging from the mock Egyptian House to the Admiral Benbow pub. There are some homes with fine frontages, while the Weslyan chapel, is still the establishment church here where the mayor goes for civic events. Dozens of West Cornish local preachers used to wait in awe for the occasion they would be asked to preach at the Chapel that gives the delightful street its name.

Having walked up and down looking for the Cornish Range on our November visit, eventually I asked someone emerging from the Admiral Benbow pub where it was. 'Tis in Chapel Street, Muzzle, mi 'andsome.'

To Bryher at Last via St Mary's and Tresco

So after a comfortable night we retrace our route through the narrow streets of Mousehole and Newlyn to the Heliport. Again, chaos, with all the people who had been 'put on the additional early flight' still waiting. *The Western Morning News* and most other papers have sold out. 'Maybe an hour, perhaps longer, but one flight has gone and will soon be back.' Time, I told Sheila, to walk to Tesco for a paper and something else she needed.

Ten minutes later: 'Could Mr and Mrs Thomas please return to the counter.' Crisis; we've been brought forward to the next flight. Sheila reappears in the nick of time, but misses part of the emergency drill. I recall the helicopter whose pilot, mesmerised in poor light, drove it straight into the sea, drowning some of the passengers. That was when British Airways ran the service. Now it is run by an independent.

There's a strong wind, and when we rise above the sea we realise that had the boat been running it would be seriously seasick-making. When winter flights are suspended a small boat occasionally takes a few people in a hurry, but we later learn that it was too rough for it today.

Not that it is exactly smooth up here. Much of the flight is through banks of fog. I hold on tight, hoping that St Mary's and Penzance terminals will not again be blotted out.

At St Mary's only four of us remain on board for the short hop to Tresco. Now relaxed, I enjoy the panorama of all five inhabited and many empty islands and sea-splashed rocks laid out like pieces of a jig-saw beneath us. From up here one sees how the smaller islands and outlying rocks offer surprising protection for the small craft plying between the chief port at Hugh Town, St Mary's, and the inhabited off isles. And it is easy to see that the islands are all that has not been drowned of former hill tops, with shallow valleys where people once tended their crops. If the sea dropped 30ft St Mary's, Tresco, Bryher and St Martin's would all be joined up again.

In a few seconds it is all there: the small fields between high hedges (though most alas now without the familiar yellow splashes of daffodils), Hugh Town's beach where many ships were crafted in the days of wood, the twin peaks of Samson, whose last residents left in 1855 but where, as in neighbouring islands, there is tell-tale evidence of early civilisations, 'early' being very relative in Scillies' long geological history. Soon, having caught a fleeting glimpse of Abbey Pool and the larger Great Pool, we descend close to the tropical gardens of Tresco Abbey.

Passing passengers waiting to fly, who have no doubt enjoyed an extra enforced day on Tresco, we jump aboard a trailer with long benches facing outward on both sides, and hold the guard rail as our tractor lurches forward, immediately to lurch backward for another tractor and trailer. Ordinary car travel is banned on Tresco. We are dropped off at New Grimsby Harbour and, thinking of what we will do when we come back to Tresco, stand in the primitive waiting room until our boat comes across the sheltered channel from Bryher to collect us.

We had planned to spend one (last) night at Hell Bay on Bryher, three on Tresco and two at Hugh Town, but a phone call to Hell Bay at Bryher brought the reassuring news that we'd still be able to enjoy it for a night, reducing our time in Tresco. 'We're used to this kind of thing, and it's organised with both hotels. And at this time of year, no extra charge.'

Hell Bay

At the end of our five minute crossing we are directed to another elementary 'taxi' with a friendly and informative driver. We climb the twisting road until we crest narrow Bryher's backbone. Descending to Hell Bay Hotel, our eyes become fixated on the restless Atlantic. They are still when we reach our hotel room. Relentless waves splash up and often completely cover great rocks, their spray never fully draining away before the next onslaught. However, there is also inland scenery including Bryher's own Great Pool, fields and cottages. The new hotel is built in several largish cottage-size units linked by a path across grass and through flowerbeds. It is idyllic.

The bedroom is one of the best-situated and equipped we have yet enjoyed; perfection at the very edge of Europe. Welcoming us back at the lounge, off reception, Philip Callan, says he used to manage the older Island Hotel at Tresco 'which now has its very definite style, while we're still discovering ours'. He was in at the beginning of Hell Bay, fighting all manner of planning and transport obstacles. The result is admirable.

Lunch of duck confit and fishcake is splendid; dinner in the dining room is devoid of even a touch of disappointment. There are not many of us, but all (including a young couple who work at the New Inn on Tresco celebrating a birthday) are as happy as you'll find in a restaurant anywhere. Sheila makes a special point of commenting on the quality and appropriateness of the wooden tables.

Why this eulogy? Because a few weeks later, Jan Moir devoted two of the *Weekend Telegraph* backpage restaurant reviews to a vicious attack on the Island Hotel and New Inn and then to an even harsher judgement of Hell Bay. There were agonies of protest when the review of the Tresco establishments appeared. That Hell Bay was found so universally appalling was beyond comprehension. Even the dining room furniture Sheila admired – and we were told that each table cost over £1,000 – is rubbished: 'The room is rather mundanely decked out in the kind of blonde wood and blue upholstery fittings that you might find in a department store cafeteria that was knocked up in a week, with change to spare from £1,000.' That is the tone set by what the *Telegraph* described as 'one of our most respected correspondents'. But much of Middle England was roused and the damage was to the *Telegraph,* not the hotels. Apparently I was among five hundred who wrote protest letters.

That Ms Moir's' partner should be so upset that newspapers come late, and muttered 'get me off these islands', suggests intentional lack of perspective. Of course bottled water is a 'rip off'; it is everywhere, though transport to the islands is bound to add to costs. We are not the only people who feel that the hyped up two-article blast has lost respect for the *Weekend Telegraph*'s back page.

Even Bryher Changes

Bryher is a very special island, rich in history, archaeology and scenic grandeur. When I was a young reporter, it was described as the oldest surviving piece of Neolithic society. Virtually nobody stayed on it because there was no hotel.

Walking between the fields and then through the village doesn't feel quite the same today as it did then. Far more visited, Bryher has lost a little of its quaintness. That is the trouble with tourist Britain: put a place under a microscope and everyone is more conscious of who and what they are with inevitable conflict between residents and visitors. How can it be otherwise when even in March a handful of visitors comment on this and that? We walked into the garden of what we assumed was a public building but turned out to be a private house. The owner politely pointed out we were trespassing. Trespass is not a word that would have been used in Bryher when I first knew it. Yet it would be extremely artificial to continue 'preserving' Bryher as it used to be. Here, as on all the islands, new residents under the spell of living on an Atlantic outpost have bought cottages once the homes of residents. Though there is still active farming, flower growing is no longer important. Without tourism there would be economic collapse.

We ponder this, gradually losing the Atlantic's roar as we pass All Saints Church, started in 1742, and descend to the sandy beach where we'd arrived, and head north past the White House (Post Office and shop, closed this afternoon) and look across to the round tower of Cromwell's Castle on Tresco – a reminder of the Scillies' strategic importance. It was built in 1651-2 after the higher King Charles's Castle (built by Henry

VIII and now a ruin with a stunning outlook across the glacial barren northern tip of Tresco) fell to the Commonwealth in the Civil War and it was realised that the higher site wasn't good enough to keep away the hostile Dutch fleet of the day. Cromwell's Castle commands the channel between Bryher and Tresco's New Grimsby Harbour.

'Perhaps it is typical of Scilly that the [top] castle is now called King Charles's Castle and the fort below Cromwell's Castle,' jokes Crispin Gill, my first newspaper boss [see *Journey*] in his *The Isles of Scilly* in the David & Charles Islands series. Hereabouts one has to be careful not to attribute the obvious meaning to names: ahead of us, only exposed at low tide, is Hangman Island, which has nothing to do with capital punishment but derived from the Old Cornish for 'the island'. Another local oddity – and the Scillies are entertainingly full of them – is a buoy which broke loose from the St Lawrence Seaway in Canada and drifted 3,000 miles to become a shipping hazard before towed and dumped on Hangman Island.

You cannot go far in the islands before thinking wrecks. As we walk back to the hotel, we have steadily to raise our voices over the roar of the Atlantic. We see how furiously it attacks Scilly Rock nearly a mile off shore. Atlantic liner *Minnehaha* struck Scilly Rock in 1910, littering the shore of Hell Bay 'with cases of everything from harmoniums to pencils'... 'the best bit of wrecking Bryher ever had'.

Before the days of radar, in the fog all too prevalent in the Western Atlantic, many ships literally became lost. Even the early *Scillonians* lost their way, hitting or becoming wedged on rocks – as recently as 1951. Earlier, on foggy days a bugler standing on Peninnis Head 'blew' to help the skipper pinpoint his position.

However, Bryher has long enjoyed a fine reputation for seamanship and, before official help arrived, its famous gigs (lengthy rowing boats designed for speed and rough water) towed in the *Minnehaha*'s two lifeboats laden with every last passenger. As on all the islands, timber from wrecks was much used in building; there are no real trees on Bryher. Seamanship is still important. Historically Bryher boats serve Tresco as well as their own island, a 100 and a 60-seater running timetabled summer services to all the other islands plus circular tours, and a fast *Cyclone* providing taxi services carrying school children, and all kinds of workers including ministers between services on different islands and increasingly affluent tourists preferring to arrange their own times for nippy crossings. 'We are very innovative,' says Mrs Cathy Stentiford, organising the daily schedules for Bryher Boat Services. With a discerning market, traffic has increased enormously. The *Cyclone* is out from 7.30am till 10.30pm most days, all special request trips.'

The Island Hotel, Tresco

Next morning we take one of their ordinary boats back to Tresco's New Grimsby Harbour, crossing the mile-long island by tractor-drawn trailer to the Island Hotel, which overlooks Old Grimsby Harbour.

'You've booked a good room anyway, but would you like to be upgraded to our best?' we are asked. Viewing three rooms involves what seems half a mile of walking along corridors familiar from previous visits. We plump for a first floor suite at the extreme sea end. There's another marvellous outlook. Again we see waves dashing against the rocks, but they are further away this time, with smooth water as far as St Martin's where we can pick out the upmarket hotel still closed for this winter. It, the Island and Hell Bay, are all among the fewer than 200 AA Top Hotels of the British Isles. Between them, the off-islands score more AA red rosettes for good food than do any of our major holiday resorts, which makes the *Telegraph*'s damning reports puzzling. But then Ms Jan Moir suggests that the Scilly air makes everyone come over middle-aged.

Not me. I feel the clock has gone back half a century. For one thing it is fresh, invigorating, seldom without a breeze. As the record of nearly a thousand wrecks testifies, the Scillies have proven hell to many mariners, but the high hotel and holiday cottage rates, not to mention difficulty in finding anywhere to stay in high season, demonstrate the islands' eternal attraction. With a temperature above 50°F on 350 days a year, and winter days mainly like London spring ones, it used to attract more out-of-season visitors. It is indeed frequently warmer than Mediterranean resorts.

I have told Sheila everything will be open at the end of March. It used to be, but is not now. While most mainland resorts enjoy longer seasons if not so pushily busy summer ones, here it is the reverse. The reason is the high cost in time and money of getting here, which discourages long weekends and short breaks.

However long the stay, at whatever time of year, I have found it easy but invigorating to slip into Scilly life. The problem is adjusting back to the mainland at the end. After surveying our suite and its outlook, we walk around Old Grimsby Harbour, 'March isn't such a bad time after all,' is Sheila's summing up.

We fancy lunch at the New Inn, but as we pass the school there is a sharp shower and we take refuge in the church, chatting to friendly, informative flower arrangers full of the joy of life, and then hasten back to the Island Hotel.

We have heard there is just one buggie that can be rented at £10 a half day. We book it for tomorrow morning's trip to the tropical gardens and, after a sandwich, content ourselves taking photographs around Old Grimsby Harbour, several with its foreground lit up with daffodils that probably years ago escaped from the commercial fields.

At dinner there are too many visitors, which usually means slower service as they settle down to chatter. For many years Southern Hemisphere English speaking staff have dominated waiting teams in remote hotels. Now it is the turn of the Eastern Europeans, especially the Polish, most of whom are excellent. Untypically one waitress purrs in suspended animation as she tells successive guests of her nationality, but we didn't hear anything as crass as Ms Jan Moir's 'where did you say you were from? Poland! How marvellous'. Neither do we find the food 'beyond grim; tough and tasteless beef, moribund lamb'. I have enjoyed every meal taken in this dining room from the first lunch on a day trip when I couldn't possibly have afforded to stay here when the hotel was newly open half a century ago. A long, low building quietly blending into the rocks, sea, harbour and its own gardens, it was then avant garde. It is hard to be uptight and critical here; though usually a newspaper fanatic, I couldn't care less if today's issues have arrived or been thrown overboard.

Off by Buggie

It is showery as we're taken to the buggie. Sheila opts to drive, but it takes her most of the morning to realise you can get into or out of reverse without having to alight from the vehicle. The buggie has two speeds: stop and go, go being somewhat violent in reverse.

Glad we haven't chosen to walk through the deep puddles of the minor eastern road, we see most of the island's few agricultural fields, go through a wood and between the Great and Abbey Pools (both great for winter and migrating birds), marvel at the size of Tresco Abbey (a private house of which more in a moment) and are halted by a red light: yes, a traffic light on Tresco. It is to stop traffic (just us) from proceeding while the helicopter we arrived on two days ago is making its turbulent morning call.

On our way to the gardens, we drive past the massive walls of Tresco Abbey from which the island is effectively governed as a private fiefdom; though the Duchy of Cornwall runs the other islands itself, Tresco has long been leased to the Dorrien-Smiths, whose current Robert we'll meet soon.

But first the chap who started it all.

The basic history of Tresco and its world-famous gardens has often been told. Though there was a short period of prosperity during the Napoleonic wars when the Scillies provided shelter for shipping on the run from privateers, thereafter things ran rapidly downhill. The Duke of Leeds, in debt and always vague about the islands, gave up his lease he had held from the Crown, and poverty and lawlessness prevailed.

> Since Scilly was Crown land, nobody could own property. Nobody who did not own property could be a JP, so there was no bench of magistrates, and therefore no law. There were no property taxes, or indeed taxes of any kind; so there was no money for public works, or indeed to escort criminals to Bodmin Assizes, or to pay their keep in Bodmin jail when they were convicted. In the absence of licensing laws any house could sell drink, and an astonishing number did.

The quote is from *Emperor Smith: The Man Who Built Scilly,* by a Tresco man, Sam Llewellyn: a well-written and brilliantly-illustrated book. Using many early travellers' hitherto unseen sketches (sketching is what people did before photography), it tells how Augustus Smith became enchanted with the idea of changing life on the islands, and after prolonged negotiations leased them from the Duchy. Improving things, often autocratically though always with what would be good for the locals in mind, was to be his full life's work.

New buildings and better infrastructure helped give employment and raise the economy with the aim that well-paid employment for all would eradicate the need for smuggling, which had long been a way of life. The objectives largely succeeded. Better living conditions were accompanied by guaranteed tenure, and it is a mark of Smith's achievement that, forty years before any kind of education became compulsory on the mainland, virtually every Scilly child attended school and studied the three Rs and a foreign language, while practical subjects included navigation for boys. It wasn't long before people realised the career benefits of education. Expectations were transformed.

Conditions had always been worse on the off-islands, where there had indeed been famine and corruption, and general disorder prevented the proceeds of a relief fund helping much. The level of hardship might be gauged from the fact that on tiny St Agnes, with scarcely half a square mile of farmable land, over-population and sub-division resulted in there being 433 separate parcels of land.

Significantly, Smith chose to live on an off-island. Though the original Tresco Abbey had been abandoned long before the Reformation, he perhaps relied on the judgement of monks to pick the best spot. He chose the island's south for his new Abbey, albeit only a private house. While the monks had been tucked away on low ground, Smith chose a higher site with a view across The Road to the Islands' capital of Hugh

Town. When he was there (before finally settling down he was often disturbingly absent), little would happen without his knowledge.

The south of Tresco was then almost as bleak as the glacial north. Not now. The thing Smith will always be best remembered for is the establishment of the gardens. To begin with it was a slow business for, even in a winter of Mediterranean temperatures, little usually survived the onslaught of Atlantic gales. Within years, shelter belts did their work. Slowly plants arrived from around the world to create what is arguably the most interesting garden in Britain, certainly without rival as a semi-tropical garden with dozens of species unknown on the mainland.

At the Famous Tropical Gardens

So, Sheila parks our buggie in an almost empty 'car' park which at busy times is filled with tractors and their passenger-carrying trailers. The loos are excellent and in the café-cum-gift and book shop we are struck by the friendliness of the staff and quality of the goods. Tresco attracts a select strata of visitors. Certainly crowds don't come here to drink and sunbathe. 'They all look like us,' says Sheila, matter-of-factly. They are (that's not a surprise) garden and bird lovers, precise over how they like their beverages, readers of books, and attracted by good though not extravagant design. I reflect how in my publishing years I was more likely to see people reading our books or hear them being discussed here than anywhere else. Everyone revels in the peace, the tame birds – I've had a thrush eat off my held-out hand in the gardens – the scenery and the walking, and the chance to relax with like-minded people anchored in their hobbies.

Buying our admission tickets and leaving our purchases till we depart, we take the new entrance across a painted bridge and are immediately pulled this way and that. A couple celebrating their golden wedding, delighted to have been given a plant by the garden to mark their special day, turn right, while we walk straight ahead to the Mediterranean Garden, backtracking to go along the Long Walk, only to be sidetracked down Lighthouse Way where a couple of young women gardeners are smiling happily as they weed a border in the sunshine.

'I love it,' says one of them. 'There's nowhere better in the world.' The other adds: 'You could say there's a problem in that we never get really on top of it: there are always challenges, but it's great. You never know what you'll be doing next day – and just look at it.' She stands up and points in a wide arc.

To which the first responds: 'Every day's different, but so are the hundreds of trees and plants. The only thing that's the same is that we're protected from the wind. And it's mild. If it drops to less than 10°C it's a crisis.'

'Mind you allow yourselves plenty of time,' says the second as we walk further down Lighthouse Way to see David Wayne's bronze of Tresco Children, the present owner's oldest two kids holding up the third. Time passes quickly. Even in March, there is much to see, camellias larger and happier than you'll find on the mainland, especially standing out, though things are in flower from many parts of the world, especially the Southern Hemisphere. One of the guide books we have bought, *Tresco Abbey Garden: A Personal and Pictorial History,* by Mike Nelhams, the garden's curator, needs six columns to list a 'sample' of plants in flower on New Year's Day and assures us: 'From the rainforests of New Zealand, the cliffs of Madeira, to the Cape of South Africa and the coast of California, the extraordinary growing conditions experienced by our plants in such a small area are to be found nowhere else in Britain, if not the world.'

Taking in the Palm Circle and Pebble Garden, we drift through an archway into a secluded area containing the ruins of the old Abbey and reflect on what life must have been like for the monks. For most of its life, the Abbey came under Tavistock's Benedictine Abbey. There were very few monks, apparently, but they controlled ecclesiastical government on the northern islands and may well have collected tolls from visiting ships, while St Mary's and St Agnes were under secular rule. Possibly the monks gave up because of piracy. We'll never know. 'But what a place to live,' says the husband of the golden wedding pair. To which Sheila responds: 'and what a place to celebrate a golden wedding.'

Up on the Middle Terrace, we spend a few peaceful minutes in the Summer House overlooking a pond and then ascend the rest of the steps to Father Neptune (a figurehead of a steamship wrecked in Scilly in 1841) who has long presided over much of the garden. Everywhere there is history, even Roman remains, and a Limpet Midden – should you be dull enough to tire of the panorama of exotic trees and plants.

There are many giant trees, and we feel so protected that it comes as something of a surprise to catch a glimpse of the sea. There is a marvellous range of interests at different heights. At our feet rare small plants thrive, many overlapping the edging onto the path. Plants flowering at the next level up include proteas, and one up again camellias, then tall bushes and so on high up into the sky.

The two great disasters that struck the gardens were in relatively recent times when happily there were the resources to restore order; it would have been much harder in the 1950s and 1960s. In 1987 there was a double whammy. A freak blizzard is especially remembered for the resounding cracks of branches breaking under the weight of wet snow, and the following frost of record intensity that killed many species. Then in 1990 the Scillies were swept by a rare hurricane. Sooner or later most gardens suffer from an extreme weather aberration so rare that it doesn't change the long-term plan; the winter now ending has been like most, lows hovering safely above 10°C and the shelter belt very effective. Though there are few visitors today – once more we pass the golden wedding couple, now pointing out a pair of parrot-like birds to another couple – in summer many day trippers come by helicopter and ship, and virtually everyone staying on the islands crowds in. What they spend keeps this 'Paradise Island' afloat.

That Buggie Again

We pop into the Shell House (the walls thickly covered with shells) and saunter down the Mediterranean Garden and the Eucalyptus Field with a sneak look into the vegetable plot before picking up our purchases and returning to the buggie.

Next stop is the store, issuing its own plastic bags, Tesco but with an R, with a rich range of foodstuffs and drinks that must make self-catering in a cottage a delight, though now customers are mainly residents buying everyday groceries. The depth of stock is justified by the store supplying the Island Hotel and New Inn (and Bryher's Hell Bay). If you own everything on the island you can make things work like that. Then we go to the New Inn. Having followed my advice to leave the buggie on the road, Sheila is told to repark. 'You'll cause a traffic hold up,' which was true as tractors with trailers arrived simultaneously in both directions. The restaurant here has a good reputation but, with slow service and extremely chunky sandwiches, we'll not come back for a bar lunch.

'Let's go to the gallery, not that I want to buy anything,' says Sheila. Surprise, though she'll blame me, we emerge with a memorable wall hanging, a cluster of shells suggesting an island in a dark blue wavy sea with discreet rows of buttons and mini-stones alternately seen as crests of waves or birds.

At the hotel's reception we naughtily ask if anyone has booked the buggie for tomorrow; normally it is rented by different people each day. 'Oh, I'm sure that will be all right.'

'Do you want to drive?' asks Sheila grudgingly. Now she backs out gently and changes gear unnoticed. We're heading back to the gardens, mainly to look at Valhalla, a large collection of ship figureheads salvaged from wrecks. The accounts of some of the wrecks are riveting while the figureheads are real works of art. Maybe canal art had its roots in ships' figureheads? Just time to walk round the Palm Circle again before returning under the over-sized tree ferns to the entrance bridge, this time to visit the exhibition centre. Here is one of the best displays of maps and interesting information I've yet seen. Noting what grows in the world's different climate zones is fascinating.

Tresco's Present 'Emperor'

One of the things the *Telegraph* attacks in the article on the island hotels was the fact that Tresco is privately owned and therefore commercially exploited. The present 'ruler' residing at the Abbey is Robert Dorrien-Smith. We start a conversation by my describing how, on a mid-summer Sunday in 1952, I was shown round the garden, deep red flowers punctuating the greenery, by his grandfather, Arthur Dorrien-Smith. A plantsman who knew every individual tree and plant, its origins and habits and exactly how it had performed for him, he held me spellbound for the first hour or so and then captive for the rest of the morning as he urged me to make more notes.

'But how long can it go on?' he asked, distressed by having to reduce the number of gardeners from twelve to six. He pointed out where maintenance had been scrimped. 'It hurts my eyes', an example of which were agapanthus, growing as weeds out of place.

They were the days when country houses and estates everywhere were under intense pressure. A thousand notable country houses were lost in the awful post-war years when farmers ripped out thousands of miles of hedgerows, wild life conservation was hardly discussed, and architects produced box-shaped monstrosities in concrete.

The Dorrien-Smiths have done what other families in their circumstances have learnt to do: live on tourism. Today's Robert Dorrien-Smith may be commercial, but his approach works. By any standard Tresco is a highly successful, one-off.

'I was only four when my grandfather died and, apart from the fact I'm a very different person, the challenges have changed totally. I'm not an expert plantsman, but love the natural shapes and textures. I suppose in a sense the two great disasters that struck the gardens were a good thing, since we had to do a huge amount of reconstruction which gave us the chance to give new purpose. Of course many of the individual trees are wonderful, but we've tried to make sense of it as a whole. We've added, too, the Mediterranean Garden, my wife's Shell House, the new entrance and so on, while respecting the past with many things the same as when you first came half a century ago.

Though it was an increasing struggle, until the early 1940s many of the great houses and gardens were kept going by city and other money poured into them from a distance. After the war that quickly became impossible. It cost a million pounds to rebuild the gardens after the two calamities, and we had to find it ourselves from our island-based activities. Restoration on that scale just couldn't have happened earlier.

Yes it's down to tourism, but we have to have a touch of realism. Early flowers and potatoes have long ceased to be economic and we only keep bullocks to mow the fields which are an important landscape feature. Yes, we sell daffodils by mail order, but it's marginal business. We can't avoid relying on tourism, but of course Tresco doesn't appeal to everyone and it is expensive to get here. Happily the great gardens are a unique draw, and it has been very satisfying adding a touch of personal colour to them. So what we attract is a keen slice of middle England.

It is a great privilege to live and bring up children in such an exotic place. But it isn't a sinecure. I've had to learn to tackle about two hundred different jobs.'

Even the Tresco boss spends much time in management meetings. The estate's jobs support a population of around two hundred. Everywhere we find enthusiastic staff, and friends with timeshares on the island highly rate the general ambience and facilities. You won't find swinging youth here – a cottage for two can cost £1,000 in high summer, and that's after you've got here – but leading a quiet island life are several of yesteryear's famous stars.

Then our third lunch on Tresco before being taken to New Grimsby for our special boat. Had we not splashed out on a special at £28, we would have had to take the day's only out-of-season service boat in early morning.

The *Cyclone* is a splendid vessel, this afternoon coxed by Mrs Stentiford's son James. We are in sheltered accommodation that certainly didn't exist earlier – and the speed is much faster. Helped by James's views on changing Scilly – 'everyone seems to need to be on a different island all the time' – in what seems only a few minutes we are walking up the steps at Hugh Town's harbour.

· V ·

QUIET WEEKEND ON ST MARY'S

Arrival Hugh Town

Hugh Town's harbour is quieter than I have ever seen it. The only vehicle with a driver on the quay is that of Tregarthen's Hotel car.

Having done the rounds of other hotels on St Mary's, I have not been at Tregarthen's since my first visit in the early 1950s, but remember the detail of the view and especially the steps to the road down which I walked to the airport mini bus for my first-ever frightening flight on the edge of a thunder storm. That was when a Twin Otter took a handful of people (who had to step on scales to be weighed) to Land's End. After the luxury on Bryher and Tresco, the hotel itself feels dated though, as one has come to expect on the islands, the food is good.

'Yes, we're very lucky in what we have here,' says Richard Larne who comes for dinner with his wife Bridget. A former prolific author, we last met them (as described in *Journey*) at Charlestown near St Austell when they were preparing 'to raise the drawbridge' because of declining mainland standards. We'll see them again tomorrow.

Anglican v Methodism

In the morning, on the edge of Hugh Town, we find ourselves mid-way between the Anglican Church and the Methodist chapel. I presume that Sheila, a Reader, would prefer the Anglican while she thinks that – as we are in Cornwall – I'd like to return to my Methodist roots. While we are persuasively trying to please each other, time runs out. Sheila makes a final effort and we find ourselves in a small traditional chapel.

Cornish Methodists [see *Journey*] were always warm, but this is exceptional. After a snappy to-the-point traditional service taken at short notice (because the advertised preacher was ill) by the primary school teacher from Tresco who has to take another service on a different island, we're more or less led by the hand to coffee by Mary Ratcliffe. She introduces us to others who want to know how long we'll be on the island, where we're staying and of course where we come from.

Having disappeared for a moment, she returns lightfootedly, and presents us with a book she rapidly autographs. *The Isles of Scilly and Beyond* is an inspirational pot-pourri of colour photographs of the islands' natural beauty from the majesty of the ocean surrounding us to the tiny flowers that grow in the heathland. Decorative line drawings, factual and faith-led captions with a Biblical quotation enliven each double-page spread. It delightfully celebrates our presence in this wonderful natural setting. How, did she come to do it?

'With difficulty. It was a steep learning curve. I couldn't find anyone to help. We were living in Chatteris in Cambridgeshire for many years but found great comfort and inspiration on regular holidays to the Scillies. That's when the idea behind the book was born, but nothing happened until we came to live here.

There are no Christian books on sale on the islands and, knowing we wouldn't find a commercial publisher, my husband decided we'd publish it privately. Then we met a mainland printer (from Hayle) holidaying here and we worked closely with him. We printed 2000 copies at £1.50 each, decided to charge £6.50 and so far have sold 800, so we aren't too badly out of pocket. But our bedroom is still uncomfortably full of boxes of books.'

Ironically in view of the earlier discussions as to where we should worship this morning, she says she is an Anglican but it 'hadn't worked out' on St Mary's, to which they moved in 1998. 'When we first came, my husband made picnics for Christian walks. We came for the support of a small community such as St Mary's gives us, and are here to help others. It's a wonderful place, though housing has become too expensive for locals starting out in life, and we under-estimated how costly it would be getting to the mainland.'

That leads to comments about the difficulty in attracting key staff, the TV series A Country Parish, recently highlighting the protracted progress of finding a head for the islands' unique five in one school. And at the time of writing there is a crisis as the island's only vet is moving to the mainland [now resolved with a German lady].

We love the book and when we return home order several for gifts to friends. And Mary has become a Friend of my Charitable Trust, and been profiled in its newsletter *Aspire*. 'I only wish that several years ago I had realised that independent advice is available for self-publishers,' she says. Not that she seems to have done badly without it.

Talking of Methodism, John Wesley, making a single rough crossing and describing Scilly as 'a barren dreary place' failed to make the impact here that he did in West Cornwall. But in the early 19th century Methodism was strong; by 1832 even the breakaway Bible Christians had chapels on three islands each with resident ministers claiming rafts of new converts following the initial success of a young woman missionary sent in answer to pleas to help the off-islands in their distress. As an example, on St Martins, a William Gibson, 'gave up the contraband trade' to become 'a burning and shining light'. In 1860 a traveller from France commented how the religious movement was 'dominated by dissenting sects' though he admitted 'the Ranters have lately produced a real reformation in morals'. Between them the two chapels of the two Methodist sects had a total of twenty more seats than the 1,274 Anglican ones in five churches on the islands. The Baptists followed, but fell out with Augustus Smith who had all their chapels closed, though the Baptists especially suited Bryher people and they lingered on here and in 1874 even built a new chapel which lasted nearly a century before its congregation finally died out.

What emotions, arguments and quarrels must be represented by those few sentences. Incidentally, until the 1934 union was accepted in Scilly, our Methodist chapel was the Bible Christian one – and still looks and feels like it. For many years it was the wont of both Weslyan and Bible Christian Methodists to attend their own services and then go to the Anglican Church, the only one allowed to hold a service at its chosen time. What is clear is that religion and education worked hand-in-hand to transform life in the islands.

Walking back to our hotel for lunch, two things strike me: how much traffic has increased since my last visit (then there was only a single taxi on St Mary's: now there are five), and how few visitors there are. Tregarthen's Hotel is only busy because it has a coach party, though the coach – as with all visitors' vehicles – has to be left on the mainland.

Changing St Mary's

After lunch, Richard and Bridget Larne collect us for a run-round the island. This reveals big changes. There is much more housing – well over 2,000 now live in the Scillies, with most of the increase on St Mary's – while agriculture has declined sharply. Only wild plants now grow in most of the small daffodil fields that generations ago were so painstakingly cleared of boulders and given protective hedges. And under some daft European rule or other, the owners of some of the few fields still with daffodils are paid not to pick them.

'In fact you could say the whole of rural St Mary's is a mess,' says Richard. 'I'm surprised the Duchy doesn't take a tougher line. Just look at that,' as we pause by a farm entrance which is positively slum-like, altogether below the standard set by the off-islands which are no longer the poor relation.

As said earlier, the Duchy of Cornwall owns all the islands apart from Tresco and much of the capital, Hugh Town. Now, even in the latter they seem busy buying up freeholds and renting holiday cottages at much higher than mainland rates. Not that the countryside can produce an encouraging economic return. As with so much of Britain, during my lifetime the Scillies have become almost totally dependent on tourism; and, as elsewhere in 'Theme Park Britain', there is undoubtedly much more for visitors to do.

'But the hotels have it too good to bother to open in March, which used to be a busy month,' says Richard. 'Though in fairness, we're packed out during the summer, and of course mainland resorts relying on short breaks have totally different economies. It costs so much, and takes so long, to get here that few people think it worthwhile just for a few days. It must be the same for most remote islands.'

Though we enjoy occasional tantalising glimpses of sea and cliff, most of the tarmac between high hedges keeps well inland.

While I have much enjoyed walking through the lanes in the past, it is only when you are well off the tarmac – and in wet weather better prepared for mud than I have been on business trips – that you reach the coast. The cliffs are stunning in places. When it has not been squelchy, I have been especially thrilled overlooking Tolls Island and following the ups and downs of the coastal path. Impressive rock formations are crashed into by the ceaseless waves round to Porth Hellick, a deep bay we pass close by as the airport comes into view.

It is only when we have passed the airport, closed on Sundays, (so there are no newspapers), that we run briefly beside the sea along crescent-shaped Old Town Bay. Hundreds of years have passed since this was the capital. Little habitation remains. When the Scillies were a popular haunt of pirates, Hugh Town on the opposite coast enjoyed the safety of being under the Star Castle. Generations of Hugh Town people still walked to church here, however, for it was only after Augustus Smith took his lease of the islands that Hugh Town's church was built – a condition imposed by the Duchy.

We pause to take a glance inside Old Town Church, only part (and that part-restored) of the original whose beginnings date back to the 13th century. Though unlocked, it is dank and dark, but still comes to life for occasional services. It is possibly the ultimate in peaceful church settings. Burials still take place here. Stupid thought maybe, but one feels the spirits of former residents must rest more serenely than in a mainland crematorium.

Then we are quickly back to the approaches to Hugh Town and park in the drive of the Larne's elevated bungalow commanding a sweeping, ever companionable panorama of land and sea.

Shipwrecking and Other Industries

Only the books, especially those of local and shipping interest, draw my eyes away from the window. I look at the new editions of titles, such as *The Shipwrecks of the Isles of Scilly,* that have been published elsewhere since I sold David & Charles, though I continued working with Richard for some years thereafter. His detailed tales of shipwrecks involving every human emotion commanded a wide readership and helped develop interest in local diving, now a thriving business.

Over tea and cake, we discuss how ships seeking shelter were wrecked all over the islands, especially on outlying rocks and reefs. And how pirates and rogue pilots deliberately escorted them in so that they might be smashed to pieces and their cargoes plundered.

Daniel Defoe wrote of 'the sands covered in people, they are charged with strange bloody and cruel dealings, even sometimes with one another, but especially with poor distressed seamen who seek for help for their lives and find the rocks themselves not more cruel and merciless than the people who range about them for their prey'. Yet, we reflect, later piloting developed into a legitimate and much-needed business.

What changes have these islands not seen? Shipbuilding on Hugh Town beach was once a major and colourful employment, though much of the wood had to be imported (the rest coming from wrecks). The introduction of iron ships put paid to that. But then, consulting Crispin Gill's *The Isles of Scilly,* I remind Richard that dairy farming was once so good that the Scillies were the first area of Britain to be free from brucellosis. That was in 1963 when all the islands' fifty nine herds (560 cattle) were clean and yielded a fat content well above mainland standards.

Bridget cuts in: 'Self dependency isn't the flavour of the day. I don't suppose many small islands elsewhere are even allowed to produce their own milk now. We're dependent on transport, but there's more in freezers here than you will find on the mainland.'

Yes, there is still a little fishing, but 'nothing like it used to be'. And you can still buy early daffodils by mail order. A cutting from *The Western Morning News* of 1954 reminds us that the isles were then 'still the capital of the daffodil kingdom of Britain'. A former colleague continued: 'Despite the best efforts of growers on the mainland and continent, nowhere can daffodils be grown that will equal those produced in the isles.' He went on to explain how the Scillonians had beaten the competition in earliness, quality, range of traditional and new varieties – and in quick transport and pioneering non-returnable boxes.

In those days the *Scillonian* ran year round, a relief ship being provided for her annual overhaul. Huge quantities of flowers, and at one time early potatoes, were transferred from ship to train at Penzance for the dash to catch the next morning's sale at Covent Garden. Now, as mentioned in the last chapter, the *Scillonian* is laid up for a long winter break. A combination of labour, picking and packing and transport costs killed the business. First to be hurt were the off-island growers, since the cost of transport even to Hugh Town before transfer to the *Scillonian* became formidable. But we have noted the details of mail-order suppliers and will undoubtedly relive our Scilly memories with their spring welcome in years to come. As in so many industries, profitable niche businesses survive when the bulk has failed. Flower sales to departing visitors at the airport is another profitable sideline.

Talking of transport, Richard asks if we have heard the news: there's talk of the government funding not merely a new *Scillonian* but a brand new wider quay, and a new quay with waiting facilities at each of the off-islands. 'The ship will operate every day of the year except Christmas and will carry both passengers and freight. The idea is that the Isles of Scilly Steamship Company will operate but not own her.'

Financing a new ship with the latest navigation aids would be beyond what the islands could now afford, not that the Steamship Company seem to have done all the right things. More expensive air travel has certainly discouraged out-of-season short breaks, and running a separate cargo vessel adds an extra layer of overheads. But then, at the end of this trip we would have liked to fly back to Bristol, and have just realised that we could have done so if only had we known that the conventional Sky Bus service – also run by the Steamship Company – has just restarted for the season. No air as opposed to helicopter services to the islands are shown in the *OAG Executive Flight Guide.*

When I wrote to her, the *OAG* editor said they had been specifically asked *not* to include details. The Steamship Company's chief executive, J Marsden, replied that that was nonsense. But the stalemate continued, no detail of any of their flights appearing during the rest of the year and beyond. How much business was lost? It reminded me of an earlier statement by Richard: 'What can you expect from a Board of farmers and other small business people with no real knowledge of transport?'

Richard adds: 'Well life is not perfect anywhere and islands have their inevitable limitations and frustrations. But [pointing out of the window] give me this anytime. If we're too laid back, it's better than the alternative. For a start, crime is minimal and, though we may feel cut off, we're right beside our excellent cottage hospital and in emergency the mainland rescue helicopter can land even in fog.'

Bridget adds: 'Well, you've done much the same thing as us, escaping to the Highlands.' Yes and no, a negative being that our High Street is not the safest place to be on a weekend evening.

So, knowing what travel we have in store for the rest of this book and privately wondering whether we'll live long enough to return to the Scillies, we say farewell to Bridget as Richard returns us to our hotel. However, that is via the Duchy office, in many ways the effective point of government, and then the pier, 'horribly congested at peak times'. The Steamship Company's J Marsden earlier agreed with me that the pier had been inadequate for many years, 'especially when it's congested with vehicles and people milling around in inclement weather with boats from the off-islands feeding into the *Scillonian*. Our difficulty is that the season's shorter and the cost of doing anything has greatly increased.'

Mumford

Next morning the centre of Hugh Town lacks one thing: people. There are cars parked, and a few on the move. There is even a bus, presumably going to the airport, mysteriously labelled Rail Replacement Service. But the pavements are empty. What must it be like in the real depths of winter, we wonder. A thin time for the shops, certainly.

Though it is hours too soon to buy today's papers, we go to the paper shop, Mumfords, who also carry a decent range of books and stationery. I knew the present owner when we worked together as journalists on *The Western Morning News*. After a successful career on various papers, he has returned to run the family business... typical of what happens to island businesses everywhere. Few Scillonians now spend their entire life stuck out in the Atlantic. 'Yes, the winter is challenging,' he says. 'We batten down. It's no use doing anything else; it's a long period without any real visitor numbers – longer than it used to be.'

When the Scillies were on my patch, Clive's father was chairman of the Council; what he said tended to be law. Clive was on the Council for a time, but it didn't suit his temperament. Then many things change through the generations. When Clive was just one, his grandfather was drowned – an all-too-common Scilly happening – and his father had a natural fear of him going to sea. 'But my three daughters row in the Scillies' famous gigs.'

Talking of the challenges facing Scilly, I say I'm amazed to hear that the Duchy of Cornwall are charging up to £1,500 for a week's summer let for property it has bought in Hugh Town. 'We're a contradictory place in so many ways,' says Clive. 'Many bird lovers, most of whom aren't wealthy, love it here but can't afford to come, but there are plenty who can afford it... but then housing has become impossible for local people, and it's getting ever harder to attract key workers. But mainlanders who have recently sold their houses for prices they couldn't have dreamed of a few years ago and want to scale-down anyway can take our prices in their stride.

It's full of contradictions. We're lovely islands and everyone wants to protect them in their natural state, yet no two people agree where to draw the line. It would certainly be all too easy for us to become over-developed, which is why I voted against extending the airport runway for larger planes, not that they have materialised.'

I spot a copy of the latest edition of *The Scillonian,* a twice-yearly publication packed with a mixture of factual reports, opinions and even creative writing – the kind of thing which reflects the various levels of island life we have met in some of the smaller Scottish islands such as Coll. How about this from the 'Bits and Pieces' feature:

> **The Chinese 'flyaway' and the lifeboat shout...**
> Fire and a lifeboat 'shout' united to scupper a Chinese Birthday meal occasion over a February weekend. The delivery of the food – ordered to come from the mainland by helicopter – was delayed when a fire SOS diverted the airport fireman who was to bring it to the mechanic of the lifeboat '*The Whiteheads*', Nathan Woodcock. It was his partner's birthday. By the time the 'Chinese' had materialised Nathan was himself at sea answering a lifeboat call... all night. Net result? A fire extinguished, a fouled trawler's prop cleared – and a very hungry mechanic...

The Scillonian, published by Mumfords, sells to many mainland and especially North American lovers of the islands, including those with family connections. Then I see Sam Llewellyn's *Hell Bay: The Classic Novel of the Isles of Scilly* which, being a sucker for regional fiction, I buy without examination.

It might not be in the top line but achieves a steady sale of 3,000 copies a year. The author is a descendant of Augustus ('Emperor') Smith, and so related to today's Robert. 'Once London had finished with it,' the Tresco Estate took over as publisher.

It is a compelling story, starting in 1829 when 'there was starvation, overcrowding and villainy' and the hero, Nicholas Power, the real name of the writer of the manuscript called *New Botallack 1835* which was discovered in the burnt-out shell of an Irish castle. It was in that year that both the hero and Augustus Smith set foot on the Scillies, the first shipwrecked, the latter planning to carve out a personal kingdom.

In this passage Nicholas Power tells of a meeting with a friend near Tresco Castle, then being built:

> David and I chatted about times past, he with a confiding air,as one recalcitrant father to another. Then he took it upon himself to show me round the house, assuming for the purpose the character and speech of Augustus Smith, Esquire, of Berkhamstead. If David was anything to go by, Smith had the manners of a Nero combined with the language of a Satanist bargee.
>
> He conducted me first through the servants' quarters and kitchens, and hence to a hall and a long drawing room with the sills of Gothic windows looking out over a terrace. The windows looked due south, across Great Rocks to St Mary's, and the distant grey houses of Hugh Town. 'And here,' said David, his face growing long and pompous under the black mop, 'Here I shall sit and count my rents and watch my subjects work like niggers in my fields for my benefit. And I will watch bloody great ships come in and unload carriages and 'orses full of lords and ladies, and I will feed them my potatoes and we will all get wet as shags in a thunderstorm, inside and out. On this 'ere table I will cheat their britches off at cards, when my carpenters 'ave made me the table. There will also be dancing girls brought over from Injer, expense irregardless. And after tea we will promenade in the gardins, as you see below.' He indicated the terraces of shattered granite running away to the left. 'In 'ere, you will find my bedroom –'

Though Nicholas has a child by Mary, 'enchantress and friend of wild things,' she won't marry him and also gives birth to Smith's child who we see her feeding at her breast after she's waved her previous lover farewell as his ship taking him away from Scilly for ever, passes Cromwell's Castle and Gimble Point.

The Isles of Scilly Steamship Company

Incidentally, I recently found an article by Clive Mumford extensively quoting a pioneer issue of *The Scillonian* reporting the building and the first nightmare journey from Scotland of the first ship of the same name. Mind you, in Scilly it's always been fondly 'the ship', rather than *Scillonian*. Realising that the economy, and especially tourism and early daffodil growing, could not safely thrive unless the islands controlled their own destiny, money was raised by many means including a house-to-house collection. 'The ship' was born of necessity.

Built in Troon, a slender low-built affair with tall chimney and with engines of 700 horse power, it set out down the Irish coast for St Mary's in January 1926. Repeatedly running out of lubricating oil and fresh water, calls had to be made at Belfast and Kingston (port for Dublin) and – also because of dangerous seas – again at Rosslare. She was however triumphantly welcomed in Scilly. Successive replacements, loved or simply put up with, have necessarily drawn little water since the approach to St Mary's is shallow. In fact one *Scillonian* managed to fix itself on rocks in a receding tide and was only floated with difficulty after passengers and cargo had been taken off. New ships are now too expensive for private companies everywhere.

But, whatever its failing, it would not be right to end without a positive note on what the Steamship Company has achieved. It came into being 'to serve the islands' and, in addition to providing basic transport for generations, has rendered much social service including rushing ill people to Penzance before the islands were served by air, carrying such essentials as the heavy equipment for the first power stations at cut rates, and encouraging cruise liners at anchor to allow their hundreds of international passengers to sample the islands for a day. This and much more is recorded in *Bridge over Lyonesse: over 70 years of the Isles of Scilly Steamship Company* published by the company. I especially enjoyed the photograph of Vic Trenwith blowing his bugle as *Scillonian II* left the islands on its last-ever voyage back to the mainland. The caption adds: 'On foggy days during the years of *Scillonian I* he would stand on Peninnis Head and "blow" so the skipper could pinpoint his position.'

The Last Hours

From Mumfords we walk up the quiet main street, conscious that we only have a few hours left on Scilly. It has to be said that, apart from the Post Office arch leading to Gibsons (generations of Scilly photographers whose famous wreck scenes appear in many books used to be based here), the main street is not grand and lacks characterful buildings though it does fit nicely together as a whole. Most of the shops certainly aren't anything to write home about. Yet that there should be a shopping centre at all is perhaps a miracle; and I reflect that, inside, some of the homes provide stylish refuge from storms, many with pieces of mahogany and other fine woods salvaged from wrecks. You cannot go far on the islands without wrecks coming into your thoughts. What I do like about the street is the way other roads and their traffic funnel in at acute angles. Even in winter, there's appreciable traffic – and there's that 'Rail Replacement' bus again – taxis particularly being noticeable though pedestrians remain elusive.

Then we climb up to Star Castle, displaying the date 1593 over its doorway. The Scillies had been planned as a rendezvous by the Spanish Armada in 1588, a few ships indeed reaching the islands. That, plus the fact that Spain was creating a naval base in Brittany, put the islands in the front line and warranted investment in defence. Another warning came in 1594 when villages round Mount's Bay were raided by marauders from four Spanish galleys. Thereafter, pirates were by far the biggest risk. The Star Castle has been involved in so much British history. In 1646, for example, Prince Charles, the future Charles II, took refuge here for six weeks.

Externally little has changed. The eight-pointed Star Castle still commands the best view on the island: it is not surprising that Old Town people steadily moved to Hugh Town for its protection. It is still occasionally referred to as The Garrison, though more specifically that means the Castle.

I could feast endlessly on the view across St Mary's Pool to Bryher, Tresco and to St Martin's with its generous ration of cultivatable land, and of course the treacherous outlying rocks. Nor should Samson, be forgotten: the island in the foreground to the west with its twin hills. Though long uninhabited (once there was a population of fifty), it remains a popular landing place for day trippers who can play Robinson Crusoe and explore the remains of old buildings. I recall that poverty was as harsh here as anywhere, the land failing to provide sufficient sustenance for the resident families. Even this little island is full of history... and secrets. Was it named after St Samson, the Celtic saint? Remains of an ancient chapel were once rumoured to have been found; more certain is the fact that the Romans occupied it, but perhaps not securely, for a hoard of coins discovered was proved to have been buried around AD400.

'A great spot,' says Sheila. 'I wouldn't want to live here and in the past it must have been grim. But it's never dull.' We watch the waves breaking fiercely on the furthest rocks, and the smooth progress of half a dozen small craft plying between islands. The early morning mist has lifted, so hopefully our afternoon helicopter will run to time. 'If it's difficult to get to the Scillies, what's it going to be like reaching some of the other islands you plan to include in the book?' she asks. But I'm too relaxed to worry. Scilly is good for making me live for the moment, breathing in the fresh air and the view... and recalling that on a quiet evening I once heard the distant melody of a ship's orchestra. For those living on the islands it was a regular occurrence in the days when everyone crossed the Atlantic by ship. Several times I have welcomed the first glimpse of Britain in the form of what from a distance seems more like a group of rocks than inhabited islands.

We go through the thick tunnel wall into what has long been a fine hotel where, yes, they'd be pleased to serve lunch. But wanting to make the most of our last hours, I suggest we first walk back to Hugh Town where we tread just above the last tide's high water-mark line of seaweed as the water again creeps up the beach. It was here that many a wooden vessel, some excellent craft, took shape with fine workmanship in the St Mary's shipbuilding days.

Looking at shells, talking to a cat loafing around more to keep itself busy than in the hope of finding a meal, time passes quickly, and we opt to have lunch at the Atlantic Hotel, whose dining room projects out over the sea at full tide.

It was just at this time years ago that I found the hotel was full of bird watchers and walkers and land-based Russians using walkie talkies to control their fishing fleet just off shore and organise the sale of catches picked up by a fast relief vessel. Today there are only a few regular drinkers in the bar; we dine alone, but again the food is good.

Then briefly back to Tregarthen's, once more soaking in the view I so vividly recall from the early 1950s, and down the steps to our taxi for the airport. It is surprisingly animated here, with people checking in, buying tickets – ouch, the price hurts – taking refreshments and purchasing daffodils. We add a bunch to our minimal hand luggage.

Journeys back to the mainland always seem speedier and (remembering to have our outward-bound delay made official for insurance purposes) once again we are in a Penzance taxi, though this time only to a nearby hotel overlooking the town and bay.

We are greeted not by the receptionist but by Thomas the cat, a Birman, whose chattiness, and especially his way of expressing disappointment when we ceased stroking or talking to him, I have noted in *For the Love of a Cat: A Publisher's Story*. Whenever we appear Thomas is waiting to greet us; later, at a gracious dinner, we hide him under our table, but it really is communication rather than food he wants. He protests when a snatch of his conversation is overheard by a waiter who grabs him – a timeless scene. That and the prospect of a leisurely train journey tomorrow helps us readjust to the mainland. I've always found it so much easier to slip into island pace than snap out of it, though with such a host of visual memories firmly recorded in my mind, perhaps I'll never come all the way back.

· VI ·

EPISODES – 1

Belstone

Among Britain's many moorland villages, none grows more naturally out of the landscape, or commands a finer sweeping view of it, than Belstone on the northern periphery of Dartmoor. Over the decades, after being in a crawling procession behind an over-taxed lorry bringing misery to Sticklepath's climbing and wandering main street and later, taking a diversion off the fast dual carriageway A30, I've stood on the edge of this village on the edge of the moor stretching my limbs, taking deep breaths of fresh air and gazing in wonderment at the panorama.

This morning, with the pub and café behind me, first I take in the River Taw in the hollow below on the first stage of its long journey to meet the sea off the North Devon coast, after its estuary merges with that of the Torridge – and then examine the panorama of the rising moor. Immediately beyond my vision is possibly the loneliest land in all southern England though, despite long campaigns to get rid of the nuisance, it is still spoilt by it being a Danger Area with live firing. But this lovely Sunday morning I can forget that. I feel close to the God of love, the source of all being, and dare I say it closer than I did in church last Sunday. This is life to be lived abundantly... or, to come down to earth, it would be if the café wasn't closed. This is our first stopping point from Bath. But then, if not for religious reasons, I welcome Sundays being different, and hope the café owners aren't so blasé about their surroundings that they fail to be refreshed by them on their day of rest. A pity our tummies cry for attention.

Sheila also delights in Belstone's position. 'Can't think why I've never been here before,' which is a clue to it's magic. (Charm would be a wrong word since it's grand rather than delicately gracious.) Though some awful new housing was built when Belstone was 'discovered' at the beginning of the 20th century, the village is seldom busy. Its admirers may see themselves as an elite group, not 'doing' the sights so much as communing with the moor, looking at it, walking across it and exploring its remains of bygone cultures we don't yet fully comprehend. The Nine Maidens stone circle, the surviving outer wall of a Bronze Age burial chamber, isn't far away, and there are other stone circles and crosses. There is some evidence, too, that the Romans were here.

Fifty to sixty people were in the embryo village at the time of Domesday. Later generations benefited from the order given by Venville rights including grazing which produced the wool for the fine woollen cloth, whose weavers over the years probably gave most of the money for the granite parish church of St Mary. Alas, this was ruinously 'modernised' in the 19th century. In other words, despite its unique physical situation, Belstone's history is typical of that of many West Country parishes. Cromwell and his men marched through here, and several Belstone men left to be among the earliest colonisers of New England. Later, there were short-lived tin and then copper mining booms.

'A stage that has seen great action,' I say to Sheila. 'And nothing living in sight,' she responds. At which moment there's a faint meow. A tabby cat with white undercarriage is in the doorway of a deserted (or is it just heavily locked-up?) building and has decided he'd like some company. He accompanies us on a short circular walk, running ahead, waiting for a stroke, and rolling, exposing his tummy. Like all cats, his ears twitch as he enjoys hearing sweet nothings. He purrs contentedly. He may not have a human soul, but surely he's part of God's creation, though I'm not going to blaspheme by saying he's been provided for my pleasure, much though he and his antics enthuse and further relax me.

Consuming some of our lunch sandwiches too early, with pussie's encouragement we walk around the block again, and take a final study of the great view. What is so obviously different here is that the main street is one-sided, looking down to Belstone Cleave, and beyond up to Belstone Tor and Cawsand Beacon, the latter at 1,799ft, high by Dartmoor standards.

Two final thoughts. The 1851 census showed that over half the 200 inhabitants were born in the parish, but by 1901 that had dropped to 38 per cent with 17 per cent born outside Devon. Now probably only one in ten people were born here, and the time will come when non-Devonians dominate as they do already in many honey-pot spots.

Second (and non-railway enthusiasts skip), one of my reasons for coming in earlier years was that a gentleman author, M D Greville, retired here and loved to be visited. In an ugly guest house where however he was thoroughly looked after, he spent his last decades steadily researching railway opening and closing dates for chronologies. He was on the wrong side of a bitter argument that continued for months; I received copies of the correspondence by the protagonists on both sides. Did a station close on the last day trains called at it, or the first day that they would have done had it not been closed? Eventually the British Railways 'closed from', usually a Monday, though the last trains called on the Saturday, was accepted, but bless him, Greville said this would cause confusion. 'Sunday isn't a *dies non*; people are born and die on it,' he pleaded. Even if you lose, fighting a cause gives purpose to many people's last years, though wisely he forgot all about railways when drawing inspiration from his daily walk on the moor.

Dungeness

The place which nature has most changed during my lifetime is undoubtedly Dungeness, between Hythe and Hastings. On my first pre-war visit, I recall Mum pointing out that, because the sea had washed up so much extra shingle, the lighthouse had become too far inland to guide the shipping passing close by. So a new one had been built closer to the sea. Now itself well inland, that it is the 'Old Lighthouse', a tourist attraction offering a bird's eye view of one of the world's largest areas of shingle, certainly Britain's greatest, and still growing. Since the first in 1615, there have indeed been five successive lighthouses.

Shingle has always been my least favourite landform. In *Journey*, I said that Suffolk's Shingle Street, where the sea constantly changes the estuary's entrance, has a hostile environment and, in stormy times, seems dangerous for those living near the edge. I also described how my boyhood fear of the sea was fostered by having to spend part of most days on our summer holidays sitting on the steeply-shelving shingle bank feet away from the waves crashing onto Hythe's beach. Mum was a Hythe girl. While generally I love the sound of the sea, the grating noise of the shingle retreating with each wave's undertow really jars.

Shingle is unstable. The sea makes light work of picking it up, robbing it here, dangerously exposing salt marshes, and dropping it there – changing rivers and blocking ports on a section of the Kent coast just as it has done along East Anglia's.

We made two pre-war visits to Dungeness, since when I've been back every decade or so. Each time the journey itself has been the main attraction: along the length of the miniature (fifteen-inch) Romney, Hythe & Dymchurch Railway, usually sitting tightly-packed with the driver on the footplate of lovely steam engines whose smells and sounds are evocative of boyhood and freedom.

This morning we've brought a good crowd of trippers from Hythe, picking up a few more families up at intermediate stations. It is a lovely mainline in miniature, full of nostalgic interest yet often delightfully matter of fact too. Except where the canal it runs along outside Hythe can actually be seen through the vegetation, the ride isn't exactly scenic.

Different but hardly memorable, except for Dungeness where the 'terminus' on the shingle is a through station on a balloon loop.

On arrival, Sheila joins me from the front coach, and we soon lose the throng as people dash to the café or fan out across the shingle. Having learnt more about the life that shingle surprisingly supports, this morning I'm more inquisitive than formerly.

If only since medieval times, shingle has steadily extended its point into the English Channel and created one of the most eerie and curious of places. Though at first impression it might seem flat and featureless, there are some 500 cuspate ridges, each abounding in life. As at Shingle Street, there is rich if patchy vegetation. Because of the sheer size, here the natural history is on a grand scale. Taking the surrounding sand dunes, salt marsh, ditches and saline lagoons into account, no fewer than 600 plants – a third of the British total – are present. There are many rarities, though we are not that familiar even with the commonest waxy leaved ones.

When one stops to study a small area in detail, it is staggering what life is going on. If it's beetles, scarce moths and spiders that turn you on, this is the place to come. It is naturally most special for birds, with the stone-curlew among breeding rarities and huge seasonal variations recorded by the RSPB. The visitors' centre's large windows overlook a flooded gravel pit which is a staging post for many migrants, expected and occasionally definitely not as strays are blown across by Atlantic gales.

As we have seen elsewhere, man also crops up everywhere. There is a village of Dungeness, though in truth only scattered huts and bungalows. On a pre-war visit, I dimly recall a greater population, with more primitive housing and bent old men struggling to cross the shingle on something like clogs. One or two pushed fish on barrows with wheels a foot or so wide. As Richard Church says in his County Book series, *Kent:* 'The scene was "tarry and ropey", more like old Pegotty and his upturned boat. Huts, fishermen's sheds... the natives move about with bits of board tied to their feet, like snowshoes, in order to ease their passage over the shingle. They are called "backstays" or "baxters".'

Drainage of some of the wetlands created rich farmland nearby. Once Dungeness had two railways, though the Southern Railway branch closed in the 1930s less than ten years after the arrival of the RH&D, which used to carry shingle as gravel for building and also fish to Hythe, and which has always brought many trippers. You can easily drive here, too, as do nearly all the workers at the nuclear power station, but it's not as much fun. The largest manmade intrusion, there are actually two power stations, though the first has been stood down and the second has only a limited life left.

Dungeness is a harsh environment, Keith Collins said in a recent newspaper article. Yet he was smitten by it when visiting it on a recent scouting mission for a film company, and bought a primitive 100-year old wooden cottage sans boundary fence to create an oasis on what English Heritage classifies as a desert, dried by continual wind. 'If there's a day when the wind doesn't blow, everyone comments on it,' he says. Adders and lizards emphasise the desert-like character of the garden. With half a million annual visitors to Dungeness, the garden, colourful in summer when it can be fiercely hot, has become its own Mecca.

War has also left its mark. As at Shingle Street, there is a Martello Tower, the first of a line eastward through Hythe. That was part of our defence system against Napoleon, as indeed was the Hythe Canal. There's a pill box from World War Two, though I couldn't find any physical reminder of PLUTO, the pipeline under the ocean, which took oil from here to the British and American invasion forces. The public are invited to see what remains of the 'Listening Ears', three large concrete structures of an experimental and not very successful pre-radar early warning system. No Sheila, there's no time to photograph it. Our train will be waiting.

As we crunch our way back, we reflect that, as is the story in so much of Britain, most things are now for pleasure. Though in the age of terrorism, it was thought prudent to close the nuclear station's tours and visitors' centre, leisure fishermen love 'the boil', a patch of the sea warmed by its waste hot water and even sewage pumped out through pipes. It attracts rich marine life and so inevitably hungry flocks of sea birds competing with the fishermen. The 'new' lighthouse I first saw as a boy is a tourist centre complete with gift shop. Even at this inhospitable place, there are gift shops everywhere, including at the RSPB and the station where our train is now being joined by returning passengers and the driver of many years, Mike Jacques, finishes a generous lunch provided by the restaurant staff.

I've one final thought to share with Sheila before we resume our very different seats. How splendid it would be if they are indeed able (as is now seriously mooted) to harness the tide here: so much better than building another nuclear power station or even barrages such as a controversial one discussed across the Severn which would interfere with much wildlife.

That I'm travelling on the locomotive, *Hercules,* is thanks to John Snell, a friend and previous general manager, standing in for his successor, Danny Martin, who is off duty. Only days ago his wife was killed in a level crossing accident while driving a train. There's been a spate of incidents with speeding cars trying to beat the 'little' train.

Though miniature, the locomotives are no mere playthings. Mike points out the crossing where the accident happened and where proper traffic control will probably now be installed, though at a cost the railway will find hard to raise.

We 'cross' the first train in the opposite direction at a new passing loop halfway along the single track to New Romney where, since drivers normally stick to their own engines, we lay over to haul the following train. Steam machines need constant watering, oiling and other servicing, the reason why for ordinary use they've now been given up almost all over the world.

'But there'll always be steam,' says Mike. It's part of our psyche. You've heard that they're building a brand new mainline Pacific from scratch? Wonderful how much steam there is, but we're one of the few lines that's always had steam. They're not cheap to maintain but you'll recognise the locos you saw as a boy. To which I add that I couldn't imagine going to Dungeness except by steam.

He is a vigilant driver and, once we're on double track beyond New Romney, is able to forecast exactly when trains in the opposite direction will first come into sight. I love it, but next time I'll have a longer layover at Dungeness for, eerie though it might be, it has far more to offer than I realised earlier in life.

The Flow Country and Georgemas Junction

In the same way that for much of my life I failed to discover the secret life of shingle so, along with many others, I dismissed the great peat blankets of Sutherland and Caithness as gloomily unattractive. When I first saw them shrouded in fog from a train en route to Wick, they seemed the nearest I had yet come to the crack of doom. Around the edges were rotting stumps of old trees of the Caledonian Forest which (except on a few islands in freshwater lochs) had died out since regeneration had been prevented by the sheep brought in to replace humans in the Highland Clearances.

When plans were announced to plant large boggy areas with trees, which meant first draining the land, my thoughts were positive: should I invest with Fountain Forestry to take advantage of the tax breaks then offered? There was something about the prospectus that didn't feel quite right. So mercifully I wasn't one who sought to benefit from what turned out to be the rapid destruction of a large slice of an eco-system that took 8,000 years to develop. With thousands of miles of drains, and the moisture taken by the trees planted over 68 square miles, the peat rapidly dried out. Gone were vast areas of 'quaking moss, where curlews and golden plovers breed and over which hen harriers drift.' The quote is from an RSPB appeal, which goes on to describe life in the boglands that survive: 'In thousands of little bog pools (known in Gaelic as Dubh lochans), otters hunt and greenshanks wade.' Where trees were planted they've been felled and left to rot, but it may take a couple of lifetimes for the peat to recover.

A well-informed campaign to prevent further damage led to an astonishingly rapid series of actions: the cessation of forest tax breaks, the creation of a separate Scottish Conservancy (now called Scottish Natural Heritage), and a reappraisal by the National Forestry Commission of what woodlands should be planted in future and how they should look. Especially with architecture and wildlife protection, things have moved on greatly since the grim immediate post-war years.

Challenges still occur, especially why not site wind turbines on peat lands? Because, answers the John Muir Trust, they would cause more damage than good to the environment. Undeveloped peatlands store huge quantities of carbon, in Scotland an estimated three billion tons. Happily the building of a massive wind farm across the peat in the North of the Isles of Lewis (see chapter XXII) has been dismissed.

But as I write this, a battle is being fought over the future of the wonderful Land's End peninsular. On one side is an alliance of Natural Britain, National Trust and local government wishing to increase biodiversity by dividing parts of West Penwith Moor into fields with the erection of long stretches of barbed wire. On the other side, there are people who see themselves as the real supporters of things natural, outraged that the prehistoric character of the bare, open moor should be tamed. Even biodiversity comes at a cost, and I'm definitely against Natural Britain et al on this. The delight is the very uninterrupted bareness of the moors capped by granite outcrops so close to the end of Britain, as far as you can get from the Flow Country with its very different kind of natural wildness.

On journeys to the far north, I now revel in the Flow Country, which in recent times has usually been bathed in sun highlighting the lochans and bird movement. The RSPB runs a nature reserve at Forsinard full of water and islets and agog with birdlife. It's fun going there, as to Dungeness, by train.

Forsinard used to be one of the passing loops with a signalbox on the lonely railway. When great blizzards blew, trains might be delayed for days, their crews earning continuous overtime, living it up at the pub. Winter trains still carry emergency rations, for this is wild country. The route is now radio controlled, and even Georgemas Junction, where the lines to Wick and Thurso diverge, is without staff.

Though nothing like as remote as the string of halts north of Helmsdale and across the Flow Country, Georgemas has always been an oddity, the junction laid out for through trains between Wick and Thurso though for most of its life none ran. When British Rail announced a cheap fare between the two termini, it embarrassingly had to admit there were no trains. For most of railway history, trains (once only two daily, now four) from the south divided here. When there was a blockage on the Flow Country, I recall being turfed off a train from Thurso at Georgemas, as were those on the Wick train. The combined load going forward by bus was fifteen passengers plus a bike and a few parcels. There was no way of warning anyone who might – admittedly unlikely – have been waiting at the string of halts.

Now a single train suffices. It goes first to Thurso and then, back through Georgemas, to Wick, at least once again offering a service between the termini. But building a short spur to avoid reversal and the double stop at Georgemas is unachievable under the divided control of our railways. While common sense generally thrives in remote areas, not so with top-heavy, centralised organisations. A final thought: the only other example I recall of a single train serving one branch after another was between the wars at Dungeness and New Romney. Maybe there are other hidden things in common between shingle and peat.

Northumbrian Rural Delight

We are resting beside a manmade lake, a reservoir, which is the most significant feature in Britain's least known National Park. With few people watching or listening to the mini-wavelets breaking on the shore, it is as calm as it is unspectacular. And I love it. What the Northumberland National Park has done is to protect a huge area of rolling mainly-wooded hills, none reaching mountain height, and to encourage walking and boating tourism. Only one main road bisects the Park through its least-attractive part. Nearly all of the minor roads up river valleys come to dead ends. This is country for exploring on foot par excellence.

This is the third time I have rested by the shore at the head of Kielder Water, and it is sad to think it might be my last, for it is the gateway to a deep peace ever harder to discover on mainland Britain. Then I think how fortunate I've been to have experienced so many parts of Remote Britain several times over. It is Sheila's first time here and she is immediately captivated by the peace. 'This is how life used to be.'

By capacity the largest artificial reservoir in Britain (Rutland Water beats it in surface area), at first it was something of a white elephant for, as Britain became less of a manufacturing nation, industry's use of water failed to rise as expected. Steadily it has come into its own, reliable with underground springs as well as the River North Tyne which it dams, maintaining a constant level. Through pipelines from the North Tyne below the dam, some water is fed to the exit point of the Derwent Reservoir in County Durham and so reaches Tyneside and Teeside by a roundabout route.

Today Kielder Water's closure would be hotly opposed, but I recall the great opposition there was to its building in the 1970s. Dated 1976, sheet 80 in my original complete OS set which has never been replaced shows it under construction. That it is of relatively recent origin is emphasised by the fact that the Border Counties Railway running alongside the North Tyne on which I took a journey well into the 1950s, had long been dismantled. Part of its course was flooded.

The woodland surrounding Kielder Water, is also manmade, the largest such in Europe. Happily I'm by no means alone in liking man's changes in the landscape. The Campaign to Protect Rural England goes so far as to award the water park the rank of Britain's most tranquil spot, an area of beauty and serenity with excellent sporting and catering facilities.

To backtrack, we spent last night in Jedburgh on the Jed Water, on the English side of the border but feeling quite Scottish. Only when we drove further south did we enjoy the full joys of rural Northumberland. By far England's most rural county, it is strangely neglected by visitors and in literature. Though *Journey* well acknowledged its string of coastal offerings, including Holy Island or Lindisfarne, its huge inland ones lack many points of special interest.

I love the delightful, gently rolling and generally still well-wooded countryside simply because, for Britain, it is so extraordinarily ordinary.

Though, especially round the edges, things are beginning to change, it is a land lacking middle-class housing, people and values. The wealthy are few but grand. Most folk spend their lives devoted to making their living. True, some farms are major enterprises, but their owners are among Britain's hardest workers. With noticeable exceptions, the arts do not flourish; bookshops are scarce. In my experience working among them a long time ago undertaking research into rural transport, the people are the salt of the earth, but different... northerners with their own distinctive way of life and dialect. Rural Northumberland definitely isn't Scottish, but neither is it quite English. For a period in its history, Berwick-upon-Tweed was indeed legally its own state, neither English nor Scottish. But though in ancient days Northumbria was a wealthy state, for a long time the county was a kind of no man's land subject to continual battling and raiding.

The paucity of rural housing has long been an issue. Landowners were reluctant to build. Though even Northumberland is not immune from remorseless national standardisation, it is still not uncommon for the next generation to wait for marriage, or at least starting a family, until they take over their parents' homes.

All these factors were evident as we journeyed south by the wiggly B6537 by Bonchester Bridge and Woffee Head, through an unspoilt landscape with long gaps between sparse villages, well-ordered farms and occasional grand houses and even castles. Over a narrow western neck of the Cheviots, we headed for Steele Road and Riccarton, once famous points on the long-closed and much-missed Waverley line between Carlisle and Edinburgh. Virtually everyone says it should never have been closed; its disappearance has cost the local economy dearly. In stages it is being expensively rebuilt south from Edinburgh, but as a commuter line it is unlikely ever to be restored throughout.

Riccarton, once junction for the Border Counties line to Hexham, was a particularly remote outpost of railway civilisation, with an inward-looking and often unhappy community, some families feuding and refusing to speak to each other for generations. With railway curiosity satisfied – oh to be eating one of those fine restaurant car lunches of yesteryear on the daily Waverley Express from Edinburgh to St Pancras via Leicester – we backtracked to the fork to the minor road to Kielder, where we are now soaking in the peace.

In such a large area, the two visitors' centres on the lake and even the Kielder Water Conference Centre for training and team building do not seem an intrusion, and neither does Kielder Castle, a 17th century hunting lodge for the Dukes of Northumberland, now a restaurant and visitors' centre for the forest.

Somehow it doesn't feel at all odd that the one major focus point in Northumberland's natural unspoilt land should be a reservoir surrounded by a manmade forest. I feel restored just being here, an hour long enough to feel the manmade landscape's rejuvenation powers. But then I've always said that nowhere more than in Britain has countryside we regard as natural been more improved by man's inspired intervention. And, while some earlier reservoirs were most unwelcome intrusions, by the 1970s planners and water engineers had a more deft touch.

So, still enjoying it, we wind along the continuing minor road roughly following the lake's irregular southern shore. Then, now following the River North Tyne (it will be much smaller when we see it near its source in chapter XXXIV) to Bellingham, a minor market town or village which I enjoyed when briefly working in these parts. The first time I arrived was on a bustling fair day on the very last special train ever to reach it.

That was from Morpeth, involving reversal at Redesmouth to join the last section of the Border Counties line then still retained for freight. The old goods station now accommodates a splendid heritage centre, where one quickly realises that much wealth was created by the rich soil both in the North Tyne valley and up the slopes.

Again following the river, we pass through Wark, one of the Northumberland villages whose transport needs I studied in depth. A fond memory is of at least two people telling me they 'warked to Wark to wark' (walked to Wark to work). There were no buses and few yet had cars. Though forestry was opening new opportunities, generally things were as primitive as could be found anywhere in the West Country in the 1950s.

The long morning has made us peckish, so we head to The George at Cholleford, romantically situated beside a weir across the North Tyne shortly before it joins the South Tyne to become the major river that flows through Hexham and Newcastle. Recently taken over by Swallow, who also swallowed two of our Nairn hotels, ran them down and went bankrupt, it is like the curate's egg: lunch OK, the gents a disgrace, the setting unbeatable.

Finally today to a far superior hotel, a favourite among Tyneside's golfers, Matfen Hall. Set in beautiful grounds towards the eastern end of Hadrian's Wall countryside. So much stone has been lost here that the wall is little more than a path, though its influence and tourist value is still considerable. I have with me an advance copy of *Journey*, and was looking forward to making a tailor we arranged to meet the first person to see the reference to himself in the book. Instantly he buries it under his tailor's bag, opens it up and insists on his own agenda.

How indifferent some people still are of books and uncurious about what might be said of themselves. Far from the typical reaction, but hurtful for the very first showing. In publishing I told my staff that every sale was a minor miracle and, though we were arch provincial publisher, we found that truer the further north and west we were from London. Ultimately we were accepted almost everywhere, but the tailor's reaction reminds me of how much grit we needed to sustain ourselves against being rebuffed in the early days.

We enjoy our remote position with excellent catering, but next morning we're back to more populated country that doesn't concern us here.

Reedham and Berney Arms

The lower part of rivers and their estuaries are great at creating corners of remoteness. One of my favourites has long been the lonely marshlands on either side of the Yare as it threads its way to the sea before reaching

Great Yarmouth (see *Journey* for considerable coverage on Norwich and Norfolk's coast).

Much of the marsh is in the civil parish of Reedham. Reedham itself is a real, and fascinating village; parts of its church, dedicated to St Edmund, King of East Anglia from 855, date back to the 13th and 14th centuries. But in a huge area there are only 400 households with just over 900 people. Fewer than the fingers of one hand live at Berney Arms, famous for its remote railway station and pub ten minutes walk away. There is no road.

When lengthy through trains still ran daily from London to Yarmouth, a few were routed via Reedham. I recall my surprise that one that I was travelling by stopped midway along a dead straight section at what must be England's most isolated 'station', a very short platform named after the pub. Passengers there have always had to use doors close to the guard's van. What a forlorn place it seemed, especially looking across the huge area of marshes to the north, through which the more direct railway route and main road to Yarmouth cross.

Since then I've had other reasons to become familiar with Reedham: to explore it and several times to take the two-car ferry that has shortened my route from Aldeburgh to Thursford. Though the other railway route from the junction at Reedham, to Lowestoft, crosses the Yare by a swing bridge, the mini-ferry still provides the only crossing for road traffic between Yarmouth and Norwich. That the river has so long denied contact between places on either side is no doubt the reason why even today there's little demand. The ferry, taking just two cars and possibly a motorbike, seems sufficient though it helps that the crossing is short. As so many ferries, each with a long history, have been made redundant, I earnestly hope this anachronism long survives. It is the kind of oddity that happily thrives in East Anglia.

In theory, Berney Arms station is even more anachronistic, but its future is surely secure, at least while the pub continues to attract crowds at peak times. True, many fewer trains now call, and they are short diesel units, but the service is well adapted for walkers, ornithologists and pub visitors, the summer Sunday service being positively generous. 'We get twenty to thirty off some trains,' says Tracey Bold, who runs the pub with her partner. 'On fine weekends, people descend from all over. Many days sixty arrive here walking along the Weavers Way, called that because of the wool trade that brought riches to Norwich and surrounding areas. Lots come just to be here, but many are bird lovers visiting the RSPB. They come for a meal, cup of tea or a drink.'

There is no road access for at least two miles, so some walking across the marshes is inevitable – from Great Yarmouth, Freethorpe, Reedham or Halvergate (the nearest point) – but you can alight from a boat at the head of Breydon Water (the Yare Estuary shared by the Bure and Waveney). It is lonesome enough on a good day. Is it not marvellous that so many people are prepared to risk the elements, winter as well as summer, to enjoy solitude?

Tracey tells the usual story. 'We came here from Birmingham, not so long ago really, but we love it. The isolation is great. No chance of our going back to city life.' She is, however, upset by 'malicious rumours' about how they've spoilt the pub, when they reckon to have taken care of the historic heritage, so far as it hadn't been damaged years ago when the wooden boards were ripped out and the old building became derelict. 'It was built in 1828 for people digging peat,' she says. 'We've had a lot of restoration work and decorating to do, but we definitely respect the heritage.'

She adds: 'Our only neighbour here is the RSPB centre, where there's normally someone staying. Everyone else has left and most of their homes have gone too, pulled down. The windmill, now with sails again, opens by appointment.'

Once the RSPB centre was a working farm – a very few survive elsewhere on the marshes – and where Sheila Hutchinson, an author, spent part of her childhood. She tells me: 'It wasn't the life that most people had. Between 1946 and 1963, we had no gas, electricity or water. We collected rainwater. My grandfather farmer never missed sending the milk churns off by train, and there was a proper postal service. There was much more here then. The windmill powered the mill, there was a row of four cottages with brick works next to it, and other homes, since pulled down. People made quite a social life. Now there's hardly anyone left, but there's greater interest in the place than ever. That's why I've been writing and publishing books about it.'

Unable immediately to contact her, I eventually bought from W H Smith what she says was one of the very last copies of *Berney Arms Remembered*. 'I printed 1,000 of this one. The first book I started with only 500 copies but they'd all gone in four weeks and I did another 750, which have also gone. One of the enjoyable things about publishing your own books is that you're close to your customers. *Berney Arms Remembered* is nearly all made up of what readers of the earlier volumes told me.'

Inevitably it is something of a scrap book, but one gets the feeling of what life was like on the marshes. She writes of the owner of lonely Lockgate Farm, whose house has long been demolished:

> Gordon was a marshman who looked after cattle and horses for Deny Wright and others. Often he would have more than a thousand cattle

to tend. He is believed to have worked the Lockgate drainage mill for a time in the 1920s and, like other marshmen, also did thistle-topping and dyke-drawing. The Addisons kept their own pigs, cows, chicken, geese, ducks, horse and dogs. Mary Ann made butter and cheese and they had a stall on Yarmouth market where they sold their produce. Gordon had a bike and cycled to Yarmouth along the Breydon wall every week to collect provisions and if Mary Ann wanted to go to the town she would go across the marshes to the Acle New Road going by horse and trap. There were about seventeen gates to go through on the trip across the marshes.

Sheila Hutchinson has now written eight books, one a year, the latest being on the neighbouring marshland: *The Lower Buer*. 'Just like the old marshlanders, I have to peddle my wares. Nobody sells better than the author, so I do regular rounds especially in Reedham. There's keen local interest, but it wouldn't work if I was dependent on the book trade.'

Snowshill

We're on our way from Ross-on-Wye to Bicester and our route includes a section of the B4077 from Toddington to Stow-on-the-Wold. There's a hint of real countryside and, on the spur of the moment without glancing at a map, I turn left and pass what Sheila soon tells me is Stanway Ash Wood. She likes to get the best out of things by closely monitoring our progress. On the other hand, I enjoy the occasional surprise – and challenge. Once I drove from a Gloucestershire village to a Norfolk one without consulting a map before or during the journey, almost entirely on minor roads navigating by railway geography as well as road signs.

'We're heading to Snowshill,' Sheila says. That rings a faint bell. Didn't Alice Mary, wife of Charles Hadfield, with whom I started David & Charles, have something to say about it... in a chapter she contributed to *The Cotswolds* edited by them jointly in our A New Study series? Though Charles soon left as fellow director, for decades he remained a valued author. And, yes, on our return, I find Alice wrote about the route along the ridgeway through Snowshill:

> It is not so long ago that this road was gated for most of its length. It certainly offers the visitor from the wide lands of the New World a glimpse of England's own outback as it was before the motor car cut it back to its present size... high up on these austere and noble wolds is Snowshill, very lonesome with a National Trust house of unusual primitive interior design.

We climb steadily past an ancient burial site on the kinder and gentler south-facing slope till we reach what seems an outstandingly pretty village with honey-coloured stone-built cottages that might have been arranged by an artist, at varying levels. There's a delightful group of them overlooking the tall war memorial in the churchyard.

However, getting out of the car, even on a relatively mild spring day, the air strikes us as distinctly crisp. Astonishingly in what most people think of as a lowland area, we're at 800ft. Snowshill is known as a place where snow lingers. We shiver looking over the steep edge of the Cotswolds. There's an expansive view, with glimpses of the route of the abandoned GWR's North Warwick line immediately beneath us, and of the rich lowland toward Evesham. Though I'd liked to have seen the collection, a lifetime's accumulation of thousands of individualistic artefacts of Charles Paget Wade, I'm almost relieved that the National Trust's Snowshill Manor isn't open. An eccentric architect as well as artist and craftsman, Wade bought the Manor, then derelict, because of its starkness, which it retains despite a few of his own additions to house everything from functional farming items like cow bells, to paintings, children's toys and things mechanical. He lived and breathed his collection, the Arts and Crafts style garden also reflecting his eclectic interests. He's buried in the churchyard. The church, among Gloucestershire's plainest, might well have suited his taste.

But without the distraction of the house, we've more time to explore this unexpected corner of Remote Britain. Once Snowshill was a place through which many people passed. Though most rural lanes and roads follow their time-honoured way, round here routes have changed significantly and few now travel through the village on their way between other places. In Snowshill itself, though we're only three miles from pressurised Broadway, there's scarcely any activity. Along the lanes to the east and south, we might as well be back in war-time days of non-existent petrol for private motoring. On the highest of these rolling wolds, we linger and stop and reverse, without seeing another vehicle. Passing places, marked with diamond shaped signs of the kind we are familiar with in Scotland, are sparingly spaced.

With a sprinkling of woodland, it is lovely countryside, the only quibble being that too many hedges have been removed to create large machinery-friendly but very non-traditional fields. Thanks to free-draining limestone, even high up on the south slope, farming is obviously profitable, with impressive farmhouses and buildings. Style isn't forgotten; there's an enormous row of laurels along one road, for example. Everything is neat: perhaps too neat for my liking. And though the only activity we see is a very large herd of sheep being rounded up, visitors clearly aren't unknown. A notice shouts: 'You are entering a working farm. Please be aware of machinery and animals.' Clearly, too, the 50-acre lavender farm attracts thousands to enjoy its rainbow of early summer colours (harvesting is late July and August) and patronise the obligatory tearoom and shop selling lavender 'and other types of gifts'. So again tourism shows its ubiquitous face. And we recall there's a large car park on the edge of Snowshill no doubt for those going to the National Trust's house at busy times.

Generally it is mixed agriculture, stock and large arable fields, a pleasant lightly-populated land of the kind it is a treat still to find in southern England. Eventually we return to the A4077, through more woods including Half Moon Plantation, rejoining it by another ancient burial place.

Then a pleasant drive through Stow-on-the-Wold and a series of minor roads to join the A4095 to reach Bicester through Kirtlington. The further east we go, the lower the hills, the more golden the Cotswold stone. It is a wealthy, not generally that remote but lovely area dotted with churches, many with spires, though some towers. What worries me is that, as villages spread, there's continual loss of agricultural land. With that plus set-aside fields and some dedicated to biofuels, it is not surprising that food prices are rising. [This was just before the onset of the recession when they fell again.]

Next day we take the train from Bicester to London for my Trust's last-ever full-scale prizegiving – nobody can go on for ever – at the English Speaking Union. On our return, we are met by Dr Martin Barnes, who takes us back to his home at Kirtlington, on the very edge of the Cotswolds. From the pleasant drawing room we look across to a very large house with a garden by Capability Brown.

In these parts a church isn't a church without spire or tower, but St Mary's tower was declared unsafe in 1770 and only replaced almost eighty years later exactly following the original Norman design – the kind of oddball detailed historical comment Martin is used to in another context, as review editor of the Railway & Canal Historical Society's *Journal*. We talk about the poor standard of many transport books. He says: 'There are two problems. One is that many albums are thrown together without sense of direction; the other that some authors write up what they research in a record office without giving it the least perspective.' My Trust runs an award scheme with the Society to encourage taking a broader view, for railways fostered or destroyed industries – coal was halved in price, milk doubled along corridors served by branch lines – and played an enormous role in population growth and distribution.

With its spacious houses and gardens, Kirtlington is the kind of village you expect to find men of influence. A noted civil engineer, Martin chairs a panel set up to help solve disputes between parties involved in preparing London to host the Olympics. 'What we do helps keep things on time.'

Next day, on our way to the Midlands, we recount our thoughts about Snowshill and are not surprised later to discover its characterful seasonal dances were also performed in other villages and have been recorded in several books on folklore.

· VII ·

THE NORTH YORKSHIRE NATIONAL PARK

Miraculously in Rosedale

On our way north through Rosedale we have paused at the village of the same name. Today it seems so like many other pretty tourist villages that a lot of people must go through it without a thought for past happenings. There is, for example, little left of the Abbey or Priory, built in one of the waves of monastic development under different Orders. Over a wide sweep of North Yorkshire the monasteries once controlled at least a third of the land area.

Essentially a farm house, the Rosedale establishment was for Cistercian nuns. Through their very act of living simply with the emphasis on manual labour, the self-sufficient Cistercians, skilled in many specialities, amassed fortunes and, at least in some neighbouring dales, practised an early form of ethnic cleansing, moving unwanted locals out of their way. Hereabouts, the Dissolution of the Monasteries seems to have made little practical difference, landowners simply carrying on developing the estates, improving agriculture and amassing wealth. Little is left of Rosedale Abbey. It was cheaper to raid its stone than quarry fresh.

Overlapping the monastic development were the beginnings of the iron-stone trade. My ever-faithful Victorian travelling companion, the county *Murray's Handbook,* wryly comments that the miner's early forges must have been a source of great annoyance to the nuns, adding that a later army of miners was served by the company's own hospital, and 'Dissenting chapels have risen in the village'. It continues: 'The works are readily shown. The ore is conveyed by a rly., along the ridge of the moors, to Ingleby Greenhow (above which there is a steep and dangerous incline).' Visitors, it says, could be carried on request.

What makes *Murray's Handbooks* so different from later guides is that they were written before (starting with the late Victorians) tourists turned their back on industry as being not quite respectable. Yet the *Handbooks* were also far sighted in their criticism. For example, the rebuilding of the modern church occupying one side of the cloisters is called 'ugly', as later generations have commonly regarded much Victorian church work. Descriptions of St Mary Parish Church of Whitby we'll see tomorrow are equally disparaging: 'so changed and filled with pews and galleries... strongly suggestive of a ship's cabin,' and today's *Rough Guide* calls it an architectural dog's dinner.

On our way up to the open moor, in one of the last pieces of woodland, I pull into a lay-by to give Sheila a break. That we are here at all, only a couple of hours later than planned, is a miracle. In the wee hours of yesterday morning, she was in increasing pain till I called the doctor, who diagnosed gall bladder and gave her a shot of morphine. Waking late from a deep sleep, she announced: 'I'm OK. We can still go. I think we should. Let's get the one o'clock train.' She was insistent.

To make things possible, our gardener quickly set south to York in Big Car, handing the keys to me in the car park of the large hotel outside York station soon after our arrival. I had cancelled our booking at the hotel and was just able to rebook the room.

The National Park's First Officer

So this morning, only slightly later than planned, we were on our way from York. I've always loved North Yorkshire and its moors, and came to know them well when publishing several books about them. I recall that publication of one was temporarily stopped by the only injunction ever actually placed on us, as opposed to a variety of threatened ones from drug manufacturers and others who our authors criticised. The injunction was at the instigation of the author of a manuscript we had rejected on the North Yorkshire Moors. We turned it down because we had an abundant supply of topographical works. However, the authors of several projected titles failed to deliver on time or at all so, when another very acceptable manuscript came along, we readily put it into production. Balancing demand and supply over many categories in a large list is always tricky – something part-time authors, easily disrupted by family problems, promotion at work, moving or taking part in elections, don't realise.

What authors *do* suspect one is making light of is their copyright. The first author had told his solicitor that nobody else could possibly write on North Yorkshire as informatively as he. When we were legally forced to submit a copy of the other work for his scrutiny, he was flabbergasted that someone knew as much. But then Yorkshire folk are keen, and there is greater literature here than for most popular areas.

Another book was *The North York Moors*, in the David & Charles Landscape Heritage series (1989). The final chapter on Modern Times was written by the then and original National Park officer, Derek Stratham, whose opening still sets today's challenge:

> Despite the changes in British society brought by the Industrial Revolution, the appearance of the countryside changed but slowly. The landscape of the Moors early in the 20th century was different in detail and degree rather than in form from the landscape of the early 19th century. The main change was the introduction of railways and heavy industry, particularly in Eskdale and Rosedale. To be sure, there had been some enclosure and improvements in farming techniques, but the basic farming systems had not changed. The pattern of moorland, dale agriculture, daleside woodland, compact villages and scattered farmsteads also seemed immutable.
>
> The ensuing decades have witnessed changes on an unprecedented scale. Fortunately, there are accurate records of most of them including photographs, films and even personal memories. Not that all rural matters have been carefully recorded. Less is known about the ownership and occupation of land today than is given for its time in the Domesday survey. There still is no accurate field survey of wildlife and not until 1975 was there an attempt to count the visitors to the Moors.

When I caught up with Derek, he explained how difficult the job had been when the National Park came into existence forty years ago. He was the County Council's assistant planning officer while 'running' the North York Moors and part of Yorkshire Dales National Parks without any professional assistance. I recall it was the same in Devon with its National Parks. Yet, being reminded of just how grim those days were for the protection of our best landscapes, still comes as something of a shock.

'It wasn't just a shortage of money but the attitude,' says Derek. 'Farmers were dead against it, and there was little general support or understanding. Some things we wanted to do right at the beginning, on day one, had to wait twenty five years. When the Park came into existence, it had more heather than Exmoor, but the only way we could stop development was by the odd purchase, for which we had special grant funds. Even in 1974, when the National Parks were given their own staff for the first time, we had no Centre. Danby Lodge, the former shooting lodge, came soon after. Not until 1997, by which time I'd retired, were the Parks made completely independent. I never saw that day though I'd worked toward it for many years.

Inevitably we lost much to farming, forestry, industry and general development. Farming seemed to get everywhere. But we did steadily get public opinion on our side, and it was pleasing that when the Parks were finally given their own authority, Parish Councils such as Helmsley's, half in and half out of the boundary, opted to come in. Attitudes have changed enormously. The farmers who were dead against open access came to realise it made little difference and, as one indication, we're just beginning to see the return of black grouse which need wild country.

The trouble is that people don't realise how intensively Britain is farmed: 83 per cent of our surface is devoted to agriculture. Only 10 per cent to forest, against Germany's 48 per cent. If we were starting with a clean slate, a third of England would be farmed, a third given to other activities, and the remaining third left totally wild. It's our population pressure, but then that's what makes it so important to retain what we can.'

In retirement, he still walks, once a month with Nick Pennington, retired from the Loch Lomond National Park. They especially love the Hornby area in the upper part of the Rye Valley: 'a mixture of steep valleys with a lot of woodland, and moorland on top. Long may it survive.'

Derek is active President of the North Yorkshire Moors Association, whose lively magazine *Voice of the Moors* shows what a splendid range of attractions are offered and how local life and business are encouraged alongside protecting the wilderness and ancient buildings and ruins. It is decidedly not a landscape in a glass case. The National Park itself publishes booklets on individual attractions and themes. There's also a user-friendly timetable of buses, including those it sponsors, and to open up access especially for walkers and explorers at weekends.

Our 4x4 from Scotland feels at home as we climb onto the open moor, where we clearly see the route of the former private mineral railway, two branches from Rosedale joined together, winding round the contours. Little evidence, however, to show that a staggering half a million tons of iron ore were carried away, most of it high grade.

Fryup and into Eskdale

The open moor is great and one has to learn to make the best of it (in truth a great deal) without being irritated by all that's been lost even since the establishment of the National Park. As the editor of the Landscape Heritage series we'll meet later says, Derek Stratham's strength lay in an ideal tempered by the art of the possible in changing days. At least there's somewhere still with space and fresh air to breathe uncompromised by any kind of development. And though this has to be a lightning trip compared with ones in my younger days, it's exhilarating to see such great and increasingly appreciated landscape.

Reaching the dramatic heads of the Dales where views all around are breathtaking, we take a diversion west around short Great Fryup Dale, passing a sign pleading us to beware of sheep and lambs, 150 of which were killed on the Park's roads last year. We pause with heads of the Dales on either side. Then down through Castleton, where several sheep in the long main street seem determined to put themselves at risk (perhaps the sign has given them too much confidence?) and half the properties are up for sale.

The Park's population has decreased considerably, only villages around its outskirts close to towns with employment opportunities showing growth. There's no doubt that the Park's enemy is agriculture and afforestation, now partly because, employing so few people, that they have ceased to provide the traditional foundation for community life. Even farmers accept that more wilderness is a good thing, yet ironically, without the hill farms and their livestock, vegetation of the wrong sort quickly gets out of hand. Up here it is easy to see why the balance is so delicate. The big question: who else but farmers are going to pay to keep large areas tidy on the verge of wilderness?

Down the Esk Valley, we enter a land of inviting pubs and grand houses and farms, and even of railway stations. Driving to Danby, by no means for the first time in my life, I pop into the station where my timetable says no trains are due, only to discover that a steam one is approaching – and is for general public use, too. The surprise is that at its eastern end, the Middlesbrough to Whitby line's four basic diesel trips are this season being supplemented by steam ones run by the North Yorkshire Moors Railway. Sheila is on the platform in the nick of time for me to snap her in front of the steam engine coming in backwards hauling several lightly-filled old-fashioned carriages. What an excellent thing. Hopefully the steam trains will have a place in next summer's timetable and, becoming better known, attract more custom. The current timetable does show that some of the trains from the North Yorkshire Moor's line now run through into Whitby. Maybe, just maybe, such common sense might spread. Who could it hurt other than officials defending their isolated status?

After a shaky start, the North Yorkshire Moors privately-owned steam railway supported by an army of enthusiasts has become a major tourist attraction, allowing a new generation of travellers to appreciate the beauty of Newton Dale, and the famous domes of the Fylingdales Early Warning Station (recall the discussion it prompted about the four minutes to decide our fate?). The steam line runs a few miles nearer the coast but parallel with Rosedale Dale through which we chose to travel this morning. One day the steam trains might even be extended to Malton, reopening the whole route closed by Beeching. That they go as far south even as Pickering is due to the National Park having given the railway a substantial incentive.

Derek Stratham tells me: 'At first the enthusiast backers only wanted a short line. We saw the possibility of trains carrying a broader range of people including walkers, and it's worked out.' Preservation serving the present? What a naughty idea it's been seen as for years.

Lunch at Lealholm and the Printed Word

Though they live in Glaisdale, we now go alongside the Esk to the next village, Lealholm, to meet Mrs Ann Bowes and her husband Allan for lunch. This is delightful, delicate country, with many individual touches. We simultaneously point out to each other a hump bridge on an adjoining road. Little did we realise until lunch that the bridge replaced a ford, and that in crossing through it their son lost his life as a sudden surge of water swept his car downstream.

Lunch is arranged that I might talk to Ann about the prizes she has won in my Trust's writing competitions. The first was for *Riding for Life: A Journey across the North of England*, which a couple of years ago won our Community Cup for the best self-published book to raise money for charity.

> We made our way along Little Fryup Dale, past Danby Castle and down the narrow lane to Duck Bridge. This is where the new raised ford was built to save wear and tear on the old historic bridge. It is where Dan drowned and it's only natural that I think of him every time I have to cross the river that claimed his life. He was such a happy, carefree character, always willing to please. I had been very blessed to be given such a son as Dan. My horse [Danny-Boy] was well named.

She calls her own imprint Fryup Press; only local people would know the name came from the hamlet we made our moorland diversion to pass through. So far the book's publication has raised £6,000 for local charities, and shows what the self-publisher can achieve with a well-focussed project. There have been two printings of a thousand copies each with 400 copies left to sell. Publicity including an appearance in ITV's Dales Diary has been crucial.

With commercial publishers cutting back on their lists, it is increasingly tempting for authors to do their own thing. Those tempted by 'Vanity' publishers, whose high charges are backed by promises seldom fulfilled, usually end up disillusioned. Vanity publishers thrive on general ignorance of how things work. On the other hand self-publishers who have grasped a simple understanding of what is involved are increasingly successful. Another of our recent winners, the first lady guard on British Rail, positively withdrew her *Railway Women* from the commercial publisher who had accepted it to organise her own layout, printing and marketing, and is far happier and better off as a result.

The trouble is that, as in so many matters, such as making financial investments, people turn to experts who have their own agenda, when actually they themselves best know what they want to achieve. With a little concentration and general advice, they can quickly find their way around the technical details. (Two booklets giving a practical overview are available free from PO Box 6055 Nairn IV12 4YB.)

Rounding off our Yorkshire trip, we will be holding our annual prizegiving in Harrogate, at which we will present Ann with the prize for our Community Newsletter/Magazine. Her achievement with *Valley News,* serving the villages in the lower Esk Valley, has been considerable. *Valley News* is mainly what we discuss over excellent food at the Shepherd's Hall at Lealholm, a quality restaurant with keen staff of the kind one expects to find where there is great inland scenery, but curiously not usually along the coast.

The need for a community magazine began as the commercial local weekly ceased including details at the very local level people look for. All over Britain it is the same, chain-owned titles usually having non-local editors. Post Office and shop closures have added to making it harder for organisers of local events to reach their audience. The four main villages served by *Valley News* all have public halls. 'But how would people know what was happening in them if we didn't spread the message?' asks Ann.

'I have to devote a fortnight of each month to collecting information, writing, doing my own typesetting and laser printing and distributing copies. In the summer I do about 200 copies, and I know they are eagerly read and used. We really do hold the community together. At present all four villages have a Post Office, but almost certainly not for much longer, and that will make us even more necessary though we might have to change our method of distribution because all four of them are important sales outlets for us.'

Charging £1.50 for a well-packed forty eight pages of A5, she has just started paying herself an honorarium. *Valley News* includes all the ingredients needed in a magazine serving a small, well-defined area: gossip, notes on country life and gardening, reports from each of the villages, a list of forthcoming events, sports news, bus times, and advertisements which are especially helpful when facilities lacking in one village are available in another.

'I suppose I'm really quite pleased with it,' says Ann. 'And do you know I'm also attending the prizegiving because you've short-listed the writers' group I belong to?' Oh yes, come to think about it, we do. But what we're not letting onto is that the Egton Bridge Writers' Group, near Whitby, will be outright winners of our Writers' Circles Anthology Trophy, for the different kinds of writing by their range of contributors has great vitality. Each year we invite four representatives each from four short-listed groups to come along, get to know each other over lunch and sit in suspense while we discuss the relative merits of their anthologies. Ironically, Egton Writers launched their annual anthology when the Post Office, then foolishly calling itself Consignia, gave grants to writers' groups. When the funding stopped, the writing continued.

Allan, a gamekeeper, has enjoyed his lunch with an occasional supportive comment, and now leads the way for our visit to the National Park's Moors Centre at Danby. The old shooting lodge is being given another make-over and is basically closed, but we learn that all kinds of events are held at what is obviously a popular gathering place and focal point for the running of the Park. The bookshop *is* open, so we spend some time reviewing what is new in local publishing and buy a selection of the brief guides produced by the National Park: excellent value at 40p. Then farewell to our lunch guests, back past the Hump Bridge replacing the ford and through the little villages served by *Valley News*, each pleasingly distinctive.

To Whitby

At Egton Bridge there's a lovely scene including a village cricket match and another of the steam trains running on Network Rail. I wish I were on the railway which keeps more intimate company with the river winding between high hills, at times almost gorge-like. We had intended to eat out but Sheila, at the end of a long day she's clearly found challenging after her trouble of not much more than 36 hours ago, is desperate to lie down. So it is an early high tea in a non-memorable but handy guest house.

The last thing Henry VIII would have had in mind when dissolving the monasteries was the creation of a new cult. By the 19th century, the cult of ruins attracted poets and painters, and in our time has given respectability to the newer appreciation of other kinds of ruins, especially the best of discarded industry. Henry VIII the founder of industrial archaeology? Hardly, but the abandoned great abbeys certainly meant that it wasn't just old castles that had a large following.

My favourite ruin has always been Tintern Abbey; Fountains and

Whitby quickly follow among a host of others mainly in the North, many in the National Parks. My top two favourites have gorgeous river settings; Whitby is famous for its position audaciously perched on a high cliff.

As well as stone being taken for new work after the Dissolution, furious storms also took their toll on Whitby Abbey – to this day used by mariners as a navigational mark. Actually there is more of it left than many of our great abbeys. Yet for me the detailed examination of the preserved state of decay it is now maintained in is less satisfying than at many others, even in Yorkshire. Part of my difficulty is the sheer complexity of the history. The English Heritage website begins:

> High on a cliff above the Yorkshire seaside town of Whitby are the gaunt, imposing remains of Whitby Abbey. Founded in 657 by St Hilda, Whitby Abbey has over the years been a bustling settlement, a kings' burial place, the setting for a historic meeting between Celtic and Roman clerics, the home of saints including the poet Caedmon, and inspiration for Bram Stoker, author of Dracula. Discover how over 2,000 years of history make the Abbey one of England's most important archaeological sites. And at the interactive visitor centre your family can interrogate personalities from the past – including Dracula!

Interrogating past characters including Dracula seems to me to trivialise it. What I stand in awe at is Whitby's trademark, ruins so exposed above the town. Is it surprising that it was a great storm, in 1763, that brought much of the nave tumbling down to be followed by the central tower in 1830? No other seaside town is more identified by anything as Whitby is by its ruined Abbey, great to look up to and (when you've recovered your breath from the climb) to use as vantage point for town, harbour and cliffs.

Arguments over aspects of the past will continue for generations, one conjecture being that the Dark Age Abbey wasn't a simple wind-swept community but a bustling, complex and sophisticated centre of its time. Naturally archaeologists have to pursue their profession, and I'll be interested to know what they say. To me, however, the magic is the sheer wonder based on a few simple facts that ignite rather than confuse my reverie – in the same way that some people feel that, with its rituals, the very early church complicated the life of Jesus and lost focus on his basic teaching.

My handful of Whitby essentials include that it was founded way back in 657 by the undoubtable St Hilda, Royal Northumbrian prince whose very name, Hild, denotes battle. Destroyed by invading Vikings soon after William the Conqueror landed in Kent, it was refounded in the following decade by one of his knights. Fifty years later it was not large enough for the rush of northern pilgrims, so the present building was started, to be abandoned or 'privatised' (which meant both) after Henry VIII's dissolution.

Remember that – the very minimal history? It is enough for me to be going on with while being free to *imagine*, to feel I'm part of the scene, to capture something of the hopes and fears of many generations of supposedly holy people (I'm sure many of them were unselfishly devout) and wonder what their feelings would have been for the souls of the fishing community that kept to itself down below by the river and harbour. For all their aestheticism, the monks enjoyed a far higher life style.

On the cliffs just below the Abbey, we are dazed by St Mary's Church but don't go inside to see its 'bizarre' interior. At the bottom of the long flight of steps, we do have time to enjoy cobbled Church Street, among the best old streets anywhere, though no longer the workplace for hundreds making delicate jet jewellery (about which more later). Like so many former working places, Whitby is now largely devoted to tourism.

George Hudson, the Railway King who had much of the north east under his thrall, built the first line to Whitby, one of the most isolated resorts to grow tourism in Victorian days cheek-by-jowl with smelly but picturesque fishing. My *Murray's Handbook* of 1882, putting the population at a sizeable 16,744, says that between 800 and 900 vessels belong to the port, among the chief benefactors of the rich herring years along England's north east coast.

In my time I've seen Whitby's fortunes sink and rise. Today it has a definite niche. Many prefer it to larger Scarborough, and certainly the likes of Bridlington. As we explore and eavesdrop this morning, it is obvious that different types of visitor mix well in the cobbled streets of the old town and along the shores of the extensive harbour from which gigantic quantities of Cleveland iron ore were once despatched and fish is still landed, if now in smaller quantities. Geography sets its seal on Whitby, crowded in but made cosy by the high cliffs on either side and with the wide river dividing it, not to mention the great position of its harbour. Everyone seems determined to cross the bridge separating the two parts... and to enjoy the fish.

'Not sure I want fish today,' says a buxom Yorkshire woman.

'Darn it woman, fish an' chips's what you come to Whitby for,' snarls her husband almost propelling her in search of it.

'Can you recommend somewhere good?' I ask a local woman pushing her shopping trolley.

'Do you want good or perfect? Lots of good ones, but you'll never beat...'

Dear me, I've forgotten that until her gall bladder is treated or removed, Sheila, so much revived today, has been told to avoid anything fried. At the recommended perfection, a large café bustling with activity, fish and chips is being carried out from the kitchen by a continuous stream of waitresses. Ours sympathises with Sheila for not being able to do the normal thing, but at least she has grilled fish and spuds.

Almost her first time in Whitby, she's impressed and wished we were staying another night. Having made ad hoc arrangements last night, however, we must move on to keep our next appointment.

As with most large resort towns, Whitby is excluded from the special planning status given to Britain's top landscapes, but the coastline north and south *is* included in the National Park and very deservedly so. To the north, the National Park stretches to the outskirts of Loftus on the way to Saltburn-by-the-Sea, a hotchpotch of a place unflatteringly described in *Journey*. This short but much-loved piece of protected coast, with the gems of Runswick Bay and Staithes, remains one of a handful of sections I have never visited. It isn't the size of Britain so much as its utter complexity that makes it a hard country to know in every detail, but then that's its special challenge.

· VIII ·

DOWN YORKSHIRE'S HERITAGE COAST

View of a Lifetime

To the south, the Park's boundary rejoins the coast close to Whitby and continues down to its southern boundary a few miles north of Scarborough. This section, as I am soon to demonstrate to Sheila, contains a mixture of gems: spectacular cliffs, and great geological and historical interest. Much can be seen from and around the hotel we're staying at the next few nights and now make straight for, though later we will backtrack to Robin Hood's Bay.

That means taking the A171, which even at moderate speed throws the car round. New Big Car is a Toyota Landcruiser we have so far driven little. I concur that, if this is a typical country road performance, it won't do, though I'd be sorry to part with it, for it has many excellent features including reliability. A fine compliment was paid by the RAC patrolman instructed where to rescue a driver but not what was his trouble: 'I knew that either you'd lost your keys or got a puncture. I've never been called out for anything else with a Toyota.' Happily very soon we realise it is the road's fault. Don't the locals object to such a roller coaster?

The Raven Hall Country House is a friendly, large hotel on a clifftop with a panoramic view across Robin Hood's Bay which both we and our friends will absorb with immense pleasure today but especially next morning in changing light: a crescent moon setting and leaving near darkness, then early morning blanket fog dissolving into drifting mist with the sun breaking through, followed by occasional blue skies allowing bright sunshine, but more frequently scattered cumuli producing a continuously changing variation of dappling. It was as though God had directed someone with imagination to control a sophisticated lighting console, though in reality no manmade lighting could equal this.

Our bedroom window looks out north west, a green field with bright yellow gorse sloping away from us in the foreground. Below is a long arc of a ribbed beach. As the tide recedes, strips of sand or, lower down, residual sea water where softer rock has worn away, lie between long, thin lines of surviving harder rock. When the tide comes in, the rollers break over the ridges in a ballet of movement. As the sea eats away the softer layers making it easier to attack the harder, the cliffs are in various states of retreat and differ sharply in height. As though that is not riveting enough, my eyes trace left to right and back again, the route of the former coastal railway between Scarborough and Whitby which, much of the way, kept closer to the coast than the road. Today only walkers experience many of the glimpses enjoyed by train passengers.

We can see a tunnel interrupting the smooth, though steeply-graded route, down from here to the village of Robin Hood's Bay, much of it on a ledge, on which the so-called permanent way was laid. What a thrill it was travelling by one of the early diesel railcars with forward seats sharing the driver's view. I covered the vast majority of Britain's then larger but fast-declining rail network and my one journey here was the most memorable of all.

Though without the same clarity of vision, in steam days passengers on heavy excursion trains when sea mist made the rails slippery had their own excitement as men and machine fought to keep the wheels moving. Failed first attempts and re-runs, some of the rails pre-sanded, weren't unusual. Only occasionally the struggle had to be given up until conditions improved, or the train divided in two.

Even when the mist lifts, the village of Robin Hood's Bay, tucked cosily under the cliffs, doesn't show up sharply until our third day, by which time we will have visited it.

Today there's little movement to be seen beyond the passage of occasional walkers, but once there was intense activity on the sea and the beach below. Except in storms, there would nearly always be vessels on the move or beached. Quarrymen would have been seen attacking selected parts of the cliffs with pick and shovel for shale containing alum. Flat-bottomed boats brought coal, potash, burnt seaweed and even stale urine needed in the complicated process at the nearby works, and took away the much lighter quantity (still hundreds of tons a year) of saleable alum. This was needed by the garment industry for making fast the colours of dyes and the tanning of leather; until the arrival of synthetics, it was the only method of fixing dyes. Britain had no other source, and wars cut off overseas ones.

In past times, also going on nearby, was the search by poorly-paid workers for the shallow black seams of the trunks of monkey-puzzle trees, washed into the sea 150 million years ago and fossilised. Though beads of up to 5,000 years old have been found, what gave jet its popularity was Queen Victoria wearing it while in mourning for Prince Albert. Once over 200 were engaged in prospecting for and collecting the jet, while in Whitby 1,500 people turned it into ornamental pieces.

The demand dropped catastrophically when Queen Victoria ceased wearing it, and anything to do with death was not the flavour of the age, any more than was enquiring into industry past and present.

Things change, and happily the National Park has devoted one of its 40p leaflets on the Heritage Coast – 'a place to care for, a place to enjoy' – entirely to how people used to earn their keep. The production of alum is described in detail, one of the largest of the abandoned works a stones-throw from us at Peak being complemented by an early cement works using quarried stone.

As though this is not enough to think about absorbing the view of a lifetime, we have to remember that millions of years ago we would actually be on the edge of a great tropical delta. This is also the dinosaur coast, the whole land mass once being near the equator. The strata are of two groups: the Lower Jurassic 'Lias Group' and the younger Middle Jurassic 'Ravenscar Group', the former laid down in warm tropical seas, the latter in a huge river delta. For the geologically minded, the leaflet on geology goes on to explain:

> The end of the upper Lias era (around 170 million years ago) was marked by a period of change which included a series of minor earth movements followed by erosion and further deposition. The first new sediments were iron rich rocks called the Dogger Formation. These rocks weather to a rusty orange colour and so stand out from the almost black Upper Lias shales. The contact between the Upper Lias and the Dogger can be clearly seen in the quarries near Ravenscar. Above the Dogger are rocks unique to Yorkshire, which were formed in a huge river estuary or delta. These are the rocks of the Ravenscar Group (previously called the Deltaic Series) which form the rugged cliffs south of Ravenscar.

Large pieces of jet fossil wood are still occasionallydiscovered, well preserved because there was little delay between the uprooting of trees in a flood or storm and their trunks being buried in sediment. An excellent showcase with a great variety of fossils in the hotel lobby displays 'millions of years of history beneath your feet', while in our bedroom is a potted history of the building itself.

Still at Raven Hall

The hotel's potted history records that there had been a Roman fort here – indeed a signal station – in the 5th century, the commanding position being ideal both for defence and the enjoyment of the view. The building has been a hotel most of the time since 1895, and is now Methodist owned, with a chapel in which occasional services are held.

An interesting notice puts it in perspective, saying the hotel is:

> Situated among inspiring remains of such cradles of faith as Whitby, Rievaulx, Byland Abbey, Mount Grace Priory; all reflecting the ancient church of these islands. And for more recent examples of how the faith has influenced the area, John Wesley visited Osmotherly eighteen times during his life, interestingly at the initial invitation of a Franciscan Friar. Today the chapel opened by Wesley in 1754, is appropriately, part of a local ecumenical parish. Specialist leaders are available on a whole host of subjects such as Celtic Christianity, Iona Liturgy and Church Music.
>
> The Christian Hotel with the Good Hope Chapel at the centre of its life: Raven Hall proudly standing on the land made famous by the Saints...

Built in 1774 by the owner of the local alum works, what was then a large mansion was left to his daughter, whose family became wealthy treating George III 'and various other loopy Royals'. Their parson son squandered everything, though happily not before he had blasted out the terraced 'hanging gardens' even closer to the cliff edge. The project included battlements and 'a cosy and well-hidden bolt hole for anyone who wished to pass signals out to sea'.

A William Hammond then arrived from London to give Raven Hall and the scattered village Victorian respectability. He built the local church and windmill, and later was a keen supporter of the Scarborough to Whitby line – subject to the trains passing close to his property being hidden in the tunnel into which the old route disappears in from view. That cost an extra £500. Opened in 1885, though not a great commercial success, the railway revolutionised local life, opening up the coast to tourists, our hotel starting trading only a few years later. Until then the cliffs had only really been appreciated by passengers on one of the occasional steamers between Scarborough and Whitby.

So in our view once there would have been steamers, giving their passengers a close view of the cliffs hard to get today – and no doubt once smugglers' boats, too. Then things turned sour. Hammond's daughters sold the property.

The Town that Never Was

The new owners, the Park Estate Company, had a great ambition: to create a vibrant new town and resort, which is actually when the name Ravenscar first came into use. The town wasn't to be. In 1911 the company went bust, only a little having been built.

Our friends still not having arrived, we drive to look at the small beginnings of the town that never was. First to the old station remains, high up and often misty (a snowdrift closed everything for six weeks in 1947), which I clearly remember calling at on my one journey shortly before its closure in 1956. A single platform and just one siding, the station, 631ft above sea level, was the highest on the magnificent, expensive line. From here it was downhill (1 in 39 in railway parlance) through the tunnel to Robin Hood's Bay. I never stand on an abandoned platform without thinking 'Our little systems have their day...' And yet we're not the only ones here. The platform is more visited than when trains called.

There's a large display with historical notes and a plan of the proposed street layout of the town that never was and details of the public auction of everything in lots after the company went under. Here is also one of the distinctive olive-green metal waymarkers used in the local waymarker scheme, the oversize ears pointing in one direction to Scarborough and the other to Robin Hood's Bay and Whitby.

Just below the station is the one square that was laid out, at the bottom of which the main shopping street was to run. Only one side of the square was completed, with a row of three storey houses. Ah, here's a tea room. Several motorbikes and a solitary pedal bike are parked outside. While the other people on the station platform scarcely responded to our greeting, the leather-clad bikers enthusiastically welcome us and draw us into their conversation over a snack. This is their regular rendezvous point, one of the café's mainstays since most visitors take a glance at the station and the abandoned start of roads and seek somewhere more successful or in a cosier setting to relax. Nearby most of the houses, including new ones, that have been built sporadically over the years are up for sale. Not a place we'd want to live. 'But we do get a lot of walkers along the Cleveland Way,' says the owner. The bikers want to know about us and our 4x4, and peel off into motorbike jargon.

The conversation suddenly takes a different turn. Leather-free Frank Thompson, a pedal cyclist from Scarborough, unable to use his motorbike since an inner ear problem, says he comes for a pedal or a walk five days a week. 'It's magic. It was chilly this morning, but the fog lifted as I arrived; what an experience. My wife has been a librarian in Scarborough for thirty five years, and I don't work now. I've no particular skill. Framing is very difficult. Few people you see going to work these days are happy. I am. But what is one to do? The Post Office and shops close early, so I come here. I love it, and it's easier now part of the old railway is absorbed into the National Cycle Network. This is very much my area. My father was Mayor of Scarborough in 1997, and my wife's aunt and uncle lived in this building when it was a house. They bought very decent second-hand furniture from the hotel where you're staying.'

His gear draped over a neighbouring chair, one of the bikers chips in with a recipe for making alum: 'Firstly, take some shale, and carefully layer it over brushwood to form a clamp. Set it alight and leave it smouldering for approximately 9-12 months.' He goes on: 'Add seaweed (potassium), urine (ammonia) and, don't ask me why, a hen's egg. The egg had to be newly laid, but the urine stale. Some of it came from locals; it was collected from their doorsteps. It was quite valuable was urine, and some was stolen.'

The nice thing about cafés, especially not of the select gentile variety, is that you never know what you'll hear next.

Then we take a quick tour of the roads laid out now nearly a century ago still with their kerbstones but never developed, and the old alum works and quarry. Then a quick visit to the shop/museum near the entrance to our hotel where diagrams of the making of alum, samples and displays bring it all to life. At the hotel, our friends Allan and Barbara Patmore have checked in. We are planning to travel together down the coast to Spurn Head, sticking out into the Humber. Like the new town, not to be, however. They've made a special effort to be here just for tonight. Allan has a foot problem, bad enough to reduce him to crawling around the room, except when making an heroic effort to reach the dining room for dinner. The geographer and historian in him won't let the disability spoil the party, or his taking in the view.

Over dinner we discuss the merits and idiosyncrasies of authors and contributors to the series Allan edited, on railways as well as landscapes, and his own books including the pioneer *Land and Leisure* of 1970. 'How things have changed,' he says. In *Journey* (p534) I quoted his piece about the great waves of development since 1800. First industrial growth, then the railways, followed by car-based suburbs. 'What I called the fourth wave, leisure, has been far more pervasive than anyone expected. The whole countryside seems to be steadily given up to it.'

I chip in that I call it Theme Park Britain. 'Yes,' says Allan. 'That's a good description. It's not just that tourist attractions and golf clubs are opening everywhere, but much of the national parks are being tamed by too many signs, car parks, paving of paths. Encouraging visitors and looking after their needs is the national priority. Getting into really wild country becomes ever harder. Perhaps one day you'll only be able to do it in Scotland. The North York Moors National Park has done its best and of course gives a good measure of protection from the worst kind of development, yet even here – and it's worse in the Dales – how does one put it? Life is being made too comfortable. It's right that people should be encouraged to come. That's good. Yet everything is in danger of becoming too organised.'

Next morning he's unable to come down to breakfast, but has enormously enjoyed looking out as the early morning mist clears to reveal sparkling detail – and the enthusiast part of him cannot help recalling special and difficult times in the workings of the local railways. When it's time to say our premature farewell, it has to be in their bedroom where again he's on his knees. The kindly hotel staff assure us they are making special arrangements to help him to his car. 'Make the most of the coast, especially Flamborough Head and of course Spurn Head. That can be the most eerie place in Britain.'

Robin Hood's Bay

Nowhere has Allan Patmore's fourth wave, the leisure revolution, made such an especially sharp impact on the village of Robin Hood's Bay. My *Murray's Handbook*, published in 1882, just three years before the coming of the railway, advises there is no conveyance. Except when an occasional steamer called, the only way of reaching it was by foot. Few from other parts would have seen the fishermen's cottages cascading down to the sea. Robin Hood's Bay was a self-contained private world, only really accessible by boat, though already somewhat changed by the alum and jade industries. It built its own boats. It landed fish, but most was reloaded to be taken by sea to Whitby. Coal and even essential groceries – though local farms supplied much – came by sea. Then boats became bigger – too large for the little harbour, and fishing migrated to Whitby.

Though now there is only a little crabbing, the Bay is a gem today, but how much more leisurely the place must have been then, how much more appealing the scene to any artist who had the persistence to spend time here. *Murray* says:

> The pedestrian will find fingerposts with R.H.B. to guide him. He should take the l. road thus indicated after leaving Hawsker. Steep descent to the Bay through the curious old quaint village of Thorpe, perched on a hill above a rivulet, some of the houses walled up perpendicularly over the stream. Note the Coracles of the fishermen here. There is no part of the Yorkshire coast more attractive to the naturalist or the artist than Robin Hood's Bay.

'The glamour of poverty,' I say as we think of how it was precisely the hard way in which fishermen earned their keep and lived primitively that made places such as Robin Hood's Bay and St Ives in Cornwall so appealing to artists. For other visitors there was also the allure of smuggling. If you believe every story about smuggling around our coasts, no excise duty would ever have been paid on imported booze – in the same way that resorts' exaggerated claims of visitor numbers suggest that up to half of Britain's total population is on holiday throughout the season's peak. Smuggling claims here are, however, authentic. Secret tunnels have been found and, in 1815, soldiers were deployed to help the Excise men unable to keep pace with the locals' knowledge of a complicated coast.

The Dinosaur Coast: Yorkshire Rocks, Reptiles and Landscape, published by the National Park for the Yorkshire Dinosaur Coast project, explains the basis of the natural beauty:

> The great arc of Robin Hood's Bay is one of the most famous and beautiful sights on the Yorkshire coast, and the village is one of the most picturesque anywhere in England. The shape of the bay comes from underlying rocks, and in particular from an odd structure that has bent the rock strata into long curves. It is these curves that make the bay, when seen from above, so remarkably graceful.
>
> During the Tertiary period, long after the Jurassic rocks of this region had been deposited, the whole area was lifted up. This happened because two of the great plates that make up the earth's crust collided, making the earth's surface buckle and fold. The area buckled upwards, forming a long arch that runs from east to west across the high moors.
>
> Robin Hood's Bay is at the eastern end of this arch... Forces from different directions have pushed against the rock strata and made it buckle upwards into a dome. The dome is curved on all sides and lends its shape to the Bay.

Allan's third wave of development, suburbia, made just a tiny impact here as a handful of incomers built houses in what was to become Upper Town above the village, near the station. They were joined by some of the better-off captains whose modest abodes were a great improvement on the cramped ones huddled above each other down by the sea at Bay as it became known.

The effect of the fourth wave, tourism, is all too clear to us this morning as we struggle to find anywhere, convenient or not, to leave Big Car. There is absolutely no possibility near the sea, and on a sunny Sunday the big car parks also overflow. There's not room enough on the pavement for the stream of people walking down. Years ago, after the arrival of an excursion train, there would have been a similar procession, but today's stream is unceasing.

Some visitors only stop briefly and move on, making room for others: such is today's short attention span even when on holiday. The really relaxed are the kids on the beach, immersed in their own small world, who haven't yet discovered the mystery of views, but a few parents snap away catching their loved-ones against the grandeur.

Most Bay homes are now second ones, many expensively rented out by the week, a few occupied rarely by their wealthy owners keeping them solely for their own occasional use. Locals cannot afford the sky-high prices and have had to rent accommodation in Whitby. Tourism may be unstoppable and the basis on which the local economy is now based, but it destroys the old or natural order. As property is modernised and many of the other reminders of Robin Hood's Bay's workaday past disappear, how can it avoid becoming increasingly self-conscious, a village in a fish bowl? (Incidentally most people fondly call it RHB. The name seems to have little or nothing to do with the famous outlaw.)

The dilemma was brilliantly portrayed in Arthur Rank's very first film, the beginning of the modern British film industry, shot here in 1935. Turn of Tide was a real life story of Bay Natives v Incomers, an incomer girl especially stirring things up.

Back at Upper Town, morning service is being held at the church backing onto the old railway station yard. On our drive here, we passed about a hundred boys and girls on their long walk from Fyling Hall School, who for thirty eight weeks a year comprise the largest part of the congregation. The boys especially were then quiet, almost glum. Out they come now – we'll overtake them again in a few minutes – joyously joking, though we can only guess whether from spiritual uplift or having 'got it over' and in expectation of lunch.

In the evening, sitting at the next window table in our Ravenscar hotel dining room with its great view of Robin Hood's Bay is its Rector looking across to his own St Stephen's House. He describes it as 'the Rectory with the best view perhaps in all Yorkshire… from our window this hotel stands out and invites us to come over'.

The Rev John Richardson has a nice sense of place and history. 'Robin Hood's Bay is a lovely village but not without problems. Except on Christmas Day, the crowds are the same. In fact getting around is even harder when the double yellow lines don't apply in winter. The old working Bay is now totally over to tourism, and even Upper Town has many second homes as well as the newly-retired moving in, though there's still a community spirit.'

With its triple-decker pulpit, the original church, Old St Stephen's at Row on the way to Whitby, was inspired by the Anglo-Catholic Oxford Movement, while forty eight years later New St Stephens in Upper Town was decidedly low church. Now in the hands of the Churches Conservation Trust (what we used to call the Redundant Churches

Fund), Old St Stephen's is open to the public in summer and evensong is held there four times a year. The schoolboys and girls attending Sunday services at the new church are a blessing for otherwise the congregation averages barely thirty. And 'one has to be all things to all men, from Anglo-Catholic to Evangelical: not always easy to keep them together.' A lovely village but undoubtedly harder to unite than single-centre ones further away from towns.

As darkness descends, those of us at neighbouring tables look out on a clear evening across the bay to the twinkling lights of RHB, as the village is fondly called, and discuss our small part in human history, our hopes and fears no doubt more ambitious than those who struggled to earn a living here in earlier times. 'But how much happier are we?'

Through Scarborough

Though superficially the cliffs to the south may look similar to those to the north, at nearby Peak sticking out into the North Sea there's a gash in the earth's surface, a fault caused by catastrophic movement. We have now reached that part of the coast with cliffs outcropping younger rocks with further faults pushing out a series of great headlands, the first of them being what Scarborough has so successfully commercialised.

Before we reach Scarborough, though, roads are again further from the sea than the old railway route, difficulty of car access being just one reason why this section of the cliff-top Cleveland Way is especially popular. We make just one diversion closer to the sea than the railway to absorb the sensational view at Rodger Trod. This is near Cloughton, whose quarries were the source of much fine limestone for buildings which blend so superbly into their setting, especially in the neighbouring inland villages. No imported Peterborough brick here.

At the approach to Scarborough, we enjoy being right beside the sea along North Bay and around the headland with its Castle and remains of an especially-well-sited Roman signal station, which brings us past the harbours to South Sands with its famous Spa. There's a lot of Scarborough, its sheer scale supporting excellent facilities, though shortly after I had stayed at it, what was then the town's most highly-rated hotel fell into the sea: there will be more drama yet along this unstable coast.

Conferences earlier in life were more enjoyable here than at most venues. And on our way out of the town we're spoilt for choice of great view points. We cannot justify lingering because, though on its own as resorts go, Scarborough is scarcely remote; anyway it was included in *Journey*, though then I forgot to mention the unique Rotunda which charmingly and practicably combines architecture, art and the science and society of its day. And don't overlook the Tabular Hills stretching 30 miles inland from Scarborough. They are another delight. There are many reasons for coming back for a break at Scarborough another year, we tell ourselves. I've always liked it. But now we have to press on down the coast.

The next of the faults has resulted in broad Clayton Bay with its long sands. The cliffs are now lower, which makes us unprepared for Filey Brigg, a curious landmass sticking out into the sea: one legend says it was the start of a bridge the devil was building to Scandinavia. Explains the excellent *The Dinosaur Coast* already quoted:

At this point the sea meets an extremely hard slab of rock known as the Birdsall Calcareous Grit. At the particular time in the Upper Jurassic when the rocks around Filey were formed, this was a shallow warm sea. The rocks being deposited were oolitic limestones, easily recognised by their bead-like grains. At some point the southern side of this area of sea was slightly lifted and a great wedge of sand poured onto the sea floor. This has survived as the bed of hard calcareous grit, about six metres thick, that forms the Brigg. Seen from the top of Carr Naze, the bed of hard grit that makes the Brigg dips to the south. Underlying the grit, visible on the north side, is a bed of oolite. Great slabs of this oolite are broken off by the sea and thrown up onto the Brigg, forming a bank of boulders.

The cliffs are not particularly high, but with a path running at the foot of the main mass leading to the lower extension it is curious in the extreme, and we can well understand how walkers get trapped by the tide.

Filey and Bridlington

Then Filey, a surprisingly stylish resort which makes me regret my earlier judgement. That was based on familiarity with a much-reproduced railway poster depicting campers who had detrained at the separate Butlin's station near the camp on spacious Hunmanby Sands. Along with other Butlin stations, it (and its triangular junction with the mainline) has long gone. Indeed it must be forty years since on a car journey I stopped at the station on a summer Saturday to look at sun-burned campers joining two trains taking them home at the end of their holiday, one to head north, the other south but avoiding Hull. I did get to know Bridlington, unashamedly popular and foolishly bracketed Filey with it.

Even Bridlington, it has to be said, is way upmarket of what it was in those difficult years after English families ceased taking the traditional fortnight by the sea. Like many other resorts, it has at least partly fought its way back. This Monday morning it is very busy, the promenade and beaches pleasant, the café's temptingly attractive. I never thought I could stay here; now I'm not so sure.

My attention is drawn by a notice of a concert at the railway station. What's this about? When I look into it, feelings are mixed. The Scarborough to Hull line has been designated a Community Railway. I'm much in favour of Community Railways in areas such as North Norfolk and Cornwall, where the active involvement of local people has led to better understanding, more detailed management and increased traffic. Stations are better kept, often with gardens, too.

However, it has long been a failure of our railways to kill a good idea by over doing it. Too many routes have been called Community Railways too rapidly, and it is hard to see how a long line .serving competing resorts, the capital of the Wolds (Driffield) and the charming old town of Beverley, with Scarborough at one end and Hull at the other, can effectively be strengthened by a common community purpose. A twice-yearly forum attended by officials maybe? Railway management is too hamfisted for different kinds of public involvement to be invited where appropriate. 'Our job is just to run trains for those who turn up,' remains the common attitude. It might just do in the London suburbs, but it's different here, and different again where the community can effectively be brought together to play an active part in generating usage. Music on the platform is hardly going to achieve that.

Flamborough Head

Then to our final fault or headland, the largest, one of the major sights of all Britain's east coast, a place where many people have been inspired and thousands of others drowned. Seven miles long, Flamborough Head is thrust out like a great whale. You can judge its importance from the large car park. 'It's a kind of Land's End, the north country one,' says a plump bow-tied man who has just slid cautiously out of his Land Rover.

'Thought that was John O'Groats,' says someone who seems more likely be his sister than wife.

'That's on the west coast, isn't it? This is the east, isn't it?'

'See what you mean. And they wouldn't have needed a dyke there would they?'

This dizzyingly inaccurate piece of geography at least refers to the fact that Danes Dyke, a two-mile long ditch isolating the seaward five square miles, might have been named after the enemy of the day though, since

Bronze Age arrowheads have been found, it could well be an earlier work than its name suggests. But then, even if John O'Groats were situated on it, the north west coast wasn't always free from the Vikings either.

The truth is that much about Flamborough Head is a mystery. Why, for example, were ships still wrecked, once one every twelve weeks, after the first lighthouse was built in 1674? Though much renovated, it is England's oldest complete surviving lighthouse, well back from the sea. But then there doesn't seem to be any proof that a light was ever lit in it. If not, why not? And why was this of all places the scene of a battle in the American War of Independence? Other sea-battles were also fought, including one in our own Civil War.

The second and taller lighthouse on this tough chalk headland is 85ft high and, though still called 'new', has been sending its warning light over a wide area of sea since 1806. It was built without resort to scaffolding. With the cliff 170ft high, at the combined height it must have been a windy place to work. Like the rest of England's lighthouses, it is now automatic but that doesn't seem to have robbed it of romance.

Inevitably one goes first to the headland, where the racing tides contribute to shipwrecks, where the elements meet, and so do past and present. It is breezy out here today, and one is not surprised that the sea has carved many caves, up to 50ft deep, into the chalk. Visibility is brilliant; eerie it must be when the foghorn sounds, its warning also spreading over a wide area and being something of a night nuisance to those who live nearest to it.

The village of Flamborough is naturally further back, but still a lonely place, and one worth exploring, as are the North and South Landings reached by steep tracks. After fierce shipwrecking storms of February 1871 which no lighthouse could prevent, the RNLI established a lifeboat at each, but in today's motorised world one suffices. At the South Landing there's a café with a daily list recording birds seen. It changes dramatically since many migrating species pause here, a huge range of species including puffins being recorded over a year. The headland is rich in flora, too.

At North Landing, we watch a girl of ten or eleven chip away pieces of rock as she searches for fossils, one of which she quickly prizes. Whether or not she should be doing that here we're not sure, but the public are invited to do it with mallet and chisel (and told what materials to bring to take the fossils safely home) in an area near Danes Dyke. This has the easiest-worked chalk in Yorkshire, responsibly for healthy farming. Altogether there is much to see here, including the RSPB reserve on the chalk cliffs at nearby Bempton. Yet it is the extreme headland that lingers in the mind: an extraordinary place where nothing seems as though it will ever change and yet so much has happened. Remote Britain personified. Yet it can still regularly be viewed by boat from Bridlington, which is more than can be said of most headlands these days.

And now, having enjoyed so many cliffs of different ages, shapes and sizes, we realise that's it. From here south, no cliffs to be met all the way to Kent, or in our case till weeks later when we're on The Gower.

· IX ·

THE YORKSHIRE WOLDS AND THEIR CRUMBLING COAST

The 'Typical' Yorkshire Wolds

Britain is such a varied country that no one part is really typical but, if I were pressed to choose one area which best sums up how we think the countryside should be, it might be the Yorkshire Wolds. Still thinly populated, often with considerable distances between villages, they are also lightly wooded. Curving hills are a prominent feature, yet nothing rises very high.

It is a gentle countryside, pleasingly mixed, always welcoming, occasionally gorgeously so, though what especially appeals to me after showcase mountains and headlands is its very ordinariness or matter of factness. There is nothing spectacular here, nothing especially memorable, but a rolling land of pleasant hills, farms, and villages where one feels it would be good to live without being over-run by tourists. Delightful. Happily not Theme Park Britain.

It is a land in which I lose my worries and feel at home without the Wow factor. Here is excellent walking, cycling and riding country. There's a 79-mile peaceful Yorkshire Wold Way from Filey to the Humber, though naturally most people only use a section. The Wolds are pepper-potted with ancient sites, gracious buildings including what might be called modest stately homes (as opposed to the Longleats and Chatsworths), churches still at the heart of their community, and where good food is both produced and sold. Farmers markets have long been a familiar feature. It is decidedly not a poor part of Yorkshire.

The Wolds occupy a large wedge-shaped area immediately south of the North Yorks. Moors National Park which is spectacular to the end and undoubtedly offers great views of the Wolds below. The Wolds narrow as they reach further south, where their eastern boundary is an almost straight line north from the Humber Bridge, excluding Hull itself. To the east of the narrowest part of the wedge lies Holderness, though to some people that conveys just the coast rather than the countryside. Away from Hull, this is superficially similar though lower lying and flatter, on clay rather than chalk and so with many differences in vegetation. It is however also what I call matter-of-fact country with well-spaced villages.

South of the broad Humber estuary, across the long high bridge, the Lincolnshire Wolds pick up the theme in much the same way. Parts are close to sea level, subject to morning mists and fogs, but the impression I gained of the Wolds, long before visiting them, was of a cold, damp land, and that is entirely wrong. Perhaps the trouble is the uninvitingness of the name, 'Wolds'.

The Concise Oxford Dictionary defines that as a place name, especially in Britain: 'a piece of high, open, uncultivated land or moor.' But that's not fair, for much is cultivated, and the Old English (from German) 'wald' meaning wooded upland isn't accurate either, for an especially delightful feature is the *scattered* woodland. It is mixed country of a kind which occurs surprisingly rarely in today's Britain. The writer Winifred Holtby describes the Wolds as 'fold upon fold of encircling hills, piled rich and golden'. 'Rolling landscape and laid-back charm, inspiration to many,' is how the guide of the East Yorkshire Tourism Association puts it. Other writers and many artists (most distinguishably David Hockney) have been inspired by the rolling chalk lands and their quiet country lanes. Artists' studio's abound, but not in an overpowering way any more than their work depicts great glamour.

Civilisation began here early (much tree clearance having been completed by 1000BC), hence the rich archaeological remains, while the Romans made the most of this part of their conquest and are responsible for some of today's road system. I have found it hard to put down a book with what sounds a somewhat forbidding title published by the University of Hull Press, but which enterprisingly captivates one's interest in our yesterdays and how they shaped our today. *An Historical Atlas of East Yorkshire* combines maps and, drawings and diagrams with an easy-to-read accessible text emphasising change (many medieval villages now deserted) and continuity. For millennia the Wolds have enjoyed the fruits of good climate, soil and an industrious population, though they did not escape the tensions between rich and poor. Sometimes that led to riots. The Wolds may always have been green, but they weren't always happy. There was indeed a viciously-divided society at the time of the Civil War.

So we go east from Bridlington along a largely-straight Roman road breathing in a pleasurable Wold sample, though at first we're close to the border where the southward sloping chalk gives way to clay. First stop is Kilham, whose straggling single street has tell-tale traces of better days. For example, outside the church, towering above the village on an eminence, is a tethering ring anchored in a stone block from the days when a cattle market was held on the street. Fairs were just one ingredient in Kilham's earlier role as capital of the Wolds.

It was the opening of a canal off the navigable River Humber that initially gave nearby Driffield a trading advantage, leading to its steady growth into the Wold's capital. Kilham steadily declined. Once it had six schools; only the C of E Primary survives. It is a pleasant little place, with light traffic passing through. A few individual businesses such as The Craft Cupboard and Old Ropery Antiques no doubt find support from residents of the pretty restored cottages and small developments of larger houses. Almost anywhere in the Wolds is reachable by commuters working in Hull and other towns on their periphery, but this countryside in not everyone's choice and, except close to Hull, pressure is far from overwhelming. There's rolling countryside to north and south. Though early man lived on hilltops – there are indeed remains of Hill Forts and many tumuli – today's villages are either in valley bottoms or near the bottom of (mainly south facing) slopes.

'A bit sad, much declined,' says Sheila suggesting we have lunch here: 'They look as though they need our business.'

'Let's go on to somewhere needing it more,' I suggest.

'I know what that means... getting lost as I starve,' she moans. I *don't* get lost... well not exactly for what does it matter which route we take from the disused airfield (think of the memories it must have generated) where the Roman road seems to peter out... providing we go north.

The scar of the airfield apart, it is very pleasant country, true chalkland Wolds. We drive on still straight but by no means steep lanes crossing the intrusion of the B1253 – not a car in sight – and an ancient earth work rapidly arriving in the metropolis of Weaverthorpe from the direction opposite to the one I expected. Metropolis? Weaverthorpe is minute, again in a shallow valley bottom. Each of the few people we meet greets us with curiosity and that noonday uncertainty: should it be Good Morning or Good Afternoon? Like Kilham, Weaverthorpe has an over-sized Norman Church and a school, again a C of E Primary, and still a Post Office cum-general store. Here there are also two pubs, both offering good Yorkshire fare and no doubt banter; ours certainly did.

Suitably fed and watered, in high spirits we agree there's time to go further north... through the excellence of the Wolds, up East Heslerton Brow to look down on the Derwent Valley and across and up to the southern rise of the North Yorks. Moors. Distances aren't huge – apart from the North Yorks. Moors, everything is small scale – so by another complicated route, navigating more by feel than map, we find the deserted medieval village of Wharram Percy where the outlines of many former houses can be traced.

Settled since pre-historic times, and after a period of prosperity from the 12th to 14th centuries, it was abandoned with many others around 1500. We can see the ruined church. More visitors seem to be here than at the live villages we went to earlier: the places that have totally died always have a fascination. The atlas mentioned earlier has a map of swathes of them in both the Wolds and Holderness, while other maps show population changes, as one might expect, increases in and near the major towns and decreases in the Wolds heartlands.

Then to Driffield, or actually Great Driffield to distinguish it from Little, almost absorbed as a suburb. The mighty tower of All Saint's Church helps guide us the last miles. Here we have a real town, clearly enjoying its status as local capital, and paying renewed respect to the creator of its success, the canal. Though we now don't have much spare time, certainly not for shopping, it is pleasant walking by the canal with its restored lock and warehouses put to new use, attracting walkers, mums handing out crusts for kids to feed the ducks, and a few sitting eating a late sandwich or pie.

Crossing the Scarborough to Hull railway by one of the few bridges, for hereabouts level crossings are the norm, we follow the Driffield Canal alongside the River Humber, a modest affair this far up. Then in flat, watery country, I am attracted by the remoteness of Skerne. Remote yes, but not quaint. The shops and school have gone, yet old cottages have been gentrified and there's considerable new building. Though sympathetically done, it's not real village-style, though again not overpowering. The church is truly rural: the main way in seems to be by a farm gate.

We're becoming tired, and realising that to avoid main roads we'll have to cross the River Humber quickly, we go map-reading across country adding another list of villages to those we've already enjoyed: Wansford, North Frodingham, Brandesburton, Sigglesthorne and Withernwick, each very different, to reach our resting place for tonight, West Carlton Guest House, a few miles from the sea at Aldbrough. Yes, we remembered to buy a bottle of wine since, though obviously a superior and certainly a comfortable establishment in deep countryside, it doesn't yet have a table licence. After a meal made with fresh local ingredients but wine from Chile, we crash out early.

Unsurprisingly, the villages have become somewhat confused in our minds. What we'll always remember is that here is a corner of England with real country, friendly people, lovely gentle scenery and good food. If only we had the time we'd be content to explore it for a month and discover the undoubted individuality of each village and its surrounds. Next year we'll be doing the same village hopping deep in the Lincolnshire countryside. 'But let's take longer,' says Sheila.

Bracing Hornsea

In the morning, our immediate destination is Hornsea. It is only my second visit, the first being around 1961 when, in common with so many others, the branch lines to Hornsea and Withernsea, sharing a common exit from Hull, were under closure threat. To enable me to travel by both, soon after arrival at Hornsea's substantial station which could shelter a thousand waiting passengers and had a grand frontage, I took a taxi along the coast to Withernsea. There was time to look around there. Not knowing how long the taxi journey would take, I saw little more of Hornsea than the station and seafront. So most of it is new to me this morning.

Though by then most passenger trains on both level-crossing-infested lines carried few passengers, and the daily goods trains were down to a handful of trucks, what was obvious was that the little resort owed almost everything to the coming of the railway in 1864 and that the impetus it created continued after it closed just a century later. Both resorts became Hull-by-the Sea, thousands of day trippers arriving on Bank Holidays and fine weekends, especially when the skies were blue and the sun warmed things up after a long period of unsettled weather at the season's start. Sometimes extra trains, each carrying hundreds of passengers, had quickly to be formed with any locomotive (passenger or goods) and rolling stock available. At least the route didn't offer much challenge: the highest point it reached between Hull and Hornsea was 66ft above sea level. There was also substantial year-round residential business as Hull businessmen started moving here.

Warming up is comparative on the east coast. It is lovely inland today but, when I ask a passer by the best way to walk to the seafront, he replies: 'You'll know when you're getting there; you'll be blown around.' We are. The bracing breeze is really stiff. There is an excellent, broad promenade along which a few of us are putting up a good pretence of enjoyment while being dashed by the erratic east coast air keeping the temperature down several degrees. Many more have either come deliberately for other attractions or to slink off to them. There's quite a lot to do besides the obvious pull of the Market Village already celebrating its silver jubilee, which puts its opening just half way through the time since I paid that fleeting visit by train and taxi.

Away from the promenade, Hornsea is bubbling with activity, the

Freeport Hornsea Outlet Shopping Village being a particular pull. Walking down the attractive garden-like path, I ask Sheila if she would like to go into any of the shops. A plumpish Yorkshire dame, distinctively if not fashionably dressed, answers for her. 'Cos you do luv; super fashion at cut-throat prices. Even Lancashire people think it's super.' A real recommendation.

Next a disappointing short trip north back toward Bridlington. The somewhat dull road keeps well inland, though there are occasional lanes down to the beaches and the small campsites exploiting them. Then, with greater interest, the two miles around Hornsea Mere, Yorkshire's largest sheet of inland water, big enough to be both a bird sanctuary and to offer sailing. After the dissolution of the Abbey, the manor and mere became Crown property until privatised by Elizabeth I. When we've completed our circumnavigation, we see an attractive café with boats for hire. 'Yorkshire Lakeland' is how a railway poster once portrayed Hornsea.Then to a newish housing estate where Bettison's Folly, Grade II listed, seems ludicrously out of place. William Bettison was a Hull brewer and newspaper owner always impatient for his dinner when returning home. But how did his servants know exactly when that would be? By looking out from the tower, high enough for them to see him coming, and dashing down to do the final preparations. At least the nouveau rich of yesteryear flung their wealth around in a way that would be remembered.

Back to the town for lunch: the choice is surprisingly difficult and we probably don't make the best. Though the coast is the main draw, inland Holderness is friendlier, badly signposted, very flat but well kept with productive farms and inviting villages. Not that much of the land was always productive. In modern times serious drainage of waterlogged areas didn't start till the 17th century.

The Famous Pottery

Before leaving Hornsea, a walk along the main street, where several shop windows detain us. 'Wanted please... a pair of old hobnail boots (size 10 or 11)... for our model in the blacksmith's workshop.' And a fantastic display of green and cream Harrod's ware made at the famous Hornsea Pottery, closed nearly ten years ago.

Back at our guest house, next morning enjoying a super breakfast and Percy the pheasant strutting round the lawn with a couple of his wives, we are joined by Mary Potts from Exeter, a devoted collector of Hornsea Pottery: 'Each time I take a day out I add another two or three. I wasn't into collecting anything with a focus until a few years ago when one day I studied a couple of organic-looking country browny-yellowish mugs I had from the famous pottery. That set me going.

Many people would call it tat, and of course it's not fine porcelain, but they're beautifully glazed, brilliantly designed and really representative of their era. I found I wasn't alone. There's a big collectors' club which meets five times a year. I try and get to the meetings.'

The Director of Grounds (and fine they are) at Exeter University, she's never been to Hornsea before. 'I've come specially to see it because of the pottery. Its closure must have hit the town badly. Hornsea is certainly not Torquay but reminds me a bit of Paignton, smaller scale. How does it survive? Anyway I'm pleased to have got here at last, seen where the factory [within the Freeport Shopping Complex] was and spend time in the Folk Museum. That's largely devoted to displaying Hornsea ware. An incredible range, and what colours. And there's an account of the story of how a small pottery in a remote seaside town became internationally famous. Alas after fifty years of pouring out enormous production, it gave up.' Yet, as witness, the museum is expanding to show off even more examples. The pottery is still doing something for the town.

I reflect that there were many potteries in Devon, but their combined output might not have equalled Hornsea's. While Hornsea ware is now being sought by an enthusiastic brand of enthusiasts, it still turns up cheaply at car boot sales. If you have any mugs, ashtrays, stylish vases or figures of people or animals from the 1950s to 1990s, check to see if they are from Hornsea. It might start you collecting.

Mary Potts puts me in touch with the pottery's famous designer, John Clappison. He is revelling in the fact that there's a collector's society, his designs are now fetching high prices, and he's even the subject of a book. 'It's recognition at last, which didn't come very easily,' he says.

His father helped set up the business in 1949; he'd been a butcher in Hull but, suffering from what today would be diagnosed as ME, he was told he'd better sell the shop and move somewhere peaceful. 'The pottery was run by two brothers, the Rawsons. After I'd gone to school and art college in Hull, going there daily by train, I joined the firm and quickly started designing mugs and vases. My designs really took off, but they treated me as a junior, with a basic salary.

They tried bringing in more senior designers, but they didn't work out. It was my designs that brought in the money. But still I wasn't properly paid. It wasn't just the money, but recognition.

So I left. Again they brought in new designers, and again that didn't work, so they started wooing me back. Though I had a spell at Royal Doulton, I spent four years at Ravenhead Glass, and in that time introduced five hundred designs there.

I must have done thousands at Hornsea: mugs and other tableware, vases, plant pots, an enormous and ever-changing range, though I didn't go in for the cute animal ones. Yes, we were remarkable. We bridged the gap between individual and mass production in a way that hardly anyone else did. The runs could be quite short but it wasn't just a few at a time.

We had a strong local following from all over East Yorkshire. We actually made more money selling seconds direct to the public. We didn't even have to pack them properly and got paid in cash. Selling to shops meant packing, delivery, invoicing, book-keeping, chasing up payment, not to mention trade discount. To encourage people to visit, we had a café and most who came to it bought the seconds. The 300 regular workers were augmented in the season. It seemed such a good model that the brothers decided to replicate it at Lancaster, with Blackpool on the doorstep. Lancaster was a carbon copy, even in size. But whereas Hornsea had started in a converted building and grew with temporary space, Lancaster had an architect-designed modern building. And while most of the workers at Hornsea had come from low-paid farm jobs, wages were much higher in Lancashire. They were paid differently for a time, but Hornsea people got to know they were getting less, so up went the costs there, too. It wasn't a happy position – the main cause of the downfall.'

Quite a story. I tell him I'm waiting for the arrival of a copy of *Gone to Pot: The life and work of John Clappison*. 'That's certainly vindication after all the bad times,' he says. Now in his seventies, he's on a high having bought a small kiln and making special items sold at meetings of the collectors' club. He's delighted, too, that Hornsea's High Street Folk Museum is expanding to enable more pieces to be displayed. But a move back to the town didn't work. 'We'd lost the rose-tinted spectacles. It wasn't the same place any more.' He now lives at Stapeley near Nantwich.

Aldbrough and the Coast

What the resorts do not say in their publicity is that the main feature of the coast south from Hornsea is its steady destruction. Hornsea itself, protected by its promenade, is built on soft boulder clay. 'One day we may be left out on a peninsular,' was one comment. Once the sea was as much as 2½ miles away. Nearly thirty settlements, including Hornsea Burton and Hornsea Beck, have been lost between Flamborough Head and Spurn Head. If Hornsea and any other protected part were made into a peninsular as the rest of the coastline retreated, at least it would make for a more interesting map. Currently, from a few miles south of Flamborough Head, it is one of Britain's longest sections of nearly straight, just slightly curved, coast. It tilts a little west of north and catches the full fury of many storms, which at high tide nibble away at the base of soft glacial clay till the rest, especially if it is sodden comes tumbling down.

Along the Withernsea road, many of whose details I do recall from that trip of branch-line days, our first stop is at Mappleton. To protect a population of only 250, sea defences have been built and an effort made to restore the sands. Previously, the sea had been consuming nearly ten feet a year here. Not only has the restoration of the sands not been very successful but, where man intervenes, there is usually a price to be paid elsewhere: increased erosion further south.

In Aldbrough's attractive village one is hardly – yet – aware of the coast, but it isn't far down a side road, still leading to a holiday camp, before there's a warning sign and the tarmac ends. It dips seaward beyond barbed wire. I've already been told that Old Aldbrough went years ago. Whole streets have disappeared in the last century and, when we park the car on the street, the car park having gone, we see the end bungalow is already boarded up in preparation for its disappearance one stormy night when the wave action will undercut the ground it's built on.

Of all the people we've met on our journeys, by far the most anxious to answer questions and talk is William Peacock. His 357 Seaside Road is now the last occupied bungalow on his side. He explains: 'We fell in love with this area when I was working for Reckitt's Blue in Hull, bought a caravan in 1960 and this bungalow in 1965. Rosie my wife died three years ago so I'm on my own now, but I still love it here, even though it's deteriorated badly. You still feel you're somewhere; it isn't just anywhere. I've seen four rows of houses fall into the sea... gun mountings from the war, bungalows, car park, café, four or five more rows of cottages... about 600 yards in my time, I suppose. The best of neighbours have gone; I may finish my time here quite on my own, though my family are good. And it's obvious that this bungalow's days are numbered, though it might just about see me out. I'm 86 now, 87 next week.'

He's full of tales... and resentment. 'What's the government doing about it? People lose their homes, their life's investment. And though I own the house, I don't own the freehold. This year my ground rent is £500 and I'm told it'll go up in stages to a staggering £1,000 supposed to be based on the value of the caravan site. But that won't be worth much when its turn comes to fall into the sea. Perhaps the freehold owner is trying to make his fortune first.'

He adds forcibly: 'Oh, first to go after the war was the Temperance Pub,' as though that explains it all. He doesn't need to say how lonely he is. He has so much to tell, he doesn't know what to say next or which pictures to show of how things used to be. The pictures are revealing: once this would have been a really sociable area. After a long talk which might have gone on all evening, I make my escape to chat to someone loading fishing gear into his van opposite. We saw him on the beach earlier. He will have come up the temporary complicated way since the proper one lies in ruins on the beach.

As Sheila comes to meet me, she's intercepted by William who has dashed out in his shirtsleeves for more company, this breezy night, blowing very wet drizzle – horizontally. Feeling sorry for him, she accompanies him back home, where with obvious pleasure he starts by calling me 'a nosy b------.' Out come the photos again.

Graham Addy, from further up Seaside Road, tells me about his catch. 'Only taking home a large coddling tonight. Had a seabass, but not legally large enough to keep so threw it back.' He sometimes goes to the bird sanctuary at Bempton, beyond Flamborough Head, for better fishing off the clifftop, though that's not allowed in the migration season. 'The birds come first. I don't mind that, but what we do object to here is getting no compensation for losing our homes. Unbelievable, isn't it, we have to pay to demolish them when they are about to go over. And it's wicked what we have to pay for ground rent based on the supposed value of land in the holiday camp. We're not a holiday camp, are we?'

A candidate in the local Council election agrees the charge should be dropped for flattening homes before they are claimed by the sea. 'We know we won't get sea defences here. That's a losing battle. But we would like the Council to consider demolishing the houses for free.'

'Holiday Homes' and B&B

All of which leaves us feeling rather sad. Nothing we can do – except send lonely William a birthday card and present [which his son later writes to say did much to cheer him up]. Many others must be in a similar situation, which directs my thoughts to something I've never seen in print or heard discussed: the marvellous way in which many working people secured holiday homes before that name was invented.

From the early 1920s, they somehow found the means to build a shack, nearly always at an inconvenient, not generally cherished, indeed often remote place where their bosses wouldn't be seen. In the days before planning controls, they used bits of huts, greenhouses, old railway trucks and worn out buses to piece together a not very comfortable retreat of the kind that later were seen as eyesores. Eyesores indeed they were, often without running water. Washing and lavatory arrangements were at best communal, sometimes a considerable way away. But how different it was from their everyday working surroundings. How they enjoyed the fresh air. Unsightly though they may have been, such shacks must have given purpose and pleasure and so prolonged life. Once this coast had many of them, but they've nearly all been cleared away or been absorbed into today's static caravan sites. And now the likes of William, who delighted in just finding 'somewhere' where he could come to life, are steadily dying out.

Much has been said about conventional tourism in Victorian and Edwardian days, and about the great holiday revolution after 1945. The exploits of the first generation of working people to find 'somewhere' became taboo because of their initial makeshift seaside escapes disturbing previous patterns and undoubtedly creating what later was seen as a planning nightmare: ribbon development of the worst kind along what had till then been pristine coast.

At breakfast again at our guest house, our final morning at what has been an outstanding successful choice, Caroline Maltas tells us: 'This was one of four farms in the group, and it was a struggle to make it pay. So we sold off the land to a neighbouring farmer, and my husband Tim trained as a special needs teacher. The house was rather big for us, and we had long talked about establishing a bed-and-breakfast. We delayed so we could do it properly. We are rated four star, and love making people feel really at home in a country setting in a part of Yorkshire many don't even realise exists.'

Though technically it's a B&B, for those who want them, evening meals are provided with consultation over the menu. They are modestly priced. A two-paged standard letter in our room headed Food Glorious Food invites us to place our breakfast order whenever convenient in the evening to be ready at whatever time we choose and with a great choice of local produce. No wonder a good repeat business is building. Though our largish bedroom may lack a touch of the 'refinement' of a four-star hotel – blow me, there's no trouser press – we have experienced less flexibility, friendliness and general well-being at up to three times the £92 we're paying a night here between us for dinner bed and breakfast. It's been great.

A specially-memorable feature is the utterly unspoilt rural position. From our bedroom we watched a beautiful spotted-woodpecker among many birds, attracted by bird feeders in the garden.

We would love to stay in places as good as West Carlton Guest House, but without a real recommendation they are risky, often being excellent in many ways but having an unforgivable eccentricity or two. The commercial guides may do basic inspections but are driven by the pressure to achieve more entries.

· X ·

TO THE MOST EERIE PLACE IN BRITAIN

'Road Ahead Subject to Erosion'

There was one thing we intended to do in Aldbrough but have forgotten: see the ancient (pre-Norman Conquest) Aldbrough Sundial. Now in St Bartholomew's Church, the language it uses is an ancient form of Anglicised Old Norse, showing how strong the Scandinavian influence must once have been. But it is time to return to the main road and continue south down this disintegrating coast to Withernsea. Taking a diversion toward the sea near Tunstall, we spot a singularly useless warning notice: 'Road ahead subject to erosion.' There's no road at all: the end has been fenced off. To the side caravans are parked on concrete, some close to jagged ends broken off in the last attack by the sea. 'A metre can go in a day,' says a glum man.

My 1882 *Murray's Handbook* optimistically speaks of a slowing of erosion due to better protection works, but the speed has accelerated and rising sea levels and increasing storms bode ill. Nothing however compared to the consequences the decline in glaciers might lead to, including a threat that a third of the world's population could be forced to move because of flooding or water shortage. And even this is small fry compared with the changes in geology and climate of millions years ago we've noted earlier along this coast. To make the point, elephant teeth have been found closeby.

Withernsea

At last Withernsea. You'll not find it in the likes of the *Rough Guide* but, according to its own website, it offers 'a wonderful blend of seaside attractions with just a touch of the wilderness about it'. It certainly has a charismatic sea front with unique castellated twin towers nicknamed The Sandcastle up the steps at the entrance to what was for a very short time the pier. Despite accidents during its building, the pier had a great opening in 1875; its ornate iron girders stretched out over 1,000ft. Only five years later, during a great storm on 28 October 1880, and after a collision with another vessel, the *Jabez* crashed into its end. The same storm ripped the sails off a coal barge trying to reach the refuge of the Humber. Driven helplessly, it punched a 250ft gap in the centre of the pier before grounding on the beach with another dozen vessels. Bodies and bits of wreckage were everywhere. A macabre detail: a special train ran from Hull to bring people to identify the drowned. Only three years later the local paper reported that the wreckage of the *Henry Parr* coming into contact with the piles of the Pier 'swept it down, span after span, with a fearful noise and brilliant display of sparks'. The pier was clearly not meant to be.

The new Valley Gardens, though too full of concrete for my liking, are a delight for children. Whether the town, with a tall lighthouse mysteriously bang in its middle, is attractive is more debateable. Very Yorkshire, very un-English, yes. Feeling slightly God forsaken at first, it's a place that might just grow on one. I'm not sure. At least it will not be Scottish even if the Scottish Jacobite Party were to win and achieve its aim of moving the Anglo-Scottish border to Flamborough, assures the front page of a free local paper.

The long-closed line by which I travelled back to Hull on my 1960s visit was built a decade before the Hornsea route. Unlike most local concerns, the company, led by a Hull merchant sponsoring it started by owning and running its own trains. It even built a grand forty-bedroom Queens Hotel next to the station with its canopy on cast-iron columns. That suggests importance, perhaps as a centre serving a prosperous hinterland, villages slightly higher than most of the lowland, with oversize churches mainly built with irregular-shaped stone blocks and with tall towers commanding huge views across the flat land and the often not so flat sea.

Think again. The villages and their churches may have spelt agricultural well-being but, before the first trains arrived, only a few hundred lived here. Though trains were ultimately to bring prosperity, even in 1891 the population was little over a thousand. Like many other Victorian seaside dreams, Withernsea was really a failure.

Few buildings of merit lined its carefully-planned broad streets. In 1873 the local paper complained of the 'dormant state' of the place: 'Plans which looked so elaborate on paper seemed to have vanished into thin air – look at the town as it now is, one long straggling irregularly built street.' The promenade and pier were built, but not much more. The hotel proved too large and costly, and soon became the hospital. (Later another hotel was called The Queens.)

By the time trains started bringing thousands of day trippers, and a serious number of Hull residents had moved here, it was too late to lay the solid foundations of a major resort: nearly everywhere the die was cast by the 1860s.

We walk along a busy street whose width, with speeding vehicles, makes it hard for pedestrians to cross. There's nothing especially to detain us, except possibly the lighthouse which is a museum. Apart from the fact it isn't open, I don't want to climb scores of steps and actually even less to gain a bird's eye view of the countryside, coast and Humber estuary. An understanding of a place gained from ground level is sometimes better left that way.

Towering 127ft among terraced houses, the lighthouse was retired in 1976 after serving for eighty two years. Belatedly filling a gap between the lighthouses of Flamborough and Spurn, and deliberately sited well away from the crumbling coast, it was built following the 1890 outcry about a captain being frozen to the rigging of his floundering ship. The lighthouse's beam shone out seventeen miles on a clear night, its Morse Code often flashing 'U', meaning 'You are standing into danger'.

As a museum it offers many things, especially a tribute to the local girl Kay Kendall and a video which includes excerpts from her 1950s films. At street level there's a café and gardens. There's a lot about the past, too.

The town's medieval church was lost to the sea and its replacement further inland was abandoned as a ruin after its roof was blown off in a 1609 storm. In the late 1850s, the shell was skilfully reroofed and restored to be today's St Nicholas'. They are used to the unusual along this coast. Even the re-roofed St Nicholas' had lead torn off it in the 1890 gale; the headstones in the churchyard are full of tales of the grim unexpected.

Withernsea's a sad place, and maybe God-forsaken isn't a wrong description, but 'might have beens' are always fascinating.

The Narrowing Land

Still heading south, we are kept mainly out of sight of the dead-straight, boring and steadily being eaten-away coast until Easington. Here the land begins to narrow between the sea and the Humber. Beyond the substantial village (a string of those further east were destroyed by the sea centuries ago) it feels almost like the end of the world. It is in fact the end of a natural gas pipeline from Norway, also connected to the North Sea's Rough gas field, now mainly used as an undersea storage area. The twin terminals can deliver up to 10 per cent of Britain's peak winter demand, the importance underlined by the fact that a fault closing it in 2004 led to an instant increase in spot-gas prices. Nearby is an Army depot and other unsightly things. Not the place for a picnic.

Only the dregs of Yorkshire left is one way of saying we still seem to be heading toward the end of the world though, as the land narrows and we're forced away from the coast, a new hazy foreign land opens up through the mist beyond extensive mud flats and the broad sweep of the mouth of the Humber. We can just make out Grimsby and Cleethorpes in a totally different environment. To the right, flat pasture land with numerous streams and drains. Ahead the last Yorkshire village, tiny Kilnsea. Old Kilnsea was washed away in medieval days, the present 1860s church incorporating some of the old stone, often so used along this retreating coast.

Nowhere has the geography changed more than at East Yorkshire's southern tip. More villages were lost even on the estuary side while, long buried under the North Sea, are the remains of Ravenser Odd, which 700 years ago returned two MPs and rivalled Grimsby as a fishing port. The tip of the peninsular which now ends at Spurn Head has had successive predecessors further out to sea. It will no doubt change again.

An Historical Atlas of East Yorkshire referred to earlier shows villages which are known to have been lost in recorded history and, using projections based on scantier evidence, where the coast might have been at different times back to about 600. At up to nearly ten feet a year, much land has been lost in the 1400 years since then. He also projects where what is now the spit to Spurn Head would successively have been. In his accompanying text, George de Boer says the very earliest reference to spits invites careful conjecture:

> The oldest of these accounts tells how Wilgils, father of St Willibrord, first bishop of Utrecht, came to 'the promontory encircled by the sea and Humber' and founded a chapel and monastery dedicated to St Andrew. Such a site, possibly on the broader tip of a peninsular with a narrow neck crossed by the tide which would cut it off from the mainland at intervals, might have seemed attractive to a community seeking solitude. It appears to have existed from c670-770 just as, 1,000 years later, the site of Angell's lighthouse lasted from c1674-1776; it too was cut off from Holderness when high spring tides crossed the neck of Spurn Point. The details given in *Egil's Saga* of his shipwreck here c950 resemble conditions at Spurn today when a northerly gale causes heavy seas to break on Spurn and the Stony Binks.
>
> Each of the five spits of this reconstruction seems to have received a name after its appearance, and each name is topographically appropriate. *Cornu vallis* (the horn of the valley) was the name in Wilgils' time, when the valley in the boulder clay near Kilnsea and

Easington would have been long enough, probably at least two miles, to justify this title. The spit on which Egil was wrecked was possibly that later named *Hrafnseyrr* or *Ravenser* (Raven's beach or sand bank), from which Olaf sailed with the remnants of the Scandinavian army defeated at Stamford Bridge in 1066. Later Ravenser became the name of the village near the tip of Holderness, and the next spit to appear was *Ravenser Odd* (the headland near Ravenser), which also became the name of the town established on it. By the time Bolingbroke landed there, the succeeding spit was called *Ravenser Spurn* or *Ravenspurn* (the spur of land near Ravenser). The new name for its successor, *Spurn Point*, is first recorded in 1675.

Sailing the Rails

On school and road atlases, millions must have noticed the oddity of Spurn sticking out into the Humber's mouth. I first did in 1938.

The next thing I discovered was that a peculiar railway ran down it. Not merely was its standard gauge laid within feet of the sea on either side, and so subject to weather interruptions, but many people travelled on it by wind power. Arriving back at Kilnsea late from an evening out, the normal train service having ceased, soldiers based at Spurn used one of the trolleys, like the old permanent way ones, fitted up with sails. Raise the sail and off they went, covering 3½ miles in as little as eight minutes. The latest book on the subject, *Sailing the Rails: A New History of Spurn and its Military Railway* (published by the Spurn Heritage Coast in Easington). Howard M Frost, says it would have felt tremendously fast travelling so close to the ground.

> A good driver (or skipper?) would be able to judge just the right moment at which to lower the sail... stopping depended on skill, but in case of problems, there was sometimes an emergency braking system. This took the form of an old railway sleeper, which was carried on the front of the trolley and could be pushed off onto the track to jam the wheels. Not surprisingly, there were some hair-raising moments.
>
> On one occasion, a small party of soldiers had borrowed a trolley to get to the Blue Bell Inn at Kilnsea. When time was called, rather the worse for wear, they boarded the trolley hoisted the sail, and set off for Spurn. Once moving they all dropped off to sleep, leaving the bogie to carry on briskly but unattended. There were big entrance gates to the fort just past the lighthouse. Just when it looked as though there would be a major collision, one soldier woke up and managed to heave off the piece of wood just in time.

Spurn has always had strategic importance, and had a large military presence in both world wars. Opened by the military in 1915, the railway seems to have been a friendly concern carrying lighthouse keepers, soldiers' wives and children, their Spurn schoolteacher and even visitors. It had its own steam engines, a stylish carriage and numerous goods vehicles, with an extensive layout at Kilnsea and Spurn, where it served its own dock. Much of the time, there was roughly an hourly train during the day. Before its opening, the postman used to walk from Easington, a round trip of fifteen miles a day. One forgets how slowly roads developed in out-of-the-way places and that, before the days of big lorries, bulldozers and dumper trucks, the first thing to happen at a large construction site was the building a tramway round it for the conveyance of sand, cement, timber, sometimes even water, and the removal of top soil and waste. It was easier to build a railway than a road to Spurn Head.

The Most Eerie Place in Britain

Nowhere in Britain, not even Land's End or John O'Groats, is more noticed and less visited than Spurn. I missed the closure of the railway in 1951 and well over half a century later am paying my first visit. As the land narrows to a mere spit, there's a gated entrance to the road replacing the railway running down it and occupying nearly all of the land above sea level.

Though cars pass freely, they are obviously recorded by the wardens of the Yorkshire Wildlife Trust. 'Up to 60,000 people come a year, 1,000 cars at holiday weekends,' says today's duty man, assistant seasonal warden Chris Gorner, who lives near Warren Cottage, the bird observatory just behind the information centre. Though a bit hut-like, this has an excellent display of leaflets and books we found useful. Chris is paid for eight months a year. Access is normally restricted in the winter. As visitor attractions go, 60,000 visitors a year isn't very many. As I say, Spurn is much known about but little seen.

'By the way,' he says to a colleague. 'How's the BBC camera team?' At which the colleague gives me a knowing grin: 'The BBC are filming.' When I was a television reporter, I was often amazed at the way the letters BBC carried such prestige, giving instant welcome and priority. And that's when the corporation was an august monopoly. Even today the BBC somehow spells superiority; ITV companies have never enjoyed the same clout.

When I say it must be a bit wild here sometimes, the reply is straightforward rather than graphic. 'Yes, the sea often comes over, washing away bits of the road but, if the school buses can't run, they usually manage to bring the children across by Land Rover along the beach,' [on the Humber side].

As we get back into the car to drive through the open gate, we're told to look out for the cowslips, but the pheasant we unexpectedly find in the road half way down isn't mentioned. There's a kestrel hovering overhead, too.

So down we drive. It's lowish tide, and on the Humber side a great expanse of sand or mud is exposed, so we'll have no worries. Even on a day like this, it is undoubtedly the most eerie place in Britain. I'd hate to be cut off on a wild night at high tide when at best there are only yards between sea and estuary. Just how much the spit changes is shown by the fact that the only two remaining sections of standard-gauge railway track are at angles to today's road alignment. Replacing sections of road is routine, especially at the north end. On the sea side the beaches, often depleted and then restored, are built of matter washed down from further up the coast including fossils from tropical times. A leaflet welcoming us to the Nature Reserve says some of the stones 'may come originally from the Pennines, Scotland or Norway'.

For ships, the enemy isn't sea but land and especially rocks. The Stony Binks, shallow shoals exposed at low tide, just off Spurn are notoriously dangerous. Before the age of reliable communication, some captains who were grounded waited hopefully for the next tide to float their ships safely off... while the locals knew the currents would almost certainly smash them to pieces and watched it happen. Throughout history, remains of wrecks have been a familiar part of the scene on the North Sea side.

So, noticing there are surprisingly few passing places, looking at waders feeding on the rich mudflats, in ten or twelve minutes we reach Spurn Head. Here there is solid, anchoring ground safely above sea level. In fact we have to walk the last few hundred yards, past a weatherworn caravan café open at weekends, to look around the most curious of all settlements. There are two groups who live here: coastguards and members of Britain's only continuously-manned lifeboat station. 'One day the road'll be totally washed away and we will be an island,' says the coastguard, but he walks off in a hurry, perhaps to go up to the look-out.

'The best place to live in all England,' says a more talkative Dave Steevoorden, who after his Dutch father died when he was young and, his mother remarried, was brought up British. 'I'm delirious about it. I've the best job in England. By the way, I'm the coxswain it's a magic spot. In winter you don't see anyone.'

He goes on: 'The Humber's very busy: 36,000 ship movements a year, around a hundred a day. Big ones including ferries, bulk oil, coal, everything to Immingham and Hull, everything to Grimsby and up to Goole and the Trent and Ouse. The VTS [Vessel Traffic Services] first opened here in 1810. That row of parked Fiestas is part of the car fleet for pilots taking boats in and out. The RNLI has seven families here, each with a crew member. In the first four months this year we've been called out fifteen times. Two crewmen had to be hospitalised.'

There have been eleven children living here, but after today there'll only be eight. A lifeboat mechanic and his family are steadily packing their belongings into a van. They are shy, maybe emotional and obviously don't want to talk, but the coxswain says they hanker after being closer to their mainland family. 'Don't go because of the kids, I told him. They'll not like it, I said, but he and his wife wanted off. Now we're looking for somebody who wants to spend time with family: there's plenty of time here, and all the kids seem to love it. There are two school buses a day. The older children go to Withernsea.'

Several lighthouses, many military buildings and much more have been demolished since Spurn Head was a target attracting the attention of German planes during the wars. Then you'd be unlikely to enjoy your own company, though the mere level of activity might have made it seem less isolated than it is today. It is good that so much has been returned to nature.

On the way down, we noticed many bushes, including sea buckthorn, with peculiar what looked like woven sacks hanging from them. Another lifeboat man now warns us that they are the cocoons of the brown-tailed moth and their caterpillars are now out in force. 'They get everywhere and cause great skin irritation. They're a health hazard. Don't think of having a picnic here today.' When we return to the car and open the door there are a couple crawling around inside. So we cautiously sift through our luggage and things left loose on the seats.

Spurn is as rich in moths (there's also a colony of the six-spot Burnet moth) and butterflies as it is in flora, with several salt-loving species at the northern extremity of their range. Migrating birds regularly include rare visitors to the UK.

We have no picnic planned anyway. We'd half looked around Withernsea to make one up, but were not impressed. So it is a pub lunch, back in Easington at The Neptune. Here there's a copy of today's *Yorkshire Post* telling about the caterpillar invasion. Just one of many things we'll always remember about Spurn. And another paper lying around projects the number of homes likely to be lost along the coast in each of the next four five-year periods: a total of sixty in twenty years, sufficient to cause much individual hardship but not enough for a national outcry.

It's a busy pub. 'You should have seen it seething at the weekends they were laying the new gas pipe from Norway,' says Maureen Naylor, who keeps it with her husband Ken. She's full of chatter asking me, since I'm interested in Remote Britain, if I've heard of Read's Island off Barton-upon-Humber. 'I used to go across in a rowing boat to relatives who farmed on it.' And: 'Our son Philip is the youngest Master Mariner Captain.' Other talk is of maritime matters as are the plaques lining the walls. 'But we're tired.' says Maureen. 'Never a day off.' [We are not surprised that, by the time I come to write this, new brooms have moved in; Christine and Paul Coupland. 'They'd had enough, but we're keen.' T'was ever so with seven days a week, fifty two weeks a year self-employed jobs giving only nominal independence.]

The 'Queen' of Holderness – and Exit

Only time for one more stop before we have to dash to Harrogate to prepare for what will be the last prizegiving in association with *Writers' News,* for our Writing Competitions.

Patrington. Even when I mention its name, it means nothing to Sheila. She's not before been to any of the places we've visited in this chapter or the last. But as we approach it, and I point to the octagonal top of the tower, she almost shouts: 'I've been here. Patrington. Why didn't you say it was Patrington?' In common with many others attracted by Beverley and its Minster, often said to be the best cathedral church of all, she came here (but no further) specially to see St Patrick's, the 'Queen of Holderness'.

Giving it five stars in his *England's Best Thousand Churches,* Simon Jenkins says: 'It is queen too of what I regard as the finest era of English Gothic, the final flowering of the Decorated style of the early 14th century before the Black Death.' I'm especially impressed by the beautifully-proportioned nave, so perfectly and harmoniously executed for the glory of God out of the wealth of the surrounding countryside. Its unity is no doubt helped by the rapidity of its construction: no time for changes of thought or fashion.

Patrington was then a thriving market town, capital of Holderness. Farming produced greater wealth than in later days, when the land became sodden, later to be drained and restored farming prosperity. A charter for a market was granted as early as 1223 to the Archbishops of York who held Patrington's rich manor (1033-1545). The remarkable thing is that the gem of the church survived through many troubled days: Black Death, climate change, the development of the port of Hull, the opening of the Hull to Withernsea railway. Though Patrington had a station, the line still took trade away. Patrington Haven couldn't possibly compete. Its link with deep water by a long, narrow channel into the curvy Patrington Channel through the sands to Hole Bars on the Humber, had already proved difficult to keep open.

Markets, fairs, the flax mill, shops closed. Patrington went into a long decline, only reversed in recent times by new housing, mainly for people working in Hull. At least there was no money to spend 'improving' the church. Somehow its great feeling of spacious calm, harmony of style and materials, has miraculously been preserved to give it recognition, among non-Monastic churches perhaps only beaten by Bristol's St Mary Redcliffe.

The name Patrington Haven is preserved by the small village beyond Patrington itself. It is the gateway to truly unvisited flat lands with little more than occasional streams and drains and scattered farms. While in the appropriate setting a view of salt water commands a premium, some of the most lonely places are also within sight of the tides.

It is certainly lonely across today's bridge over the silted channel on Sunk Island. With an extensive system of lanes and much reclaimed land, this is now very much part of the mainland, the name Sunk Island now being that of a small hamlet, beyond which it is possible to make one's way to the estuary. Though we could be in the outskirts of Hull in half an hour, nothing feels more remote. Estuaries impose their own will on the landscape and where people live. This is part of their magic.

And soon we will be making our way into anything but Remote Britain. As our farewell, a quote from Yorkshire novelist Valerie Wood, always attracted by river settings. Rosa of *Rosa's Island* (Sunk Island) is playing twag or truant, and has to hide in the ditches marking field boundaries as she progresses toward salt water.

> She gazed up into the vast infinite sky. It was so wide and boundless and made her feel so small. There were no hills or undulations to obscure the landscape, no trees against the sky-line, only acres of rolling farmland and a wide canopy of drifting clouds floating against a back-drop of pale blue and meeting a slender finger of brown river, and beyond that the low grey line of Lincolnshire, at the horizon...
>
> How did Ma know which ship ma da would be on? She wondered. There are so many. Some she recognized as coal barges, making their slow way upriver. Some were fishing smacks coming in fully laden with cod and haddock from the northern fishing grounds and others were merchant ships from all countries of the world.
>
> From her position at Hawkins Point she saw a coggy boat pulling

towards the narrow channel which once led to Patrington Haven, but which now petered out to an inlet, close to where they had crossed in Henry's boat.

· XI ·

GOWER

Peninsula and AONB Britain

There are many categories in which the glories of Britain's landscapes can be divided. Islands, Coasts, National Park and Mountains immediately come to mind. Much less popular are Peninsulas and Areas of Outstanding Natural Beauty, but both of these are worthy of study.

Among peninsulas, Scotland's Kintyre, England's Wirral, Purbeck, the Lizard and Land's End and, in Wales, Lleyn and Gower are readily recalled. They are an extremely varied bunch, but all are relatively isolated, reached by indirect land routes, while the sea's influence has naturally been strong. Some bear the characteristics of an island, thus both Purbeck and Portland (visited in chapter XX) include Isle in their name.

Once I had thought of writing a section or even a whole book on British Peninsulas but, though they have much in common, the differences (as between the industrial Wirral and Lleyn, the next going anti-clockwise round our coast) are too great to attract a marketable audience. There is predictably no peninsula society or grouping.

Turning to Areas of Outstanding Natural Beauty (AONBs, though many mistakenly confuse the order of the middle letters), that there isn't yet a marketable audience is for a different reason. They just aren't well enough known either as a natural thematic group, or many even individually themselves.

I have to admit that I have only recently studied the booklet issued by the National Association to which all the assorted forty nine in England, Wales and Northern Ireland belong. *Explore Your Natural Beauty* explains the Association's role and briefly each of the areas. It makes the point that many people visiting them do not realise they 'are in a protected landscape'.

The Association is a useful co-ordinator between the individual AONBs and government and environmental agencies such as Natural England (which absorbed English Nature and the Rural Development Service). That the role of countryside organisations, other than perhaps that of the National Trust, is not popularly understood, is partly because of their changes and complex names and abbreviations.

The AONBs started fifty years ago, each nominated by the National Parks Commission, as a kind of half-way house. Many of them are less-tourist dominated areas. People go about their life and work less under the microscope and with fewer restrictions than in the National Parks.

Especially in South East England, some are not at all remote, but are areas where relative solitude and fresh air can be enjoyed – and to which it is worth taking a camera. Others such as Cannock Chase are small enclaves of delightful countryside, and many more – especially the coastal ones – have the very best scenery in a generally picturesque land. One or two, such as Bodmin Moor and the North Pennines, might possibly have become fully-fledged National Parks. Some – the Shropshire Hills, Forest of Bowland, Lincolnshire Wolds and Hampshire are examples – are hopefully gaining better appreciation as a result of being included in the list.

The AONBs are controlled in a variety of ways, planning powers not totally transferred as in the National Parks but strengthened, putting the brakes on the worst kinds of development. We will see in the Lincolnshire Wolds (chapter XXX) how it works at its best, the Wolds being an excellent example of a gorgeous and varied rare piece of upland in a generally flat land, quietly enjoyed by thousands with special interests, yet not swamped by Theme Park Britain. Farming and traditional country life prosper. In that case there is a separate AONB planning officer liasing with several district councils. In other cases councils administrate the enhanced powers themselves.

On Bodmin Moor (chapter XXVIII), we will note how even mention of the possibility of this, the third of the West Country's great moorlands, becoming a National Park, has farmers almost foaming at the mouth, while the AONB (and the associated coastal areas) quietly goes about the task of co-ordinating planning and attracting sensible tourism.

Two things are evident. The AONBs have generally worked well and command local respect; and they cover much of our stunning but less-visited landscapes. While most lovers of Britain could reel off the names of the National Parks – who can forget the Lake District, the Peak District or Dartmoor? – very few of us could recite more than a few names of the AONBs – and you are unlikely to hear questions about them in a quiz programme. Most readers will be surprised by some in the following list of the English and Welsh ones. The Northern Ireland ones, though magnificent, don't qualify for inclusion in Remote Britain. Scotland has only recently established National Parks and has no AONBs.

Though I have indicated the portions of certain areas in England and Wales included, not the whole of all the others are completely in an AONB.

In England: Arnside and Silverdale, Blackdown Hills, Cannock Chase, Chichester Harbour, Chilterns, Cornwall (mainly coastal plus Bodmin Moor), Cotswolds, Cranbourne Chase and West Wiltshire Downs, Dedham Vale, Dorset (roughly half), East Devon, Forest of Bowland, High Weald, Howardian Hills, Isle of Wight (mainly the west), Isles of Scilly, Kent Downs, Lincolnshire Wolds, Malvern Hills, Mendip Hills, Nidderdale, Norfolk Coast, North Devon (coastal areas), North Pennines, North Wessex Downs, Northumberland Coast, Quantock Hills, Shropshire Hills, Solway Coast, South Devon (mainly coast), South Downs, Suffolk Coast and Heaths, Surrey Hills, Tamar Valley. In Wales: Clwydian Range, Gower, Isle of Anglesey (mainly coastal), Lleyn, Wye Valley.

The illustrated booklet is available from the National Association of Areas of Outstanding Natural Beauty, Cotswolds Heritage Centre, Old Police Station, Northleach GL54 3JH, and more is explained on the website: http://www.aonb.org.uk

To Gower (Not The Gower)

We set off once more from Bath across the new Severn Bridge and along the M4 toward its western end. Skirting Swansea's much-changed dock area, I note where Swansea Victoria terminus used to be, and where the pioneer single track of the Swansea & Mumbles Railway once ran alongside the (at this point) double-track LMS heading for Llandrindod Wells, Craven Arms and Shrewsbury.

Though relatives and friends often spoke of their happy holidays in Gower, my only visit was in the late 1950s by the Swansea & Mumbles shortly before it closed. A real pioneer, it opened in 1806 (24 years before the Liverpool & Manchester) as a toll tramway along a road. Mineral traffic was supplemented by passengers, carried in horse-drawn trams. Steam trains began in 1860, traffic boosted by the Sunday Closing Act. No Welsh pubs were open for ordinary business, but *bona fide* travellers arriving by train were welcomed by Mumbles's busy ones.

At busy weekends, even the long trains of double-deck carriages lacked sufficient seats, and often many passengers stood on the open top deck or clung Indian-style to railings outside the carriages on the lower one. Especially busy were boat trains connecting with paddle steamers including trips to Ilfracombe.

The line was electrified in 1929 and, though bus competition soon hurt, frequent two-deck trams coupled together continued carrying summer crowds. My trip on swaying trams coupled together possibly gave me and many others a false first impression of Gower – and I recall being made to feel an uncomfortable intruder when I referred to 'The Gower' (hated as it's not a proper translation of the Welsh) and to the tram. Locally, even a single car, stopping at stations, was known as a train.

It has taken the preparation of this book for me to see the whole of Gower, which admirably fits into three of my categories of landscape: it is a real peninsula, has a fantastically-varied coastline and is also an AONB, in fact – because it was seen to be especially under threat – the first to be created half a century ago. The unexpected publication of a long New Naturalist volume on so small an area has also given impetus to planning our trip.

While I'm delighted that Collins have so enthusiastically regenerated the New Naturalist series, there are drawbacks. An informal collectors' club has grown, guaranteeing successful publishing at high prices. With lavish use of colour, now much cheaper, superficially the titles look great, but editorial control, which technology cannot make cheaper, is not as good as in the early days. The result is an enormous difference between volumes – in their approach, organisation and even in details such as how notes are presented. Some authors blind us with science, unwilling or unable to address the intelligent layman, which was the series initial hallmark.

Gower is a model of its kind, its author, Jonathan Mullard, having as much skill in conveying his enthusiasm for, as he has knowledge of, the peninsula. Eventually the title will surely outsell less worthy volumes even on more popular subjects. Always judge a book by its long-term sales.

A keen collector himself with an almost complete set – his own is the 99th – he describes the New Naturalist as 'a wonderful but uneven resource and inspiration especially for amateur naturalists', and goes on to tell me of earlier volumes whose quality he aimed to match, and those he definitely wouldn't want to emulate. A naturalist from his earliest days, he spent a considerable part of his career in Gower and became the only full-time planner in the AONB, not replaced since planning is now undertaken (it has to be said sympathetically) by the district council, the City and County of Swansea. Jonathan and I had several long telephone talks, and hoped we could meet up on Gower, but it wasn't to be. He is now director of Park Management in the Northumberland National Park, and with me living in the North of Scotland, finding a mutually-convenient date wasn't possible.

He pulled some strings to make my visit a success, however, and bubbles with delight about what the AONB status has achieved for

Gower. 'Every AONB is of course different, but Gower particularly so,' he says. 'It is governed from Swansea, and its borders have always been industrial. Though it is separated from the rest of Wales by Swansea, it hasn't been overrun by it. It remains a land set apart, a separate and special place, with complex geology and landscape types, and a sharp historical division between Welsh and English-speaking parts. It's an incredible mixture you'll find fascinating. Enjoy it.'

Naturally I learned much from the book itself. Norman settlers claimed much of the best land, and an easy way of telling which language is spoken is by studying field patterns. Large fields around villages are generally in English-speaking lower areas, while small irregular fields around a single farm on the higher central areas indicate Welsh. Like Arran, described as Scotland in miniature, Gower has some of almost every kind of landscape and many geologists and school trips (over 500 annually) visit it. It is important to naturalists, too, with great bird life and plant rarities. From badgers to rare woodmice, mammal life abounds. There are otters on every water, while all the British species of bats are probably here. Walkers adore Gower and, for archaeologists, interest starts with eighty three listed monuments.

The website (headed City and County of Swansea) Gower: Area of Outstanding Natural Beauty is also helpful. 'The complex geology gives a wide variety of scenery in a relatively small area... from the south coast's superb carboniferous limestone scenery at Worms Head and Oxwich Bay to the salt-marshes and dune systems in the north. Inland... large areas of common, dominated by a sandstone heath ridge include the soaring sweep of Cefn Bryn. Secluded valleys have rich deciduous woodland and the traditional agricultural landscape is a patchwork of fields characterised by walls, stone-faced banks and hedgerows.' But possibly the best introduction of all is that in *The Story of Gower* by Wendy Hughes, in a series of concise guides to areas of Wales. It exactly echoes my feelings as I try to get to grips with it.

> The Gower Peninsula has such a unique combination of natural beauty, history, and customs, that at first sight it is impossible for the visitor to appreciate its full potential. In an area that is no more than sixteen miles long by seven miles wide, and narrowing to just four miles, the scenes change like a kaleidoscope, leaving the observer spellbound in awed wonder. The scenery transforms from neatly bordered fields to wild rugged moorlands, from sheltered bays that once hid the activities of smugglers, to bleak isolated cliff tops, scene of the wreckers and their wicked activities. The impressive churches cast their solemn eyes down on the tiny cottages, that could tell countless tales of mystery and suspense. Nature too is not forgotten

with its unique abundance of rare flowers, bird sanctuaries and the fishing industries.

Fairyhill

Armed with books, notes and maps, and prepared for a steep learning curve, we have decided to stay inland at Fairyhill, near Reynoldston. Distances are short – the whole of Gower fits into less than a quarter of a single OS Landranger sheet – and from here we can radiate out. Rounding the bay toward Mumbles, with low tide exposing a massive area of mud and sand, we eventually leave the route of the old railway which I clearly recall after sixty years. I reflect that everywhere the congested but companiable 'tripper days' of yesteryear are but a memory. Sundays in Mumbles are less boisterous, and today's fewer tourists spread themselves out more evenly not just so much seeking 'fun' as engaging in a hobby.

Finally leaving Swansea's built-up area, we take a minor road to join the A4188 for a short distance before heading north, enjoying a fine view south to Oxwich Bay, reaching Reynoldston across an open common passing close to a prehistoric burial site. Already we have experienced great contrasts. The hotel at Fairyhill is in woodland; we turn into a drive just before an intriguing lane through the trees, which we later take as the first part of a circular walk, and also enjoy the hotel's spacious informal garden with a brook running along its bottom. Memorably peaceful and enjoyable, the hotel serves good food, starting with a light lunch before (at Jonathan Mullard's suggestion) another author, Harold E Grenfell, calls to take me on tour.

He's seriously intent on making me share his love and understanding of Gower, based on years living and working on it in many different roles. He is president of the Gower Society, one of the most influential and largest amenity societies, and another of Britain's firsts. Also Fellow and South Wales representative of the Royal Photographic Society, he has published two outstanding collections of his work. He inscribes a gift copy of *Gower Images,* a gallery of exquisite black-and-white photographs of a powerful and historic landscape home to a huge range of wildlife. Many are detail in close-up with minimal captions. They really touch Gower's very heartbeat. And I purchased a copy of *Gower in Focus:* 'One man's response – intellectual, artistic and personal – to "What does Gower mean to me?" ' This is a Gower Society publication.

Few areas have so many dedicated enthusiasts guiding them. 'Occasionally the Gower Society is seen as a nuisance, but not often these days,' he says. 'The AONB has been a major help but with all

AONBs it's all in the detail. We've won major battles: stopping a Butlin's camp in Rhossili Bay, a 400ft radar mast on Rhossili Down, saving Oxwich Castle from being cut down to just 6ft and, maybe, given up to the sea. There's more to do, of course, the firing range in the north being an especial nuisance, but today's threat isn't of hugely inappropriate development so much as the solicitors and other professional people of Swansea wanting to live in this desirable landscape. I always tell those going to West Wales that Gower is somewhere they should pass on the way to Pembrokeshire'. He concludes: 'We're just too small and delicate to take great crowds.'

On the Road with Harold Grenfell

So we set off on one of the most fascinating and complicated trips for this book. As Wendy Hughes, quoted above, says, it is impossible to absorb it all at first sight and, as well as respecting his love for this surprisingly-unknown corner of Wales, I'm particularly grateful for Harold's guidance. 'You're right to say it's Wales in miniature,' he enthuses. 'We have a little of everything here.'

Yesterday morning I would have dreaded having to live in Gower. By tonight I can think of many far worse possibilities, except I'd never cope with the Welsh names, some of which have been through many changes making reading about past days a nightmare for a dyslexic Englishman.

'You see, we're not just a peninsula but have a great inland with moors or downs,' says Harold as we pass Arthur's Stone, the prehistoric burial site we noted on the way to Fairyhill. The millstone grit here is very hard, once used for grinding stones. 'There's one there split maybe 2,500 years ago. I think it might have been for a millstone but somehow they gave up on the idea.' Soon we pass Broad Pool, fringed with small yellow fringed water lilies only found naturally in East Anglia but looking very much at home having been introduced in the 1940s. The pool is a clay-plugged depression on limestone and was one of the earliest nature reserves to be established.

Beyond Broad Pool, we soon head north west. 'You'll note that as we get closer to Swansea, the grazing is less good.' We touch the coal measures, and see a road built for traction engines to haul strings of coal-filled carts.

This brings us to Llanrhidian, an estuarine village – we are now in North Gower – once a centre for sheep rearing and home weaving with two mills, both closed. There's been considerable new building, though the village centre remains distinctive. The Church of St Illtyd

Back to Rhossili Bay and The Worm

Bright and early next morning, we study the OS and note many prehistoric and other features that abound in Rhossili Bay and Downs, and read about the Bronze Age cairns and ditches and the much later cliff forts – and a lost village discovered by a National Trust archaeological excavation. No part of Gower is without interest, but here it overwhelms. The beach is undoubtedly one of Britain's finest. A third of a million visitors see it annually.

Again in sunshine, at mid-tide, the scene grabs us. Few car parks are better placed, with nearby toilets, National Trust shop and café. First we walk along the pleasantly busy but uncrowded path, our eyes always to the right taking in the line of breaking rollers. We pass the site of an abandoned coastguard lookout and scramble down to the rocks at the beginning of the mile-long Worms Head Nature Reserve which ends in the serpentine-like promontory of Worms Head itself, locally known as The Worm.

We didn't take note of the tide time before setting off and, at our age, certainly don't want to be cut off – and the guide warns there have been fatalities on the slippery rocks. In truth, though it's exhilarating, with declining agility I'll be relieved to be back on solid ground. With wild flowers, especially banks of thrift, screaming birds, pounding waves, irregular rocks, we're unlikely ever to forget our walk back along what is the beginning of the Gower Way to the car park area. Lambs are playing their usual 'king of the castle' routine, sure-footedly jostling for prime position on a little green knoll between the path and sharp cliff edge.

The arc of the bay is five miles long. We clearly pick out detail on Burry Holms, the tidal island at the far end whose ruins include a medieval monastery and Iron Age earthwork. There are less than a score of people on the long white sands, and perhaps half that number surfing; but what would a Butlin's camp have done? By now it might anyway have been closed, for the days of mass British tourism, which seriously threatened Gower's character in the decades immediately after the war, have passed into memory. As in other areas of fine landscape, more people come and go than ever, but most pay a day trip to Gower or spend only a night or so on it. This is the age of moving on.

We now see the tide is receding and catch a glimpse of the rotting ribs of the wrecked *Helvetia*, driven ashore in 1887. Some of its wood helped furnish local homes. Other wrecks, when the beach would have been agog with activity, were of the 'dollar ship' which was carrying the dowry of a Portuguese princess who became the Queen to Charles II, and of the *City of Bristol*, a paddle steamer which came to grief on a voyage from Waterford in 1840.

The track beginning to run alongside the beach terminates on a shelf halfway along at what used to be Rhossili Rectory. The tale is told that, on his way to church one Sunday in 1898, to his astonishment the Rector saw a long trail of people making their way to the beach. 'I soon perceived the rocket apparatus... I officiated to an almost empty church.' A 2,000-ton steamer en route from Dieppe to Llanelli had been wrecked and, as along the North Cornwall coast, clergy had to accept that parishioners couldn't resist the lure of finding something to ease their poverty.

Renovated, the old Rectory is now a much-prized, isolated National Trust holiday house. There's no through road. Rhossili Bay is somewhere to visit specially as have we this morning. We linger over the view between the National Trust shop, having tea and a snack at the café and before reluctantly departing.

Next morning we make our way out of Gower, back to the north coast via Llanrhidian and alongside the line of the old LNWR/LMS into Gowerton. At the tamer end of the peninsula, we head north in order to go to West Wales.

The Final Word

The final word goes to Jonathan Mullard, whose New Naturalist *Gower* has been a constant companion. At its very end, he questions whether it was right that the Gower Society's wish to see full National Park status hadn't been granted. He explains that, while the AONB has checked the worst kind of development, resources are stretched, the Welsh AONBs not receiving the funding of their English counterparts. It might not be too late for a National Park, he suggests.

I hate to disagree but, because of Gower's proximity to a large population, the enhanced status might actually attract more pressure than it could deter. Its compact subtlety might be better served as now in an AONB. The campaign should surely be to secure a belated successor to the independent planner that Jonathan himself was. It would cost far less than a National Park for so small an area.

One thing is sure: the battle for Gower's soul will not end soon. May it long be a special place protected from being over-run but fascinating those who quietly appreciate it. If you have not yet discovered it, pay a visit for a day or two but, to make the most of your visit, first read about it, for there's a great deal to absorb.

· XII ·

WEST WALES

Have You Ever Been to Tenby?

The very name West Wales conjures up an image of a different blend of things familiar and things not. For some reason, West Wales doesn't mean the Cambrian Coast, but particularly Pembrokeshire, 'Little England beyond Wales'. Though little Welsh might be spoken, I've never found it particularly English, just its own thing at one end of the Great Western Railway.

On many occasions while heading back to the West Country, a term the GWR never used on its destination boards, for it was always specifically Penzance or some other place, I saw that the last coaches of the lengthy trains leaving at fifty five minutes past alternate hours, proudly boasted 'West Wales'. At Swansea, they became the front coaches after much of the train including restaurant car was left behind. There was another reversal at Carmarthen.

Though Penzance is further, trains to Pembrokeshire's four terminals served by through trains took considerably longer. Only the boat train to Fishguard Harbour sometimes bypassed Swansea and Carmarthen. Technically Fishguard Harbour was 'at the end of the line' but, apart from the Irish bound, many fewer travelled there than down the slow lines to Pembroke Dock, Neyland and Milford Haven. One of the features of West Wales is that it has no real centre. There are now few through trains, and roads remain poor. I recall excruciatingly slow journeys and, later on this trip, in touring so much of Britain's extremities, the greatest delay we suffered was going through Haverfordwest. Pembrokeshire has always been poorly signposted, too.

Other memories are naturally of the superb coastline, but at best indifferent hotels. As a boy in the war, my napkin ring was from Tenby displaying its coat of arms. In the days of famous one-line jokes whose sheer familiarity had audiences giggling, such as ITMA's 'Can I do you now, sir?' and Jack Warner's 'Mind my bike', 'Have you ever been to Tenby?' became a family joke.

With poor service and high prices, I'll never forget my disappointment on my first visit in the 1950s. When sandwiches and snacks couldn't be readily bought from a shop, my hotel 'packed lunch', consisting of three small sandwiches and an apple, cost more than a delicious four-course restaurant car lunch. Tenby and the Cambrian Coast's Barmouth are where I've been ripped off more than anywhere else in the British Isles. Decades later, when British Rail offered special early and late packages to extend the seasons of popular resorts, Tenby had to be dropped from the scheme because its hotels were mainly closed out of the core period.

Come to think about it, my father's answer to 'Have you ever been to Tenby?' was that he wished he hadn't. There were excellent hotels in West Wales, some long-favoured by relatives in coastal villages, whose charm isn't second rate to Cornwall's.

Lively farming, including early potatoes, tractors at the head of lengthy convoys, friendly people but long waits while locals concluded their conversation at shops, and churches with disproportionately tall towers are among other familiar images of this corner of Remote Britain. And it does always feel remote, leisurely, out of the rat race. Even in the days when pride in the job remained strong, railwaymen were unusually laid back. It never has paid to be in a hurry in West Wales.

Laugharne and Dylan Thomas

There still being no bridge over the River Towy below Carmarthen, our journey to English-speaking Wales is indirect and slow, and it has started drizzling. First stop is at Laugharne, on the west bank of the Taf which joins the Towy shortly before reaching the sea where at low tide there is a huge area of sand and mud. Laugharne, the inspiration for *Under Milk Wood,* was Dylan Thomas's final home. I recall cricket-reporting John Arlott who, having been a D&C author, became a close friend, telling me many stories about Dylan who he held in great respect. For example, in the days when radio newsreaders wore formal evening dress, once Dylan was too drunk to take his rostered duty, and John – never himself abstemious – took over. Afterwards, Dylan gave a reasoned but semi-humorous resumé of his performance. Damaging your health but enjoying good conversation with excessive drinking seems to have been *de rigueur* for creative people at the sharp end.

How important is Dylan Thomas to Laugharne today? Not as much as I expected. Says the local bookseller, George Tremlett: 'We're off the beaten track and don't get that many visitors anyway, but quite a few come because of him, but he doesn't make much difference to my business because there isn't much available about him... his poems of course, something on the boathouse which I expect you'll visit. But no popular souvenir.' He adds: 'By the way, if you're going to see the gazebo where Dylan worked and the boathouse – it's not a very nice day for it – don't worry about parking on the yellow lines. Our traffic warden mysteriously disappeared years ago. As for my business, it is 70 per cent on the Internet. That's what justifies a stock of 60,000 titles. Laugharne is a lovely laid-back village, just into where English is spoken. You crossed the border between the Welsh and English areas a few miles back.'

Corran Books is named after the river that flows into the Taf under Laugharne Castle. It's been described as a bookshop that's 'as long as many a high street'. Relaxed over where we've parked, Sheila, who has been prepared to drive off should she have spotted the traffic warden we now know doesn't exist, joins us, and we descend down the chain of stone-walled rooms packed with books, including the working library of an alternative medicine writer and many Welsh and Anglo-Welsh titles and Celtic ones – plus a huge selection of old records and maps and prints. One could happily spend all day here, but content ourselves buying a few books including the *Poems (Everyman's Poetry)* edition of Dylan Thomas's work. It is selected and edited by Walford Davies who, in his introduction, says of the poetry that first produced fame united Welshness to intricate verse forms familiar in the Bible, the repetitive units bringing pressure to bear on a single word.

> What we have here, at base, is an endless appetite for the essential musicality of language – what Thomas once called 'the colour of saying' – the auditory power that language can have in and for itself. In another magical phrase, he called it the need for poetry to be 'heavy in tare, though nimble'. This weight and density of texture and musical movement were exactly what was reacted against after his death by the more 'intellectual' English poets of the 1950s, such as Philip Larkin, Donald Davie and John Wain, enamoured of more modest verse-forms, of understatement and irony. These in fact were often poets who, a decade earlier, when they themselves were starting to write in the early 1940s, had admired Thomas above all others. He was, after all, only marginally older. Thomas's early death made him doubly potent: his exciting poetic skills were, within a decade, both emulated and reacted against.

Under Milk Wood came later when Thomas himself had changed direction into something more austere, but even it has lost the widespread popularity I recall it enjoying up to thirty years ago.

We've a long way to go, but before setting off again, hurry in driving rain down a narrow lane to Dylan Thomas's home, his famous summerhouse whose view overlooking the river must have soothed and inspired – and briefly to the boathouse.

There are no other visitors and, when I question a few people going back up the lane, they are locals in a hurry to get out of the rain and don't seem particularly interested in the poet. Sixty years have passed since his death and he was only at this restful spot a few years, yet *Under Milk Wood,* showing how people lived, played and misbehaved in a small Welsh town, must have featured local characters and attitudes. Now it is better known among lovers of literature than travellers, categories with surprising little overlap.

There'd be much to do here on a fine day and, even on this gloomy morning, we cannot help noticing the fine Georgian townhouses. There's a slight aura of mystery, or is it just that there's probably a lot more going on behind the scenes than is evident in this slightly quaint and antiquated yet very much alive small town? It has the last surviving British medieval corporation, founded back in 1291. The leader, the Portreve, appropriately wears a traditional chain of gold cockle-shells.

The Castle, described by Dylan Thomas in his typically oblique way as 'brown as owls', started as one of a string of Norman fortifications built to subdue the Welsh, but was enlarged into a solid, square home providing extravagant luxury in the 13th and 14th centuries. It played a pivotal role in the Civil War, and then fell into the romantic ruin we just glance at today. Another place of interest I'd love to have seen is the rare open field system still in active, traditional production.

Tenby and Manorbier

We continue along the coast to Pendine with its great beach where land speed records were achieved in the 1920s, and are celebrated by the Museum of Speed. Parry Thomas died when his car went out of control at 180mph. The car was rescued and is still occasionally driven on the beach.

Ouch! Even reading about the lesser weaver fish which thrive in shallow water and are Britain's only venomous dorsal fish whose sting is excruciatingly painful sends me into a shudder. Then we wend our way to the A477 and, having already agreed not to risk another possible culinary disappointment in Tenby, keep to it.

In fairness I see that the better hotels in the beautifully-situated triangular-shaped resort bounded by cliffs on two sides receive reasonable AA percentage ratings but, for whatever reason, one comes to love some places and not others. I would however once more have enjoyed taking the short ferry to Caldey Island where there's a monastery with an involved history. The first monks came in the 6th century – the settlement possibly ending with Viking raids in the 10th century. In the 12th century the Benedictines from St Dogmaels established a priory.

They naturally left at the 1536 Dissolution of the Monastery, but in 1906 an Anglican group of Benedictines built the present Abbey, towering Italianesque style above the village. In 1913 they became Roman Catholics but, with financial problems, left in 1925. Four years later Cistercians re-established a presence in Wales that had been missing since the Dissolution, before which they had thirteen monasteries. The strict, contemplative newcomers in turn found it hard going economically, and in the 1980s looked as though they might fail.

That the community is now thriving is due to a new balance being struck between deep spirituality and a more open approach, visitors now welcome except on Sundays. Substantial funds have been raised through the sale of the island's most popular souvenir, perfume distilled by the monks from the island's generous flora. Honey and other produce are sold at the shop, too. The monks also farm, but that's never easy on an island. They live and work alongside the small village and the marvellous bird life, Caldey Island hosting numerous migrants as well as its own resident species.

We work our way back to the coast by a series of lanes; we would anyway have been forced inland again (as is the coastal path) by a firing range – until we descend to Manorbier of happy memories. Time for sandwiches, Sheila pleading patience until we climb to a seat just under the castle and can enjoy looking down onto the little half-circular beach below and engage in that everlasting seaside pastime of people watching. Coast walkers come into sight almost on the horizon on the way-marked path and descend at different rates down the steps to the beach which, as the tide comes in, will soon be totally submerged.

The few narrow streets of the village below are intriguing, while all around us are wild flowers – and banks of bright gorse. On the hills frolicking lambs playing together make sudden dashes to their mums. The walls above us are well-preserved, the Norman castle being a highly-defended fine home. We would have paused longer but for the cool wind – and realising we still have a long way to go.

Britain's only Coastal National Park

We are now well into Britain's only Coastal National Park, which to me seems to be a great success. A linear park has natural disadvantages, but the best has been made of what it stands for. It is not continuous but from whichever direction you enter one of its sections, look carefully and you'll see the fruits of half a century of taking special care of the landscape. And unprecedented numbers are experiencing being at peace along the great cliffs, taking in the beaches and coves, rocks and islands, from the Heritage Coast footpath.

Unlike Gower, here there's scale and, though there's pride (or snobbery) among those who complete the entire route, it is assumed most won't. By publishing a leaflet with timetables of the special bus service calling at possible starting and ending points, and another on calling points and their facilities, the National Park has made it easy to enjoy short sections.

As in Gower, while the great days of tourists flocking to popular resorts may be over, visitors' individual interests, be they the coastal path, prehistoric, Celtic, castles, natural history, crafts, good food and even gardening, are well catered for. Some of today's visitors are of the kind who hopefully might buy this title, which certainly would not have been the case among those who dominated in the postwar decades. Though some of their successors come back to enjoy peace and their hobbies, most now sun themselves in the Med.

If I have one complaint, it is that in an area that has never been Welsh speaking, all publicity is dual language, inconveniencing the vast majority for the benefit of what here is a tiny minority. Constantly I find myself turning over leaflets irritated by looking at Welsh headings and, worse, pictures with Welsh captions. As in the North of Scotland, we appreciate bi-lingual notices in Gaelic-speaking areas – it is part of the character – but not having them foisted on us where learning Gaelic is a cult among a handful of English speakers.

Broad Haven, Lily Ponds and St Govan's Chapel

We miss what is probably the best part of the coastal path from which I once enjoyed Stackpole's mini harbour and the fine beach at Barafundle Bay, usually quiet since there is no road access, and drive straight to the Castlemartin peninsula, parking in the National Trust's almost full car park at Broad Haven, beyond Bosherston. Then a walk round the western pond, the best of the trio of famous lily ponds, artificially created in the 18th century for coarse fishing (and you can still buy a licence to fish). With their reed-fringed, irregular shapes, they now look delightfully natural and much frequented by otters and wildfowl. The abundant lilies are just showing their first flowers, the yellow coming out first. A monstrous digger with shovel is working on one bank dredging sand and spreading it over land. In the last year the National Trust has spent £30,000 on dredging to ensure the ponds' future.

A notice at the bus stop of the special bus serving intermediate spots for coastal path walkers exhorts us 'To Keep the Pembroke Coast Special'. Another notice pleads that used fishing lines be placed into a tube-shaped bin to protect the swans and other birds.

Nearby at Broad Haven South, not to be confused with another Broad Haven near St David's, (after we've passed a huge private café) is another NT car park whose attendant, Glarre Rycroft, tells me he's a proud holder of the director general's award for recruiting the most members at one of their car parks. 'I was made redundant twelve years ago at the Texaco refinery. I love it here and most people are great, many really interesting, but last year a colleague died of a heart attack after arguing with someone who wouldn't pay his £3 parking ticket, which includes use of the toilet. This is really a lovely place.' Such enthusiasm. He adds: 'Perhaps like most people coming to Little England Beyond Wales, you don't realise that Welsh was once spoken: it's only a thousand years since it was.'

After gazing down on the surfing sands of Broad Haven and across at the tall Stackpole rocks just off shore, we move onto another car park to walk along a path with frequent gates on a limestone shelf from which the cliffs drop almost vertically into the sea. It is not hard to tell that this is the land of legends. Jokingly, we try creating our own, but they're not as good as that of St Govan choosing to be buried on the spot after he'd been attacked by a gang of hooligans. The cliffs opened up to receive his body and refolded around him to preserve it.

I peer down to St Govan's chapel; Sheila still has the energy to walk down and back up the seventy six steep steps to the chapel which only contains an altar, and even more steps down toward the sea. She bounds back telling me what a great view I've missed with lonely crags and exposed strata. Anything only one of us enjoys is automatically in a class of its own, though it must be a very unusual spot, fascinating even what I can see of it peering down from the top.

Ammunition, Gas, Oil and Wreck

Then into a land where romantic tradition is buried by the ghastly. Going west, only the coastal path itself is available to the public. The path must be why the great tract of land strewn with spent military hardware is still technically within the National Park. Along our road, which is sometimes closed, there are dire warnings of occasional 'Live Firing in Progress', and live ammunition being a hazard in the fields on either side. We leave the trunk road at Lamphey scarcely noticing the village or realising there's a ruined Bishop's Palace here. It will be mentioned later.

Most of the remainder of the south coast peninsular terminating at Angle is devoted to a huge new gas terminal and its associated works. A fleet of supertankers will ship gas as frozen liquid (–160°C) from Qatar on the Arabian peninsula. A fifth of the UK's gas needs will be supplied from here, each of the storage tanks big enough to accommodate the Royal Albert Hall.

At the far end, Angle is a one-street village of coloured cottages and welcoming pubs overlooking the entrance to one of Britain's finest harbours, Milford Sound – Nelson said 'The finest of all'. Opposite the entrance is St Ann's Head at the tip of one of Britain's least-visited, secretive peninsulas, off which are the bird-lovers paradises of Skomer Island and Skokholm Island and, further out a mere thin line as seen from the mainland, flat Grass Holm sometimes seeming almost half buried by its 70,000 gannets.

From a previous visit, I realise how wild a place St Ann's Head can be. It is among the windiest spots in Britain – gale force on average almost three days a month – while tides sweep rapidly in and out of the huge and deeply-penetrating, many-branched waters of Milford Sound. There had already been a long history of wrecks and it should have been obvious that, as the oil industry grew with large tankers making frequent visits, the rocks were waiting to claim a truly major victim. Though it happened well after my first visit when I learnt about earlier wrecks, I cannot claim to have foretold it.

It was in February 1996 that the fully-laden *Sea Empress* carrying 72,000 tons of crude oil came to grief making world headlines, not only for the scale of the spillage but also the shoddy way in which the crisis was handled and local people were treated – some forcibly evacuated – and kept in the dark about what was happening.

It was nine days before a clean up operation fully started. Harrowing were the pictures of the sufferings of sea birds and seals that frequently popped up on our television screens. The lovely coastal fauna also suffered major loss. Happily there is nothing left of the disaster to see today, and undoubtedly lessons were learnt. In particular, the oil companies found they had to deal with a better-organised public, whose opposition to a new controversial kind of process led to the closure of one refinery.

Now heading for Pembroke, as we make our way back along our peninsula, we see just how vast the industry's impact has been. It dominates both shores of Milford Haven with many square miles of refineries, oil tanks and other installations. The other side of the coin is the huge employment and spending power it has brought, though they in turn have changed the very character of the under-developed area I recall from my first visit. Pembroke itself then seemed especially sleepy. Though certainly not the town most affected, it has grown, its road traffic enormously.

Friday Afternoon Hold-ups

At what admittedly is usually the week's busiest time everywhere, late afternoon on Friday, it is grid locked. We move along under the castle wall one or two car-lengths at a time. Every parking space is tightly jammed, a few vehicles double parked. The castle, the key one in the line of Norman strongholds, was built to impress and control Pembrokeshire, though by an agreement this far-flung corner of the conquered land effectively retaining considerable 'independence' – the Earls of Pembroke held on to tough feudal rule from afar. In its active days the castle was never really controlled by the Welsh. It cost Cromwell a great deal in delay and resources to control it. Above us, as we try to crawl a few feet at a time, it looks huge, grey, forbidding.

Once we clear Pembroke, a couple of miles further on we virtually bypass Pembroke Dock, built with a grid street system to serve the Admiralty's Dockyard. Pembroke Dock has endured some lean times but has especially benefited from oil. I'd hoped we might be delayed on the bridge to Neyland, for there are great views of the tidal system on both sides. Beyond the water the bridge also crosses the abandoned railway route to Neyland. After alighting from the train at Pembroke Dock, you might soon see another arriving at Neyland. As the crow flies the two termini were barely a mile apart. Though served by a branch off the Milford Haven branch, Neyland was where the nightly sleeping car used to end up.

Then it is a slow journey into Haverfordwest where we suffer what seemed an interminable delay, sometimes stationary for five minutes on end. 'Rather soulless' is the *Rough Guide's* view of what is the region's largest but not most prosperous town. Despite all the time in the world to examine each foot of the way (there are actually a few really attractive buildings and it is said to be a good market centre) we do not yearn to return.

When at last we're free of Haverfordwest, it is good to be out in the rolling farmland, but the traffic is still heavy and overtaking difficult. So we're tired by the time we reach our destination: St David's. Now there's a demonstration of how a good hotel can be wondrously welcoming and relaxing. The Warpool Court (AA 79 per cent and two rosettes) makes a great home for our long weekend in what is only a glorified village with an oversize cathedral.

Expectations were raised when the hotel's brochure was received weeks ago. It tells us:

> The contemporary visitor discovers a small community surrounded by a peninsula of magical natural beauty which has inspired some of the world's most famous artists. The hotel commands a southerly outlook over one of the most beautiful coastal stretches in Europe. The view across the delightful lawned gardens reveals the gentle sweep of St Brides Bay and the offshore islands. This is a haven of peace at the heart of the Pembrokeshire Coast National Park.

The brochure photograph made us fall in love with the amazing view from our room which, at the beginning of this weekend of beautiful sunshine in this little corner of Britain while rain falls virtually elsewhere, looks in real life exactly as captured on camera.

· XIII ·

ST DAVID'S AND CARDIGAN

Smallest City, Largest Cathedral

For me the peninsula with Britain's tiniest city (the only British one wholly within a National Park) and Wales's largest cathedral is a place to stand and stare, enjoying the magnificent light and great, varied natural and manmade beauty, feeling close to the Divine in a non-analytical way. It is always a privilege to be here, especially in such lovely weather not being experienced by the rest of Britain.

Writing a prologue to the book I've been reading, *St Davids Peninsula*, James Nicholas, former Archdruid of Wales and National Chaired Bard, emphasises what a great privilege it was to be being brought up in St David's. He says that the genius of the land 'eludes definition, but we may have a sense of understanding when we look at the variety of exciting images which abound here.' He adds that all are related to place 'and are sometimes of a mystical nature'.

He goes on to describe looking at the coastal path through a series of places with deeply-Welsh names 'which not only appeal to the ear but have an unfailing quality to excite the imagination. These names remind us of the relation between land and language reaching back to the Age of the Saints.'

There he has the advantage over me. My name might sound Welsh, and indeed I have Welsh ancestry, but my dyslexia makes spelling some English names complicated enough, and I physically shrink when trying to cope with the mixture of Celtic, Welsh and other names that take up so much space on the map with their lls, ws and ys. And if I learn to spell them, I still don't recognise them when they're pronounced by Welsh-speaking people. But as soon as I give up the battle, lost in wonder and awe, I feel myself growing as one is taught to in the Alexander Technique, tall and erect, at peace with a magical landscape and history by which I can be fascinated without totally comprehending. However, as he hopes, the book certainly helps me 'to discover the land anew but also to realise its genius and hence a noble heritage'. I have to do it in my own way, no doubt missing much but revelling in it all the same as I suspect do most visitors from outside Wales.

Says the Dean of St David's Cathedral, J Wyn Evans, in his introduction to the same book:

> Mesolithic hunters and Neolithic farmers; Celtic monks and medieval pilgrims; Viking raiders and Norman lords; Modern tourists and visitors; all these have made their way, in their turn and in their generation, to this windswept peninsula where the land juts out into the Atlantic. This landscape, its hills and beaches has from very remote times and for differing reasons, drawn human beings to the far West. Some, like David, the patron saint of Wales, have come here to be close to God in the sheltered valley where St David's Cathedral stands today. Others, like William the Conqueror and countless others since, have made pilgrimages to that sacred spot to which two journeys counted as one in Rome; others of his followers, more typically, pinned down the country with a chain of fortresses. In our own day, others come by their hundreds to the Pembrokeshire Coast National Park. They come to an area of outstanding beauty where land and sea meet together to form a unique landscape, blending history, myth and legend.

I notice that the book, in the top rank of local publications anywhere, is self-published and illustrated with superb photographs by the author, Jacki Sime. It is nicely arranged in thematic subjects with intriguing chapter headings such as Raiders, Invaders, Traders and Saints, with interesting sub-headings, in this case Mesolithic Hunters, Neolithic Farmers, Beaker Folk, Irish Celts, The Romans and the Demetae, King Arthur, History and Legends, David The Water Drinker, The First Foundations, Viking Raiders and Norman Lords, The Black Book, Land and Wealth, The New Pilgrims. That list alone tells us much. There are useful reference features, too. While the text is good, the photographs are truly world class, catching the land in many moods, and making excellent use of light and shadows, especially in early morning and dusk scenes. I'm growing curious about Jacki Sime.

Meantime we take her advice following a suggested walking route through the mini-city. Though it is smaller than many villages, it is nearly all centre with scant suburbs. So it is full of interest, with a couple of narrow streets off the main one and quite a few shops including galleries and those offering local crafts, cafés, pubs and other public buildings. There is even a short section of one-way streets and, as I've found on previous visits, the main road running through the centre is almost continuously busy during trading hours, drivers searching hard for somewhere to park as though this were Swansea or Cardiff.

We've both been to the cathedral several times before and will leave visiting it till a service tomorrow, but – concentrating on the outside – are still surprised by its size and the depth of the valley accommodating it so close to the ancient, narrow streets. The scale of the ruined Bishop's Palace is almost obscene, speaking of the church's former greed, wealth and power especially in the Middle Ages when a pilgrimage here scored half of one to Rome on the eternal scale. Moreover, there was another Bishop's Palace at Lamphey, near Pembroke – their country retreat, would you believe it. Both bear the decisive imprint of Bishop Henry de Gower (1328-47). As the website says, it was he who built 'St David's Great Hall which remains undoubtedly the finest range... he brought a graceful unity to the palace which takes command of the beholder's eye though designed to impress important guests of which there were many.' The same applied at Lamphey, now also a tourist attraction, though it is here in St David's that a series of building bishops, as rich as any Middle-Age landowner, created a unity of medieval buildings with no equal in Wales.

Two other points impress us about the outside: the tilt from east to west has only been partially controlled by massive buttresses (the problem wasn't helped by a slight earthquake shaking it up in 1247), and the height of the tower (125ft), of gold-and-purple stone, rather more colourful than the rest of the enormous veritable village ostensibly devoted to God.

There's an interesting relationship between the sloping nave and the height of the tower. As we have enjoyed seeing from our hotel, the surrounding windswept heath soon ends with the sea, the highway that carried raiders and invaders. The cathedral was built in a hollow so that its obligatory fine tower couldn't be seen from a ship. That meant choosing a marshy site in a hollow by the bubbling river which didn't give the best foundations. And speaking of greed, the tower has clocks on only three sides, because those living to the north wouldn't pay for the privilege of being able to see the time.

Though the Great Hall is a ruin and little of the once impressive perimeter wall, and only one of four gates survive, it is fairly easy to imagine what life would have been like here at the height of the Church's power. The monks endured long days but it is doubtful if they went hungry and, while the Bishops no doubt sincerely raised money to the glory of God, they undoubtedly enjoyed some of the trappings of power.

To get back to the 'city centre', we have to climb thirty nine steps, or the Thirty Nine Articles since they're named after Thomas Cramer's Anglian tenets. Sheila, who bustled back up far more steps yesterday, finds it tricky to build up a rhythm on the wide steps... or, is it because she's desperate for a coffee.

That has us making straight for Pebbles Café and Gallery. Only after refreshment when we look round the gallery with stunning photographs on display does the penny drop that this is Jacki Sime's base from which her book was self-published. She's finished an early stint this morning and gone off duty (or is perhaps busy with her camera) but, when I catch up with her, she indeed proves interesting.

Partly brought up in St David's and partly in Dawlish, Devon, she was a child-prodigy photographer. First inspired by taking pictures when she was eight, then taking and printing her own photographs when she should have been studying for A-levels at sixteen, winning a college place to study photography but deciding to do it in real (which meant commercial) life and opening her first gallery when she was just twenty one, she has never been one to hang about. Her writing grew out of taking pictures which remains her passion: 'I'm still hanging in there mainly using film, digital only occasionally.' The present gallery is linked to the café run by her long-standing partner; they have two children beginning to prove their worth to the business.

'The Dean encouraged me, almost pushed me, into writing and publishing the book. Having to make all the publishing decisions was something quite different. We knew there'd be good support. I've now sold 12,000 copies, but they nearly all go the Cathedral bookshop, the National Trust, the National Park's visitors' centre and my own gallery. As for the book trade, forget it. The chains make it difficult for you to get orders and don't pay until you've chased hard. We do get some bookshop orders which we supply, but we don't encourage them for they're not very worthwhile. There are many direct orders by mail, but the ideal is just supplying a handful of supportive customers.

'If that sounds all straightforward, there were many challenges. I suffer from something like dyslexia, especially struggling to know my right from my left, so when I was writing my text I had to check directions very carefully. And the printer I chose did a batch of thousands perfect bound that started falling to pieces, so several thousand copies were printed that couldn't be used. Altogether it's been very worthwhile, but my second book, of my photograph work, is being published for me.' (Perfect bound books rely on glue to hold the pages in place... as with the telephone directory which can be dangled from a single page. As I found myself with a paperback edition of the popular *Crossing's Guide to Dartmoor*, a bad batch of glue causes chaos, books falling apart in customers' hands.)

Jacki's photographic genius might come from her maternal grandmother, the wife of a missionary in Madagascar for many years who illustrated her own books with glass plates which are prized possessions today. Having already done a photographic trip to the Arctic, she is keen to find a TV or other sponsor for a visit to Madagascar to compare how things are now with what her grandma wrote about and illustrated in her day.

St Davids Peninsula, which remains our constant companion while we explore, is published by her Pebble Books at St David's SA62 6SP. If you are planning a visit, read it thoroughly alongside OS Landranger sheet 157 in advance.

The café has recommended a nearby delicatessen where we buy a sandwich for our lunch, first walking round the town once more, popping into shops and galleries. I comment that it only seems like yesterday that hotel breaks automatically included lunch, while today few of their restaurants are even open except on Sundays. The Edwardians followed the Victorians with many-course meals twice daily and appetites to match, yet it is our generation that is overweight. What causes obesity? Is it lack of balance in the diet, junk food, sugary drinks?

We eat delicious crab sandwiches, once more enjoying the expansive view of a kind not seen elsewhere: an uneven but flattish treeless heathland, little cultivated, rising high in the north and hiding the sea behind it, while west and south, though the coast isn't continuously clear, there's a beckoning deep blue sea. There's access to the coastal path from the hotel's extensive gardens. However, after yesterday's exertions we fall asleep over our books.

When I am jolted back to life, I find myself asking if St David would approve of today's cathedral. But who was David (or Dewi)? We know tantalisingly little about him or why he should be the only Welsh saint revered beyond Wales, celebrated each first of March. We don't even know why we Davids wear a daffodil (or leek) on that morning.

David was a powerful character, certainly: an austere monk and 6th century bishop who only drank water, founded many monasteries including some in Brittany. But it was only in the 12th century that he became Patron Saint of Wales. Much of the early writing about him is allegorical or propaganda. Least of all do we know about his birth, its date or circumstances, but I'll come back to that when Sheila might have an excuse to run down more steps on our exploration of the sun-drenched peninsula.

Onto the Peninsula

We start by going the short distance to St Non. What brings people here is not so much the cliff scenery and bird life, great though they are, but the tradition or is it legend of St Non. She was a nun at Ty Gwyn, near

Whitesands Bay who was seduced (or was it raped?) by a prince. The 'information' comes only from the 11th century (that's over five centuries after his death) life of St David by Rhygfarch.

St David's prince father was supposedly out hunting when he came across the pretty nun. Her own father was deeply upset by her pregnancy and planned to kill both her and the unborn baby. As the moment of birth approached, Non fought her way through thunder and lightening to the coast. In the pain of labour she grasped one of the standing stones so firmly that it took imprints of her fingers and split in two. As David was born, a spring of pure water gushed from the ground. Still flowing, St Non's Well inevitably became a place of pilgrimage. It remains such, with a modern retreat centre busy on the cliffs. Nearby and easily accessible from the road (and on foot by a path from our hotel garden) are the ruined chapel and well, both with explanatory plaques. This afternoon we have them peacefully to ourselves. But there is only a handful of steps down to the well.

The rape version might have been invented to clear Non's name, but anyway it seems likely that the Patron Saint of Wales was born out of wedlock. Many Welsh legends, for example that any form of interference with a standing stone caused elemental disturbance, are woven into the story. Jacki Sime gives a fuller account and describes many other such legends in her book.

The whole of the peninsula is virtually drowned in fable, and we can only guess what people believed at different times. It is part and parcel of Wales's enduring Christianity, which began early with the arrival of the first saints across the Irish Sea and retains something of the more colourful experiences and legends of each successive age. Again, I can but stand and stare, feeling close to God without understanding quite why. Then many of the emotional Welsh are more prone to break into song celebrating legends than to approach them critically.

Next we take two separate lanes both ending at quays. The first, reached through a gentle valley with a stream, is Port Clais, once St David's commercial harbour on a narrow creek and the place where the saint is said to have been baptised. Now it's only for pleasure boating. The second is named after Justinian, a 6th century hermit and martyr of Ramsey Island, for which this is the starting point of most boat trips. There's a hut from which to buy ferry tickets, a ruined chapel and a lifeboat station, but nothing more other than a car park, empty this afternoon.

We look across to the island, less than two miles long but narrower with very different east and west coasts. This famous sea-bird sanctuary belongs to the RSPB. Living alongside the birds – and we can clearly see a cloud of them circling overhead – is a herd of red deer.

Finally this afternoon we visit Whitesands Bay, a popular resort with camps and cafés and surfers taking full advantage of the North Cornwall-style Atlantic breakers leisurely rolling in. I've just read a newspaper listing of the new wave of good eateries by the sea, predictably concentrating on Southern England and the West Country. Certainly nothing Welsh, and you wouldn't come here for good food, welcome though our cuppa is. Activity bubbles all around with families continually going to the beach or returning – one little boy stubbornly refusing to come like a Westie who hasn't finished sniffing.

To the north, only the coastal path braves it around St David's Head with its Iron Age fortress on the cliff. There must be a lot more legends there and around Carn Llidi, the high crag we see from our hotel to which we return by the road which will eventually lead us toward Fishguard. Happily that's not till the day after tomorrow – still not long enough to begin to do St David's and the peninsula full justice.

Cathedral Service and St Brides Bay

Before breakfast next morning – and a lovely one it is – we descend the steps to enter the Cathedral for the early Communion. When we walk in from the bright sunshine, it doesn't seem so spacious as from the outside; first impressions are of narrowness. Then walking along the nave to the choir stalls, we feel the considerable slope. Only a dozen and a half of us are at the service, half Welsh, the rest mainly English, though with an Australian or two. It is a friendly little congregation, and the priest has time to ask how the regulars are faring and where we strangers hail from. We're the latest in a very long line of visitors, most in the early days far more distinguished.

After the short service, the organ coming to life for the next one, we have time to look round. There are many handsome features, though St David's wouldn't score highly in our ranking of the many cathedrals we've visited at home and around the world. The special excitement has to be its remoteness, quite out of scale with the village-like city it serves. And we marvel that St David made such an impression that this is virtually the Welsh equivalent to England's Canterbury Cathedral and HQ of the long-disestablished Church in Wales.

At peace and full of the joy of life, after a breakfast which will also serve as lunch, we start off through Solva on the Haverfordwest road, to make our way south along St Brides Bay on the west-facing coast. First stop is at Nolton Haven. Slightly inland the village is delightfully-situated, and near the beach is what might well claim to be the most-picturesquely-placed holiday cottage in all Wales. The beach itself is pebbly, and there's a pebble ridge to restrain high-tide waves from flooding the car park. The tall waves break with almost deafening fury, but surfers are no doubt discouraged by the shingle. There's always something unexpected to see: here it is part of the route of a tramway which once brought coal from a local colliery down to a sheltered jetty. As we have seen elsewhere, even much of the winning and transport of coal was once romantic.

Enjoying the contrast of the white spray off the breakers with the deep blue of sky and sea, we soon reach another Broad Haven, where there is a large number of houses. Happening to meet the manager of the Post Office which is within the mini-Londis supermarket we're told: 'This is a great place to live, perfect for retired people, but there are many council staff, doctors, hospital workers and so on who commute mainly to Haverfordwest.'

I ask about the Post Office's future. 'Logic says we'll survive, for it's a busy place and the nearest other Post Office is a community one, only part-time. But who knows with the government so little in tune with the countryside, wanting to make it easier to build out-of-town supermarkets and extend homes.'

Broad Haven is surprisingly large, definitely not subtle, but the next place, Little Haven, with a narrow sandy bay, really catches our imagination. What with the Atlantic rollers, the bent trees dramatically showing the direction of the prevailing wind, and people sheltering their ice cream cornets under their spare hand, it is all quite Cornish... and, like many Cornish havens has a cosy touch to it too.

We drive through pleasant but fairly ordinary countryside two thirds of the way to Haverfordwest before returning via Nolton Haven. Then back along the coast road we came by. There's no doubt that the coast is Pembrokeshire's distinguished attraction and especially so in this area with the National Park boundary never far inland.

Eventually we're back on the main road that was so crowded on Friday, making our last stop of the day at Solva, parking in the wooded valley to sample the coastal path back toward Newgate Sands. The cliff top walking is relatively easy here, but the experience one to die for. As one guidebook says, it's very Celtic. We feel a part of the history of this relatively unknown corner of Britain, the 'genius' (as the former Archdruid of Wales put it) of the land, cliffs and sea, somehow making the Age of the Saints feel very real and recent. It's been another afternoon well spent and one ever to remember.

To Fishguard

On several occasions over the last half century I've stayed at the little Cardiganshire resort of Gwbert-on-Sea and driven to St David's for the day. That's quite an undertaking. On a crisp Monday morning when everything seems well with us and the world, on a one-way journey there, we need be in no hurry and can enjoy exploring minor roads and spending time out of the car.

We've scarcely left St David's before, abandoning the busy main road, we take the minor one close to the coast, and soon sidetrack off that to tumble into tiny Abereiddi, with its stony black beach. On grim days when the Atlantic gales train the branches of trees to point uniformly inland, the little place can seem the epitome of dullness, but it is welcoming enough in this morning's sunshine. Its blue lagoon, as much violet as blue, stuns with its brightness.

All around are industrial relics, including the remains of a tramway that brought slate from a long-abandoned quarry down over the hill. The lagoon itself is a former quarry, blasted open for safety reasons. In winter, with frequent gales and rain, it wouldn't have been much fun for those working in harsh conditions and poorly housed, but for us there's always romance in how people struggled to earn a living against the odds – and a fascination in the ruins.

The coastal path going east is especially challenging with high cliffs – and fossils galore. It takes us to remote mini Porthgain, with ruins of a slate quarry, brickworks and cottages tightly packed in around the quay. Pity it is nowhere near lunch time, for it is said that the best pub in Pembrokeshire is here – and a second one renowned for seafood. That shows how popular the coastal path has become, but here's yet another place where industry has been replaced by tourism.

Next comes Abermawr with shingle beach and woodlands. Unlikely though it now seems, Brunel planned to establish a railway as well as a cable terminus here.

Big Car, on its way back from Bath to Scotland, bounces along the minor road to Abercastle, another place where slate – and coal and farm produce – were exported in the 'good old days' of small rural industries offering appallingly low wages. No doubt life was a struggle, yet every last person would have been an individual if not a 'character' with great local comradeship though probably with frequent disputes and quarrels. Today's harbour is packed with yachts. How often can they safely venture into the Atlantic?

Though this is still Pembrokeshire, we're back in Welsh-speaking country (though the proportion of Welsh speakers steadily declines) and a land where past and present, fact, legend and superstition mingle. There's a 4,500-year old burial chamber, and another challenging section of the coastal path but, again in the car, we're a mile or so inland as we bump along a narrow lane between high hedges. We catch occasional glimpses of the shimmering sea and pass ancient burial places, but what we'll remember most is the full glory of the spring flowers. As we head toward Strumble Head, the Wicklow Mountains come into sight. We are as close to Ireland as you can get in Wales... and there is a ferry bound for Fishguard.

That is where we now hasten, for it's already getting past lunch time. First through curiously-named Stop and Call, once a separate village, but now part of Goodwick's suburban sprawl, and then along the flat area created for the railway terminal by blasting away 1.6 million tons of rock. This was generally regarded as the South Wales end of the GWR: a huge area and once a busy station. Today many more drive here to catch the Rosslare Ferry than join it as foot passengers.

Though there is talk of reopening Goodwick & Fishguard station, better situated for both villages, and improving the sparse train service, thoughts are more naturally of past glories... and ambitions. The spacious terminus was built mainly for Atlantic liners. Though the breakwater, which used up the blasted stone, was necessary for protection, it caused silting. Hopes were born to die. The few liners such as the *Mauretania* that called had to transfer their passengers and mail by tender.

One piece of former GWR property has been expensively restored: the hotel, the smallest of the railway's total of only four, looking down on the station and across the bay. It is again the area's premier one, and serves a decent if not cheap bar snack.

There was once a thriving herring fishery and we see where cattle as well as humans landed from Ireland and, where in postwar years, a daily Motorail train brought a string of cars bound for Ireland. Nearby, in 1912, the first plane across the Irish Sea took off on its flight of 100 minutes. But the area's most-noted event was the last 'invasion' of Britain by a comically disorganised rabble of semi-intoxicated Franco-Irish troops in 1797. Legend may be stronger than fact, but the invaders' surrender is said to have been caused by their mistaking the traditional Welsh dress of a hundred or so advancing women for the British soldiers' uniform of the day.

What does seem to be true is that a local cobbler, Jemima Nicholas, alone captured fourteen French soldiers. The 'Welsh heroine' is vividly portrayed in the Fishguard Tapestry which can be seen in a hall near the town centre. Though scarcely justifying comparison with the Bayeaux Tapestry, it is not only fascinating but demonstrates the lively spirit of enterprise that has thrived here (at least in prolonged spurts) for centuries. Fishguard with Goodwick have contributed much to Welsh and British life. Jemima Nicholas has a monument at the Parish Church, where coincidentally, at a London conference, one of the most powerful Christian speakers we've ever been inspired by, was incumbent.

There is certainly a burst of enterprise and self-confidence right now, with much renewal and many local initiatives for a place of just over 3,000 people. Though I didn't care much for it when queuing for our turn to join the Rosslare Ferry on a stormy, rainy evening many years ago, Fishguard has grown on me and wouldn't be a bad centre for a holiday. There are really two Fishguards and technically the harbour is in Goodwick. The small Lower Town with many holiday cottages to the east enjoys a commanding view over the harbour and beyond.

To Gwbert-on-Sea

Though there's no doubt that it is the coastline that is Pembrokeshire's greatest gift, a few inland areas also have special qualities. I've always wanted to explore the deep valley of the River Gwaun, Europe's oldest glacial vale. On days like this, we are always tempted to include more than we comfortably can. No matter. Though we're getting tired, why not collect another landscape memory?

Leaving Fishguard by the B4313, we're soon into a quite different environment. To retain intimacy with the winding river, several times we descend the steep hillside and climb up the other side. Close to the river there's green lushness, but it doesn't spread far up the rugged stone-strewn sides. Habitation is confined to the bottom and, emphasising the valley's remoteness, it is said that some people still celebrate New Year in mid-January, sticking to the pre-1752 calendar. There are not many places so accessible yet so remote that offer a stronger feeling of stepping back into history. If staying in Fishguard, this is just one of the areas deserving exploration in greater depth.

We make our way back to the coast almost due north along a minor road that doesn't make much effort to follow the contours. At the highest point, we're away from habitation, even the small villages with their tiny little churches of the valley we've left behind seeming to be in a quite different world, though in minutes we could be back beside the Gwaun or in Fishguard. As in so many empty high areas, there's evidence of ancient man's activity when the climate was kinder and primitive farming could be practised without the need to clear forest. Especially there are burial sites. We wonder just what the burial ceremony would have been like: so many yesterdays across a wide span of history being experienced today.

As we descend there's a fine view over Fishguard Bay flanked by dramatic Dinas Head to the east. Only the coastal path goes round it, but we get close to Cwm yr Eglwys, tucked cosily around its small beach. Though it is claimed that it is warmer and drier than anywhere else locally, the ruined church demonstrates it is not immune to the Atlantic's anger. The great storm of 1859 felled all but the belfry and west wall. Well over a hundred ships were wrecked. Some of the victims must be buried in the churchyard, but we cannot identify any grave. Except in storm, Cwm yr Eglwys is a charming but, for its size, a rather busy place, the ruined 12th century church seemingly more of a pull than those of the same age still active today.

Having crossed it earlier, we head east on the A487 (T), resisting stopping in what has always struck me as an unexpectedly interesting Newport, an ancient small town between the end of Newport Bay and Carningli Common, the remains of an old volcano splattered with ancient sites. The high land's name is based on the belief that St Brynach lived there in contemplation with angels. Making another excellent centre, the town is surprisingly little spoilt by the allegedly trunk nature of the A487(T), but I've always been in a hurry in a queue of vehicles and never patronised its attractive shops and cafés. This is certainly Remote Britain – and sparsely populated, yet it teems with social life.

Sheila yawns and drops off, as we finally leave Britain's only Coastal National Park whose one major inland sweep includes the areas we've just explored, and cross the old county border into Cardiganshire. Sheila is still sleepy as we pass through the former county town, a major administrative centre which once supported a branch railway I used in splendid non-corridor isolation in what seems like a different incarnation. There's so much activity and enterprise, with some distinguished buildings and real streets, that it comes as something of a shock to realise that only 4,000 people live here. Very much its own place, Cardigan has an independent spirit and is about as Welsh as anywhere the length of the Principality's west-facing coast. Welsh is widely spoken.

'Are we there yet?' asks Sheila, jerked back to life by stopping and starting in traffic. Yes, we're about to turn onto the B road to Gwbert-on-Sea. The Teifi Estuary soon comes into sight and we drive alongside it, with golf links on the inland side, to reach the Cliff Hotel, high on a cliff just facing the open sea.

It was in the mid-1950s that, travelling with a male relation, I came across the hotel toward the end of a busy day. Instantly I fell in love with its position. We checked that they had two single rooms, but before going to them we walked across the field to the cliff top, enjoying the view of the tidal estuary exposing a large area of firm sand twice daily. It seemed magic. It still does.

In truth the building would be more at home in Bournemouth than here, and today's planners wouldn't approve such a stark design, the pure white of the walls adding to conspicuousness. Over the years the quality of everything from welcome to bedding and food has been distinctly variable. It seemed fine on my first visit when one assumed the bathroom was down the corridor; now it is benefiting from another of its periodic makeovers. The brochure says it remains 'one of the most luxurious hotels in the area attracting visitors from the UK, Europe and America' though, like the receptionist, the first visitor we meet is Australian.

I've long wanted to bring Sheila here and now, over fifty years since my first and twenty since my last visit, I'm delighted to be back. To celebrate, we walk across the field to cliff top. It's sunny. It always has been on my visits. It's invigorating as ever, and over the next few days we delight in watching the tide sweep in and out, families playing on the sands, and look across to the other side of the river where there's a glimpse of the extreme end of the Pembrokeshire Coastal National Park – not that there's not good coastal scenery continuing north. We feel child-like on the cliffs though, at our age, realistically this could be one of many last visits to favourite places. That spurs us to make the most of it. At last a snooze, and then fine dinner and another walk along the cliffs with a bouncy young lab anxious to include us among his owners.

Up the Teifi to Newcastle Emlyn

Next morning provides an opportunity to do something I've planned since I was a teenager: visit the small town of Newcastle Emlyn. It is too late by fifty six years to fulfil my original intention, to travel by train on the branch from Pencader. Only by the skin of my teeth did I manage to travel on the long single-track 'main' line with steep gradients from Aberystwyth through Pencader to Carmarthen. It was pioneered by the Manchester & Milford Railway which proposed a trunk route but didn't succeed even in completing the single line between Aberystwyth and Carmarthen.

Today I'm still curious why so small a place as Newcastle Emlyn (1,500 people even including Adpar across the river) could ever have justified its own railway. Part of the explanation is that the terminus had a through platform in expectation of building on to Cardigan; the rest is that the opening year was 1896, just as building rural railways slowed down on the threshold of the motor age.

A through Cardigan-Pencader route would have followed the River Teifi the whole way, far more closely than we can setting off from Cardigan by road. But down a side road, after crossing an abandoned railway, a goods extension of the Cardigan branch, we reach Cilgerran – and spot the castle's tower among the trees on the rim of the river's deep gorge. The castle was rebuilt by a Norman baron after the 1109 abduction of the Welsh 'Helen of Troy' by an over-amorous Owain, son of the Prince of Powys, which stirred up much of Wales. The area, favoured by man since prehistoric days, continued to be hotly disputed so the new castle was no mere decoration. In more peaceful times when Turner visited and painted it, the dramatically-situated castle was already the soft ruin we see preserved today. Maintaining ruins in the same state of decrepitude has become an art form.

We then make our way back to the river opposite Llechryd and are surprised to find ourselves running alongside an old canal. On returning home and consulting *The Canals of South Wales and the Border* by Charles Hadfield (the Charles of David & Charles), I discover that it was built back in 1772 to help navigation, mainly up the river, to a tin plate works a few miles further on. We're in another fine piece of intricately beautiful scenery with ancient monuments, industrial remains and pretty villages... and brimming with legends.

There are sharp bends as we follow the river into Newcastle Emlyn, a romantic under-sized nearly, all-centre town with little suburb. There are surprisingly fine tall buildings and again an air of enterprise with everyone greeting each other in Welsh and no doubt knowing everyone else's business. There are keen tourists, too; we join a few who are enjoying looking down on the river. Another ruined castle commanding an even better view than we have from the outdoor tables of a new café serving a tasty choice of lunch dishes.

Between courses, we read about the Wyvern of Newcastle Emlyn. On a crowded fair day, Wyvern the winged viper breathed fire and smoke causing terror as it alighted on the castle walls. A brave soldier waded into the Teifi floating a red cloak downstream and shot the beast on its underside. Catching sight of the cloak, in its death throes it shrieked, attacked it and poisoned the fish with its venom.

The castle is on high ground on an elbow of the fast-flowing river's double bend. Newcastle Emlyn has an enviable position and is thoroughly likeable and full of interesting detail. The market hall and clock tower are specially worth photographing, while the map indicates the sites of the first printing press, old grammar school, milestone of 1841, old shirt factory, power station, tannery, flannel mill, railway station and dragon maze. There may be less activity here than formerly, but it feels prosperous, the private shops offering first-class produce. While tourists are well catered for, Newcastle Emlyn is still basically a place for the Welsh to live, work, pray and amuse themselves. As centre to a flourishing farming area, it especially comes to life on Friday market day.

I'm delighted to be here, yet there is always a qualification at the back of my mind in such Welsh-speaking gems. While the Welsh majority may smile, they make it very clear you're not one of them. Though we don't have to struggle to make ourselves understood, for the English it can almost feel more foreign than parts of the Continent. That never happens even in remotest Scotland where the grandeur of the scenery may be utterly unfamiliar but it is far easier to be part of the local scene. Yet the more remote and Welsh-speaking the area, the more I love the countryside.

On our way back from Cardigan, we take the opposite bank to our hotel's. First stop is St Dogmaels, where we see what little remains of the Tironian abbey, once among the richest in Wales and, continuing toward the sea, go along a steep and very narrow lane which almost turns back on itself near the National Park's border.

Turning round and then passing other vehicles is difficult, our white hotel, the prominent landmark across the sands, perpetually coming in and out of view. This really is a difficult lane, but soon we're down, almost at sea level and park on the sands. We cross the road for a refreshing cuppa at the modern café and then a walk on the firm sands. It would be hard not to be in a relaxed holiday mode. It takes a surprising time to go around the estuary, crossing near Cardigan, and get back to our hotel. Then another walk on the cliffs. This is a lovely, memorable spot and, like listening to a familiar piece of recorded music, looking at the scenery reminds me of the thoughts I had when first experiencing it.

Along the Coast to New Quay

There is a hectic jigsaw of villages, roads and lanes, many leading, though not always at all directly, to the sea. Signposting isn't great and some hedges are high and overgrown, so we get vaguely lost several times during the morning, but there's no hurry and the wild flowers softly compel us to take it easy. We remind ourselves that, when life was tough in the early and mid 19th century, thousands emigrated from this coast.

First stop is Aberporth, with a pair of sandy beaches attracting summer crowds who are sometimes blessed by sightings of bottlenose dolphins. There is a bronze sculpture of a leaping dolphin in what used to be a busy herring port. It retains commercial crab and lobster along with leisure fishing, and still has something of a traditional atmosphere along with its modern cottages. Mixing with the visitors and locals are staff from the ParcAberporth research centre, famous for developing UAVs (unmanned aerial vehicles). The downside is that the resort's over-popularity is said to encourage high prices.

A mile further on, tiny Tresaith is a smaller, cosier Cornish-like hamlet with a small beach from which the roar of the Atlantic breakers is almost deafening. Next Llangrannog, the older part in a steep valley, the holiday area below a waterfall spread out along a pretty beach where everything apart from 'Bed-and-Breakfast' is in Welsh. The Welsh language is regaining importance in this area, with virtually all young people able to use it. 'This is too good not to photograph,' says Sheila, regretting that our camera has been left at our hotel. So she buys an instant one and instantly uses it half up.

The nearby Post Office has a notice that might have been better addressed to the Welsh: 'Please respect the privacy of the customer in front of you.' Its keeper bemoans having to wait so long to hear of its fate in the cut backs: 'I'll tell you one thing. Without the Post Office, the shop won't survive. It's difficult enough getting small quantities. When we only want a few pounds of carrots we have to order many kilos. It's hard to look after your customers.' We notice empty produce bins, but then there are productive gardens and smallholdings nearby.

Finally New Quay, another place I've long wanted to visit. It's bigger and brasher than I'd imagined, a touch of the much larger Cornish Newquay about it, with camp sites, cheap cafés, parking problems, and an earlier commercial and shipbuilding history. But until postwar holidays with pay, it was a more sedate, intimate place mainly of densely-packed cottages where everyone knew what their neighbours were about. It rivals Laugharne we visited on the way to Gower in its claim for having been the model for *Under Milk Wood*. Dylan Thomas and his family lived here till the mid 1940s; there's even a Dylan Thomas Boathouse.

The family left, almost driven out, as a result of an alleged attempt on Thomas's life following a fight in a pub. A soldier newly back from the war, taking the portrait of an immoral village rather too literally, accused him of a ménage à trois with his and his own wife and fired a bullet at his rented home. He was charged with attempted murder, though acquitted.

There is certainly much to do in New Quay as well as taking your bucket and spade down to the beach. The situation is gorgeous and, especially along the rocky coast, there are walks that quickly get you away from activity. In a storm it might again be akin to the Cornish Newquay. Two busy lifeboats are maintained here, the only ones between

Cardigan and Aberystwyth, not the most benign part of our coastline.

After a quick bite, we make our way back to Gwbert-on-Sea, enjoying an exhilarating final cliff walk and early to bed. Tomorrow will be a long drive through many kinds of scenery to Oswestry (see chapter XXVII). Though I don't want to live in Wales, we've had a marvellous time in some of its more remote areas since we first crossed the border. There are plenty more awaiting later exploration, including the coast around Aberaeron, the next resort up the coast from New Quay where Georgian terraces show that seaside development started much earlier and the GWR had a branch from Llampeter.

· XIV ·

TO THE SHETLAND ISLES

Fair Isle: First Casualty

Happy thoughts of our tour of Shetland will always be with us, but the first thing memorably different has been the difficulty in making arrangements. While Hertz will rent me a car as long as I have a driving licence, no Shetland car renter will. Arranging cover through our Nairn broker is straightforward but, when the specific vehicle insured is rendered unusable by a *young* driver, last-minute panic from which our Nairn broker emerges triumphant.

Herrislea House Hotel, at which we plan to stay the first night phones profusely to apologise they cannot honour our booking while, when we check at the Lerwick Hotel, they have no record and anyway are overbooked.

Next, unlike Britain, much of which has been flooded, in Shetland irrigation systems are in full blast and summer dryness encourages fog. Suffering occasional distinctly off days, Sheila is still waiting for her gall bladder to be removed. I'm nervous of being stranded on Fair Isle, a frequent risk. So I call the new American owner (of more in a moment) of the bed-and-breakfast where we're going to stay. He tries to be reassuring: there's always the twelve-seater boat which runs certain days; it only takes two and a half hours when it's not rough. 'Anyway, the rescue helicopter flies unless the fog is really bad.' That hardly puts my mind at rest, and neither does Fair Isle's well-known weather forecaster, David Wheeler, who the day before we are due to fly, says: 'Its classic conditions for fog, no south westers for weeks. Everything is unpredictable on Fair Isle, but for what it's worth the morning plane didn't run today.'

Having fulfilled every last engagement in Yorkshire immediately after her first bad attack, Sheila – game for anything – hates the idea of cancelling our Fair Isle visit, so I justify doing so by saying I'm worried that the rest of our arrangements might be thrown into disarray at the peak of the islands' short, sharp season. 'I so wanted to go to Fair Isle.' Hopefully one day we will for, having discovered so much about it, I've a strong feeling for it: Britain's remotest lived-on island, famed for its knitting patterns and mention in shipping weather forecasts.

Fair Isle's seventy one people live on a tiny speck of land about 25 miles south west of the tip of mainland Shetland, just half way to the Orkneys. Nearly surrounded by cliffs, some spectacular, the island has a stormy though equitable climate. The scene of many shipwrecks, its history goes back 5,000 years. No piece of land has been more intensively and fruitfully worked over by archaeologists; there are fourteen scheduled monuments. No island is more visited by migrant birds using it as a staging post. Tourism is largely bird-driven, the Observatory being the only eating place. Besides it and bed-and-breakfast tourism, employment opportunities are scant and, as on all small islands, the enterprising fulfil a variety of functions.

Fair Isle knitting? There's one machine loom 'more complicated than mechanised'. The work is hand finished, and mainly framed for sale in the island's only shop. A few knit traditionally, not a great money spinner. Crofting is mainly rough pasture. There's a little fishing when the weather permits. An enterprising museum is seen by nearly all visiting the island, including those from occasional calling cruise ships who outnumber residents. There's a communications centre – and weather forecasting. David Wheeler's website forecasts cover all the Northern Isles; reports are well-read in the *Shetland Times*. He's been the professional observer for forty five years: 'The trend is definitely warmer, though the top summer temperature just 17°C. With very high humidity even that feels sweltering.' Rainfall, though recorded on 266 days, is only 40 inches.

The school, now with six primary and three nursery children, periodically struggles to attract a head teacher, and so does the National Trust to find tenants for vacant homes. Advertising for two families hit the headlines in the States, accounting for seventy of ninety four applications. Great has been the publicity given to the choice of Tom and Liz Hyndman and their six-year-old son Henry from Saratoga Springs, Upper New York.

Says Tom of the successive journalists visiting them: 'They all come to do pieces about us being in culture shock, but they're the ones in shock. After a short interview, they go crazy about having to wait – with the possibility of real delay before they can get off the island. They're so wound up that it's they who need sympathy. We've adjusted well and love it, and aren't alone in that: a quarter of the residents have no relations here. The nature's wonderful. Henry loves watching people ringing birds in our back yard. It's a natural resting place for birds. There are no trees for them to hide.' A hat maker by trade, he's delighted he's been asked to produce a special mitre for the new Bishop of Aberdeen, who wants all his robes made in his Diocese. This sets Tom on a new track, making one-off hats, some with puffin or gannet themes. A few are stocked in the shop, while others are ordered online. No production line now.

'There's so much tradition from this tiny island – Fair Isle knitting: Polar explorers, mountain climbers, royals, they all wear it, though everyone imitates it. It's just the place to be creative, but things move slowly and you just have to get used to waiting for materials.'

Some time after our aborted trip, on the telephone his wife Liz confirms: 'A year now and yes it's great... funny how easy it is to get out of compulsive consumerism. When we went to the mainland, we were soon drawn back into it, but really relieved to get home. How you live your life is what counts here. Tom already knows the bird life well enough to call the Observatory if a rarity has landed.'

Britain?

There is a mistake above, which happened naturally, but has deliberately been left: at the beginning of the chapter's third paragraph, I compared Shetland's weather with Britain's. Local people are unlikely to spot it, for they don't feel in the least British. It is not that they particularly seek independence; they just *feel* independent. While the Western Isles we will visit soon are totally different from the rest of Scotland, the people and their traditions are undoubtedly Scottish. Not here. The Norse influence, and today's links with Norway, are close. Bergen is nearer than Edinburgh, as indeed are the Faroes. The isolation and the unique geology and the climate have bred a distinctive culture.

Brussels, London, Edinburgh may hold the purse strings and add irksome regulations, 'but you have to be governed somehow'. Real independence, how people think, talk and spend their time, isn't deeply affected by government – something that possibly other parts of the world could beneficially realise, but then so often the issue is racial and that's not in the least the case here. Look what it costs and how long it takes to take a car to Aberdeen and you begin to understand.

Though we live only eight miles from Inverness airport, it is still a formidable journey to Shetland, with a thick mist threatening to turn into an aircraft-stopping haar. At the intermediate call in Orkney, we only see below us just before landing. If it's like that here, might we be turned back from Sumburgh? However, the sun shines on Sumburgh Head, Shetland's southern tip, showing up the cliffs in sharp relief. The twenty-minute drive along Shetland's fastest road also reveals cliffs and a variety of distinctive local scenery.

Lerwick

Spirits rise, and do so more when we arrive in Lerwick en fête and we just squeeze the car into a space near the Queens Hotel, where the friendly receptionist has been able to find a sea-facing room for both the nights we can now spend in the island capital. From the bedroom, we watch shipping activity including the ferry to and from Bressay, the largish island opposite. The coldest part of Shetland, it affords Lerwick considerable shelter. We have only a two minute walk to Victorian Pier. Coinciding with dozens of yachts in the annual Bergen-Lerwick race tied up on either side, there's a great Flavour of Shetland, the culmination of celebrations beginning with the Johnsmas Foy marking the arrival of the Dutch fishing fleet, a turning point in the port's prosperity (and that of Bressay) over a century ago.

A thronged quiz is being broadcast live. Another crowd watches a cookery demonstration. In a third marquee, a teller of traditional stories, dressed as an ancient Norseman holding an axe lovingly rather than threateningly, has dozens of children spellbound. Local caterers and hotels show what they have to offer. Delicious fresh seafood is being eaten at a large indoor-outdoor area without a vacant chair. There are exhibits by craftpeople and a bookbinder. So much to take part in, eat, buy. Such jollity.

On cruises, twice I've spent a long day here, landing by tender at this pier which then seemed somewhat bleak. On those occasions I saw enough of the capital and Mainland and on the second, driving the length of Yell, to realise just how different Shetland is from anything at home or abroad. But now it is in a totally new, utterly lighthearted mode. Winters are long, summers short so, in late June, metaphorically and literally on the small proportion of land that yields it, hay is being made while it can.

Islands do this: we have to pinch ourselves to realise we only left home a few hours ago. 'Shop while you may,' I tell Sheila, for there are more places to do it in Lerwick than in the whole of the rest of island group. So, in one of the craft booths, she quickly admires jumpers with very original ideas based on deep colours made by Barbara Ibister. Though pleased to have the sale, she admiringly takes a last glimpse of her creation as she carefully wraps it: a zip-up stylish black garment with a scrolly red pattern with lighter flecks made of fine wool with alpaca and silk.

'I've been doing it all my life,' she says. 'It's a way of life, giving women a touch of independence when they're home-bound with children. It's always been a home industry, now with knitting machines. I can make two a week, absolute maximum. Useful income, not a fortune.'

Then I buy some great cards from Photography & Hand Made Shetland Felt, combining a chatty Donna Smith's two hobbies. And, bringing two odd spare chairs together, we squeeze into the open air part of the food stall, and select our fish platter from a wondrous range: prawns, lobster, fresh and smoked salmon, crab meat and claws. Everyone is smiling. Only one thing stops full summer enjoyment: while not cold, neither is it warm enough for dresses. Yet the scene is animated: crowds on the pier, many taking part in the race proudly showing off their yachts, a host of small craft moving around the harbour, busy road traffic. We wonder what the Viking Parade scheduled for later involves.

When we walk along the Esplanade, such is the friendliness that, if we pause a moment, someone asks if we need help; people wave on the town bus service. After looking up at Fort Charlotte we see the Bressay ferry, a substantial vessel, arrive with two cars and half a dozen shoppers. 'It can't pay,' I say, to which a local joins in 'Course it doesn't; jobs for the boys who hope Bressay folk will go on rejecting a causeway'. A landlink would undoubtedly turn Bressay into a dormitory for Lerwick. At breakfast we watched nine cars descend by sundry lanes to take the 'rush hour' ferry.

One of the joys of islands is the general lack of coach tours, but I've long enjoyed seeing small parties in the vintage vehicles of Classique Tours, and talked with some of the keen passengers I've met in various hotels over the years. There on the Esplanade is an empty Classique Tours coach with driver. On the spur of the moment I climb up. Luck; he's the firm's owner, David Dean, gentle and obviously nearing retirement, but not shy:

'We were basically a garage in Paisley and could only do charters before bus deregulation in 1980. I used to have seven drivers but now it's only one besides me, and next year just me. Then that'll be it. EU regulations have killed it. Drivers aren't allowed to work more than seven days on the trot and, because of the distances, we've always done week or longer tours.

Anyway the time to see the islands was in the 1950s when they were just opening up and local life was unspoilt. I felt like suing my parents for not having me earlier. It's been immensely enjoyable meeting all the old characters, just sad to see the roads getting wider and busier. Of course the scenery is still magnificent, and the wild life... and there are still great old buddies who remember the more colourful days when people's expectations, particularly in housing, weren't so great.'

Classique Tours, another colourful institution sadly on the way out. There'll never be another like it. The present passengers' successors will surely drive themselves and miss much. 'I'll miss our regulars who come year by year,' says David. 'It's been a great experience sharing my love for the islands with them.'

At dinner with a grandstand view, most tables are taken by yachtsmen speaking Norwegian among themselves. As often happens, people are less insular at breakfast, several Norwegians from other tables annotating what a woman next to us is keen to explain about the race. 'Twenty hours each way, though we were delayed by lack of wind at the start. It's good eating on land after a full day at sea, but the big thing is dinner on Saturday night. By the way, Belgians have joined in this year.'

Though we'd a number of alternatives mapped out, including a walk on Bressay, and possibly crossing it to visit the great nature reserve of Noss, the day slips by as we explore Lerwick: a town of considerable individuality. A few of the shops, including Harry's waterfront department store (London has Harrods, Edinburgh Jenners, Shetland Harry's says a lively leaflet) are almost museum pieces still serving their customers well. Other shops are plain. Few exciting. The narrow, stone-blocked part of Commercial Street running parallel with the Esplanade is of another age. In two days we saunter up and down it four or five times, always enjoying the glimpse of the steps down to the Esplanade. The *Shetland Times's* bookshop has long been enterprising, offering rich treasure in a way independents can rarely afford to do when competing against a chain. No chain bookseller here (though a girl who serves us at ubiquitous Boots says Shetland can be lonely for young incomers and, with regret, is returning south).

The range of books on Shetland is incredible, and so are the sales many achieve. Two large new titles are on special offer; scores are listed in a catalogue. Though there's never been a proper railway, someone's even produced a work on the short quarry and other industrial lines. The 'islands' Viking legacy, archaeology and geology are especially well covered, with a steady sprinkling of books by outsiders giving their impressions, the message always being that this is no more Scotland than it is England. I recall the hundreds of copies of *Shetland* in D&C Island series sold here.

The author, James R Nicolson, a true Shetlander, kindly drove me round parts of Mainland when I made my first cruise call. Among the places we visited was a fertile valley; it took years before I realised how untypical it was. While we were there, two-thirds of the cars we passed came from Iceland or the Faroes. A new mini-cruiser cum-car ferry had just established a route between the three island groups, with astonishing initial success. The novelty soon wore out, however, and the Shetlands were abandoned, but are now again currently served by

Smyril Line from Torshaven in the Faroes. We saw the large cruise-like ship come in yesterday, though the latest *Shetland Times* reports that next year Shetland is again being dropped. Also this morning we saw the spacious Northlink ferry from Aberdeen, at the season's peak without a spare space. Having to attend a sudden funeral or meeting, or being stuck because of weather disruptions, causes many problems.

Evening on Trondra

It was publishing James's Nicolson's *Shetland* that first gave me insight into the remarkable islands. Fifteen are still inhabited. Though some of the smaller ones suffer, the overall population has climbed back to 22,000, largely thanks to oil. Not only does it give direct employment, but the penny a metric ton disturbance royalty negotiated by the Council has allowed many improvement schemes including roads and schools with swimming pools. Only farmers have reason not to be confident: the soil is thin, the little arable cultivation really a hobby, sheep not worth rearing for freezers have long been full of lamb and it is illegal to subsidise transport. Tourism is thriving, but with a short summer peak when temperatures are relatively low. Only bird lovers really take advantage of the generally mild winters. Occasional storms can be grim.

Apart from the dramatic scenery and unique general ambience, many tourists are attracted by three things: the rich bird life, with many sightings unique to the islands; the extraordinarily rich archaeological heritage (the islands were settled early, and industry and agriculture have caused less disturbance than elsewhere); and finally the geology. Of course that is the main reason for the scenery, but thousands come each year to study it in its own right. When you realise the islands are all that remains of the tops of a great mountain chain, you just begin to understand that the rocks are old... in fact among the very oldest in the world, turned into extraordinary shapes by glaciation and millions of years of the sea's vicious attacks. As geological maps hanging in many public places clearly show, the geology is complicated with an unusually strong north-to-south pattern of parallel bands. Glaciation wore away some rocks quicker than others while, as the ice melted, relieved of its pressure, the land rose. The sea did the rest. It still nibbles away, resulting in some of the world's finest cliffs of weird shapes, caves, blowholes. When it breaks through hard rock, it gobbles softer ones inland. Nowhere in Shetland is more than three miles from the sea. The total length of coastline is an incredible 900 miles. Here is a passage from James's *Shetland:*

Shetland is divided into blocks by several faults, one of which, the

> Walls boundary fault, is the northern extension of the Scottish Great Glen fault. The central block, the 'backbone' of Shetland, consists of Schist, Gneiss and blue-grey limestone, originally sediments laid down on an ancient sea-floor, then folded, uplifted and recrystallised under intense pressure during the Caledonian orogeny or mountain-building period more than 420 million years ago. These rocks appear today as parallel bands of varying hardness, giving a pronounced north-south grain to the hills, valleys and voes of the larger islands.

James Nicolson, is suffering from Alzheimer's disease. So Robert, his son, has invited us home after dinner. Where the land mass is narrow, it is a short, complicated and hilly route from east coast to west coast, Robert explains where we are, and tells us about his dad. He astonishes me by saying he was born after publication of *Shetland.*

'Dad always had a pen in his hand, always researching and writing. He was trained as a geologist and had a spell in Sierra Leone, a culture shock from Shetland, but this is where he belonged and what he cared about. After Sierra Leone he was a fisherman before turning writer. He didn't have a grand office, just an old Imperial on which he wrote eleven books and regular contributions to the *Shetland Times* and also *Shetland Life*. That magazine has never been the same without him. He really knew Shetland. As an example, when South Havra became uninhabited in 1923, he had the presence of mind to talk to the old people about the way of life they'd given up. He still remembers a lot of the history, but not more recent happenings. We enjoy each other's company, but you visiting would have been hard for him.'

From his home overlooking the east coast of the bridge-connected Isle of Trondra, Robert takes a daily hour's journey (half by car, half by ferry) to the east coast island of Whalsay, one of Shetland's most vibrant communities. There he works at the fish-processing (mainly salmon and shellfish) factory, once a whaling station. Though the emphasis has changed, shellfish and farmed salmon now being more important, fishing remains vital. The Da Haaf Fishery College at Scalloway, which we passed close to on our journey across the island, is 'an anchor' and has a brilliant restaurant. And: 'When you visit Scalloway, do enjoy the first glance of it with its castle... and the memorial to those who lost their lives rescuing wartime Norwegian refugees on the "Shetland Bus" which was based there because of its repairing facilities. The Queen of Norway has just paid a visit. Scalloway was in the front line, such an interesting place, the former island capital.

I'm a Shetlander through and through and couldn't possibly live elsewhere. It is an interesting society. There's nowhere in all Shetland I wouldn't feel comfortable calling on someone for a cup of tea.'

His grandfather was from Papa Stour, a west coast volcanic island with Britain's most dramatic sea caves but a population down to the low twenties, where Christmas and New Year are still celebrated on the old calendar twelve days later then in the rest of the world.

Having put the new baby to bed, his wife Rhona joins us. She's also a true Shetlander. Her grandfather was a Lerwick poet 'with a great sense of joy – real fun. He really touched people. When he died I was only ten. Grown fishermen were in tears.'

Soon we find ourselves talking Christianity. As in most of Scottish islands, its early arrival has been well documented, but our subject is Christianity today. 'It has more relevance to life, a practical Christianity. We're Pentecostal but our church will take anyone. The Western Isles are where we were a century ago.'

Rhona says they have a weekly home group meeting: 'eighteen of us, and not just a cosy little group. It's a Christian group, but the door is open to anyone. We see many more random acts of generosity in Shetland than you'll find elsewhere: that's what we want to pass on to our children. We want to make this place closer to God.' We asked a big band to play for a disco, but were first told "impossible without booze". But it worked. The best party night we've ever had. People have been quiet too long; alcohol is a big problem.'

Time passes quickly, and soon we're again at the front door, enjoying the view, the sense of place and history. 'The problem is, people don't want to stunt progress, but how do we retain traditional values?' asks Robert. When I point to a grindstone used as a feature in the garden, I'm told it used to be used as a weight for haddock lines tied by women – which unleashes a repertoire of recollections of fishing and fishing tragedies.'

The Burras and Scalloway

Next morning we again make the eight mile cross-island journey across Mainland and the bridge to Trondra on the way to the Burras. These are wonderful examples of Shetland's north-to-south-strip geological pattern: islands of hard rock dangling down with smaller bits dangling off them further south with deeply penetrating voes (dead-end lochs) and sounds on either side. Populations are healthy, the early 1970s bridges opening up all sorts of possibilities including commuting to Lerwick and ferry-free retirement. What we most notice is the wealth of successful, specialised fishing: fish farms and smart fishing craft. There are also flashy cars parked outside posh bungalows and chalet-style Norwegian houses with steeply-pitched roofs. There's growing support for the annual 'flag day'. The Shetland-Norwegian inspired flags, blowing in the wind with the white cross (the vertical well left of centre) on a blue background make quite a point. All this in a grand land and seascape.

We could live here, we say, and are delighted by the setting of Hamnavoe, West Burra's mini-capital, where we park opposite the Post Office (more pension cash needed) looking down on the picturesque, busy little harbour. Until 1971, the journey to mainland was by boat to Scalloway. Not merely the bridges, but oil money has greatly improved local amenities, making general standards in Britain seem primitive. There's strong community life, with an especially active history group; one is not surprised to learn that the island has an early Christian site – or that South Havra, the extra piece dangling south of West Burra has long been uninhabited. People were once attracted by its fertile high ground and children and livestock used to be tethered, as still happens on a few fertile patches high above some Norwegian fjords.

Near the small bridge to East Burra there's an Outdoor Centre available to voluntary groups and a marina for visiting boats. East Burra is less developed. We enjoy the dramatic glimpse of the broad Sound separating it from the Cliff Hills of Mainland, largely uninhabited at its narrow point.

Then, remembering to savour the castle-topped view, we approach the gem of Scalloway, Shetland's ancient capital built around a curved sheltered bay where the Vikings landed. There's much to see and eat here – fish at the Fishing School or from the chip shop beside the castle. I love the contrast between old and new. The 1600 castle, stronghold of the Stewart's who forced change from Norse to Scots rule, looks down on the extensive modern fishing harbour and school, while new and old homes jostle with traditional and trendy shops. Within a few years of the castle's completion, Earl Patrick Stewart and his son were executed. The castle was occupied by Cromwell's troops before falling into disrepair, though in World War Two ammunition was stored in it and there's an interpretive centre – if you can take your eyes off the view. We snap the imaginative Shetland Bus memorial topped with a boat; the museum is rich in detail about the dangerous operation. A hundred were lost in storms or enemy attacks.

Links with Norway are also evident at newly-opened Yeatland Books in Main Street whose owner has just moved from Bridge of Allan. The shop is a bit of a mess yet, but is to be extended and will undoubtedly attract those interested in the Viking legacy and the Shetland Bus among other aspects of Shetland history. 'I'm sure it's the right place for me to be,' says Andrew. There's already fascinating stock.

We explore the extended quays with their huge fish works. Every inch of berthing is used; goodness knows how many million pounds' worth of boats are tied up. It was fishing that revived Scalloway's economy after general trade had drifted to Lerwick. A recent *Fishing News* is substantially devoted to its success and hopes. And much was the pleasure here when a Spanish gill-netter was escorted into Lerwick by the Scottish Fisheries Protection Agency and its catch inspected. Rightly or wrongly, it has long been felt the Spaniards compete unfairly.

Southern Comfort

Next, we branch off the trunk road south to take the B9122 with west coast views including St Ninian's Isle, near where the ruined church said to have been founded by the saint who brought Christianity to Shetland. Even a mere 5,000 geological years ago, the sea level was 30ft lower, and one result has been the formation of spits, known locally as ayres and by geologist as tombolos. The spit with Atlantic rollers crashing on either side connecting St Ninian's Isle to the mainland is perhaps the most fascinating. And what joy in 1958 when a schoolboy discovered silver treasure; not in the ruined church but under a slab of an earlier one. The designs have been incorporated into many items of modern island jewellery.

Beyond the Bay of Scousburgh, we reach tonight's resting place, Spiggie House commanding a grandstand view of the large Loch of Spiggie. Closely watched by baa-ing sheep, we walk down the steep hill, before returning to dinner and comfort. Though Lerwick was bursting at the seams, there's hardly anyone here. We're warmly treated by Evelyn and Pete Scrivener who have just sold before moving south: 'It's been good, but we need something different,' the sentiments of many who have been tied down by continuous long days.

Before going to sleep I enjoy J W Irvine's self-published *Good Old Days* – colourful days, maybe, but scarcely comfortable – among the books for visitors' use. Then a scan of the week's *Shetland Times,* dominated by marine affairs, fishing, oil and local transport-related. A breakdown in the Bressay ferry carrying morning commuters has strengthened the case for a causeway with bridge, but others feel that would encourage drugs import to Lerwick. Norwegians are becoming the largest shareholders in Shetland's biggest company. Ferries should be free, say campaigners. There was actually a bomb scare at Sumburgh airport when a couple of passengers left their luggage unattended to take a last walk on the beach. The paper, incidentally, has its own resident archaeologist.

Next morning, Sunday, we begin with a leisurely drive to the north shore of Loch of Spiggie, across the short barrier between loch and sea, and then along the western and southern sides. Unusually deep red campions decorate the verges. There are birds on the road, flying and hundreds on the RSPB-controlled loch, once an arm of the sea. The range will be far greater in autumn and winter when visitors from the north include numerous whooper swans. There's rich trout fishing, too. We note the marshland famous for its flora separating the Loch of Spiggie from the smaller Loch of Brow. South now with a glimpse of Quendale Water Mill (restored 1860s overshot mill with dam), cashing in on tourism with shop as well as tours, and past a number of well-cultivated gardens (rare in the Shetlands) to the sandy circular Bay of Quendale. Every view of the sea is utterly different. Nearby rests the rusting remains of *Braer,* the massive oil tanker whose disastrous destruction was headline news in the early days of 1992.

Then back through what are probably regarded as a series of townships, but come near to being ribbon development, to the main road. Next along a narrow and now little-used road past abandoned barracks to the west of the grandly-titled West Voe of Sumburgh. Alighting at the desolate end, we quickly return seeking the shelter of the car: especially during the nesting season, the Arctic skua's speciality is dive bombing intruders. They're capable of causing real injury.

Though some may see it as just the place where their plane lands before they head north, South Mainland is full of attractions. Almost at the end of the airport's runway is Old Scatness, one of Shetland's key recent archaeological finds. Visitors are invited to pretend they are Picts or Vikings, reliving history in an Iron Age broch and village. It is well done with plenty to interest the light-hearted and serious-minded alike.

Round the airport, and out towards Sumburgh Head, topped by a Stevenson lighthouse, we join a keen band of ornithologists with binoculars and cameras peering down on a noisy bird city lacking police to retain law and order. While some birds are patiently sitting on their nests or going about their rightful business, noisy squabbles, and thefts by skuas are incessant. Razorbills, fulmars, eider, guillemot, gannets, shags, kittiwakes – and, from our height, looking really petite, comic little puffins shuffling in and out of their crevice nests. 'First time I've seen them,' says a thrilled Sheila.

Now north, and east off the main road to welcoming Hoswick area with a light lunch at the visitors' centre. It has obviously been busy, and we see why: a party of German visitors off a cruise ship are just climbing back into their coach. Across the road is the Hoswick Woollen Mill open on a Sunday specially for the cruise visitors. The manager, Rosemary Gourdie, obviously having been busy now has time to explain that spun wool is measured and, with charts and sizes, delivered to homeworkers who use double-size knitting machines to produce ovals without seams.

She continues: 'Today they are nearly all older people; the young one's go out to work. Cuffs and neckbands are grafted on. Back here my son washes them at a high temperature to prevent shrinkage, though we recommend they are never hot-washed again. I put on the buttons. We also buy in some ready-finished things entirely done by homeworkers, some very original work. Shetland wool gives gorgeous colours, though people with soft skin find it hard, so we also do children's garments in lambswool and buy in fine mohair.'

We're welcomed at the pier by the son of the skipper of the open tourist ferry to the uninhabited island of Mousa. 'Coming?' asks the lad celebrating his twelfth birthday doing man's work. Sheila fancies going, though first drives me back to our hotel where I long for a Sunday afternoon nap. She returns full of enthusiasm for Mousa's broch, the best-preserved of about 120 Iron Age towers around Shetland, one of whose purposes was to provide a ring of communication when the islands were becoming more dangerous. With a series of intermediate galleries in the dark interior (industrial-type torches provided), visitors can climb the narrow uneven steps to spot the neighbouring, not-so-well preserved broch on Mainland.

Dinner guest is Allen Fraser, a Met weather forecaster for thirty four years, now a keen geologist, who has just returned from a day's guiding. 'I love showing people who've never been here just how different Shetland is with its archaeology, extraordinary geology and scenery. You see all the rocks of Scotland in a small area. And with the great faults, especially in the north, you can really tell what happened to some of them, metamorphosed, as they were bent upwards when the continents collided all those million years ago. Non-geologists have to be told that today's islands are just the remaining tops of some of the world's oldest rocks. It's easier to understand the rising water level when you explain that peat is often found under the sea. Whatever your fancy, there's so much of interest in Shetland. Those I guide for a day are never bored, and neither am I.' His wife has left the island for a few days and he's grateful not to have to get his own Sunday meal.

Then he's back to geology. 'You know the central backbone of Shetland thrown up 400 million years ago would have been as high as today's Himalayas. Imagine the grandeur, and the erosion that has taken place to reduce the ancient Caledonian Mountain chain to what it is today.'

Heading North

It is time to start the journey north, but with time for deviations. The first is through one of the rare east-west valleys from Easter Quarff to Wester Quarff with a glimpse across the sound separating the Burras just where a tributary sound separates East Burra from Trondra. Next through the fertile Tingwall Valley first shown to me by *Shetland's* author. This is one of several valleys with Shetland's best land, based on a floor of calcite marble, limestone transformed by heat and pressure of former ages and in recent centuries extensively quarried for lime. We can see remains of the old kilns where peat was used for the fire.

An eight-seater plane is landing at the small airport for internal services, with an intriguing timetable varying by day of the week, it provides a lifeline for remote off-islands such as Out Skerries (with a one pupil secondary school said to cost £80,000 a year), Papa Stour (where apart from one family all twenty five residents are incomers) and Foula (fifteen miles out in the Atlantic whose storms can isolate it for weeks) as well as more-visited but physically more remote Fair Isle. This is the plane we should have taken there.

Then up the main A70, avoiding Lerwick, we branch west heading to Walls, exploring the peninsula where Mainland is widest. First stop is opposite long Weisdale Voe and beside wind-swept Loch of Hellister under the cliff-like Hill of Hellister: the names are totally unfamiliar but, especially driving north, we are becoming used to a dominating if not domineering landscape. We hurry into the shelter of Shetland Jewellery. Not as famed as Orkney's silverware, Shetland's jewellers usefully contribute to the economy; eleven work here. Owner Ken Rae says his father started the firm in 1953; he took over nine years ago. The speciality naturally is Celtic jewellery: 'The genuine thing, not what comes from China masquerading as Celtic but having nothing to identify it. Dad was totally committed to original work based on authentic designs.

We're holding our own. There's a growing interest in Celtic and Norse designs, and our loyal regular customers of course want genuine things. We make some with an explanatory note. Only 20 per cent is sold in Shetland. The US, Canada and Australia are strong markets. Often we're asked to do a special commission.'

Noting the shop supports other local enterprises, including Shetland soap, made by handicapped people, we retire to the small café to discuss possible purchases. A gold chain with Celtic pendant and matching earrings in yellow and white gold will do nicely for Australian daughter-in-law. I cannot resist buying Sheila a silver spoon for her small collection. It is a mini-replica of one of that schoolboy's discovery of a hoard of ecclesiastical silver on St Ninian's Isle in the 1950s – a communion spoon from about AD800. The accompanying letter says: 'The dog's head lapping a bowl is a rare eucharistic symbol, possibly suggesting the humility with which Christians should approach the Holy Eucharist.'

The staff are a happy bunch. As we leave they give us the universal greeting of those you are only ever likely to see once: 'See you soon.' We press on, almost turning back on ourselves at the head of Weisdale Voe, and go west through a heady loch-and-hill landscape with sparse population, obviously little visited but much loved by the more adventurous of the fishing and boating fraternities. Yachting days must be few – as are special points of interest for tourists, the *Shetland Visitor* brochure being reduced to telling us we will find 'a butcher and licensed grocers, stocking a wide range of goods including fresh meat and fresh-baked bread. Autogas is now available and this is also the community Post Office.' In other words, country for pioneers.

We reach the pleasant little maritime village of Walls, and then – pioneers – get lost in a land of few road junctions and fewer understandable signposts. The trouble might be that we've taken a road built since my 1976 edition of OS sheet No 3. Well, how often do you use the four sheets needed to cover Shetland? Another excuse: the top half of the sheet is very confusable with the bottom. One thing is certain: though it is more of the same kind of mixture of hills between fresh and salt water, it is not the least boring. How I pity those who say that when you have seen one or two hills, lochs or beaches, you've seen them all.

Now sure of our position, we pass along what the OS calls Trona Scord to the pier by Ness of Melby and have what will probably be our only glimpse ever of hugely-indented Papa Stour. Then a long mesmerising journey, broken by pauses for a few indescribably fascinating views, by Aith ultimately to join the trunk A970. Mountains still tower over us as we head west along a firth. Then Brae, giving the impression of an unfinished shanty town but our destination for tonight.

Over a decade ago, tentatively reunited having not been in touch since we were boy and girlfriend together in the early 1950s, Sheila and I came here for lunch at the Busta House Hotel on our way back from the island of Yell when on the second of the cruise visits mentioned earlier, when Sheila and I who had been girl and boyfriend in the 1950s were tentatively together not having been in touch for 45 years. Either of us might have said it, or perhaps we just thought it? 'Might we ever come back to stay here?' It seemed a nice hotel, a true Shetland rarity, a quality country house hotel just beyond Brae with trees if not woodland just outside the village. So here we are overlooking yet another voe, a host of memories of travelling together meanwhile accumulated.

· XV ·

THE FAR NORTH OF BRITAIN AND BACK

North and Wild

With its stepped gables giving it a slightly superior look, Busta House is still a treat in an unlikely position. Nestling under its sloping car park, it was built as a laird's house. Over hundreds of years it has been well maintained and tactfully extended, and unobtrusively turned into a comfortable hotel. Dinner guests, assembling in the long drawing room, are a mixture of visitors each with a different reason for exploring the north, and individualistic locals using it as reliable watering hole. We all greet each other: just the set who would have belonged to one of my country book clubs of former days.

In the morning, unhurriedly once again we head north on the A970, expectations of an interesting drive heightened by another glimpse at the two extraordinary OS sheets covering our route to the A970's extremity. First though across an isthmus where arms of the Atlantic and North Sea almost join: it is said you can throw stones to pop in the water on either side. Then a brief diversion across the bridge to barren, little-inhabited Muckle Roe.

We pass an OS view point at quaintly marked Burn of Magaster. There isn't much traffic anyway but, as we pass a few side roads and scattered houses, it becomes progressively lighter. Time seems to have stood still: letter boxes are beside red telephone kiosks as they used to be when the Post Office controlled both. We take just one more side road to little seaside Hillswick. They are re-erecting a wooden hotel just arrived from Norway and, after a five-year battle, a Burmese family has been granted permission to stay: it says much about the harmony of Shetland that 6,000 islanders signed a petition supporting them. Then on to view the relatively calm Atlantic which in its frequent rough moods breaks off slabs of rock and tosses them inland. This is the coast of natural arches, outrageous pinnacles, explored only by the hardy or foolhardy. At one point rocks have landed in a natural amphitheatre making it look like a quarry.

The further north we head up the A970, the wilder and less inhabited it becomes, but is still capable of surprises, such as at The Brig. Tied up at the pier reached by a steep descent, there's a big cream-and-red ship, the Lerwick-registered *The Altaire*. Curious, I walk up the gangplank and shout. Though the lights are on, nobody hears; no sign of life at all. How long it is since someone walked up, or down the gangway we'll never know. There was no sign of life, even a car, when we looked again on our return journey, just large bundles of cord are stored in containers.

Only a few not very cosy miles yet to go. Everything hereabouts needs protecting from all sides; cemeteries are surrounded by high walls. Other than birds, at peak times many of them migrants, what wildlife can live here? I recall a passage headed 'A surprisingly fragile ecosystem' in the New Naturalist *The Natural History of Shetland,* (1980) by R J Berry and J L Johnston.

> Shetland is an isolated group of islands where many species have very small populations and no adjacent reservoir for replacement; furthermore, some species, both terrestrial and marine, are close to either the northern or southern limits of their distribution, and this means they are in a delicate position within the ecosystem and may easily be displaced. Two further points have a bearing on how carefully we must treat the local environment: 1. There are only 681 vascular plant species in the islands compared with some 2241 for the whole of Britain. A similar species poverty occurs in virtually every other group from phytoplankton to terrestrial mammals. Such a species-poor ecosystem is inherently vulnerable, as a lack of diversity normally means a lack of stability. 2. Compared with the rest of Britain, the climate and especially factors associated with wind, is severe; while the growing season, as a result of the islands' northerly latitude, is extremely short. Disturbance to plant cover can rapidly lead to erosion which may take many years to heal.

Collecting the New Naturalist series has become something of a cult. That interest in the islands was thin at the time of publication has resulted in *Shetland* (and also *Orkney*) being expensive rarities. I've only just succeeded in obtaining a copy. Though, says the author, planning has generally been sensible and there has been a long tradition of open access combined with responsibility, the book does not make comfortable reading and shows how close to the edge much of Britain must be, or was at least until the present climate change which may enable wine to be produced further north as it once was along the Greenland coast. Climate change, however, will also undoubtedly speed the sea's ability to gobble up the islands.

Naturally things are most fragile in the remoter off-islands. One sad tale of species scarcity comes from Fetlar. There was much excitement in the 1970s when Snowy Owls made it their southernmost breeding choice. One randy male however saw off all rivals – and then died leaving forlorn wives until there were no residents left. Unexpected discoveries, such as of a rare moth in Unst, and curious adaptations add to the interest. The commoner Ghost moth is so called because in the rest of Britain the females go for the male's pure whiteness. In Shetland the ghostly appearance is obscured by brown tints. They normally mate in July in darkness but, here in high summer where it is perpetually light, white would attract predators.

Standing Stones are a reminder of past cultures, going back over 2,000 years, while there's recently been excitement over the discovery of a well-preserved 5,000 year old skeleton. Areas we regard as remote today were on the highway of those times, the sea, and there is considerable evidence of prehistoric trading. North Roe is Mainland's last community, though there's life beyond, and even beyond the end of the road, which peters into tracks. The short north coast, and the extreme west coast, also have caves and stacks and banks of steep cliffs chiselled out by the Atlantic. Allen Fraser, the geologist we met in the last chapter, makes an elegant contribution to the *Shetland Visitor* tourist guide, saying of Mainland's far north:

> From Mavis Grind to North Roe you can see how huge masses of magma squeezed, forced and eventually punched their way up through the crust beneath an ancient continent. Ronas Hill and the cliffs of Muckle Roe formed from these magmas, now exposed after millions of years of erosion, get their dramatic red colour from the abundance of the mineral potassium feldspar within the rocks.
>
> From North Roe you can walk back across rocks hundreds of millions then billions of years old. You can stop at the place where Neolithic man made his tools and see around you how ice formed the landscape and then travel on to find the remnants of trees that once grew by a lake some 120,000 years ago before the last Ice Age.

Lit up by afternoon sunshine, the mountains and lochs stand out sharply on our return non-stop journey. Back in Brae, we overshoot the hotel to fill up with petrol. Pumps are few and far between, it isn't sensible to run low. Then sumptuous afternoon tea in our hotel's long lounge.

Sullom Voe and Yell

Next morning, before heading even further north, we go east to Sullom Voe. The very name spells Shetland's prosperity, conveying to most not the voe as in penetrating water, but the oil terminal. Safely situated in protective water and unseen by most tourists, it is where the black gold pours in and is processed, though shipped away for refinement. Even with some oil now coming in from Atlantic rigs, overall tonnage has long past its peak. There's activity enough, however. In both directions we are delayed by traffic lights so aircraft can land at Scasta airfield. There's some military as well as oil traffic, but no timetabled civilian flights.

We cannot get close enough to the terminal really to study it, but the scale is large, and the speed with which it was created is demonstrated by the frontier-like buildings, some now empty, thrown up to house the workforce in the immediate area as well as at Brae. Sullom is one of the few voes which still has regular shipping. Once the coast was lined with piers where the old steamships called, older people readily recalling the days that they provided the only way to reach outlying areas of Mainland as well as the Northern Isles. 'If you'd just arrived from somewhere else, you certainly had time to adjust,' one told me. 'Mind you, it was very companionable. People from different parts generally knew each other better then.' Another told me that, returning from Hong Kong, it used to take less time to set foot on Mainland Shetland than the rest of the journey home to Unst. All history seems to be here. About 7,000 years ago the greatest tsunami known to have reached Scotland as a twenty metre wave. Caused by a giant underwater avalanche off the Norwegian coast, and reaching the English border, it struck especially hard on the northern shore of Sullom Voe around Maggie Kettle's Loch where peat, vegetation and stones high up the land are tell-tale evidence.

Now we're off to the Northern Isles, three of them: Yell, which Sheila and I visited on that cruise call years ago; Unst with the furthest north point of Britain; and Fetlar, the unlikely 'garden of Shetland'. Departure for all is from Toft, not a name well known around Britain but served by two large vessels on the short crossing to Yell. After paying the modest fare, we climb steep stairs to a bridge-like spacious sitting area with an automatic machine for refreshments and are absorbed by the islanders' conversation. Everyone still seems to know everyone – and, more importantly to know *about* them. Being surprised, even if feigned, is good etiquette, though it's perfectly in order to amaze others with the same tales.

I will not add to the unkind things writers have said about Yell. Certainly it is a plain island, but the fast road enables reliable tight scheduling between the ferry routes. Last time, we explored more widely, taking in the only real settlement of Mid Yell. Basic, yes, with few facilities and little accommodation, but its eighty or so inhabitants are said to love their secure isolation. Life is certainly easier than in 1841 when it was 'congested' with nearly 800 eking out an existence in far greater isolation. Yell has always suffered from poor soil, and there's never been an economic case to develop a port on one of the penetrating voes, so little seen that German U-boats sheltered in them. Then to Gutcher where our next ferry is waiting at the pier.

Unst

The pier is for the even shorter crossing to Belmont near the southern tip of Unst. There are two ferries on this route, too, though they also serve Fetlar. It is rough and the wind is rising: we hear a discussion as to whether the Fetlar service will survive the rest of the day, the approach to that island's pier at Harman's Ness being exposed. We see a ferry coming from there making heavy weather. The Unst and Fetlar ferries are free even for vehicles (you can reserve space): oil money wisely spent to help the economy after the RAF left Unst in the lurch in the early 1990s.

The one thing worse than the military occupying prime landscapes is when they suddenly withdraw, leaving fragile economies in tatters. Tatters is perhaps an exaggeration for Unst, but a third of its population disappeared when just into the new millennium, the early warning station closed and the RAF withdrew. Because it was closer to northern rigs than any other, off-shore workers used to transfer from plane to helicopter at the little airport, which also had timetabled flights from Sumburgh. Now it is used only in emergencies. Only 700 people are left on Unst; less than 100 on Fetlar. Add Yell's population, and the three islands' total of well under 1,000 have four substantial car ferries to support them: or less than 250 people per vessel. But then there was once a railway coal truck for every fifty Britons.

Off the ferry at Belmont, after passing a loch with wavelets driven by the gusty wind, we take the first side road to east-coast Uyeasound: a small place now, but once the scene of intense activity. A Hanseatic trading port in the 1400s and important in Unst's herring boom, of which more in a moment, even during the war it was still served by the coastal *Earl of Zetland* from Lerwick. In fact she only narrowly survived a bomb attack here. The now uninhabited island of Uyea opposite also has a history stretching across civilisations. In Unst, we begin to feel, it's going to be hard to get away from ghosts of the past.

Returning to the main road, we only go a short distance north before taking a lane down to the west coast of caves and rocky islands, one with the remains of a broch. There are remains of another on the northern tip of Yell which we can also just see, while we passed yet another near the ferry terminal. Those ancients certainly knew how to organise themselves.

On the way back to the main road, after a stop to let Sheila pat a group of Shetland ponies, for the second time we pass a group of students digging. Intrigued, I squeeze the car into a gateway and climb over a wire fence to see what is happening. A stylish young lady steps forward to explain they're students from Bradford University working on a Viking longhouse dig. 'Very exciting, we've found lots already.' She praises the living conditions, too. That apart from the fact that she'd stepped forward since 'you seemed lost', and that she's not the person in charge, is all I can reliably quote, for later in the day the wind clean blew away my notes. They were on a few sheets torn out of a perforated mini-notebook in readiness for transferring their content to the regular notebook left in the car.

The *Shetland Times* comes to the rescue: 'During the last few days the Viking Unst team have also begun to uncover a longhouse site beside the road at Underhoull. The site is one of two in the field and is close to the broch site. There is a third longhouse in the field below which was dug in the 1960s.'

Later a copy of the report of the Bradford group arrives. The dig, under the supervision of Alan Braby, has found several hundred artefacts in the initial trenching under unusually thick peat. Pollen analysis might confirm that the house was abandoned because of climate change. Also 'a hugely exciting discovery that has become known as the "Little Man" – a unique steatite carving of a human figure.' Much more beside but, lest winter weather damage it, the floor will not be excavated until next summer. With a score of Viking longhouses now discovered on Unst alone, we'll steadily know more about ancient lifestyles and climate change: painstaking business largely undertaken by purposeful students.

We are soon also aware that Unst is its own geological paradise. To the west, the impermeable ancient rocks are blanketed with peat. Especially at the north west, with the Hermaness National Nature Reserve, cliffs are world class and include some of the world's most ancient rocks, thrust up billions rather than millions of years ago and – when not covered by ice – continually chiselled away by the ferocious Atlantic in more recent millennia. The east is quite different, seemingly covered by a load of rubble which is actually weathered serpentine, with veins of iron chromate, and black and green jasper. The broken-up serpentine is best studied in the Keen of Hamar National Nature Reserve, where the stones can be seen clearly sorted by size. In fact they are constantly moving and, if interfered with, quickly reform themselves into strips. Their progress downhill at a few centimetres a year is caused by repeated freezing and thawing – even at less than 200ft above sea level. The peat, and the poor soil yielded by serpentine, support very different *fauna* with rarities. Between the two main geological bands there is a complex 'dislocation' zone.

Quarrying and mining have frequently been on the agenda. Chrome was once shipped – 50,000 tons of it over the years – to Glasgow. Only stone quarries are still active – apart from a talc one, unique in Britain. The talc is layered in a deep quarry, the white stuff being even harder to get off our shoes than Cornish china clay. Not fine enough for medical use, it is used in ceramics and cosmetics. Loaded into occasional lorries which dump it on top of a quayside pile ready for taking away by ship, It is the only serious cargo now handled at the island's capital, Baltasound. Yet:

> In the early years of this 20th century as many as 750 of these [larger] boats have been engaged to fish here, and on the first Sunday of June each displayed a great coloured streamer from her foremast, and made a wonderfully gay scene: 1500 masts and 750 flags lining the two sides of the harbour, with a background of thousands upon thousands of herring barrels built up along the shores, acres upon acres of green grass covered by brown fishing nets, each 'fleet' with its 60 or so individual nets laid neatly one on the other with the sixty rows of corks spaced three or four feet apart.

The quotation comes from Charles Sandison's *The Sixareen and her Racing Descendants*, published by *The Shetland Times*. Thousands of seasonal workers were housed and fed in primitive huts. Though there is some evidence of busier times such as lots of abandoned piers, it's hard to grasp the sheer scale of it in a township now of only some 200-300 souls. The hotel looks as though it has enjoyed happier days; we find a large store, lavish for today's trade: Baltasound has something of the feel of a theatre with only a few staff around between performances. Over the centuries there have been many grand presentations and, however vicariously, I feel privileged to sample the experience. The theatre's curtain may never rise again. If not in tatters, the economy is under strain, unhealthily dependent on tourism, mainly based on the geology, fauna and birdlife, museums and ancient relics. If only more people came. Britain's most northerly island is rapidly dismissed by most tourists, Scottish as well as Sassenachs, yet is full of interest. The locals couldn't be more welcoming, though it has to be admitted accommodation is a bit of a problem.

Time to check in at Buness House, now a B&B run by the island's laird and his wife, David and Jennifer Edmonston. Customers are 'house guests'. Our large bedroom used to be the nursery its walls covered by a colourful collage of all sorts of Victoriana. The private bathroom is next door, the owners' room facing us down the end of the corridor. Breakfast and dinner are served a touch haphazardly in the conservatory, guests and family eating together. We learn much about local life. Hot on opinion, Jennifer sets the topics: rumour has it that, standing up for lairds, she killed a conversation about the Clearances by saying there never were such things, only people voluntarily moving and leaving others in the lurch.

Boat Haven and Heritage Centre Trust

In June and July 1905, when the herring fishing was at its peak, it employed 8,000 people in and around Baltasound. Not an inch of berthing space was spare; on the quay were thousands of barrels waiting to be filled by the herring girls. Baltasound was once Europe's chief herring port. The herring years were 1879-1913 though, after the local peak in 1905 or 1906, Lerwick and Stornoway became more important. Just a few of the things we learn during an afternoon visit to Unst Boat Haven, a few miles north, at the coastal village of Haroldswick, part of an extraordinarily active Unst Heritage Centre Trust. As fascinating as any mainland transport museum, we wish we had allocated it much more time. The part-time custodian, Robert Hughson, revels in taking us round the substantial collection of craft.

'It wasn't just London that was remote; everywhere was, except Norway and the Faroes, easily reached by sea. Unst fishermen had to do things for themselves, and needed sturdy boats that suited the local conditions and the changing trade, a lot depending on what fish they were catching and how far out they had to go.'

Before the herring boom, the most prized fish were ling, caught well out at sea. Haaf or deep-sea fishing in open boats, was year round and in all but the worst weather. Profits seesawed; most eked out an existence, fighting debt rather than making real money. To begin with Norwegian boats were bought in kit form. That changed around 1840, when Unst began to get good Scotch larch and build its own boats. Says Robert:

'Fishermen were not at all well off. Things had to be kept cheap and simple, for which read pretty crude. What fortitude those fishermen possessed, what tragedies when sudden storms occasionally sank their boats: one horrid day five failed to return.'

Most of the crew on those early boats were needed to row. Only one actually caught the fish. The ultimate was the larger sixareen with a keel of at least 20ft which, with its traditional squaresail, remained popular, though as much for racing as fishing, during the

20th century. The museum's version is a replica, but I find myself returning to it spellbound. Says Charles Sandison in his *The Sixareen*:

> Sometimes a sixareen was said to become 'sea-loose', implying the conditions in which she was travelling so fast that the 'fluid' under her became a mixture of air and water, and the noise made was said to be as if 'she were being drawn through a beach of pebbles'. When the sail was reduced she would become normal again.

By the height of the herring boom, steam boats with proper shelter were normal. The museum has photographs illustrating the theme in the quotation on page 201. Along with the overcrowding and everything that went with it – no piped water on the island till 1957 – the herring business at least guaranteed Baltasound a few summer weeks of prosperity.

As well as the boats and the historical photographs, there are artefacts such as tools and herring baskets, and a study room full of documents. There's a lot, too, on earlier times, including the ancient Hanseatic trade – and much of human interest I should love to have pursued more deeply.

A counter assistant at Nairn Post Office has been one person telling us about Unst. Dinner guest is her sister, Rhoda Hughson, who turns out to be sister-in-law to Robert at the Boat Haven. Not much time for private conversation while everyone is presided over by Jennifer, but we're a bit on our own for coffee and say we've enjoyed the Boat Haven. 'What times. The herring business was colossal,' she says. 'But did you realise how difficult it was to dry that enormous quantity of fish? After August it often meant keeping them in salt to dry out the following season. And for those who went out in the open boats, what luxury it must have seemed when they began to have a little covered area to shelter in.'

Memories come floating back: how her father-in-law had once carved a model of a sixareen out of serpentine, local lumps of which were once prized, but not these days. She was Britain's most northerly head teacher at Haroldswick School, with its own history and traditions, which closed its doors for the last time in 1997. Of her own idyllic childhood on the island... and the time she moved to secondary school in Lerwick, spending term times in a hostel with girls from all the outlying islands. 'We got to know all about their islands through our gossip,' she says. 'The one I'd not been to until last year was Fair Isle. I stayed there recently with a girl who was in that hostel. Despite it being all those years ago, we still really knew each other.'

Next day Rhoda helps us make the most of a morning's exploration. We're in a thick cloud heading north as we climb the hill, Saxa Vord, where the unofficial British wind speed record of 177mph was recorded before the anemometer was clean blown away. Not that we see much today. As we approach the 1,000ft, I have to slow to walking speed. Dropping down the other side, visibility improves, and soon we're looking across the Burra Firth to the Hermaness National Nature Reserve on the next peninsular. Drizzly and very windy, it's not exactly cosy. Yet over 100,000 sea birds will have busy breeding over there, including 25,000 pairs of puffins and, perhaps more remarkably, a healthy increase in the number of Bonxies, or Great skuas, once on the point of extinction, with a very few confined to here and Foula. There are also Arctic skuas and Arctic terns among the rest of the rich bird mix – and the rare moth found hardly anywhere else.

'The last house in Britain,' says Rhoda, pointing to a holiday let as we near the end of our peninsular. Beyond and opposite are great cliffs, and off Hermaness isolated great rocks, the largest topped by Muckle Flugga lighthouse standing out crystal clear. One of many island lighthouses built by the Stevenson family, it was visited by Robert Louis Stevenson whose *Treasure Island* was clearly inspired by Unst. The map of the imaginary tropical island is very similar in outline.

On the way back, we visit the former RAF base, Saxa Vord, named after the hill, expensively converted by an entrepreneur into a mixture of hostel (where the archaeological students are staying), B&B, retail outlet and restaurant, with an imposing entrance, hall and corridor with brand new carpet, doors and toilets. Late morning coffee is welcome, though choice of something light to eat limited: the chef has walked out, gone for good. No, they can't do lunch, not even soup and a sandwich. The entrepreneur isn't going to get his money back if customers are turned away like this.

Then the Heritage Centre itself of which Rhoda is an active trustee: here one could spend several days learning about Unst life. I assemble a mental miscellany. By special arrangement one can land on a helipad at Muckle Flugga's lighthouse, which has become something of an interpretative centre; once the keepers signalled when the sea seemed safe for an open boat to reach them. Unst is famous for its wee Shetland ponies which are far more frequently seen here than on Mainland. When a Russian trawler went aground, the locals quickly salvaged what they could, especially wood for doors, but the Russians rushed in to prevent more people eyeing what might have been more than an innocent fishing boat. Unst was bombed several times during the war. And, inevitably, the sad tale of decrofting and emigration.

I am especially impressed by the Centre's involvement with the fine lace knitting which once employed a goodly proportion of Unst's women as home workers. There are excellent displays, the Centre itself has published *A Stitch in Time: Unst's fine lace knitting,* and classes are organised for today's hobby practitioners. The book tells us that a thousand yards of yarn comes from an ounce of wool. A finely-knitted five-ft square shawl containing one and a third million stitches weighs only 2½ ounces. Even a six-ft square can be drawn through a wedding ring. Scarves 'of every variety of pattern and shape', gloves, stockings and cravats were once produced as well as shawls. It was so obsessive that 'you see them busy knitting when footing their way through the marshes, with creels on their backs'. Direct orders, more profitable than going through middlemen; were obtained by woman doing colourful work placing themselves where they would be seen by visitors.

Christine Brown concludes:

> As I researched the story of the spinning and knitting industry up to the present day, I was impressed by the skill of the women who pioneered lace knitting, inventing intricate patterns, and passing them on to their daughters, leaving a legacy which must not be allowed to die out.

Remembering we must tell her sister what an interesting time she gave us, it's time to say farewell to Rhoda. In the afternoon we drive once more to Haroldswick past the best-preserved yet discovered longhouse (currently under tarpaulins) where there's just been an open day. Then north again, this time close to the east coast with terrific views of cliffs and stacks. At the end of the road at Skaw, we meet another 'most northerly' house. As at Land's End and John O'Groats, it is last this and last that.

At dinner our hosts question us about what we've seen. Jennifer says they own the Hermaness Reserve and have done much to preserve the natural island. Quieter David scarcely seems like a laird. It is he who has to rush to deal with an overflowing saucepan. Next morning it's hard work getting our bill: 'Very complicated.' With helpful or not computer, perhaps quite a comedown for a laird to have to issue one at all.

While waiting, I wonder what kind of a future Unst faces. The need is more cutting publicity backed by better accommodation, but which comes first? With good visitor numbers this year compared with recent seasons, to some extent they're already on the job, particularly planning to publicise a ring of Viking longhouses and other sites to give visitors a coherent insight into different ancient times. They were by no means all bad. Surprisingly early in their history, at least some people lived well and healthily with sound teeth and great respect for their forefathers. I'd love to be able to come back in say a hundred years and then a thousand years from now.

Fetlar

Our last island is more reminiscent of Cornwall than most of Shetland, though more because of its lushness and abundance of summer flowers than its serpentinite outcrops (only the Lizard peninsula has as good) and the geological accident of there also being a patch of kaolin (china clay). Its varied coast is magnificent, with natural arches, caves and stacks – and a great Cornish-like sandy beach. Birdlife and history are very much northern. A huge area in the north is an RSPB reserve, closed during the breeding season when it is home among many others to a large colony of Arctic skuas. Breeding, over-wintering or just passing through, the bird list is formidable and includes a couple of species seen at the extreme southern tip, as well as more at the northern limit, of their range.

An historical curiosity is the (scant) remains of a metre wide wall which once crossed the island, separating different tribes and apparently keeping peace for centuries before the conquering Vikings (Fetlar is the nearest landfall to Norway) arrived and must have been delighted by the quality of the land. They counted it as two islands, on either side of the great divide. In later times, the story is the more familiar one of depopulation. Fetlar was the first part of Shetland to be substantially cleared of people to make way for more profitable sheep. A cruel detail: the laird, used stone from the 'cleared' cottages in a round-tower folly built as an adjunct to his extraordinarily unaesthetic rambling castellated concoction of a home. We see the house in disrepair, the folly intact, by the first road junction coming off the ferry, the point at which we join the islands only classified road.

The entire island offers only one alternative route. We leave the B9088 (hardly a need to remember its number) to swing south, seeing the beach that many English Channel resorts would dearly love but on a sunny June morning no human in sight. At Houbie, the mini-centre where everything happens, we are shown into a spotlessly clean room at the Gord B&B by the lady who, with her partner, also runs the adjoining island shop, only part-time even in June, though with an excellent stock – and a window stuffed with revealing notices. One says the island nurse is away on leave and what to do in an emergency. Sounds a bit complicated.

Then to lunch at a Community retreat well-known in Shetland: The Society of Our Lady of the Isles, or SOLI. On a recent evening in Nairn, I descended our steps to the promenade and bumped into Mother Agnes, who is also an Anglican priest, with a member of our church who regularly visits the retreat. They came in for coffee. We have enjoyed Mother Agnes's first four books and, a great cat lover, she has studiously read my *For the Love of a Cat* given her by the friend.

Near the remains of a broch on the first peninsular heading west, Soli's HQ including chapel, with a summoning bell by the front door, is in a reasonably conventional building, next to which there are individual hermitages (bed, prayer desk and kitchenette) for those on retreat. Leading us to a small room overlooking an arm of the sea called Wick of Tresta, Mother Agnes says: 'We've "come out" today,' apparently a rare occurrence in honour of our visit. 'We' includes an 84-year-old Sibyl who prepared the delightful meal and bubbles with enthusiasm: 'When the advance copy of Mother's *first* book came through the letterbox, I was vacuuming. I just left the vacuum till I'd read every word.'

Mother Agnes explains: 'Fetlar is a wonderful place to feel near to God and to contemplate. I felt things should be written down; I write better than I talk. I'm quite a hermit. I think in bed, and write slowly two hours at a time. I never share my thoughts till they are on paper: no writer should.

'The population has halved during the twenty three years I've been here. People used to stay. One man never left Fetlar in his life. Another, taken ill, was driven to Lerwick and, when just getting there, asked "What part of Fetlar is this?" But the young ones today, though they may only plan to leave the island for a bit, don't come back. So our little Community is important for the economy; we're very much part of the island... even for those who don't quite understand our perennial journey with God.'

She revels in the way her four books have spread her message, the island's message too though, as with so many authors, she regrets the first titles are out of print. Here is an extract from her latest, *For Love Alone*, with her thoughts on her boat journey on the way to officiate at a wedding.

I must tell the young couple that under those earthly crusts of ours we were love, and that every one of us was made in the image of love, for Love was God. For me, there was nothing more important in the whole world or in our lives than this love; not hope, not joy, not peace or any other thing, for love encapsulated and was the ultimate of all things. Our life was a being called forward in love by Love himself to participate in a journey of love; and for us as religious, our vows were as binding as any marriage, for ultimately our binding became a binding with Love himself.

> In my mind, I longed to share with the young couple and the congregation in church something of this journey of love. In Shetland, of course, there was much journeying, for there were many islands,

> and in order to travel from one island to another one had to take a boat. On a summer's day this could be idyllic with glassy waters, puffins, incredible views, reflections and, sometimes, extraordinary sights. One day I was lucky enough to be able to lean over the rails and watch five killer whales hardly a boat-length away. However, up here in the far north it was on the whole either winter or summer, with little spring or autumn between, and as you will imagine, generally the winter was as wild as the summer was calm.

Even with spiritual-based activity, today growth is the watchword. SOLI is going to expand. Mother Agnes drives us to the higher ground of the next peninsula where a new centre is planned. The view is broader, even more splendid, indeed a place for contemplation, though perhaps yet more cut off. She combines driving force – it *will* happen – with her deep explorative contemplation.

After she drops us, we take the side roads we've not yet seen, and then enjoy the livestock and flowers around the B&B before a splendid meal in the dining room. We'll not be leaving Fetlar hungry. After dinner, we go east once more and, until the midges become overpowering, walk round the Loch of Funzie (pronounced Finnie), possibly the only place in Britain to see tiny red-necked phalaropes. They were said to have been here last night... but not now.

A Rush to Nairn

We wake, planning to spend next night at Sumburgh: a formidable journey with two ferries. On vastly improved roads, it goes like clockwork, a changing kaleidoscope of scenery very different than we're used to anywhere on the mainland. There's time for a leisurely bar lunch back at Brae's Busta Hotel, memories of which now include the company of top primary school boys and girls from the island of Whalsay. They're terribly end-of-school-year excited, incredibly well behaved and know exactly what they want to order, having to hold themselves back until it's their turn when they speak with confidence. Their teachers lightly supervising them are great, too. 'Only one worry. We must get the afternoon ferry back.' In September the older children will commute daily to a mainland secondary school – and may not be as well behaved when teenagers.

We leave still with no feeling of urgency, but the dramatic miles slip by. Even after we have filled up the car ready to return it at the airport, we find time to walk around the mini-supermarket opposite. But, as we approach Sumburgh, I see that the last plane to Inverness is still on the ground. 'We could have caught that,' I say to Sheila, with no thought of actually taking it.

'Do you want to?' she asks.

Suddenly I recall her gall bladder. Perhaps because the strain of knowing that things could go wrong, thoughts of the nurse being off Fetlar last night, whatever, I panic: oh to get home. (When the gall bladder is removed a few days later, the surgeon said it was in a bad way and could have flared up at any moment.)

Yes, there's space. No, the return halves of our tomorrow's apex tickets aren't valid. Yes, there's time to issue new more expensive ones – and just to cancel the hotel. But hurry, everyone else has gone through security. Security: nightmare. Unknown to us, a new rule allowing only one piece of hand luggage, *including* handbag and even book, has come in since we arrived only just over a week ago. 'Hurry, but I need to have another look in that case.' And more questions. Hurry: departure is already late.

How foolish we can be. Only a remarkably clear view of the Orkneys seen from north, west, south and east begins to calm us. Because we're late, and there's another plane landing, we're circling on hold. The extra miles on this last British Airways internal service we'll ever use (all shortly to be taken over by others) are hopefully paid for by our extra tickets.

'Never again,' says a stressed Sheila, and I nod agreement. But as we go to bed: 'What a wonderful trip. What a pity even so few Scots ever see Shetland. It's an eye opener.'

But 'I've never fancied Shetland,' is all we get when we extol its virtues to staff and friends. How foolish can others also be.

[A recent survey nominated the Shetlands, with little unemployment and long life expectancy, as the best place to live in Scotland.]

· XVI ·

HEREFORDSHIRE

English Treat

While we love living in Scotland, we miss the gentler, intimate English scenery, the cosy villages with their neat churches and pubs, the intricate field systems across the gentle sloping landscape, with occasional woods and specimen trees. On another journey from Bath, everything is a treat, and certainly in great contrast to our last expedition to the Western Isles. In Little Car, we have the enthusiasm of kids as we travel to Herefordshire on our way through the jewel of Ledbury. True to form, Sheila soon demands we return for a night on a later trip: I share her enthusiasm.

I had forgotten how many black-and-white buildings survive, including nicely overhanging examples. The Market House on stilts and 16th century cobbled Church Lane are world class. Sheila has not been here before, so we take a leisurely second circuit as she points out how upmarket the town is, with high-class individual shops. 'Yes, we must come back,' she says, I suspect as she's seen not merely fine buildings but shop windows with clothes to drool over.

Everywhere there are Land Rovers: three in front of us, two behind... and another two parked over there. Land Rovers, no doubt along with Agas, are a way of life. Describing itself as 'a character country railway station offering a high quality local information service plus mail order railticket sales nationwide' – trains include an occasional express to Paddington – the station is privately run by a stationmaster, a rank long generally consigned to history.

Now along a quiet B road of the kind that survives better in West Worcestershire, Hereford and parts of Shropshire than in most of rural England, to Bromyard, which I last explored on foot just before its railway (always a rural byway) closed. Not that its loss seems to have mattered, for clearly Bromyard also flourishes and even supports a lively Conquest Theatre, no doubt drawing its audiences from many towns and villages. This is the kind of area where people have their doctor in one place, dentist in another, hairdresser in a third and vary where they shop and take their entertainment – no doubt by Land Rover. Between arable fields there are still successful apple orchards and a few hops, though these have declined in Herefordshire almost as rapidly as in Kent.

That property prices have risen hereabouts is demonstrated by the fact that the same clerk to the then Bromyard Rural District Council, who bought its offices for £35,000 in 1964, is now organising their repurchase by the Town Council for £700,000. Local government reorganisation has proved costly in Herefordshire in many ways. The marriage of Herefordshire and Worcestershire between 1973 and 1999 was a particular mistake. 'The Malvern Hills are a mental as well as physical barrier,' was one comment when I stopped to ask passers-by a few questions.

Since then Hereford has become the only complete English county unitary authority, giving rise to a new generation of grass-root town councils which are linked through a Herefordshire Market Town Forum. The town clerks and a few councillors from each (now including Hereford itself) meet regularly to pool ideas and experiences. Another popular plan is merging the Primary Care Trust into the County Council. 'The ageing population sets the agenda,' was a comment. Aged or not, it's certainly vocal – led by an energetic County Council leader. 'We're out on a limb so need to be heard,' echoed a group of several older men. On a limb but distinctly not withering. Probably nowhere else in Britain are farming and farmers so dominant. Good luck to them.

Still heading north, we are even more off the beaten track with signposts to villages I have never heard of, such as Edvin Ralph, the combined names of two former friends who fought a bloody duel over a girl said to have been fatally-wounded when she threw herself between them. This is remote, certainly generally unknown, Britain: it is on no direct route or in danger of receiving overspill population. Though hardly anywhere is development overwhelming, you do not go far between homes, most of them stylish. A perfect place to live. 'Don't extol it too much,' said more than one person we chatted with. 'We don't want city people coming in and demanding a motorway,' added another. It is indeed motorwayless Britain.

Tenbury Wells

The countryside does not change as we cross into Worcestershire, nearly at our journey's end. I love collecting minor spas, and for years have wondered what Tenbury Wells is like. It was a place that as a young man I had intended to visit by train, but branchlines were closed more rapidly than time and money could keep pace with. More recently, I have often thought how good it would be if the Severn Valley Railway could reopen the line that ran through the town, turning Bewdley into the first real preserved railway junction. While that might have been too ambitious anyway, it certainly will not happen after this year's Midland floods caused over £2million damage to the main Severn Valley line, the miles of track swept away happily being speedily restored thanks to generous support for the emergency fund.

Unspoilt Spa

What we do not realise until tomorrow is that Tenbury Wells was one of the main sufferers in the floods, for we make straight for tonight's hotel, Cadmore Lodge, described as a couple of miles west of Tenbury. We run up over a dozen miles before realising we are following directions from the wrong road. Elusive, Cadmore Lodge certainly is, in deeply satisfying country close to one of Britain's principal tree growers.

The hotel itself is prettily situated on a large lake, or rather manmade pond. Purpose-built and fairly modern, it is an odd find, possibly more interested in corporate events and its health spa than casual visitors. It is not that the staff were unfriendly, or the dinner poor, but somehow it didn't quite seem to come together. Loose tiles spoilt the neatness of the outlook from our window. Breakfast wasn't so hot, the owner, doing everything, saying he was busy and not bothering to replenish the only soft fruit, a bowl of mass-catering grapefruit segments. 'There's fruit juice and cereal,' he told a later arrival. Though we enjoyed a family of swans repeatedly climbing out of and returning to the lake, we've no desire to return.

On the borders of Herefordshire, Worcestershire and Shropshire, Tenbury Wells is perfectly situated for exploration of much of England's best and least-spoilt inland scenery, including Wenlock Edge visited in *Journey*. Unlike Ledbury, the town is no architectural gem. It is however very friendly: we only had to look forward and back to receive offers of help, and people of all walks seemed happy to greet each other. Indeed some peered at us wondering if they knew us. We felt we could fit in here.

Walking along the pavement glancing at the shops, we realise that literally dozens of masons, carpenters, shopfitters and decorators are at work, their parked vehicles (into which flooded remnants are being loaded and from which brand new timber and fittings taken out) causing traffic jams, especially as there is a constant flow of tractors pulling heavy trailers loaded high with potatoes.

Most shops are still closed after the inundation. Attention-grabbing notices tell their stories of disaster and plans for restoration. A few cafés and hairdressers have been able to restart trading more rapidly than those whose stocks were destroyed, but there is much work still to be done in a pub whose bar has been reduced to a masonry shell.

One is perhaps used to small bookshops not being the tidiest of places, but Books, Books, Books, bravely open and with a group of good-natured browsers, is beyond a joke: carpetless, chaotic. It is going to take more than a flood to destroy the spirit of the owner, though.

'We're all in it together,' says Mrs Diana Ryan. 'Almost the whole town was wiped out, and not for the first time. There is a long history of the River Teme doing this, but this was a nasty one and, just as we were beginning to recover, it goes and does it again.' Yet, while we had heard much of problems in the south west Midlands down to Tewkesbury, there was no mention of Tenbury Wells in any news bulletin I heard or paper I read. 'Typical,' says Mrs Ryan. 'Isn't it?' she asks customers. 'Absolutely,' they confirm. 'We're seen as too small to matter. But we love each other here: a great community spirit.'

Small independent bookshops find it hard enough to cope with the deep discounting especially of the bestselling titles of the moment, so perhaps it didn't matter that the floods coincided with the publication of the final Harry Potter? 'Oh, we have our supporters.' I jokingly ask if any came by canoe for their copy. 'As a matter of fact, I did have to deliver a copy by boat.'

She is a lady after my own heart. She honours what we achieved at David & Charles, and hates the present personality cult. 'We ran a stall at the Ludlow Food Fair, and I was delighted that nobody bought a book by Gordon Ramsay. Values are still more traditional around here. It isn't how famous the author is but the quality of the book, and we still delight in drawing the attention of regulars to what we think they might like, even if it is a book about horses or tractors. We're a very rural community. All those tractors going through are carrying potatoes for Tyrrells chips. It's a heavy potato harvest: the rain swelled them but it's dried out OK for the harvest.'

New shelving is about to be delivered, but I admire the very personally-chosen stock that wasn't destroyed and cannot resist buying a few titles, including (in an unlikely setting) the latest volume by the former Bishop of Edinburgh, Richard Holloway: *Looking in the Distance: The human search for meaning.* (See *Journey*.) 'Well, I was right that someone would buy it,' says Mrs Ryan. Having paid for the books and told her to add the change to her restoration fund (other customers put coins in the box, too, which you cannot see happening in Waterstones), we ask if we can take a photograph. That involves considerable movement of heaters, fans and cardboard boxes,

Apart from the building trades hard at work and the constant passage of the potato tractors, the town is quiet; at the Post Office, all three clerks are eager to serve... and a rich source of local information. 'There's been a serious flood here about once a century but, with climate change, will that mean two, three or four a century?' asks one of them. Built on the river's flood plain, Tenbury has provided a major river crossing point since the Iron Age. Said to be Britains fastest flowing river, the Teme, at the town's northern end dividing Shropshire and Worcestershire rises rapidly with exceptional rain. The tributary Kyle Brook skirting the east of the town has seriously eroded its banks, temporarily shored up while debris such as tree trunks and shopping carts has been left behind as it subsided from raging torrent to gentle brook.

So we are not surprised that the Spa on the brook's banks is closed. We cannot get further than the entrance. 'Sorry, dear, I don't have a key, and anyway it's dangerous,' says the receptionist when I ask if she might be able to open the door of the 32 by 30ft Pump Room with its 'handsome fountain'. I've been wanting to see it all these years and can't, but thoughts quickly change to sympathy for the hundreds who have really suffered. The disaster wasn't meant to be, since the town's website, at the time of writing still not updated, after recording the destruction of the bridge in 1615, that of the church in 1770, and flooding up to ceiling height in some houses in 1886, optimistically adds: 'Nowadays however, the river authorities seem to have solved the problem of diverting the water.'

Spa status came late, too late to make much economic impact: along with other minor spas ranging from Scotland's Strathpeffer to a string of them south of Builth Wells in Wales, it is little more than a curiosity. That the building would be worth visiting is however emphasised by its individual 'Chinese Gothic' exterior, said to have been based on its Birmingham designer's elaborate greenhouse. Sponsored by the Tenbury Improvement Company of ambitious ideas, it is a pioneer pre-fabricated affair, the Birmingham-made wrought-iron sheets of the extraordinary outline of a series of pagodas rapidly being assembled in position. One is perhaps pleased it never attracted more than a handful of old dears, for Tenbury Wells's merit is surely that it is so rare, unselfconscious kind of a place. The most westerly town in Worcestershire, with its jumble of buildings, only a few such as the oval Round Market having special merit (the joy is the lack of modern monstrosities), it has more of a feel of a little-known Welsh market town than an English place. Yet failed Spas always seem to retain a little of the atmosphere they sought to generate.

This is how most small country towns used to be, relying on the surrounding agriculture, though there are many fewer orchards and hop plantations than even in the recent past, leave alone Elizabethan days when the Worcestershire Tapestry now in the Victoria Museum was assembled. It contains the lines:

Heare hills doo lift their heads aloft
From whence sweet springs doo flowe,
Whose moisture good doth firtil make
The vallies couchte belowe.
Heare goodly orchards planted are
In fruite which doo abound;
Thine ey wolde make thine hart rejoice
To see so pleasant ground.

Roundabout to 'Welsh' Kington

In almost every direction there is rich, unspoilt country. We greatly enjoy our roundabout route, not to Knighton further up the Teme but to Kington, just missing Presteigne and indeed Wales.

On the Shropshire side of the Teme, near the former railway junction of Woofferton, we quickly become confused between Orleton to the east of the B4631 and Orleton Common to the west. A young mum pushing a pram kindly studies our OS to point out where we have gone wrong: in doing a second circuit, we will be wrong again if we pass a caravan site (what an inappropriate place for one). Arguing about how to interpret her instructions (Sheila was of course right) we climb steeply to near The Goggin (but if we get there again we will also be wrong) until happily we can turn left with the reassurance of a sign to Leinthall Earls.

This is a wonderful hillside road through thick woodland though the surface is much damaged by the constant dripping from the trees, and it is extremely narrow with few passing places. Don't linger between them, I warn Sheila; but too late. A Land Rover comes up closely facing us, trying to force our retreat. The road being very narrow between soft ground under a wet bank on one side and a big drop on the other, Little Car's performance isn't great, and not made easier by the Land Rover impatiently edging towards us. I get out to direct, but at that moment the Land Rover shoots back to a passing place very close to where it had stopped in the first place. If cars can hate each other they surely did. Little Car is offended by the Land Rover's superiority. The occupants scowl at each other.

Though we would seem to be in utter Remote Britain, we don't go far between gateways to extensive up-market properties. Like its sister, Leinthall Starkes, and in common with dozens of other Hereford villages, Leinthall Earls is little more than a collection of farms, though a lively notice board gives useful information about what is happening in the district. I could live here, but not without a car and someone to drive it if I became unable to do so myself. But then more of us drive into old age. It is mainly those who never learned to drive who are in trouble. Overlooking steeply-contoured Leinthall Common, we drop down into the Lugg Valley and suffer an A road (a Roman one at that) for a couple of miles to Mortimer Cross, from where it is a straightforward mainly B road job to Kington.

First impressions can be misleading. The floral welcome on the roundabout at the approach to Kington suggest beauty and class. The small town has neither. Friendly, yes, and perhaps a rare example of classlessness, for everyone seemed at one, joking on the pavements and using the same small and obviously declining range of shops other than perhaps the nucleus of 'Alternatives', such as Kyrstals, Inner Secrets and a tattooing specialist (and there is a wide choice of therapies). In many ways it is a most basic, ordinary place. The large ironmonger (sadly an estate agent is offering it for sale) and the mini-department store Pennels of Kington ('Next week we'll have completed 170 years of uninterrupted trading') are period pieces.

The reason we have come is to stay at the Burton Hotel run by John Richardson, the son of one of my D&C directors, Gerry, who once treated us to a weekend at John's former hotel, the Castle Pool in Hereford. That had to be sold when his marriage broke up. He had, however, already purchased the Burton, which we visited for lunch during that weekend. I recall it as a dark, rather unwelcoming establishment in drastic need of attention. Now it boasts three AA stars at 73 per cent, not a bad achievement albeit the *AA Hotel Guide* awkwardly places it opposite Hereford's Castle (the former Castle Pool) which has gone up market, and is one of the top Inspectors' Choices with four red stars and three rosettes. I am dying to know how John coped with the loss of the greater hotel and the uphill struggle to make the Burton succeed in an unlikely town, where another hotel has long given up the ghost. Like Tenbury Wells, Kington doesn't appear in the *Rough Guide*, so is unlikely to be over-run with tourists.

Elated that he thinks the new chef he has appointed moments ago will go down well, John launches forth: 'I love it. Kington is a real place with real people and what keeps me going is that they seem to love the way we serve them. The best thing I did was to knock the public and the lounge bars into one, so when people look in they can see straight through to the far side of the building. All kinds come for a drink, a cup of coffee, a light lunch, leisurely afternoon tea or a snack at any time. It is a great common denominator in a place which isn't rolling in money.

'It was tough at the start; we tried to sell it a couple of times. Persistence and the new bar have paid off, though in truth what really made the difference was me coming to live here full time. You have to be one of the community. Recently, we've given the town a swimming pool as part of our leisure centre; that cost a great deal, but the returns have exceeded expectations.

'The hotel is making money now. We've already improved many bedrooms, the bathrooms especially, and next we want to add ten to the existing sixteen bedrooms plus six 2-bedroom chalets. That should attract new business and hopefully improve the occupancy rate which isn't that good yet. It will certainly make it more attractive for visitors. Yes, we do get them, especially walkers, for Offa's Dyke goes through here; its wonderful walking country and handy for so many places such as Llandindrod Wells, Hay-on-Wye, Builth Wells. We get people from those places to meals. 'We'll never be the greatest in the world, but we're accepted by the community and couldn't possibly betray it.'

John, or JR as I discover he is universally referred to in his beloved community, has found his niche, which is more than some supposedly successful people do. And he's full of praise for his dad. 'When I told him I wanted to run a hotel, he said to me, "well you're never going to be a lawyer or accountant, so why not," and he rounded up support from the family for Castle Pool which we ran for sixteen years.

He was fully behind the Burton too, and I was so glad he was able to perform the opening ceremony for the leisure centre with the mayor. It was only days before his last stroke deprived him of speech.' It is still a family affair since, though confined to hospital and unable to speak, Gerry continues taking an active interest, and it transpires that it was John's new wife who showed us to our room.

Next morning we explore the town in more depth and note that the bakers, greengrocers and especially two enterprising butchers offer first class fare at keen prices. They obviously like their food in Kington. The dentist, we see, has gone to Leominster, though his excuse for leaving empty premises cannot be the familiar one: 'Supermarkets have ruined the town,' which we hear at least half a dozen times. There's still a Tuesday cattle market, though. The Market House and the clock tower are among the few buildings really worth examining, but we are much impressed by the welcome in the new Kington Centre which houses the library and Council services and offers photocopying and internet access. There's also an obviously much-used notice board.

It is not surprising it feels Welsh – the border is only three miles away – since it used to be in Wales. The locals naturally took the side of the

Welsh when they attacked the occupying English in 1055, but retreated when a large English force was being assembled for counter attack. Edward the Confessor decreed that the local estates should be forfeited.

The bookshop is closed even during the limited hours it says it's open. It looks another right mess and the reason is the same as in Tenbury Wells: flood, though this time caused by a burst pipe. When I catch up with him, Peter Newman, the owner, describes the horror and confirms the business is mainly by email. 'It's useful to have a retail outlet, but we're only open three hours on Monday to Friday mornings, plus Saturday afternoons. I spend most afternoons packing up and despatching books.' Formerly in the Birmingham tube-making business, he moved from Worcestershire to Kington because property was cheaper and began the bookselling experimentally, only taking the shop and going full-time when it showed signs of working. The speciality is books on local history, on Wales and all British counties and regions, and industrial archaeology... so quite a few D&C titles, 'always useful'.

His wife, Elizabeth, speaks of the 'state of war' that existed during the unhappy marriage of Herefordshire and Worcestershire. At first she says, the revived Town Council was pretty unpopular, so she and three friends put themselves forward as councillors, forcing the first election for years. That they all got elected was due to the fact that there was a cock up in the nomination papers of some of the serving councillors. 'I think we've made quite a difference, but the real success is the Hereford Market Town Forum at which the clerks and a few councillors from each, discuss policy and share experience. It works; there is no longer a state of war.'

She's less enthusiastic about the attitude in Kington itself: 'definitely negative, as it is at places like Hay-on-Wye and Knighton. When something good happens, there's always some objection. It's not a bad place to live, but I do wish people were more positive. Things are however slowly changing with more incomers, especially from South East England because property is so much cheaper here, even the big properties marketed by the specialists advertising in *Country Life*. It's also easy to rent since there are many fewer owner occupiers than in most places.'

She is full of praise for the local government model Hereford is setting as the only English unitary County Council, with town councils having real if limited power and working well together. 'Roger Philips is a good County Council leader, a small farmer but brilliant speaker. At the Regional Assembly, people say, "Wow, you've got a lively one there".'

She knows her stuff. When I order a copy of the book on the local railways saying that Beeching came too rapidly for me to be able to travel on those lines before being closed she says: 'But it wasn't Beeching. It went a decade earlier – in 1955.' And that after temporary closure during a coal crisis and closure delayed several years by admin argument. It shows my age for I recall looking at the services in the new timetables year after many a year. It seemed an interesting little system, Kington once being at a rail crossroads, though only one of the four routes out of it had as much as half a dozen (the rest only three) daily trains. 'The trouble was that the connection with the mainline was at Leominster while most people wanted to go to Hereford.'

The book is by J B Sinclair and Dr R W D Fenn, who have collaborated on other, mainly ecclesiastical titles. It's rich in social background and anecdotes, among the best on rural byways – but a pity they had to call it *The Facility of Locomotion* as opposed to the sub-title *The Kington Railways*. The obvious, descriptive title, easy to remember and look up, always the best – if you want sales.

A route to Hereford would have been of much greater use than that to Leominster, while the continuation through even more remote country to New Radnor (which had ambitions well beyond its rustic capabilities) was never popular. With lines also to Eardisley and Presteigne, Kington had too many railways, all inconvenient with poor connections. It spelt what an Urban District councillor described as 'the beginning of deurbanisation'. The authors tell us:

> The railway failed to revive either New Radnor or Presteigne's flagging prosperity and Kington fared little better. In 1861, four years after the opening of the line from Leominster, the population of Kington was 2,178, but by 1901 it had declined to 1,944, 1,819 in 1911, and 1,688 in 1921. In 1863 the vicar of Kington expressed his conviction that the railway would tend to promote the success of the town: he did not look to it as a means for carrying people away from the town as much as a means of bringing them into it. But he was mistaken. The taste for travel developed by cheap day tickets also helped to establish depopulation as the on-going scourge of Radnorshire and the border. Its accessibility gave many the ambition to move away to more prosperous or attractive areas. No doubt when A W Gamage gave up his shop in Kington High Street and travelled to London and set up his famous store in High Holborn, he went by train. Moreover, the gentry could now have goods and furnishings sent down from London in a greater and more fashionable selection, and their dealings with local shopkeepers and tradesmen declined. Even Meredith's iron foundry, Kington's largest industrial undertaking and which had supplied some of the original tramway, barely survived the century.

The brave expectation expressed anonymously in the *Hereford Times* in 1862 that the railway would restore the little town of Kington to its former prestige so that it would again be 'the eye of Radnorshire' was never fulfilled.

Patronage of ordinary trains was thin, the colourful memories being of several specials on Sheep Fair day and Sunday School outings and occasional long day excursions to Rhyl or Barry Island. I was interested to note that GWR 0-4-2 tank, now well-loved on the South Devon Railway of which I am Patron, spent much of her life as one of the Kington 'coffee pots' – and in the light of what is happening to Post Offices now, it is amusing to note that the local MP, fighting closure, asked Parliament that, since village Post Offices and telephone kiosks weren't closed because they were uneconomic, why pick on branch lines?

Leaving Kington, whose shops are on a par with those of our home town of Nairn, only over four times as large, it seems extraordinary that for half the lifetime of older people it boasted both Urban and Rural District Councils. There hasn't been time to explore what is obviously marvellous high walking country to the north, but even as we head south to Hereford it is surprising how we drop almost continuously if not very steeply for many miles, with great views down to the wide, flat Wye Valley and beyond to the Black Mountains and the hilly country north of Monmouth. The road is truly rural until we are within a few miles of Hereford, the villages, with their squat church towers, little spoilt by development. Fine houses and gardens abound, only an abundance of roadside notices, many inviting the purchase of organic produce, threatening to get out of hand. The signposts are always worth noting in rural Herefordshire: Kinnersley, Yazor, Wormsley, Mansell Gamage, Mansell Lacy (under Merryhill Wood), Credenhill (under Credenhill Park Wood), Weobley featured in *Journey*. Real, real countryside, beautiful to see and very productive.

Credenhill Park, on a steep slope topped by an Iron Age hill fort, is one of a cluster of Herefordshire woods that have recently come into the ownership of the Woodland Trust. Back in 1306 the manor kept rabbits and deer in it. Traditional coppicing continued until well into the 20th century when, as in so many ancient woods, the character was changed by the introduction of conifers, though a few more acres of more natural woodland still survive in the north west corner. There's now careful management while the public are invited to park their cars and explore the paths, trees and wildlife – and walk up to the hill fort. A small project, but a snapshot of what is happening in much of Britain. Visitors include local regulars and school trips as well as those, like us, exploring this unspoilt area.

Hereford: As County Towns Used To Be

Though the crowded, awkward junctions on the relief road cutting through part of the city are among the worst in Britain, once you are in its small heart, Hereford feels as county towns used to. While country people come in for market, shopping and much else, most of the traffic on the ring road is simply passing by. Having promised ourselves a couple of relaxing days, we go straight to the Castle Hotel once run by JR who we've seen improving the fortunes of the Burton at Kington. We are luxuriously spoilt. I love the setting, at the right angle of a typical Hereford street, each building telling a real tale. Our bedroom overlooks the garden and Castle Pool, the castle being a picturesque ruin. And it is only a short walk through parkland to the Cathedral.

First we wander into the shopping area, and blend into the crowd swollen by market day. A group of farmers are bemoaning the price of sheep. People chatter away pressing against the stalls, some of whose obviously local country holders seem sincerely convinced they are offering the bargain of a lifetime. I love it: just like Newton Abbot market when I delivered produce from my fruit farm a good fifty years ago, though then people didn't raise their voices above the crowd to be heard on mobile phones.

It is fascinating to see where the country set take their lunch. A few still drift to the Green Dragon, once a fine hotel, but two small cafés seem to be so good that even farmers are prepared to wait for a table, while – Hereford not being totally immune to wider trends – others graze on the hoof. Knowing we're in for a three rosette dinner tonight (we were not disappointed) we do that, too: cheap but tasty, if no doubt with more than the daily recommended intake of salt.

After a snooze, back over the meadows to the Cathedral, through the impressive double porch for evensong with the Cathedral choir. With Elgar's influence, music is a great tradition. Somehow I've always felt that Hereford Cathedral is more of a piece than those of the other Three Choirs Festival, Gloucester and Worcester. Though abounding in historical features, it is with its wholeness that Hereford Cathedral wins; I feel totally at home among the small congregation with more locals than visitors. It is not my very favourite cathedral but none fits its surroundings better looking as it does like a slightly overgrown, village church.

Next day we examine it in greater detail, and study the Mappa Mundi (what brilliant colour and detail) and the famous Chained Library, both part of the Cathedral treasure. We are not surprised to learn that the tradition of chaining books persisted longer here than elsewhere... and when Sheila returns from 8am Communion next morning she reports that, based on the Book of Common Prayer, it was more traditional and complete than she has experienced in many years.

The rest of our full day in Hereford is devoted to leisurely walking round and re-experiencing the city, enjoying the Wye as it winds its way through and the view of the Cathedral from the narrow old bridge with the pedestrian refuges in its abutments – though the best view (and most familiar photograph) is from the modern replacement to include this picturesque one.

Life and Death at Much Dewchurch

Next morning first stop heading south is at Much Dewchurch in the rich farming and fruit growing areas on either side of the B4348 between Ross-on-Wye and Hay-on-Wye. It is my first visit since the burial in the churchyard of John Mcfarlane, father of my grandson Mathew whose ashes, after his tragic death through a drug overdose were later scattered here. Until his dad's death, Mathew went to what used to be the village school, but had become a Steiner school, beside the church and pub in a showpiece tiny village, though not one especially visited except by parents of kids at the Steiner School. After that, he came to live with me in Scotland for a few years, before moving to Devon to be close to his mother, Alyss my daughter. He seemed to be doing well in the roofing business when he lost his life. That is something one never gets over; indeed I've been afraid to come back here too quickly. I recall every detail of his father's funeral, the cloud and the breeze, the mourners, the words of the priest, except the exact spot of burial which would anyway have looked different when there was only a mound of earth around it.

One of the church wardens happens to arrive and helps us find the modest memorial to two lives lost prematurely. There is still a question: why? And what more (or less) might I have done to allow Mathew to reach his twentieth birthday? Sheila and I hold hands and at least know they were happy together, father and son, enjoying being part of Hereford rural life. On visits over the years the last of them now nearly fifteen years ago, I got to know some of their friends, seeing them for the last time in the pub after the father's burial. Such is life... and death.

Death is certainly no stranger here. Legend has it that St David was born here in the year AD500 and the Norman parish church is named after him. Much Dewchurch has been a Christian parish since Roman times in AD314. Records show that when the Black Death reached here in the year 1348, no less than three vicars held the parish within that one year.

At the entrance to Bryngwyn [a large house once employing fifteen

> gardeners] was Wormelow Tump, a burial mound that was reputed to cover the remains of Mordred, the nephew of King Arthur, who was murdered by his uncle at Gamber Head (three quarters of a mile along the Hereford road towards Monmouth from Wormelow). Legend has it that no-one was supposed to have been able to step round or across this mound twice in the same number of paces. Unfortunately the tumulus was removed for road widening last century.

The quotation comes from the *Herefordshire Village Book*, compiled and co-published by the Herefordshire Federation of Women's Institutes. As one might expect in what is virtually an anthology, entries vary sharply in length and the information they impart, the unevenness balanced by a joyful spontaneity with a nice variety of openings. Studious editing wouldn't have paid, though with such communal efforts it is always worth giving a good brief requesting that a few essentials are covered.

· XVII ·

WALES IS WALES: A POWERFUL BRAND

Which Way Round the Black Mountains?

For more than half a century I have enjoyed long journeys through rural Wales. At first they were by train; now uasually by car frequently paralleling the abandoned tracks from which, with young eyes, I saw an even less-developed landscape. Later I recall mulling over alternative road routes from the Severn Bridge to North West Wales. Some, especially toward the journey's end, were through marvellously off-the-beat hilly country. One image has especially stuck in my mind: a broad canvas of the insignificant road winding down the mountain ahead, crossing the half-mile-wide river plain below, and threading its way up the next hill or mountain. No other car in sight.

It is as pleasing as any British landscape. Wales may lack Scotland's awe-inspiring mountain passes and the juxtaposition of vertical land and deep loch, or the cosiness of much of England's scenery. Wales is Wales with a very different feel. Away from the industrial cities and valleys, with the relatively few inland main roads, the honey-pot coastal showpieces and Snowdonia, by today's standards Wales is delightfully underdeveloped. And decidedly under-appreciated. I am talking mainly of an extended Mid-Wales, the great land area, in which we can perhaps include the Black Mountains and Brecon Beacons, where a small minority of people live or take their holidays. Most of it is as natural as one can now find, an un-self-conscious landscape in which personally I feel free rather than exalted. While possibly never looking forward as eagerly to Welsh holidays as much as Scottish ones, which in West Country days spelt glamour, trips across the empty heart of Wales have always been heartily refreshing. After a time I pine for them as much as I do for West Country cliffs and moors, and Scottish firths and lochs.

Tomorrow we have an appointment near Merthyr Tydfil with a hotel booked close by. We're in no hurry, so where shall we go? Having flirted with Wales for the last couple of days (the brand stretches across though soon diminishes beyond the border) we now have time really to get into the Land of my Fathers.

'How about Llangorse Lake where I used to take parties of school children on adventure holidays?' asks Sheila. Why not? However, when I do mental geography, the mass of the Black Mountains seem to be bang in the way, and I find myself weighing up whether we should make a northern or southern sweep around the Black Mountains and Brecon Beacons, and find myself curiously resentful that we don't have to be back in Much Dewchurch tonight so can't accomplish a complete circuit in the day. Out by the Golden Valley, Hay-on-Wye, Three Cocks and Talgarth (what memories they evoke) and back by Crickhowell and cross-country to Pontrilas. But there's another problem: they are all in *Journey*. So, coming back to reality, we do the obvious and head quickly to the main road down to the outskirts of Abergavenny, the pivot point of many an interesting route, to give us more time for new exploration later.

Little Car braves competitive lorries, but we are kept sane by the wonderful outline of the Black Mountains, which seem almost to hum in their glory, and the less exuberant mountains concealing the industrial valleys to the south. Through Crickhowell and, in a few miles along the Usk Valley with contours tightly-packed on both sides, we are soon back in B road Britain heading north, following the OS of unpronounceable names, soon seeing the lake's southern arm down below to our west.

Llangorse is one thing, but discovering the road down to the lake another. Sheila hadn't remembered it was so elusive. When found it is a minor not to mention soggy affair. At the lake's car park it is just about possible to reach the loo without paddling. The boat piers are well under water; the lake has substantially increased its normal size. The season's campers have long gone; unwatched by anyone but us, a woman heads to the water with an otter on a lead.

Swathes of migrating birds and a family of swans add interest to a lovely if hardly summerish scene. The kids always enjoyed it, says Sheila; but it was never this watery. Through the wind and the lapping of water – little waves ripple along the piers between moored boats standing proud – we listen hard trying to tell different bird songs. Even when not overlapping its banks, it is a big lake and, away from the camp and caravan site and the piers, surrounded by farmland.

Through the Brecon Beacons

From Llangorse we head west through Llanfihangel Talyllyn to plain Talyllyn and get involved with the route of a long-abandoned railway and even with a Roman road (not too many of them around here), and then very narrow lanes with high hedges which seem to be leading to nowhere. Somehow we manage a complete circle between high Devon-like hedges. We're trapped in Remote Britain!

We had been told that the hotel we have in mind for lunch is north of the A40, but when we get a mobile signal we learn that Peterstone Court is actually on it at Llanhamlach. Fifteen minutes later we look for a place in the crowded car park. The hotel is seething, though whether with a special party or a collection of families happening to be out for a pleasant autumn day, we never discover. It is far more upmarket than we expected – 'the style is friendly and informal without any unnecessary fuss' – on the banks of the Usk. There's no room in the dining room, 'but we can fit you in the conservatory,' where we welcome a tasty two-rosette meal efficiently served though mainly we are left with our own company. Certainly somewhere worth coming back to, with eye-catching scenery in every direction.

By going a very short distance toward Brecon we escape the traffic by taking the B4558, crossing the Monmouthshire & Brecon Canal, pleasingly taking on a useful new life for today's pleasure boating folk, and then south east to reach Talybont or Talybont-on-Usk as the GWR called it. I last came this way on a slow all-station train from Newport, panting for breath on its way up to Brecon, though I changed at Talyllyn Junction for Moat Lane Junction for a further change for Aberystwyth: a memorable journey, enhanced on the way to Moat Lane Junction by a Welsh professional comedian coming into my non-corridor compartment and enjoying joking privately. 'Don't need company,' he announced hanging up his socks in the window and displaying his bare feet when we ran into a station crowded with women going to market. It worked. We were left alone.

Talybont-on-Usk was once calling point for a summer Saturday 'express' from Barry to Llandrindod Wells; in those days it didn't take so many passengers to cover the cost of staff wages. One definition of railways used indeed to be 'a source of employment'. If only the future could have been foretold and modernisation undertaken when affordable, most lines (but especially the longer rural ones such as those of Mid-Wales) might still be running with a skeleton labour force and probably better used to boot.

Now south by unclassified roads through a slice of the Brecon Beacons: a delight enhanced by the beauty of manmade reservoirs which do something to make up for the lack of natural lakes in Wales. First comes Talybont Reservoir filling the bottom of a valley with contours packed tightly together though, from the road, because we are in woods actually alongside this reservoir, we can only clearly see the rather unnatural ends. Even though the railway ran on a ledge closer to the water, it was also mainly only trees one could see.

Then by genuine mountain road we ascend to nearly 2,000ft but still look up to the peaks before dropping down to run beside several more reservoirs, the longest of which is Pen-tŵyn down to Pontsticill. The Brecon Mountain Railway, a short steam-preserved section of the old line, runs on the opposite bank. According to the timetable we should see a train, the very last of the season and visibility is good but, as so often happened when passing alongside country railways in my younger days, there isn't a whiff of steam.

Into the Valleys

Gently we ease ourselves down through the start of industrialisation to the A465 Heads of the Valleys road. We revel in the way we have crossed the Beacons, but I recall that the section from Talybont to here was a mere fraction of that train journey once possible from Newport to Aberystwyth.

I particularly recall the huffing and puffing as we struggled up out of the valley to Dowlais Top, at which station the GWR timetable advertised that a public telephone was available. If you were stranded, it might have been very welcome. The 1930s timetable also advised that it was about half a mile from Dowlais (Cae Harris), where horses, carriages and motor cars could be loaded or unloaded, a facility also provided at Dowlais Central (reached by a branch connection from Pant into the train on the journey I took). A fourth station, Dowlais High Street, was LMS served, though was included in the GWR timetable. All in what was virtually a suburb of Merthyr Tydfil with its own complicated system, emphasising how utterly different life was and how lucky we older people were to catch the Railway Age's final hours before the postwar explosion of road traffic. Though car ownership spread slowly in the Valleys, only one train service to Merthyr survives.

Back to today, going west we soon switch north on the A470 through a watery environment to Nant-ddu on the banks of the Taff. Much of the car park of Nant-ddu Lodge is flooded and we have to search for a vacant space where we can alight without getting wet feet. A curious establishment, it boasts its history stretches back 200 years yet strikes us as trying to be ultra modern. Its roadside position appeals mainly to lone businessmen trying to achieve as much as possible during the shortest time away from home. They arrive breathless, order dinner brusquely, catch up on their records between courses, and rush off to bed. Their mobile is always beside them but they are curt on calls. This is the new sterile work ethic, lacking the sociability among commercial men of the road of yesteryear who happily ate communally at a table headed by a 'father'. If the food was not as imaginative, it was certainly better digested. Now there are also lone women, but keeping even more to themselves and seldom welcoming conversational overture. It's more relaxed at breakfast, though, when a greater number eat at the same time and joke around the self-help buffet.

After a wet night, everything gleams in the sunshine, experience suggests is too bright to last. To make the most of it, we drive up the main road towards Brecon. Only a few miles to the west of yesterday's route through the Brecon Beacons, it is better engineered and a hundred times busier, so doesn't seem as intimate. Yet the empty mountains with tops over 2,000ft come right down to the Taff's valley's bottom which the road largely fills, though a couple of reservoirs have somehow been accommodated. It is magnificent; our arms are constantly gyrating as we point out features to each other. Turning back just short of Brecon, we have the advantage of seeing it in both directions, as always the light as well as the shapes looking quite different. We see that the Mountain Rescue Centre has come to life, and hope nobody is in trouble. This is empty Wales, at its best, a huge contrast with what we will soon see in the packed valleys.

For a Picture at Merthyr Tydfil

Over the years I must have received thousands of letters from readers (as well as authors and book club members and magazine subscribers) but never once do I recall one from the Valleys – until Clive Crowley of Trelewis, near Merthyr Tydfil, wrote with appreciation of *Journey* and a postcard-size colour reproduction of a painting of passengers clambering over rocks between trains because of a breach in Brunel's Sea Wall between Dawlish and Teignmouth. This, I at first believe, is totally different from others I've seen. When I enquired if he had sent it inviting my interest in acquiring it, he replied that it deserved a new, appreciative owner. Would I like to visit? So here we go.

Skirting Merthyr Tydfil, we opt for the single-carriage road to the east of the Taff rather than the newish expressway down to Cardiff roughly half way down to Pontypridd, turning east through Treharris to Trelewis in a tributary valley. Clive Crowley is outside his terraced house surveying the world, obviously waiting for us.

Comfortable the house isn't; my request to use the toilet causes positive embarrassment. It soon transpires that Clive needs money to fight the damp which threatens his continuing to live in his parents' old home. But it is also quickly clear that he reads broadly and has a deep knowledge of literature and much else. The one thing he has not done is to move away from where he has always lived though the very raison d'être for such villages as this has long disappeared.

And that is what is different about the Valleys. They're a world apart, in a sense one of the remotest spots in Britain. That is why people there don't write letters to authors and publishers and, though they may occasionally sun themselves in Spain, they have little knowledge of, or even interest in, the rest of Britain. Illiterate by no means. There is still greater love of poetry and choral singing (probably better Bible knowledge too) than anywhere else. When you mix with them, they are welcoming, warm-hearted... on their own ground, which often means just in their own valley.

I've enjoyed many splendid occasions with them. Yet these days I find the Valleys sad, Hamlet's missing ghost here being the coal mines and especially the miners and the coal trains snaking their way down, often on both banks of rivers. Even in the 1980s, when offered a tailor-made treat on rails in Wales, I chose a day out by coal train, and wonderful the comradeship and the organisation were. The end of coal here and elsewhere happened so suddenly. These days the Valleys must live largely in the past. They no longer suffer old-fashioned poverty – most homes seem to have been improved, and take-aways abound – but colour comes from the memories of older people who actually went down the mine and from tradition. How long can they survive purposefully without fresh commercial or other input? The service industries thrive as elsewhere, but what refreshes the individuality other than the Valleys' unique geography? And can that be enough?

We have an exceptionally interesting conversation with Clive before he brings out the picture. There's a long delay before either of us dares mention a price. Oh, he needs money badly, and we appreciate why. When I baulk at what he's striking out for, he throws in a lovely locally-painted picture of the Taff Valley Railway Station at Pontypridd in 1867, which I'm delighted to add to the Welsh content of my transport gallery (hall, landing and stairs)... and, as we prepare to go, he throws in a Scottish print. He's actually generous, just needful, and he's so decent that it seems a privilege to help him.

On leaving, under a bridge built on the slope, we instantly get lost in a very wet mini-valley with ferns growing everywhere. There being nobody else about, Sheila says: 'Remote Britain!' Instead of the dual carriageway down to Cardiff, we make our way over a succession of tops between valleys. Every time one does this, it emphasises how utterly unique the geography is, and why, especially in pre-motor days, marrying the girl even in the next valley was different if not disloyal – and why musical, religious and other traditions varied between valleys. They were self-contained mini-worlds, their populations only mingling at sporting and other events, mainly in Cardiff or down by the sea at Barry Island. I shall never forget the consternation when, hoping to experience rails in two valleys on the same trip, at the terminus of the first I enquired about a taxi over the top to the next one.

Magor Motorway Services

From this hidden secret for most Britons, we emerge near Newport. What contrast. Last time we travelled east on the M4, we found ourselves appreciating what seemed the unusually classy Magor Motorway Services, just west of where traffic for the two Severn Bridges separates. It's hard to feel remote (even quiet) in any motorway station, but at least we felt civilised in one of only two run by a small and seemingly caring concern. But having recently found a series of highly critical reports about falling standards and lack of hygiene on the station's website, we skip it today and hope the cheese sandwiches bought in Kington yesterday might toast for a late lunch in our Bath flat.

This is being written back home in Scotland with two things to add. Firstly, I'm curious about Magor Motorway Services and send a letter asking if they'd like to comment. Half an hour ago, First Motorway Service's managing director, Rob Millar, phoned. Interesting comments:

'Of course mistakes will happen when you run a 24-hour operation, being all thing to all men, from the many regulars who love us, such as a couple travelling to their holiday home in Pembrokeshire who are always using us, to vandals like the one who recently threw a bottle of tomato ketchup at a cash machine. But I don't believe our standards have dropped. We had a very unfair report in *Which?* which annoyed our regulars. For example, it said that we had a poor cold selection. When we sent a video of what we offer every day, they admitted they hadn't been right, but corrections like that never get into print. The damage is done.

We have to live with people's comments on the website, but they are not all accurate. There's often a hidden agenda. One customer wrote his entry because we wouldn't give a refund. We felt he was seeking it unfairly, just making up a complaint in the hope of getting money back. A member of staff at one of the big operators might be a softer touch and agree to a refund; we are small enough to look at each case individually. We really do care and I think it shows. Instead of crowding in lots of franchises, we only have two restaurants. In the main one we'll cook individual orders at quiet times, but people are in a hurry and it's just not possible at busy ones. Somebody complained there was no spaghetti bolognaise but it's not one of our menu items. You cannot possibly offer everything.

I'm from a retail background where everyone's normally out for themselves. But in this business we actually want competitors to do well, for bad newspaper headlines hurt us all. Like the old railway sandwich, service stations are easy targets. We are one of only two independents. Our other station is Bolton West Services, while the one-off Tebay, with its farm shop run by someone with farming background, has a great reputation. It's a pity there isn't room for more independents, but it's a mature business now since there are no longer gaps to be filled and no new motorways are being built.'

And that Sea Wall Picture

The other thing to comment on is the Sea Wall picture which I've not yet hung but am studying in detail while actually typing this. I stand to type, and above the filing cabinet on which the machine rests there's a cherished relic of former technology: a montage of four copper blocks of letterpress printing days. They are of the jacket of my volume on *The West Country* in the Regional Railway History series: using skill now nearly disappeared, I love telling which blocks carry the four different colours that used to be standard in colour-printing before the days of lithography.

Both the books and my newly-purchased pictures show passengers clambering over rocks between trains drawn by broad-gauge South Devon Railway saddle tanks on either side of the line's blockage, but whereas the familiar one (and others I recall) is painted from the perspective of the railway's sea edge, this new view is seen from the cliff's edge and looks out to sea, with waves breaking well inland of a breach where the permanent way has clean disappeared.

Fascinating detail. Skip the last paragraphs of this chapter if you're not interested. In the familiar scene, the engines are facing the blockage; in this one, they have backed their trains to within feet of the yawning gap. 'Health and Safety,' I find myself muttering. While the authorities have thoughtfully provided a couple of temporary lights in the familiar scene, there are none in this new picture which is unsigned and might well be the work of an unknown amateur. His perspective and people are generally good, and there is the merit of having a close-up of the Clerk before erosion cost him his hat; the headland, the Parson, looks down on the Clerk (a small vertical rock sticking out of the sea). While the early carriages are accurate enough, artistic licence has driven a westerly gale-tossed sea much higher up the cliff near the entrance to Parson's

Tunnel, than the height of the two-coach train parked just outside its mouth.

Then I realise what I call the new picture is also inaccurate in that it shows double track when it was single. Perhaps the whole thing is a figment of the artist's imagination, for the book's cover correctly shows people clambering over a rockfall in 1852 and the first breach in the Crimean winter of 1854 was near Teignmouth.

But hold on. When belatedly I consult the fifth edition of my book written in the 1950s, behold, in the inside black-and-white plates is a reproduction of the very picture I have just bought under the one also used in colour on the jacket. The caption: 'A breach of the sea wall outside the Teignmouth end of Parson's Tunnel in February 1855.'

Yes, there was such a breach, and the pictures are at different locations on quite separate occasions. So have I paid expensively for what is only a print of a familiar scene, or do I, as Clive Crowley thought, have an original? That I'm not skilled enough to tell, and what matter? I shall greatly enjoy it, and will always think kindly of Clive and of the Valleys when doing so. Meanwhile we're busy planning another trip to Wales.

PLATE I: Isles of Scilly. *Top,* Mary Ratcliffe at Hugh Town, St Mary's (p 66); *Middle left and right,* transport on Tresco (chapter IV); *Bottom,* Tresco's tropical garden around the ruins of the old monastery (p 59)

PLATE 2: North Yorshire Coast. *Top,* unusual enterprise, private steam train on national track (p 99); *Middle,* view of Robin Hood's Bay from Raven Hall Country House Hotel (p 106); *Bottom,* the town that never was, except for this just below a preserved platform of long-closed railway (p 109)

PLATE 3: Crumbling coast of the Yorkshire Wolds. *Top,* now on the edge in Aldbrough; *Middle,* and the next home to go, boarded up but still taxed (p 128); *Bottom,* Spurn Point. Most has fallen into the sea, but odd sections of the track survive of the 'Sail Rail' to England's most eerie place (p 135)

PLATE 4: Gower and West Wales. *Top left,* 'Mr Gower,' Harold Grenfell (p 147); *Top centre,* award-winning National Trust car park attendant, Glarre Rycroft (p 159); *Top right,* steps down to St Govan's chapel (p 158); *Middle,* path to Worms Head (p 146); *Bottom,* not much of a hotel to look at but great for looking from (p 174)

PLATE 5: Bookshops. *Top,* newly established Yeatland Books, Scalloway (p 189); *Middle,* 'we're all in it together,' at Books, Books, Books at Tenbury Wells (p 213); *Bottom,* Liz Drew has a farewell glass of wine at The Bookshop at the Tinners Rabbit, Ulverston (p 482)

PLATE 6: Shetland. *Top left,* Barbara Ibister (p 183); *Top right,* Mother Agnes (p 207); *Middle,* Fetlar's guest house, restaurant, general store, PO and meeting place (p 206); *Bottom,* Whalsay children at Busta House Hotel, Brae (p 195)

PLATE 7: Shetland. *Top,* interview at longship dig on Unst (p 200). Other recent Northern Isles discoveries include a prehistoric 'cathedral' in Orkney; *Middle,* Unst's boat museum; *Bottom,* only one actually caught the fish on a sixareen (p 203)

PLATE 8: Episodes. *Top,* Kinema in the Woods, Woodhall Spa (p 347); *Middle,* Sheila eventually emerges from a tunnel linking a pair of prehistoric homes on Papa Westray (p 348); *Bottom,* with daughter Alyss at Turf Lock, entrance to Britain's oldest ship canal, with hotel in background (p 353)

PLATE 9: South Coast Islands. *Top,* inside the period signal box on the Isle of Wight's steam railway (p 251); *Middle,* low tide transport from Burgh Island, Devon (p 238); *Bottom,* Art Deco bedroom furniture, Burgh Island Hotel (p 237)

PLATE 10: *Top left,* bronze fishergirl, Stornaway (p 285); *Top right,* Chris Bavostock; *Middle,* 'light relief' black houses (p 294); *Bottom,* 'guest house, not hotel' Baile-na-Cille (p 283)

PLATE II: Western Isles. *Top,* the only ferry on the 120 miles top to bottom of the Western Isles; *Middle,* one of the new causeways; *Bottom left,* glamorous granny (p 298); *Bottom right,* Bill Lawson (p 302)

PLATE 12: Wye Valley. *Top,* the classic view of woodlands and old railway bridge, interviewing George Peterken (p 410); *Middle,* once business and religious centre, now tourist attraction (p 407); *Bottom,* looking down on lower valley toward Chepstow

PLATE 13: Lincolnshire. *Top left,* Canon John Wickstead on reclaimed sea bank 'at the end of nowhere'(p 388); *Top right,* Reader David Beeton outside a rare fen shop (p 379); *Middle left,* could only be Lincolnshire; *Middle right,* Tennyson's birthplace, Somersby where his father was vicar; *Bottom,* Grimsby's iconic landmark in the distance with Jane Gammond beside abandoned fish piers (p 402)

PLATE 14: East of the Lakes. *Top,* milecastle at Hadrian's Wall; *Middle,* Garrigill Post Office and guest house (p 452); *Bottom left,* Angela Jouneika at her Edwardian Rock Garden (p 456); *Bottom right,* Tracy, landlady of the Tan Inn, Britain's highest pub, with dung shovel and Izzy the sheep (p 400)

PLATE 15: West and South of the Lakes. *Top,* 'Patrick of the Hills' at Muncaster Castle (p 468); *Middle left,* wedding party of Americans at Walney Island reserve (p 476); *Middle right,* distant view of Piel Island (p 474); *Bottom,* at last a cruise on Ullswater (p 484)

PLATE 16: In the footsteps of the Queen Mother. *Top,* the Queen Mother's sitting room at Glamis Castle with her great friend Lady Strathmore (p 432); *Middle,* Castle of Mey taken looking back from Pentland Firth (p 442); *Bottom,* Newly arrived from Land's End at John O'Groats (p 441)

· XVIII ·

SMALL ISLANDS: FROM THAMES TO BRISTOL CHANNEL

Death at Canvey

Apart from the Isles of Scilly (chapters IV and V), Southern England is not rich in islands. Moreover nearly all the so-called islands have either long land boundaries or strong road connections to the mainland that at first it would seem they lack the individualism one expects from land totally surrounded by sea.

Thus, at least on casual acquaintance, Canvey Island with its 35,000 residents and busy roads in the lower Thames Estuary is little different from adjoining parts of Essex. However, such is Britain's geography and nature that such expectations are almost invariably wrong. The greatest individuality we discover in this trio of chapters might be in the 'Isle' with the longest land boundary, though Essex's other islands discussed in chapter XXXVII have great character.

In passing Canvey Island, 25 miles from London, off the coast between Basildon and Southend-on-Sea, is best known for the loss of fifty eight lives in the East Coast floods of early 1953. Only an area round the highest point at Canvey Village wasn't much affected. The Red Cow pub, used as rescue headquarters, was renamed the King Canute.

Sheppey

Moving south of the Thames, though the bridge over the navigable Swale has caused much trouble and is now in its third manifestation, Sheerness on the Isle of Sheppey can still be reached by electric trains as well as by the A249. There is little island-like about the busy port town itself, but nearby Queenborough at least has distinct maritime charm and the village of Minster, with a Rural Seaside Award, was named after a Royal Saxon Benedictine Abbey where the 7th century Queen Saxburga was the first abbess. It once crowned the hilltop. The long-closed nine-mile Sheppey Light Railway to what was then the old shack and bus body straggling resort of Leysdown, was a real island oddity I'd love to have seen, though today's improved resort apes its mainland counterparts.

What does feel eerily remote is the marshland along the southern coast between the sub (island within an island) Elmley Island and the Isle of Harty (both part of Sheppey) overlooking the equally remote marshlands of Kent's northern coast south of the Swale to the east of Whitstable. Bird interest abounds, with two sanctuaries attracting many ornithologists. Even before you get out of your car at Elmley Conservation Trust you can see lapwings, redshanks and widgeon close by. Go to a nearby hide and there is much more – often ceaseless activity, the sky filled with a great variety of land and sea birds. It is so remote I have to pinch myself to realise I'm in the crowded South East.

Three Quasi Isles

So to the South Coast proper where, starting from the east, the first three islands in a row are more like peninsulas dropping down from the mainland than the genuine thing. The first of the trio, Thorney Island, bridged across the Great Deep separating it from the mainland, has during most of modern times largely been occupied by an RAF airport though now land has been reclaimed for farming. It has, however, always been possible to walk around its peripheral path – except when a section is flooded by a very high tide. Even today that's all you can do for the military jealously cornered much of the rest. Along with parts of Selsey (which, though with a long land boundary, feels more island-like: see *Journey*), Hayling Island and a small area of mainland, and much of Chichester's harbour, Thorney is in an Area of Outstanding Natural Beauty. 'Beauty' is open to question, but certainly different.

Thorney figures in the Domesday Book and in ecclesiastical history. Because the Rector had prior entitlement to complicated tithes, in the 1300s the poor residents were excused royal taxes. But don't be confused by another Thorney Island built of silt in the Thames estuary first colonised by the Romans. Its Abbey Church, started when it was a pretty unhealthy place, is none other than today's Westminster Abbey.

Hayling Island is different. Though it is surrounded by water, traffic pours across the narrow bridge bringing staying visitors and day trippers and taking residents to work, shop or whatever on the mainland. With nearly 17,000 locals and ceaseless visitors, the T-shaped island, six miles wide and four long, has a considerable road system and offers many open-air and indoor attractions from a great (though partly artificial) beach, windsurfing and a whole range of other sports to a tourist railway along the seafront and drama by the amateur theatrical group in the converted former goods station. The resort certainly works to keep its visitors happy, though the proximity of Portsmouth means most shoppers spend their money off the island.

Other than by the overworked bridge, the only way of getting to and from Hayling is by the Portsmouth ferry whose future is threatened by poor patronage. That is what killed the railway in 1963, passengers being especially scarce during the long winter. Because of the weak railway bridge from the mainland, only the London, Brighton & South Coast Railway's Terrier tank locomotives could be used. We'll come across the Terrier tanks again on the Isle of Wight.

Family memories of Hayling are enjoying a delightful sunny day on the beach not realising that despite the haze and breeze, bare flesh was being over-cooked, leading to mild sun stroke. And a final comment: while Hayling can well be dismissed as a quasi island, being bounded by the sea precisely defines who lives on it. That leads to a much stronger community feeling than would be found if the same number of people lived in a similar area on the mainland. (The island is far smaller than in ancient times, for there's been much erosion.)

The last one in our trio is Portsea Island which few people outside the area will even have heard of – as distinct from its principal place, Portsmouth. With a long land boundary – the triangular railway and motorway junctions well separated – it is crowded with Portsmouth and Southsea, along with Fratton and Eastney. While the land approaches are pretty awful, Portsmouth – or 'Pompey' – has a real maritime character. Much bombed in the war, Portsmouth has been a major naval base since Henry VII established the world's first dry dock here, and today it's a major commercial port, too. From our hotel on Southsea seafront we watch more passenger ships simultaneously on the move than you'd see anywhere else in Britain. The large vessels of the rival routes to France and Spain are joined by the smaller Channel Island ferries and foot and car ferries to the Isle of Wight. In built-up areas it is easy to forget you are on a so-called island, or even a peninsula, but not that the sea is close – unless perhaps you're shopping, maybe in one of Britain's finest independent department stores.

Burgh Island

Skipping islands deserving more detail (following two chapters) we move to that which is probably the one more people hope to spend a night on than any other in the British Isles. It had long been on my wish list, and so it had been for everyone else staying at the Burgh Island Hotel on the night we had chosen.

Built in 1929 in the then fashionable jazz style, the hotel had already become famous as the haunt of film stars and others of note when it was twice abandoned and left to the elements for a total of seventeen years. Capitalising on the way it caught the imagination and created a marvellous marketing opportunity, current owners Tony Orchard and Deborah Clark have restored and developed it in its original art deco style. The result is that probably even London's Ritz or Claridges do not have such a pool of would-be British patrons waiting for a special occasion or other excuse to visit, albeit most only for a single night.

It was the most expensive night ever for us. Was it worth it? Undoubtedly. For a start there is the romantic location. We had to phone where there's a reliable mobile signal at delightful St Ann's Chapel (still with busy shop and Post Office) for the code to let us into the private garage area and be met by a Land Rover whose driver soon whipped us across the sand and up the steep irregular drive to the hotel's entrance. Burgh is a tidal island, and by bed time we were surrounded by sea.

It is a hilly though minute (twenty acre) island topped by a hill with a hut used in the 17th century by Huers who looked out for shoals of pilchards and raised the cry to alert fishermen. Vegetation is windswept, showing that sometimes it is extremely rough, though not today when, immediately after arrival, we start off on an island circuit by overlooking the natural saltwater swimming pool in a high-cliffed bay close to the hotel. Though the island isn't without its fascination, most memorable are the views of the cliffs and fields of the mainland, from our height seen more clearly than from a boat. We return by tennis courts carved out of the hillside (there are many sporting facilities within the hotel) and the Pilchard Inn. This is run jointly with the hotel by Tony and Deborah who own the entire island and are resiting footpaths and generally applying green principles.

'AD1336' displays the Pilchard. It must have a few stories to tell. The front bar is reserved for hotel guests and regulars who come across from Bigbury-on-Sea, the nearest mainland pub being much further away. Foxes also come across the sand for refreshment: rabbits abound on the island, which also provides considerable bird and wildlife interest though there are no real trees and the hotel's kitchen garden has to be on the mainland.

So to our bedroom, like the other twenty four, named after a 1920s or 1930s personality: Jessie Matthews, child dancer who later captured the hearts of lovers of musical comedy for her performances on stage, film and television.

The whole hotel is wonderfully of a piece, consistently art deco, everything with angular and triangular furniture and decorations.

The co-ordinated detail is splendid. Our restful bedroom has recessed pelmet lighting, and a dressing table of unimaginable curiosity. It winds up to take little space, but when fully rolled out the stool which was tucked away in the middle emerges conveniently opposite the dressing table itself with its stepped glass cover. The bathroom has an octagonal stepped basin and loo, with period taps.

There are many delightful touches throughout the hotel; nothing shoddy or in need of updating from the point of utility. It is wonderfully and consistently off beat art deco.

'We try to create the atmosphere of an ocean liner,' the manager Chantel Thomas, an Australian tells me, when I say I've come without cufflinks. An extra £32, but they'll be a nice memento.

I ask: 'What's it like being here year round?'

'No two days are the same. We're busy most of the time, with weddings and special parties especially in winter, and the changes in the weather are amazing. I suppose I have a bit of a love-hate relationship with the island. I'm usually very happy, but every now and then I discover I haven't been off it for ages. And if I get itchy feet, of course it's just when the tides are in at the wrong time and we can't use the sea tractor because the wind is too strong.'

Then, pressed for a comment on how such a high standard is maintained and where the staff comes from, she admits that while she likes them, 'the local people can be a bit too laid back for the superlative standards we aspire to'.

Most staff we met were from far away including Poland and the Czech Republic... but it was just the time that, especially with the sinking pound, better opportunities were beginning to call the Eastern Europeans back home. First it was Irish, then Australians, New Zealanders, and South Africans, now Eastern Europeans. With rising unemployment at home and restrictions on non-EU immigration, perhaps we'll see a return to British staff in hotels? If so, will they work as hard and care as much as the Polish or most from the Southern Hemisphere before them?

Chantel is full of enthusiasm for the owners. 'He's an architect dedicated to making the hotel physically perfect. She's an aviation lawyer. They have children at school in Exeter and appear most weekends mucking in where there's a need.' To which I might add they are first class communicators and publicists.

Over tea (served without charge at any time) and later pre-dinner drink, guests explain their reasons for being here. 'Something we've wanted to do for years,' says Ivor Hill, a retired technical support officer for ICI from the Vale of Glamorgan. 'There's only one Burgh Island Hotel, and it's marvellous.' One couple were celebrating their Ruby wedding: 'A special place for a special occasion.' Another woman had brought her aunt to celebrate her eightieth birthday. 'Just grand,' says the old lady. 'You won't hear anyone grumble.'

My cufflinks and all, we make our way to the restful and spacious ballroom for dinner. The chairs have chrome framework with cane seats and backs. The sideboards are stepped works of art. On a quiet Monday evening, just a dozen couples are around the periphery. We all glance at each other's dress. Except at special parties, on land I have never before seen everyone dressed as on a formal night at sea – though here it's more quality than glitter.

'It's lovely,' purrs Sheila. We are all very much our own people, apart from the eightieth birthday celebrant and her niece, everyone was with spouse. No children. Under fives are anyway banned. And if you prefer not to dress black tie, they'll gladly serve you in another room or the Pilchard Inn.

The dinner itself exudes quality ingredients and cooking rather than seeking to impress. Nowhere would a Baked Alaska Parade be less appropriate, though I'm sure they are capable of giving private parties whatever kind of celebration desired. My especial culinary memory is of chilled cheese parfait with warm fig and parmesan biscuit. Gently mouth watering.

And so to a good night's sleep. Our written confirmation warned we might have to be off the island by 9.00am or wait another six hours, the period each tide floods the way to the mainland. But the forecast is fine with just a light breeze, so we can enjoy a late breakfast and cross by the famous sea tractor. In the 1930s, this was a truly weird contraption, briefly appearing (1935) in a DVD the hotel sells. Today's Mark 3 tractor has over-sized wheels with a raised platform, seventeen steps up. Up to thirty passengers, all standing, in daylight, twenty after dark.

On this lovely crisp late summer morning, I delight in seeing the tide come in, steadily covering the sand. When there is already a sizeable channel, several people still wading across, trousers and skirts held high, have suddenly to retrace their steps since the water is deepest on the island side.

The tide that gives this outpost its character, comes at a cost. The public can pay to come across for £1.50 each way but gawkers are distinctly not allowed in the hotel whose front door is kept locked. Guests have their own special crossing. This involves a driver taking us down to sea tractor and transferring our luggage, driving us through the gentle rippling waves, and transferring luggage to another Land Rover for our short climb back to the garage.

Back in our own Little Car, after climbing up through sprawling

Bigbury-on-Sea, we pause for a glance at the impressive white hotel across the water on South Devon's only inhabited island (though in recent times only by hotel and pub). The image is famous from television and newspaper coverage, for Burgh Island seems ever in the news. There is a calendar of events such as a round-the-island swim not to mention all the special events and visitors at the hotel. An excellent website too. It is only twenty hours since we caught our first glimpse yesterday. Time definitely not wasted.

Now through Devon's narrow sunken lanes and down to Aveton Gifford, with a diversion once more to enjoy its picturesque narrow street not built for the motor age, and back to the A38 which played so important a role in my earlier life. 'We did it,' we burst out, it being Burgh Island Hotel.

Lundy

Finally, the most isolated English island that a substantial number of people visit. Essentially a narrow piece of granite, Lundy intrigues and inspires. It is many years since I made my only trip, by one of the Campbell Steamers that used to criss-cross the Bristol Channel during the summer. But the memory has not faded. There were several hundred passengers. Transferring us by small boat from ship to the foot of the steep path up to the plateau was challenging. Periods when powerful waves prevented progress taxed patience.

Once we had climbed up in a series of crocodiles to the top, about 400ft up, there was more than enough space for us to spread out and enjoy our individual exploration choices in some solitude. Though only half a mile wide, the island is 3 ½ miles long, so a walk round the periphery takes a couple of hours. The views of the cliffs, the clear sea below and of the Welsh and north Devon coast are fantastic.

In common with most of the day trippers, I had only previously seen Lundy on the horizon from various points of the Bristol Channel coasts. Looking back in retrospect, I'm amazed by the complex history and the intricate system of walks across the island. A huge surprise is the old granite quarry which supplied part of the Thames Embankment and the basic stonework for many Devon churches, and the row of ruined quarrymen's houses. The earlier history especially fascinates me. Though we know little about him, primitive man has left many traces including pots, flints and burial mounds.

Is it not incredible that, throughout Britain, even when the population was maybe a tenth of today's, every speck of land was inhabited and exploited?

The first mention of the name, Lundi, meaning puffin island, was in the Orkneyingasaga; it was a good choice, an ideal location from which Scandinavian pirates could raid ships heading to both shores of the Bristol Channel. In the 12th century it was owned by the Mariscos, after whom today's island tavern is named. They pirated any ship they could catch up with and board. After William de Marisco was hanged, French and Spanish pirates took over. An island near which much of Britain's trade passed was just too tempting.

In a dramatic change, Lundy then became nicknamed 'The Kingdom of Heaven'. It was bought in 1834 by a William Hudson Heaven who declared it a 'free island' and successfully removed it from the control of the mainland judiciary. Then came the Victorian industrialisation; transferring granite to waiting boats must have been a tricky job.

When the quarry closed, the quarrymen's cottages were left to nature, along with the old church and the square keep of Marisco Castle, and Hudson's home, an 'incongruous piece of Georgian architecture in desolate surroundings'. Yes, there is a surprising amount to see as well as the natural grandeur.

On my visit, after several hours of walking, we retire to the warmth of the overcrowded Marisco Tavern, where they've always been used to rushes between long sojourns. Everyone wants to warm up, have a drink and buy samples of the famous puffin stamps needed in addition to the Post Office ones before going down the slope – hoping the transfer back to the ship now anchored further off will not be too hair raising.

In those days, like us, most visitors went for a few hours by the occasional steamer. The regular boat, from Bideford or Instow, was a rough-and-ready affair taking up to half a day. If you had to go on business, as did Sheila's father to carry out a Ministry of Agriculture inspection of the only farm, it might mean hiring a fishing vessel.

Excited by the prospect of a different kind of trip, Sheila's mother went along. The experience has long been part of family folklore. Setting out from Instow, they – surprise – encountered rough water making it impossible to proceed or return. The night was spent roughing it in Clovelly Roads. No proper bedding, but images etched into all our minds of the skipper steadily adding garments on top of them as the temperature plunged in the wee hours. As the storm abated, they reached Lundy at breakfast time and were welcomed with typical island hospitality by the farmer about to be inspected.

My attempts to pay a second visit failed, usually because of a combination of weather and having to book ahead on the normal small boat, once because of technical trouble on the *MS Balmoral*. With a BBC colleague, we reported to the captain, who explained he'd only enough battery power to enable the ship to be moved to a more sheltered position along Ilfracombe's quay – after it had been lightened by the disembarkation of the mass of passengers and wouldn't draw so much water. Though the Welsh passengers had been told the trip to Lundy was off, those on the quay hadn't, which caused much confusion. The 'station' manager eventually joined us in the ship's 'restaurant'.

'Have the passengers been told what's happening?' asked the captain.

'Yes. They know they'll not get to Lundy. Not today.'

'But do they know what's happening to them?'

'Happening to them? Oh. No, not yet. I suppose they'll want to get home some time. Um. Yes, buses, that's the answer. Buses. After lunch I'll have to think about how we're going to get them. Lots of buses to take them home – all the way to Swansea – that's the answer.'

South Wales people were still wandering around like lost sheep when my colleague and I left to do another improvised broadcast, from the stepped slope of Clovelly's main street thronged with holidaymakers, the luggage of those staying overnight being taken down by sledge.

Getting to Lundy is now much easier. Currently the *MS Oldenburgh* has capacity for 267 passengers with bar, buffet, shop and even information centre. From Bideford or Ilfracombe, it takes only two hours. There is even a Lundy Shore Office on Bideford's Quay and a helicopter alternative is available.

The Landmark Trust, who now run the island on lease from the National Trust, offers a range of accommodation from the 13th century castle to the old lighthouse and a fisherman's chalet. The only problem is that only bookings for entire weeks are accepted until two weeks ahead. That usually rules out shorter stays in the season. Bird interest is intense (trapping and ringing is mainly a winter occupation), with the excitement of appearances of unusual birds blown over from America in Atlantic gales. The annual reports of the Lundy Field Society make interesting reading. Lundy also offers night skies without light pollution, clear water diving and is home to Britain's first marine life reserve.

Peaceful and timeless: Lundy compels many to return, some several times a year. Because of the numbers, it cannot feel quite as remote as it once did, but it is certainly more pristine than in its industrial days and even when a hotel struggled for survival before the war. 'More a way of life than going on holiday,' a friend who never goes anywhere but Lundy tells me. 'There's a great social side to it, too, because the same people usually return at the same time and you get to know them really well through sharing bird and other interest and not being tempted by dance floors, pub-crawling or eating out. And we don't rough it these days.

It's being very cut off that makes it different. One is very conscious of the weather.'

Many more people will hear Lundy mentioned in weather forecasts and see it in the distance than will ever land at the only possible spot at the south east and climb up the steep path to the plateau. Incidentally the rhyme

From Hartland Point to Lundy light
Is a watery grave by day or night

refers to the original lighthouse on the plateau top, where fog too frequently blotted out the light, resulting in shipwrecks. It was replaced by lower lighthouses at the northern and southern tips and, as already mentioned, it now offers visitor accommodation, occasionally up in the mist but, when the sun shines, having the best views of all.

· XIX ·

THE ISLE OF WIGHT

Across to Yarmouth and on to Ventnor

Almost a mini-kingdom with its own County Council, varied landscape and great variety of towns and villages, railways, red squirrels, dialect and way of life, and full of archaeological remains and historical and literary associations (Tennyson and Dickens wrote while here), the Isle of Wight is a real island by any definition.

The difficult part of our journey is getting to Lymington, especially getting lost in Bournemouth. All is then relaxingly straightforward. The reference number given by our hotel for our 'free' ticket (cut-price maybe but no doubt included in our tariff) instantly yields the forward and return parts. There's orderly queuing to board the ferry, with time to buy a civilised sandwich from the terminal café, and a smooth, rapid crossing with Little Car on the mezzanine deck while we enjoy a hot drink on the bridge deck.

The Isle of Wight is so full of contrasts that first impressions are meaningless. Facts say more. Though only 147 square miles, it has over 500 miles of excellent footpaths, a 62-mile cycle route, bridleways that have been in continuous use since the Stone Age, an electric and a steam railway. Above all, a huge contrast in land and seascapes. It is full of the unexpected.

Yarmouth, where we disembark, is an encouraging gateway, neighbouring larger Freshwater full of its own contrasts, the Needles Pleasure Park downright inappropriate (you have to walk across Tennyson Down to get close to the Needles themselves), while the West Coast road, partly along the white cliffs is sheer delight. It is so spectacular in the afternoon's early autumn sunshine that we stop just off the tarmac to soak in warmth and view. The only disappointment is that the coast view doesn't stretch back to the Needles. Much of the Isle of Wight is now designated an Area of Outstanding Natural Beauty. It is a pity it didn't happen earlier, for some intrusive development, such as the Needles Pleasure Park, would surely have been prevented.

I've only been to the Isle of Wight once before, fifty years ago for the

BBC, but I have the clearest of later memories of going on deck on a departing *QE2* trip when the moon popped out from behind a cloud to reveal in stunning detail the declining line of remnants of white cliffs with a lighthouse at the end. Though the Needles are nowhere near the ship's route round the south of the island, I'm certain the memory is accurate. In the moonlight the distance must have seemed foreshortened. Don't die without having seen the Needles.

On our leisurely way to Ventnor, we stop occasionally, including at a village in search of an ice cream. It is that kind of day. But nothing worth eating. The scenery makes up for it. Blackgang Chine – the original road went in a landslip in the early 1960s – is another over-commercialised disappointment. Better is to come.

Bending through Niton and a tunnel of trees, we are on the short southern coast. Passing the entrance to Ventnor Botanic Gardens which we say we'll return to tomorrow, we find our Royal Hotel without a search. Set among some of the large Victorian houses that shout that this was a very special place to live, it is a great hotel. AA four star 76 per cent and two rosettes. Opened in 1832, though extended since, like so many, it fell on bad times in the 1970s and in 1982 for the first time closed for the winter. It's now privately owned, much improved and very busy. Having a cream afternoon tea in the garden, we feel we are on holiday, by no means always the case when researching these chapters.

Full of energy after tea, Sheila walks down to the harbour and back up the steep hill, while I enjoy talking with the guy who was coming to dinner but has asked for an earlier meeting as he's still getting over a cold: John Metcalfe, in charge of island tourism. He's more enthusiastic and communicative than any other council official I've met in recent years. Facts and perspectives pour from his lips:

'At high tide we're smaller than Rutland, just 138,000 population, but with 360 daily ferry crossings and a hundred tourist attractions. Much has improved in recent years, especially with top hotels and restaurants. Even fifteen years ago it was hard to get a decent meal. If I had to name a single feature that makes the island attractive it would be its great variety of scenery and towns and villages in so compact an area.

We've an advantage over mainland holiday areas because, working with the ferry operators, we have precise counts of visitors. Over a quarter of them are aged over sixty, so it's important to protect traditional values, but nearly 100,000 crossed for the two major music festivals this year, and Britain's largest walking festival, the cycling festival which has just finished, and the extreme sports festival – it drew over 30,000 – are all vitally important. The perception that the island is behind the times is itself outdated. We've an excellent website which helps a lot, and work closely with the Chamber of Commerce. Some 58 per cent of the island is an Area of Outstanding Natural Beauty, and we've a fine heritage coastline. Another thing: the island is increasingly known for its own organic food. It all adds to the value of tourism, now about £330 million a year.

Our towns and villages are hugely varied. I live here in Ventnor, and love it. Parking is the problem, but quality hotels like this are flourishing, at some other places such as Yarmouth, while Sandown and Shanklin haven't totally given up their character as more traditional bucket-and-spade resorts. Some accommodation there may be still a bit tired but much has improved, and Sandown's Dinosaur Isle is in the top museum league.

Yachting is the chief draw at Cowes; no big hotels there so regatta time sees people renting out their houses. Ryde, still a big entry port, has developed as a social centre. It's where the young people go for their evenings out. The capital, Newport, with 40,000 people, is a traditional market, administrative and shopping town, but it has some gems such as the Roman Villa and nearby Carisbrooke Castle where King Charles was imprisoned. And, not far away, Queen Victoria's favourite home, Osborne House, now English Heritage, is one of our biggest attractions.'

Problems? 'The perennial one is the second homes, mainly owned by people from the South East, but they do bring in a lot of money. There's a need for a good hotel in Cowes; the Medina Estuary has great appeal. Everyone and everything having to come by ferry obviously puts prices up, but hotels offer excellent online bargains inclusive of ferry and being surrounded by sea is what makes us different – with a wonderful community spirit and sense of belonging and scores of local societies.'

Then he talks about his job. 'Our main spending used to be on the official guide book, but that's now left to a private business. We're more concerned with strategy and co-ordination, accepting that the pace of life on an island will always be different but encouraging enterprise and balancing the different strata of the tourist industry.

'Above all, of course, making the most of our natural heritage, for instance realising that, when it is exposed, the unstable blue slipper clay underlying many of the cliffs leads to falls, but that's what helps make us the country's biggest source of dinosaur remains. And our climate; especially down by the sea in Ventnor, there's nowhere milder in Britain.'

On his way out, regretting he's had to cancel dinner, he gives me his mobile number: 'Call at any time.' When did you last hear that from a council official?

'He seems a nice chap but I'm still glad we can have dinner on our own,' says Sheila who is back from the harbour in sparkling mood. Dinner was indeed a lovely occasion, Sheila especially enjoying the scallops.

At 1.30am, with violent sickness and then diarrhoea, she's ready to die. 'I'll never eat scallops again, I promise.' It probably wasn't the hotel's fault that possibly there was just one scallop that had such poison, but Sheila stays in bed all day, not even enjoying our sea view. First I go shopping, for a rehydration powder among other items. The town centre has real character. I like its mix of traditional shops among small multiple branch stores – and a friendliness not often met with south of London. The main street is one-way, so my return to the hotel is almost by the harbour. A quick check on Sheila and off again.

Botanic Garden

In every way, the Botanic Garden surpassed expectation. First the position. The car park is at road level, the garden on the sheltered Undercliffe below, sheltered even from the sea on the south. It's down two stairways or lifts, where there's a visitors' centre including a restaurant and exhibition. First I go to the latter: absorbing. I learn that only fifteen kinds of grain prevent world starvation and that, though there are a thousand other plants which (or whose fruits) we eat, international trade is concentrated on just two hundred species. So why is my annual seed order so complicated?

There's a fantastic mini-climate down here, and I'm soon enjoying being back in New Zealand with a selection of many of the 80 per cent of its plants that are unique. Though planted less than twenty years ago, the trees around the lawn are immensely high. While New Zealand has even more of a Mediterranean climate, fog and other dampness come to the rescue here. A seat invites me to linger and I read about the Botanic Garden's history – quite a story.

For the best part of a century the Royal National Hospital for Diseases was here, a special refuge for tuberculosis sufferers. Antibiotics rendered it redundant and it fell into disuse and such poor condition that it was demolished, in 1969. There were then pleasure gardens, but soon that famous plantsman, Sir Robert Hillier (see *Journey*) recognised the site's potential and, with suitable windbreaks quickly established, planted up the whole 22-acre site largely with specimens he'd brought back from many overseas expeditions and propagated at his Romsey nursery.

For the first decade all went brilliantly, but the mid-1980s were cruel. In 1985 Hillier died without leaving his thoughts about the future. The winter of 1986/7 was the coldest here for 150 years and (as at Tresco) much of what wasn't killed by frost was uprooted in the Great Storm of October 1987. Apart from a handful of trees such as a Brown Turkey fig which, like the one I used to grow, fruits 'sometimes', there was a clean sweep.

It was decided to devote much of the site to a series of zone-based mini-gardens, of which the New Zealand is the largest with the joy that it brings together trees and shrubs you wouldn't normally see at the same time.

The herb garden is a delight, too, but I can miss the hydrangea dell: I was delighted to be told by my son Gareth (see next chapter) that he's inherited my dislike for flambuoyant hydrangeas and passed it onto his son. Curious how many of our likes and dislikes are in the plant world. Thus, while some Britons devotedly struggle to grow agapanthus in pots, in California they are often dismissed as ugly weeds.

That brings me to a yellow diamond-shaped Kangaroo warning sign announcing the Australian section. A little boy of four or five refuses to walk a step further. No, he's not frightened of kangaroos; he's heard about them and is going to wait to see one. Poor lad, he's so excitedly determined. When told they're not actually here but in Australia he dismisses the notice as a cheat and demands to be taken to Australia – instantly. Then I chuckle seeing that the Australian garden appropriately overlooks a cricket field with a match in play. I expect to find the eucalyptus trees or gums, but other Australian species also have a story to tell.

On the far side beyond the American collection – not so satisfactory because the plants come from such different climatic zones – there's an inviting link to the coastal path. Open access to the garden is perhaps why there's no charge beyond a modest parking one. It is Council run, backed by a lively Friends who happen to be holding their 21st birthday celebrations. David Kelley is keenly inviting visitors to fill in a square in a huge sheet of paper (one is already completely filled) by contributing £10 per pane of glass for a new Temperate House. 'Write clearly,' he says, 'a calligrapher will copy every name into a book to be kept inside it.' He explains that it will replace the hot house where steaming up glasses delay those wearing them from enjoying the exotic plants, but the plants themselves are suffering from too little light coming through the polythene. Alan Titmarsh, who as a young man twenty one years ago opened the old house, has already been photographed buying his pane of glass to launch the new appeal.

'We need a Temperate House because, though we're level with Tresco, about once a decade there's a damaging frost. The new house will protect some more delicate species and also bring on possible replacements. The estimated cost is £4.5 million, and that'll take some finding, over the next years. The Friends – yes it's our 21st today – have an excellent relationship with the Council who run the garden. We help in all kinds of ways, including practical work; there are only eight or nine full-time gardeners.'

Here is another example of how common sense still thrives in communities surrounded by sea who simply have to be largely self-sufficient. I love this garden, the friendliness of paid and voluntary staff, and wish I could purchase a few of the plants on sale. They'd be dead by the time we're back in Scotland, but I do acquire an experimental packet or two of seeds.

Sheila is still in bed, and grimaces when I suggest something to eat. I have a quick sandwich, and rejoin Little Car.

Electric and Steam Railway

Once Ventnor had two stations, one for Shanklin, Sandown and Ryde, a route I travelled by steam on my first visit – departing trains immediately went into a long, smoky tunnel – the other for Newport (which by then had already been closed). To test the remaining 8½ miles of the national system, I'm driving to Shanklin. The remnant is now electrified, the home of vintage London Underground trains back in their traditional maroon livery.

A curious sensation sitting on an Underground train on an island... and having a talkative conductor. 'Oh, yes, we're a friendly crowd; with only fifty staff you can't afford to fall out with anyone. Of course a route of only eight miles can't possibly pay, but we take a lot of money from passengers going to the mainland, and without us there'd be many fewer on trains at Portsmouth Harbour, So, though South West Trains have to have us, they also need us.'

There's a good sea view before Lake ('the only lake without water,' explains a dad to his son), but we dive inland to Sandown, the island's most popular resort. I recall that on my previous visit I saw a special steam-hauled train of two luggage vans for PLA, letters which have little meaning today but once spelt convenience for the millions who took their holidays by train: Passenger Luggage in Advance. Just one of so many facilities not to be found on today's near-porterless railways.

At Brading I note the abandoned island platform where passengers from Ryde to Bembridge changed sides for the branch line train. Bembridge is the island's largest place I've still never been to; there's said to be a great community spirit there – and has the island's last surviving windmill.

The last part of the journey abounds with railway interest. Smallbrook Junction, once just the point where the routes to Ventnor and Newport/Cowes diverged, has sprouted a new exchange platform between the Island Railway and the Isle of Wight Steam Railway I'll be visiting tomorrow. Soon we pass a south-bound electric train on a section of double track that's been retained, and I enjoy the increasing rarity of semaphore signalling at St John's Road, the first of three Ryde stations. Then through a tunnel. It was because this was subject to flooding and the track needed raising that the line was electrified using the former Underground trains, not as high as standard rolling stock. Lots of passengers alight at all three stations. Esplanade serves the hovercraft to Southsea, and at the terminus, Pier, most passengers transfer to the fast (eighteen minutes) connecting catamaran to Portsmouth Harbour.

The last section along the pier feels something of a relic: the tracks of the former parallel tramway have long been taken up, and the other Island Railway track has rusted out of use. Yet, now also road connected, the pier head is as busy as at most times in its history except on peak days in the 1950s when most Britons could afford a holiday but took it at home.

Many stayed in Ryde itself, an elegant Victorian resort and now a bustling multi-faceted town of 30,000. It boasts of great sands (the railway pier is among Britain's longest in order to reach deep enough water), famous regatta and carnival, theatre for live music, ice rink, speedway and other sports facilities – and these days especially – a wide range of restaurants and pubs. There's excellent shopping ranging from numerous antique and bric-a-brac stores to the island's only Tesco.

Wanting to get back to Sheila, I'm soon on the return train absorbing a crowd from the mainland. Now we 'cross' the Ryde-bound train at the loop in Sandown station, an oddity being that roughly twenty and then forty minutes elapse between trains in what at first seems a half-hourly service. Back in Little Car I then briefly explore steep routes to Luccombe Village and Chine, and Ventnor's charming suburb of Bonchurch. With its sharp corners, gradients and views, even the main road is pretty exhilarating.

Feeling better next morning, Sheila comes down to a bowl of porridge for breakfast and a taxi is ordered to take her to Yarmouth where we are spending tonight and we will meet for lunch. There's little traffic on the main road this sunny Sunday morning, so I take my time soaking up of the coastal views. Once more I drive slowly past the two large thatch-roofed pubs in Shanklin and I am almost pleased I have to wait at the traffic lights allowing only one-way passage through the narrows.

At Sandown, my route is past the pier and the great sandy beach which helped make it a major resort for traditional family holidays. The pier has been shortened; fifty years ago I went to the hall that used to be at its end for a summer show featuring Cyril Fletcher. How differently we all dressed in those days when most men still wore a hat. There is a surprising range of highly-rated busy hotels as well as the many boarding houses, the latter's season virtually over. Quality equals a longer season.

Back on the main road, a few miles shy of Ryde, I turn into a more intimate countryside with scattered woods and small fertile fields and go almost to the main Ryde-Newport road before turning back through the long village of Haven Street, much of it a long way from its station to which I'm heading.

This is the headquarters of the Isle of Wight Steam Railway, whose progress I've long watched and admired from afar. Says its guide book: 'It is difficult to say anything complimentary about the Newport Junction Railway', part of which has been brought back to life. Opening of the original was refused several times, for the work was shoddy...and the line went bankrupt.

It was not until the Southern Railway absorbed the extensive miscellany of island routes at the 1923 Grouping that universal enterprise was enjoyed throughout the island's extensive system, albeit the rolling stock and motive power were largely mainland leftovers. I recall the spurts of speed the Brighton Terriers achieved between stiff gradients, speed restrictions and station stops. At busy times, it was five or six across in the narrow non-corridor compartments. But it worked, handling huge summer Saturday crowds, especially in the immediate postwar years. Yet within a decade of nationalisation, nearly all had gone.

I recall passing another train on the opposite side of Haven Street's narrow island platform which, fifty years on, but with the same boyish enthusiasm, I approach over a level crossing. I'm greeted by the general manager, Peter Vail, and the commercial manager, Jim Lowe. We get into a first class compartment in a carriage, built even before my father was born, for the trip to Smallbrook Junction and back. Perfection. Roger Macdonald, the guard, making the fourth person of our group, we talk railway history, getting the balance right between the nostalgic experience and the business needed to support an expensive living museum, personalities and human oddities – and the scenery. Unlike so many of today's railways, especially south of London, there aren't endless trees blocking out the view, for it is recognised that people buying a journey for pleasure need to enjoy the countryside, gentle farmland to the north and rolling downland to the south.

'Keeping the view open comes at a cost, but it's necessary,' says

Peter. With a non-railway admin experience, he has been brought in to ensure viability by creating new business opportunities. Jim is all for these helping to balance the books. 'The railway is at the centre, but there's an event every week of the season. Last weekend our field by the station hosted the Ford Classic Car Club; now there's a wine festival in our new block, you'll see it when we're back at Haven Street.' I can't help noticing that both of them are keen, if not anxious, to see how many people transfer from the Island Railway at Smallbrook Junction. Roger the guard is more philosophical. He was a real railwayman for thirty three years, before being thrown in at the deep end here in 1995. 'You learn that no two days are the same and just look after those you've got on board,' he says. He is sometimes guard, sometimes signalman.

'The good thing about the island is that we all help each other,' says Peter. 'Many come over specially for one of our events, and that gives the Wightlink ferries traffic, and they give us a subsidy. The Island Railway gives us traffic and we give then some; there's an Island Liner ticket £12 or £6 for a child, giving unlimited travel. My brief is to increase income; though I'm not a railway enthusiast in the ordinary sense, I'm very keen about the experience we offer, and of course we carry passengers to events such as the popular Island Steam Show held in our field, and those coming for the traction engines can't help getting interested in the trains. And they all eat at our café and see our shop. With nineteen full-time paid staff, the railway barely pays, but the special events take our income to nearly £1 million and then we're OK.'

Robert the guard points out the island's highest point and Jim says they're proud they print their own old-fashioned Edmonton tickets on two machines bought from British Rail. Interestingly, almost one in five travel first class 'making it a real experience'.

At Haven Street the wine festival is celebrating island wines, including samples from Corsica, Majorca as well as several IOW (Isle of Wight) vineyards. Then to the signalbox. Wow, only a sixteen-lever frame. At South Molton where I unofficially learnt signalling, the Great Western, ever conscious of safety and not strapped for cash as they were in the IOW, needed thirty two for a similar layout, but with safety or trap points to derail trains in preference to allowing a run-away to crash into another train. Stuart Duddy (there's a picture of him talking to the Queen when she paid a visit) is on duty and thinks the GWR was odd as well as wasteful. Sometimes he's rostered as the daily operating manager or guard, offering variety rarely found in the commercial world.

The train which we've got off has meanwhile gone on to Wootton, the part of the route first rescued, after teenagers from London formed a group to save a Terrier and a few carriages while the real railway was still running. A great success story giving happiness in many different ways. But new roads and buildings prevent any chance of reopening through to Newport, once a railway crossroads though with a pretty basic station inconveniently situated. The guide book's 1959 picture of trains at the island platform taken from the top of the old gas works is so fascinating that I keep turning back for a further look.

To Yarmouth via Cowes

From the station I make my way through narrow lanes south to ridgeway Arreton Down and then down through Downend to the island's most complicated network of fast roads around Newport, at the head of the long Medina Estuary.

Driving myself between places I've only previously done by train, and that half a century ago, is a familiar but still thought-provoking experience. Memories are crystal clear of trips along railways closed well before the majority of people alive today were born. In this particular case, it was alongside the broadening estuary and past a line of coasters unloading coal and everything else, from food to furniture, needed on the island. Now it nearly all comes by lorry on a ferry. As has happened at so many places, shipping has largely been replaced by marinas, docks by luxury housing. The old railway has become a footpath, but by car it is now hard to get a good view of the estuary. While most rail fans rave about old steam engines, to me the magic of the country railway largely lay in the way it offered an alternative and so often more hands-on view, especially of rivers, and of estuaries when docks were docks, as opposed to the gentrified housing with de rigueur Victorian-style lamp posts.

Far more vessels enter the river these days but, apart from the Southampton ferries, they are nearly all pleasure craft. Cowes lives on its obsession with sailing. Many of the shops in the narrow streets are devoted to it.

The first luxury vessel built on the Medina, was for Queen Elizabeth I. Royals of all ages have been extravagant spenders but have often also incidentally stimulated employment. Boat building became a staple industry that still thrives. And Osborne House, where, after major building works, Queen Victoria spent many happy summers reigning over an elaborate household, is now a popular tourist attraction run by English Heritage. There are really two Cowes, connected by a chain ferry. Osborne House is just outside East Cowes.

On my way back from West Cowes, the most noticeable buildings are a trio of prisons, including Parkhurst. Before Newport I turn off the ugly road system and head to Yarmouth. What many felt was the best of the branch lines, from Newport to Yarmouth and on to Freshwater, is now also a cycle track, preserving its totally different range of views.

Now lacking time to make diversions to taste the complicated Newton River estuary system, I enjoy the lovely outlook across the eastern Solent before slipping into Yarmouth. In the seething mini-shopping centre, the pace is that of pedestrians too thick to make a way ahead. The George, the island's only AA Inspectors' Choice hotel, happily invites me to leave the car keys for valet parking.

Sheila has had a good morning and is eager for lunch. But the first taste has her running back to bed. A few hours later she's so unwell that I call a doctor. Then island luck. Though there's only a handful of shops, a pharmacy is opposite the hotel whose owner says he'll see the doctor when he calls and will gladly wait in case a prescription is needed, which it is. Staying here was to be our last night treat on the island, but the doctor says we can't possibly return tomorrow. Without being asked, the hotel sympathetically cuts the room rate for the second night.

Brighstone and back to Yarmouth

With an extra morning, I decide to get to know one village, choosing Brighstone, just a mile inland from the west coast road, in preference to the popular and more self-consciously pretty Godshill, well inland from Shanklin through which Sheila came by taxi yesterday.

In Freshwater, I take a wrong turn and, with thoughts of Tennyson who once lived here, land back at the car park of the commercialised Needles Pleasure Park. At least the mistake gives me a chance to wend my way through an intriguing network of lanes back to the proper route at Freshwater Bay, which I was reading about last night. It is a super place to pause. Though not as much a resort as formerly (all over the country hotels are being converted for residential use) it is highly picturesque, and famous for rock erosion in fanciful shapes around it. Tennyson Down over which you can walk to view the Needles rises sharply above it ending in spectacular white cliffs with a touch of that lovely edge-of-the-world feel. Glorious. There's even a great crop of teasels.

Driving round gently curving Compton Bay to Hanover Point, I pop into the National Trust car park and read that: 'Over five million years ago, there was a series of rivers and lagoons where dinosaur-like Iguanodon roamed leaving their footprints in the mud and preserved as casts.' There's a charge of £1.50 even for a moment's parking, a notice saying that the Isle of Wight Council's permits (allowing parking anywhere for a sensible fee) are not valid.

In a few minutes I'm in Brighstone. First call is to the thatched

Post Office. 'Escaped the latest round of cuts, but who knows,' says the postmaster. Then, next door to the National Trust's homely museum of Victorian domestic and farming life and the Trust's only island shop, also thatched. 'Ye Olde Shoppe' at that. The thatched group with 'Mind Your Head' doorways is much admired and photographed. Encouraged by a friendly assistant, and realising I've not yet collected the usual pile of local publications, I leave with three titles and, thanks to the helpful assistant, details of how to contact their creators.

The first is the most specialised but has personal appeal: Helen Butler's *Red Squirrels on the Isle of Wight*. When I call her from Nairn after I've had time to read it, I say I've just seen a baby red climb the wire to our bird feeder and hang by back-paw toenails while grasping a nut between its front paws.

The island and the north of Scotland remain free of greys, whose arrival usually heralds a rapid disappearance of our native reds. We discuss a story in today's paper saying that a few reds have now been found to be immune to the virus which is carried but does not affect the greys and which is supposed to be the chief cause of 'ethnic cleansing'. There is possible hope of a vaccine though quite how our reds could be caught without cruelty isn't clear.

'I simply love the reds,' says Helen, whose enterprising little book discusses their behaviour and life cycle in considerable depth, with many beautiful photographs. Dedicated to all supporters of the Wight Squirrel Project, her main tool in encouraging interest and support for the reds, there are nice little boxes of 'Squirrel facts':

> Fossil remains of the red squirrel found in Britain were dated at between 7,000 and 10,000 years old. Red squirrels were widespread over the whole of the British Isles after the last Ice Age.
>
> Squirrels rapidly declined during timber shortages in the 15th and 16th centuries. During the 18th century Scottish red squirrel numbers plummeted almost to the point of extinction. The reason is unknown.
>
> By 1900 numbers were high. Between 1900 and 1925 reds suffered a dramatic decline in the British Isles. Natural disease cycles exacerbated by overcrowding, food shortage, bad weather, habitat destruction and pressure from grey squirrels, all contributed. Timber requirements for the Second World War and a series of harsh winters hastened the decline. Greys expanded, being better suited to exploit broadleaved woodland.

Helen used a desktop publishing system to lay out the text and colour pictures and obtained printing estimates from several local firms. 'The first 2,000 sold out so I did another 2,000, keeping the stock in a little bedroom. Though there is a local distributor, I make most of the sales myself. A lot go at shows, and my talks sell seventy or eighty a year.'

Most Haunted Island by Gay Baldwin is full of spooky tales, including the ghosts of Osborne House. 'I've now done seven island ghost books,' says Gay, a journalist on the island weekly. 'At first I had to take hold of myself to write, self-publish and sell copies. The seven have now sold about 7,000 copies each, so a total of 50,000 which I'm sure will eventually double. I've steadily built up a head of steam: readers of one book tell you stories for another, the titles help sell each other and, as you get better known, it's easier to get attention, stocked and invited to give talks. Several titles make it worthwhile treating the website seriously, and meeting people at launch parties in a haunted place has led to my starting ghost walks.

Like a small industry, it's become self-perpetuating. But I have to remember it's the ghostly happenings that drive the interest. It genuinely seems that the island is the most haunted part of Britain. I defy anyone to say it's all rubbish.' Remembering Dr Johnson's answer to a woman who asked if he believed in ghosts, 'No madam, but I'm afraid of them,' I'm not about to challenge Gay since so many well-known people have experienced something.

Steve Gascoigne is in fact the photographer rather than writer of the most popular of my trio: *The Isle of Wight: Gem of the Solent.* His pictures are renowned for clarity of mood and detail. Each is a masterpiece, literally opening people's eyes to the island's unique majesty.

Having been in the photographic business in Coventry for twenty years, when he moved to the island creativity was spawned by his delight in the scenery and complemented by practical commercialism. Prints of many of the pictures can be found in island galleries and gift shops, a 60 by 40-inch print commanding £360. Few islands have been so brilliantly portrayed; looking at the book while writing this makes me itch to return.

A bright morning, a jovial atmosphere in Brighstone. A Parcel Force van is delivering to the Post Office: 'What, you've brought me a parcel of spare money,' jokes the postmaster. 'You say it's your first time here?' asks someone who has overheard me talking in the National Trust shop. 'Wonderful village; but then West Wight is always tops, less crowded, nicer people.' Passing the pub – oddly named, or so it first seemed, The Three Bishops – I make for the tearoom, surprisingly large and pretty nearly filling the former garden of the house to which it is attached. It's doing a roaring trade.

Choice of treat with morning tea is difficult. 'They're all wonderful,' says a bonny woman who having demolished a tart is about to attack a slice of fruit cake. 'Stranger? Everyone here will tell you that the west of the Island is best.' Tuning into conversations at several tables is entertaining; a harassed young man is continuously henpecked; I wonder if he's listening to the next table where coincidentally they're talking about a man 'well rid of her; given him nothing but trouble. If he doesn't go from the frying pan into the fire with another tartar, he'll be in heaven'.

There is a mixture of villagers, others from neighbouring places and mainlanders, one couple talking about the parish church opposite, my next call. Outside there's a notice explaining the pub's name. Three former incumbents became Bishop: hymn writer Thomas Ken, at Bath & Wells; Samuel Wilberforce, anti-slavery campaigner, at Oxford, later Winchester; and George Moberly, whose fifteen children made considerable impact in the village, at Salisbury. Inside there is a mural devoted to their memory. Another interesting clergyman was William Fox, one of the founding fathers of the study of fossils. A long-serving curate apparently with light church duties, he spent most of his time delving into the local cliffs. Much of his collection is still in the British Museum.

Though there had been earlier failed attempts, the island was actually the last part of England to be Christianised. Even so, there's been a church here for over 800 years. Founded as the village eventually grew following the Dark Ages after the disappearance of the Romans, it has a great sense of continuity. There's much to see, from Norman arches and a dual wagon roof supported by central pillars, to a smooth 21st century limestone floor with underfloor heating. I like the neat round of chairs in the 16th century Waytes chapel adjacent to the east of the chancel, an intimate setting for weekday communion services. I also enjoy the brilliant colours of the ancient Good Samaritan window, and the memorial to lifeboat men who gave their lives in the great storm of 1888, whose trail of destruction is recorded in so many places I've visited. Though the village is slightly inland and lacks the stunning views commanded by the west coast road, it has strong associations with the sea, fishing and shipwrecks. The beams of the chapel are believed to have come from a shipwreck.

Did I notice the little building by the doctors' surgery, asks the Rector, Rev Malcolm Williams. 'It used to be the Rector's stable. Occasionally in the morning, he'd find the horse sweating from a hard night's work – and a barrel of brandy under straw by way of thanks for its use.' When I'm sceptical about smuggling (with every seaside village throughout the land boasting of daring feats) he says: 'Well, two graves have the skull and crossbones trademark of smugglers.' He adds: 'It's a friendly village

– and lively church, with an average Sunday congregation of 140. Really outward looking, too.'

With an unusually interesting bookstall for a village church, it is so well run as even to afford a part-time administrator. But above all a place of peace, where I contemplate my place in the greater scheme. Just one moan. In my youth we had real local produce, fruit, vegetables and flowers displayed at Harvest Festival. Now, even in the countryside, among the genuine things, there's a line of tins of foreign fruit and a pack of Tesco pre-wrapped carrots.

So back to Yarmouth for another sandwich lunch. Sheila's medicine beginning to work, we're able to enjoy an afternoon tea and then a walk around. The lifeboat, we notice, is of the larger all-weather Severn Class allocated to stations where it can be kept ready afloat and, with a speed of 25 knots and a range of 250 nautical miles, might have to stay at sea for a considerable period. Wreck and rescue figure prominently in island history and folklore – and still do.

Making our way to the pier, we see the back of Yarmouth Castle (English Heritage, but already closed for the day), with Henry VIII's artillery fortification and gunners' lodgings, gun platform and powder magazine. The longest wooden pier in England, its future was uncertain as its greenheart wood had been systematically eaten away from the inside by gribbles. A feature is a seat with mock over-sized gribbles chewing away. A recent refurbishment has been made possible by a Lottery grant and local donations, each recorded in large lettering on successive planks.

'Just six days after they'd finished the repairs, the Paddle Steamer *Waverley* crashed into it,' says a talkative David Groves of Freshwater fishing at the pier end. He shows us the corner pile she's ripped. 'Next day she did the same thing at Worthing.' It is a lovely old ship, the world's last surviving sea-going paddle steamer I've twice chartered for company events, but these are not her first accidents.

'It will be bass for the next six weeks, but bream finishes at the end of October. We get mackerel, whiting, skate and much else from the pier. A fishing licence is £27 a year; not a bad bargain. But no fishing Wednesday evenings; they're for the sailing club.'

Next day I notice how I'm exchanging 'Good Mornings' with strangers as though we were in Scotland. The island way of life is distinctive, more natural. People have to work hard, often combining several jobs to make a decent living. Enterprise and island loyalty abound and are no doubt very necessary. We're taking back a few samples of the local delicacies including a round box of soft cheese. Others have patronised local craftsmen. For its value system, if no other reason, the Isle of Wight qualifies as Remote Britain; I love the mini-kingdom with such great scenery, history, everything compacted so intimately.

The return ferry trip is routine except that the captain points out the first of a new larger class on her trials. 'I've tried her; she handles very well,' he tells us. The present ferries will make their own way to new use in Australia. 'Wouldn't want to be on one of them in a gale half-way there,' says Sheila. Today's journey is trial enough for her.

· XX ·

PURBECK TO PORTLAND

The Isle of Purbeck

Purbeck, though always called the Isle of Purbeck, is actually a peninsula, surrounded on two sides by the sea and one by Poole Harbour. There is no unanimity of opinion on what constitutes the fourth side, but many people believe that, apart from a 300-yard section, it is river, mainly the Frome. What everybody agrees is that including Isle in the name is justified because it is so different, cut off. The island feel is strongest to the east, toward the irregular coast of Poole Harbour, overlooking Brownsea Island. Sizeable Brownsea, National Trust owned, with great birdlife, a haven for red squirrels and birthplace of the Scout movement after Baden Powell led a group on it in 1907, is indeed a genuine island and historically part of Purbeck.

The island feeling is emphasised if Purbeck is approached by the chain ferry across the narrow mouth of Poole Harbour. Recently we enjoyed a visit to Poole, staying at Sandbanks, reputed to have Britain's most expensive houses. Our hotel overlooked the ferry, the gateway to a different world, with fewer people, less wealth but greater individuality... not that Sandbank's estate agents will agree that anywhere is better placed than it, particularly for guaranteed uninterrupted views over Poole Harbour. Only Sydney has a larger natural harbour.

On that trip, we took the chain ferry and went to Swanage. Beautifully situated between cliffs, but largely abandoned by family holidaymakers who now prefer the Med, it is not quite sure what kind of a resort it now wants to be. Sometimes described as low key, it has character, but not much upmarket accommodation. The largest town actually within Purbeck, it isn't a business centre either, since most people look to Wareham, though across the River Frome and so just beyond the border.

On this occasion, I'm with Gareth my son over from Australia for a few days relaxation before the furious activity of the Frankfurt Book Fair. With Sheila, we had a perfect night at Stock Hill Country Hotel and Restaurant, privately-owned and personally managed. Now, just Gareth and I, having come through Wareham, take the first turn off the spine road to Corfe Castle and Swanage. We meander down a largely single-track lane, with a job lot of obviously Scottish 'Passing Place' signs. There is a plague of grey squirrels. They are everywhere, half a dozen often in sight, a few dead by the roadside. Coincidentally, the front page of today's *Telegraph* carries a story about a scheme to sterilise the greys in an attempt to save our remaining reds. We love the reds [or did until the night before writing this they dug up newly-planted bulbs] in our garden in Nairn but know that the greys are encroaching north a few miles a year. They cannot live together; the greys always win.

First stop is the car park of the Arne RSPB Reserve. The Wednesday volunteer, Bill Jordan is just the man to put things in perspective. Formerly a Cambridge botanist, he moved to enjoy better natural history country and enthusiastically extols the merits of this eastern part of Purbeck:

'The OS have divided the UK into ten kilometre squares, and the one in which we are now standing has the greatest habitat diversity of any: chalk, heath, river valley meadows, rough grass, mudflats, shingle, conifer and deciduous woods. Added to that there's a long history of industry: clay and oil, Purbeck and Portland limestone, all still active. So, helped by the work done by the RSPB and others, there's a great diversity of plants, rare invertebrates, butterflies, just about everything.

'But [pointing to the car park already pretty full, mid-week mid-morning] it's the birds that most people come for. The famous success has been the Dartford warbler, once down to ten breeding pairs here, in danger of becoming extinct nationwide. Since the RSPB arrived in 1965, that's been increased to fifty breeding pairs, nationally one to two thousand birds. It's recovered. Bird life is good at all times, but richest in winter when large numbers of avocets are a special attraction and there'll be up to 25,000 wading birds, ducks and geese in Poole Harbour.' Picking up a leaflet on the reserve he points to the fact file: 'More than 220 bird species, 31 mammals, nearly 850 moths, 33 butterflies, 23 dragon-flies, nearly 500 flowering plants.'

While one might have expected the area overlooking Poole Harbour (access only on foot) to be well protected, the outstanding achievement has been retaining one of England's largest areas of remaining lowland heathland. Nearly four-fifths of such land has been lost in England, and what survives represents quite a proportion of Europe's total. Created by man with woodland clearances over 4,000 years ago, it used to be sustained by grazing, burning, cutting turf for fuel, using heather for thatching and road building, gorse for bakers' ovens and animal food. Left to nature, gorse and then trees would take over. A museum piece, perhaps, but who dare say it is not worthwhile?

We take a different route across the heath on this crisp autumn morning and see groups of men studying, ready with tripods to snap anything that moves. Pausing while crossing Hartland Moor, only a few feet above sea level, reading the Nature Reserve notice I am quickly joined by some men. One in particular is anxious to amplify its message:

'I often come here, it's unique. You can see creatures you won't see anywhere else,' said the well-preserved agile elderly chap from Poole. 'You simply can't beat it. It's an Area of Outstanding Natural Beauty and so on, but in a class of its own. Where else, only a few miles across the water from a big conurbation, do you find this: a unique environment with its specialised wildlife – birds, insects, dragonflies, everything, and some of the richest birdlife in the world? Where else can you watch about 300 avocets follow the tide as I did on the Wych Channel? Added to that, it's an area rich in ancient history, industrial archaeology and flourishing clay quarrying, the largest UK on-shore oil field and, down towards Swanage, both Purbeck and Portland stone cutting.'

He was so vocal that I forgot to ask him his name, so he may never know his enthusiasm has made it in print. As we seek to escape walking down one of the three abandoned narrow-gauge clay tramways that reached piers on Poole Harbour, he adds: 'That's where clay used to run down to Middlebere Quay on the Wych Channel... and by the way there's lots of human interest stuff too in Purbeck. Enid Blyton had her Famous Five here. While she was married, she came on holiday with another man who subsequently became her new husband.'

Resuming our journey, Gareth says: 'It's always the men who get together in their groups to feel they are really connected through their hobbies and interests. We've hardly seen a woman. If they come along at all, bet they're socialising. They feel connected without the need to research, study or photograph.'

Then, passing a notice telling how to distinguish deer from front-end or back-end profiles, and a farm at which carts and wagons are repaired or restored, Purbeck design a speciality, we make our way to BP's Wytch Farm. This is the gathering installation for the unique oil field which used to produce 111,000 barrels a day but is now down to 23,000. Though still declining, it remains viable. The glory is that unless you search for it, you wouldn't know it was there... any more than I saw any sign of the several large ball clay pits that together produce over 100,000 tons annually. Though woodland encroachment is carefully prevented elsewhere, everything, every last 'nodding donkey' scattered around the oil field, is discreetly hidden by trees.

'We've cared from the beginning' BP's Susie Baverstock tells me. At the start of her career, well qualified and keen, she's spokesperson for environmental, scientific and planning issues. She even organises guided walks. *Living with the Heath,* an excellent guide published by Wessex Archaeology, is among the publications she gives me along with BP's own *Landscape on Loan* carrying the Wytch Farm Promise: 'To develop and operate the oil field whilst safeguarding the integrity of the landscape, taking care to monitor all aspects of each phase to ensure that the landscape on loan to BP for the life of the oilfield will be returned untarnished to the Purbecks.'

From the nodding donkeys that pump it up, oil arrives by underground pipelines and, after separating butane and propane, is despatched in crude form by a sixteen-inch diameter 56-mile long pipeline to BP's Hamble terminal on Southampton Water. That journey, passing through a series of valve stations, takes over twenty four hours.

Then we make our way to the new Norden Park-&-Ride station on the Swanage Steam Railway. Though the next train isn't due for the best part of an hour, cars are arriving at the already well-used park. 'Don't you want to go?' asks Gareth. Not today, though I admire what the volunteers have achieved, bringing a fascinating route back to life and adding a valuable attraction for Swanage's visitors. The romanticism of the steam railway is epitomised by its great viaduct giving an extra dimension to the glorious view of Corfe Castle, the ruined castle itself atop the hill above one of Dorset's most charming villages. Happy though he may be in New South Wales, the sight obviously touches Gareth's feelings for his English heritage.

Corfe Castle has its own station, but next to the new Park-&-Ride at Norden is the Purbeck Mineral & Mining Museum, which has recreated a short operational narrow-gauge system and will soon display *Secondus,* one of the hard-worked locomotives that used to haul the clay to the quays. It is also hoped to recreate a typical entrance to a ball clay drift mine with working winch gear and a rake of underground tubs.

John Rowley, one of the founders, tells me: 'It's been a bit uphill, but very worthwhile. It will add interest to the holidaymakers taking a steam train by showing them how huge quantities of stone, clay and oil were once carried on the Swanage branch. Freight traffic has all gone. At least that makes it easier for the Steam Railway to connect up with the mainline.'

China clay is granite decomposed where it is quarried. With a quite different character, ball clay was washed down millions of years ago into basins such as the Bovey Basin near Newton Abbot and this Wareham Basin.

The rarer ball clays are more easily malleable and nearly white when fired at high temperatures. They are the fine ceramic clays of porcelain, though also used in innumerable everyday products. Long safeguarded from development as a vital national asset, Purbeck's deep deposits are distributed in what were once hollows over a wide, flat area and, like the oil industry, have to be worked in an environmentally friendly way... indeed have been since well before the area was given special protective status. When I first visited the azure Blue Pool at Furzebrook in the 1960s, it was already a popular tourist attraction: a delightful sight, once a ball clay quarry, as indeed was Decoy Lake around which I used to take a daily walk at Newton Abbot.

The Newton Abbot-based Ball Clay Heritage Society takes equal interest in Purbeck, Newton Abbot and in North Devon's Petrockstow Basin in a remote area between Torrington and Hatherleigh. It collects and preserves stories and photographs of the working, transport and uses of the clays. The ball clay name comes from the traditional way of cutting it in cubes at the bottom of a pit. Because of the clay's high plasticity the cubes held together, but after being handled several times the corners became knocked and the cubes turned into balls. Though now worked in large quarries, mines were once common, including near Petrockstow where I recall alighting from my private 'train' (a truck) on the internal narrow-gauge railway system to climb down a long ladder whose slippery sides were the rails used by empty tubs that slid down and full ones pulled up under the control of ropes.

Moving on, the Purbeck Hills are a ridge with steep sides a few miles inland from the famous coastline. There are substantial outcrops of Purbeck stone, sometimes called marble because of its deep colour, and the whiter Portland stone, both privately quarried. Though again, you hardly see it, industry seems to crop up everywhere. Just one BP nodding donkey is commonly seen, near the coast. Two truck loads of oil a week are still taken from an old well near Kimmeridge Bay and the oil-shaley Kimmeridge Ledges, another part of Purbeck with rare insects and plants. Says BP's Susie Baverstock: 'It's a text-book well. Geology students flock to see the spectacular natural dome. The well cuts down through the earth, opened up through erosion.' But then the whole Dorset Jurassic Coast is a geological magnet.

Back at Corfe Castle, half way between Wareham and Swanage on the spine road, we thought we'd head west along the ridgeway. The Army has other ideas. Povington Hill is closed, as it frequently is for live firing. In much of remoter Britain, the military are still huge land occupiers and disrupters of civilian life. Close to this great heritage coast, the village of Tyneham was evacuated in 1943 and, though token restoration has been achieved for visitors when allowed in, has never been a village again. It's really disgraceful that, except at weekends and school holidays, people are usually forced to take a long detour inland, though what we see while doing so is full of interest: all the sweetcorn cut save one lonely tall square in the middle. Perhaps the farmer has thoughtfully left the last piece to allow wildlife to escape. There are lovely trees starting to turn colour and – toward the coast –glorious glimpses of the ridge the Army stops us reaching.

At a pub we find two large parties of women gossiping away. The wives of some of the men we saw exercising their hobbies earlier? 'I told you,' says Gareth. 'Those men wouldn't have felt important enough, well adequately connected anyway, just partying away like that.' Then, passing Army tanks on manoeuvres even here – there's a tank museum – via Wool down to the picture-postcard of West Lulworth.

Lulworth Crumple

Each time I come I'm stunned by Lulworth's beauty and detail. Encouraged by a lively *West Lulworth Village & Country Trails* leaflet, we start by walking up to the familiar view spot. At first one simply enjoys the horseshoe bay, created when the sea broke through a fault in the line of hard rock and quickly devoured the softer rock beyond. After minutes of satisfying astonishment, next it is compulsive study of the convoluted strata, some of Europe's most folded. One wonders at the sheer might that must have bent the hardest rocks that will survive much longer than any trace of this book or for that matter Shakespeare's work or conceivably even mankind.

Just thinking about the Lulworth Crumple is frightening, though I enjoy reading about it. In the 1970s in a D&C's *Geology Explained in Dorset,* John W Perkins wrote:

> Excitement must be compounded on excitement when the student continues to Stair Hole and Lulworth for the upturned and faulted beds... the rucking of the Lulworth Crumple.
>
> Stair Hole is a modern example of how the local coast received its detailed shape. Here the sea has eroded through joints in the Portland Stone, widening them into arches. The most westerly have already collapsed into the sea to form an open gap. Once the limestone wall is breached the Purbeck and Wealden behind it are soon removed. Much of this erosion is due to the Wealden's inherent instability. Great slips and flows occur as the inner slopes tumble over each other to present themselves to the sea for destruction and are then sucked away through the arches. The same process accounts for St Oswald's Bay, Lulworth Cove, Mupe and Worbarrow Bays – once the originally continuous outcrop of Portland Beds between

Durdle Door and Gad Cliff was breached...

On reaching the beach at Lulworth Cove, the first cliffs are in the Upper Greensand. Look for some brickwork of an old limekiln. The Greensand outcrop ends just beyond it. In the Chalk which follows, the *plenus* Marl is readily identifiable, cut out upwards by a Group 5 fault. The rest of the back of the cove is in Middle Chalk dipping 40-60° north, but about two-thirds of the way up the cliff face an undulating break can be traced – the outcrop of a Group 4 fault, and above it are beds of Upper Chalk, overturned and dipping 108° north!

Next we take a cream tea in the garden of our hotel, warmer this October than much of June to September. We watch people returning from Stair Hole and some probably from the spectacular archway of Durdle Door, buy an ice cream and drive off. Famous Durdle Door is the subject of an excellent website by Ian West:

The natural arch of Durdle Door has been cut by the sea through the almost vertical Purbeck Caps and the top of the Portland Freestone. From the landward side, the Portland Stone is hardly visible and the surfaces here are mainly those of the Purbeck stromatolitic limestones (the Soft Cap), like those of the Fossil Forest. Holes left by the late Jurassic trees are visible. The soft Wealden strata, thin here partly because of strike faulting, have been eroded away on this side except for a narrow connecting peninsula protected by some extent by the wall of stone. Originally there was Kimmeridge Clay seaward of Durdle Door but these relatively soft strata have been easily removed by the sea.

There is parking closer to Durdle Door, but the cliff walk is exhilarating. I've often enjoyed the features of this exceptional but unstable coast, now a World Heritage Site, yielding a rich crop of fossils. This afternoon, however, Gareth is still recovering from jet lag and gentle leisure is the priority, though first there's time to revive memories of earlier explorations vicariously by studying the OS map, with its horrid DANGER AREA in red close to the coast.

While hating its presence, the military has prevented much undesirable development. As John Perkins puts it, bullets are less unfriendly than humans to wildlife.

Our choice is a gentle stroll through the traffic free lower village with its cottages of stone walls, some with roofs of thatch, and gardens blooming late after the wet summer and good autumn. Gareth discovers an inviting fish restaurant where we book for a rare off-duty evening together.

The Isle of Portland

For keen watchers of horror movies who also happen to be interested in scenery, Portland might have a special appeal. Treeless, and never beautiful, it has been seriously mucked up by man. Paying his first visit, Gareth was truly shocked. Had Sheila been with us, it would have been one rare place to which she did not demand to return. Yet Portland is a real one-off and certainly not devoid of character. Four miles long by up to a mile and a half wide, it dangles into the English Channel from Chesil Beach which is a manmade causeway south of Weymouth and is home to around 13,000 people. They are contented, reasonably prosperous. There is little crime. But while I'm usually happy when surrounded by sea, I'll be relieved when this visit is over.

The approaches through a duller part of Weymouth aren't inspiring, while first impressions of Portland prepare one for what is to come. We cross the bridge onto the causeway and run parallel with a tall bank of over-size stones at the eastern end of the Chesil Bank. The stones get progressively smaller until, near Abbotsbury, they are down to marble-size. The large ones, piled up almost into a wall here, are about as inviting as the abandoned quarries we will soon see. The bridge, incidentally, is over the lively channel into the Fleet, the long stretch of water inland of the Chesil Bank, over which there used to be a ferry. The Ferry Inn is still in business. Technically Portland isn't an island since it's anchored by Chesil Bank, though hardly anyone can walk on the shingle all the way via Abbotsbury.

Fortuneswell, the first place we come to, strikes us as particularly unwelcoming. Though it is overlooked by the forbidding Tudor Castle, we cannot help looking up to what may well be the least-appropriately sited of many blocks of flats that over the years I've felt should never have got past the planners. Highly obtrusive, it is huge, determined not to be missed. 'Quality built space in a superb waterside location,' says a notice. The developers will, correctly, say they have rescued a former naval building, that it looks better than it did, and that the apartments will fetch high prices. The estate agents will join in emphasising that the owners will be less interested in the external appearance than in the fantastic view they will command over the broad expanses of the manmade breakwater with its three gaps for shipping. One of the many pieces of drama enacted here was the sinking of the veteran (1899) *Hood* to prevent U-boats using the southern entry in World War Two.

Near the converted apartment block is the Weymouth & Portland National Sailing Academy, itself scarcely discreet while, at the time of our visit, work has just started on the redevelopment of Osprey Quay, a 600-berth marina with an extension with more facilities for yachtsmen. This furious activity is in preparation for the 2012 Olympic Games which will do much to put Portland on the map. From raised ground, the view of the races in the harbour will certainly be spectacular. A new main road will improve access to the island and that certainly is needed.

The Olympics are also giving a shot in the arm to Portland's traditional activity: selling its very self, its stone. 'It's brilliant,' says Andrew Jackson, manager of one of the two quarry companies: '350,000 to 400,000 tons this year and no end in sight.' Because of its workability, durability and appearance of the better grades, Portland Stone has been used around the world for centuries. Christopher Wren took delivery of over six million tons of it in London's rebuilding (including fifty churches) after the Great Fire. Buckingham Palace and the United Nations Building in New York are just two in the line-up of famous names using the stone. Wars have often increased demand: after World War Two, a batch of the very stone that had been set aside for Wren hundreds of years earlier was used to repair St Paul's, while the Cenotaph and thousands of headstones of soldiers graves are made of it. So were the navy-inspired breakwaters enclosing the harbour, Britain's largest manmade one: five million tons of it, much hewn by convicts. Most of Portland's older houses including the terraces awkward to modernise at Fortuneswell and the other villages have thick walls of the stone, the poorer grades which have a stark, yellow-greyish appearance. And other naval buildings, prisons on the island (Portland might be law-abiding, but its remoteness has long made it a good place to bang up offenders) and churches and chapels.

It is hard to get away from stone. We pass under an arch of the Merchants Railway, a standard-gauge line opened in 1826 (only the year after the pioneer Stockton & Darlington) built to bring stone down from the quarries 400ft above sea level past the prison to Castletown Pier. Water transport has always been preferred for long-distances, including into the heart of London. The railway passed the prison and, though normally only carrying stone, I tell Gareth that once visitors were allowed to use it on Sundays – the kind of useless information enthusiasts collect. I also explain that since the island stations were called 'Portland' and 'Easton', I'd assumed that Portland was an actual place as well as the island name. People would have to have walked from 'Portland' to their several villages.

Confusingly, the hilly northern end of the island is called Underhill and the flatter lower part, beyond a dividing hill, Tophill. The stone is mainly found at the extremity where the strata declines very gently until Portland Bill itself. This is an eerie not to mention windy spot. Cars are almost outnumbered by coaches full of people doing the rounds of 'attractions' where they can be left to explore and take refreshment. For me the interesting thing is actually to have made it to the Bill, for on clear mornings (the ones usually followed by rain), it could just be seen on the skyline from the third-floor clifftop flat I once had at Budleigh Salterton. I recall many an argument, most Budleigh folk adamantly decreeing I couldn't possibly see it which, at a lower level, they couldn't because of the earth's curvature.

Before starting our return journey, I pop to the toilet, where the urinal is awash with dead daddy-longlegs, a reminder perhaps that Portland (like the rest of Dorset's Jurassic Coast) has rich insect life and rare plants thriving with minimal competition on poor soil. Portland Bill eerie? It depends on your view, but bleak and windy certainly. Pausing only a couple of hours a day, the tides race past the island's tip at a wicked rate. Sailors give the Bill a clear berth.

On the way back, we pass many deserted quarries, Titwell converted into a small sculpture park, and several with special scientific interest because of their unique wildlife. Also a few large ones open such as a deep pit of Stone Firms Ltd near Southwell controlled by Andy Jackson where we peer down to what seem Lilliputian vehicles and men beavering away below.

I wouldn't consider even taking a holiday let alone living here, but the Portlanders we meet are happy people. 'With the sea all round what more could you want?' is a common theme when I speak to folk, most of whom have lived here all their lives. There are certainly few of the mainland's problems, even few overseas immigrants. 'I tell you, it's great.' says our quarry manager friend. 'Sea, good sunshine, pure air, companionship. We'll never move.' And when I question him about the stone extraction, he assures me the supply is endless.

The locals are proud to be hosting the Olympic watersports, but fear that the new luxury accommodation might bring in too many outsiders, who have never been really welcome. Thomas Hardy, who set his *Well Beloved* here and drew the island into other novels, called it the Island of Slingers after the way the locals used slings to aim stones at would-be invaders. Because of its similarities with that other naval stronghold, Hardy also called it the Gibraltar of the North.

Surrounded by sea, like fishermen, many natives still have superstitions. Don't mention rabbits; it's unlucky. They can be referred to as bunnies or underground mutton, never rabbits. This may have arisen centuries ago from quarry workers spotting the things before a rock fall. Certainly if a rabbit were seen in a quarry, until recent times the quarrymen downed tools. If that seems a bit primitive, as perhaps does the island as a whole, amenities are by no means lacking. That is clear from just looking and listening, but confirmed in a roundabout way when at a mini-market with a news-stand I ask the girl at the till if there's a local paper.

'Only the evening one,' she says. No local weekly?

'No. Nothing. Oh, a free monthly, but we don't stock it because everyone gets it delivered free.' She's just destroyed her last copy and cannot remember its address so, proffering a pound coin, I ask if she'll kindly post me a copy of the next issue when she's done with it.

When it arrives, it turns out to be the thickest, most prosperous community magazine or newsletter I've yet seen, eighty A4 pages. It could well have won our £1,000 annual competition (whose final winner we met in the North Yorkshire Moors) we've had to abandon for lack of entries. There are dozens of pages of advertisements, including many for local events and eating places. Nearly all the ads are of Portland enterprises; there is obviously keen support for local business.

Surely there's enough advertising to support an island weekly. Papers indeed still serve populations of Portland's size and smaller, even where there isn't such geographical separation. The owner-editor, Jan Davey, tells me how it began.

'The evening *Dorset Echo* used to be everything to us, but blotted its copybook when it said it wouldn't publish more protest letters about Weymouth Council's scheme to tip sewage into our beautiful bay. People felt as though their views were being suppressed, so my late husband who was a printer published a free news-sheet. It just grew from there. It's become a real business; you couldn't do the amount of work involved without it being profitable.'

Her husband was a stationer looking for somewhere to transfer to without wholesale competition when their eyes lighted on Portland. Though they were divorced some years before he died, it is still a family business, their son now setting the ads, quite a task. The printing is done by contract using the same people they employed. A dozen or so paperboys deliver most of the monthly 5,800 copies, while she covers outlying areas herself. 'People soon complain if their copy hasn't arrived.'

She's a mine of information on local topical themes. Portland has steadily recovered from being abandoned by the Royal Navy, the new marina will be a boon but again people are worried about what a rush of incomers might do to the island. A new experience is having lots of Poles, if only temporarily, working on the large block's conversion into flats. Local fishing prospers, but tensions are still strong between Underhill and Tophill, south and north of the dividing hill. And again:

'Everyone loves it here; it's good to be part of it.'

Personal Remoteness

Gareth and I however find ourselves loosening up as we cross the bridge back to the mainland – 'interesting but I'll not want to see it again' – knowing that once we've cleared Weymouth we can take a leisurely cross-country journey back to Bath. Gareth might have preferred seeing more of the Jurassic Coast but, for better or worse, Portland was high up my shopping list and he's used to following the work.

However, we've only gone a few miles toward Hardy's Egdon Heath when he asks if I could go back to an old bridge, closed since it has been replaced by the new road. When we alight and stand by it, a bollard blocking all but cycle traffic, I recall that a little time ago Sheila had requested a similar thing – at this exact spot.

The peaceful scene of river, arch of the old bridge, trees and irregular fields, instantly relaxes us. How often have I promised myself to spend more time gazing at inland moving water for, much though we love, indeed are anchored, by the sea, it isn't everything. This is personal remoteness which, if only you can park conveniently just off the road, doesn't take an age to work its spell. What matters in life? For us during the best minutes of our trip together, simply the way autumnal leaves fall off the trees, glide down to the river and are swept along by the current.

'Remember Favourite River?' asks Gareth. Yes indeed – evening picnics on a stone bank of the Dart. Only bird song and occasional leaping salmon splashing back into the water augmented the rhythmic sweet sound of the young, fast-flowing Dart. Come to think of it, that was when the family could be guaranteed to be at one wrapped up in private solitude.

· XXI ·

TO THE DIFFERENT WORLD OF THE WESTERN ISLES

Common Themes and Problems

Most Britons who travel at all in their home country, at least once in a lifetime, experience a touch of the Hebrides: the Inner ones such as Mull and Skye. Many fewer venture further west into the very different world or worlds of the Outer Hebrides. Today they are usually called the Western Isles though, outside Scotland, many people still know them better by their old name.

If there is a single part of Britain I hope more discerning people might visit as the result of reading this book, it would be these islands. Today with only a single short ferry crossing, it is a 140-mile drive from the northern tip of Lewis to Eriskay.

It is truly a journey across the ocean for at high tide, even in fine weather, you are very conscious of salt water lapping the causeways. There are many scenic and cultural contrasts. Some parts are much more Gaelic speaking than others, while the extreme Protestantism in the north is replaced by ardent Roman Catholicism in the south. It was explained to me: 'Your religion is decided by where you happen to be born.'

Very individual though each island is, there are common themes. The small farms or crofts barely supported the population even in ordinary times. The Napoleonic Wars brought a brief period of prosperity. When vital minerals for manufacturers became harder to obtain from overseas, huge quantities of kelp (seaweed) were burned, the ash providing an alternative source. Though seaweed still has commercial uses, after the Battle of Waterloo, that market collapsed – just as the population had expanded to an unviable danger point.

Then came the potato blight of the 1840s, when emigration scarcely balanced births. Next, the powerful landlords realised their estates could run more profitably with sheep, needing few people to tend them. Humans were an unnecessary commodity. The harshness of the Clearances, when thousands of thatched cottages were set alight or demolished, knew no bounds. The poor people worked closely together to make the best of damnable circumstances.

Memories of those grim times remain a strong part of oral tradition, and to this day there is still an exceptional closeness among the sparse, generally much-reduced island populations.

Another common theme is the islands versus the rest of Britain. On the one hand the great wilderness areas are seen by outsiders as the perfect place for wind turbines or (in the case of Harris) a mega stone quarry. On the other, farmers have the preservation of rarities foisted upon them. They feel that when species (for instance, corncrake, choughs and Britain's rarest bumblebee, the great yellow) have been carelessly lost elsewhere, it is hard to be expected to down tools to save the rest. On a mini-scale, it is the same as the 'civilised' West saying that developing countries should not clear their forests because they are the only major ones surviving. Certainly the islands have rich and in many ways unique wildlife, whose guarding leads to much conflict, but also attracts substantial numbers of bird lovers and specialist naturalists.

The islanders are deeply attached to their land, always have an eye on the sea, have deep emotional involvement with song and poetry, and produce wonderful craftswork. It is to be expected we will meet real personalities.

Two other common themes could be noted: more estates will probably sell freeholds to their tenants, some of whom are already holding their breath; and the difficulty of attracting more women to the isles to help balance the population and stimulate activity.

Our Route via Skye

So I wake up in Nairn, excited that for the third, and probably last, time I am going to make the journey down the length of the main islands. For Sheila, it will be a first.

We could fly from nearby Inverness to Stornoway in Lewis, the only real town on the entire chain, or even to Benbecula. But they don't like renting cars to the over seventies and, because the Western Isles are notorious for their rapid weather changes, Sheila has announced she wants to take everything but the kitchen sink. The 4x4 anyway comes into its own on such rare major Scottish trips; normally it does less mileage than Little Car kept in Bath.

So off we go, via Inverness and Dingwall, stopping to pick up sandwiches at what used to be a filling station but, like so many others in rural areas, has succumbed to commercial pressures. The catering side happily continues. I am familiar with every bend in the road, and know the exact point at which the road and famous Skye Railway to Kyle of Lochalsh start running alongside each other. In its early days, the railway carried fishing boats (in competition with the Caledonian Canal), offering a quick and safe switch from east to west coast or vice versa.

We follow the railway virtually all the way to Kyle of Lochalsh, and then cross over the sea to Skye, by the bridge now – after a monumental political battle – free of tolls.

Raasay and Portree

The journey through Skye isn't brisk, but the glimpses of the majestic Cuillins to the left and Raasay to the right keep us alert. Seeing a ferry crossing to Raasay whets our appetite for a visit we are going to pay on our return.

We pause in Portree, Skye's capital, where today a vibrant European market is being held in the central square. With Skye prospering from a wave of incomers, and the town itself growing rapidly, there are enough good shops to give Sheila a breath of retail therapy before withdrawal symptoms inevitable strike on the outer islands. Anyway, we always seem to buy all our rainwear and stout shoes here.

Then we eat our sandwiches with that lovely view of cottages in the harbour area in their pastel colours reminiscent of Mull's Tobermory. Oh, I miss the MacBraynes steamer that overnighted here before making its daily round trip to Raasay, Kyle of Lochalsh and Mallaig, where it connected with West Highland Railway trains. The smooth sail between Kyle and Mallaig, Skye one side and mainland the other, was especially precious. Then few people arrived by car; the main road was a single-track lane with occasional passing places. To be sure, we couldn't then do what we are doing today, but there was something very special about the old ship with sheep and cattle, mail and cargo in profusion but plentiful passenger space with separate restaurants for the two classes. Today we're all in a hurry, but we have lost much of the pleasure of more leisurely days.

Uig and the Ferry

We head north and west again, back on North West Skye's Trotternish Peninsula featured in *Journey*. We pause to take in the sunbathed almost circular Uig Bay before checking in at the ferry queue.

The roll-on, roll-off ferry has a complicated rota. Sometimes it goes to Tarbert on Harris (our destination today) and others to Lochmaddy on

North Uist (from which we plan to return). There are also still occasional Tarbert-Lochmaddy runs completing the triangle, though we will use the popular new, shorter route between Harris and North Uist.

The last time I was here, boarding the then pioneer roll-on, roll-off ferry gave a sense of occasion. You could still rent a cabin with beds even for a day crossing. Now everything is everyday. Bog standard. There's now not a single cabin in the entire MacBrayne fleet. Once out of their cars and up the stairs, people go straight to the formal seating, the bar or the self-service restaurant.

One moment we are stationary, the next moving at a fair lick. With the new faster vessel, it takes only a little over an hour and a half, with land in sight throughout. While visitors abound in Skye, few are making this journey. Locals and lorry drivers exchange the latest gossip. 'It will be good to be back where I belong,' says (or intones in her soft voice) a young freckled ginger-haired woman. 'It's just too busy over there,' which I take to mean Skye, Scotland, Britain, Europe, the lot. If you regard the pace of life in Harris as normal, everywhere else must indeed seem out of sync.

It is a fantastic rocky approach to Harris. As we thread between many craggy islands, we have a fine view of a particularly barren part of southern Harris to the left. If we knew exactly at what angle to look, we could see Plocrapool which we will visit when we return to Harris after the trip around Lewis. To the right, when visible between outcrops, is the large island of Scalpay with signs of new building along the main road. Scalpay's economy has been transformed since it was connected to the mainland by causeway. Throughout Scottish island groups, the chief island is always Mainland.

Gradually the sea narrows until the only place left to go is Tarbert pier. Tarbert means a narrow piece of land between two waters, in this case both long sea lochs. Indeed if the sea level continues to rise, the connection might have to be by causeway.

The uninitiated assume this is where Harris and Lewis join, but Harris extends considerably northward: its mountains, across which there is only one through road, provide the boundary. Both islands have some of the oldest rocks in Europe, but while earthless, bare rock (plus the lochs of trapped water) account for most of the surface of Harris, Lewis generally has a softer appearance, many of its hills gently hummocky, and there is a large flattish northern area deeply covered in peat.

Driving onto an island is a thrill of a very particular kind. On the last land before America, we are full of curiosity. Every minute brings fresh thoughts. Have you noticed how journeys out to islands always seem longer than the return?

Ardhasaig

One is used to leaving a ferry terminal in a queue but, despite Tarbert being minute, the traffic gets thicker and then we are delayed by parked vehicles. It is the day of Tarbert's Agricultural Show, 'the day of the year'. We are brought to a prolonged stop by the field in which it is all happening. There are joyous shrieks from the kids, people milling round blethering away, with a general carnival atmosphere presided over by the master-of-ceremonies or whatever they call him on the echoing tannoy. If only we could be there.

In a strange kind of way we do become part of it, for someone we are to meet later at Plocrapool, mentioned for the second time in this chapter, is with great acclaim, declared the island's Glamorous Granny. Later we will tease her about the award – whose popularity emphasises the respect accorded older people on the Western Isles.

Having crossed the Minch, we are now running alongside Loch A Siar, an inlet of the Atlantic, until we see a petrol station, where we have been told to turn left. The Ardhasaig House Hotel is in a hollow immediately beneath us. It proves a great choice; so much so that at the end of her very first night on the Western Isles Sheila announces she wants to come back 'soon'.

One is quickly reminded that things are different here. Many of the people aren't a bit like you expect them to be or accord in the least to first impressions. 'I'm the only one who cooks,' says the owner, Katie Macaskill. 'Though the girls cut the carrots'.

She looks far too young to have spent a dozen years in a bank in Stornoway before opening the hotel in 2004. We are not surprised to hear that the building was already in the family, for family ramifications are famously involved in these parts. It was self-catering flats when she took over and added a sixth bedroom. Nothing unusual in that, and our bedroom, the only one available when we booked, isn't large. At first, too, the meal arrangements feel a tad regimented. But perfection. Absolute perfection. We have never anywhere had a more imaginative meal of absolutely first class ingredients.

'I love setting high standards with different kinds of cooking; it is my passion,' she says. Ingredients are sourced seriously, the chief supplier being in Glasgow. Spain, Italy and France are all part of the supply chain. Fish is local; if there are good langoustines, the fisherman phones to make a deal while still out at sea.

'It is a serious commitment. From April to November, it's 6am to midnight.' The staff are all local girls; Jenny, who serves us dinner, is a psychology student at Glasgow. They are an enthusiastic bunch, as indeed are the guests. 'Marvellous place,' says an Englishman of the hotel.

St Kilda

The Englishman has just returned from a twelve hour trip to St Kilda with two Japanese visitors. They look distinctly the worse for wear but are determined to make the most of their last dinner. The owner of the twelve-seater boat phones at the crack of dawn to say if conditions are 'fit' for anyone wanting to go that day.

Says the Englishman: 'The boat is a bit primitive. The toilet, such as it is, involves going outside. It's hard not to feel sick if not actually being so, but how else do you get to enjoy the magic of St Kilda unless going on one of those occasional over-priced cruises which land too many people at once?' He waxes eloquent: 'Getting there is an ordeal, but arriving is unforgettable. Hirta, the largest island with the village (evacuated in 1930 after more than 2,000 years of human struggle), was shrouded in fog which suddenly lifted – and there it was: the semi-circular ring of high peaks surrounding the village street and cottages and the almost circular bay. Stunning. It must have been a harsh place to live.'

The ultimate in Remote Britain and a World Heritage site, St Kilda is somewhere we would love to go. However, apart from the fact that at the best of times Sheila is a poor sailor, and I scarcely relish the physical challenge, there is already a vast literature on St Kilda, its lifestyle, how men climbed the dangerous cliffs to catch the sea birds that were the staple diet, the daily 'Parliament' meeting of the working men to set parameters, and the way that the tradition of rubbing earth into the umbilical cord at birth caused frequent tetanus, effectively reducing the population. So much that it is hard to be original. Here is a quote from one book, Monica Weller's *Voyage to St Kilda:*

> We steamed directly to Village Bay on Hirta. It was a grand vision. The semi circular bay. The hundreds of beehive like cleits cluttering the hillside behind the clear remains of the village street. The strange skinny brown sheep dotted around the scene. The thousands of sea birds forming a skin over the protective cliffs either side of the bay. A scene virtually indescribable. But the faces of the intrepid travellers and the crew told the whole story. A seven hour sea trip had focused our thoughts. The excitement and fear. The sickness. The detailed discussions and expectations. All the emotions, so obviously different for each member of our party, had been smoothed into one of unified awe and amazement. Moments of silence. Eyes close to tears. Smiles of satisfaction.

What a life those hardy, self-reliant residents must have both enjoyed and endured. They had to be tough yet, in the isolation experienced in remote communities such as Tristan da Cunha (where older people still refuse to meet those off rare visiting cruise ships) they had low resistance to germs. Men paying occasional visits to other islands both succumbed to disease themselves and brought it back home. On several occasions, such as after smallpox and influenza outbreaks, the male population was especially hit and recovered only slowly.

I deeply regret not having gone when younger. The quality of light captured by many of the excellent Colin Baxter photographs, in his *St Kilda,* especially of the amphitheatre of Village Bay, has encouraged many more younger people to take the trip.

Rough Track, Super Breakfast and a Garage

After the fantastic dinner, all taken together, and still thinking of what life must have been like on St Kilda, we go exploring along a rough track past a pier where there is still active small-scale fishing, and under a serious hill, until it goes no further. We then climb to the top of modest Gob á Champa where the Atlantic air is as fresh as the view of sea, cliff and rocks.

Always in view is a tall gaunt chimney across the water at Bunavoneader. A well-known landmark, it is the desiccating chimney of works where whale meat was chopped up and dried. Built by Norwegians in 1895, the factory closed during World War One, but was reopened for a few years as part of grandiose short-lived schemes by Lord Leverhulme, discussed later. It stands as sinister memorial not only to failed enterprise but to the days when the sea's largest mammals, cruelly-harpooned, were dragged ashore here. But we quickly put those thoughts behind us and again lose ourselves in the majestic setting. As the sun sinks I find myself whistling 'The day thou gavest, Lord, is ended'.

The temperature also drops, so it is back to the hotel. Katie is still at work on view in her spotless kitchen. The girls, though, have finished the washing up and gone home. Who could resist the offer of a nightcap?

'I hate getting up so early when I've been working late seven days a week,' says Katie next morning. Before breakfast she has already checked her six cattle and forty sheep. Getting to the table on time and paying the bill may be a ritual, but don't for a moment think that breakfast is an anti-climax after dinner. It is better than any I rated for my *Breakfast Book* of many years ago. Readers who think porridge is just porridge should try Katie's.

Hardly anything in the Western Isles makes the national hotel and restaurant guides, but *Eating out; Places to eat in the Western Isles,* distributed locally, shows what a revolution there has been in recent decades. Then menus used to be spartan, once literally a choice between lamb or mutton. I recall a lively debate on their relative merits: 'Not the same thing at all.' There is also an excellent leaflet on the *Outer Hebrides Speciality Food Trail,* showing how much better today's self-caterers are served.

Our fuel being low, and with a Lewis Sabbath ahead, we call at the petrol station where somehow they know where we've been staying. It's in the same family, of course; and it isn't just a petrol station but a serious grocer, ironmonger, newsagent and offers a range of medicines, books, maps, cloth and clothing – all in a typical island unhurried friendly way. Surprise, we end up buying much more that the fuel and sandwiches we intended.

To Lewis

And now we have a formidable drive. Close examination of the Ordnance Survey sheet No 13 makes one dizzy. Between pinkish areas where crazy contours are packed in tightly, are others where blue water dominates. As the crow flies (if it *could* keep straight flight through the mountains) we are going to spend tonight little more than twenty miles away. By the only road it is a real slog. It indeed involves going off OS 13. We have to take the main road to Stornoway for all but its final five miles. At least it is now something like a road much of the way, and a decent lane the rest. In the 1950s one's hand was constantly on the gear lever, frequently having to go into reverse.

The scenery, especially above long Loch Seaforth with its own mini-mountainous Seaforth Island, is incomparable with anything English. Later on, for miles we pass scattered housing, settlement after settlement. Land fit to build on is so scarce that few homes are more than a stone's throw from the road. On the mainland, it would be called ribbon development, but here it has its own curious attraction: Look: a shop – and a bus stop!

· XXII ·

CONTRASTS IN LEWIS

The Callanish Stones

Going west across the island, we gobble up the miles on an almost straight and only gently undulating road through open featureless country where there is bitter opposition to erecting dozens of wind turbines. Surely, the argument goes – and I find it hard to disagree – we need to retain some areas that are just nothing.

This is the land of peat, still worked for fuel, but less intensively than before. Years ago, at the eastern end, Stornoway people combined a holiday in a glorified hut (many with personal embellishments) with harvesting their peat for the coming winter. I find myself curiously resentful that there are far fewer such holiday homes today. Wherever one goes, eccentricities are on their way out. But then again I love open nothingness.

'It will be good to get there,' says Sheila at the road junction at Garynahine. But the sun is out, and we are now only a couple of miles from the Callanish Standing Stones, the one sight nobody visiting Lewis should miss. We'll see them now without threat of rain, giving us a second possible viewing after the weekend.

I had never heard of their existence when first driving past on a misty evening in the 1960s, when they could be seen faintly from the main road which then passed closely by. I recall getting my camera out to walk up to them when a passing motorist hooted and said I should leave it behind as I'd be bound to waste film in the poor light... a hangover from the days of austerity when waste was universally despised. As it happens a shot of the Stones looked mystical.

The greater thrill then was seeing the Stones themselves: the Stonehenge of the north without the restrictions already imposed on Salisbury Plain. Pure magic. Nobody else around. No car park, boundary fence or even notice to tell visitors what they were. Ancient, prehistoric obviously, and almost certainly related to spiritual ritual involving the sun and/or the stars.

I don't know that after this visit we will be much wiser, but I thoroughly approve of the tactful way in which today's far greater number of visitors are handled by Historic Scotland. The small car park is tucked under a slope, as are the visitors' centre and toilets. There is an unobtrusive gravel walk up to the Stones, where one can commune with them and what they stand for, and – without distraction – reflect on our own place in the universe. Among a dozen or so people walking peacefully around the Stones, only one loud American needs to be given a wide berth as she says what it reminds her of back home.

First impressions, even on repeat visits, are always telling. What power, what organisation and effort, and what astronomical understanding must have been poured into the creation of the central circle and the rows of stones forming a cross beyond. One is a steadily widening avenue between stones. What majesty: the tallest stones stretch towards the sky dwarfing humans. The great central monolith almost touches the sky. If nothing were known of the background, thousands would still make the pilgrimage to this lonely spot on the west coast of the largest of the Western Isles.

But what we are told is also fascinating. The Stones were probably laid out 5,000 years ago, that is about 3000BC, when there was an active cult religion supported by agricultural prosperity. The climate was better; cereals were grown abundantly. Much has survived not only around Callanish but at a variety of neighbouring satellite sites because, when the climate deteriorated, everything was covered in deep peat.

That was about 800BC: 'Look at the landscape and think of between 150 and 200 generations of continuous farming and worship before Christ was born,' says Historic Scotland's official souvenir guide. The importance of the Stones was recognised at the beginning of modern times. Then peat, well over a yard deep, was removed from above what once was and is now again ground level. Elsewhere, many secrets are still hidden beneath the peat, for boundaries of the prehistoric field system are below today's water level. The guide tells us that the main site is 'a cross-shaped setting, centred on a ring of stones containing a central monolith and a small chambered cairn'. Eleven satellites sites are listed; a splendid aerial photograph shows many of them, as well as remains of 19th century field systems.

Clearly there was a connection between the Stone's remarkable setting in the landscape and astronomical events. One special point to remember: 'Every 18.6 years, viewed from the main avenue, the moon dances low over the hills to the south, sets, and then gleams bright within the silhouette of the stone circle as it passes a notch in the horizon.'

Personally that is all I want to know, for the splendour and the imagination it sets free can only be compromised by mathematical formulae.

'Stupendous,' says Sheila as reluctantly we return to the visitors' centre. That the café is better than those at most tourist attractions is no doubt because it is not under such pressure. Though I might hark back to the days when you just found the Stones and walked in without any tourist artefacts, you are still very much an individual. The unhurried staff have time to discuss the well-prepared dishes.

A family at the next table have also been studying the guide book. 'I'll never forget Callanish,' says the father.

'You're out of date, Dad,' corrects his daughter. 'It is pronounced Calanais without the h. It's Gaelic and that's how it is going to be spelt on the next Ordnance Survey. Magnus Magnusson says so here.' So we found he does, in his introduction, adding 'And a good thing too'.

'Maybe,' says Dad. 'But when they take down the familiar spelling from signposts and leave us to find our way with unrecognisable and unpronounceable names, I wonder if they want us here at all.' Also true. Where does one draw the line? I still use the familiar Callanish, but that won't please the Gaels.

While we are cogitating that, the mum has picked up the guide and puts her oar in. 'Anyway, however it is spelt, they say it should be pronounced Kalanish with the h.' At which point we decide it is time to resume our journey.

Great Bernera

And what a journey. Beyond the junction with the way we came, at Garynahine, we are on a wandering road, improved here and there, climbing hills but threading between their tops, veering to avoid fresh water lochs and rivers. It is generally not at peace with itself. As happens almost wherever we travel in Remote Britain, we wish we had time to shoot up the admittedly few side roads – especially for me to pay a repeat visit and introduce Sheila to the bridge to Great Bernera. Once on the island, the road splits into half a dozen routes, each of which offers treasure. The bridge was built in 1953, after the islanders had threatened to dynamite a hillside to do the job themselves.

Bernera people have a history of action. A monument in the form of a cairn by the bridge records how, in 1874, local crofters began the process of attaining legal rights. Some 150 of them marched to the castle at Stornaway to protest about the eviction notices served on fifty six families. Typically the owner of Lewis, Sir James Matheson, said it was up to his factor. The protest had actually been peaceful, but three men were still brought to trial. Though they little realised it, their case was to change history. They were found not guilty, the eviction notices were withdrawn and – greatest achievement – the factor replaced.

Greater Bernara is full of interest. There is a famous lobster fishery, innumerable fresh lochs and inlets of the sea and very scattered townships. It probably has Scotland's smallest Post Office, a tiny hut doubling as community shop for essentials. We read that it has just been entered in a new Post Office competition for the most innovative branch; among those it will compete against are a Post Office at the back of a church and one in a pub, both these examples being in Orkney.

Should you run out of interest on Great Bernera, for the sailor at least there are outlying islands starting with Little Bernera. While Great may have seen its population halve, Little (though once it produced corn) hasn't been home to anyone for more than a century. Further out to sea are the Flannans, best known for the 1900 disappearance of its three lighthouse keepers, a mystery which has never been fathomed.

To Timsgarry

We continue to turn this way and that, wondering how great is the proportion of Scotland's land area covered by fresh water compared with the all-British less than a single per cent. But when we reach the southern tip of Little Loch Roag, that is salt water, part of the West Coast's safest harbour system. At that point we turn sharply from a westerly to a northerly direction, running beside Little Loch Roag for some miles before going through a grim glen made even less charming by the spoilations of man. At its end we are almost at our destination: Timsgarry, where my helpful publisher told us there is an hotel whose situation and food make it doubly worth staying at.

With little other sign of habitation, we call at the shop. As we have seen, people in these parts are used to having to fight for themselves. When the commercial one closed a few years ago, folk clubbed together to form this Community Shop and Post Office.

'It works,' says the manager Elaine Newton, adding: 'Most of the staff are locals, part-time, but paid the minimum wage. A great advantage is that the Co-op supports us. We're allowed to order from them and get good prices.' But there are items like luxury chocolate you wouldn't find in a typical Co-op. Tomorrow being Sunday, when the hotel will be closed for lunch and there will be nowhere else open, we arm ourselves with more provisions than we really need, plus local reading matter. The shop deserves supporting.

Guest House, not Hotel

Elaine gives us directions to Baile-na-Cille: over a cattle grid down a steep track. We see it beside a great bay with backcloth of humpy mountains. The tide is out, exposing acres of silver sand. But tight against what we call the hotel and its garden, there is a serpentine channel of deep blue water still flowing out to the distant sea. Bright sun brings out the colours sharply.

Because of the shape, and other cars and a boat, parking arrangements aren't easy; and when we walk in we discover the place is empty. Then we see a scrawled note advising us of our bedroom. 'Not very smart' is possibly a kind description; it is obviously much lived in as a family home. It is higgledy-piggledy and, though by no means dirty, certainly doesn't sparkle as do many classy Scottish hotels.

When he returns in early evening after a day on the boat, the owner, Richard Gillin, disabuses us. 'We're not a hotel. If you run a hotel, you have to put up with whoever decides to stay. We're a guest house, and if I don't like somebody, I can tell them to leave.' Guests, we discover, are to obey rules, notably all tumbling into the dining room sharply at mealtimes. It is not always convenient to serve dinner at all. Breakfast time depends on what the boss is planning for the day. It is scarcely your normal up-market set-up. It closes each autumn so that Richard and his wife Joanna, who flies helicopters, (there are many aeronautical books and artefacts) can spend a couple of months in America.

They fell in love with Baile-na-Cille on their 1980 honeymoon. The building began as the manse for a now-closed church; we have what was the priest's bedroom. It was a run-down bed-and-breakfast when the Gillins took over; in their early years they worked closely with the founder of Scarista House in Harris, the pioneer light of good food on the then dark Western Isles.

Now, the compensation: the food is as exquisite as the view. Both much appreciated by the other guests, who find it all very companionable. Dinner delightfully ends with perfectly-timed soufflés ready to accept orange and apricot sauces.

Sunday is another bright day. We walk locally soaking in more of the view from different angles and exploring the not-very-tidy garden, only taking the car for a short spin to the end of the road at Brenish. The cars we pass going the other way are all Continental: four German and one (furiously driven) French. As meaningless an observation as I am sure are many so-called surveys.

There's wonderful cliff scenery; but what really surprises us is the amount of new homes being built, and one or two older ones being extended. If the population is increasing even this modest amount at the end of what is a cul-de-sac all the way from the junction near the Callanish Standing Stones, themselves pretty remote, what hope is there of preserving tranquillity in crowded southern England?

For all its eccentricity, we love Baile-na-Cille, and after an early final breakfast (Sir has to go to town, and since he's a great chef we all oblige by being punctual) we leave more relaxed than we arrived. 'A hotel I'd like to come back to' says Sheila. 'Guest house,' I correct her.

Stornoway, Island Capital

I used to think that Stornoway, the only piece of real urban development on the Western Isles, was more like a rural slum than a town. Certainly it has had its problems. My earlier visits bring back memories of uncomfortable hotels and the bookshop that was often closed because the owner was what is referred to in the Highlands and Islands as being 'under the weather'. A consultant friend recalled that, when he was an intern at the hospital, because the ambulance driver was thus incapacitated, he had himself to drive to the west coast to pick up a patient with suspected acute appendicitis. Having helped wheel the patient on a bed into the operating theatre, he returned (now in his gown) to see him jump up protesting: 'I'll not be operated on by the ambulance driver.'

Another suspect thing was the bribability of officials. While presenting an early publishing proposition to a member of the council staff I had invited to dinner, he interrupted: 'Don't bother with more details; this fine dinner is enough to get my support.'

More recent memories are of reading about the plight of the Western Isles Council, and plea for government help, after it had foolishly borrowed from one bank to lend back to another at a higher rate. Higher rate comes with risk. The second bank went notoriously bust. And as we were planning this visit, the local Health Board was in crisis, with almost daily news of intrigue and members resigning. A couple of weeks ago, the Scottish Health Minister and two others paying a special visit to discuss the problems were locked out of a meeting they had travelled specially to attend. They waited in vain in gale and drizzle for the door of the Health Board's HQ to be unlocked. The latest troubles are that the Arnish fabrication yard, one of the largest employers, is about to go bust, while the airport is closed for the controller's meal time as there is no relief. Among those diverted? The Scottish First Minister coming to discuss the provision of more reliable transport.

But either my memory was wrong, or in the twenty plus years since I was last here, Stornoway has pulled itself up. Though booze and drugs are a real problem, the town presents itself as a friendly, well-ordered place, as visits to today's Baltic Bookshop, and rival outlet selling books, Hebridean Jewellery, quickly confirm. Though small, with a population of only 600, it's a real town: island capital, admin and commercial centre, with solid buildings.

Its situation is stunning. The road out to the airport first passes a large park around the castle – gifted to the town by Lord Leverhulme (featured later) – and then skirts the picturesque inner harbour before turning back on itself to go along the outer harbour with great sea views. Entering the great natural harbour is a relief for passengers thrown about in a storm across the Minch. Not long ago, unable to turn into the harbour, the ferry from Ullapool was driven into the wild Atlantic where crew and passengers were frightened and sick.

The spacious new terminal for the twice-daily service is one of many improvements of recent years. On the harbourside, we pause in admiration at a recently-created life-size bronze of a fisher-girl gutting herrings, a reminder of the days when up to 600 sailing vessels of the herring fleet would be crowded in for a few weeks before the herrings and the girls moved on. (Stornoway Amenity Trust's *The Herring Girls in Stornoway: A lifestyle gone but not forgotten* brings those harsh but colourful days back to life in words and pictures.) Over the years the harbour has given employment to many but also seen great sadness; storms have wrecked countless ships.

Though facilities may now be over generous, all kinds of cargoes are handled. This afternoon tenders are ferrying in passengers from a visiting cruise ship, the 11,162 ton *Calzopos* whose last call was Invergordon; had we been home we would have seen her passage in and out of the Cromarty Firth.

'What's the thing to do now we've got here?' asks an American irritably.

'What's the shopping like?' asks her friend.

They will certainly be welcome by shopkeepers. Though it is sunny, the breeze is likely to drive the visitors indoors. Then we overhear a snatch of conversation between someone just landed and a local. 'Say, is it really cold here even in the summer?'

The reply: 'We don't get really hot weather here. It's like this most of the time, pleasant for people, not too warm. Those who need heat go to the Mediterranean.'

That reminds us that we're running out of time to meet Eve Evans, who runs a B&B at Gress on the east coast a few miles north of Stornoway. We occasionally meet her in Nairn to which she is hoping to move... if only she can sell her house. Western Isles prices are low, even in the Stornoway area. That is one reason why mainland retired people trading down are helping stem the population decline. But even when offered cheaply, traditional homes like Eve's are slow to move. When eventually I apologise to her for not being able to see her as planned, she explains: 'Life's good here in many ways, but I don't feel I can face another winter like this year's. The storms were unbelievable, one after the other; frightening. You feel so trapped. And it would be nice to have it a bit warmer.'

Sauntering up and down the main street, we see several of today's few fishing trawlers tied up by the castle in the park across the water: a pretty picture, but we wonder how long they have been there. The town's architectural heritage owes much to former fishing prosperity; the old bank buildings are particularly fine. Among the shops, we notice that The Iron Lady offers a superior pressing service Mondays to Fridays from noon. A florist delivers fresh flowers throughout the island daily. (I recall that in the past flowers had to be ordered from Inverness.) A house agent offers houses from £40,000 and a new bungalow at £45,000, but crofts which until recently sold for £500 now fetch £60,000 to £70,000. That is because under the latest change in crofting law (a croft is sometimes described as a parcel of land wrapped up in legislation) it is easier to sell them as building land. Then, in this town of unwholesome food, we see a café's menu: Chips, Chip Butty, Cheeky Chips (small chips plus a sausage), Chips & Gravy, Chips & Gravy with Curry, Cheeseburger & Chips, Chickenburger & Chips. Not much else. But a hotel which was pretty rough when I stayed in it forty years ago has been smartened up.

Then back to our hotel where incidentally, during a bar lunch, we watched the gardener still persecuted by midges though dressed up as though going to the front line. Come early in the season to avoid being bitten. The hotel, a newish, standard business one, is far better than any used to be anywhere on the island.

Voice of the Island

Dinner guest isn't a council official but Francis Thompson, who I've known since planning his *Harris and Lewis* in the David & Charles 'Islands' series. First published in 1968, it was reprinted several times as Francis wrote further titles for the series. It is good to see that several including *Harris and Lewis* are back in print, in an edition making good use of colour.

A gentle person, Francis (or Frank as he likes to be called) is kind and helpful. He lives and breathes his islands, especially Lewis. Incomers are changing the nature of life, he says. Yet the locals are rock solid in their beliefs. As elsewhere in Lewis, the Free Church attracts the largest support – greater than the Church of Scotland. But the splinter Free Church Continuing also has considerable support in some areas. He explains the complexity of divisions in the Presbyterian Church, The Wee Frees, the arch-defenders of the Sabbath, are the Free Presbyterians. Throughout Lewis, everything in playgrounds is routinely locked up on Sundays.

Lewis still has a slaughterhouse, but it only opens in the autumn. The Norwegians have taken over the fish industry whose processing works on Scalpay employs forty while Oban's is finished. Traditional Harris Tweed, is fighting a losing battle. The 850 weavers of the mid-1960s is down to between 100 and 200 [now fewer, see note in square brackets next chapter]. But 'progress' means there's vastly more housing in Stornoway and surrounding areas, especially on the Eye Peninsular beyond the airport to the east. Stornoway is no longer 'quite its own place' as it was in the days of isolation when many genuinely thought it was the best town in the world except possibly Dublin. But it has had its share of disasters, notably the loss of 205 men returning from war service in the 1918 wreck of *Iolair* on rocks just outside the harbour. Virtually every island family was affected.

Talking more personally, Frank is surprised that his *Harris and Lewis* has sold only marginally better than *The Uists and Barra*. Before he came to dinner, he spent the day as a guide on a coach tour for visitors off the cruise liner. He reminds me that he used to teach electronic engineering at Stornoway College. But we're quickly back to talking about Lewis and its harsh history, especially the days at the end of the 19th century when most crofters only survived on destitution relief. Families were large and the land couldn't support them.

The harsh environment, with high unemployment persisting till this day, or the isolation in the long winters, or tragic shipwrecks? Which was responsible for the melancholia suffered by many in their mid-life? Let us end by quoting his book which in a passage includes its own quote:

> Today, the island folk are reputed to be gloomy with a black, depressive attitude towards life. The editor of the *Stornoway Gazette* has pointed out: 'We cannot understand a people and why they act as they do unless we know the content of their memories. We cannot understand the paradox of the naturally gay in heart seeking religious consolation in a grim and gritty Calvinism. We cannot understand why Lewis, which clothes the world in colourful tweeds, clothes most of the women in nothing but black. The young have found the island a much more kindly place. They have never been forced

by circumstances to choose between predestination and despair.'

To take account of matters beyond the material level is inherent in the Gaelic Celt. Celtic poetry and song, legend and folklore, all so alive with fancy and so sympathetic towards the things of nature, reflect the inborn sensitivity and character of the present-day Highlander and Islander. Fiction's caricature of the island-dweller (not only in Harris and Lewis, but in the other islands) has been taken by another society with a different cultural background, with insufficient knowledge of historical facts, as being virtually authentic. The Western Isles have had more than their share of 'observers' who have failed to penetrate to the inner Gael. Only with a knowledge of the background, social, cultural, ethnic, historical and so on, can the 'larger than life' islander be seen in perspective – as a normal human being.

Back to the West

With last night's conversation and that quote very much in mind we start across a largely uninhabited, plain peat land – only enlivened by yellow ragwort growing out of control here as in most of Britain – on a journey of 30 miles to the far north west. 'No wind factory on Lewis' demands a placard. I've already commented on that, but I've been set thinking again. To outsiders, the wide open area might seem an ideal choice for green energy. But does everywhere have to be 'used'?

Then I read the Bishop of Argyle and the Isles, The Rt Rev Martin Shaw, saying that local feelings have been 'effectively sidelined'. It was frightening to imagine the 181 turbines planned between Stornoway and the end of the road at Barvas. 'We must cherish and protect the wild and unspoilt places. It would be disparaging to lose the moorland which gives the people of Lewis a constant reminder of what there is to lose in the natural world. This awe-inspiring moorland has a unique light and atmosphere, created by its place being on the edge of the North Atlantic.' Hard to disagree with the Bishop over that.

At Barvas, we replenish our diesel and turn right onto one of the most extraordinary roads in Britain. Running a mile or so from the coast, and with occasional glimpses of the open Atlantic, it passes through innumerable scattered settlements, some with housing stretching towards the sea. These townships may be isolated, but we are told that people, indigenous and in-comers, happily pull together. Certainly churches play an important role; curious, we pause to check which particular denomination is most popular. The buildings of the Continuing Free Church, sometimes spoken of as the 'Free Church, Continuing', seem well-together (and have large car parks). So for that matter is the majority of the housing, new buildings often being beside old abandoned ones, though about a quarter of old homes are totally abandoned, their ground taken over by a neighbour.

The land of this coastal strip isn't as useless as that of the first part of today's journey, but neither is it first class. In what was once classified as a Congested District, large and largely destitute families were crowded in with inadequate protection for themselves and their crops against the constant onslaught of Atlantic gales. Today we see small groups of sheep, which don't need much attention but are not very profitable, on some of the narrow green strips between houses.

Years ago I took the not very good road from Stornoway up the east coast past Gress to where it peters out, beyond which the ragged cliffs are inaccessible. If this is the east coast (the east being the more tame on almost all islands) what must the north west extremity be like, I wondered, thinking of the mainland's north western extremity at wild, unpopulated Cape Wrath.

I suppose that at some point I must have consulted the map; indeed, often waiting in the car in the West Country, I studied details of all island road systems. Yet somehow the image of desolation has remained with me, so this morning, in virgin territory, I am amazed that, as we head to the Port of Ness, there is a complicated road system supporting what seems like a town-like population.

The Butt of Lewis

Taking a left turn, we pass Lionel School currently with 106 pupils, sixty four primary, forty two secondary up to second year only, and a super website. (In all Lewis there are 2,708 pupils in state schools, out of a total of 3,891 in the whole island chain.) Next, we park at an inviting café with interesting crafts for sale. This is Eoropie Tea Room. No sooner have we sat down than we are joined by a young man who has just alighted off a bus from Stornoway.

Astonishingly, in this remote corner there are eight such buses a day, though some only come off the main road by request. All over Harris and Lewis there are buses of many different hues; hardly anywhere is without a service. Details are included of a daily service from the Port of Ness to Eriskay slipway, the long north-to-south journey we will be starting after lunch.

By mainland standards, the Local Community Transport Schemes co-ordinated by the Council, who publish a joint timetable with every kind of information you could wish, is just too sensible. There are excellent bus shelters too. We have all become so used to public transport not actually serving the public with goodwill and common sense. When bus co-ordination can be done so well, it is a shame that so many people in more populated rural areas suffer unnecessarily. In many ways – like helping your neighbours – the rest of the country could learn from Remote Britain.

We walk to the Butt of Lewis, a majestic headland projecting both west and north. Naturally, there is a lighthouse on the tip: built high above the grey rocks, incongruously it is in red brick. Many whales have been seen rounding the cliffs, as of course many ships do, though giving the rocks a wide berth. Even during our visit the perspective is constantly changing. We wonder if the lighthouse keepers who manned the light until it went automatic in 1988 fully appreciated their kaleidoscopic outlook.

Even this, we have to remind ourselves, isn't actually the final piece of Britain. The sizeable island of Rona is stuck 44 miles NNE off the Butt. Continuously inhabited for 700 years, and with good growing land, it was given a chapel by St Ronan (don't ask for definitive biographical detail) in the 8th century. In 1680 there was a contented population of five families. A year later, thanks to rats from a ship invading and eating all the food and the only bull being stolen by visiting seamen, all were dead – not realised until a party from St Kilda (100 miles away) were wrecked there. It took them seven months to build a boat out of driftwood and alert the mainland.

Fresh people went out to Rona: the last two to live on this outpost were found dead in 1885. However, the fleeces of sheep are still harvested there in summer, and it is possible to arrange a boat to see the ruins of what is one of the three oldest known buildings of the Celtic church. These details come from Hamish Haswell-Smith's *The Scottish Islands: A Comprehensive Guide to Every Scottish Island* – a substantial and truly fascinating work.

On our walk back to the car, still enjoying the cliffs, by the one large bay we pass (and photograph) the young Englishman who had got off the bus and joined us at the café. He is Chris Bavostock. 'The transport is fantastic,' he says, 'though you need to get your head around the possibilities. I worked out today's programme at my B&B at Gress last night.'

'Would you be staying with Eve Evans?' I ask him.

'How do you know?'

We didn't, but there won't be many B&Bs in Gress. We send Eve a greeting for this evening, which we later hear was well received.

Next we head to the Port of Ness, but only go a few yards before stopping at an intriguing gateway to a long green path through croft land leading to what the OS indicates is an ancient monument (restored). The fascinating website of Teampall Mholuaidh (or St Moluag's Episcopal Church) says: 'This small and ancient church has a plethora of legends and traditions associated with it, making it one of the most important mysterious sites on the Isle of Lewis.' It probably dates from the 16th century with some of the legends suggesting earlier foundations. Having fallen into ruin in the 19th century, it was restored in 1912. Open between Easter Day and October, it attracts visitors from around the world. It has no heat or light, so a different chapel is used for services at other times.

Especially enduring among many traditions is the church's power as a place of healing. In 1630, it was said that those who couldn't come themselves 'were to cut out the portion of their lame arms or legs in wood with the form of their sores and wounds thereof and send them to the saint where I have seen them lying on the altar of the chapel'. Later, it was especially those with mental problems who came to be cured. After they had walked seven times round the building and drunk from St Ronan's Well they had to go to sleep in the church for the cure to be effective.

This is only one of several old chapels in the area and there are many other ancient remains. Probably the Vikings consolidated themselves here early, and more local names have Norse origins than elsewhere. But then the Vikings were said to have tried towing the land back to Norway. When pulled the towrope lurched which broke the land into its different islands.

The Port of Ness

Opened in the 1930s, the pretty harbour at Port of Ness immediately suffered from being clogged by sand driven north and west around the Butt of Lewis. Though it could seldom operate smoothly as a fishing port, it is the traditional starting point for those setting out for Rona. Last year it was cleared of the accumulated sand of generations, exposing the original slipway – for how long, local residents are watching with interest.

Historically best known for the skills of its seamen, and once boat building, the Port of Ness offers a surprising range of interests for the visitor. There is a heritage centre, an arts and music centre, galleries and a welcoming inn. No doubt many who journey to this remote corner are surprised to find so much, and those early in the season must delight in the thrift matting the clifftops and abundance of colourful flowers on patches of machair, the highly fertile sandbuilt areas just inland from beaches and sand dunes especially those facing into the prevailing wind.

We are attracted by Callicvol, a small centre offering various activities.

It is a useful contact point for the Book Trust, which encourages research on the islands and also publishes a growing list of island titles.

Its private collection of Scottish and especially Scottish island books has been described as 'the best in its field put together by an individual'. It belongs to Michael Robson, who greets us. 'I started collecting books on Scotland when I was still at school, I wanted to share what I have with others to encourage interest in our history. Most who use it are visitors including academics rather than local people, but some of the residents come on the trips I lead to islands for the Book Trust.' (We're already on an island but, as in other island groups, the largest landmass is seen as the mainland.)

Upstairs his wife, Janet, exudes enthusiasm, running a large quilting exhibition; there are imaginative, even fantastic, designs, many drawing inspiration from the local scene. There are also quilts of very original designs for sale.

'Welcome back,' says the tearoom owner when we return for lunch. 'You know I only opened nine weeks ago. Hope to open year-round, but will see. We only moved here from Derby seven years ago. 'Escaped to give us a better life.'

Before eating, our fancy is taken by a simple impressionist painting of the Callanish Stones. It is somehow more spiritual, not to mention cheaper, than the grander ones we saw when actually there. It hangs in our bedroom over one of two prehistoric houses we saw on Orkney's Papa Westray (see page 348). In pencil and watercolour, it is the work of the Elderberry Craft Club and cost us £30. As we see for ourselves time and again touring the islands, art is very much an everyday accessible thing.

Then we briefly return to the Port of Ness to start our journey down the island chain.

· XXIII ·

SOUTH TO HARRIS

Two Tweed Mills and a Black House Village

The direct journey from Port of Ness down the island chain to the slipway for the Barra Ferry on Eriskay may be only 140 miles, but it is hard to imagine many doing it without stops or deviations. By the time we get to that slipway we will have driven over twice as far, around 300 miles and enjoyed ourselves immensely.

We rapidly retrace our route to the road junction at Barvas, beyond which we continue paralleling the coast. Between Barvas and the Callanish Standing Stones, the coastal strip is rich in prehistoric and other remains, among the more recent being several preserved settlements of black houses. It is also a traditional area for Harris Tweed, woven into the islands' culture. It is said to have started in 1846 when Lady Dunmore, widow of the Earl of Dunmore, asked Harris weavers to copy the Murray tartan in rich Tweed.

The 'congested district' still supports quite a population. We enjoy some of the side roads leading down to the sea or terminating shy of it. A couple run alongside fresh water lochs. Their ends offer a wide range of sea and cliff scenery including sandy coves. One road, taken at random, leads us to Shawbost; we stop at Carnan Mill. It has a very sad feel to it, obviously having seen better days. Trying to find someone to talk to, I notice a big range of rolls of Harris Tweed, lovely bright designs, being sold off at knock-down prices.

Eventually I'm led to the manager, Derek Murray. He is not a happy man, for the mill will soon be closed. 'We had sixty five workers here till recently. There are only twenty five left, but we are still in trade,' he says, describing the show-case exhibition in Paris where they will soon make a presentation.

'We're remote and transport and fuel costs have overtaken us, not to mention cut-price competition from China where they pay workers a bowl of rice. The industry itself won't die in my time, but it is becoming a small niche business, totally dependent on design.'

Apart from the mill we will visit later this afternoon, there is only one major manufacturer, the KM Mill in Stornoway. [It was sold to an English company a few weeks later.] When in a few months, the last workers are given their cards, the remaining production will go to Stornoway. 'They call it progress,' says Derek Murray. I think of all the mills (paper, textile, leather and others) I wrote about as a young journalist which have closed, some turned into housing or converted to tourist attractions. Somehow I doubt that this ungracious mill will attract people as does the nearby 'Click' mill, the last in working order of a type once common in the Western Isles. The millstone clicks when turned by a waterwheel on a vertical axis. [A year later, after the new owner of the KM Mill in Stornoway cut back on its range of patterns and rejected orders for others, hope was suddenly revived for private mills. The mill at Shawbost reopened and has done well. Then the large Stornoway mill was closed putting many out of work in favour of jackets produced in China. 'Once again, people come here, feed us a pile of rubbish, saying one thing and then doing another,' a newspaper headline said quoting a representative of the weavers condemning the action.]

Then we go down to the end of the road overlooking a sandy bay and a thin semi-circle strip of shingle separating salt water from a fresh water loch – an area otters are often seen if you wait patiently for longer than we have today.

After the dying mill, the abandoned village of black houses we visit next seems light relief. It is hard, though, not to share the suffering there must have been when the last group of them was forcibly abandoned, well within living memory. Humans, animals and barn were under a single thatched roof with a hole to let out the smoke. It was economical and, until well after World War Two, few would have thought it curious – leave alone imagining that the black houses along this coast would one day attract tourists.

The cycle of abandonment, restoration and tourist attraction seems ever shorter. Though some are now improved as holiday cottages, I feel I'm still invading the privacy of the cottagers peering in. Even by immediate post-war standards, the black houses were primitive, but people were content, the community spirit great. At Gearrannan, the last people were moved into council housing in 1974. OK, the cottages couldn't be left abandoned indefinitely, and one can hardly expect restoration not to be followed quickly by use. A notice says:

> Today you might not meet anyone else on the way, but let your mind go back to a time when cattle and sheep were herded, peat was cut and mills and stills were kept busy with grain from the crofts. People have lived their lives in this area for a thousand years and more.

Take a walk through history as you enjoy the rugged beauty surrounding you.

There is an oval bay beyond the village, with great cliff walks on either side. That to the north passes the site of a pair of promontory forts, while further on at Dalmore, after a big storm in 1982, a Bronze Age settlement was discovered. Ancient burial grounds abound along the coast.

At Carloway Mills, we have an appointment with the manager, Stephen Mackay. Embarrassment: he's away on a medical appointment. It shall be revealed: we experienced more difficulty with appointments being kept in the Western Isles than all the travel undertaken for *Journey*. The relaxed lifestyle? Yes, but sometimes geography, for medical appointments and business meetings mean long, sometimes unpredictably long trips. And twice my failure to grasp sufficient geographical detail led to my being made to feel foolish. Well, you do if you invite someone for a quick dinner and are told it would involve a long drive on both sides of an hour's ferry crossing. I can perhaps blame that particular instance on dyslexia, for similar looking Gaelic names were confused.

So Stephen's wife, shows us round buildings, obviously less used than formerly but still with reasonable activity. 'We're the only privately-owned mill outside the Stornoway company: a bit of a struggle, but we survive on our designs.' They are truly vibrant. Sheila examines several longingly.

When I catch up with Stephen later, he says that making the cloth from yarn (spun by homeworkers) starts in January and usually finishes around mid-summer. Earlier this year it was down to part-time operation, but business has picked up. The industry is obviously in a much reduced state than thirty years ago when the Harris Tweed Association commissioned David & Charles to produce a book about it.

'Everything was different then,' says Stephen. 'And not just Harris Tweed. Crofting paid: now it is only £10 or £12 a lamb; most people have given it up and taken jobs. Then we used to be snowed in two weeks a year; now it's two days. But there are more storms. People hear about them in the weather forecasts and pity us. But those who settle here never want to leave. It's an excellent place to bring up children. Yes, the January storms were unbelievable, but they are still the exception. It's a brilliant place to be, but jobs aren't easy. There used to be a large fishery here, but that's gone, too. Crofting is finished, and back at the mill we have to compete against Marks & Spencer's improved tailoring, Edinburgh Woollen Mill's knock down prices, and of course China. Yet people still love our designs.'

The loss of this mill would cause widespread disruption. For one thing, virtually all the local voluntary firemen work in it. May it thrive. But Carloway has been used to being hurt and somehow people still smile. Despite high unemployment and the need for many to work away from home, it is very much today's place. From the head of Loch Carloway we explore its extent and, among other roads, we take that leading in to the somewhat rough Pentland Road. [The Harris Tweed industry is continually in the news with further developments. As mentioned in the last chapter, eventually I gave up on attempts to include later details.]

Railway to Carloway

'At least you won't be able to write about railways,' a friend said when hearing we were exploring the islands. Wrong. We drive a short distance onto the Pentland Road, whose other end indeed we skirted on our way into Stornoway yesterday. It was laid out to take trains. In the mid-1890s, the Pentland Railway was planned as a cheap Light Railway providing an almost straight route across a featureless landscape from Stornoway to Carloway. Carloway's prosperity suddenly declined with its fishing trade just as Light Railways were losing their vogue. Lord Pentland had already sunk considerable capital into the project, so it wasn't totally abandoned but became a third-class road. Though theoretically the Pentland Road is the shortest way from Stornoway to the west coast, few people drive it, for it is narrow, rough, and pot-holed.

There would actually be enough railway history in the Scottish islands to fill a book. For instance, the abandonment of the Sanday Light Railway has just been announced. In its seven year existence on the remote northern Orkney off-island it has carried 25,000 passengers. Mull's short passenger-carrying line continues to offer a convenient way to visit a castle while, back in the Orkneys, on Hoy, hidden away from German eyes, there was a large base much of whose harbour standard-gauge trackwork survives. Raasay had an inclined mineral line and, as in the rest of Britain, there were small narrow-gauge systems adding charm to the quarries they served. And that is before one starts on grandiose schemes, especially in Skye, for lines whose first sod was never cut.

It is not far from Carloway to tonight's hotel, Doune Braes, on the road south wandering between hills and fresh water locks. After dinner we drive the short circuit through a scattered population to Tolsta Chaolais close to salt-water East Loch Roag, returning by the main road. This is the life. Despite the obvious disadvantages, no wonder people don't want to leave and new folk are being attracted. In such isolation, community facilities are vital and we hear of several village halls being rebuilt or upgraded.

It feels as though we have already been on holiday for weeks. Just before leaving home, I had a telephone call from a West Country writer saying that generally he has been happy when it is time to return from holidays, but that has never applied to Scottish ones whose ends he always hated.

In the morning we continue heading south, past more black houses at Callanish, where we take what will probably be our last-ever glance at the extraordinary standing stones. In my late-seventies, I cannot possibly return to everywhere I've enjoyed; it is not morbid to wonder if that's it while continuing to enjoy a rich library of memories.

Down through Harris

Then, having been to Stornoway and the Port of Ness, at the road junction at Garynahine we rejoin our original route from Harris. The return journey gives quite different views and combinations of light. So we say farewell to Lewis and slip down the Harris mountains to the outskirts of Tarbert, stopping again to refuel at the multi-purpose garage at Ardhasaig, overlooking the hotel where we spent our first night. We're recognised with 'How did you get on in Lewis?' as though it were a foreign land.

Not having bought a roll of tweed at Carloway Mills, Sheila is delighted to learn that the one she's settled on for a suit comes from there. It is measured out with confident precision by the man who has served us diesel and sold us sandwiches and newspapers. Katie from the hotel was in recently, so he even knows what tonight's menu will be, though by dinner time we'll be a lot further on.

We have decided to call on the Glamorous Granny we heard announced as we passed the agricultural show. That means taking the winding, up-and-down East Coast road, of which I have strong memories from 1968, the year that Francis Thompson's *Harris & Lewis* was published. On a particularly challenging piece of narrow trackway, I asked my daughter to look up something in the index. Just as I was about to crest a summit, being prepared to go sharp left, right or (unlikely) straight on, she replied: 'There isn't an index.' This was an advance copy from the binders. The text came to an even working of pages without the index, which was on a separate section. Had it been left out of the thousands of copies about to be distributed?

It took hours to telephone the binders, for the call had to be routed via a series of operators and, if any were engaged, 'Please try again' was said with resignation. Then one pressed Button B to get the advance minimum three-minute payment back. Older readers may recall the noise that made.

When eventually I did get through, the sacrifice of time proved worthwhile. The whole edition, packed and about to be despatched, was minus index. Every copy had to be unpacked, unjacketed and disbound. To this day, if I find a book without an index that should have one, I picture the harsh, rocky landscape overlooking a coast of rough-hewn complexity with scattered rocky isles which you could appreciate from the telephone kiosk – which happily nobody else came along to use.

Isolated though we now feel, the east coast of Harris was of special concern to the Congested Districts Board. There was little productive land to be shared out, and the few large sheep farmers were not about to reduce the size of their wandering herds. Many folk emigrated; fishing for herring was the only semi-reliable way of earning money, though scanty crofting provided a supplement for some.

Impossibly hostile though it seems, much fishing (especially shell fishing) holds its own along the coast. As in so many places, tourism has come to the rescue, while every year a few retired people from elsewhere who earlier fell in love with the rugged area move here. A scattering use computer skills to earn a living. And there is still sufficient demand for the traditional home-based production of Harris Tweed and retailing of Lewis-based tweed to fill a handful of mouths. One way and another, the economy is more diverse and probably livelier than ever, but the harsh landscape and the remoteness aren't for the faint hearted.

The Glamorous Granny

So we twist and turn along what is called the Golden Road, presumably because it was expensive to build. Though somewhat improved since the 1950s, it is still an adventure. When we reach Plocrapool, we discover Glamorous Granny, Katie Campbell, presiding in style over her second hand seventy-year-old loom in a glorified shed on the edge of the low cliff near her home. Her card offers weaving demonstrations (coach tours welcome), parking and toilets. Nowhere in the world will you find a loo with a more compulsive outlook of rocks and sea. (I spell Plocrapool as on my edition of the OS, but it has various spellings. On Katie's card it is Plockropool.)

Katie is as used to posing with feet and hands on the machine as was Marion (1909-1996), the subject of Gisela Vogler's *A Harris Way of Life*, which I have already read with fascination. Setting the scene, it tells us:

> By the turn of the 20th century crofting families in theHighlands were usually big... poverty was common, money was very scarce, but there

> was always plenty of food. Fish, `the main diet all the year, was eaten either fresh or salted, and was also rock-dried for winter provisions. Sheep were killed for special occasions like New Year so that there would be enough food for all those that called in and at the time of the Communions where many visitors were expected, and consumed fresh or salted mutton. On the east side of Harris with the poor grazing there, fishing went hand in hand with croft work, and became an important support contributing both food and cash.

Katie looks so like the Marion in the book that at first I assumed she was her daughter. Appearances as well as family ramifications run deep in the islands. In fact Marion was Katie's husband's aunt. For years they had their workplaces side by side. Their involvement began after Marion's father died in a fishing accident in a blizzard. From a young age Katie helped Marion. Then she and her husband, another fisherman but also with expertise in Harris Tweed, decided to set up their own business in 1967. Just as well since that is when herring suddenly disappeared.

As she uses both her feet and hands to add a few more rows in a variety of deep colours, I ask if it is skilled work.

'Not really. The skill is in picking the colour combinations: design is all important. Of course, it takes a while to set up a new design.'

Perhaps the real skill is in people management. She relishes hosting or conducting a works (or is it a shop) full of visitors, whether they are seeing her as a craftswoman, a survival of more colourful times, or seriously buying. There's no artificial modesty when (every few minutes) she is asked to pose for a snap. However, the title Glamour Granny makes her a touch bashful: 'I've fourteen grandchildren.' Two belong to her daughter, Katherine who, while her mum is being snapped over the loom, runs around answering queries and serving customers.

Among the customers is a lady from Georgia, who goes out of her way to tell us all that she's originally from New York. The 12oz crochet wool she buys seems to fill a substantial bag. Ruth Grant from Lumsden in Aberdeenshire, is writing about the political background of the survival of the Roman Catholics in post-Reformation Scotland (1560-1600). 'A very interesting subject that's not been researched.'

Everyone learns everyone's business. A van driver delivering a heap of Harris Tweed jackets joins in and wants to know why I'm writing in a notebook. I ask Katherine, who has her own loom in a separate room, if she and her mother ever quarrel. Mother answers first: 'When stocks get low she's at me to produce more.'

'We only argue about colours; I like really bright ones,' says Katherine, who is obviously determined to make a go of the business. Making cloth

– 660 threads including stronger ones for the edges and up to 90 yards long – on a traditional hand loom is obviously slow. But Katie deprecates the double width introduced in the factories to increase productivity when Harris Tweed first met stiff competition. 'It's too wide.'

Even during our visit the takings mount up. The cloth and small items made on the premises are obviously popular, but much is bought in and then sold, including jackets and a colourful piece which could be a hanging or a wrap. We fancy it to hang over our bed. Katherine lovingly wraps it.

It was made in the small village of Drinishader which we passed through immediately before reaching Plocrapool. ' It was only the second thing I ever made,' Yvonne Roberts told me later. 'Because I was a beginner, it's actually acrylic, though I do them in Harris Tweed now and you'd hardly know the difference.' It depicts the sandy bay at Scarista where we are staying for the next few nights. Originally from Huddersfield, Yvonne says that sadly they are thinking of returning to the mainland.

'We love it here and had hoped to settle. There are two problems. My husband has to work out of doors in all weathers; if only he could get a workshop, just a garage; that would probably keep us both here. The other thing is health. Harris is good in many ways. Education, for example, is fine. But the NHS isn't always. I've a bad back and, though there's a small hospital in Tarbert, it usually means Stornoway. That wouldn't be too bad if you could get appointments and they were kept. The last time I saw the specialist from Inverness he said he wouldn't be coming any more. If we had to leave, we'd be very upset.'

Lord Leverhulme's Legacy

We continue turning and twisting, rising and sinking, with bare rock growing out of many inland lochs and white horses on the crazily indented coast emphasising that this is not a naturally hospitable part of the world. Yet there is considerable evidence of recent building. 'People will do a lot for a view,' says Sheila. So they will. There are ample signs of civilised living. Cars parked in drives are certainly not those of down-and-outs. And there's another isolated but posh shop selling a wide selection of tweeds and crafts.

After a particularly crazy piece of road, at the minute settlement of Ardvey (where a tidal pool that must have once have worked a mill is indicated on the OS), we turn right for a splendid drive across to the west coast. We go along the shore of several lochs and around the tightly-packed contours of mountains whose bottoms are more rounded than their irregular dizzy heights. That brings us to the coast at Leverburgh, not where they made the early soap flakes and washing powders but named after the man who did.

The story of Lord Leverhulme's connections with the islands is involved. He bought Lewis in 1918, and embarked on an ambitious plan to improve Stornoway and its harbour to benefit the local population and supply his MacFisheries, which also operated from several established mainland ports and (as older readers will recall) eventually had branches throughout the land. He also set about dividing large farms into smaller units for crofters. Then, always impetuous, he decided to pull out of Lewis to move into even poorer Harris. As a parting gift, the Lewis crofters had title to their land, while Stornoway's castle and grounds were made over to the town.

In Harris, the small port of Obbe was transformed and renamed Leverburgh (though the small harbour is still shown as Obbe). Unlike Stornoway, it lacked a natural harbour. One had to be blasted out. Quays, fish processing plant, a tweed mill and even roads were part of the master rejuvenation plan. It all came to an abrupt end when Leverhulme died after a visit to the Congo. That was 1925. His estate cut and ran, a mere £5,000 being raised from the sale of all scrap at Leverburgh. There is no tall chimney here such as we saw from Ardhasaig (last chapter) but one permanent improvement remains in daily use – the blasted out deep harbour which serves the new roll-on-roll-off ferry to Berneray we will be using in a few days.

From whatever angle, physical or psychological, Leverburgh is odd. We will pass it several times in the next few days, and never without a thought about what Lord Leverhulme achieved in many ways, and how much more might have happened had he been more at peace with himself and of course lived longer. While to this day his name is greatly respected in Lewis, the memory passed down as part of the folklore of Harris is how money was wasted and everything stopped. That perhaps suits the Harris outlook, for through the ages help from outside has seldom proved reliable – and didn't the very thing named after it – Harris Tweed – get stolen by Lewis.

Scarista

Now driving north, we turn inland to cut off the small, hilly peninsula jutting out into the Atlantic terminating with Toe Head – and there is the magnificent sandy beach at Scarista. I've soaked up this view before when staying at Scarista House in its original ownership yet, however sharply you conjure up an image from memory, when you come back a great landscape always exceeds expectation. The large, empty sandy beach, has a deep pool even at low tide next to the peninsular, while coast and islands (especially Taransay of which more later) add their own brilliant touches in the sharp sunshine.

Judging by the cars scattered around outside, and the correct English-speak in the dining room, Scarista House is still an establishment place. It is the only Lewis/Harris hotel in the *AA Guide*. It has good if unusual rooms and the food served by friendly local girls in the twin dining rooms is as perfect as ever: limited choice, superb cooking, informal atmosphere. A delighted honeymoon couple say they are next going to a luxury hotel near Nairn; they will find that a lot more formal.

Our only use of the car next day is a morning trip to Leverburgh and back. Deserted industrial place it might be but, even as mourners crowd into a church, one of the several denominations of Presbyterianism, in the sunshine everything looks great. The warm welcome accorded the gent in front of me and to me at the Post Office is followed by both our pensions being refused. The first gent can't understand it at all. Having made two attempts, I recall that I've been using the security code of another card. If I try again, it might unleash yet another attempt to persuade me to have the pension paid direct into my bank.

Says the assistant, still smiling: 'They're doing everything they can to kill Post Offices. But will you be all right; can you manage dear?' In another shop window there is a notice saying that the long-awaited bridge to Scalpay will soon be open; it was – nine years ago. A vintage Classique coach passes with another load of visitors touring in style. And at one of those far-between but diverse shops, we buy a paper, book, sandwiches, medicine and have coffee in its upstairs café, looking out at a man peacefully sitting in a boat parked on an oval tidal inlet.

Bill Lawson's Race Against Time

Half way back to Scarista, then to the Old Schoolhouse Exhibition Centre in Northton to meet one of those remarkable people who creatively and sensibly exploit an idea perhaps only possible in remote areas with development grants. Bill Lawson, who taught law for a long period in a varied career, first came to Harris as a teenage backpacker. While on the mainland he was troubled that, as older folk died, it became harder to piece together genealogies and knowledge of how people used to live and work. He taught himself Gaelic and in 1981 became project leader of an EU-funded programme, allowing him to develop the Old School as an exhibition centre and base for various activities, including his research and writing.

He's a veritable one-man industry. His website gives a hint: 'Books, genealogy research, events and walks,' it begins, listing titles published and a further half dozen in preparation. Yet, he tells me:

'I don't see myself as a writer. What drives me is oral traditions. There's a great temptation among those looking back on different ages to concentrate on artefacts and to write distilled history, everything put in English. What concerns me are the *people,* the folk who lived in past ages, different conditions with hopes and fears quite unlike ours – what it was like for them, how they related to the landscape, the crofts, the islands now without any humans left. I learnt Gaelic because I wanted to tap into the great oral tradition before it was too late. You could say I'm running a race against time. Though I'll never retire, my great hope is that others will follow with other ideas – including the history of individual crofts – when I have to leave off.'

In enthusiastic flow, he adds: 'Not all historians like oral input, perhaps because it is more likely to be accurate than written history and contradicts favourite theories. But it is "hands on"; it brings things to life. But then of course you want to put it in permanent form, and that means writing.

And when you hear what went on in the impoverished islands, nothing surprises you. Census and church records help. We can now date much back accurately to 1750, and know for example that the peak time for infant mortality was 1890 in Lewis and 1911 in Harris. In Victorian times, a couple would have six or seven kids most of whom lived to become parents, each with eight kids of their own. The register of deaths decreases dramatically in the late 1850s, which is the time that population pressure was beginning to be eased by emigration.'

That word emigration conveys strong meaning. In the centre's exhibition hall, large panels with maps of eastern Canada and the United States show the exact spots in which locals settled. Thereafter what happened in Canada and America had more local relevance than goings on in mainland Britain.

Many of the panels are poignant, a common theme being how islanders helped each other in adversity with inadequate resources. Help from churches was varied but vital; many forced to leave were given assisted passages.

In many ways resources are still scarce today, and we're impressed with the way the Old School has been adapted to serve different purposes. For example, the exhibition panels are removable so that space can be created for concerts. There is a steady flow of visitors, undertaking research, looking at displays, buying books or just using the toilets.

One of the titles I buy is *The Isle of Taransay*. The actual Isle can be seen from the window. This is where a television series 'Castaway' first showed a group playing Robinson Crusoe. In common with many of Bill's books, this one is divided into episodes, most of which begin 'The year is...' The first episode is dated about AD300, when the climate was going through a bad patch and, short of land, mainland tribes were seeking pastures new. Watching out for attackers and hiding the women and cattle when a distant beacon was lit as a warning had become a well-rehearsed procedure. Episodes telling of ups and downs, surprisingly good times between awful ones, till we reach 'The year is 1971' and learn of the forced evacuation of the last three residents.

After a sandwich back at the hotel, we set out on foot still in glorious sunshine. It is a convoluted way to the great sandy beach, down a low cliff and over dunes held together by marram. We have to jump over a stream, running fast but disappearing into the sand long before it reaches the sea. The sand along this coast consists of shells finely ground by Atlantic gales. It is this rich sand, blown inland which feeds the highly-productive and, in the spring, colourful machair.

The whole place is ours: not another person for hours: pure magic as successive breaking waves throw up white spray adding to the colourful contrasts. Though it is hard to hear each other, the rhythmic sound is stirring.

Even the golf course is laid out on gentle-sloping machair and must be a picture when the flowers burst out in spring. Over a drink in the bar, each evening the contented visitors exchange details of their varied days of exploring an unknown land full of surprises. 'And it's still our own country,' says a very English man in a tartan kilt bought as a novelty this afternoon.

Rodel, Clearance and Church

My bedtime reading causes irritation. Bill Lawson's *Harris in History and Legend* can be thoroughly recommended apart from one detail. Not merely is there no index of places (there are good ones of people and themes) but chapter titles and running heads use Gaelic names. Stupid I may be, but I cannot get my head round Tarasaigs, Caol na Hearadh and na Baigh. So it is with difficulty that I find this piece about how in 1779 Captain Alexander MacLeod settled at Rodel at the southern tip of Harris.

> He was a different type of landowner: a businessman, much more interested in commerce than in the status of a clan chieftain. He had made his money as the captain of an East Indiaman clipper and set up fishing stations all along the east coast of the Bays and encouraged

fishermen to settle there:not just people from the machair but from all over the islands and the west coast of Scotland. He built piers and a net factory in Roghadal and, most important of all, he built himself a new house beside the pier, in one of the most beautiful spots on the whole island. To have a resident landlord, interested in making a success of a local industry, was a new experience for Harris. John Knox visited Roghadal on his tour of the Hebrides in 1786 and was full of praise for his work.

The success of Captain Alexander's schemes did not last; the tax laws were against them for a start. It is said that on one occasion a ship laden with salt had to land its cargo hurriedly at Roghadal because of bad weather. Salt at that time had to be checked for tax at Steornabhagh, and the excise insisted that the cargo be loaded again at Roghadal, taken to Steornabhagh, unloaded again there to be measured for tax, loaded again, brought back to Harris and unloaded once more! In any case, Captain Alexander found, like Lord Leverhulme a century and a half later, that you cannot rely on herring; for years you will get a good catch, and then suddenly, for no apparent reason, they disappear for a year or two.

As so often happens, Alexander's son and his son after him were not made the same. Edinburgh was the place for them. The grandson only visited Rodel once, and that was to plan emptying it. This is a piece of evidence given to the Napier Commission enquiring into crofting in 1883:

> I will tell you how Rodel was cleared. There were 150 hearths in Rodel. Forty of these paid rent. When young MacLeod came home with his newly-married wife to Rodel he went away to show his wife the place, and twenty of the women of Rodel came and met them, and danced a reel before them, so glad were they to see them. By the time the year was out – twelve months from that day – these twenty women were weeping and wailing; their houses being unroofed and their fires quenched by order of the estate.

Over the years I have read much about the infamous Clearances, but somehow it is only when you are actually on the ground and consider the thing in mini-scale does the sheer commercial audacity and cruelty sink in.

Next morning, a sun-soaked Rodel looks great: that is what is left of it. We will return in a moment to the large church we have just passed wondering how on earth it came to be built for so little habitation. Of course, it wasn't, for the land at Rodel had real soil, infinitely more productive than most of Harris. Over 150 families earned their living on it until it was stolen from them without mercy.

Another piece of evidence:

> I saw my mother with her youngest child taken out of the house in a blanket, and laid down at the side of a dyke, and the place pulled down. My mother was in child-bed at the time. The child was born only the previous night, and my father asked MacLeod, who was the proprietor at the time, whether he would not allow them to remain in the house for a few days, but permission was not given, only he came to the dykeside where she lay, and asked what this was, and when he was told, he asked him to lift her up and remove her to an empty barn.

Convincing though such evidence might sound to us, the Commissioner's effectiveness was blunted by the more polished presentations of how the powerful but utterly selfish landlords saw things.

Long ago, Rodel House, built for the good Alexander MacLeod, became a hotel but, apart from the bar, has been closed for years. We see how it has now been thoroughly upgraded for the new generation of discerning visitors.

So back to the church. The finest and most interesting building in all the Western Isles, it sits atop a small hill. Its impressively tall tower is built on an outcrop of rock at a higher level than the nave, choir and two transceptal aisles. The local stone glistens in the sun, while the imported decorated black schist which ornaments it, especially the tower, tell of hefty investment. After walking all round the outside with glorious views of Loch Rodel and of where so many people used to live and earn their livelihood, some of them buried in the churchyard (still in use), we are taken aback by what we see inside. It has long ceased to be an active church, so there's a spacious, empty stone floor, but what history and what wealth, and confidence in his privileged position on earth and in heaven Alasdair Crotach, eighth Chief of the MacLeods of Harris, must have had.

After the collapse of the Lordship of the Isles, the rival chiefs built themselves churches for their own burial rather than have their remains join those in the Lordship graveyard on Iona. Rodel was a natural choice for Alasdair Crotach. It had been picked by early Christians and before that by Pagans for their defensive look-out and rituals. Several standing stones can be seen from the churchyard. And when the chiefs of the MacLeods (whose badge is included in the tower's decoration) moved to Dunvegan on Skye, Rodel remained their ecclesiastical centre. Rough though it often was, the sea was the natural highway. Across it came the masons and the decorative stone from Mull, while the design was obviously partly inspired by Iona.

So we are drawn to Alasdair Crotach's tomb, built in 1528 though he lived for two further decades. The tomb and the archway of the wall into which it is recessed depict all human life and Christianity: a castle, bishop, Virgin and Child, St Clements to whom the church is dedicated, a galley under sail, hunting scene. There are six panels each with a pair of apostles, while the figure of Alasdair Crotach is clad in chainmail and holds a sword. At the head are lions, with a lizard or probably stylised greyhound at the foot. Says the inscription: 'This tomb was prepared by Lord Alexander son of William MacLeod Lord of Dunvegan in the year of our Lord 1528.'

Wow: there are more memorials and much more of interest, but this tomb says it all. Another visitor is now sharing the church with us, a German: 'This is my third summer visit to make sense of myself. I don't get time to think in Munich.'

After Rodel, we're back on the east coast Golden Road passing what they call the Bays heading north to the point at which our southerly direction ended on our way to Scarista. It is more of the same, up and down, sharp turns, through a bare rocky landscape with occasional views of the shredded coast of long bays littered with rocks and rocky islands. Harsh country, where only a handful of people lived on mini-crofts, most of their erratic living coming from fishing. 'Small places that kept three families in comfort where there are now eight,' was a comment after many Rodel people were dumped here, reducing all to subsistence level. Times are happily better now; we notice more new building.

At the junction at Ardvey, we turn west and follow the same mountain road across the island. It is not shown on the AA Large Scale Atlas which, like most, only includes the Western Isles on a smaller scale as a periphery oddity. As reception fails we cannot finish listening to Berlioz's *The Trojans* on Radio 3: hearing its first part will always conjure up visions of the Bays on the Golden Road where reception was crystal clear.

[As this went to press, Harris people voted 730 to 311 in favour of the island becoming Scotland's third National Park. Duncan MacPherson, the land manager for the community trust that owns most of the Gaelic-speaking Harris said that 300 people had died and just eighty seven had been born since 2001: 'A frightening loss of population, not sustainable. At that rate, in 30 years we will be down to 1,000 people.']

· XXIV ·

FOUR CAUSEWAYS AND A FERRY

Prince Charles's Berneray

Next day we wait in Leverburgh's vibrant quayside restaurant for the roll-on-roll-off ferry to Berneray. To the disgust of many in Lewis and Harris, it recently started a Sunday service; the first passengers were greeted with admonishing stickers and posters with biblical texts. Uist and Benbecula people welcome it since it makes possible Sunday afternoon visits to people in hospital at Stornoway.

The route is almost as indirect as the Golden Road. We thread through islands and rocks, the angle from which the sun shines constantly changing. It takes less than an hour, not much more than a third of the time of the former route (still with an occasional service) between Tarbert and Lochmaddy. Though we can occasionally see the open Atlantic, a variety of headlands, islands and rocks give considerable shelter.

We land on Berneray's east coast, at the harbour built in 1989, just ten years before the opening of the causeway to North Uist. Technically part of Harris, Berneray is now the only inhabited island in the Sound of Harris, but there are interesting historic sites on several of the others, and memories of how people from Pabbay and Berneray entered the same church through separate doors.

'It still has a small island feeling about it,' says Sheila as we begin to explore. 'Just one village shop.'

New, however, is the Historical Society and Information Centre. Ena, the woman in charge, says her uncle John 'started Bill Lawson off'. She adds: 'I'm against the causeway. We used to police ourselves; now we have to be politically correct and report to the police.' Most of the displays relate to the pre-causeway days, when 'you'd see Prince Charles playing cricket. You know, he was a regular visitor experiencing the island way, living as one of us.' The island accorded what must be rare royal privacy – as did the Queen's private charter of the *Hebridean Princess* for her first cruise since the Royal Yacht *Britannia* was laid up.

The neat little historical guide shows that Berneray's history follows familiar lines. Ancient sites abound especially on the west coast machair and on high cliffs at the wild north east. Though only three miles long by one and a half wide, there was once a population of 712, six times that of today. The end of the kelp industry after the Battle of Waterloo brought the first hardship; then a combination of the 1845 failure of the staple potatoes and the vicious Clearances. In 1845 a few were paid in food rather than properly employed to build what is still called Destitution Road. But in some respects Berneray has always been different. There is no peat (men used to go to other islands to cut their fuel), and inland from possibly the finest beaches in Britain there is a large fertile area.

We drive across it on a narrow concrete road with barley waving in the wind on either side. When we turn the car by a rough piece of ground, we hear the unmistakable rasping cry of the corncrake, a bird often heard but seldom seen. Once found as a summer visitor all over Britain, it is now only heard ('sightings' are counted by hearings of the males) on the islands and a few mainland extremities. The RSPB is running a concerted campaign to revive it, and today most island farmers do corncrake-friendly harvests, starting in the middle of a field and working outward.

Suddenly there's a nasty squall. Berneray is one of several islands which boasts you can enjoy all four seasons in a day. It is, incidentally, just half way between London and Iceland, and every few decades a great Atlantic storm actually changes the west coast's shape.

The Sea is all Islands; The Land all Water

The journey down through the islands linked by causeways is one that can only be appreciated by actually taking it. A detailed account of the route would quickly become a boring catalogue. My memories of doing it three times (though with more causeways adding extra islands to the string this time) are of the land and water never being quite where you expect them. As an old saying puts it, the sea is all islands, and the land all water.

Briefly, across the newish causeway to North Uist, where a notice warns that otters cross, one enters an entirely different land, even less cultivatable and prosperous than Harris. At times grim but never boring, it has fewer people and cars and hardly anything approaching even an embryo town. Sunshine, which I have always seemed to enjoy, obviously helps. So do surprising details, for instance the varying proportions of white and pink waterlilies now in full bloom in the more sheltered (or only just more sheltered corners of larger) freshwater lochs.

The first side trip we take, east to Cheese Bay, makes the point splendidly: salt water is full of islands, dozens of them, while, where salt water does not penetrate, fresh water fills much of the landscape.

Since we will have to come back to it later, we don't deviate for Lochmaddy but head west through an amazing terrain along a road being modernised: a painful business with short sections like a race track, others (controlled by lights) currently disturbed by the contractors, and others again still in their native (or near native) state as little more than undulating, winding trackways. Then it is south until we do an arc incorporating several different pieces of causeway, leaping from island to island including Grimsay with its own road system. We are warned of storm danger as well as otters. The causeways are much narrower than that from Berneray and the parapets have not been repaired since winter storms. At high tide on rough days, it must feel positively unsafe. There have been perpetual cries for improvements since three generations of a family were swept off to their deaths in a January storm on another causeway.

On Benbecula, the flat Dark Island, we take the loop round by the airport, where because of a strong military presence, there is the largest concentration of population and commercial activities on the southern islands. We watch a handful of passengers take the second and last daily flight to Glasgow. 'But we also have planes from Stornoway, and a daily one from Inverness,' says a counter clerk.

It is a simpler though still narrow causeway to South Uist. Before the causeways there were of course fords, with horses and carts, though poor people walked. That was only possible for an hour on either side of low tide, and many were drowned, either losing their way as the tide came in or because storms kept too much water in the deep channel for it to be safe to cross at all. Much else has been improved; where the old road has survived alongside a new stretch, it looks pitifully titchy. At one point we see three generations of road beside each other, the middle one soon being abandoned as not having been improved enough.

Though a series of mountains rise majestically to our east – the highest in truly isolated country over 2,000ft high – our journey through South Uist is mainly on fairly level ground inland from the wide band of machair, down the west coast which supports most of the population. Fascinating it remains, though not quite as unusual as it used to be. Among other things, there are fewer shrines, celebrating miraculous sightings and cures, though the Roman Catholic priest remains by far the most important person in most townships. Protestants are in a small minority, but there's never been sectarianism and all join in the calendar of social events which knit the scattered community together.

'People Say We Have Nothing Here, But...'

Changing to yet another OS map, at Daliburgh crossroads we turn left and pass our umpteenth loch (which we would also have done had we turned right or gone straight on) for the road to Lochboisdale. This seems even more dreary, not to mention run down, than on previous visits. I recall a soaking-wet Sunday spent almost entirely in the Lochboisdale Hotel, with the compensation of the good company of sports fishermen round a cosy fire and outstanding food, which of course fishermen and golfers demand. That is why so many Scottish hotels are good. Here the fishermen steadily disappeared, and the hotel went bankrupt.

This we only learn from the owner who (after we have waited at reception and looked all over the place for someone) shows us to our nicely-refurbished room looking down the rock-strewn sea loch. 'It had been closed for three years when I bought it – an enormous restoration challenge,' he says. He's not going to be helped by the fact that on a Saturday in high season there are few others staying. A two-day wedding still in progress is good news, though he could have done without a waitress getting drunk the first night.

With people shouting over a loud television football report, and the wedding party lolling over most seats, we opt for dinner in the adjoining conservatory. This surprises, if not puts out, the lass behind the counter. No effort is made to take our order, and I have to return to the bar and suffer another long wait as people endlessly need their glasses refilled. Then there's time to have leisurely consumed a four-course meal before any food arrives. It is scarcely edible. The only other couple who have insisted on a full meal say that no way will they eat here tomorrow. We arrange to book at another hotel, inland. Yet we feel guiltily sorry for the owner.

Long though we have been stuck at table, it is still broad daylight. Strolling up the sad street with run-down buildings, we are followed by two men from the bar. One is in a hurry and rushes on. The other holding a glass of beer announces: 'I know I'm drunk but I'm serious. People say we have nothing here, but we have everything here – the best place on earth.' He asks where we have been, and when we mention Lewis he adds:

'Father was the lighthouse keeper at the Butt of Lewis. I had to rush up every forty five minutes to turn the mechanism that shows the light. Now it's automatic; fine, except that if the electricity is off it doesn't reset itself. It was a well-known target; a Messerschmidt fired at the light. The Germans flew over here too. My son saw the ghost of a World War pilot with his peak cap.'

As though that's not enough entertainment, we enjoy the notices in several of the shops that have not given up the ghost, notably the butcher, and go down to the quay to see fishing boats come in, one after another, and unload the finest lobsters. Apart from a few sold on the quayside to those who have popped along in their cars to pay cash to the fisherman for a weekend treat, all are bound for France. Pity it isn't the night before we go home.

Finally to Eriskay

Next morning we return to the crossroads at Daliburgh and travel south to the end of the main road, at the attractive Pollachar Inn, where we think we might stop for Sunday lunch on our way back. We spend a few moments looking across to Eriskay, half a dozen uninhabited islands, some with sheep on them, and to the northern peninsular of Barra which was once cut off by a storm and certain to be so again as sea levels rise. Then east along the coast road to the longest of this journey's causeways to Eriskay. It was not opened until September 2002; there's another warning about otters.

Years ago I received a manuscript from an Eriskay MacBraynes captain. Though it was never quite publishable, we corresponded and on several occasions he phoned me, rousing my curiosity about what was then a very isolated island. Wondering if I could trace him, though not knowing his name, as we drive up a hill I decide to ask the first person we see.

'Oh, that was Angus Eddy MacInnes. He was my next door neighbour. He was a deep sea man before he went to MacBraynes. He didn't keep good health and he has died. So you were the publisher. Fancy that.' This as though it were confirmation that the publisher the captain talked about did actually exist. 'Eriskay used to be an island of seafarers. They earned a better living than had they stayed at home. MacInnes's brother is at sea but lives next door when home. I'm on a coastal fishing vessel, usually home. Next week I've got a great niece coming to live with me for a year. She's the relief teacher.'

Then without seeing another person we could have stopped to ask, we top the hill and drop down the other side to drive quickly to see the ferry waiting at its sheltered berth at the end of Eriskay's only safe bay.

This, then, near the bottom of our sixth island, is the end of the north to south journey on the road across the sea. It is the most extraordinary of all journeys of that kind of length in Britain. If only more Britons, even Scots, had an ambition to make it.

For a moment we are torn between keeping to plan and renewing our acquaintance with Barra for the afternoon, but watch the vessel leave with a handful of cars. We've more yet to see on Eriskay before we have to start going back part of the way we have come.

Eriskay

Eriskay is delightful, the areas served by roads much softer than a glance at the map suggests. There are grand vistas, and everywhere flowers and butterflies. The people are friendly... and talkative. They all seem to expect us to want to know their views on the causeway. 'Yes, we can escape now, even if there's a storm, but there isn't so much togetherness as when we only had each other to help,' says another former seaman we meet while gazing over to South Uist. 'Yes, many of us went to sea; it was the thing to do. Yes, the bosses knew that if you came from Eriskay you had a good tradition.'

We ask the way to the pub, The Politician. 'Everyone misses it,' says a man spending Sunday morning tending his neat garden, something you wouldn't expect to see in the Western Isles thirty years ago. 'You've passed it; can't miss it on your way back. So what do you think of the island? He's dying to tell us why he's here.

'When we lived on the Wirral this used to be our holiday cottage and we loved it. Upgrading it so we could be here always – that was tough. Everything eventually had to come on the small ferry. No way would we consider moving back. It's so friendly here.' That togetherness, I reflect, is a hang over from the harsher days of the lucky ones sleeping under the same roofs as their livestock and the less fortunate suffering hunger and illness before being forced off their island. To put it in perspective, for most of the lifetimes of my father and myself, five islands per decade have lost the last people living on them. Will things remain as friendly in better, less isolated times for those on the remaining inhabited islands?

There's certainly no evidence of lack of togetherness today for, as we park at The Politician, someone else asks where we're from and do we know the story of the ship the pub's named after. We do in part, especially that the islanders' helped themselves to whisky after the shipwreck that inspired Compton Mackenzie's *Whisky Galore*, a most enjoyable and remarkable tale.

'She was 7,900 tons, and I can tell you where best to see the point where she was wrecked. *Whisky Galore* makes it sound very innocent; none of its characters went to prison, but some of our people did. Like many others, I used to prefer whisky to milk even at breakfast.' We see him enjoying a wee dram while we have an enjoyable chatty lunch in the bar.

We are served by Joe Campbell who says his family own this and the Pollachar Inn (where we had originally thought of returning to for lunch). 'They're great locations. They look out on each other across the water.' I mention the late Captain MacInnes, my would-be author, and his neighbour.

'Now, there's an interesting situation. Did he tell you his great niece is coming to stay and him a lifelong bachelor? How they'll get on for a whole year... I don't know.'

He tells us about the various wrecks that have taken place around Eriskay. That of *The Politician* figures largely in the old newspapers and magazines on the walls.

'It was an accident that needn't have happened; the crew were saved. In 1944, that was, when whisky was scarce, so it was a godsend, though they were very harsh on those they picked as ring leaders.

Yes, the story is good for the pub's trade, but the film was made in Barra where Compton Mackenzie lived for a time. True, some of the crew were landed at Barra, some at South Uist, but the wreck really belongs to us.'

On our way back, we take the road to the north shore and walk up a hill to look across to the little island of Calvay, opposite Rosinish at Eriskay's north east tip, where *The Politician* suffered its fatal injury. Then back over the Sound of Eriskay by causeway with a bridge section through which the currents still pass. At the Pollachar Inn, a last glimpse of The Politician and further across the water to Barra, before returning to Lochboisdale, where the butcher is doing brisk business with Sunday newspapers.

Farewell to Lochboisdale

There is little Sunday observance on South Uist. Sunday boats have always been welcome and after we return from dinner we see people gather on the quay to see in the four-times-a-week ferry from Oban. Tonight only nine vehicles, mainly heavy lorries, roll off, many fewer than when I was last here, though more than the four including mine (which had to be swung off after being driven on to a net) when I first visited in the mid-1960s. Then we called at Tobermory, Tiree, Coll and Barra, long stops at each, giving time to stretch one's legs on land, even to go shopping. The days of such leisurely stopping services have long past. Tonight's ferry has just called at Barra's Castlebay, and then only for ten minutes. Now almost all goods are carried in heavy lorries which take moments to drive off. Over twelve hours on the ferry have been reduced to six and a half.

Happy memories linger of the more leisurely crossings, every meal of the day taken in the restaurant. But this traditional route from Oban is still long and expensive (over £100 for a car), and there is rejoicing that soon it will be switched to Mallaig, saving overall time and expense though meaning a longer road journey south. 'I reckon Lewis people will drive here to save going via Ullapool or Skye,' someone on the quayside says. Within fifteen minutes of arrival, the gangway is removed and the ship sleeps.

Next morning it takes slightly longer to bring her back to life. From our bedroom and then the dining room, we watch the crew board, followed by a few cars and vans and a handful of pedestrian passengers. The ferry leaves sharply at half past seven, taking a careful course through islands and rocks. Anyone going by train to Glasgow won't be there until gone half past nine tonight.

Soon we're off, too. Passing through North Lochboisdale, I recall that a neighbour, Col Charles Cameron, brother of the Camerons' clan chief, ran a business here that most of its life was known as Alginate Industries Ltd. Opened in 1935, and followed by factories in North Uist and Lewis, it revived commercial interest in seaweed, both rockweed and the tangle washed up on the shore, that had largely lain dormant since the collapse of the kelp industry over a century earlier.

Used in a variety of things from ice cream and orangeade to transparent foil and alginate yarn, the demand was specially strong in the final years of World War Two and the immediate aftermath. The tale is told that in 1945 the local collectors – paid piecemeal – weren't sufficiently active to sustain the factory's output. Air-dried weed had to be flown in from Ireland. Though there was no local resentment, the lesson was learned and thereafter South Uist folk collected the weed more assiduously.

'It was an interesting industry,' Col Cameron told me later, 'but we sold to the Americans in 1979, and things didn't work out with them. I left in 1980 and the Lochboisdale factory was closed in 1981. The others had already gone.'

Our first stop is outside the hotel at which we had enjoyed dinner with the other couple as refugees from our own hotel. We are intrigued by a mobile carpet showroom parked outside. We ask if we can look around: 'No problem, no rush here,' says John MacDonald beckoning us in.

'Plenty of time. When I'm out on the road for a week or more, some days there are no customers at all; others I have three new customers. It's worth it. I joke that they might be able to buy it cheaper from Littlewoods, but they won't get the choice on their doorstep.'

Fitted out just like a carpet showroom, and an offshoot of a Stornoway business, it is one of many niche services in the islands. He visits all settlements reachable by causeway. He must enjoy many experiences and insights to a very different way of life. He has spent the weekend in the comfort of the hotel (we noticed him at dinner) but shows us where he dosses down in the back of his cab when on the road.

North along the Machair

When it is possible, we stay off the main road and run close to the sea. How I'd hate to live out here! Especially for those of us who enjoy villages and small towns with a proper nucleus, it is a planning nightmare, the secret of course being that each home is on its own small plot of the fertile machair.

Sand dunes generally hide the sea; when we clamber over them, the beach looks like a battleground. Storms have dumped debris, from both sides of the Atlantic. Though some of the wide strip of rich machair is attractive, and will have been truly colourful with spring flowers until a few weeks ago, even beyond the sand dunes there's debris blown in by recent storms. Nobody seems to think of removing human detritus such as rusting cars. Piles of garbage ooze from black plastic sacks pulled to pieces by seagulls. There are numerous shallow fresh-water lochs, but they also attract yesterday's unwanteds, while houses – occupied and abandoned again with decaying remnants of cars and tractors – are scattered seemingly indiscriminately between patches of barley. At nowhere at all, there is a large, modern Roman Catholic church; it smells musty.

Modern bungalows, small barley plots, a few cattle, lochs, abandoned older houses and the remaining walls of others which have long lost their roofs, unsigned road junctions, occasional thistles, ragwort and other flowers (but again we're too late for the brilliant spring flowering), sheep, a statue on a pillar ('Our Lady of the Isles'), ... it goes on and on. Only in scale does it differ much from the townships of the rest of the islands and indeed parts of the mainland west coast, but in such a remote area frequently buffeted by storms, the very concept of everyone living on their own self-contained plot over such a wide area without a real centre sends the shudders down me.

No wonder anyone we stop to ask a question is delighted to share our company. Yet, I reflect, I'd prefer to live here than in featureless English suburbia where people are reluctant to greet each other. And though it is not much seen in the physical evidence of buildings, there is in fact a lively social life. Certainly there's more money than in the machair elsewhere. Which is bad news for the great yellow bumblebee, confined to the islands' machair and a toehold on Sutherland. It has suffered a decline of 95 per cent in the last fifty years, though it was never widely distributed. Its survival even on its favourite machair is said to be under threat from a variety of economic and land management pressures. It really is large (females have a wingspan of 4cm) and yellow. At the time of writing, an expert investigation is being launched to save it.

Prosperity is the last thing that people had in mind at the time of the Clearances. As Francis Thompson says, getting rid of people from the land owned by General Gordon of South Uist, Benbecula and Barra was unrivalled in brutality. He considered himself 'neither legally nor morally bound to support a population reduced to poverty by the will of Providence'. He quotes a note from a Catherine MacPhee from Lochdar in South Uist:

> I have seen the women putting the children in the carts which were being sent from Benbecula and the Lochdar to Loch Boisdale, while their husbands lay bound in the pens and were weeping beside them, without power to give them a helping hand, though the women themselves were crying aloud and their little children wailing to break their hearts. I have seen the big strong men, the champions of the country-side, the stalwarts of the world, being bound on Loch Boisdale quay and cast into the ship as would be done to a batch of horses or cattle in the boat, the bailiffs and the ground-officers and the constables and the police gathered behind them in pursuit of them. The God of life and He only knows all the loathsome work of men on that day.

Even in prehistoric times this concentration of machair supported above-average populations. Under Norwegian ownership the Vikings had a greater civilisation than then existed in Edinburgh. Some of the broken-down walls we have seen might have been remnants of wheelhouses, so called because stone piers radiate out from the central hearth dividing the outer area into eight or more compartments; and tiny islands in many of the lochs were once topped with duns or small forts. There are remains of all kinds – scattered in the rest of the mixture of this and that but no resemblance of a village – that seems to go on forever.

At Howmore we realise that a broken down wall surrounded by old graves mainly in the form of a cross is a medieval survival. This is different! There are in fact four chapels, one dedicated to St Columba, in this group probably founded in the early days of Scottish Christianity. Most were destroyed in the Scottish Reformation. Once this was a monastery much visited by scholars even from the Continent. A flock of birds –

and birds are everywhere along the coast – helps decorate a bewitching scene. A neatly thatched crofter's cottage has been incorporated into a youth hostel. When one personally remembers the time that hundreds of homes were of low single storey with thatched roofs, it comes as a surprise that Howmore now boasts the largest surviving group. Another surprise is that at the Reformation Howmore turned Protestant, an island within what to this day remains a Roman Catholic stronghold. There isn't a person in sight during our brief visit.

Jeweller Extraordinaire

When eventually we do find a shop, clearly signposted down another piece of dead-flat, complicated road system, of all things it is a jewellery centre. It would be hard to come up with a less likely place for a major workshop, shop and office – the headquarters of Hebridean Jewellery, a branch of which we saw in Stornoway.

Why here? John Hart explains that not only does he like the area but it serves him well.

'The difficulty for anyone setting up in business is to find somewhere to do it. My father was a well-known maker of Celtic jewellery and I studied the subject. I always wanted to do my own thing, design and manufacture, but there wasn't even a shed to be found... till one day a crofter let me have a tin hut for £10 a week. That was great as a starting point. You can't welcome the public in a tin hut, so I began by having to sell everything to the trade. There've been many ups and downs since then, but mercifully more ups.

When I was able to get this site, we could begin selling direct to the public. You make more profit and get paid quicker that way and meeting your customer helps tell you what they like and why. Now we've a branch in Fort William as well as Stornoway.

My father gave me his designs when he retired, but I design a lot myself. Sometimes an idea just comes, or I remember an old design or idea, or a customer sets me thinking. Celtic designs are our bread and butter, but I like to experiment too.'

Sheila loves it; so do I, spotting a gold broach pendant, richer in detail than anything we have seen elsewhere that would be just perfect for Benny, our Australian daughter-in-law, as a Christmas present. I do an inward 'ouch' when I hear the price. John smiles; he's the complete businessman with a love of design and manufacture, has to make money to survive, likes giving satisfaction – and loves publicity. (Here it is: www.hebrideanjewellery.co.uk) Among the ten permanent staff there are six craftsmen working in an area of sparse opportunity. The main building was put up in 1981, but it has been extended since – and there's a substantial café with books and quality souvenirs. What attracts customers to so remote a place?

'A few find us by chance; the signposting definitely pays. A few who have visited the branches seek us out. And you'd be surprised how many from overseas, especially North America, still have connections here. Some local people are occasional buyers, especially at Christmas but more help support the restaurant. We stay open year round.' For those living isolated on the machair, it must indeed be a delightful oasis for a coffee, light lunch or tea. Students help with peak summer demand. Much of the baking comes from nearby Kildonan, on one of the many roads from the main road down towards the sea, which crosses Loch Kildonan, famous for trout fishing.

There is a good sprinkling of customers, several of whom share with us in seeing how sheet silver is cut with a fine saw, heated and poured into a mould in which over and under impressions have been made from the prototype. That still leaves much fine work to be done by hand with the concentrated flame of a microwelder and a sharp metal instrument under a magnifying glass. A girl briefly acknowledges our interest before resuming total concentration. Polishing follows. That makes it sound simple; in practice it takes a long time to learn the basic craft. And it is all dependent on the right mixture of design for changing tastes. Upstairs is the room in which, sometimes after a walk, John develops his ideas and translates them into artefacts. 'It's exhilarating when it comes right.'

On the way out, we pause by the attractive range of books. No copy of *Buddhism for Sheep* can be sold closer to the beasts who would supposedly benefit from it.

Returning to the main road, without at first realising it we cross the causeway (it looks more like a raised path across a small bridge) from which the family of five from three generations, were washed away in their two cars while trying to escape from their flooded home. In Stornoway the wind peaked at 120mph; down here it went as high as 160mph. There were great storms two January's running. This lovely summer morning, it is hard to realise the fright that must have caused, though we do see quite a bit of evidence of damage.

So back across the South Ford, opened as much for defence as local interests in 1943, though still nicknamed 'O'Regan's Bridge' after the Roman Catholic priest who had long agitated for it. We're sorry not to have been able to spend more time in South Uist. A large island, 22 miles long by 6 to 8 wide. It is so different that one cannot help being fascinated: each time I have visited I have felt very much the outsider.

· XXV ·

BENBECULA AND NORTH UIST

The Dark Isle

When I'm asked what part of Britain I like best, I reply 'Where I am'. Best of course does not necessarily mean where I want to settle, but where I might enjoy a holiday, the wild scenery, or about which am perhaps just curious. When we arrive back in Benbecula, I'm certainly no less curious than in extraordinary South Uist. I cannot refrain from using two of the quotes used by our friend Francis Thompson in his *The Uists and Barra*. Both are about Benbecula, roughly a rectangular, 6 by 9 miles but deeply indented by the sea and full of water. I have almost said it before regarding the whole southern island chain, but John McCulloch speaks specifically of Benbecula:

> The sea here is all islands, and the land all lakes. That which is not rock is sand; and that which is not mud is bog; that which is not bog is lake; that which is not lake is sea; and the whole is a labyrinth of islands, peninsulas, promontories, bays and channels.

The other quote is by a sportsman complaining about how the locals spoilt his fun:

> Much of the pleasure of shooting in the Outer Hebrides is spoilt by the conduct of the crofters. It is not conducive to sport to be followed by a gang of men and ordered out of the country, nor is it pleasant to be cursed in Gaelic by a crowd of irate old women, even if you do not understand every word they say. They accused us of shooting their horses and sheep, filled in the pits which we dug in the sandhills for geese, shouted to put up the geese we were stalking, cut up the canvas and broke the seats of our folding-boat, and tried in every possible way to spoil our sport.

Visitors of all kinds are more than welcome today and, if there is strife, it is mainly in the background, caused by the large military presence, which mainly means English folk. Knowing they will only be based here for a limited time discourages them paying even lip service to Gaelic or even the Scots' way of expressing things in English. Like military families posted in any strange place, they tend to keep to themselves.

What the military have done is create activity, which especially helps the catering and building trades. That, plus the fact that with its airport Benbecula, or to be precise Balivanich, is a convenient commercial service and medical centre for the Uists. With its fewer crofts and large uninhabited eastern areas, the island relies increasingly on the military and its central service role. Of course this has grown especially since the opening of the causeways. Balivanich only became a post town in 1962, since when it has steadily sucked business away from Lochboisdale and Lochmaddy.

The Dark Island Hotel gives us a good lunch, we top up on diesel, buy a newspaper at the airport. And on our way out, we stop at the much-advertised Benbecula Baker. The shop has already closed for the day, but they are pleased to sell us some of its delicious goodies through the back door. None of Balivanich is particularly attractive, but it works – and many a local family is grateful that there is enough employment to prevent the men folk having to absent themselves.

Traditionally Benbecula also serves as a barrier between Protestant North and Catholic South Uist. In common with other islands, it has many historic sites, but one's overall impression of the flat built-up area round Balivanich is one of depression. It would make a fascinating social study, though.

So to the North Ford, whose opening by the Queen Mother was in 1960, not until seventeen years after that of the South Ford. In total much longer than the South Ford, it jumps from island to island in a semi-circle of separate causeways and bridges totalling several miles. The afternoon sunshine brilliantly lights up the exotic setting of sea, sand, islands, ill-defined land, hills and flat areas of which a third is lakes. On one side of the great bay chiefly of sand except at high tides are the runways of Benbecula airport; on the other Caranish and the ruins of its ancient temple after which our hotel is named.

Caranish

At our hotel, Temple View, in a main-road township, compulsively I watch the scattered traffic. In the evening, it is mainly heading for the link to Benbecula. Long after the ruined temple on the hill had passed its heyday, there were scarcely any decent tracks leave alone roads or causeways. Yet here, it is thought, was the very first university.

Early Christianity made such an impact in the Western Isles that much of what we know still comes from handed-down oral tradition. There was a church here in the 12th century. It fell into ruins, was rebuilt and then destroyed in about 1581 after the Reformation. Partly restored in the 19th century, little has been done in recent decades to prevent it tumbling apart again. We are shocked by its condition. It is indeed extremely hard to reach. One supposes there are so many ancient sites around the islands that it is hard to justify careful maintenance of all; yet this temple clearly has special significance. Memory has been passed down of features which have long disappeared.

On the knoll, near where one of the many battles between clans was fought, it commands a fantastic outlook, including the rich land at the northern end of Baleshare and the sand dunes which years ago overwhelmed the fertile machair of the southern part.

Before dinner, we decide to recross the first part of the North Ford, and do the circuit of Grimsay; its fishing village of Kallin is a favourite haunt of artists. Full of expensive craft, the harbour exudes success. Lorries leave regularly loaded with lobsters and other fish for Spain and Italy. The introduction of salt-water tanks has proved of great benefit, since the supply can be better regulated and everything is fresh at the moment of despatch.

Then back to the main road and, thinking once more of the hazards of crossing before the completion of the causeway. Back on the northern shore near Caranish, we note the point at which MacBraynes buses turned. Between tides passengers frequently suffered long delays before there was enough water for a ferry, or the tide was out far enough for carts or pedestrians. The single carriage with lay-bys now seems inadequate, but what a difference it must have made in 1960.

Flora to Dinner

Flora Macdonald is already waiting in the hotel's conservatory. Her smart contemporary appearance, her hair put up, and her general vivaciousness, go along with a lifetime's ambition to ensure old island ways and crafts are not forgotten. Though initially surprised by my invitation, she is not shy.

'I love old things. I'm into restoration – piloting ideas to inspire other people to do the same. I'm interested in everything my ancestors did, such as using herbs and plants for dyes. Nobody would take me on for a job I'd want, so eventually I took a four-year course at Glasgow in community arts and graduated at fifty three. I've started writing stories in Gaelic for the BBC, I've taught Gaelic, started two local-history groups, and in front of my house I'm using a bothy, a single-man's home, what I call a sheiling, as a museum for my weaving. I run a B&B; people love it here. So I'm pretty busy. I do workshops on dyes and am going to write a book about them. I also sketch – a few minutes every day – and grow vegetables.

I came from an island where people are individuals, caring towards each other, good community support. You can't escape from an island, or certainly couldn't before the causeways. It is important that you retain your heritage. If you don't, who are you? I could always feel the difference between me and mainland people.'

I tell her I have recently read a book on lichens, and ask her about their use in dyes. 'With clear air, we've plenty of lichens here, everywhere,' she starts. 'I still spoon the black lichen off the rocks in the old way. It's magic, for depending on how long you steep it in the pot it gives you a variety of shades from a pale apricot to tan and dark brown. It leaves a lovely perfume; it's fast and doesn't need fixing.
The original brown of all Harris Tweed came this way, but that's before there were machine looms and it was a household industry.'

Old man's beard lichen, a cobwebby kind of thing, gives yellow, as does turmeric, there's a lovely blue from red cabbage, elderberries and their flowers are especially good for pink. She simply loves it all. I ask if she uses a traditional three legged pot to steep. Once most local people did, resting the pot on a rock and lighting a fire underneath. She says no, but I wouldn't put it beyond her to seek one out.

It is perhaps not surprising that employers were reluctant to take her on but, though steeped in the past, she's not the quaint old lady I'd half expected, but very much today's person, revelling in her dinner, asking us penetrating questions, trawling for people we know in common... and won't dream of a lift home. Quite a character!

Books Old and New

After a final glance at the dwindling evening inter-isle traffic, I compare the original 1974 edition of Francis Thompson's *The Uists and Barra* with the 1999 one. It reveals much about the changing publishing scene. The modern, larger page size (but many fewer pages) edition is infinitely more handsome, with truly great photographs by Derek Croucher. Several of the double-page pictures of sea that is all rock, and land all water, are world class. No reference is made to the earlier edition; reprinted several times. By yesterday's bibliographical standards, this is plain naughty. I recall that, before the chains took over, some of the great individual bookshops of yesteryear refused to stock titles that broke the rules. Who can afford to be fussy about finer points in today's intense competition?

Much though I enjoy looking at the modern edition, I find myself constantly referring to the older version because it says so much more. The new text, quarrying from the first, is well written, but, with so little space and so many different islands to cover, Francis has inevitably been beaten by the two-way pull between describing overall themes and the individual islands. The original has many more facts and figures, more about the great families and feuds, details of the Clearances, and especially about social life, something I used to encourage 'Islands' authors to take seriously.

But then in the quarter century between the editions, the islands came in from the cold. Outright hardship has largely disappeared with few now living in primitive conditions. And the population is no longer in freefall. People confidently plan for a future. In other words, the subject is less exotic though the landscape still is – and that can be better shown pictorially with good captions. Another difference is that the illustrations of the old edition include good reproductions of historic subjects only available in monochrome. Not wishing to compromise its all-colour approach, the modern edition only includes postage stamp size reproductions.

Being a single island title, Bill Lawson's *North Uist in History and Legend* avoids the problem of the two-way pull between different islands and themes. It goes unashamedly for themes. Studying the machairs, shores, lochs and so on works well because most of each happens to be concentrated in a geographical area. And, praise be, the chapter headings have their English spelling in parenthesis. It is all black and white. When colour is given preference, often the text becomes secondary, 'illustrating' the pictures, a dilemma shown in all types of publications. Narrative railway history, however well written, fails against rich colour even if the reader is told much less, and maybe less accurately.

So while the general public seems to have an even-shorter attention span, demonstrated by increasingly shorter 'takes' in TV programmes, happily there is a growing reaction, with a noticeable minority enjoying prolonged concentration. Indeed, my 700-page *Journey* sold well, better than the publisher expected, and has been reprinted and sold out as a paperback, while the average length of novels is rising dramatically.

Back to Francis Thompson and Bill Lawson. Here is an example of how Francis tells us much in a brief way:

> Even a cursory glance at the map will reveal one of the problems of island living: inter-island access. Up until the 1940s the islands were wholly dependent on small cargo ships delivering lifeline essentials and exporting the island produce. These ships, called 'puffers', were built with flat bottoms so that they could be stranded deliberately on the sandy beaches and stony shores to discharge their cargo.

> Travelling between the islands of North Uist, Benbecula and South Uist meant hiring a horse-drawn cart to take one across the fords at low tides, accompanied by an expert guide. The dangers inherent in these ford crossings were summed up in the Gaelic prayer, *Faothail mhath dhuibh* (A good ford to you).

With over 230 pages, Bill doesn't need to be in such a hurry and his systematic coverage has room for extensive use of contemporary quotations. This is from John M MacDonald talking of the North Ford:

> I have stood on the vast stretch of white sands, through which flows the salt water river that joins the Minch and the Atlantic Ocean, and watched droves of cattle plunge into the water until nothing could be seen of them but their shaggy backs and long horns. The drovers followed them on foot, after taking off their lower garments, tying them into tidy bundles and hugging them under their arms. Their nailed boots were tied together by the laces and hung round their necks. The water at its deepest covered the men close up to their ribs, and at this point they always took the precaution of hanging on to the tail of the nearest pony or cow.
>
> The riders on horseback, often two on the same pony, also plunged into the water, lifting their legs high to save a wetting. Carriages drawn by two horses, dog-carts, gigs and crofters' carts were all packed to their utmost carrying capacity, for it is a recognised rule never to refuse a 'lift' to anyone waiting to cross the ford.

The Anatomy of North Uist

At breakfast next morning we discuss island life with the hotel's owner, Harvey McLean-Ross. In common with many others, he is full of confidence for the future of North Uist. 'Though all island house prices are low, they are as expensive here as in Stornoway. People want to come here, but finding a house is difficult. For one thing, there are no For Sale boards; nobody likes to let their neighbours know they are moving. It is especially difficult to find a house with a sea view. Crofters worked outside all day in full view of the sea, and at night what they wanted was protection from storms.

But there'll be building as there are road improvements; road engineers have helped keep us busy in the winter. Our difficulty is finding staff. Without the Poles we'd be in trouble.'

Our lively Polish waitress says she enjoys the work but finds leisure time difficult. 'I don't want to be in a big place, but it's just so isolated here, difficult to make friends. There are very few of my age around.'

Before getting into the car for a final day of island exploring, we consider a few facts. North Uist is 18 miles from north to south, 13 at broadest from east to west. Before the worst of the Clearances, the population had been 3,870. The 2001 census recorded just 1,271, no more than you'll find in some single mainland factories and schools. Knowing who is who is certainly a lot easier than on the mainland. Through personal friendships and friends of friends, and those we are meeting on this trip, we feel we know of at least half of the North Writers group.

The capital, such as it is, Lochmaddy, is at the end of a sea loch of the same name which astonishingly has a coastline stretching over 300 miles encompassing several safe harbours. Loch Eport, another of the complex eastern indentations left by the last Ice Age, virtually cuts the island in two, only falling short of meeting a western sea loch by a quarter of a mile. Despite a considerable area taken up by steep mountains and hills, of great geological antiquity, a third of North Uist is water. Shallow Loch Scadavay has a shore line of 50 miles and contains well over 100 islands, many with relics of duns or fortified homes.

Not surprisingly, geographers, geologists and nature lovers make up a sizeable proportion of visitors. Twitchers are seldom disappointed. Archaeologists are exhausted before they can visit all the hundreds of ancient sites including ruined churches, burial chambers, standing stones and even stone circles.

Road Ends

Though the sandy beaches on the north west are among the best in the world, you'll have to bring your own deckchair and even ice cream. A tour by one of the Paisley-based Classique vintage coaches is as close as you'll get to a package holiday.

Having seen it from a distance, and read about its curious story, first we go across a small causeway to Baleshare, at high tide an island. At the north (the south being abandoned to sand dunes) the crofts are as productive as any we have seen, and there is obviously great community spirit. At the end of the road there isn't much to see (the sea being behind the dunes) until, bless me, we hit upon a sculpture and a sculptured seat. 'The Road Ends Community Sculpture Project aims to encourage communities to celebrate their identities, history and spirit by working with an artist to create an art work set in the landscape.'

'Reflections' by Colin Mackenzie is a sculpture echoed by the ceramic-tiled seat. Both mirror the shapes and colours of the surroundings. The images of sheep and footprints refer to the pre-causeway crossing over the sands.

Though at first it didn't seem a pretty setting, around us we have pampas grass, white daisies, fuchsias, wild potentillas and montbretia. The severity of the January storm can be told from the tiles torn off the seat, not yet fully repaired. In North Uist and indeed much of the Western Isles, art is part of everyday life. Many people invite you into their homes to see their art work, usually for sale at very reasonable prices. Again, art, music, poetry are universally embraced.

Northern Circuit

Time to get going, to the road junction close to where North Uist is nearly divided into two islands, and then round the 35-mile circuit back to it. Though we explore a few roads down to the sea, including those on either side of the nature reserve run by the RSPB at Balranald, there isn't time to keep near the coast and take the one steep mountain cut-off, or even one of the half dozen or so minor routes that go so far up the north-westerly range before petering out.

Along the way we stop for diesel, paper and other items from one of those rare but vital jack-of-all-trades garages/shops. Naturally we are expected to say exactly what we are doing and are given friendly advice. With mountains on one side and the sea on the other, just as we pass a bus – even here there is a reasonable service – a golden eagle hovers into sight with what looks like a small bird in its claws.

Turning east along the north coast, we quickly come across the vast expanse of Vallay Strand and spot the long ford across to Vallay Island. Grenitote, with access to more great empty sandy beaches, is home to Pauline and Robert Prior-Pitt, friends of my sister we had hoped to see but who are away. Though relative newcomers to the island, it has already deeply anchored them. Pauline is the island bard whose work crops up in exhibitions and publications. In what other part of the world, with so little and so scattered population, would poetry readings attract viable audiences? Next we're at the junction of the road with the causeway to Berneray. When we have a chance to drive a road a second time we wish we could do the whole trip over again. The lighting changes constantly this morning. Every second, cumulus clouds briskly and variously subdue the sunlight.

Lochmaddy

Lochmaddy, the port, has always been between two worlds. The first Uist packet station and Post Office opened here in 1802, though as late as 1841 the population was only 144. Parcel post began in 1883 and flourished until shops developed at Balivanich on Benbecula. Then those on the mainland sending support for their families could do so in money rather than goods. With all the comings and goings, English was usually the language of the playground. The local hospital had a reputation for excellence until health facilities were concentrated at Balivanich. Alginate Industries had one of their processing factories here, for the harbour system produces outstanding seaweed.

Now the Lochmaddy Hotel obviously struggles. In high summer, only one other person is having lunch, a science teacher from Manchester, touring the islands by motorcycle for the third time. Between trips to places such as Cambodia, Rome and Vietnam, he enjoys discovering our home-grown ancient relics. 'It may not be what the travel agents see as exotic, but I'll tell you one thing,' he confides. 'You're more your own person here than practically anywhere else. There's air and time and space: grand.'

So to our last island call, as interesting as any. Lochmaddy's Taigh Chearsabhagh's Museum and Arts Centre. It includes public toilets (no vandalism in fourteen years), Post Office, café, book and art shop, aquarium, lecture hall, workshops and exhibition rooms... and more. In a land of so few public buildings, how sensible to combine other things with the basic museum and art gallery. I say basic not to imply that the facilities are sparse (they aren't) but what it is primarily about. The council pays £14,000 a year for the toilets, almost certainly less than free-standing ones would cost, and in this friendly atmosphere they are more likely to be respected. The café is franchised. Even so, the museum and art gallery have fourteen employees, full and part-time (some job sharers), which makes it one of the largest employers on the island.

Manager of the enterprise is Norman Macleod. North Uist born, he had no English till he was five and, after completing his education in Aberdeen, worked offshore flying out of the most northerly Shetland island of Unst. He came back sixteen years ago, was one of the museum's original directors and became manager in 1994. He has been behind the increase in the number of annual visitors of from 14,000 to 35,000 in an island of 1,200 residents. Locals do however count, giving great support, especially in winter. Everything stays open year round.

Norman's most telling words: 'Art is not a dirty word in the islands.' The project was community led from the start, the local history and art associations nominating most of the directors, while there are two community ones. The Western Isles Council, Scottish Arts Council and Lottery Fund provide much of the funding, but trading income is considerable.

'It works through enthusiasm and detail. Every penny has to count;

we're a hard-headed business within a charitable trust. It's a model beginning to attract attention and get us awards. The other day I had Croatian TV here to show people what we do. Every inch has to pull its weight.'

Taking us round, he shows how much of the space is multi-functional; he draws curtains so that the lecture hall is now a cinema. We see three separate art exhibitions (sometimes there are four), dark room and photographic facilities, print workshop and studio space and visiting students. On the museum side, there are ancient artefacts and meaningful display boards. The bookshop is well stocked.

School children come to do their art, and so do Fulbright scholars for residences of a week or three months. The centre, which even has bedrooms, runs a one-year diploma course (this year twenty students) validating a second year course which it is hoped will also run here in association with Lews College, the third being done on the mainland.

Creative activity with artists, printmakers, students, school children, museum visitors, people drawing out their pension from the Post Office before morning coffee in the café: the mixture is a joy to behold.

'Everyone has to learn to work together in remote islands,' says Norman. 'There's a ring of centres in Western and Northern Scotland that I can just walk into and expect co-operation; you wouldn't get that between Glasgow and Edinburgh. Who feeds the fish in the aquarium? I do. The café exhibits two pictures each by people selected by the Uist Art Association. It gives them a kick, and like much else on display can be bought.

On the mainland nine out of ten art students fall off the line at the end of their course and will never create. We give a full exhibition of students' work every year. It is the practical thing to do.'

There is an annual Fred Macaulay Memorial Lecture in English or Gaelic, attended by our friend Sybil, the widow of Fred whose work, including expanding the BBC's Gaelic coverage, was featured in *Journey*, while we see that Pauline Prior-Pitt is shortly to lead a poetry workshop. Many familiar titles are displayed in the bookshop. And it's all in a converted and extended former inn, opened in 1741, which must have many a tale to tell as the gateway to the southern islands then just tentatively beginning to be integrated with mainland Scotland. In the historical perspective (there were both Iron and Bronze Age civilisations), what has happened on North Uist since then is only a blip.

It has just been reported how the tractor of a crofter, Donald MacLellan half fell through a hole into the Iron Age. In fact into an Iron Age site. The exciting discovery is probably of a wheelhouse. Another announcement says that a wheelhouse will anyway be recreated in

Lochmaddy as a tourist attraction. They are the circular structures with interior walls radiating from a central hearth. [Next year, handed in to Taigh-Chearsabhagh were two Roman coins found on a beach. Until now there has hardly been any evidence of Roman activity in the Outer Hebrides. Might history have been rewritten?]

Another piece of news that will have special impact on both the Uists is that the first educational manager for Gaelic has been appointed. One way and another, there's a new feeling of confidence, especially in Lochmaddy, small and spread out though it is.

For us it is back to Temple View Hotel at Caranish for a refreshing night. Next morning we return to Lochmaddy for the ferry back to Skye. At the terminal I cogitate about the setting for so many happy reunitings between sad and, especially in times of war, final farewells. The sail out of the complex of harbours makes a great finale for us. Never have we enjoyed a trip better. Many images of the island chain will live with us forever, and I hope this account of our travels will inspire more to venture here.

· XXVI ·

ISLANDS AND MAINLAND: COMMON THEME

Back on Skye

Next morning, back on Skye after a leisurely trip down the side of Loch Snizort, soon after turning to go up the opposite side we call for lunch at the Skeabost Hotel. 'It looks a dump,' says Sheila as we navigate a weed-infested drive.

It used to be the best on Skye, a beacon in a dark land. Not now. We don't stay. The hotel has been taken over by a company that's gone bust. So lunch is a pub snack. Then to the small Edinbane Pottery where we order a set of miniature quaichs on saucers with a wood ash glaze. They'll do nicely for a mini-serving of soup at dinner parties. Stuart Whatley, the owner, tells us his interesting story. Childhood was on the one-farm island of Pabbay, just off Skye opposite Broadford.

'When I was ten, I remember Dad digging a trench half way across our 300-acre island and his being excited at discovering boulder clay, With experiment, a homemade little wheel and a book on pottery, he started turning out respectable pots. Later I remember the exciting moment when we added up what the pots had been sold for and said "We could make a living at this". Dad had had a heart attack, and then the Nissen hut at the centre of the farm, with tractor and everything, went up in smoke. Pabay was wonderful, but I had to go away to school in Portree and didn't want that to happen to my children.

So in 1972 we came to Edinbane, and set up the pottery in what had been a Bentley garage. And here we are nearly forty years later. During that time, Skye's population dropped to around 6,000 and now it's back to 10,000. There are craft shops everywhere, but we were virtually the first.

I've only one regret. The Highland & Island Development Board [predecessors of Highland & Island Enterprise] wanted us to grow. That turned me into manager and salesman. I didn't like it. So we returned to being small. With just my wife and one other, perhaps two in high season, I'm relaxed, content.

As those who've tried it commercially have found out, making a living at potting isn't easy, but with passing traffic to Dunvegan Castle and our website, we're able to sell virtually everything retail. We get full price, know what our customers want and don't have to bow to the fickle opinion of shops or press for payment. We have fun and sleep at night, and aren't the only ones who've found Skye just the place to do what you really want to do.'

Next to Dunvegan, Skye's largest west coast village: a pretty little place, once a major part with a daily steamship to Oban. Today's purely pleasure boat-trips stay mainly within sheltered Loch Dunvegan. What most people come to see is the Castle, Scotland's oldest, from the 13th century the seat of Clan MacLeod. It has a fearsome dungeon, and exhibits enough if you're into things like a lock of Bonnie Prince Charlie's hair and a pin cushion embroidered by the famous Flora MacDonald (not the one who came to dinner in North Uist).

The Castle's position overlooking the loch with sheltered gardens and woodland, couldn't be more romantic and the controlling power was awesome. But when I toured it once in the 1950s I recall vowing that I'd never return. From the start I have always disliked the way Scotland's troubled history is commercialised; here it seemed crass. I enjoy the setting and the part it played in history without joining a host of gawkers. My aversion is accepted more than perhaps understood by Sheila.

Three Chimneys and Talisker

So we press on up the peninsula to tonight's resting place, a tourist trap of another kind, the one and only Three Chimneys or to be precise the Three Chimneys & House Over-By. It makes the most of its reputation with three red rosettes. We wonder if it were say miles miles outside a Midland town, there'd be a need to book weeks in advance. The fascination is the very luxury of exquisite meals in remoteness.

Reception is enthusiastic and anything but crass. In Over-By there are six suites, all with views across Loch Dunvegan. Ours is spaciously intriguing on two levels with a light that comes on automatically when the steps up from the lounge and bathroom areas to the sleeping one are approached. The bed is gloriously inviting, the whole décor up with the gods – but we're here for a purpose, and are quickly back in the car.

It emphasises how very overcrowded towns are when populations as small as Skye's are spread over a vast 'inhabited' area. As we head further up the eastern side of Loch Dunvegan, we pass settlement after settlement, with houses and bungalows, admittedly a thin line of them, much of the way. It is the same when we take the branch road to the west. Near lush Glendale with Glen Dale hosting a short but vigorous river, the road splits again. Even when approaching the end of these smaller roads, there are rows of habitations.

Looking up to the peninsula's two mountains, MacLeod's Table North and South, still in brilliant sunshine we soak up the blue Loch Dunvegan and heather-covered pink land beyond before returning via Glendale. Here I stop on the spur of the moment to open a conversation with a rugged middle-aged gent 'Aye, we've room to breathe here.' He's more interested in me than he'll allow me to be in him, though he softens when told we live in Scotland. 'Ah, Nairn. That's near the airport: I flew down to London from there once.' Dalcross, 8 miles from us, is the 'local' airport even for Skye. Those who have to pay occasional day visits to London on business, have to set off in the very wee hours to catch the 'red eye' first plane.

He seems a happy soul making a living doing this and that. Though not quite the 'Hell of London', he couldn't possibly live somewhere as busy as Nairn. Here everyone knows everyone so he tells us about those driving past, what they're like and who their neighbours are. It is easier to start such conversations than wind them up. When we do succeed, off to our nest in Over-By.

In the small bar before dinner a young Scottish family are celebrating a birthday; Three Chimneys fetches in people from far and wide. The cooking is of the highest order, with a few simple, quality and mainly local ingredients complementing each other without the screaming competition of tastes indulged in by so many show-piece restaurants. To find this in a far corner of Skye is remarkable, though throughout the island cuisine and other catering standards have changed dramatically since the poor years immediately after the war. Service is the best matter of fact; none of your 'welcome to our wonderful restaurant'. Breakfast, with homemade baking and an array of local fish, meats and cheeses, sets you up for the day.

Then a spectacular drive south. Just avoiding Dunvegan our route is determined by the sea's successive fjord-like inlets. There is little habitation where the mountains come close down to the sea, but each of the gentler peninsulas has been actively colonised. One day, possibly, when desirable sites run out, Skye might again seem crowded as it did as a 'congested district' before the Clearances when there were too many mouths to feed. Even in my lifetime, ruined buildings are much less in evidence. Planning permission is granted where there's been former habitation, so ruins are cleared, their materials reused. In the 1950s I recall someone saying that Skye was far too sad a place for a relaxed holiday. Not today.

We play hide and seek with Loch Bracadale, whose coastline including uninhabited islands stretches 60 miles. After tiny Bracadale village, we join long Loch Harport, though forced to climb through the empty inland as the cliffs along its northern edge are too precipitous for a road. There's a great view of the Loch's head and the Cuillins just before we turn sharply to travel close to the southern shore. Our immediate destination is Carbost: or to be precise Skye's only single-malt distillery, Talisker. The website has a great beginning:

> The shape of the Isles of Skye is notoriously hard to describe, perhaps because it comprises a series of peninsulas sticking out in various directions that happen to come together untidily and chaotically at their inner ends. On one of the stumpier peninsulas projecting west the attractive village of Carbost straggles down the line of the B8009 as it descends the hillside above Loch Harport, from the church at its south eastern end to Talisker Distillery at its north western. A track along the shore here brings you to the old pier that was once Carbost's main means of contact with the outside world.

It goes on to emphasise that even where the road seems to end, it simply turns and climbs into a further world beyond. Getting right to the end of a peninsula is always more complicated and time-consuming than expected.

Then it tells us that the very name Talisker, as in the malt, has a special ring. Known as 'the lava of the Cuillins', it is characterised by 'a powerful and peppery taste that has more than a hint of the sea in it and is moderately peaty... even the ten-year-old bottled at 45.8 per cent alcohol is consistently regarded by the experts as one of the very best single malt whiskies.'

Though the season is scarcely over, there's only one other car in the visitors' centre's huge car park, its passengers and ourselves being the only people looking round the displays of artefacts and printed matter. Staff are cheerfully informative and enthuse when a purchase is considered.

A small bottle will make an excellent gift for a Sassenach whisky devotee and, though she prefers non-peaty ones, Sheila can't resist a dram for herself. The barley comes from the Black Isle since the soil and climate wouldn't suit it here, though the distillery's founder started (as did so many businessmen) by cruelly forcing people out of their crofts.

'Ah, that was a very long time ago, sir. I think we can forget it now,' says a slightly pained assistant. Memories handed down are perhaps still too poignant to be treated lightly, though you can have a good thrash over Bonnie Prince Charlie's ambitions and death. Not yet however about the deep wound the English victory inflicted on Scottish culture such as the outlawing of the kilt.

Now to somewhere totally different. Or is it? For though the landscape and the local life it determines are always individual, it is hard to get away from the common themes: hunger, the Clearances, rich lairds and remaining tenants still struggling, better communications helping attract newcomers who make communities more vibrant.

Raasay

After once more enjoying the spectacular mountain pass across Skye, at Sconser on the main road to Portree, we are the first of only three cars on the ferry for the short crossing to the Isle of Raasay. This was the first small island I ever called at on the MacBrayne ship which did the Portree-Raasay-Kyle of Lochalsh-Mallaig run. The return was frequently delayed waiting for a late-running train on the West Highland line. Except for a private boat, it was Raasay's only connection with the outside world, and great was the activity around the pier when people, mail, livestock and goods of all kinds were loaded and unloaded. Many of the islanders came along to make it a social occasion.

Our fifteen minute crossing on the fourth of today's seven ferries is much enlivened when the captain draws attention to the school of dolphins running alongside us. And, almost as soon as we start the car, Sheila points out an otter paddling along on its back. 'And another.' The pier being part way to Raasay's southern shore, this is where we head first, with a great view of the rugged Scalpay abruptly rising to nearly 1,300ft – a small island, owned by a merchant banker and farmed by his sons who cherish the herd of red deer.

Raasay's only hotel is quiet at the end of a busy but short season. The Post Office and its shop at Inverarish is agog with activity. The more remote the community, the greater the number of visits most people seem to make to the business at its heart. Here you'd never guess the island's total population is under 200.

Over a sandwich in our bedroom, I reflect that in many ways Raasay, again with some familiar themes, has been a perverse island. Part of it somehow missed glaciation and plants killed off elsewhere survived here. Though the MacLeods were generally Protestant and the Skye ones naturally supported the government, the Jacobite Raasay branch, in what was their usual out-of-step way, keenly supported Bonnie Prince Charlie. A hundred men, and twenty six of the island's famous Pipers, went to Culloden. After his disastrous defeat, the Pretender was smuggled here and later secretly taken to Loch Broom where he hoped he would be rescued by the French. Raasay was severely punished, many properties including Raasay House being raised to the ground, though the MacLeods were allowed to spend their fortune on reconstruction.

Prosperity returned, the population peaked at over 900. Then starvation, the Clearances – and the death of the Pipers and other music at the end of the 19th century when the Free Church tightened its grip. Dancing and poetry were banned. After the MacLeods had disappeared, Raasay House became a hotel, until in 1960 it was purchased by someone who neglected it and its surrounds. He did nothing even when it was ransacked and everything valuable including an extensive library stolen. Eventually the Highlands & Islands Development Board bought it for an adventure centre, at the same time converting another house into our hotel.

In other ways, officialdom has served Raasay poorly. Highly departmentalised, the Inverness County Council of yore was more concerned with saving money than with long-term prosperity. School closures and lack of roads countered other efforts. What is best known is that when the Council failed to provide a road to the north end, Calum MacLeod built it himself: two hilly miles with grit and determination. In all weathers it took nearly twenty years in his fifties and sixties.

That's where we head now, up an empty moorland, initially with views towards Skye, but then down a steep hill to the ruins of Brochel Castle on the east coast. Calum's road starts here, up a steep hill at a narrow point of Raasay and down an even steeper one back to the west coast. Oh dear, half expecting to be catapulted into the sea, for the first time ever I'm suffering vertigo at the wheel. So we turn back without reaching the road's end. Sadly, by the time Calum reached his home at Arnish, the school, Post Office and everything else had gone. He and his wife were the last people out.

In his *Calum's Road,* Roger Hutchinson quotes from an interview with two former residents who say:

> When you saw Calum when he was working on the road that's all that was on his mind. He would ask your opinion of things, and then he would tell you: 'The big rock that's more or less at the fank there at Tarbert – enough gravel there, boy, to cover the road, a bhalaich, from Castle to Fladda.'
>
> That was the type of thing he was seeing. He was foreseeing where he was going to get everything. The boys that used to go over to do the boring and the blasting for him once every six weeks or so, they were saying to themselves, 'Och, that will keep him going for two or three months'. But by the time they went back, there was nothing – not a stone was to be seen. It was all in place in the road. You can

see his stonework still. It was terrific altogether. It seems practically impossible to do. For years he went off in the morning, his wife Lexie would say, with his piece in his bag, and she wouldn't see him again until dark. He was determined to build that road.

Oh there was marvellous talent, you know. The work he put in there is unbelievable, and with no modern equipment – just the barrow and the pick and the shovel. It was marvellous. And the way he built it up there at Tarbert, his stonework is something to be admired. It's amazing when you take it all in.

So, as with the long island of Rona to its north, Raasay's north end is now without ordinary population. The gentler and more fertile southern end offers diverse scenery and a variety of activities, some based at Raasay House, now an outdoor or adventure centre. We approach it through a patch of slowly decaying woodland and then under the clock tower by the stables. Everything is a bit run down: the clock hasn't worked properly since the day in 1914 thirty six Raasay men left for the Great War, only fourteen of them to return.

After poking our heads into pretty basic accommodation, we're met by a girl who says the season's over and the café closed, but she'll willingly make us a cup of tea. We enjoy it looking out at the grand view of Skye, little has changed since centuries ago it must have attracted the branch of the MacLeod family to build their home here. Throughout the period of the Scottish and English school holidays (to the benefit of Scottish tourism, they only overlap a little), there's been a full complement of children enjoying a wide range of activities.

No kids next year, however; the house is to undergo a thorough overhaul. The derelict state of the woods is urgently in need of regeneration, and the garden tidied up too, to dispel the impression that things are in final decline. In an ancient burial ground in the woods are the remains of St Moluag's chapel. St Moluag founded the monastery on Lismore, normally reached from Oban. Boswell, staying at Raasay House with Dr Johnson, found 'something comfortable in the thought of being so near a piece of consecrated ground'.

At dinner in the hotel bar, with the owners' now taking their own holiday, the young people provide a very edible meal with friendly banter including ourselves, one other couple staying and a handful of locals enjoying a social dram. Though communications have been much improved, it is clear that the ferry trip adds to costs and deters much of the activity there would be if there were a causeway, not that one has been seriously mooted or might be practical. 'We just hope things don't catch fire,' says a local to the other visitors. 'The fire engine has to come across the ferry. There are standby arrangements but you never can tell with fire.'

'Must feel like living on an outpost,' says the husband of the other couple.

'Don't know about that. We're fine here; it's just the authorities. They never understand. Never have, never will.' Which might have been said on virtually all small islands, or for that matter much of Scotland's west coast mainland. But he then blames visitors for the season being so short. Raasay v the rest.

We take the next day gently, walking through the woods alongside the rushing Inverarish Burn and only using the car for a drive through Raasay Forest, over the summit and down steeply to the east coast where, under packed contours, before it finally gives up, the road looks out to the ancient hills of the mainland's Applecross peninsula. That's where we'll be heading to tomorrow.

On our way back we explore what can still be seen of the old iron mine, which flourished in World War One. Little now remains of the curiously-sloping bridge which carries its steeply-inclined railway down to the transhipment quay. The village was extended to house mine workers, whose number was once swollen by Italian prisoners of war. Soon, however, the price of iron ore dropped ending Raasay's flirtation with heavy industry.

Elgol and Soay

Next morning, back on Skye, though we really should head straight back to the mainland, I cannot resist taking the single-track road from Broadford to Elgol (See *Journey*). It has everything: changing scenery under the domineering Cuillins, salt water, early history, industrial archaeology, an active marble quarry, and a string of tourist traps including several cafés, the last of which, just before the road's final drop down to the sea, has a view to die for. There's one island in the panorama that on previous visits I seem to have missed. That's because it is the closest, almost as much below my caveman's natural long-sight vision as the beach. But last night I read a small book about it: *The Soay of our Forefathers* by Laurance Reed, from one of today's group of small Edinburgh publishers. It includes this quote from an islander to his MP in 1937:

> We sincerely trust that you will be able to get this boon granted to us, otherwise we are not prepared to face another winter on the Island. The miseries and hardships of the last are too fresh in our memory. There is only one of two things to be done, either another mail steamer or else take us off the Island and settle us somewhere

in the Empire where we will get a chance of living decently.

Largely due to the lack of a regular boat service, there had been pleas for evacuation as early as the 1880s. Owned by the MacLeods of Dunvegan from the 13th century, Soay had already had many challenging times when over a hundred people were dumped on it, those cleared off their crofts in Skye who wouldn't emigrate to America. That only a few had previously lived on Soay was because of its poor soil. The newcomers just about survived mainly on fishing from the sheltered harbour that almost cuts the dumbbell-shaped island in two.

In 1944, the MacLeods sold it to Gavin Maxwell, later famous for his wildlife writing, who used it for shark fishing. A 'factory' was erected to process the oil, but the price slumped. The unsuccessful venture is vividly described in Maxwell's first book, *Harpoon at a Venture*. Those who enjoy his later *Ring of Bright Water*, of which more than a million copies were sold, will be sad to know that even today the number of harmless basking sharks in Hebridean waters remains depleted as the result of a few years of intensive killing.

Maxwell lost heavily and there was little joy for his partner, Tex Geddes, who struggled to continue for a brief period. He bought some of the crofts from Maxwell, and the rest from the remaining islanders after they were eventually evacuated on 20 June 1953. That caused a flurry of media activity with echoes of the 1930s evacuation of St Kilda. Because of a legal quarrel and tenant improvement rights, the purchase bankrupted Geddes. However, the island's next owner, Dr Michael Gilbertson, generously gave him lifetime tenure of a farm and finding his feet, he was eventually able to buy the island back, though he died a few years later.

Gazing down on the island, I imagine some of the emotions caused by all these and many other mainly religious-based happenings. Though the harbour inlet is clear enough, it is difficult to pick out details. MacBraynes refused to make night calls because it was hard for captains to see clearly under the shadow of the Cuillins. I don't know who owns the island today, but wish them better luck. The last I heard it was up for sale at less than the price of a good detached house in a London suburb.

The Highlands' Prettiest Village?

Now we set off along the single-track road to Broadford, following the coast and, in a fraction of the old ferry time, across the Kyle by the bridge (after a great protest campaign now toll free) to Kyle of Lochalsh. From the car park with a view, I glance at the railway station.

That makes me angry, so a digression.

In my transport gallery I have a painting of the station when real trains with an observation car in summer brought large crowds and the freight yard was packed. Now there are just two-car everyday Sprinters, many seats having the view obscured by window pillars.

Nearly all regular traffic has long disappeared. A host of places whose postal addresses were By Garve or By Achnasheen now have direct roads and bus services and, unless there's real point in doing so, today's traveller without a car to Portree takes the fast through bus. The only possible justification for retaining the long, expensive Kyle line is because its beauty is well known. But encouraging tourists to enjoy fine views is not part of ScotRail's remit.

I'd be as sad as anyone to see the railway go. There'd be an outcry if it did. The chances of common sense prevailing are, however, as negligible as the winter train's loadings. If only a New Zealand example could be followed. Generally that country's slow narrow-gauge railways serve few passengers, and the three daily railcars across the Southern Alps were poorly patronised. Replaced by a single daily proper tourist train, seats with sheepskin rugs, a broadcast commentary and decent catering, large numbers are carried. The trip is included in many coach and other tours.

We follow the railway north from Kyle until forced to take higher ground before descending to Plockton. Pretty as in 'pretty village' is a word generally used comparatively, certainly earlier in this and the preceding chapters. Plockton is *definitively* pretty. With well-cared for gardens and palm trees and other lush vegetation, it is gentle and good-natured as well as good looking. Its secret? It faces east, sheltered from Atlantic winds, the curse of the west coast. The lake-like sea loch whose gentle waves lap Plockton's shores has many lovely inlets and islets. It is perfect.

Plockton, a planned village, was created especially for fishing. Now, like so many places to which they are easily lured, it fishes for tourists. The lake-like environment and softness against a stunning mountain backcloth encourages boating, gardening, sitting, eating out of doors... and it attracts picturesque Highland cattle, too. It seems perfectly natural that there are often painters at their canvasses dotted around the scene. One day there may even be a Plockton School of Art.

While the Highland cattle as always look benevolent, so today do most humans soaking up the sunshine. 'A bit of Scotland, a bit of Cornwall,' says Sheila, but most of the visitors are Scottish, and the conversation very much so. Hence an intense interest in other people's affairs.

That is what made the TV series of 1995-7 about the laid-back detective

Hamish Macbeth, with his wee Westie, Jock, so successful. Busybodies featured strongly in Lochdubh (Plockton) and its majestic backcloth. In the same way that crowds still go to Holmfirth to see where Norah Batty and the rest of the characters of Last of the Summer Wine have their pranks, so they poured into Plockton. Well over a decade since the final episode of Hamish Macbeth was shown, it has naturally quietened off, but the memory lingers of a soft, colourful place.

Our well-rated Haven Hotel seems in a bit of turmoil with change of ownership and staff problems, so we opt for dinner at the Plockton Inn's fish restaurant which does us proud in a suitably relaxed way. As bed time approaches and the warmth lingers on, we take a last walk along the main street. The calm water is still lit by the sunset. Many front doors are wide open, some residents sitting on chairs on the pavement. 'Not a bad place to live,' I say to one. 'The best,' she replies. A few are having late picnics or wee drams in their gardens opposite their homes on the other side of the street. Only clouds of midges send us scurrying to bed.

Via Applecross to Torridon

Next day's long journey starts by paralleling the railway along the southern shores of Loch Carron, rounding its head, and back along the north shore through Lochcarron village, turning north as we touch Loch Kishorn. Then onto Britain's steepest and most challenging road, over the Bealach na Ba or Pass of the Cattle that continually zig-zags in its struggle to gain height. 'Not advised for learner drivers' is one of the statements on the warning notice. There are unbelievable views, but all that concentrating drivers see is the next zig-zag. Descending, it is alarming looking down and seeing umpteen zig-zags with a host of cars slowly coming toward you. I love the story of a timid passenger in the early days of motoring.

'Do many cars go over on this road?' she enquired fearfully,

'Oh yes, especially in summer,' replied the driver,

presuming going over meant over the summit, not tipping over. The passenger moved to the middle of the car and held tight.

Originally a route for cattle drovers, it became one of the last Parliamentary roads, built for strategic rather than social or economic reasons, paid for by Parliament with a statutory contribution from the laird. Back in the early 1820s workers from Applecross, to which having 'gone over' we now make a spectacular descent, would have counted themselves lucky to be paid a shilling a day.

The whole area, with rocks up to 75 million years old, deer, eagles and outstanding walking country, is known as the Applecross Peninsula. The more remote you are, the more likely there is to be an ancient Christian site. The Gaelic for Applecross means sanctuary. In 673, Maelrubha, a monk from Ireland's Bangor, established his monastery here, sometimes said to have been only second in importance to Iona in the spread of Christianity into Scotland. No road, then, and only a small native population mainly no doubt living on fishing, though there has always been some cultivatable ground.

Applecross is a pleasing little centre which predictably attracts its quota of incomers, welcome if sometimes found to be overbearing in their insistence that what they think is the traditional way of doing things should be preserved. There is certainly a strong community spirit and interest in the past.

For nearly 140 years after the opening of the Parliamentary steep road across the Pass of the Cattle, it was the only one by which Applecross could be reached. Applecross and Toscaig at the peninsula's bottom were frequently cut off when the pass over the top was closed. 'When I bought my house at Ardheslaig, Shieldaig, about 5 miles to the east, was where the road from the east ended; it didn't go through to Applecross,' says Liz Pritchard who we meet later in connection with somebody else's book.

'I was still teaching in the south, and there was a ford I had to cross, always hoping it would be possible when I arrived on holiday but not too worried about being marooned when it was time to go back. Things were very different then. The other day I was flatteringly introduced to a newcomer as the original White Settler. Now there are many from the south, Scottish and English, very welcome and a blessing to the community provided they don't try and take things over. Occasionally there's been trouble with that.' As there was at Lochdubh (Plockton) in the episode of Hamish Macbeth we enjoyed on DVD the evening before this was written. In the story the newcomers naturally had their comeuppance.

We are heading to one of the Highlands' most civilised hotels. Though not so self-consciously grand as to call itself a destination in itself, it actually is for many who come for a few days cosseted in splendid scenery. The Loch Torridon Country House Hotel (three red stars and two rosettes) is gloriously situated, an elegant Victorian shooting lodge, about nowhere By Achnasheen, with friendly staff, great meals, seclusion – and a panoramic view of water and mountain like a painting capturing the very essence of the Highlands, though the real thing has the advantage of constantly changing light. The gatepost says 'where spirits soar and eagles fly' and, in unlikely territory, there is a productive garden with an unusual gardener, Helen Christie who says, that after coming to the area as a National Trust volunteer, she was the only one to apply to an advertisement. 'When I came in 1998, you couldn't see there was a garden. I'm getting there. I hope to get a cookery book going on what we grow here and how the chef uses it.'

This is excellent walking country, with nature trails, and a log fire to unwind by when you return. May it long remain a family-owned hotel. A book on offer at reception assuages curiosity about the area and its natural history, a 432-page self-published *Torridon: the Nature of the Place* is by Chris Lowe, who for many years has spent his holidays in the area. Living in the south himself, his marketing strategy includes giving Liz Pritchard (mentioned earlier) an incentive to achieve local sales. 'It's amazing how many have sold since it came out five years ago,' she says. 'It has opened lots of people's minds: showing the locals what interest there is in the area and persuading many visitors to look more deeply.' It is also stocked by the shop at the hamlet of Torridon across the water. I like the way Chris uses sentences in boxes to draw people into the text. Here are a few examples, one sentence each, I've brought together:

Plants on Torridon soils need all the help they can get!

Now many metres above the level of the highest tides, bands of shingle can be seen gently sloping down from obviously marine eroded glacial drift and even what were once sea cliffs.

Successive waves of Celtic people washed over the British Isles for a period of over seven hundred years and a map of their tribal kingdoms looks like a patchwork quilt.

Sir Hector Mackenzie's runner used to cover the 60 miles between Gairloch and Dingwall (the nearest Post Office) between Monday and Wednesday, set off back on Thursday and hand over the mail on Saturday.

Spending the next morning walking locally, after lunch we take the winding road on the northern shore of Upper Loch Torridon, catching a glimpse of Inveralligin with its pier below and then climbing steeply through really mountainous country before dropping even more steeply to reach Upper and then Lower Diabaig. Lower Diabaig, where the road peters out, overlooks Loch Diabaig, again with a pier which in past times would have been its front door. My framed map of the LMS of about 1923 or 1924 shows it served by several steamer routes. Then you had to be truly adventurous to reach here by car. Inland there is a vast treeless, roadless, humanless region, with a multitude of unnamed short rivers: a score flow into a single freshwater loch between two mountain ranges.

Throughout there have been views in every direction, but the OS correctly points out a special one as, on our way back, we begin to lose height towards where we now branch off to slip down to Inveralligin: a few houses, Post Office and pier with a handful of small craft. Has so small a place a website? Yes. And no. There is one, with a space for a photograph (can someone supply it?) and an invitation to write a description 'of the town'. We know the ideal person to do that: the chap (presumably male) who makes use of the sheltered mini-climate to exploit a vegetable patch still with much to harvest.

Part of the produce is sold from a covered self-help 'The Veggie Table' with an oversize notice begging 'Weigh Pay & Takeaway', besides which is an imaginative list of items and prices, and an invitation to walk around the garden. Just the chap for the job of attracting more visitors (and veggie buyers).

Even in a minute place like this, the historical themes are the same, with great poverty, cruelty, loss of population and amenities. Will the Post Office be open even by the time this book is published? Yet something tells me that Inveralligin, where there is reasonably sheltered boating and you can even grow veggies, has a bright future.

· XXVII ·

EPISODES – 2

Mablethorpe and Woodhall Spa

We're staying close to Lincoln's grand (Britain's third largest) Cathedral, 'uphill' above the endless flat below. I love the city, a long way from any other, yet perhaps too busy to qualify as remote. Today, however, we're using it as base from which to go to a couple of places to the east whose very different reputations have long fascinated me.

Flat roads are not necessarily straight and remoteness attracts tat as well as quality. At the end of a slow drive, Sheila asks: 'Why on earth have we come here?' Mablethorpe, we find, is down market from Skegness. The official guide lumps them together in *The Fun Coast*.

Unless you're a crackpot author, the only reason for coming must be to eat unhealthy food – cheap according to zealous menus – and rapidly to part with holiday cash. There are many amusement parks, and don't forget Bingoland and Tanland. The architecture? Forget it. Attention is any way distracted by large signs – like 'SUM-FING 4 ALL' – vying for attention.

A hideous protective wall keeps out rogue waves and hides the sea. When you find the beach, though blue-flag and two miles long, it is as boring as they get. To take a glance we drive up the wall, literally by a ramp to a small car park. One of the advertising claims is actually fair: it's a resort for all seasons. It may be bracing like Skegness, but it's seldom fit for people used to today's heated homes to lull around outside. There are more indoor attractions than anywhere else I've seen. That at least has the merit of attracting trippers all year, mainly from East Midland cities. So there's economic success.

Perhaps we're not able to comprehend the nature of what the website calls a 'charming resort' and missed the 'super range of charming shops', though we understand the appeal to kids – and no doubt the summer illuminations and carnival are special. But we're off without having spent sixpence; only a proverbial (these days free) penny.

The exit south is on a winding road mainly close to the gigantic wall preventing communion with the North Sea. As we strike inland, we note that nice little villages soon begin. I can't imagine too many of those living in the gracious houses of Alford, known for its working five-sail watermill and music and craft fairs, going to Mablethorpe for Sunday lunch.

Then into pretty, undulating country with neat farms and villages, our first taste of the Lincolnshire Wolds and what's known as Poacher Country. Amused to be told to engage low gear for a short 13 per cent descent, we take a series of lanes through Tetford where the Scarecrow Festival lasts three days, but everything else is understated.

Then into a larger place with tree-lined avenues, pine woods and spacious Edwardian houses. Is this Bournemouth or, with half-timbered hotels, is it Droitwich Spa? This is certainly not the Lincolnshire I'd expected. Indeed it's the county's oddball, which makes it the more worth visiting. What immediately strike me are the people: relaxed, smiling, friendly.

Woodhall Spa. It breeds articulate people. The community website spells out a host of initiatives ranging from restoring the original Spa – half-heartedly discussed for decades – to preventing the closure of the camping site, and listing events and achievements such as the heritage trail through the conservation area and the tarmaced walk and cycleway along the abandoned railway which offers great water views. Of the opening ceremony for one section it says: 'At least 200 people processed, on foot and by bike together with a jazz band, from the ribbon cutting at Bardney to Bardney Lock. On the viaduct there was a marquee providing much needed shade and a hog roast.'

Woodhall Spa is an ambitious little place full of surprises. Our first call is at the Book Fayre offering a mixture of second hand and new titles. 'I wondered who might buy those,' says the owner, Kathryn Fairs when, as well as a title of local interest, I proffer copies of several of the alternative gospels I'm studying. As someone else comes in, she looks up to greet them personally. When I tell her of my involvement with the book trade, she immediately volunteers a trade discount. 'I love the business. My customers are great people,' she enthuses.

Later she sends me a copy of a title she's commissioned and published: *The Woodhall Spa Guide*, by Edward Mayor. A model of its kind, it demonstrates what can be sensibly compressed into a hundred text-led but well-illustrated pages.

Then we do the rounds, briefly calling at the excellent cottage museum doubling as information centre, and going on to two of the hotels. Everywhere there are photographs of the colourful pre-war 1914 days when there were through carriages from King's Cross. At the end of Broadway, the striking Golf Hotel (the village has two golf courses and the National Golf Centre) has tapped its own supply of the bromo-iodine water that first made the place famous and, having given up on the hope of the original being resurrected, runs its own spa. 'Highly half-timbered' is one description of the distinctive building, agog with activity this afternoon, as is the Woodhall Spa Hotel, also half-timbered and on Broadway.

Round the corner, the Petwood Hotel is even more splendid. It was built as home for Grace, the socialite daughter of Maple furniture fortune, when she was in the middle of a divorce in 1905. The building's name comes from oak being her 'pet wood'. There's a superb staircase, up which the very best of Maple's furniture was carried. Grace remarried, Captain (later Sir) Archibald Weighall, an MP, and changes were made to create a Jacobean-style home for lavish entertainment. In the mid-thirties, when tax problems forced them to give up the house, they helped its conversion into a stylish hotel, commandeered only a few years later for an officers' mess for locally-based squadrons including 617, the Dambusters. Back as an hotel, it has changed hands several times, now flourishing in private ownership, offering superb service and making the most of past associations.

Everyone greets me when I go to the bar. It is like going into a real officers' mess. In a congenial atmosphere, with much 617 Squadron memorabilia on the walls, there's inevitably conversation about Barnes Wallis's clever invention of the bouncing bomb, one of which is on display in the village.

'I've always wanted to come here,' says an upright, elderly gent. 'You have to admire them.'

'It's long been on my list, too,' replies another. 'I remember how their success cheered us up when the war wasn't going too well.' When he asks where I'm from and I say Nairn, he replies: 'RAF Kinloss. Did a stint there, but that was after the war. Nimrods now.' We see them take off from our garden seven miles away.

In a wood close by, the old Spa is a sorry sight. That it came into existence at all was by curious accident. They were unsuccessfully prospecting for coal (how different the village would have been if it been found) when a fissure was pierced and water bubbled to the surface. That was in the early 1820s. A farmer noticing that ailing animals seemed to be cured by drinking it led to it being analysed – and declared Europe's finest curative bromo-iodine water.

'Taking the water' led to rapid growth. Though hotels seem to be on a generous scale today, once there were more. The 150-bedroom Victoria, with pleasure gardens, bandstand copying that in South Kensington Gardens, and a pavilion (now the Kinema in the Woods) and tea room, burnt down on Easter Day 1920. More grievous were the direct hits which demolished the Royal Hydro Hotel in August 1943. The Germans knew that the village had military significance, though most billeted here were away that night. The loss included an extensive shopping arcade wrapped round one of Britain's largest glazed winter gardens. However, after 1945, the village's popularity declined and the other hotels struggled.

Then to the Kinema in the Woods, one of the oldest surviving anywhere. As it is not going to be open till this evening, we won't experience its unique front-projection system or hear the Compton Organ, but we're shown around and buy a book about it. 'There aren't many villages with a cinema let alone one as large as this,' says our guide. 'It's amazing how local people support us, though many come from miles away. There's always interest.' The frequently-changing programme offers new films, re-runs of old favourites and rarities.

Much though I love eccentric spas, I've never quite understood the commercial drive that so quickly followed the discovery of foul-tasting curative water. Before 1914, even German aristocracy had faith in it and sometimes outnumbered other guests at the Royal Hotel. Though it wouldn't have been realised at the time, with spas as well as holiday resorts, what mattered was an early start – when building grand hotels was affordable, which it ceased to be well before the end of Victorian days. Not a single large, well-balanced holiday town has ever been created off the railway system. However, the future seems brighter here than at most minor spas.

Now back to Lincoln, getting horribly lost in the complicated road system trying to find the down hill restaurant where we've booked dinner before returning to our up hill base. What a day of contrasts.

Papa Westray, Orkney

Having recently landed on a grass runway, we are at the Knap of Howar on the tiny Orcadian island of Papa Westray looking at a pair of ancient houses. Built around 3800BC and older than the Egyptian pyramids, they are Europe's oldest known standing architecture.

People were smaller in those days, and we hadn't yet read the website's note about the internal link between the pair: 'Watch your heads!' Wondering why Sheila is taking so long while I'm waiting to snap her emerging, she comes out dizzy having nearly knocked herself unconscious. (Plate 8)

Few people come to see this historical marvel, for Papa Westray, one of the most northerly islands of the Orkneys, is distinctly remote.

Far better known, and a World Heritage site, is Skara Brae on Orkney's Mainland: a Stone Age village, or as I like to think of it, the world's first housing estate. Each of the connected houses has a hearth, stone beds and a two-shelf stone dresser for precious items. Part of the fascination – and the excellent state of repair – is due to the fact that for thousands of years it was buried. The belief is that it was over-run by sand about 4,000 years ago while still occupied. Then all knowledge of it was lost until another great storm uncovered it in 1850.

Within the terms of the length of human life, it is hard fully to grasp: the Knap of Howar pair were abandoned for almost as many centuries as they were occupied before Skara Brae came into existence. Another thing, the Knap of Howar remained unknown for a century after Skara Brae emerged from the sand. Then the older pair of dwellings were also revealed (1929) when a gale blew away the sand that had cocooned them.

I love Orkney and its different, more agricultural and entrepreneurial way of life than found on most island groups – and not least its people. But I've written at such lengths about other islands that much more might deter mainland readers. And somehow our Orkney experiences have been unusually personal. Before returning to the miniscule Papa Westray to focus on just one island, suffice it to say that, though Orkney and Shetland share much of the same long (a hazelnut shell was recently dated as between 8820 and 6600BC) history, they are totally different in landscape, wildlife and human kind. Yes, oil has also had an impact on Orkney, but is physically confined to the terminal from the North Sea on the island of Flotta in the semi-enclosed sea of Scapa Flow. Most of the workers commute by boat.

Scapa Flow is where the navy was substantially based in World War One and where, in World War Two, a German submarine lethally penetrated. The Churchill Barriers were built to close vital gaps by linking the Mainland to the southern islands. The first of these is tiny Lamb Holm, where over 100,000 visitors a year are attracted to the Italian Chapel, a Nissen hut made perfect by prisoners of war, improvising with the limited materials at their disposal. Though there is huge natural history and especially ornithological interest, most of the other tourist pulls are ancient remains, including Maes Howe, the Stones of Stenness, and the Ring o' Brodgar, all world class. Orkney is easily accessible, with an extensive and civilised Mainland and excellent ferries and air services to a host of highly individual small islands.

We chose Papa Westray for its remoteness and population struggling at less than seventy. The first impression is how well things work. We have an instant transfer to the hotel, part of the islanders' co-operative enterprise embracing hotel and restaurant, bunk house, shop and petrol station, and immediately feel at home. The complex staff rota includes mostly women of working age. Meals are timely and enjoyable, the atmosphere relaxed. Everything is spotless. Possible to rent a car? Yes, just £10. No formalities. The keys are in it.

Just one problem. The petrol tank registers empty and the petrol pump has already long closed for the day. Providentially, the postman notices our dilemma and stops his motorbike to help. 'No problem. Follow me', he says and tells us to change to another car parked in a driveway. Though Papay, as the locals affectionately call it, is only a mile or so wide, it is four long, and we don't want to be cut off at the far end or have our sightseeing curtailed.

Our first stop is at the rather stark new pier built with the aid of European Union money for the twice-weekly car ferry from Kirkwall. The posh recycling bins (more sophisticated than we have on the mainland) are also EU funded. But in all its glory the EU couldn't create the greatest attraction nearby: the most gorgeous display of orchids we've ever seen. We gaze and gaze... and think of what we have lost with the spraying of mainland verges.

Some of this might be taken to make fun of Papay. Not so. It's a lovely, thoroughly up-together island largely devoted to agriculture, both arable and cattle. There's evidence that the ancient pair of homes were for farmers who grew grain and kept stock while also fishing – fish no doubt more plentiful in those days. There's an ancient water mill, and an excellent traditional steading with doo'cot and old bothy which for three centuries has been home to the island's owners, the Trait family.

After the Disruption, when most working people left the Church of Scotland, Papa Westray was the first place in Scotland to have a chapel ready to hand over to the new Free Church. The laird, George Trait, paid for it, but his daughter Anne made the actual presentation, in 1844. The chapel is dedicated to her, not to a saint in what has been nicknamed the 'priest island', probably where Christianity arrived in Orkney.

Nearly a century later, in 1929, the rival brands of Presbyterianism joined their small congregations, and now St Anne's is the Parish Kirk. We note the times of the once-a-week service conducted by the minister from larger Westray, to which there is a regular passenger ferry.

Margit Fassbember, a German, is the unexpected postmistress in the nearby settlement of Daybreak. Once afraid of dogs, she's here because she fell in love with one, a border collie. They're on their second now, lively and prone to barking. Margit and her husband, once university teachers in Germany, combine the usual island spectrum of tasks. The Post Office doubles up as craft shop, and sells her knitting – 'I make traditional socks that were once sent all over the world, especially to the Hudson Bay Company in Canada, and there's a new demand' – relief postman, helping at a club for the elderly, and so on. 'We adore it here. You're an individual in a friendly society; everyone's nice and polite.'

Then we drive down a picturesque sandy track along the sheltered east coast shore lined with tall grasses to the old pier, where lobster boats are anchored and passage is available to the Holm of Papa, the island opposite giving protection. Uninhabited except for the long dead, this has a number of classic burial chambers and is thought to be where once all Papay folk were buried.

Gravestones from the more recent past are in profusion beside the old parish church of St Boniface on the opposite coast. Though long abandoned, it has been restored and used for occasional summer services and concerts. We explore what, apart from St Magnus Cathedral, is the only Orkney church to survive the Reformation. I wonder about St Boniface (AD675 to 754), English but best remembered as a German missionary and archbishop who established many churches at the site of ancient brochs as is the case here, before he was murdered by pagans while waiting to confirm novices. All around is evidence of human life and death covering the period from the 12th century BC to the 6th century AD.

Among the sixty ancient monuments on the island, there's special interest in the ruins of St Tredwell chapel on a headland overlooking the Loch of St Tredwell. Legend says that Tredwell was an 8th century Celtic girl hermit living here. When Nechtan, King of the Picts, was roused to passion by her eyes and tried to rape her, she tore them out, proving that spirituality is all. Blinded, she went on to become an abbess and was canonised and the chapel dedicated to her became a place of pilgrimage among those seeking restored sight.

Before there's time even to glance at the uninhabited north with its RSPB reserve, which attracts many tourists, we've had to return to the hotel and are soon again in the transit van. 'See you soon,' they say as we leave.

Ancient houses, pier, chapels... we've been on our own everywhere and even the 'airport' is deserted, though the 'terminal', a hut, is unlocked. Feeling skittish, Sheila weighs herself on an ancient Avery machine, but what it registers has little to do with reality. The phone rings. We ignore it. It rings again. Better answer it?

'Mr Thomas? Hoped it would be you. This is Kirkwall. You've a tight connection, so would you mind weighing your baggage?' We oblige and hope any inaccuracy won't matter.

On the way up, with no passengers for Westray, we flew non-stop, depriving us of experiencing the world's shortest commercial flight, less than two minutes from Westray to Papa Westray. Now, looking over to Westray, we see our plane has just taken off – when a Land Rover arrives (driven by our friend the postman) and hooks itself to the trailer which acts as fire engine. As broadcasters know, just under two minutes (the flight's length) is time for many thoughts: even in Papa Westray, which we've fallen in love with, we could have done with more than the nearly two days we allowed; the timetable of the inter-islands air service using just one plane for morning and tea-time flights from Kirkwall has daily variations opening many journey possibilities; a shame more people don't holiday in Orkney...

The only passengers on the flight, we sit behind the pilot who, tipping the plane, shows us stunning cliff scenery. Then we follow the plane from Shetland we'll be catching for Inverness. We take off fifteen minutes after touching down.

Footnote. Since our visit, Papa Westray's population has increased slightly and there are a number of new projects. There's also a handsome self-propelled fire engine.

In addition to the many islands featuring in this work and in *Journey*, I also love two other islands with great agricultural foundations: large Islay (famous for ancient crosses, distilleries and birdlife) which including a day trip across the narrow sound to Jura took me a whole week thoroughly to explore; and tiny Gigha, only half an hour's ferry ride from Kintyre and easily explored on foot in twenty four hours.

I'm often asked which are my favourite islands. For what? Arran is Scotland in miniature; Skye lives up to its fame; gentler Mull has splendid variety, a great wee capital in Tobermory and is access to magical Iona; the Orkneys are a delightful group whose variety can be tasted in a short time. But the more islands you get to know, the more you want to explore... the chain of the Western Isles, Shetland and the utterly varied one-offs of the Inner Hebrides... While the Isle of Wight fits into half an OS Landranger sheet, Shetland, the Orkneys and Western Isles need a dozen sheets between them.

The Turf on the Exe

Having parked Little Car near Powderham Church, we (Sheila, daughter Alyss and I) are walking along a well-established footpath recently widened and added to the National Cycle Network beside the Exe. The mainline from Paddington to Penzance is only a field or two away. The trains we first hear are however on the Exmouth branch well over a mile distant on the other side of the river. Sound carries with amazing clarity across rivers at peace between tides and when a mainline train passes close by, it is almost silent. It is travelling at a snail's pace, and it soon becomes clear that it is delaying the following train, which is also crawling. Then we see a gang of around twenty five men on the track though not working. Mystery.

This is a walk I used to take back in steam days when you could enjoy a greater variety of trains and see clearly into their windows to gauge the number travelling. Before the days of air conditioning, some folk poked their heads out, for Powderham is the point at which speed restrictions start for the curves where the railway meets salt water. Down the Exe, along the Sea Wall through Dawlish, and up the Teign.

No doubt with a childhood too dominated by my railway obsession, Alyss, in a large loose red anorak, making the most of her height, shows she's not interested. Between conversations, she dives into her private world, or rather sees things through the lens of her camera, delighting in the symphony of blue between sky, river and distant sea. She excels at atmospheric photography, which I encourage her to add to her sources of income. Life is tough for a single mum.

Last night we spent with her and Joshua, the creative but tiring four-year-old fruit of the romance between Alyss and Stephen (see *Journey*) which didn't lead to them staying together long. 'Families' have become almost a swear word today, expressing so many older people's frustration of the consequences of the volcanic relationships between today's young, though in truth Alyss is in her second half century, a psychologist to boot.

Once ships reached the heart of Exeter by the river, but Countess Weir was deliberately built by the Earls of Devon to force traffic to use their port of Topsham where they raked in dues. Opened in 1566, the canal allowed coasters to reach Exeter. Improved several times, it was not until 1824 that it was lengthened to give easier access at this lower point on the Exe. Though displaying the name Turf Hotel, today, with no bedrooms it is now known as The Turf. Built to house lock keepers, it also provided basic refreshment to ships' crews.

Exeter remained a busy port until the 1960s. The opening of the swing bridge at Countess Weir incidentally seriously delayed peak holiday traffic in the days I reported so that it sometimes took two hours to traverse the notorious Exeter bypass, and so that the city centre was jammed with traffic attempting to bypass the bypass. By the 1970s, the only substantial vessel then going out into the Exe from the canal was a sewerage boat, on which I once took a trip for the BBC to describe life aboard – comfortable if smelly – and just where the sewage was dumped... a favourite spot for fishermen.

Deprived of its raison d'être, The Turf fell into disrepair, and the canal owners, the City Council, planned demolition. However, it was actually Teignbridge District Council's support of the bid of David Goddard of Exeter Maritime Museum (which alas closed for lack of funds) to list it as an historic building. Like so many former industrial-based things, when forcibly restored, it was for leisure, and its clientele has gone distinctly upmarket

There's a commotion as we arrive. A couple of burley railtrack workers kitted out in bright yellow are desperate to find the driver of a council (presumably Teignbridge) van left blocking access to the railway. 'We must find him quickly; there's a broken rail and until we can repair it the timetable will suffer.' It does throughout our stay. Though there aren't many of them on a weekday mid-morning, successive customers want to know what's going on. While the couple of railtrack workers are searching the area for the driver, many others idle time away even between the passage of crawling trains. Their lorry that cannot get through has the heavy equipment needed to effect the repair.

When one of her grown-up sons relieves her at the bar, Ginny Redfern, who runs the Turf with her husband Clive, joins us for morning refreshment. Because of the sons, there are no longer rooms to let. 'We used to do bed-and-breakfast but now we couldn't cope. This is a funny place. It's so quiet much of the year that we only open when the weather's good and we feel like it, though, if we're here at all, we open at weekends. From Easter to October we can be mobbed and it's very hard to cope.

It's been even busier since the cycleway was opened, but people come every which way. The sixty one-seater *Sea Dream* makes several daily trips from Topsham's quay, there's the Topsham pedestrian ferry, and a ferry service down the canal from Double Locks with a bus connection from City Basin. Others like you walk from Powderham, or park by the railway line at Swan's Nest, Exminster, and these days there's even a car park less than a mile from here though there are just nineteen designated places. Sometimes we think we're nowhere, then suddenly we're the centre of it all.'

She shows me the extensive summer lunch and more ambitious summer evening menus. They cater for special parties, too, including at Christmas 'if we're here'.

Clive arrives with Rufus and Rocket, lively Jack Russells. 'They're very dog orientated,' puts in an elderly gent at the bar. To prove the point soon Poppy, a Labrador cross belonging to one of the son's girlfriends threatens to knock our coffee off the table with her waggling tail. 'It's brilliant here now', he adds, 'but before Clive came it used to be a very part-time pub. And the last lock keepers, they were some characters.'

'In theory we're our own bosses,' explains Clive. 'We can wind the business up or down as we like, but the bills go on all the time. A comfortable living, but we've got to work at it, and keep on improving it. The menus, for instance; they're increasingly based on the best local ingredients we can get, and the play area and barbecues with great river views cost a bit to improve too. Expensive building to maintain; it's timber-framed, and nothing is bang upright.'

'That's what I like about it,' says Alyss, who has a penchant for the historic irregular.

'Even the slate roof eats money,' says Clive.

Alyss looks at her watch and fidgets. She's a client to see in Totnes 'and it'll take forty five minutes just to get back to the car'. So, warmed up physically and psychologically, we leave one of England's most fascinating pubs, trains on the upline still crawling. (Phone 01395 833128 for The Turf's opening and route details.)

Two Country Hotels on the Border

We're spending the night at the Pen-y-Dyffryn Country Hotel, included in the excellent Welsh Rarebits Hotels of Distinction booklet, which shows how dramatically Welsh catering has improved in my lifetime. 'Not sure it's actually in Wales,' says Sheila looking at the map. We've had a lovely journey from Machynlleth: Wales at its best, with bare green mountain tops rising above the tree line, pretty villages with welcoming pubs and, it seemed, fresh beauty at every turn, especially as we came nearer to Oswestry.

'I'd like to stay in the land of my fathers one more night.' So: 'Are we still in Wales?' I ask as we check in. 'No, but your car in our car park is. And the view from your room will be of Wales as seen from England.' Here's another for my collection of hotels on the border. Then I read that the 'hotel straddles the Wales/England border in a landscape that speaks volumes of the way in which the two countries historically went their separate ways. Drive west from Oswestry on an arrow-straight road that lances through the Shropshire countryside and within a few minutes you round a corner to be plunged unexpectedly into a rollercoaster of steep hills and deep valleys.'

The hotel presides over the ancient border marked by Offa's Dyke. My body may be in England nurtured by quality food sensibly cooked, but my soul and most of my vision are still in Wales, to which I quickly return to collect something from the boot. A leaflet in the folder in our room tells us that when the new parish of Rhydycroesau was created in

1844, it straddled the border. The church was on the Welsh side. The first rector, Robert Williams, was a Celtic scholar, showing impartiality by producing *The Biographical Dictionary of Eminent Welshmen* followed by the first dictionary of Cornish. When the Church of Wales was disestablished in 1920, the congregation, decidedly not Celtic, voted to stay in the Church of England, which became one of a handful in Wales. Later the Rectory was sold off, and had several uses including a restaurant before Miles and Audrey Hunter (it was Audrey who greeted us and told us we were in England but the car in Wales) turned it into this stylish hotel. There's a friendly, family atmosphere. The tall dark waitress is the girlfriend of one of their sons, and they speak highly of a Polish couple on the staff.

Over a drink in the lounge before dinner, a Welsh couple tell us they come every year: 'We like their style of cooking, and it is very comfortable. Remote to the feel, but in fact handy for many things. Anyway each day the breakfast menu suggests things to do for the day.'

Dinner is a real occasion, our room delightful. But what I'll always especially remember is the multi-layered view deep into rural Wales: hills with sheep and cattle on fields of varying steepness and woods sweeping up and down other hillsides. Even in the intriguing terraced garden, I find it hard to take my eyes off the view across the road, or is it lane. Does border country set out to show itself off? Hardly, I think, but this one is particular fun, and we'd have liked to spend longer at the hotel.

That crossing the border can bring disappointment as well as joy is well remembered from what it used to be like as you drove into Devon on the A303 from Somerset. The road instantly deteriorated, and progress round endless curves with narrow bridges and steep hills was so frustrating there wasn't emotion to spare for the scenery.

Devon is – just – where our other border hotel is. A lovely hotel, too, about which more in a moment, but again memorable for a huge view, this time in fact across two borders, with Dorset in the foreground and Somerset beyond.

It is the kind of view that could be used for a challenging jigsaw puzzle. Though there are a few distinctive points, for the most part it is a patchwork of farms, small woods, and odd pieces of lanes hard to trace as through routes. Open, expansive, it is as different as it could be from the first hotel's or for that matter any Scottish view.

I can't take my eyes off it, and – yes – I can sincerely say that it is possible to distinguish between the lush Devon we're in, rolling West Dorset though the hills (or 'Dorset Knobs') are not so sharp this far north and west, and Somerset descending to its broad marshland plain beyond. In a short drive through villages of all three counties next morning, Sheila is more or less convinced I'm not exaggerating. Hereabouts, Dorset wins our votes for being the most liveable in.

Our Dorset choice of place to visit is Beaminster, once a full-blown town but, ignored by railways, now just a village at the head of the tranquil vale of the River Brit. But remoter Dorset has many delightful parts. I've always loved the journey on what used to be one of Britain's finest railways, the Waterloo-Exeter route as, now reduced to single track, it passes through Dorset with two separate sections, a wedge of Somerset inbetween. There's gently rolling, uncrowded countryside, with only a few modest market towns, virtually all the way west of Salisbury.

That we are at the Fairwater Head Hotel, near Hawkchurch is because it's run by Adam and Carrie Southwell, whose hospitality we were delighted by at the Prince Hall Hotel, near Princetown (see *Journey*). Then they were tenants of the Duchy of Cornwall; now they're the proud owners of a near-perfect hotel (AA three stars, two rosettes). How are they doing? The posh car in an otherwise empty car park as we arrived mid-afternoon (often the hotel owners' is the most upmarket) suggests not too badly.

'It's very different,' says Adam. 'Obviously a lot milder and closer to things. There I was doing fifty miles a day mainly taking the boys to and fro. Much easier here.' Over a pre-dinner drink on the terrace, I comment on the county borders. 'We have a Somerset postcode, Dorset phone code and pay Devon rates,' he says. 'You'll not find many hotels in such a tranquil setting in its own garden and with a great view.' To which I might add, don't attempt to find it without directions, though many attracted by Lyme Regis, only four miles away, prefer to stay here, and it is the only AA hotel listed under Axminster.

As to Hawkchurch, the postal address, it's a pretty little village of about 300 people sometimes known as the 'village of roses' since roses planted on walls by a 19th century rector still make a colourful splash. But it has lost its shop and Post Office, and today's residents include commuters to London.

Stanley, Falkland Islands

We are in the Upland Goose, struggling with what seems like a wartime school lunch: soggy meat and mushy peas. They don't do sandwiches or salads. Frozen peas are seen as new fangled: 'People like mushy.' The Americans off our cruise ship can't face them. 'This is barbaric,' mutters one man used to having his whims served back home. Then a seaman from our ship advises us to stay where we are till further notice. 'There's a storm and we've had to suspend the tender operation.' A local puts in: 'That might mean you'll have to spend the night on the school floor. It happened with a cruise ship only a few months ago.'

The first time I had heard of the Upland Goose was when it was the only overseas hostelry included in the list of British Best Western hotels. Bizarre? Hang on. As a serious war was fought to prove, the Falklands *are* Britain, part of the scraggy remains of Empire and not an independent member of the Commonwealth.

Between my first learning about the Upland Goose and that war, I'd become publisher to the Falkland Isles Development Corporation, and sold them many books, especially *Falklands* in the 'Islands' series. By mail and phone, I'd got to know the author Ian J Strange and worried about his safety during the Argentine invasion and forced retreat. Come to think about it, a consignment of books were en route to the islands when the invasion happened. It made an unusual claim on the Export Guarantee scheme that then existed to help small exporters.

Ian, on New Island, has not been able to join us for lunch, but I've had a busy morning meeting an interesting bunch of people. On the in-bound tender, we sat next to Sir Rex Hunt who was the colourful Governor of the Falklands when the Argentinians invaded, and who wrote a book about his experiences for me. It was much censored by Whitehall who wouldn't allow any criticism of the armed forces or Maggie Thatcher. However, it sold well, and boosted Rex's demand as an after-dinner speaker. He's drawn large audiences as lecturer on our ship. This is the first time he's been back. I watched him disappear into the old London black taxi used for State occasions.

I was met by a former staff member, Rosemary Wilkinson. The only Falklands subscriber to *Writers' News,* she handed me a copy of the latest issue, published since we left home. Over a cup of coffee, she also gave me a splendid jumper I still wear when 'Falklands weather' hits the Moray Firth: the pattern is of rows of penguins in the undyed natural wool of black lambs. She says: 'It takes me nearly a day to get here from our isolated farm on West Falkland, but we're so much happier than we were in congested Britain. Not that we aren't British mind you.

We're remote, windswept, barren but beautiful. Never regretted that we all came here from Devon in 1979, that's Clive, me and our three sons. Our farm, cattle as well as sheep, is called Dunnose Head. Clive my husband bought a good kit house and we've imported our own generator – it's important to keep the freezer going – and we use bottled gas. We have regular phone check-ups with the doctor – everyone has a government medicine chest – and he visits camp [outlying settlements] several times a year and can land on our strip in an emergency. So don't be sorry for us! But transport is difficult. Heavy items have to be floated in on a spring tide.'

Then Rosemary's son Alistair drove us up a seriously windblown hill to look at a colony of small Magellanic penguins, known as Jackass because of their braying noise, in their mini-nests, hollows beaked out of the earth. After that, to the editor of the local 'newspaper', the A4 *Penguin News*. Jim Stevens was a sub-editor on the *Western Evening Herald* of whose reporting staff joint with *The Western Morning News* I was a member. Marvellous how small facial expressions are immediately recognised many years later in a totally different environment. He was a nice guy, particular about detail.

Before lunch we also had time for the tourist tour. In high summer and, surprisingly, further from the South Pole than we are at home from the north, the first noticeable thing is the pathetic lupins struggling at a quarter of the height of ours in Nairn which is further from the Equator. But then the Antarctic is the sixth frozen continent shedding cooling icebergs. We noticed that the small church is the Cathedral of the South Atlantic: some diocese for the Bishop to get around. With a cruise ship in town, both windows of the Post Office were open; we naturally bought a set of the colourful local stamps. But there was little on offer in the handful of rather dreary shops scattered along the waterfront main street we saw so often on our TV screens during the war.

Though sorry I wasn't able to take up an official postwar invitation to visit this reconquered outpost of Britain, I couldn't live here. As we finish our lunch and wait for news about the tender service, I reflect that only 1,800 people are spread across an area the size of Wales – and that the Britons living most remotely are not actually in their home country but represent it in every corner of the former Empire or working in outrageous conditions, whaling in Antarctic seas or fishing off the Icelandic coast.

And, after sailing across the ocean with the protection of an Albatross for five days, we later call at Tristan da Cunha, the comparative isolation is emphasised when a young nurse tells me: 'Yes, I've travelled. I've been to the Falklands, but I couldn't cope with Stanley and all those shops.'

Eventually we are told the tender service is resumed, but it will be pretty rough. I put on my new penguin jumper. 'Where did you get that?' asks an American sitting opposite me on the tossing boat, accusingly. When I explain it was a gift, like a spoilt child, she cries: 'That's not fair. There was no shopping at all. A whole cruise port and nothing to show for it.'

It has to be said that my visit was far longer ago than any other recorded in these pages, and is included to be different and to emphasise perspective. In their modest way, the Falklands are booming. Many more cruise ships now call. The number of Stanley's shops has more than doubled and I'm told there's now real competition for custom. Stanley has mushroomed and the islands'overall population has reached 3,000. Fishing has become serious and brings in cash, and there's off-shore oil exploration.

Another winner is greatly expanded natural history tourism. On New Island, Ian Strange has founded and runs the New Island Conservation Trust, a Falklands first, and has even written a 160-page book, *The New Island*. It tells of how badly early traders and hunters hurt wildlife, and how control has been unified with splendid results, especially for the Black-browed Albatross which, with the Falkland Flightless Steamer Ducks and Gentoo Penguins, breed in profusion. (www.falklandswildlife.com.)

On much larger West Falklands, Rosemary Wilkinson is over the moon having won funding through the Foreign & Colonial Office's Economic Diversity Programme for a purpose-built woolcraft workshop. 'I've nicknamed it the Rookery, since it is by the sea (amazing views out of the big windows). We'll have lots of activity, not just me producing stuff to sell but visitors flying in from the military base by helicopter. They are noisy things, but maybe that's preferable to the smell of the penguin rookery.' (www.falklandwool.com Dunnose Head Farm)

So even the wild, rugged Falklands are moving forward. Soon Rosemary and her husband will find going to Stanley for shopping much easier than our going to Edinburgh. The world over, everyone escaping from crowds to remote places, immediately wants better communications, more visitors and so on, but there's no chance of these most isolated of Britons becoming over-run by neighbours.

· XXVIII ·

BODMIN MOOR

The Undiscovered Gem

When I lived with Dartmoor on my doorstep, I frequently compared it and Bodmin Moor and became increasingly fascinated. Smaller, far less visited and talked or written about and more accessible by road and easy track, it was yet the more mysterious. There was no surprise that it captured the imagination of Daphne du Maurier. Jamaica Inn which, on the main A30 bisecting the moor, has, ever since her book been one of the few 'honey-pots' for tourists, noticed far more than Brown Willy, at 1,357ft the moor's highest point.

Whenever I went to that other famous spot, Dozmary Pool, I enjoyed its gentle wavelets and experienced its undoubted magic out of sight of any other human. I loved genuine Dartmoor people, with whom for one reason or another I often mixed though, with frequent controversies (Military, Prison, the stringent 'stop all development' campaigning of Lady Sayer, routing of the very same A30 south of Okehampton), opinions were often black and white. Bodmin Moor equivalents were more pragmatic, gentler, though not a whit less colourful.

Talk of Bodmin Moor becoming a National Park quickly died, and today a mere mention of such status upsets its keenest residents and the few visitors and incoming residents who really love and appreciate it. That the standard books on Cornwall go into great detail about the coasts, but include little about it, is good in their eyes.

'The shutters are down on any form of publicity,' a prominent member of the Commoner's Association tells me. 'We're belligerent.'

She ceased threatening to put the phone down when I asked if that had anything to do with a recent controversial BBC film on badgers and other wild things on the moor. 'I deliberately made a point of not seeing it,' I say.

'Well done you,' she replies. 'Absolute rubbish.' When I express sympathy, she softens more, saying: 'The tragedy is the media haven't really shown an interest in what matters: using financial incentives to reduce stock levels on the moor, for instance.' Now relaxing, she continues: 'Travellers of long ago described the moor as brown, but we have loved it for its greenness. Then "experts" dangle incentives we're foolish enough to take; times were tough. By reducing stock levels, vegetation of the wrong kind doesn't get eaten, spreads and dies, brown. As soon as the period we're tied to is over, we'll flood the moor with stock again, and hopefully we'll get it back to green.'

But will that pay? We're back to the urgent question of who is going to take care of the appearance of Britain's countryside if it's not farmers? 'And there's not much profit in farming. Holdings are being merged. We'll probably be down to only a dozen Commoners, but they'll be really Cornish. Low returns will keep out the others. It'll probably be OK, but it will be despite, and not because of, government policy.'

As we will see, there's been a lot of diversification, mainly small scale, including growing organic produce and catering for visitors in the fight to survive. 'The young ones find it too tough to spend their lives on the moor, but it's still what anchors them.'

Bodmin Moor is as resilient as the Cornish. Caring newcomers are not so much accepted as 'Cornishised'. They tell you more forcibly than the locals that the name shouldn't be Bodmin Moor (for it has little to do with the town of Bodmin) but Fowey Moor. 'But perhaps not,' adds one: 'We don't want to be seen as another Dartmoor or Exmoor. That might happen if we were named after a river. But it really is Fowey Moor, the place where the river starts just like the Dart and the Exe.' It was the Ordnance Survey who first labelled it Bodmin Moor, apparently without consultation.

'Biding its Time'

Once more we're at what for decades I've jokingly called Cornwall's Piccadilly Circus: Congdon's Shop. There's not been a shop there in the many decades I've known it, and there's little else beside a junction of pretty insignificant roads. But it has long been a point of interest on journeys to the best of Cornwall. When living in South Devon, I reached it by crossing Dartmoor and a series of lanes, including a little-used crossing of the Tamar, on my way to magic coastal places such as Boscastle as well as Bodmin Moor. This Sunday morning, having taken the fast A30 from Exeter, bypassing Launceston and dropping down the B3254, as usual we discover absolutely nothing is happening at Congdon's Shop. Now '1 miles right to North Hill and 400yds right again, Trebatha...' I love such directions.

E V (Ernest) Thompson, the novelist, we're calling on before taking him and his wife Celia out to lunch, lives in a delightful long house.

Their warm welcome is sealed by the diminutive timid Siamese soon making friends. There's an aura of peace. 'There's a sense of belonging,' says Celia. 'It's timeless, feels just right,' adds Ernest who has written two books about the moor in addition to many novels.

In area, Bodmin Moor is tiny, being little more than ten miles in both length and breadth, increasingly fragmented by farming needs and split into two unequal parts by the A30 trunk road. Despite this, Bodmin Moor is a place with a magical quality that has been recognised by writers, poets and historians for as long as such men and women have existed.

It is a silent, yet very real and starkly beautiful living museum, holding the secrets of the people who have lived, loved, worked and died here for perhaps some 7,000 years. It is a place that possesses a remarkable air of timelessness. A prime example of nature 'biding its time'. It has seen man come and go, taking back its own when the time is right, yet acknowledging the past in its own inimitable way.

To strike out across the coarse grass of the moor, leaving behind the grey-stone moorside hamlets is to stride back into history. For those who seek its past it is here to be discovered. From the flint-flake microliths of Stone Age man, to the roofless skeletal remains of 19th century mine buildings. It also possesses a tranquillity that is rare in today's world.

What we hear next is how extremely untranquil their earlier lives have been. In Ernest's case, bombed out in London, Naval postings abroad, police including vice squad, investigator with BOAC, Hong Kong's Police narcotic bureau, security in Rhodesia... Soon after he returned to Britain, trying to earn his living writing short stories, and also selling many, he went 'heroically broke'. Their first child on the way, his wife ill, he earned what he could sweeping floors at a local china clay works. 'We had a tiny cottage and arrived in the coldest winter in living memory but, when we "escaped" to London, I knew I wanted to come back,' says Celia.

A turning point for Ernest was weeks of walking the moor recovering from an illness. He recalls many moorland characters and, inspired by the old mine engine houses surrounding the high moor, developed a strong interest in man's achievements and failures. An ancient clay pipe he dug up in the garden led to unravelling many secrets about how the clay, quarried on the moor, was used locally.

Then breakthrough. In 1977 his first novel, *Chase the Wind,* rapidly sold an astonishing 500,000 copies, later followed by a further 200,000. It won the year's contest for the best historical novel. It has just gone into a further reprint but, in tougher publishing days, that means only

1,000 copies. Many of his novels draw heavily on Bodmin Moor. 'Where fact and fiction merge,' puts in Celia. In his *Discovering Bodmin Moor,* he speaks of Dozmary Pool as 'this dark, brooding, reed-fringed basin of water, a mile in circumference, about 900ft above sea level' being 'woven into the moor's fabric, factually and in legend'.

Time to disturb the smallest Siamese I've ever seen and make our way to North Hill's Racehorse Inn. Almost fighting to reach the bar, and having to shout to be heard, we're relieved quickly to be shown to our table in the less frantic restaurant. A super traditional beef and Yorkshire pudding Sunday lunch, a real occasion for us as well as for the three generations of the large birthday party.

Like all writers, Ernest says he's constantly under pressure to appear at public events. I say I sympathise and won't even mention something I'd half had in mind. We're so relaxed, enthusiastic about life and writing, and writing and life that, as the dessert comes up, he asks what it was I had in mind. The upshot: he's to present the fiction prizes at what will be the very last prizegiving of our Charitable Trust, independently run by ourselves this year and back at our old venue, London's English Speaking Union. As he presents prizes, he'll no doubt warn that, while writing them is excellent practice, short stories don't really pay.

'The Best Bog I've Ever Seen'

Chris Blount, an old colleague in BBC days introduced in *Journey,* has kindly suggested a few contacts. (We once did a jolly broadcast together in the guard's van of a clay train on the Wenfordbridge goods-only line we'll come across in a moment.) Among them is a Mrs Bousfield. Though there are only two Bousfields in the area, the phone number he's given me is for the wrong one. However, having discovered that and rung off, I immediately called back to arrange to see her: she had sounded so interesting. Directions for finding her inevitably start with Congdon's (long-closed) Shop, but we've already done that so it only takes a couple of minutes to cross the bridge in Middlewood and turn sharply right up a steep, rough, boxed-in lane to a tiny lodge and parking area for a nursery garden called Bregover Plants where it peters out to a moorland track.

We're welcomed by Jen, the 'wrong' Mrs Bousfield, Pete her husband, and his mother, another Mrs Bousfield – 'they're like buses, none at all and then three in a row'. We have hardly settled down when Percy, a large brown Burmese with the loudest, most insistent feline voice I've ever heard, announces his arrival – delightfully enthusiastic and (once in diminuendo) relaxing.

Jen is part-time librarian at Launceston College and runs the nursery, not yet open for the season, growing alpines and other hardy plants at 500ft above sea level in the wettest place in Cornwall. Pete, once head of art now part-time, after-hours teacher at Launceston College, produces unique moor-inspired relief scenes in many shapes on medium density fibreboard with subtle acrylic colours. Some are sold by word of mouth, others retail. Jen, on the other hand, is licensed to help increase the dormouse population by building little nest boxes with their holes facing the tree trunks up which they happily run. They have Commoners' rights (for a head of cattle and five sheep). Their lives are busy with work, and a passionate love of where they live that typifies Cornwall's more remote parts. Possibly they are in line to join the successors to the old moorland characters they enthuse about.

Their conversation ranges widely. Some of the earliest people in Cornwall lived on the moor when the climate was kinder but the risk from invaders greater. There's a ring of tumuli around Brown Willy and many other pre-historic remains. At Wimalford, an axe factory has been found; the flints came by sea from Beer Head in Devon. The Anglo-Saxons developed better weapons to handle woodland but there's evidence of Cornish and Anglo-Saxon villages co-existing and even of peaceful trading with each other. As elsewhere, after the Black Death which thinned the population and, encouraged by the deteriorating climate, people started drifting down from the high land for an easier life: some of the ancient field patterns are still discernable, with one field that's never been ploughed.

A fascinating map of the moor's former lifestyles and remains, published by the Cornwall County Council's archaeological unit, is carefully unfolded. 'Of course,' says Pete, 'things moved from north to south, between the moor and the nearest coast. You can still tell that from today's dialects. The turnpike, which is now the A30 smack across Bodmin Moor, came much later.'

Back to farming and the land. Though many of the moorland farms have long disappeared, a few staunchly survive including a couple at Ten Men's Moor, so named after ten real men whose names are still known. That's where the Bousfields' land runs up to. The crop in their field was once gorse for firing the old cloan ovens.

Once the Duchy of Cornwall owned much land, but it is now nearly all privately owned. Because of the merging of holdings, there are fewer Commoners, fighting a battle against officials who don't understand. 'The grazing balance is very fine,' says Jen. 'At Wimalford there's a wonderful marsh formed from old peat cuttings. The area now has special protection so peat cutting has had to stop, but that might well mean there's no marsh to replace the present one. It isn't realised that most habitats are actually manmade,' a theme I say is familiar to us on our travels around Remote Britain. They delight in the moor's oddities. A photographer on a Cornwall Botanical Group outing, on reaching Wimalford, said with great delight: 'The best bog I've ever seen.' A tributary of the River Lynher which it joins at nearby Berriowbridge delights in the name Raven's Drinking. It starts with a waterfall fed by a marsh. In the 1976 drought the waterfall dried out, though water could still be heard underground, but wetter times have steadily replenished it. And once sufficient alluvial gold was sifted from the Lynher to make wedding rings for a landowner's several daughters.

Around the Heart of the Moor

Back by Congdon's Shop, we cross the A30 as an irrelevance, and saunter through Polyphant, Altarnun and Bowithick as near as we'll get to Brown Willy. Though there's less of Bodmin Moor north than south of the A30, the upland strewn with granite is perhaps the moor's heart with Brown Willy, the source of the Fowey and the De Lank rivers and rich archaeological remains. It often seems that, the more remote the country, the more English history has been played out, though in truth this might just be that it's easier to see the wood for the trees without layers of later development.

The enterprise of Neolithic man (4500-2500BC) who developed axes to clear trees and started settled farming, the early arrival of Christianity, the Black Death, society divided in the Civil War, and all-conquering early Methodism: they all speak to us on the moor and its villages. Altarnun especially breathes Cornishness, past and present. With its 109ft tower, the church is the acknowledged 'cathedral of the moor'. Though mainly 15th century, partly built of granite lying around that didn't need quarrying, there are traces of the original Norman building including the font, while outside the gate is a 6th century Celtic cross. Visit on a Thursday in summer, when there's a welcoming spread in the church hall for visitors and locals. It is a bit of a showpiece village with granite cottages and colourful gardens. In a field below the vicarage, there's the holy well of St Nonna, a bowsening pool into which lunatics were plunged and then preached at in the church till cured, says the legend.

Back on our journey past Brown Willy, we join the A39 from Bude and are soon driving through stretched-out Camelford, as individual and as Cornish as capital of any small district. There's nasty new development, but a good core of traditional architecture our successors would truly treasure. In reporting days I enjoyed the comradeship that Camelford exuded (warmer than in coastal areas), but to save moving about we're spending several days just off the moor at Washaway on the Wadebridge-Bodmin road. The Trehellas House Hotel, takes pride in our succession of visitors, phone calls and pleas for help. The gardens of nearby Pencarrow House are just coming into bloom.

Cornish Publisher

First visitor at breakfast next morning is Michael Williams, who has recently sold his Bossiney Books, strongly Cornish-based specialising in quality paperbacks. He published both E V Thompson's illustrated books on the moor and lends me his file copies as they're now scarce. 'A novelist who really understands how the moor came to be as it is,' he says.

'Publishing is a disease. I was in the hotel business, did a few booklets for fun, and overnight it seems it's forty years on and I have had hundreds of authors work with me. Looking me in the eye, he adds: 'You felt you had to move away from Devon; I know how hard it would have been seeing David & Charles's new owner get rid off staff. I wasn't on the same scale, so I'm still here, enjoying Bodmin Moor, writing newspaper articles about it. I started journalism with sports reports at an old penny a line. That was for the *Western Guardian* for which I still write a weekly 1,000 words.' An article about memories of magic and religion are brought back by a favourite walk appearing in the next day's regional *The Western Morning News*.

He's fascinated by the paranormal; he's 'definitely' seen a ghost in the older part of Jamaica Inn. Describing himself as an all-rounder, he's also a publishing consultant, on the Board of the Cornish Gorseth, into animal welfare and an inveterate local explorer. He talks of the 'creative chemistry of the moor', and how it shares with Dartmoor in having more ghosts than anywhere else outside London.

'Bodmin Moor is my joy. Without a National Park or a Lady Sayer so publicly coming to its defence, it has survived amazingly well. Though smaller in scale than Dartmoor, it's a real wilderness and much more varied, harder to get to understand. I hope some of our books helped. You know, when I started there was far too little published on Cornwall but, by the time I finished, too much. Once W H Smith were our friends, but they ended up an enemy. You wouldn't go to Smiths for local books today.

Bodmin Moor has inspired novelists, poets and painters such as Charles Simpson, who went around by motorcycle with materials in the sidecar. He famously illustrated C E Vulliamy's *Unknown Cornwall.* I sometimes feel he's still around there with me... in the places you feel you're the last person in Cornwall.' While saying all this, Michael is enjoying his breakfast. In Cornwall it's always easier to switch in and out of reality. And anyway what is real? Isn't it natural that Christianity caught root here and in other Celtic lands before it penetrated the big cities? 'It's thinner here,' is how it is sometimes expressed. A bit like the Biblical desert.

Let us leave Michael with two brief quotations from recent outpourings:

> In a curious way Bodmin Moor challenges you not to accept everything at face value; it presents a landscape which prompts questions and analysis. Why, for example, has a small village like Altarnun so many phantoms? Are the rivers, the stream and the pools factors in the haunted reputation? Dame Daphne du Maurier once said, while standing in a field on the edge of the moor, that she felt like 'an astronaut in time'. There is certainly a timeless quality about the place and it is quite possible that a ghost is simply a footprint in time. Interestingly, some spirits manifest themselves very quickly after what we call death. When I first met Princess Narisa of Thailand at her old family home at Tredethy, Helland Bridge, she told me that on the night her mother passed away she was seen by people on the other side of the valley.
>
> The tors of Bodmin Moor defy generalisation. Truth is they have distinct characters. Some are smooth and sleek. Others are peaked with granite crowns. Rough Tor and Brown Willy, the two highest points in all Cornwall, are beautifully proportioned and inevitably dominate the landscape, but... smaller, lesser known tors have their qualities too and, among them, is a special favourite. Alex Tor beyond St Breward. Heading for a farmstead called the Candras, you suddenly find yourself in unusual terrain, littered with granite boulders. It is as if some angry giant, perched on top of Alex Tor, has flung them widely on the ground below.

St Breward

Having enjoyed our visit to the 'wrong' Mrs Bousfield, St Breward Post Office tells us that the right one is away on holiday, but I can buy her *A History of St Brewards: The life of a moorland village.* This is a model of what a local book should be. Though I catch up with her later, what she says is best included here.

'My husband, a retired Eton housemaster, and I lived on a farm in the parish. I inherited a huge batch of paperwork from someone who had taken great interest in unearthing things about the village. It took me a year to sort them out, and then a group of us decided we'd produce a history. We went to a course on writing local history and were inspired to think about what effect man has had on the landscape, and what effect the landscape has had on man.

A member of the team each wrote different chapters. I did some, but my main task was editing the work as it came in and filling gaps. Farming was the hardest nut to crack, done by retired BBC producer Paddy O'Keith, whose roots were here. She was marvellous, visiting farmers and telling them she knew nothing and opening them up.

I'd decided it had to be a hardback with a square spine that would last generations on people's shelves. People here don't "belong to buy books" as they say in Cornwall, so the price had to be keen, which meant publishing it myself. What that boiled down to was sales. We had a marvellous launch party, the contributors down one side of a long table, buyers the other. The first copies were autographed by every contributor. I visited the church and noted the names and addresses in the visitor's book, especially those who said something about their roots being here and sold almost as many copies to the descendants of those who migrated as I did to locals.'

Published in 1988, the first 800 copies went in months, and was reprinted the same year. The demand continued with second-hand prices of £30. So in 1999 there was a third printing of about 600, all but a hundred sold. She's eighty five, on her own now, and has moved into a flat in Wadebridge. 'But my heart is still in St Breward. It's a wonderful place.'

So here we are, buying the book at the friendly Post Office cum tearoom, 'though for lunch you might do better at the inn'. The Old Inn Freehouse Restaurant is famous for its moorland grills. A talkative group of carers are being rewarded in the restaurant, and the bar being busy, we share a table.

Les Saunders from nearby St Tudy soon tells me he's writing a family history, how he regrets Cornwall has become less sports minded ('one of our two racetracks closed, wrestling has gone and today's Rugger players go to Bath'), but how generally good life is locally. Then he and his wife talk about local characters, past and present, while Sheila has a Madras curry and I go unorthodox with mushrooms stuffed with Cornish brie followed by a Cornish cream tea. 'In what order me handsome?' The pub, the highest in Cornwall, offers a huge menu and range of daily specials.

St Breward is a long, drawn-out village, continuing well beyond the pub. Like many other places with Celtic origins, it began as a series of farm settlements and has steadily filled itself in. The population is about the same as two hundred years ago, new building being offset by fewer people per household. There's another shop close to the Post Office, pub, school, even a clean public toilet... the complete village, all older buildings in granite. Not being on the way to anywhere, there's only a little tourism. Locals and incomers love it equally – for its sense of community, its position and fine views. There's never been an overwhelming influx of incomers, so those who come are rapidly assimilated and as, elsewhere in Remote Britain, soon find themselves playing a leading role. In the relaxed atmosphere everyone seems pleased to answer questions. But throughout history there have been troubled times. At the Methodist Church, below the Post Office, we read the notice about how a young man was killed when the earlier building received a direct hit in 1943. A stone in the wall records the opening of the new building by that great character of yesteryear, Isaac Foot. The church still attracts a good congregation while there's a lively Friends of the 12th century Parish Church – another highest in Cornwall – named after the 6th century Celtic Saint Branwalder ('Raven Lord'). Things seem naturally to thrive in this village.

Bodmin & Wadebridge Railway

A traditional source of employment was at the nearby De Lank quarry close to the river of the same name on the edge of the real moor. It was the first place I saw granite being cut and polished for prestige buildings and monuments – when I profiled it in the 1950s. Then there was a large workforce. I recall the bumpy approach road I again take through a cutting, and how most of the cut granite was let gently down a steep incline to the Wenfordbridge railway station. The remains of a triangular-shaped bridge which used to carry the steep track are still there, but there's only a little activity around the quarry today.

Though it never had a passenger service, parcels could be delivered or collected from Wenfordbridge station, though the chief traffic was china clay, which left by the trainload. Recently there have been hopes of reopening the clay works and railway, but the trackbed was converted into part of the popular Camel Trail, which includes the delightful route of the old line from Wadebridge to Padstow. Convert something into a tourist attraction and it is hard to get it back to its former use. Though it was said that path/cycleway and railway could both be accommodated, the ministerial consideration of a public enquiry ruled against reopening.

Now making our way through almost secret, partly wooded, country full of streams and bridges toward Blisland, I'm able to take several glances at the Wenfordbridge section of the Trail and admit it might lose something of its intimacy if the trackbed, partly overlooking the Camel, partly in a cutting, were widened. The goods trains used to squeal round the sharp bends; in steam days only an ancient 2-4-0 Beattie tank, built in the year of the collapse of Gladstone's first government, was allowed to use it. I remember how it stopped half way along for the tank to be refilled by gravity.

What has optimistically been called the Bodmin & Wenford Railway has retitled itself the Bodmin & Wadebridge after a pioneer private concern that played a vital role in preventing the Great Western having a Cornish monopoly. Among visitors to our hotel, Martin Webster, the leading light, explained the concentration of effort to reopen to Wadebridge. It already links with Bodmin Parkway on the mainline. Wadebridge was once railway minded, its engine shed housing an amazing assortment including a West Country Pacific, needed to haul the full length *Atlantic Coast Express* on summer Saturdays, the only time the string of stations serving remote communities down from Launceston really came to life.

'We've achieved much but we're too far from any conurbation to be among the busiest,' says Martin, hoping that the permanent loan of a T9 might bring in the people. T9s or Greyhounds were a delightful old mainline class that, despite their age, still ran down from Launceston in the postwar years. I wish them success.

Blisland

Continuing our journey, now well off the high moor, lovely Blisland appropriately welcomes with a fine piece of granite celebrating the millennium. It could survive all through the next and beyond. There are daffodils around the base of trees and children's swings on the spacious green which, with the church and village hall (formerly school and county library) opposite, present an unusually soft face for Cornwall.

All it needs to complete the magic is a tearoom, though just out of the village there's a community shop, new school and surprisingly an 'industrial estate' with three units. No tearoom on the green, but the hall advertises bingo with refreshments, proceeds in aid of the churchyard grass-cutting fund. So that's why it is so tidy.

Blisland has seven of Cornwall's 360 wayside crosses, pagan in origin but given a Christian role with the addition of a cross engraved by early converts. The church, basically Norman, vividly reveals the last thousand years of taste and style of establishment worship. 'As a restoration –

even improvement – of a medieval church, this can hardly be bettered' is a quote from John Betjeman in a leaflet describing St Protus and St Hyacinth. There is much to see including an outstanding (whether you like them or not) rood scene stretching right across the church and high pulpit. My final glimpse is of the fine parallel wagon roofs with bosses. In the right hands, timber seems almost as endurable as granite.

Two More Enthusiasts

Back in our hotel next morning, the first visitor is Oliver Howes who I've invited to breakfast simply to find out about his website. Well-illustrated and informative, it covers an enormous range of Bodmin Moor topics including the Copper Trail, a 60-mile route around the circumference passing many picturesque industrial ruins including the ageing engine houses of old copper mines.

'Bodmin Moor is my love,' he says. It's easy to get to Brown Willy from Camelford, yet there are places where you can see nothing but countryside. You can see all the hot spots in a day; away from them it's wonderfully remote.' He first fell in love with Cornwall as personal guide driving discerning Americans around England. A digital camera was then put to excellent use.

'The website is for love. I don't want to be 'Googleised', don't want to make money out of it and certainly not to have it disfigured with other people's ads. I'm afraid the desire to interfere may be too strong; I'm told I've got to reduce the length. It's a circular thing: I go for a walk to relax, take out the camera, come home and start writing just to share what I've seen.' Perhaps he'll be forced into putting Oliver's Travels into book form. If so, I'll be a buyer.

Inevitably when David Attwell, North Cornwall District Council's Coast and Countryside Manager visits, mention is made of *Cream Teas and Concrete,* a television programme of the early 1990s which featured a councillor boasting that they loved bungalows and caravans more than the scenery. 'A lot's changed since then. We're now known for encouraging excellence in tourism. We control 464 square miles, with 80,000 residents, half of them in towns, so the rural areas have the very lowest English densities.

Though we look after a long stretch of coast and do things like hand-picking litter off the beaches, Bodmin Moor is a gem in our crown. It needs special care. Some tourism is welcome in the surrounding villages but it's quality, not quantity we're encouraging. Wet and mild, the moor is a workaday place, the best Bronze Age landscape in Europe – very much an archaeological landscape – settled surprisingly early because of its light tree cover, many of the woods surviving till the late 1770s and early 1800s when there were new "intakes". There's still evidence of the medieval strip field system, lots of hamlets below the remains of hill forts neatly surviving in the modern landscape.

After the Black Death, when most people moved down off the high ground, the Commoners (mainly landowners around the periphery) have controlled most of the moor. The system has evolved over thousands of years. It's dangerous when outsiders impose rules on it, dangerous suddenly to reverse things too.

You can over-graze, while under-grazing might let the gorse go rampant. I myself keep Devon Cattle on the moor, but I don't make any money. It's hard for outsiders to understand the passion and commitment, but they're very real.'

Many years ago my eyes opened when I first went to Rough Tor, an easy one to reach. As David Attwell says: 'Between the car park and the Tor there's 6,000 years of history including the rings of a Neolithic hill fort.' A very Cornish note is that the ceremonial hill was used for a few of the popular teetotal gatherings in the 19th century, often accompanied by drunken revels organised by the equally militant non-abstainers.

Reflecting on my quite frequent visits from the 1950s to the 1970s, the politics of the commons, with some maybe necessary but ham-fisted government enquiries and intervention, comes across as complicated as that of the Scottish crofts. But then we keep on meeting (and hearing about many other) well-balanced, intelligent people giving their best to the moor. Nowhere else have we quite met this level of commitment.

David says he lives at Temple, planned as our first stopping point next morning.

As Enjoyable an Inland Journey as Any

Today's journey is as varied as it is interesting; we've never had a more enjoyable one in inland Southern England. It starts by heading toward Bodmin, bumping across the former level crossing over the Wenfordbridge goods line. Already several walkers have parked their cars to set off along the trail; only on the crossing itself are the rails still awkwardly in position.

Bodmin was once Cornwall's capital, hard to reach; 'Out of the world and into Bodmin,' is reputed to have originated with judges hating crossing the moor in pre-turnpike days. We however are quickly whisked north east by the A30, which somehow hasn't much damaged the moor nor shows it off to best advantage. We feel the real spirit of the moor as we divert to Temple, an insignificant moorland hamlet with a romantic history and much-visited church.

Inevitably we're back to the early days of Christianity. Pilgrims from Ireland, fearful of being shipwrecked going round Land's End, came up the Camel to Wadebridge and struck across the moor to join the Fowey Valley down to Fowey, whose harbour offered ready access to many English and continental ports. The original 12th century church was built by the Templars (who gave their name to the hamlet) as a safe resting place. Then, in the 16th century, it became the Cornish equivalent to Gretna Green: imagine eloping couples wandering across a foggy, boggy moor to find it, get married and, fait accomplit, hasten back to civilisation.

In 1753 such marriages became illegal, the congregation dissipated, services ceased, and after a century the building lay in ruins. Eventually a restoration fund was started and a little of the original building, and a lot more of its stone, were incorporated in as close a replica as possible. Reconsecration was in 1883. We see the engraved crosses of the Templars and, just inside the entrance, the old Norman font. The churchyard is an oasis for small birds and flowers in otherwise pretty bleak country. There's a feeling of utter peace, timelessness.

Cardinham, across the moor closer to Bodmin, also tells the story of Irish missionaries, its church being named after St Meubred, whose body was returned after he was beheaded in Rome. And halfway between Temple and Cardinham lies the farm of possibly the most famous of today's Bodmin Moor's residents: Robin Hanbury-Tenison, explorer, author, film-maker and, in his campaigning role, president of the Camel Valley & Bodmin Moor Protection Society. 'I'll never be a local,' he says. 'I've only been here half a century.' But, judging from many comments I've heard, he's pretty universally liked and respected, certainly not aloof. Though he's away on exploration much of the time, he and his wife offer bed-and-breakfast at their Cabilla Manor.

He's off on exploration now, but when I first approached him he sent a manuscript of a chapter on the moor he's written for *The Character of the English Countryside*. It starts:

> I have never wanted to live anywhere else and, during all my travels around the world, it has been the magnet that has drawn me home to friends and family. It is a strange place, fragmented sweeps of open moorland interspersed with farmland and deep, wooded valleys. Within its 25,000 or so hectares can be found a rich microcosm of much that is best about the British countryside.
>
> There are high tors rising to Brown Willy, Cornwall's 'mountain', at 420 metres. Craggy outcrops of granite are worn into weird shapes by the weather and the moor can be a frightening place on a wild

foggy night when, riding through the half light, Daphne du Maurier's stories of smugglers and murder seem all too real. Jamaica Inn is still the pub at the centre where Commoners meet to discuss their problems in front of a roaring fire on winter evenings.

We're only back on the A30 for a short time before leaving it at Bolventor. No, we're not heading for Jamaica Inn, but cannot resist a haunting glimpse of Dozmary Pool before switching to the delightful minor road down the Fowey Valley. The river is in full spate, not overflowing as a road sign warns is a risk, but bowling along, spraying itself over rocks and a weir, as though it might be punished for not quickly reaching the estuary. My opinion is strengthened that it's England's most under-appreciated river, though as we lose height, lusher vegetation begins to interrupt our view. Lower down, the deep valley threaded by the A38, is known as the Glyn Valley and most wouldn't know the river was there at all. Even the estuary is amazingly private till Fowey's great china-clay docks begin.

At a farm entrance there's a secret pool which must be a breeding spot for lesser river life. I gaze in its still waters amazed it needs a notice saying fishing isn't allowed. At the discreetly-tucked-away car park for Golitha Falls, there's only one other vehicle, and that's because the driver wants the toilet. The falls are in full flush, unseen. In the damp atmosphere, many ferns and mosses thrive.

At the crossroads, we turn left for Minions, half way between the Fowey and the Lynher. 'I'm hungry,' says Sheila, pointing out we're now only a stone's throw from the places, including North Hill's Racehorse Inn, where we spent much of Sunday. OK, I agree, but let's go to St Cleer. We find a brilliant delicatessen, but its staff hesitate to recommend the pub, while an extraordinarily talkative policeman, assures us there's little trouble on this beat, but says we'd do better at Minions – at another supposedly highest pub in Cornwall.

I especially enjoy the journey back by a different route. All around us, in the high, open moorland, are abandoned engine houses and other remains of mining and quarrying, while the place names, Crow's Nest, Tokenbury Corner, Railway Terrace (now usually called Darite) Cheesering and Minions itself, are redolent of railway history. Linking with the Liskeard & Looe Union Canal at Moorswater, the Liskeard & Caradon Railway thrived on mineral traffic. Early guide books tell that, loaded with tin ore and granite, trucks came one after another down an incline by gravity at the day's end. Horses took them back.

Later the Looe Canal Company took over a modernised and extended system to and around the moor. Not licensed to carry passengers, with Cornish ingenuity, the railway took them free provided they carried an umbrella or parcel for which a charge was levied.

The doyen of Cornish historians, A K Hamilton Ellis, relates how in the 1840s miners rapidly increased the populations of the local villages until they resembled the mining camps of America's Far West, and how lively pubs became after Saturday pay day. Soon rival brands of Methodist chapels opened everywhere, substantially reducing the number of heavy drinkers. The granite chapels, now mainly converted to private homes, are as much part of the truly Cornish scene as the gaunt engine houses, stone crosses, scattered boulders, and those, famously piled one upon another, above Minions called The Cheesering, and the set of three circles of standing stones known as the Hurlers. The latter are said to be a group of local miners who dared to play the local game of hurling on the Sabbath. They were turned into stone pillars to set an example. Not only are the immediate surroundings as interesting as they are perhaps desolate, but there are expansive long-distance views, with a glimpse of Dartmoor.

And that, after one of our best-ever short visits to Cornwall and another excellent pub lunch, is where we head, reluctant to leave Bodmin Moor but still enjoying the dip down to New Bridge over the River Lynher, another under-valued river with a mysterious, largely unseen estuary system, and up to Callington (once a real back-water but now a growing dormitory for Plymouth), down again through Gunnislake to cross the Tamar and then to Tavistock. Dartmoor glistens in the sun but I cannot yet get Bodmin Moor out of my mind as we hasten to a Devon village to see Alyss and grandson, Joshua.

· XXIX ·

FLAT LINCOLNSHIRE

Least-known England

Writing this book has taken us to areas which, in common with most people, we would otherwise have ignored. And, while it is obvious that we should go to off-beat islands, a big surprise is that hitherto I've missed much of Cambridgeshire and especially Lincolnshire... both where only the county towns (especially the university and cathedral respectively) attract disproportionate interest.

I've been collecting books of regional, county and local interest most of my life, buying volumes in out-of-print series (including my favourite *Murray's Handbooks* from a mere old sixpence a time for years) and new titles as they appeared. I have a considerable collection on both East Anglia and North East England, but scarcely anything on Lincolnshire. This was not because of my being selective but because of what was available, publicised and reviewed. Murray himself, broad-minded among guidebook writers of the day, says of the journey from Cambridge to Wisbech: 'The sole object of interest, as generally in Cambridgeshire, are the churches.' Apart from the engineering of the drainage, most the Fens are generally dismissed as uninteresting, though a large region, 'almost the dimensions of a province', with the country's richest agricultural land.

When we told friends we were going to explore the Fens, it was regarded as eccentric. When I mentioned Grimsby, one said: 'Grimsby, whatever is there to see in Grimsby?' This lack of interest in England's least-visited area is almost unbelievable. Yes, Tennyson might have been born there, but he soon left it, didn't he? The best I could muster up among friends was that one had been taken to Cleethorpes as a child: 'But I don't think it's the kind of place people go to today.' The withdrawal years ago of what had been a good service of through trains to London perhaps confirms that. Skegness is better known, but there's general ignorance of where exactly it is and, after a slow journey to reach it, no resort's visitors are less curious about the surrounding countryside.

For an inveterate traveller, I've hardly done better myself. Apart from

Cambridge, Ely and Lincoln, I've made only brief incursions and know the region less well than any other part of Britain. Worse, until recently (when we went to Mablethorpe and Woodhall Spa: chapter XXVII) I didn't realise that there are attractive Wolds in Lincolnshire as in Yorkshire... the valley of the broad Humber simply being an interruption between the two.

Because we are going to an area where I know no-one and there aren't always suitable hotels where we want to stay, planning is unusually troublesome. But read on and share our delight in exploring this generally ignored corner of our country, finding great contrasts in landscapes and in how people live and work. Rarely have I been more surprised.

Avoiding duplication with *Journey,* I'll not reintroduce Vermuyden and the story of how the Fens were drained though, in passing, I wish that when visiting Ely we had been to Wicken Fen, nine miles to the south, where the country's oldest nature reserve preserves a chunk of undrained land cultivated in the traditional way. The more you see, inevitably the more you miss and, even at seventy eight, I hope there'll be another time. Also to be seen, and possibly even more natural, with tall reed beds and mature trees, is the smaller (200ha) Woodwalton Fen National Nature Reserve, a fragment of medieval black soil fen in deepest Cambridgeshire.

Wisbech, Capital of the Fens

Our starting point, still well into Cambridgeshire, though most of our time will be in Lincolnshire, is where *Journey* left off at Wisbech. We reach here by a roundabout route, refamiliarising ourselves with the fen landscape to visit the Gatehouse, about all that survives of the once powerful Benedictine Ramsey Abbey that drew wealth from a swathe of the rich land, this part-productive even though it was then subject to floods.

And here's a secret: the journey is being done in Little Car, our Micra, which is being replaced in Bath and is to become our second vehicle in Scotland, where it will seldom go further than a mile or so to the supermarket or church. Making the best of it on this final tour involves keeping our luggage neat and tidy... without any possibility of giving a lift to anyone. Little Car: you have served us nobly in Bath and around the West Country – and developed quite a character. Take us home safely to Scotland where we'll use you more often, saving starting up Big Car for local trips. Little Car began this journey by taking us to Bicester and waiting while we went by train to London for our last-ever big prizegiving for my Trust's writing competitions (which are now reduced just to the Self-Publishing and writers' groups Anthology Trophy) and has since brought us here via Leamington Spa.

'What time is dinner?' we ask reception on arrival at 6pm at a curious Elme Hall, Elm being a few miles outside Wisbech. Though last night we had a good dinner with family at the Dolphin in a beautiful waterside setting in St Ives, lunch was light and we're peckish.

'We've already stopped serving food.' And there doesn't seem anywhere else they can recommend. Then the Japanese owner-manager takes over, says she'll take our bags up and cook us a meal. 'What would you like?'

Our bedroom is spacious but odd, plastered with notices warning of this and that. There's over-sized furniture and the bathroom isn't the most convenient. The beds are comfortable, though, and the Japanese owner couldn't be more considerate. Though food on Sundays normally finishes at 6pm, there's a table of four other well-satisfied residents. Our steaks are among the best we've ever tasted. Later the Japanese lady tells us she is holding the fort while her English husband is in hospital fighting cancer. Though we kept our thoughts to ourselves, we feel guilty at finding anything amiss.

The setting on a roundabout isn't the easiest and next morning we go the wrong way toward Outwell, only a couple of miles away where we stayed for *Journey,* before correctly heading back to Wisbech. That is a lively little town of about 20,000 and an active port, if not as busy as in the 19th century when larger vessels could reach it and Midland coal and Worcestershire salt were among cargoes brought by inland waterway for export. Return loads included Baltic timber. Pleasure craft supplement today's ships to maintain the waterfront as Wisbech's window on the world, and many industrial firms flourish along it. The town has ancient buildings and other attractions, but for me its character – as undoubtedly its historic importance – is determined by the port where silt is a continuing enemy. All the rivers emptying into the Wash still carry silt and the boundary between water and land continues to change.

Along with Ely and March, Wisbech frequently crops up in history, but that of the Fens they serve is much less known. Predictably we note that, though he quickly fortified Wisbech, it was the last part of the country to be tamed by William the Conqueror.

Next morning we head north to tiny Tydd St Mary to meet David Beeton, who is a Reader at the church (as is Sheila in Nairn) we found through the Diocesan network. When I phoned out of the blue, he was immediately welcoming, saying he'd like nothing better than to show us round the core of the Fens. And when I explained we only had a tiny car with luggage piled on the back seat, he instantly volunteered to drive us.

New Holland

'Yes, we're on the edge of a very different world here,' says David. 'Come and see for yourself.' One reason he was so immediately friendly was mentioned in chapter III, namely that I was visiting his area at the suggestion of the Bishop of Truro, who had earlier been the popular Suffragan Bishop of Grantham and had soaked in New Holland's different way of life.

Soon we're crossing a flat land of incredibly deep ditches crossed by few bridges, of great open skies, large fields, scattered poplars and an occasional different tree, poor cottages, (a few derelict that will never be lived in again, others repaired and even extended). Everywhere there are buzzing tractors, mainly working on the dark alluvial soil, which yields much of our food. Cereals, fruit and vegetables, even flowers, cut and for seed and daffodil bulbs: they are grown by the ton, many delivered to 'vegetable factories' such as the one in Chatteris, and obviously are profitable. Right now Sweet Williams make quite a show, though obviously mainly grown for seed. 'Flowers are known as special work,' says David.

We are in deep into the Fens where I've not quite penetrated before, and quickly realise the truth of the statement that fenmen are different, independent. A higher proportion are self-employed than you'll find elsewhere. Few go in for fancy homes or traditional trappings. Their success is best told by their tractors. Not surprisingly, by far the largest commercial premises we see during the tour is a supplier of tractors and their implements.

Though we are not far away from towns, this feels as remote as you get, certainly different, some land well below high tide level. Before man intervened and drained the Fens, causing the land to dry out and sink and so create extra drainage difficulties until powerful steam engines seriously aided the work of the rivers and artificial channels and ditches, it was really cut off, the Fen Tigers of pure Anglo-Saxon stock fighting for a living dependent as much on catching fish and water birds as growing crops.

My *Murray's Handbook* goes to town in its usual way freely quoting from others to portray a vivid picture:

Round the borders of the Fens there lived a thin and haggard population of 'Fen-slodgers,' called 'yellow bellies' in other districts, who derived a precarious subsistence from fowling and fishing. They were described by writers of the time as 'a rude and almost barbarous sort of lazy and beggarly people'. Disease always hung over the district, ready to pounce upon the half-starved fenmen. Camden spoke of the country between Lincoln and Cambridge as 'a vast morass, inhabited by fenmen, a kind of people, according to the nature of the place where they dwell, who, walking high upon stilts, apply their minds to grazing, fishing, or fowling.' The proverb of 'Cambridgeshire camels' doubtless originated in this old practice of stilt-walking in the Fens; the fenmen, like the inhabitants of the Landes, mounting upon high stilts to spy out their flocks across the dead level. But the flocks of the fenmen consisted principally of geese, which were called the 'fenmen's treasure'...

> In the oldest reclaimed district of Holland (Lincolnshire), containing many village churches, the inhabitants, in wet seasons, were under the necessity of rowing to church in their boats. In the other less reclaimed parts of the Fens the inhabitants were much worse off. 'In the winter time,' said Dugdale, 'when the ice is only strong enough to hinder the passage of boats, and yet not able to bear a man, the inhabitants upon the hards and banks within the Fens could have no help of food, nor comfort for body or soul; no woman aid in her travail, no means to baptize a child or partake of the Communion, nor supply of any necessity saving what these poor desolate places do afford.'

Though there was inevitably widespread opposition to what would dramatically change people's lives, it isn't hard to realise just how challenging life and the aches and pains must have been when the water was 'putrid and muddy, yea, full of loathsome vermin'. If you could stay dry yourself, your home, however primitive, would have been continually threatened by flood or shrinkage. Shrinkage is why, to this day, there are few quality buildings or really old ones of any kind – apart from churches expensively built with deep foundations on slightly higher ground, which does exist since, though the Fens are proverbially likened to pancakes, they do undulate slightly.

David drives us through South Holland through a repetitive, rectangular landscape of field and ditch, some fields having an extra diagonal ditch or two. The OS is packed with thin blue lines. He tells us about his family's involvement with agriculture and how things have changed. 'Once 40 to 60 acres made a reasonable living; now it's 400 or 500. There are many fewer people involved, more efficient perhaps, but not so colourful when everything had to be done by hand and the workers were real characters.

My grandfather said he wouldn't for his life have missed working with the hand-fed threshing machines. Threshing was a social occasion. When he started in 1925, he called it "a boundless expanse of freedom". In those days there was little outside interference. With today's councils, only the sky is free.'

He explains: 'The level of fields was actually lowered when earth was collected to raise the banks, which have served their purpose. I've never seen it flooded.

Once sugar beet was important, but nearly all the factories have closed. Potatoes and sugar beet used to be carried by the narrow-gauge light railways to the nearest proper railway siding. Rails were easy to lay and avoided potholes. They said that a small truck laden with 5 tons could be pushed by hand.'

One of the potato railways was a major concern: the 2ft-gauge Fleet Light Railway stretched 12 miles, from Moulton, Whaplode, Holbeach Drove and Gedney Dyke to Sutton Bridge at the outlet of the River Nene where the dock has incidentally been restored.

There are few houses and many fewer we'd be happy living in. Several are boarded up, one in the act of falling down. David says that when a lightly-built one collapsed, the rubble could have been carried in a wheelbarrow. With the decline in labour and proper roads, today there's no need for houses in the remotest parts, and generally the planners are happy to see old property demolished. Only if it is an old rarity does it have to be preserved. Traffic is sparse, mainly tractors and lorries.

When I say I'm finding the geography difficult, I'm told that it takes years to come to grips with it. For one thing, most places have two names, those with the same main one aren't always at all close together. The addition of Drove indicates where cattle were once driven, usually over a bridge across a watercourse, but can be miles apart from other places with the same basic name, and a village's fen is by no means automatically close to it.

As has so often struck me, the flatter the countryside, the more the bends on the road. 'On one stretch, there are forty nine in 2½ miles,' says David. Added to that, with so few bridges farmers often have a long way to go between two points close together as the crow flies.

A series of identical concrete bridges – one, a mistake, leading to nowhere – were built as a work-creation scheme in the 1930s. Having seen a kingfisher fly along well below road level, we stop by one of the standard bridges to peer down into the deep ditch with lazy water: its own universe with wildlife galore which no doubt lives for the present or its next meal. 'There'll be lots of newts deep down there,' says David. I cogitate on the Fen's yesterdays and its future, which I presume largely depends on the profitability of the crops it grows.

Threat from the Edges

Wrong. Though we're not on the main road, as we get nearer to Peterborough we become conscious that things are gradually changing. Parson Grove is where we first see greater prosperity, with a range of greenhouses and polytunnels, and some better housing. Making our way north to Gedney Hill, I stop to talk to someone working on extending a home. He turns out to be Peter Tourle, a retired builder from Kent who has recently moved, using his practical skills to create a better nest.

'We sold out at a good price in Kent and have money in the bank as well as a better place to live. We've been made very welcome and have a far better lifestyle. There's space to breathe here, yet we can be in Peterborough in half an hour and, if we wanted to, could catch a fast train and have a full day in London. Our friends thought we were cutting ourselves off; in a sense we have because we don't really want to go back but just enjoy it here. It looks remote, but really isn't.'

David Beeton comments: 'There are a lot more like him, economic fugitives from the South East where all their wealth was tied up in their home. They can sell it, and buy or usually build somewhere almost twice the size with a bigger garden for half the price.'

That is demonstrated forcibly when we turn a corner, at the next village, Holbeach Drove, first pausing to listen to, watch and smell a couple of splendidly-preserved traction engines possibly making their way to a rally. When the engines disappear out of sight, we see more of what might become the norm over vast areas: lovely houses and bungalows in spacious, well-kept gardens, some reached by their own mini-bridge across a ditch. It would be very desirable property in Godalming or Guildford. The trouble is that it doesn't fit here. About whether or not that matters, opinions will differ sharply, but the threat to the traditional way of life on the Fens is obvious. The richest land in the country quickly produces fine gardens with trees to die for and, with proper understanding and foundations, these homes are not going rapidly to fall apart. They create their own desirable environment, but it isn't the natural one and the Fens are not large enough to survive sustained attacks that will rob them of their individuality.

Though looking somewhat suspicious with notebook on the pavement, I manage to talk to a couple of the incomers. Their story is the same: twice as much space for half the price, a healthier and better lifestyle, and no wish whatsoever to return.

There's a large shop on the corner at Holbeach Drove selling everything from petrol to papers and pet food, no doubt with a slow turnover of a large stock. So far we've seen only a few smaller shops today; but the keeper of this mini-emporium isn't happy. She says: 'The incomers are out all day, and go to Tesco for their weekly shop. But they'd grumble if I wasn't here to sell them the odd thing they've forgotten or need in a hurry. It's a hard job, fifteen hours a day, little passing trade, regulars coming from a widespread area. But then, we're remote aren't we?'

Holbeach Drove and neighbouring Whaplode Drove were two of the villages the Bishop of Truro had suggested I see: 'Nobody goes there,' he said. Why should anyone? Ultimately probably only for one reason: to live more cheaply and enjoy a good life around a village nucleus. Already a few go to Peterborough to work, and many commuters have worse journeys to London than it would be from here. Admittedly at a cost, frequent non-stop trains to Kings Cross defy geography.

So probably the future of much of the Fens doesn't depend so much on the profitability of agriculture as I had surmised while peering down to the deep ditch near the bridge where we stopped to look round, but on the state of the national economy. Only boom times usually create economic fugitives. Even with occasional recessions, eventually the Fens may lose their claim to having one of the largest proportions of natives among the population. The fact that for centuries there's been an almost cathedral-like church at tiny Whaplode Drove may show that this has long been a more prosperous area but that hasn't affected its, maybe self-imposed, isolation.

For the second time in twenty four hours, we're peckish without the prospect of food, other than a sandwich we bought for later on. On arriving at the one sizeable pub-cum-restaurant, we're dismayed to find it's closed on Mondays. David says there's no other pub around where we'd get anything decent. 'The quickest thing will be to go back home and see what there is there.' So back to Tydd St Mary, where cheese, a lovely cake and a cuppa supplement our sandwiches, while we talk more about the Fens and David and Sheila swap notes about their preaching duties in extremely different environments.

Tydd St Mary itself has quite a history. Just five miles from the Wash, though in Lincolnshire, it is close to both Cambridgeshire and Norfolk. As you come in from the Fens, the church's slender light stone spire 'rises serenely from an island of trees'. Though most of the church is 14th and 15th century, an earlier rector is thought to have been the only Englishman who became Pope. It must then have become a more desirable place for, from the beginning of the 16th century, nearly all the rectors died in office, while self-employed small farmers and trades people accounted for an unusually high proportion of the inhabitants.

Boston's Ups and Downs

We drive north across the South Holland Main Drain to Long Sutton, to join the A17, missing both Long Sutton Bridge (where we had been told the quay has been reopened) and Holbeach to Boston for a happy evening. The journey takes us along the edge of the Fens, much of the time on marshy country, especially as we cross the broad River Welland, which higher up skirts the bulb town of Spalding and drains a large area of the Fens.

In Boston, we're still very conscious of the Fens, and nowhere more so than from the window of our bedroom at the White Hart Hotel, in the main street. We look out on the river called The Haven. It is tidal but, since water is held back by a great sluice gate at high tide and released at low, it is not immediately clear where we are in the cycle. The pair of swans don't seem to notice. Beyond the river is more land where drainage is all important. Boston may be near the northern fringe of the Fens, but it is still very much part of it. We love the view, and relax – that is once we have successfully followed the complex directions to the hotel car park.

Boston's fortune has risen and fallen many times. It was late gaining any importance, since nearby ports had the maritime business. That was dramatically changed by a great flood in 1014, which diverted the River Witham into The Haven. Soon Boston became one of the 'staple towns', licensed for imports and exports, the latter being mainly of wool. For a period, richly trading with Flanders, it was England's second most important port, long before Britain began looking westward to the Atlantic and that distinction fell to Bristol.

There followed a long gloomy period. The Haven silted up. Fortunes were not restored until the drainage of the Fens brought two benefits: the town served an increasingly prosperous hinterland, and navigation was improved by the scouring of silt by water, held back at high tide, released in a rush by opening sluice gates.

Changing road and railway geography also had a major effect. For a brief time Boston was on the trunk railway north, and when it lost that distinction it became a thriving local railway centre. Now only the extraordinarily indirect branch to Skegness passes through its widely-separated platforms, the legacy of busier days. Slow it may be, but the journey offers a kaleidoscope of unusual terrain.

Sheila has been talking about Boston's most famous landmark, looking out both across the Fens and to sea. Once a light from it guided travellers in from the Fens and ships into The Haven: The Boston Stump, the tower, high but with a blunt top somehow looking as though it should continue higher yet. This was an addition to the medieval parish church of St Botolph.

We can't help seeing The Stump from afar, but we decide to make our way to its base, keeping as close as we can to the river. We gaze up, and then notice that on the church's south west buttress there's a marvellous record of flood heights: more evidence that weather extremes didn't begin with global warming. Looking up the river there's what at first sight what looks like a bridge, but is a massive sluice gate.

Inside the spacious church what specially gains my attention is the early 17th century pulpit. In the days when preaching the orthodox word of the church was all important, and anyone who rebelled was in trouble, congregations rapidly increased as John Cotton (whose appointment coincided with the new pulpit) preached a different word, even daring to encourage those who couldn't stand the intolerance of the day to go to the new Boston in Massachusetts. Several of the original *Mayflower* Pilgrim Fathers had been briefly imprisoned for trying to leave for Holland to escape that intolerance. It was an offence to leave the country without authority. John Cotton himself later felt he had to emigrate and became a leading figure in the new Boston.

Intolerance seems to have shown itself in various forms over the years. The Civil War was especially bitter here, the initial leader of draining the local Fens, Lord Lindsey, being shot in a battle. As the result, the old order continued for decades. An interesting throwback to those watery days is that a local bedding manufacturer still uses feathers from water fowl.

Today we see Boston on a high, with many Eastern European workers apparently happily at work, but what would it be like if unemployment suddenly rises, as again seems possible? While crews of ships from many lands have long been familiar here, they haven't all been welcome in the pubs, and quite recently there were near race riots when the locals turned on Portuguese supporters after England was knocked out of the 2006 World Cup.

Perhaps I have that in mind as, later we find the market square filled with boisterous youngsters attracted by an equally noisy fair. 'Are you scared?' asks Sheila as I approach a policeman. No, I'm just thoughtful, but want to ask if he could direct us to a new Italian restaurant that's been recommended. He and his colleague don't merely do that but enthusiastically review what we can expect on the menu and its quality. Modern and fine.

There's a lot more to do in Boston such as follow the pre-1014 route of the River Witham and the course that ships leaving the modernised quay have to take to avoid sandbanks. The workaday town has both interesting and dull old streets some of which we ramble down after dinner. But on these trips we have to be selective and possibly a full fortnight's holiday still wouldn't be enough to study everything in and around the town.

To the End of Nowhere

Next morning we drive back down the A17, realising how dramatically it marks the border between the Fens to the west and the Marshes to the east. It is in fact built along a slight (in places only inches high) silt ridge. There's a series of small former ports that used to be reached by rivers, Holbeach being the largest. With about 8,000 people, it feels like a large village but qualifies as a town since it gained market fair rights as early as 1525. Its port ultimately became buried in a sewer, nicknamed The Stinker.

To emphasise the town's border nature, the OS clearly marks Holbeach Fen to the west and Holbeach Marsh to the east, the latter having fewer roads and greater gaps between settlements. Plain Holbeach is a considerable distance from Holbeach Drove already introduced, but to the east are a crop of lesser Holbeaches: Clough (meaning sluice), Bank, Hurn and St Marks.

Passing the town's substantial St Mary's Church with its spire rising to such a height that it must be seen from large areas of both Fen and Marsh, we call at the vicarage. The Rev Canon John Wickstead is another contact made through the Diocesan network, and has offered to take us to what the map suggests might feel like the end of the world.

With family milling around in the hall, he shepherds us to his book-lined study. A tall, athletic, amiable man, he's obviously a serious thinker and reader. Though raised in the Trent Valley and beginning his career as a teacher, since he was ordained aged thirty eight he's been posted in flat Lincolnshire and has come to know it well and enjoy its quirks and those of some of his colleagues and others.

'The Marshes are a particularly deprived area,' he says. 'The isolation of the towns and villages along the coast causes special problems. When I was vicar of Skegness, the church was fine but I found the town very draining.'

Flower festivals are important in this area, and there's one at his church at present. So he can be back for an event connected with it without having to rush us, he suggests we go now 'through nowhere to its end' or what we have nicknamed the end of the world. Little Car with excess luggage resting at the vicarage, again we're passengers.

We follow the A17 to Fleet Hargate, another former little port, turning off near Gedney to head north. The church, almost cathedral-like, looks like a liner floating on the Fens when you see it coming from the east, says John. 'When it was built, for miles around all there would have been were sheep.'

The wool they produced and the cloth made from it spelt wealth, and that's what would have gone out in the little ships. Wherever one goes in England, over-size churches means they were built with money from sheep... in eastern England well before arable cultivation became important.

Except that it is flat, we are in an environment quite different and obviously harsher than the Fens. 'What used to be the main landmarks here were water towers of startling design, but they're nearly all gone,' says John. The next village is tiny Lutton, its church being the only one on the medieval sea bank. Monks reclaimed the land before moving on to the Fens where they found living easier and more productive.

John tells us about two previous vicars. 'One set up a vestment-making business in a prefab which still thrives in this most unlikely of places. When the other was moved to an inland parish of flat Lincolnshire, he famously said that he was leaving "from the end of nowhere to go to the middle of nowhere".'

We wander across Lutton Marsh, where the land has been reclaimed more recently and is clearly more fragile. Incidentally, the term 'reclaimed' is misleading, since it obviously involves areas that, at least in historic times, have always been sea. It is as though in his search for new land man assumes the sea was God's mistake.

At our destination, about a mile south of Gedney Drove End, we walk up onto the sea bank. Certainly it feels like the end. In fact it is pretty horrible, partly because it is obviously newish, partly because, though the sea has been artificially kept back, at low tide it is still a long way away. The expanse between us and the waves is marked 'Danger Area'.

'You'll notice that the further from the sea, the lower the land,' says John. 'That's caused by silt, sometimes an enemy, sometimes man's friend. See, the new enclosures already have silt lined up.'

To our right is the mouth of the Nene, again artificial. The OS labels it 'Nene outlet cut'. Where the water from the Fens surges out to the sea, there's an artificial island with a small reservoir on it. On the other side of the Nene, the Peter Scott Way goes all the way to King's Lynn. And we are only a few miles from the church with the tall tower at Terrington St Clement where our trip for *Journey* coming up the coast ended. Here, as there, the Marsh doesn't even yield flint, so all building materials have to be brought in.

Bird life is about the only thing other than the distant sea that's not artificial. Among the birds we spot is a white egret. Seldom common, we see the odd one or two in many places.

RAF Holbeach Bombing Range adds to the general gloomy tone. This is a fascinating area, but when I think there are no high cliffs going south before Hastings, I'm glad I was brought up in upland Britain and right now could gladly swap places with one of the headlands of the North Cornish coast. 'It's not surprising that people are taciturn in these parts,' says John out on this rough and ready but effective modern sea bank.

After this, as we drive into the village of Gedney Drove End, the pub called the Wild Fowler on the Wash seems more than unusually inviting. But what again takes my attention is new housing. And again I talk with a few of the incomers, as I also do later on a modern estate at Holbeach St Marks. True to pattern, they are all happy: 'better environment', 'space to breathe', 'friendly neighbours' and 'much better value' repeatedly come up. Is living in built-up Britain so horrible that people are moving even into really remote spots like this? Just one man did regret that Gedney Drove End's only shop closed at Christmas, but that seemed a minor irritation when you could be in Holbeach with its choice of shops in twenty minutes, no longer than it takes to reach a shopping centre from much of suburban Surrey.

So for us it is also back to the Roman-cum-medieval sea bank five or six miles inland, and to Holbeach itself, where there are indeed good shops and eating places, but the traffic is heavy and parking difficult.

Yes, if you take root here, there are obvious attractions, and I love people who as it were grow out of their landscape and take a keen interest in it and the inhabitants, long-settled or incomers, as John clearly does. He's been an excellent guide, and over the phone is helpful in answering a couple of supplementary queries. It is a pity we're unlikely to meet again; but that's travel.

· XXX ·

HILLY LINCOLNSHIRE

The Surprising Wolds

Next morning, when I say to Sheila: 'Why don't we go for morning coffee in Skegness,' it doesn't provoke much reaction. Separately, years ago, both of us quite enjoyed a different kind of night there. I went by a crowded summer weekend train by bits of different routes the rest of which have long been abandoned, their link involving a sudden turn of well over 100 degrees between sections of straight track. But when I add: 'Then we could go onto Mablethorpe for lunch,' she knows I'm teasing. Our guide yesterday, Canon Wickstead, described it as a dreadful place.

Where we are really going should give us a pleasant surprise. Though the Fens and Marshes are totally different from each other, the Lincolnshire Wolds are a world apart... the highest land anywhere in the east of England from Kent to Yorkshire. Those who dismiss all Lincolnshire as boringly flat find that hard to believe. Lincolnshire is in fact an extremely diverse county. The Wolds are a little known treasure; delectable is not too romantic a word to describe them.

Travelling up the B1182, and having seen Coningsby airfield (the village we bypass is home to the Battle of Britain Memorial Flight), we notice that the countryside ahead is changing. Soon, on the A153, we intersect the route of our previous journey from Mablethorpe to Woodhall Spa (chapter XXVII) finding ourselves close to Woodhall Spa. We then run parallel to the Horncastle Canal, closed but still attractive. Packed with antique and bric-a-brac shops and where the Romans were particularly active, Horncastle is a fascinating little town, one of several around the Wolds. We enjoy exploring it briefly – and sitting for a few minutes by the old canal.

Heading north again, we admire a sharp escarpment to the north east. We then drive along a short section of disconnected Roman road going from east to west; there's another short section of it, just under the escarpment, heading to the coast along a route not closely followed by any main road today. It used to link Lincoln with Ingoldmells, a port long eroded, and salt-making works on the coast.

We're in a lightly-populated land of rolling countryside, obviously fertile, especially in the deep, and often wide, valley bottoms with frolicking streams. Unspoilt, it's Remote Britain par excellence. I can't help thinking how nearer big cities such a landscape would be more full of people, houses and roads. When you see this, the thought of what we've lost elsewhere is deeply upsetting, though quickly I put that behind me and revel in the magic of this particular landscape.

Once there were many more people, a special attraction being that the Wolds have one of Britain's richest concentrations of abandoned villages. A deterioration in the climate, Black Death, famine, the rise of the wool industry making sheep more profitable: they all played a part in medieval days. Abandoned monasteries, castles, some with moats, stately homes... they're all here, but what concentrates our minds is the patchwork of hills, valleys, lanes and tracks of today's little-exploited countryside.

Somewhere on the journey (or was it tomorrow's? – it doesn't much matter because it is the experience, rather than exactly where one is, that counts) we walk round the humps and bumps of one of the many villages. What were the people's thoughts about their place in history, and about the 'Deadmen's Graves', the long burial chambers of the earliest farmers, the oldest of which go back four millennium before Christ? Some of the medieval strip-fields are close by the deserted villages, though there's the catch that medieval and later, even 19th century ones can be mistaken for one another.

The story behind the burial barrows, narrow but surprisingly long humps, occasionally above the skyline, is both gruesome and calls for respect. Bodies were defleshed, because it was the bones, separated and carefully arranged, that were seen as having spiritual and memorial qualities. Religious celebrations may have taken place around the barrows acting as a kind of pre-Christian church.

At Scamblesby we go into The Green Man for a drink. Green Man? You can see him carved in wood and stone in churches, but he's also celebrated in pagan ways and, in forests and woodland, he's associated with legends, such as that of Robin Hood. The landscape reveals much, including military and industrial remains of many ages, but hides a great deal more, much of which will never be known. It is a humbling yet joyous landscape in which (in a way I never suspected could happen in Lincolnshire) I feel much at home. There seems to be little population and, in the tightly-packed villages, a welcome absence of holiday homes. There are hardly any items offered for sale along the road found in most of Britain.

Time for another diversion: from Scamblesby down to the start of the next steep hill, Red Hill, where we park and eat our sandwiches looking down across to where we've come from... and much further afield too. Particularly with our thirst already assuaged, never ever did a sandwich taste better. For once I don't eat too quickly. This is a complex landscape, yet it feels singularly of a piece.

We've been sent an advance parcel of information relating to the Area of Outstanding Natural Beauty, designated five years ago, and I recall that one of the excellent series of booklets (actually a large sheet folded to make a dozen well-displayed pages, a different thematic map for each) is on the Wolds' complicated geology.

As one might expect, the landscape is largely down to glaciation. During the Ice Age, the Wolds must have totally disappeared under ice which stretched down roughly to the course of the M4. As it grinded slowly south, massive quantities of rock were broken and redeposited. Then came tundra-like conditions, and a sudden temperature increase until it was warmer than today.

Over 100,000 years later, the Little Ice Age blocked the Humber immediately to the north, but only the Wolds' valleys were glaciated. Among the changes wrought was the broadening of valley bottoms, rounding of lower hill tops, and again the moving of materials ('erratics') from as far away as Scotland and even Norway. At places where there are steep hills, it is also possible to see the different underlying rocks (alluvial sands and solid chalk, clay and ironstones and various sandstones) packed closely together shown up by colour or lushness. A humbling landscape, yes, and perfect for walking, full of interest for nature lovers and archaeologists as well as geologists.

Among the industrial archaeological relics are naturally the abandoned routes of old railways and, now heading to Donington on Bain, we pass its old station yard on that from Lincoln and Bardney heading toward Louth. Once a railway crossroads, in common with so many market towns, Louth is now trainless, though – as in so many cases – a group of railway enthusiasts are running steam trains over a restored part of one route.

It is still nearly a mile into Donington on Bain, one of the Wold's larger villages with the first shop we've seen since leaving Horncastle, six miles from here as also is Louth. The owner's life scarcely seems idyllic: 'I'm here from 6.30am to 8.30pm every day, just one day off a year, and that's for thirty four years. There's a second shop with the Post Office, a school, play school, church and a lovely pub. We have it all. It's very hard work running a country store, just selling a little of this and that. Many people go into one of the towns.' The keeper of the shop with Post Office has 'only been here twenty five years, making me one of the longest-staying people in the village. There are about 250 people, nearly all incomers... just a few real locals like a couple of elderly sisters living by themselves.'

Though the Viking Way passes through the village in the valley of the River Bain, main roads don't, but the nearby towns can be reached in not much more than fifteen minutes. The area was livelier when it was more self-contained in past centuries: one tell-tale sign is that, with Norman beginnings, St Andrew's Church lost its north aisle as long ago as 1779.

Soon we're in Louth's outskirts and a snooze before my visitor arrives.

Administering the AONB

Meeting us at our hotel in the early evening, so he can get home for dinner with his family, is Steve Jack, the manager of the Lincolnshire Wolds Country Services. This co-ordinates the running of the Lincolnshire Wolds AONB on behalf of the several councils, parts of whose areas it covers. While waiting for him, I read the succinct summary of its aims on the front cover of its Management Plan:

> The Lincolnshire Wolds will continue to be a vibrant living and working landscape through the primary influence of sustainable agriculture, forestry and land management. It will retain its unique and nationally important sense of place: an area of open rolling hills, dramatic views, farmed fields changing with the seasons, tranquil valleys, woodland, pasture, streams and attractive villages.
>
> The Wolds' natural and cultural heritage will be well known, enjoyed and widely respected by both residents and visitors. It will continue to provide a place of tranquillity and inspiration for those fortunate enough to visit the area, whilst meeting the economic, social and environmental needs of those who live and work there.

Steve Jack is a good example of the newer no-nonsense men and women to whom the future of Britain's best landscapes is now entrusted. There's idealism backed by excitement, a clear understanding of practicalities with none of the 'aren't they lucky to have me' status-seeking attitude of some of the old gang who competed with the landscape to be centre stage.

'It's a glorious, intricate landscape, highly fertile and intensively farmed. It's not really natural for, ever since man arrived on the scene, it has been changing, but what we can say is that it is surprisingly thinly populated, where even on a bank holiday you can walk all day literally without seeing a car. In the 1930s superbikes were roaring through it most weekends; that's not allowed now.

The villages are charming. We're lucky that there's so far been such little development, but naturally there's pressure for some, notably in-filling in the built-up areas, and we can't stop that entirely. But it can be controlled, and we can insist that traditional local materials are used. This is not the place for innovative buildings. There are few second homes, so we're free of that pressure from which many rural areas suffer. That's a big factor, making it easier to support what the residents need.

The Lincolnshire Wolds are precious, but that's partly because they're so productive, and lively farming supports other local businesses which are also part of the character. Another good thing is that there are no special honey-pot areas drawing great crowds, but an extensive network of rights of way wandering through the woods, along the ridges and down the valleys. That makes it easy to encourage visitors who really appreciate it as it is. Supporting the right kind of tourism is an important part of our remit. We still have pockets of poverty, especially to the west, and must think of encouraging jobs.'

When I congratulate him on the quality of the publicity leaflets, especially the co-ordinated series of fold-out booklets in the *Wonders of the Wolds* series, he smiles and says: 'You see how we specially play to people's special interests, be they wildlife, archaeology, the rituals and religions of the past, enjoying the fine tradition of local produce, walking or just exploring the very different villages and the few great houses.

With just 12,000 people living in our 216 square miles, there's obviously not a vast infrastructure and it's a question of making the most of traditional things. So even churches with great heritage value are working together. We watch planning tightly, and have to be aware of some pressures, especially those from Lincoln's growth and the rising price of property there. But our task is largely about getting things done on the ground, bottom-up working based on good dialogue, be it restoring a hedge or involving schools in specific projects.'

The AONB is run on a shoestring, with a team of only six part-time officers, including two project workers, a specialist in chalk streams which are a powerful ingredient of the countryside mix, a sustainable development officer and an admin officer. As Steve says, on that basis, 'We can't help working closely together.' Three quarters of the costs are borne by Natural England. 'Small was ever beautiful.' Something it seems the National Health Service has been slow to grasp.

Louth, How Small Towns Used To Be

'How do you like Louth?' Steve Jack asks. 'It still doesn't have a major out-of-town supermarket. There are lots of lovely individual shops, a joy really.' We explain we've only just arrived at the hotel, but after an early dinner will go into the town, with time to do so again tomorrow. As he gets up to leave, he adds that, though the NFU and Country Landowners' Association had initial reservations, today most people seem happy with what is happening with the AONB – and that, once more, agricultural prosperity is the basic foundation.

The way from our hotel into the town is partly alongside a stream where once there'd obviously been a water mill. The centre is compact but complex, too, with streets, some of them narrow and twisting, meeting at different angles and no obvious through street. Parking is easy, in a small car park bang in the middle by the market hall with its odd high tower competing for attention with the 295ft steeple of the parish church.

Louth's history is summarised in the *Town Guide*, supplemented by David Robinson's Louth now and then website and his books including one he's just finishing on the Wolds. A geographer, he's long played a role in protecting the local heritage.

The town started early. At Domesday there were 600 residents. It grew as a trading centre serving Wolds and Marshes but was set back by its leading role in the Lincolnshire Rising, a protest against Henry VIII's plan to rob the church of its valuables, producing the rebuke 'ye rude commons of one of the most brute and beastlie shires in the whole realm'. The ringleaders, including the vicar were hanged, drawn and quartered at Tyburn. The Civil War depressed things more here than generally too. Trade only revived with the opening of the turnpike and (in 1770) especially the canal. A dockland, separated from the town, developed on quite a scale.

The town's independent character today is due partly to the early foundations, to the church (which warrants a three-page entry, and many references in the introduction, in *Lincolnshire* in Pevsner's Building of England series), and also has much to do with its geographical isolation and the prosperity of the surrounding area.

Louth is how towns used to be when friendship and service to attract and retain regular customers were more important than the immediate bottom line... when shopkeepers loved seeing customers' children grow up and hear about them after they'd left home and, for their part, the customers felt terribly guilty if swapping allegiance from one butcher or baker to another. The town clerk, solicitors and small traders had time for morning coffee and perhaps discussed how soon they might dare remind a member of the aristocracy that they hadn't paid their bill for months. I'm just old enough to realise what it would have been like in most small towns when, for instance, hot cross buns were bought fresh first thing on Good Friday and Mum's weekly shopping list began with 3lb of butter and 2lb of lard, but the first line on the invoice stated '1lb Cadbury's milk chocolate, gratis.'

I can't be the only visitor induced into such nostalgia by Louth. I'd greatly enjoy a holiday here, and it would make an excellent base from which to explore parts of the Fens as well as the Lincolnshire and Yorkshire Wolds. We loved the Yorkshire ones, but these, for which Louth serves as capital, are even better though small, a narrow wedge-shaped band running north west to south east.

Tennyson's Birthplace and the Bluestone Heath Road

After a second walk round Louth, we head to Tennyson's birthplace, the tiny hamlet of Somersby. First to South Ormsby, then by Brinkhill, Harrington Hall (a great house whose gardens are busy on four open days each summer) and Bag Enderby, every turn, climb and descent surprising.

Amazingly, we are Somersby's only visitors. When I think of the major role Wordsworth plays in the Lake District's tourist industry, and even more how Stratford-upon-Avon exploits Shakespeare, remembering that, after Shakespeare, Tennyson is the second most frequently quoted poet in the *Oxford Dictionary of Quotations*, why should this be? Is Tennyson (possibly our most popular Poet Laureate ever) so out of fashion, or is Somersby so out of the way that people don't trouble to go there? Both reasons probably tell, but the latter is certainly the chief. As we saw in chapter XIX, Tennyson is far better remembered on the Isle of Wight where he later made his home. Yet it is usually the birthplace and where the famous were raised that are commemorated.

Of one thing there is no doubt: Tennyson's character and interests were heavily determined by his love of the countryside around Somersby, where his father was vicar. The church is now one of nearly a dozen in the South Ormsby group, with a complicated rota, with services at most churches at least twice monthly. Some drive or even walk between neighbouring parishes. The group's newsletter is called *Tennyson's Chronicle*.

Appointed in 1808, George Clayton Tennyson, was also vicar of Bag Enderby, only half a mile away. Then there was a combined population of around 200. Thanks to the mechanisation of agriculture and older people dying off, now there are just forty. The shops and most cottages that the Tennysons would have known have fallen or been pulled down. With colourful country people and smaller farms, it might then have seemed more rural. John Large says in his self-published *Stories from the Fens and Wolds:*

> At the age of ten Alfred mastered Pope's *Homer* and wrote hundreds of lines in imitation. This was followed by 6,000 lines based on Walter Scott. By the time he was fourteen he had completed a play in blank verse.
>
> The children used to play complex games of invasion in the rectory garden and surrounding fields, involving stone-throwing attackers and equally determined defenders. They always looked scruffy, and Alfred in particular had a reputation for his down-at-heel appearance, with a mop of unruly dark hair that was seldom washed or brushed. None of them had any real regard for fashion, although they did mix socially to some extent for they attended dances at Spilsby and Horncastle.
>
> The daughter of a neighbouring landowner was probably being rather generous in her description of the family: 'The Tennysons are not easy to describe. There was a natural grandeur and simplicity about them; a streak of impish mischief and a love of the gruesome. Delightfully unconventional, they were never like ordinary people; even their dress and walk seemed different.'
>
> The family was liked well enough by the village, but was considered distinctly odd, as indeed it was. The children knew the villagers intimately, for they often used to visit the poorer cottages, particularly Alfred. For a while the three oldest boys had attended the village school, a rough old building which had once been the village bath house. It was closed by the farmer who owned the land, as he claimed the children were disturbing his pheasants.

Tennyson's grandfather, a maverick aristocrat, disapproved of his son taking the cloth, disinherited and ignored him, creating inevitable tensions from which the grandchildren suffered. Alfred was the fourth of twelve. When his grandmother died, Alfred sent what he had penned about her to his estranged grandfather, who awarded him ten shillings: 'The first money you have earned by your poetry, and, take my word for it, it will be your last.' Though well educated, Alfred's early success was meagre. His father's early death meant abandoning Cambridge and, as head of a declining family as siblings left, he arranged a local move from the Rectory which had to be given up. Then the last sibling had to be committed to an asylum. In 1837 Tennyson left Somersby, never it seemed to return.

He suffered other blows, notably the death of his great college friend Arthur Hallam. *In Memoriam,* written to calm his hurt, records his saying farewell to Somersby in 1837:

We leave the well-beloved place
Where first we gazed upon the sky;
The roofs that heard our earliest cry
Will shelter one of stranger race.
I turn to go; my feet are set
To leave the pleasant fields and farms;
They mix in one another's arms
To one pure image of regret.

The future Poet Laureate's fortunes changed slowly and erratically, serious respect first earned by *In Memoriam,* still loved by many of us for its huge range of topics, some of them everyday and critics might say pedestrian, but united in a great whole. When local people later heard of what his poetry had earned, they were predictably unbelieving.

When dining with Queen Victoria on the Isle of Wight, no doubt Tennyson thought (if he didn't actually talk) about those formative days... as we do looking at the cream-coloured Somersby House, the former Rectory and, across the road from the church, the embattled manor house with its curious square towers. We also look at the brook and the bridge across it which, as the hamlet's strongest lad, Alfred sometimes prevented other boys using, the quarry and especially at the compact 15th century sandstone church on raised ground and almost surrounded by trees.

Described by Pevsner as of no special interest, it's unpretentiously pleasant. We buy two of John Large's booklets, read the discreet display about Tennyson, look at his bust, and sit – there is only room for about eighty – leisurely meditating. I especially connect with the first poet I came to love and occasionally quote. The quarry, an outcrop of Spilsby sandstone, which weathers all too easily but turns to a lovely soft khaki green, was recently specially reopened to produce stone needed to repair the church.

An hour or more has passed and still we're the only visitors. 'I'm not surprised,' says John Large, self-publisher of the booklets already mentioned when I catch up with him later. 'The Wolds are an undiscovered treasure, one of the very last uncommercialised parts of England. One reason is that the big landowners don't like visitors: pheasants are more important to them than people. Even the Tennyson association attracts few to Somersby. The church is one of the main outlets for my *The Tennyson Family and Their Villages,* but it's only 75 copies a year.'

A retired teacher with 'an aptitude to become closely associated with the places where I've lived or have strong associations', he does his own selling to churches, museums and tearooms, and a scattering of shops in the surrounding market towns. Some titles are reprinted, regularly, but that might be as few as fifty a time. 'I write, edit and do the layout, the printing is done by a local firm with a state-of-the-art photocopier giving a sharp image and also sorting the pages, and I staple, store and sell. But when I've left an area, such as the New Forest where I was brought up, it's hard to keep the sales going. There's not much money in it, but it's a good thing to do and there's little risk. Even for a new title I only do 200 copies. That's what's good about this simple production method; but you can't use any old photocopier.'

One of his first titles, *The Wesleys*, commemorates another famous Lincolnshire family and its local associations. Epworth is a better known but also little-visited village we had hoped to see but lacked time. 'It's a flat, marshy part around there and not very attractive,' says John. The booklet reminds us that John and Charles Wesleys' father, Samuel, had been brought up by the persecuted non-conformists and trained for their ministry but then switched allegiance to the Church of England. His first living was at South Ormsby:

> By dedicating one of his works to Queen Mary he was able to acquire a rather better living at Epworth, in the north-west corner of the county, and moved the family to a thatched wood and plaster tenement of a building which passed for the parsonage. As a preacher he was plain-spoken, ever ready to rebuke iniquity, and as his parishioners were a thievish, lawless lot, he soon caused offence. Twice his house was set on fire, and his cattle injured.

The Wesleys, including John (whose founding of the Methodist Church was almost accidental and who once preached locally) and Charles (the great hymn writer) would have been familiar with Tennyson's birthplace.

From Somersby we make our way back by South Ormsby to the fourteen-mile Bluestone Heath Road striking north west roughly following the course of an ancient ridge trail along the spine of the Wolds. There's a marvellous viewpoint commanding us to eat our sandwiches once more in the best of situations.

Then we soon come to the north west escarpment we had looked up to on our initial drive to Louth. By the time we've covered the whole ridge road, we've picked off many landmarks including Lincoln Cathedral and the Boston Stump. If I had to name the most enjoyable, uncrowded, unclassified road in Remote Britain, this must surely be it, at least on a day of good visiblility. It is a road for those with long sight or caveman's eyes.

We spot many little villages and their churches, a couple of ancient burial mounds, fields that have been thrown together in the mechanical age, and abandoned wartime airfields. If only we knew where to look we'd see ancient battlefields, too. Peaceful as it is today, the Wolds have seen their fair share of bitterness fought at the cost of much humanity.

There's so much past, so much let go, but we can only guess how the view has changed over the years. What stands out sharply is the compactness of most of the villages, with little development around their periphery – apart, that is, from a couple of lines of ugly council houses of the immediate postwar years, placed prominently, beyond the edges of many villages – blots on the landscape throughout Britain.

The ridge road avoids us having to return to Louth. By North Ormsby, in totally different terrain from South, we're soon off the Wolds and whisked by main road into the busy roundabout-infested approaches to Grimsby. On this trip we happily miss out Cleethorpes and the whole Fun Coast, another of Lincolnshire's many faces.

Grimsby. Where Cod was the Currency

For its size (roughly 100,000) Grimsby, or Great Grimsby to give it the full name, is almost certainly the least-visited town in Britain. Not counting a train trip through it on the way to Cleethorpes, it is by far the largest place I've never been to, yet because of my interest in the history of commercial fishing, I've read much about it, and have also heard a lot from a Devon friend brought up there in the war.

'It was a two-centre town, "them and us", the fishing section being entirely working class though a few homes in the mainly slum area were beautifully kept, and many people's ambition was to move out,' says Dr Gordon Langley. That's followed by: 'We were an isolated community, 40 miles from anywhere and never went further than Cleethorpes, almost part of Grimsby'; 'lots of things were different, everyone cycled and, with their fathers so often away at sea, schools let children out at lunch time on Fridays to collect the weekly wage packet,' and 'we had a couple of major air raids, one of which burnt out the mile-long wooden fish dock'.

But the thing he especially remembers is the outcry when 'a piece and a pennyworth' went up from three old pence to four. People were shocked beyond belief. The very foundations were rocked. If that could happen, then nothing remained certain.

Cod was everything. The crews of the deep-sea trawlers fishing off Iceland, earning their keep in the remotest possible way, were central players in an immense range of activities that brought prosperity. The middle-men with their clerks auctioning the fish, the army of porters, railway staff whose job it was to get the fish away quickly and reliably, ice makers, dredgers and their crews keeping the essential channel open, the gutters and the salters: they were all involved in the business, which supported a vast range of shopkeepers, blacksmiths, cobblers and other artisans. Earnings rose and fell along with those of the skippers and crews.

Despite seamen being called up, fuel shortages and mines laid by the Germans at the mouth of the Humber, business continued in the war, if not quite as usual, then only with nuisances seen as temporary. But that 'a piece' of cod should cost 3d instead of 2d: that was revolution.

'Cod was the currency,' says Gordon. 'The whole economy, everyone's wages were dependent on it and everyone ate it. The docks were out of bounds, and anyone found with a cod down their trousers would be for the high jump. Fish and chips were consumed in vast quantities by the whole working class part of the town.'

Gordon's own family and their neighbours typified social change. 'Until I was ten or eleven, we lived centrally among the skippers, their crews and the artisans. My grandfather who came to Grimsby as an illiterate orphan, was apprenticed and eventually became a mate on a trawler, while a skipper lived next door. In the early mornings we were woken up by the beat of the clogs of the dock labourers going to work. But my father had academic leanings and became a teacher. Education was generally seen as the best escape route. Then we moved out into a better area. Others had already done so in the 1930s. Though Grimsby is still a two-centre town, the rigidity of the old days gradually broke down.

To this day there's still a great community spirit, which jazz, the earliest popular entertainment, encouraged. And there's always been keen competition with Hull. We boasted that we were the most important fishing port by value, though Hull claimed it on quantity. In Grimsby, the early-morning unloading of fish was done by lumpers; in Hull they were bobbers. Though Hull was technically nearer, before the road bridge of recent times, few people went there and we always said we were 40 miles from anywhere.'

Gordon and I have long promised ourselves a visit to Grimsby together but, with busy diaries and awkward journeys, it hasn't worked out. So he's suggested his cousin, Jane Gammond, might help, and she and her husband, Michael, exuding interest in and loyalty to Grimsby, collect us from our hotel and show us round.

The Fish Docks and Heritage Centre

We recap that in the 1950s there were 500 trawlers tied up several deep along the three fish docks. Today, there is only a fraction of that number and a single side of one dock is used. In common with all fishing ports, Grimsby has been badly hurt by tight quotas. Yet, more fish comes here than ever... incredibly no less than five times the total of the UK's fishing quota. Most of it is from Iceland.

In the cod war of 1973, Royal Navy frigates clashed with Icelandic gunboats, but in the end the island was allowed to extend its territorial waters to 200 miles around the coast, since when it has carefully looked after its fish stocks free from foreign competition. Some also comes from the Faroes and Norway. Since fish catching is seasonal, four-fifths of what is processed is nitrogen-tunnel frozen to ensure the flesh retains plumpness and moisture as well as flavour. With numerous gutters, each with their own knife, making Grimsby a heavily-armed place, fish processing is one of the main ways in which today's living is earned. On the back of that, other food industries have been attracted. There are about 500 of them, offering almost everything edible.

'Birds Eye have announced they're pulling out, but it won't make much difference,' says Michael, to which Jane adds: 'Things are always changing. The port used to be almost all fish, but now Danish butter and bacon, Baltic timber and Volkswagens come in while British-made Toyotas go out.'

Even the almost deserted mile-long docksides and the general air of decay convey romance. It is easier to tell what things would have been like in the port's heyday, when it was sometimes possible to jump from boat to boat all the way between the long piers, than it will be if the plan goes ahead to convert it all to yet more of Britain's vast stock of luxury dwellings beside water where commercial ships once visited.

Our guides point out the tall tower which will no doubt be preserved as Grimsby's iconic landmark, on our way here it seemed to pierce the sky but, seen from the decaying dock side, looks more like a pencil. 'It once housed the hydraulic engines which opened and closed the dock gates,' says Michael. 'Until then the port had been tidal.'

Standing amid the dereliction, nothing at all moving on the water, he pronounces: 'It's sad, and it certainly reminds one of how important Grimsby used to be.'

'But they'll be pleased to have a more modern fish-processing plant,' says Jane. Currently it's in Victorian buildings behind the harbour, the smell overwhelmingly telling what's going on there. [Icelandic trawler crews are delighted to have started unloading their catches in Grimsby

– giving the fish docks a level of activity not enjoyed for many a year – because it means they are being paid promptly. As explained in the main text, the fish was anyway being routed here, but not by the individual trawler load, for processing. The change is a consequence of Iceland faring especially badly in the financial crisis.]

Then we move on to the Fishing Heritage Centre. This is superbly done, as lifelike as any industrial museum I've seen. There is much to do, listen to and even smell, as well as a great deal to see, eat and buy: top of its class.

The human figures are so realistic that I actually ask one if he can point me to the loo. Several of the figures are on the preserved *Perseverance,* one of three shrimpers built in Boston in 1914. In an extended summer, a small beam-trawl was used to catch shrimps and prawns off the coast, while in winter 'long lines' sought North Sea cod.

A plaque explains that she was restored by unemployed people as part of a community programme: 'Her name (and that of her two sister ships) is reputedly from the motto of the Society of Oddfellows, "Providence, Unity and Perseverance" to satisfy fishing superstitions.' There are friendly staff to answer questions and help enthuse the younger visitors especially about how things used to work.

The museum now offers corporate entertainment, with special emphasis on fish and food. It earns a feature in *Food and Drink Network UK,* the periodical emphasising that Grimsby is the Food Town of Europe, with among other things the continent's largest cold-storage facilities. At the end of our tour, we join those enjoying the offerings of the everyday café: 'It's always good here,' says Jane, who recalls memories of our Devon friend, Gordon Langley, 'part of family life here till he left for university. My and Gordon's grandfathers were brothers. It's hard to realise how different things would have been here when they were young.'

Finally I pop to the shop to buy a copy of *Grimsby: The story of the world's greatest fishing port,* a substantial, well-ordered volume by Peter Chapman. The backbone is the story of how the population increased from 1,000 to 63,000 in the 19th century, rapid expansion continuing well into the 20th century. Though always seen as a modern town, Grimsby had early beginnings, and sophisticated facilities mingled with primitive ones – as they still do.

Speaking of primitive, the great galleried Flottergate chapel, a highly ornate, quality building, was possibly the most expensive and best-ever Primitive Methodist edifice in the country... just one hint of the self-confident spirit behind Grimsby's rise.

With Jane and Sheila chatting away in the back, Michael drives us briefly through the 'other town', the substantial but more ordinary commercial and shopping heart, and then back to our suburban hotel. Here we part company, grateful for their help as they have been pleased to show off their town.

Little Car across the Humber Bridge

We transfer to Little Car, still with luggage piled on the back seat. Having had an easy time so far in Lincolnshire, 'she' (vehicles are always feminine, and Little Car very much so), still on her way to live in Scotland, hurries along main roads to the Humber Bridge. We skirt Immingham, whose container port has greatly eclipsed Grimsby in terms of tonnage, and the flat lands to the north. There's a fascinating country between Lincoln and the Humber, Scunthorpe in its middle, which I've never seen... though I did once visit the port of Goole, further inland (45 miles from the sea), where the pedestrian picks his way alongside water as in Venice.

In *Journey* I recalled a trip by train to New Holland, then an isolated terminus, with paddle steamer connection to Hull. Today's trains bypass it to reach Barton-on-Humber, with a bus connection over the long bridge. The services are not busy, and road traffic is light for, when areas have been so separated by a wide strip of water crossed by only an occasional ferry, it takes a long time for new links to be forged. An attempt at integrating lands on both sides into a Greater Humberside was a hopeless failure. One thing is indisputable: though under-used, in terms of its cost, the bridge is a fine piece of engineering. The Humber is a truly major river with many different environments and rich bird life. With its tributaries (including the Derwent, Ouse and Trent) it drains a fifth of all England, while its ports account for around 14 per cent of the UK's international trade. It is a turbulent estuary, Hull itself being a surprising, often choppy, 22 miles inland from Spurn Point.

For us, however, Hull is a total journey of barely 20 miles – but it might almost be in different countries. Then onto York to spend the night with Allan and Barbara Patmore, who also spent a night with us at Raven Hall (chapter VIII). Allan's disability which began showing itself then and prevented them coming with us down to Spurn Point stretching out into the Humber, has become more serious, and tonight might be the last time we see each other in Yorkshire. Their house is on the depressed market; they're planning to move to Chesterfield to be close to their daughter.

One way and another the last few days have emphasised the shortness of our innings on earth.

· XXXI ·

THE WYE VALLEY

From the Highlands to the Wye

In almost twenty hours of continuous travel, we have sampled a huge range of scenery, from the splendour of the outskirts of the Cairngorms, to the lit-up industrialisation around Warrington Bank Quay, one of the numerous places the sleeper was delayed on an unusually late run. We endure wet Monday morning congestion in London, and yet again are poorly treated by First Great Western.

Once Paddington, the start of the Great Way West, meant fast, smooth trains with excellent catering. Though schedules have been eased, we start late and become later. Platform discipline is atrocious. As we lose a couple more minutes at Swindon, I recall a railway friend telling me that agency staff are now sometimes used at central control here: 'They don't even know their basic geography.'

Sheila says she hates going by Great Western because I complain how things have gone down hill; but she misses the serving of proper food. Again this morning, 'the trolley attendant hasn't turned up'. And now they want to take off the buffet car. First Great Western are in the doldrums but trying to fight their way back.

Then the sun comes out, the edge of the Wiltshire Downs look its best, and when we glide into Georgian Bath, it is soaked in sunshine. Taxi to our flat, a quick repack, and by car once again across the broad Severn estuary by the original bridge, skirting Chepstow, alongside its racecourse and, still in sunshine, up the Wye Valley to its pièce de résistance: Tintern Abbey.

Now we can relax. The sight of Tintern Abbey beside the tidal Wye refreshes the spirits. No matter how often you see it, in sun or rain, the Abbey, carefully preserved in the same state of ruin and, apart from the roof, amazingly complete, surpasses expectation. How well those monks chose their sites before the days of guide books and organised transport.

The road was not built for today's traffic, yet I hope they never improve it. Full of surprises, including a long elevated curved section edged by overhanging woodland, it is one of our national treasures. Ideally it should be declassified and speed restricted throughout as happens on some National Park roads.

Redbrook and the Lower Gorge

So once more to Redbrook, where generations have passed since the river was coloured red by the waste from metal works. The inevitable glance at what remains of the railway reminds one of how much faster change takes place today than formerly. At the end of the 1940s, I recall my father saying that the same type of Great Western steam engine was making exactly the same shunt it was doing at that precise time half a century earlier when he first visited his grandfather in Redbrook. It was then a very different, close-knit industrial community, not as now home to commuters from Monmouth.

Great grandfather Thomas Thomas was a successful 'tinman' who, as he progressed through roll-turner to works manager, lived in style and sent my grandfather to Monmouth Grammar School to which he walked daily. Since Redbrook has changed so much and it's well over a century since he died, there's no point in enquiring which of the double-fronted houses was his. My father remembered Thomas Thomas (whose own father was also Thomas Thomas) in home-spun garments with scull cap and white patriarchal beard, a teetotal singer who led his choir in raising money for his little Methodist chapel.

Cornish copper was shipped to Chepstow and transferred to the Wye Valley flat-bottomed trows to be smelted at Redbrook in one of the works 'whose fires gleam in red, blue and yellow flames, and blaze up through lofty chimneys'. In 1692 there were sixteen furnaces at Redbrook, but copper smelting ceased by the end of the 18th century and tin plating took over. Redbrook then produced the world's thinnest metal sheets. In 1961, after nearly two centuries, the last of the works, still using the traditional hand method, succumbed to competition from big strip mills putting its 150 men out of work.

With thoughts of those very different Redbrook days, we backtrack, enjoying views of the valley from the other direction. As we pass Tintern Abbey again, we notice the tide is running out fast. So to Lower Wyndcliff Wood, above Prior's Reach.

A notice welcomes us to the peaceful and picturesque wood and, across the road, to the 365 steps up to the Eagle's Nest. The high walk along the cliffs was made in the middle of the 18th century, when comparing romantic or picturesque scenery was the rage among travelling society. The Eagle's Nest look-out point followed in 1828, 'for the Duke of

Beaufort at a time when such dramatic view points were fashionable'. It is an exciting, if strenuous to reach, walk through 'an example of the Wye Valley gorge woodlands with ancient hanging beech and yew, as well as lime, ash and hazel coppice'.

Looking down, we follow the river's course by the horseshoe bend toward Chepstow. In the haze, it takes time to confirm that in the distance we're looking at cliffs – 'the sheer limestone cliffs below the curtain walls of Chepstow Castle' – not buildings high above the river's opposite bank. It is hard to believe that much of Monmouth's and Herefordshire's commercial traffic once fought its way up the river. Trade was heavily dependent on the tide. Eventually traffic was mainly confined to lower reaches, where the last of several weirs, built to raise the water level in selected reaches, was dismantled in 1930.

We have discovered a 'new' or restored, if small, piece of Remote Britain: incredibly peaceful, the border between the cultures of England and Wales, with the start of Offa's Dyke Path one side and the Wye Valley Path the other, and much evidence of former greater human activity – industry, transport, religion, tourism. To the Romans, who fully colonised the Wye Valley, it wouldn't have seemed at all remote. Throughout the monks' days the river was the natural highway. Later industrialisation saw the river positively congested. Now, in the little low tide mid-channel, there's only a solitary motor boat moored.

Tintern and its Abbey

Then back to our original northerly direction, we finally stop at the hotel opposite the Abbey for dinner and a night at rest without wheels under us. The Abbey Hotel isn't great, but friendly – and amazingly cheap. We soon discover why: it recently went bankrupt and is being run on behalf of the debtor bank. 'If we can fill the rooms, people will buy meals and drinks,' explains the keen temporary manager.

'But I'm afraid we're having sandwiches.'

'Yes, but you're clutching glasses of wine; it all helps.' The reason for sandwiches, hurriedly made in Bath, is that we know we're in for a surfeit of meals, at ten different hotels in twelve nights, on a long and complicated journey, some in busy but most in yet another part of Remote Britain.

Our hotel's joy is its proximity to the Abbey. We savour every change of mood and colour in an evening of light showers between declining sunlight. First thing next morning, we walk to the Abbey under a glowering sky. Many people are disappointed by the approach past a miscellany of buildings, but it was worse having to run the gauntlet of hovels and their uncouth occupants when the Abbey was first treasured as a ruin.

Founded as early as 1131 by the Cistercians, who loved remote, riverine locations to civilise and develop in their own ways, it was the first of the Welsh abbeys and has always been among the largest. Built of local stone, which has clearly proved durable, it was first dissolved in 1536. Then the White Monks took over both Abbey and the rich farming estates and developed them further.

The river always played a vital role in the Abbey's active life: for transport and trade, fresh water, carrying away waste, fishing, powering water mills and other machinery, providing the challenge to improve drainage along adjacent land and, no doubt, above all for feeling close to God. There were reverine disputes, too. In 1330, the creation of a new weir made it hard to take supplies to Monmouth Castle, but water bailiffs who attempted to interfere were attacked by monk-led locals.

The Dissolution of the Monasteries naturally gave the local economy a serious jolt though also offering new opportunities. The Abbey and most of its rich lands went to the Dukes of Beaufort. A few visitors had been attracted to the Wye Valley since Roman days but, it was not until the romanticisation of ruins that Tintern attracted widespread attention... so much so that the Dukes were persuaded to maintain the roofless Abbey in the state it was then in and has remained, more or less, since. That doesn't seem to have pleased everyone. Some delighted in ivy growing out of the walls which modified 'hurtful' regularity and might eventually cause more ruinous perfection. We will go into more detail later about the Wye Valley Tour which inspired tourists, and especially painters and poets.

What hopes, opinions, schemings, fears have been experienced in this cherished spot over the best part of a millennium.

Even in outline the story is full of irony. It was the very plenitude of coal from nearby Welsh pits that led to the building of pioneer tramways giving a more direct outlet to the sea. That, plus the working out of the local mines, meant less traffic going down the Wye. Though there have always been local stone quarries, as already indicated, the lower valley's industrial expertise concentrated on processing imported minerals. Men and horses along a new towpath, struggled to bring the laden trows upstream, agitating them to get past banks or rocks even at normal high tide.

When the Wye Valley's own branch line was opened in 1876, not merely had the great days of industry passed but so had the Wye Valley Tour for the cream of creative society. The trains ran through a green and pleasant land carrying more conventional Victorian tourists.

I recall great train journeys in the 1950s on the long-abandoned railway, and the lengthy walk from the station (now a council-owned tourist attraction) along what was once a quiet road to the Abbey. Apart from an occasional Sunday School outing or other excursion train, for whose long layover a third platform was provided, the branch line was never busy. Compared with today, few people even glimpsed the Abbey, and there certainly wasn't anything like our barrage of hotel, B&B and restaurant notices.

Today there's much nostalgia about the long-closed railway – and, decades after it was last used, the towpath has disappeared into the dense vegetation of the banks of the lower Wye that has helped turn it into the 'new' piece of Remote Britain we celebrated. Only the Abbey itself has maintained its respect; for much of its length, even the river plays second fiddle.

These are some of my thoughts as we walk to the Abbey early next morning. What stories are evoked by those vast walls, the eaves of the roof ends still towering high. The scale is almost unbelievable. It's raining and there are few others around which adds to our sense of awe.

With the guidance of the outstandingly useful *Tintern Abbey* guide, published by Welsh Historic Monuments, we follow how the building replacing earlier ones developed over many decades – and wonder at the contrast between the stark simplicity of some of the masonry and the delicate bar tracery of some of the best windows. Like most we pause to take in the great west window, whose stonework has survived remarkably intact. It is a perfect example of the Decorated style strongly influenced by late 13th century London work. That the monks were not at all insular is shown by a map of the routes between the Cistercian's greater (especially in France) and lesser establishments (many in the western half of Britain). The long daily life of the monks is well described. The simpler winter timetable starts with rising at 2.30am with two periods for work between many different ways of paying homage to God ending with Compline at 6.15pm before bed fifteen minutes later.

Applauding the unobtrusive explanatory notices, in a heavy downpour we have to scuttle to the shop for shelter. It's not long before a superb 'tree of life' tapestry in outstandingly brilliant colours, catches Sheila's eye. 'Too expensive,' she says, but in the rain 'it's fun just looking'. (Actually I order it by telephone later for her birthday.)

New Naturalist

The publisher Billy (Sir William) Collins once confided that his more financially-orientated colleagues weren't too keen on the New Naturalist series. 'I just think we should do them', he said, though later the output was reduced and standards cut. I've commented before that, out of say a dozen titles by David & Charles published on a typical release date, it was usually obvious that the book that would ultimately be most cherished and command a high second-hand price was not that which would immediately sell best. Often, it seemed, there was an inverse ratio. But in the very long term, things can sometimes right themselves. Collecting New Naturalists (whose scarce titles fetch hundreds) has become a cult thing, justifying more new titles at prices – currently £50 – that, even taking inflation into account, would have been impossible while Collins were still independent and less commercially pushy.

Hot on the heels of *Gower* has come the *Wye Valley*, by George Peterken, that rare being who knows his subject thoroughly and explains it clearly for the intelligent layman. The 105th in the series, it is as good as any. He deals with detail down to lichens on the Abbey walls without losing perspective or our interest. The text bowls along with enthusiasm born of love and command of his subject. I wish I had had him as an author. He would have needed little rescuing by editors.

My pleasure in reading it has prompted this visit to view the Wye Valley with deeper understanding. So we drive back to Redbrook to meet George and his wife Susan, who has also just had a book published, on the Wye Valley's landscapes in painting. Talking in the car park, overlooking the river, there's one point of dissention. Will The Boat Inn, reached by walking across the old railway bridge (once used by trespassing Welsh to get a drink on Sunday), be suitable for a talk over a meal? No, we conclude. It's almost too genuine an old pub for our purposes, but I'm glad to have seen it and certainly to have crossed the bridge again, the first time on foot which I doubt my forefathers ever did.

Redbrook's other pub being closed today, we have to go slightly inland, enjoying industrial remains, including the abutments of the bridge that once took coal up and tin down an industrial railway. Our destination: the Ostrich Inn at Newland; there used to be an ostrich farm here when they enjoyed a short-lived British popularity.

As we unwind, we discuss the woods we visited last evening. George says: 'Down there the Wye Gorge is incredibly remote these days. Industry has gone, the Wye is little seen from the water or its banks, and it is far more wooded than it used to be. A very special part of the valley.

On the cliffs, the ancient mixed woods have hardly changed since before Neolithic days. We know that from analysing the pollens of up to five thousand years ago in bores taken from estuarine margins. That's exciting. In parts of the gorge, as at Redbrook, there are fields by the river and on the higher land, but the cliffs between have been left alone for an incredibly long time. You can't walk down some of the cliffs with their boulders without risking turning an ankle.

In Roman days there'd have been hunting along the valley, and on the English side there was a medieval forest. But then the whole valley is a kind of no man's land between England and Wales – and also the natural boundary between lowland and upland Britain. Even today you can't help sensing you're in border country. Go east or west and it's soon very different. Most valleys go on attracting development, but not this; it is remarkably peaceful, a buffer zone which more and more people appreciate and want to see left unspoilt. There's a campaign to introduce traffic calming. The busyness of the main road, especially with drivers rushing along it as a through route morning and early evening, is our greatest threat. I'd love to see the road declassified, speed brought down. It would be a tragedy if it were turned into a decent road.'

I ask about the Valley's status as an Area of Outstanding Natural Beauty. 'Uniquely it ignores official boundaries,' says a gentle, balding George, with a smile. 'That's the Wye for you. But despite that it has worked quite well, with a number of local forums devoted to grassland projects, for example. Several views have been opened up and there are useful publicity leaflets, and schools are involved. The valley has genuinely seemed to come before politics.'

I then ask him about his New Naturalist book, but first a quote from his opening chapter starting with a comment on the whole river below Hereford, which incidentally laden boats once reached – in stages, progress only possible at high tide:

> South of Hereford any other river would flow in a broadening channel through an industrial city into a wide estuary, but not the Wye. Instead, in an extraordinary transformation, this mature lowland river flows directly into the hills. More surprising still, after sweeping past the Bicknors, it flows out into the lowlands, only to turn back again into the hills. Thus, from Symonds Yat Rock, a glance to the east shows the famous view of the Wye flowing out between Coppet and Huntsham Hills, but a glance to the west shows it flowing back in again below the Doward. Thereafter, it runs through a wooded defile past great cliffs and limestone pillars to Monmouth. Winding sinuously between steep wooded banks, it eventually reaches Tintern, below which the cliffs again stand out among the woods. This, the lower gorge, finishes against sheer limestone cliffs below the curtain walls of Chepstow Castle. Then, after passing the new Chepstow bandstand and abandoned wartime shipyards,

the river flows unnoticed into the Severn.

That is the Wye, arguably the finest and least spoiled of all the major rivers of Britain. It is also the 'unknown' river, for, despite its qualities, it has attracted relatively little attention. Indeed, it is probably less famous now than it was nearly 240 years ago, when a parish priest from the New Forest hired a boat at Ross, drifted down to Chepstow, wrote his *Observations on the River Wye...* and thereby established the Wye Tour.

With splendid food, we relax over a map to follow comments on many valley topics, including the huge literature it generates. There's a fascinating volume published by Monmouth Borough Museums Service on *The Water Powered Industries of the Lower Wye Valley* (S D Coates) which will have a dedicated band of readers but will not feature on many Londoners' Christmas wish list. Another title George mentions I'd like to read is Colin Green's *The Severn Traders: The West Country Trows and Trowmen.* George lists many others in his own book's bibliography. Then I am wrong footed by congratulating him on being an unusually good author for an academic. He denies he's one at all. 'I have many dealings with them, but I'm a woodland specialist – something between research and conservation – and most of the time I'm connecting with ordinary people.

It's been a good subject for a career. I've been involved in the whole movement of better appreciation of woodlands and our native trees. Living close to it, it's almost by accident that I've come to know the Wye Valley so well. It's marvellous and with a rich landscape and history – and special woodland interest. The book was fun to write and illustrate with nearly 200 colour photographs. The readers I had in mind were interested ordinary people. I tried to make it accessible. The first edition was 4,000 hardback and 2,000 paperback but they're already reprinting 800 hardbacks, so it's done quite well for something of that length and price level.'

Picturesque Beauty

It wasn't exactly a snappy title, but it had enormous influence: *Observations on the River Wye... relative chiefly to Picturesque Beauty; made in the summer of the Year 1770.* Inspired by a trip on the river – the author told a friend: 'If you have never navigated the Wye, you have seen nothing' – the Rev William Gilpin secured his place in history. After a slow start, by 1780 the book (one of the earliest of such publications) had run through five editions.

The picturesque was already on the ascendancy, and the lucky coincidence of his two-day journey taking place not long before the Napoleonic Wars, when Europe was closed to tourists, led to an influx, small in modern terms, but of influential people and especially writers and artists. Unlike the other famous 'Tours' of the day in the Lake District and Scotland, the Wye's was relatively short and easy to reach – and the river offered the ideal vantage point in the age when 'Picturesque' was a complex art form.

Because of a chance remark by George Peterken to his wife Susan that it was time the Wye Valley Art Society took an interest in the valley's picturesque element, a special art exhibition was held to encourage contemporary re-interpretation of the old artists. 'Then it occurred to me that there might be a book in it,' says Susan as we finish our meal. *Landscapes of the Wye Valley Tour* is a handsome paperback with fine reproductions of many of the works displayed at the exhibition as well as pictures and prints from the days of the Wye Valley Tour. I purchase a signed copy inscribed with the date and Redbrook-on-Wye (though elsewhere I follow the OS in calling it just Redbrook). It includes four of her own vivid images.

'The art exhibition was ambitious for a small society,' says Susan, 'but it worked well, with an excellent entry. The disappointment is that, for those who've become more aware of its river's charm, there are now no regular boats. Anyway, it's hard to persuade people to leave their cars.' In the book she records how 'the Lower Wye Valley became appreciated for the contrast between neat regulated fields and rocky cliffs,' best seen from the water, where even the fiery forges, whose sparks were compared to fireworks, could add to the sense of the picturesque. One writer said that Redbrook's works 'gave animation to the romantic scenery' – an illusive thought missing both earlier and later in history when industry was generally seen as a blanket deterrent.

Susan discusses the development of the picturesque, especially in painting. The old paintings still make considerable impact. Turner was preceded by at least seven other well-known artists, but the pictures by today's artists selected from the exhibition bring an original interpretation to historic themes. The book is one I'm reluctant to file away.

Its core is an illustrated tour of the river, in which we learn not only about the preferred picturesque places but how those on the Wye Valley Tour were fed and watered, what it cost and what the boats and boatmen were like. The tourists' various reactions make fascinating reading, too. While many were beyond the sublime, some were excessively fussy. She naturally discusses the contribution made by poets, including Coleridge – and Wordsworth who made this late addition to his *In Memoriam:*

Then twice a day the Severn fills,

The salt seawater passes by
And hushes half the babbling Wye,
And makes a silence in the hills.

I am particularly interested in the final chapter on changing attitudes to landscape. Its full enjoyment was always confined to a small minority, it being assumed that the mass of people actually living in lovely country would take it for granted and that 'ordinary' visitors from elsewhere couldn't possibly do it justice. Leith Ritchie, author of *The Wye Valley and its Associates: a Picturesque Ramble,* snobberly said that to understand our own scenery, including the Wye, the visitor had first to have toured abroad, which in those days was only possible by the well-heeled who could afford time as well as expense.

I put it to Susan that it is perhaps because of such snobbery that any effort to help ordinary working people enjoy today's scenery has resulted in tourists often rushing past the best as they hop from one commercialised 'honey-pot' to another.

'You're probably right,' she says. 'The picturesque was a cult among the privileged, though no less interesting for that. Anyway, the picturesque has been watered down generally into today's more general love of scenery without taking it so seriously. And today people rush to the coast or the moors of the National Parks – that is if they stay in this country at all. The Wye Valley isn't today's fashion, which is why it's so unspoilt.'

George adds: 'Yes, and though there's a far greater minority interest in geology as there is in trees and woodland, our education system doesn't help encourage any real understanding of what Britain has to offer, and books about the local countryside often tell you less about what it's actually like than do railway ones describing and illustrating routes.'

I put in: 'Our nature has become very urban. It shows even among most country people' and then reflect that once we had a domestic helper who'd been brought up on a farm but was amazed when presented with peas to shell. Though no doubt assuming they grew somehow, she'd only taken them frozen out of packets.

To the Most Typical View

The Ostrich is the kind of pub you would come back to if in the district. Now, however, we travel higher. In his book, George has a photograph of a view from Highbury Farm which 'summarises the gorge. There may be more dramatic views, but not one telling you so much. It's certainly far better than the view from Yat Rock... but it's a bit less accessible and getting there can be a bit rough – and I hope I can remember the way.'

Since Little Car is full of luggage, all four of us have to travel in his car: up an extraordinary steep, rutted narrow track on a ledge along the hillside where you dread meeting an opposing lorry. Bump, bump, through lush vegetation with occasional revealing glimpses of the river below, until – yes, we've turned correctly – we park and climb into a gently sloping field, for our final approach, avoiding marshy land as best we can. And there it is far below us: the 19th century railway bridge over the timeless Wye, which disappears after curving again between the cliffs. Though some of the cliffs rise straight out of the river, here there are fields before the wooded cliffs. There are also many fields on top of where we are. As the monks found at Tintern, this is good land, and the woods had their uses. Coppicing leaving high stools yielded a timber crop for many specialist uses.

The visual impact of the wooded cliffs is dramatic. The village of Redbrook straddles underneath us. From such a view you can tell much about the local history, geology and flora. (See plate 12)

In the corner of the field where I'm taking notes and Sheila is photographing us, George points out: 'The trees by the bridge are sycamores. Beyond them and beyond the big field with the millennium field just showing, the river is lined by alders. As the woods start rising with native woodland, limes are punching through like cumulus cloud. There are just a few tightly-packed 1970s conifers in sight, but thankfully most of them have gone.'

As we get back to the car, we walk a bit further up the ledge we drove up to look down on what George says is technically called a relict hedge bordering the ordinary woodland. 'They are old limes which spread into the hedge and have been left. Nobody would actually plant limes in a hedge.' Another term is woodland ghost. He can tell which trees were last coppiced fifty or seventy years ago 'but really very little has changed in 5,000 years since pre-Neolithic days. That's the real thing about these steep wooded cliffs.'

It becomes ever clearer how much George knows and cares about his trees: his career has suited him to perfection. As we start our descent, he suddenly says: 'By the way, I've been meaning to tell you that a turning point for me was reading the pioneer work you published by Colin Tubbs on *The Ecology of the New Forest.* There was hardly anything like that then taking the overall view'. And I comment that the first book I bought with my own pocket money was on British woods. Published much earlier, it would be too general and out of date for those seriously interested today, but I cherish it for having started to open my eyes.

Symonds Yat

Not merely is the Wye an under-appreciated river but, of those who make a point of seeing something of it, a quite disproportionate number make for Symonds Yat. Though scarcely warranting such singling out, it is undoubtedly a lovely stretch. The OS marks the famous view point high up on the narrow neck of land where the river virtually doubles back on itself. It is, however, hard to gain a real sense of the character of the river either from the viewpoint or by the road approaches on either bank.

Naughtily leaving our car in a hotel's private car park on the Welsh side, I feel we're just too late. The view from the train which passed along the opposite bank offered a far richer perspective, though best of all would have been a journey actually on the water from the Severn at least to Ross-on-Wye. That has rarely been possible for the last century and is something most of us will never experience.

What we can do, and promise ourselves we will when we're less pushed for time and the weather is kinder (it is back to heavy showers), or we are properly equipped for rain, is to take this section of the Wye Valley Path, which threads through the gorge on the bed of the old railway. Through incredibly varied landscapes, most of the 136-mile path closely follows the river, but south from Ross-on-Wye it strikes inland through hilly wooded country to regain the river where it flows under the bridge before Symonds Yat, near Goodrich.

It thus avoids the very part of the river most seen and enjoyed by motorists: gently wandering, fast flowing but no wider than a broad canal. I've often loved seeing it from the car. The road is further away, giving a clearer view, than at the approach to Monmouth where the traffic is anyway pushy. But as a lowland river, it gives not the least indication of how it will shortly behave going around the horseshoe bend at Symonds Yat and progressing downstream through a series of other gorges before marrying the Severn. The river out of sight of traffic is always better.

Over the years I've come to love the whole Wye. It gives character to so many places, such as Builth Wells and Hay-on-Wye and other little 'on Wyes' before it flows into Hereford to become centrepiece of a cathedral city. Some of the upper Wye features in *Journey*. Here I've concentrated on the lower Wye, where it is undoubtedly the most extraordinary of our major rivers.

Though there is nobody else about, we're concerned about continuing to leave Little Car in the private car park, so I make the ferry an excuse to call at the hotel. The ferry is shown on the latest OS, but the boat has obviously been tied up for some time and there's no timetable or notice. 'I know nothing,' in broken English, is the receptionist's response to my enquiry. I'm fobbed off with a brochure. If the ferry has closed, it will further isolate settlements on the other side; Symonds Yat station was once well used. Bridges are few, and where the river largely encircles a district, it almost turns it into an enclave of Remote Britain.

When we leave the hotel, a boat sets off with a handful of passengers on another of its short trips around the horseshoe. That is certainly better than nothing on the water, but not much. Our side remains totally dead. So looking across to the footpath on the railway route, we gaze, listen, breathe and commune with the river and think of its changing fortunes over the centuries. It has perhaps served man better than man has treated it, yet in the long run it has survived remarkably undamaged. Maybe the real battle for its soul has yet to be fought? Who knows, and now it's put me too much at ease to care.

· XXXII ·

THROUGH THE GLENS

A Touch of Frost

When there are clear skies in late spring and early autumn, weather forecasters warn there might be a touch of frost in Scottish glens. What do southern English people think? How wild are the glens that they are punished when their own gardens have long been frost free? Whatever they imagine, it is almost certainly less happy than the reality.

Late or early frosts are usually caused by relative lowness. Especially near day break, cold air pours down from steep hills to the gentle valley bottom, from which there is nowhere lower for it to continue draining. It is trapped in a 'frost pocket'.

Most glens were cut by glaciers in the ice ages, and deeper yet by rivers. When we go through a glen, it is usually in the company of the river. Though populations are sparse, vegetation is little different from what you'd find in most British river valleys. It is only when you study the very occasional vegetable garden and look for runner beans that you realise that the growing season is short; corn for eating off the cob isn't an option. It doesn't get going soon enough. Potatoes have to be planted late but are still worthwhile growing, if not commercially. Brassicas thrive, as do turnips and swedes, which swap their names north of the border, though turnips (English swedes) are more frequently called neeps to go along with tatties (spuds in English) to accompany haggis.

So how many glens are there that they warrant mention in national weather forecasts? My faithful *Murray's Handbook*, the Scottish edition of 1894, considerably thumbed through during my long ownership, lists 135, many more than do most later guides. That – though only just over half of the 267 lochs – shows that there are glens in profusion. The actual number, if painstakingly totted up from large-scale OS maps, would be far greater. The AA road atlas manages fewer than a hundred. Added to which are the broader Straths, valleys generally with greater flood plains. *Murray* has forty eight of them. There is a lot of geography in Scotland.

Hidden in these figures is something of the history of Scottish tourism and, to a lesser extent, economic development in the last century and a bit. That the Scottish title is of a later date than most of my prized *Murray's Handbooks* is simply because Scotland, especially its remoter areas, was late to be opened up to tourists. The railways came late to and through the Highlands. It was because of Queen Victoria's infatuation with Scottish scenery, and her purchase of Balmoral, that the popular development of tourist routes followed. But how enthusiastically MacBraynes and the old railway companies did the job. By 1894 *Murray* included an incredible range of train, coach and steamer services, many to places you cannot reach today unless by car – but you can't drive on lochs (sea and freshwater) that once had regular steamers.

In many glens, the tide of explorers has receded. Even private coach tours do not venture up many. Relatively few are covered by today's guides. Local websites come to the rescue of the curious. It is perhaps a metaphorical touch of frost.

Great Diversity

Though they are all river valleys, the glens are hugely diversified. Many stretch fifteen, twenty or more miles. The archetypal one rises gently beside its tree-lined river, the road sometimes across a field or two of the flood plain, until the hills get higher and closer and continuing the road would be expensive – or might disturb the game. Tracks usually continue higher, sometimes past ruined habitation and even a castle, since many glens were the homes of the wealthy and influential, and it was vital to protect the mountain passes that now only climbers see but through which marauding armies could descend. Wherever you go in Scotland, there are reminders of Dr Johnson's famous statement that, when they are not fighting the English, the Scots fight among themselves.

Some glens are part of today's through routes. To reach the starting point of one we are specially visiting for this chapter, today we use three – Glen of Rothes, Glen Rinnes and Glen Livet – in distillery country.

The beautiful cross-country route avoids the dreaded, accident-prone A9 from Perth to the North which, passes parallel with the railway, through Glen Garry to reach the summit at Drumochter and then descends through Glen Truim. Living in the north, we tend to take the glens for granted, yet each is special even if some confusingly share the same name. There are three Glen Begs, nothing to do with each other. Go to, or look up, a glen and be prepared for generous doses of superstitions and Scottish family history and quarrels.

Even within individual glens there is confusing name duplication. Glen Roy, just south of the Great Glen not far from Spean Bridge, has a cluster of hills in the tough walking country in its headwaters, and three of them are called Carn Dearg. For good measure, there are a couple of identically-named lochs. Roy is a very individual glen close to, but utterly off, the beaten track. Among geologists, it is best known for its 'parallel roads', clearly etched successive heights of the glaciers that once filled it.

Other glens can only be reached from their highest point and descend to salt water, where once there might have been a boat connection. Others terminate at a lonely hotel or sporting lodge. Some are through fairly gentle country with low hills, while others have successive mountains of over 1,000ft, the Munros steadily ticked off by 'Munro baggers'.

Many of the rivers that made the glens are fed by lochs where rainfall has been collected, so the 'run' is fairly constant. Some pause to pass through their own lochs, fed by tributary streams, before proceeding in a more stately fashion with greater flow. There were once regular ferries across a few of them, while others have rope bridges not always in the best condition.

Other glens have spate rivers, rising and falling rapidly according to rainfall. Often they are fed by waterfalls and, after a downpour, it is a joy to trace white water spurting down hundreds of feet from high ground, sometimes leaping mid-air before hitting rock again. Though floods can occur on most glens, most regular are those with spate rivers whose fishermen have to bide their time until perfect conditions yield rich catches.

Still other glens are private affairs, roadless, seen only by keen walkers and fishermen – who swear they are the best of all, full of natural character, little spoilt by man. Many penetrate the circumference of the Grampians.

Today's agriculture is limited to the valley bottoms but, sheep used to roam many hills, while the Forestry Commission planted other huge areas with uniform conifers climbing to the highest economic level. In some cases that meant destroying the bare line of hill tops which is now more widely aesthetically appreciated. Especial damage was done in South West Scotland's Galloway. Everywhere, replanting now is usually with mixed woods including, if not exclusively, native trees... one of the ways in which things have improved.

Ownership of the glens is a thorny question. A few of the historic families have survived their own problems and death duties, but many estates have been broken up or radically reduced. Happily the planning system has checked new roads and excessive development. Today, some of the best glens are supported by the 'new' money of the southerners who have made fortunes in finance or property and enjoy being 'laird', though rarely visiting their seat. It has frequently been put to me that nowadays sporting estates need 'money thrown at them'.

A personal dilemma. I love grouse, whose shooting has long been a way of life in upland Scotland. The holiday season traditionally reached its crescendo on the Glorious Twelfth (of August), the beginning of shooting. The pressure put on the old Highland Railway is legendary at Perth, carriages brought by three rival companies were shunted into lengthy 'caravan trains'. With two or more engines, the processions, carrying a cross-section of the cream of society, made their leisurely way up the single track to Inverness, often arriving hours late.

It has only been the research for this chapter that has made me realise how artificial the grouse moors are: how much competing vegetation, animals and birds are killed to give the grouse a chance in their chosen heather patches. My love of grouse has turned to disgust: how can I possibly be prepared for that sacrifice for the sake of my taste buds?

Then I was told that if grouse shooting ended, the way of life killed, the lairds who subsidise it would give up, gamekeepers lose their jobs, land be abandoned, everyone worse off.

Especially in their upper parts, many glens only have a handful of people employed locally – almost all directly or indirectly by the sporting estates. Many are without shops or schools, and the last churches struggle. Yet there is purpose and determination, often a great community spirit which at its best supports community centres. It would surely be a shame to see the glens emptied. I am not a vegetarian but hate things being killed, especially unnecessarily ceremoniously as in fox hunting. Should I keep grouse off the menu or once more enjoy it?

Glen Esk

On today's journey, now south of Banchory, having climbed through Glen Dyke and Bridge of Dyke and followed Water of Dyke, we find ourselves alone on a narrow road across a bare mountain before a steep descent into tamer country at Fettercairn. Still on a B-road going west, we miss the sign for Glen Esk. The trouble, perhaps, is because we're not joining the glen at its beginning. It goes further south to the dual-carriageway A90, and some claim a bit even beyond that, as the River North Esk makes its independent way to the sea just north of Montrose.

So, we head up the most easterly of the Angus glens to penetrate the Grampians on a narrow, well-maintained road with recently-renewed fencing. We follow the tree-lined North Esk, sometimes close by, occasionally across a field. It is beautifully-kept mixed countryside, the fields, the river famous for fine salmon and trout, mixed woodlands – all in pristine condition. Only the map confirms there's no through road or way out, not at least by car, though there are tributary glens and mountain foot passes.

Once the Dalhousie Estates owned the whole glen as it still does the top end. Much of the lower has been sold. We pass a succession of builders' vans: the new owner of part of the southern glen is restoring and improving everything, from buildings to gates and fences. There are also vehicles returning from the water works at Loch Lee, which supplies much of Angus. But scarcely a car, and certainly no coach. Glen Esk, not listed even in my *Murray*, ignored by most tourists past and present, has never had the popularity of parallel Glen Clova. Fifteen miles long, it is however, not a bad glen with which to start our detailed sampling.

Amazing in view of the paucity of homes, at the glen's minute capital of Tarfside, two thirds of the way up there is still a lively primary school, and a Retreat Craft Shop & Folk Museum, established many years ago by the Dalhousie Estates. Even better, it has a café.

The centre, in a former shooting lodge with new additions, is run by an award-winning community trust, and for nearly half a century has provided part-time work, and an outlet for home-grown produce, baking and craftswork, especially for women of the glen. We have the museum (themed in a series of separate rooms) to ourselves, the recreated kitchen clearly reminding us of our age, for many of the domestic artefacts are just what we or our friends, certainly our older aunts, used. Wireless sets designed as contemporary works of art are familiar too; they used to take a long time to warm up. In contrast, staff in the café are pushed to cope with a small crowd, some tucking into an early high tea, others like us relaxing with a cuppa and cake.

At the next table, a three-year old lad catches my attention and giggles as I appear from behind a handkerchief with which I now and then cover my face. He is Jack but, more important, his dad, Andy Malcolm, having tucked into a substantial meal, enjoys telling us about his work as under-game keeper and deer stalker in Dalhousie's Invermark Estate at the glen's top. There are seventeen in the primary school, he says. Once it had been down to nine. 'There aren't many full-time jobs in the upper glen: only three tenant farmers and six full-time game-keepers. All the water workers live elsewhere and just visit, and a few who live, in the glen commute out of it.

If houses at the south end come on the market, they go to incomers at inflated prices. At the top, the Invermark Estate, where I work, guests like to be out in the wilds – they love the deer being fed in front of the game lodge – and development is strictly controlled. To create the least damage to the environment, after being shot deer are brought out on horseback.'

Far happier in his work than almost anyone one meets in crowded areas, he's been in the job twenty years but uses his holidays to explore other remote Scottish areas, mainly by boat on the west coast. Scotland, he says, is full of surprises but nowhere ultimately beats where he works though, like many others, he's disturbed by the low number of grouse in recent years. Though marauding birds and animals can be kept away, the weather cannot be controlled and, in the wet, ticks are a particular problem. Happily, however: 'Steadily grouse are nesting among the heather on higher ground where there are fewer ticks.'

If the glen seems fit for royalty, it has often welcomed them. Only a few weeks before his death, in 1861 Prince Albert accompanied Queen Victoria when they followed an ancient track north across the mountains to Ballater. The Queen Mother from Glamis, where the next chapter begins, came for the shooting. At the point where Glen Esk divides into two lesser glens, we have to park and explore on foot. Heading to the top of Loch Lee, we pass a couple of fascinating buildings. The older is Invermark Castle, an excessively tall tower house. With a look-out turret near the top, it hasn't changed since the days when the great had to put up with the inconvenience of living uncomfortably to keep safe. Raiders were all too likely to descend through a mountain pass though, if they were unable to take the occupants by surprise, with no way into the high fortress, they must have felt they'd wasted their time. No way can we get in either – without waiting for the trees growing out of the walls to bring the whole thing down. In a few centuries it may be an explorable collapsed ruin. Though much younger itself, Glenlee Parish Church, astonishingly one of four churches, in the glen, reminds that Christianity was brought to the Esk by St Drostan at the start of the 600s. We know more about St Drostan as founder of churches on either side of the Moray Firth under Aberdeen's Monastery of Deer, often wrongly attributed to St Columba.

That there is much more to Glen Esk (or any other for that matter) than you can possibly learn in an afternoon was brought home when a newcomer to Nairn Jim Parker-Jarvis, happened to mention that he had recently retired from farming on the rich land at the southern end, and that his father-in-law had been factor to the Earl of Dalhousie on the great Dalhousie Estates.

'He didn't live in the factor's house because he wanted to retain his independence, and toward the end of his life made the proud boast that he had factored, shot on or valued every field in Angus. But then the Dalhhousies once boasted they could walk exclusively on their own land from the county border to the sea.'

'A bit of an exaggeration,' the present Earl Dalhousie tells me. 'There were huge estates, yes, but not without a break,' Once there were 150,000 acres. Successive death duties has reduced that to 55,000 acres. The Earl commands a thriving if complex business. There are three castles: Brechin, Edzell and Invermark. Unlike the latter, Brechin Castle, long changed from its defensive role into family home with superb gardens, is now also a business centre with a staff of ninety. There's a visitors' and garden centre along with a restaurant... one of many places where contact is made with tourists for, in addition to farming, forestry and property letting, the shooting lodges and other upmarket holiday accommodation are of vital importance. As in so much of Britain, it comes down to bums on beds. As the estate's website puts it, its land still runs 'from the fertile Vale of Strathmore to the heather moorlands and mountains of Invermark where the hills rise to 3,000ft at Mount Keen, Scotland's most easterly Munro'.

I say that changing economics must challenge Lairds?

'Very much so', agrees Lord Dalhousie. 'Some have found it very difficult. I'd spent fifteen years in the City before my dad became ill and I returned to take over. It was becoming obvious we couldn't survive on farming, so we diversified, cut back on the farming with many fewer working on the land but added new shooting and equestrian operations and a lively garden centre with café. We're still looking for new opportunities – and with higher prices the agricultural scene has brightened. Yes, I'm very busy but it's enjoyable; I get involved in all sorts of things. It is RAF at Leuchers later today, celebrating the beginning of radar.'

Glen Clova

Then a quick dash up the parallel Glen Clova. Confusingly its river is also an Esk, the River South Esk which reaches the sea in Montrose Bay without ever getting near its compatriot. They are not the only Scottish rivers to have the same name other than the prefix which have nothing to do with each other. England is a land of few but large river systems; Scotland one with numerous short rivers but few great ones. To demonstrate their independence, the North and South River Esks have a more rugged, little-visited glen cut by West Water between them.

Though there is even less sign of habitation, Glen Clova's mountain scenery has always made it popular, uncomfortably so at peak weekends. The mountains feel impenetrable even before the road splits into two, rejoining at the mini-village of Clova. There's an unofficial one way system to prevent passing places gumming up.

My *Murray* goes to town. Assuming we're interested in the owners of castles and estates and their legal feuds – and, naturally, the glen's role in sundry battles, it continues in its typical prose: 'From Clova to the head of the glen the scenery is incomparably finer. The hills draw nearer and are rugged in the extreme.'

My framed early map of the LMS railway shows a motor coach route connecting with the short branch to Kirriemuir whose trains ran on to Forfar, once a busy junction. Not merely has the main line and all its branches long since disappeared, but bus services are not great. You either drive or hitch-hike up Glen Clova.

Without doubt it is a show-piece, the camp site near the ranger station being used as overflow when the car park is full. Solitude is easily found, however: many leave their transport for hours while they climb into the mountains, explore Glendoll Forest or the Corrie Fee National Nature Reserve, where our own arctic alpines flourish. Away from the road and you're quickly unwinding, communing with nature.

Glen Coe

A couple of weeks later, we take an old friend to Onich near Ballachulish in readiness for the last pair of our sample glens. Inevitably the journey is through more glens, especially (after passing Laggan and Loch Laggan) Glen Spean. At Tulloch I always look at the point at which the West Highland Railway joins the road. It takes a much more interesting route, down the Spean's gorge at Monessie Falls, to reach Fort William.

Though the line's extension from Fort William to Mallaig with its popular *Jacobite* daily summer steam train receives greater publicity, in my view the most spectacular of all British rail journeys is that across bleak Rannoch Moor, alongside Loch Treig and down into Tulloch and Fort William. On Rannoch Moor there is no habitation, Corrour station is roadless, and the road from the east to Rannoch station itself simply reaches it and dies. The route's mood changes with the skies. I recall waterfalls, rainbows, deer, snow-topped Ben Nevis and its outline seen from the sleeper on a clear June morning, and in autumn Rannoch Moor lit up by the moon between spasmodic blizzard bursts.

Still about travel, while we're in Onich there's a renewed plea to replace the nearby ferry across the Corran Narrows. The road avoiding the ferry crossing adds a 40-mile trip round Loch Eil described in *Journey*. The justification for a fixed link? The price of fuel, always high in the Ardnamurchan and Morven peninsulas. There are surely more fundamental reasons. Even exploratory work would cost £1.5 million, so it will not happen. In Norway and Denmark, where the value system with a longer perspective, is different, bridges and tunnels are more freely built.

Glen Coe. The very name makes one shudder. The ingredients? An A road, wide but winding, with long convoys behind slow-climbing lorries, possibly the grandest mountain pass in all Scotland's ever-changeable skies. And always the shameful memory not so much of how people lost their lives in the glen's infamous massacre, but how the crime broke the basic ethos of Scottish hospitality.

Though the MacDonalds were notorious for keeping stolen cattle in their mountain hide out, and regularly sacked the property of the rival Campbells, that could never justify their murder in cold blood mainly by the very government troops who had enjoyed their hospitality for weeks. Moreover, when in August 1691, King William III/II offered a pardon to all clans who had taken part in the 1689 Jacobite uprising, conditional on an oath of loyalty being sworn, the deadline was only missed because the MacDonalds mistook the place at which it was to be administered. And then, in a blizzard, the whole thing went wrong. Many trying to escape died of exposure.

The Scots were outraged. Even those who don't fully appreciate the details know Coe as uniquely the glen of shame. On wet days, of which there are many, black skies enhance the feeling of gloom, despondency.

It was on such a day that, many years ago, a party of five friends felt they could no longer cope in their caravan and extravagantly, as they thought, took a cottage in Glencoe village to dry out. However, the mean accommodation with its lean-to shack of a kitchen, was itself ringing damp, and took two of the party a couple of days to clean up and dry out before the others could move in. Miserable memories of all sorts.

On our way from the peaceful lochside haven of Onich Hotel, we cross the bridge over the mouth of Loch Leven (most of my life having to go round it has taken ages) and drive along the route of the branch line from Oban closed half a century ago. I clearly recall alighting at the terminus on an extremely wet day to find the landscape dominated by black slate quarries and piles of dark cut slate, awaiting transport. Soon the slate industry closed, too.

We go into Glencoe village which we enter past a large, boarded-up hotel. There's not much in the village these days, but a notice on the door of the Post Office, itself now no doubt threatened, lists the achievements of the community council – including caring for the gardens of the hotel until hopefully it is rebuilt.

Then up Glen Coe, with few signs of civilisation apart from the Mountain Rescue and National Trust Centres and the old inn. Only faith, map and memory assure us there is a way through. Repeatedly, at every turn for miles, other peaks appear which seem impenetrable. What things must have been like in the Ice Age can be guessed at by the large piles of scree giving the bottoms of the glacial-cut cliffs a slightly curved, softening effect. No buildings, but plenty of people, peering down to the river deep below and even descending to it by a steep track. Of Glen Coe's pulling power there is no doubt. There's a good website referring to a regular newsletter with latest news and offers. But the last word goes to Lord Macaulay, taken from my *Murray* who charmingly had the habit of including a small anthology element in his *Handbooks*.

> In the Gaelic tongue Glen Coe signifies the Glen of Weeping; and in truth, that pass is the most dreary and melancholy of all the Scottish passes – the very Valley of the Shadow of Death. Mists and storms brood over it through the greater part of the finest summer; and even on those rare days when the sun is bright, and when there is no cloud in the sky, the impression made by the landscape is sad and awful.

Joined for a short time by the route of Wade's old military road, which climbs by what seems an even less achievable and steeper way from salt water at Kinlochleven, we're 1,000ft up on the open soggy plateau of Rannoch Moor. Soon, however, we turn right and enter an incredibly different environment.

Glen Etive

Most modern guide books omit the (usually) quiet world of Glen Etive but, in steamer and railway days, it formed part of one of the most popular circuits for visitors. Train from Oban after early breakfast, steamer to the end of Loch Etive always praised for its magnificent mountain views, coach up the glen and back via Glen Coe to the train at Ballachulish in time for high tea.

As soon as we are on the single-track road fenced in by mountains alongside the River Etive, we forget all about Glen Coe, wars and everything disturbing. This is peace.

After a wet spell, the river jumps and gurgles, fed by acrobatic waterfalls tumbling off the towering mountain whose bare rocks sparkle in sunshine. For the first few miles, there is little else to see but mesmerising river, mountain and waterfall, but at Dalness things change. There's the start to great mountain passes on either side, while the extensive woodlands have mixed replanting replacing dreadful all-conifer plantations. There's a large laird's house where we see two masons taking great care rebuilding a wall, and a scattering of holiday homes and cottages. This is a cherished environment we'll find out more about in a moment. The few tourists now drive more slowly to take it all in, but the traffic scarcely warrants the 'Fresh Eggs For Sale' notice. It is the year of the foxglove; they're thriving everywhere.

The Royal Mail van on its daily trip may be less costly than the three boats a week run for the Post Office, even in winter, well into the 1960s... but still impossibly expensive for a 'company' expected to deliver universally, in competition with new operators who pick and choose who they serve and how.

With a still-widening valley and massive woods, there's said to be excellent fishing on both banks of the Etive. The pair of 2-mile beats are rotated between the shooting lodges adjacent to stately Dalness House and, further on, Glen Etive House – from which Etive loch head can be seen.

Fourteen miles after turning into the glen, we're at the end of the road: a rough turning circle by an abandoned pier with rotting timbers at drunken angles, and roofless storage buildings. I conjure up what the scene would have been like when a paddle steamer (I can almost hear her whistle as she comes into sight) and horse-drawn coaches exchanged passengers and mail, and heavy goods coming by water were stowed under cover. There's no boat of any kind to be found, in the water or on land. Another car arrives: 'Is this all we've come to see?' The end of the road, everything?

Back at Dalness, I stop to speak to the 'masons'. They're not in the building trade at all, but adaptable gamekeepers, who happily tell me about the glen – less than twenty people in the lower glen, these days a few incomers, 'happily all Scots' – but so far as the sport is concerned refer me to the headman who manages it all in the laird's usual absence.

Alistair Hunter has been here thirty six years and is a confident mine of information. He commands five full-time and four part-time gamekeepers. No grouse, but deer stalking and rich fishing (£4,000 for a week's permit) when the river is sufficiently high (forty weeks a year). Because of its fierce spates, a costly hatchery with spawning bed had to be replaced by a smaller but better protected one.

Says Alistair: 'We ourselves don't do forestry but it's good to see the 1960s conifers – 4,000 acres which had a huge impact on the landscape – being steadily felled and replaced with native species. A lot has changed. Most of the time the glen is quieter. The sheep have gone. The Glasgow Holiday crowd go abroad. The Outward Bound School has closed, as did our little school in the middle eighties. My two children were its last, and in his final year my boy had an excellent teacher from South Uist to himself.

Times have changed and we have to be realistic. Apart from fish and game and a few holiday cottages, there's no income. The glen attracts mountain cyclists, Munro baggers and naturalists looking for rare plants; but they don't spend. We used to have a West Highland ranger who did Glen Etive, but when he left he wasn't replaced. We've asked for rubbish bins at the head of the loch. Though in theory we attract tourists, they're given no facilities. Like so many places we've suffered from violent swings of the pendulum, especially in agriculture and the kind of visitor.

Now there's something new in the glen called vandalism. At busy weekends van loads of Glasgow youths bring their drink and probably drugs to the lochhead. We have to take our boats down by trailer, because we can't leave them there or they'd be vandalised. It's a grand loch, especially the upper part, but it's not like it used to be when people did the circuit by steamer, coach and train. All that went when they closed the railway to Ballachulish. Many changes, and I'll see more yet, but the glen is for ever. It always survives, triumphant.'

· XXXIII ·

IN THE FOOTSTEPS OF THE QUEEN MOTHER

Castle to Castle

The popularity of the Queen Mother, and the esteem in which she is still held, are continually brought home to us on a journey in her footsteps. It begins at Glamis Castle, near Dundee, where she spent her childhood and much of her character was formed; continues to Balmoral Castle on the Dee where she enjoyed a few late summer holidays with her husband, King George VI and, after his death, had her own home on the estate; and on to the Castle of Mey in Caithness which, after she had been widowed, she bought and developed in her own inimitable style as a remarkable extra 'royal' home.

It is a formidable journey of nearly 250 miles, including, for us, a small detour to Nairn for a break to catch up with things at home for a few days. The Queen Mother occasionally made the journey by car and, at least once by train, but usually arrived in the far north by air at Wick airport, where she received an ecstatic welcome. But then, including exploring widely from all three castles, she knew her Scotland intimately.

The journey is one of incredible beauty, some of it in remote wilderness. There's great historical interest, too, with numerous castles, still lived in or ruined. It is not a journey to be hurried. Done continuously by car, it almost fills a day. Anyone driving it even once will remember it for life.

From an early age the Queen Mother was used to moving between homes, in the tradition of the great families, making the most of journeys and renewing familiarity with staff and local friends. This no doubt helped develop her astonishing memory, not merely for people and places but realising their special qualities and seeing them clearly in the broad perspective. What also emerges as we meet those who knew her was her great love of family, some of whose complex links go back centuries.

Few people have lived history more fully. Her own contribution has scarcely been minimal. The first twice, she declined the Duke of York's proposal of marriage because she was unsure she could handle being a member of the royal family and when she finally accepted, she could have had no inkling of Edward's abdication. Yet as George VI's Queen, not merely was she soon immensely popular but, in the view of some of her contemporaries, might actually have saved the monarchy and prevented further constitutional pain.

She brought colour and warmth to Buckingham Palace. That made a colossal difference in the war. Ever unphased, perhaps her most famous remark was that she was glad bombs were falling nearby as it made it easier to look East Enders in the eye. We'll hear much that adds flesh to that skeleton on our journey, though in no sense is this a formal portrait of the great lady.

At heart the Queen Mother was a country girl, delighting in natural things and country ways and traditions. She was able to extract much from London and its State occasions, but was never more relaxed than in rural Scotland.

Glamis Village, Post Office and the Dowager Countess of Strathmore

Having spent the first of three nights at Castleton House Hotel, fully deserving the *AA Hotel Guide's* highly-rated Inspectors' Choice, first stop next morning is Glamis Village and sole shop whose Post Office is under threat.

'We're certainly not going to die for lack of support,' says Anne Nicoll who runs it with her husband Hugh: 'But without the Post Office, keeping a small shop alive is much harder. We're a real village, not a commuter one, growing with four hundred people and several businesses, and others who work from home – and Glamis Castle just around the corner.'

The Post Office has been used by many Royals; the Duke of York chose to register Princess Margaret's birth there. Closure is being opposed by the Dowager Countess of Strathmore, related by marriage to the Queen Mother who, she tells the Press, would have been horrified by closure. A leaflet has been produced by Glamis & Area Community Council, and a petition signed by several hundred people. I congratulate the owners on their broad stock of groceries and gifts, and next day we return for tea and homemade cake in the little tea room, part of the varied enterprise at the heart of village life. If a small sum is saved by closing the Post Office and destabilising the shop, the real loss to the community would be far greater, but that's not what today's economics are about.

As the result of a previous postmaster, Bill Dougan, telling friends that visitors often asked for a book about the village, the 'Glamis Publishing Group' was formed and *Glamis: A Village History* was published in 2000. There's a foreword by the Queen Mother:

> I am so pleased that this excellent historic record of Glamis Village has been compiled for the Millennium, as I feel strongly that it is important for us all to know about the past, not only of one's country but also of the local area in which we live...
>
> There has always been a strong and happy link between the Castle and the village, and I have precious memories of delightful childhood days and visits to Mr Burns the postmaster to buy sweets at his shop and later on when I started the Girl Guides.

However times change and things come and go like the railway, but it is wonderful to know that the village and its community is flourishing today and I send to you all my heartfelt good wishes for the years ahead.

Still on sale at the Post Office, it is a model of its kind.

Though the royal interest obviously helps sales, it is very much the story of an everyday village, from Roman and Pictish times, through the 8th century visit of St Fergus (an Irish Bishop who brought Christianity to the area) and the Jacobite Rebellion of 1745, to the times of better-recorded history and pioneer photography.

Street scenes of various vintages, the school, mill and employment, especially farming, the ice-bound curling pond of 1906, the railway, the Glamis Hotel before it became The Strathmore Arms... the picture emerges of a purposeful village proud of the Castle and its royal connections without being overpowered by them.

A cheerful Lady Strathmore greets us at the top of a few steps leading to the front door of nearby Glamis House, the home of her widowhood set in a beautiful, imaginatively-maintained garden. It commands a great view of the outlyers of the Cairngorms. 'I will lift up mine eyes unto the hills,' she says, citing the opening line of Psalm 121. 'If I ever feel sad, it's a surprising help.' She gets us refreshments; informality reigns. Despite well-publicised family problems, she's determined to make of life what she can.

When her husband unexpectedly became Earl of Strathmore and inherited Glamis Castle, the Queen Mother delighted in their plan to restore it to its former glory and make its living quarters into a comfortable home. 'We moved in at Easter 1975,' she says adding when I perhaps look puzzled: 'The Queen Mother was my late husband's aunt... she was very helpful with her enthusiasm and advice.

The home had meant a great deal to her, with such happy memories. She was just fourteen when the First World War broke out and the Castle was commandeered as a convalescent home for injured troops. Her mother not being well, she seems to have become the chief organiser, and she obviously meant much to those recuperating. Over the years many, especially from Australia and New Zealand, returned to refresh their memories and show their families where they'd been cared for.

As ninth of ten children, even in early childhood she'd been very resourceful, making her own entertainment with her younger brother, David. They were so much younger than the rest of them. They got up to many pranks. They drove round in a Phaeton and kept a pig in the round turret on the lawn. When the lawn was being cut one day, she suddenly dashed out on its back hotly pursued by David. When I take you round the Castle, we'll find memories everywhere.'

In more contemplative mood, she adds: 'You know the Queen Mother would have been a great person anyway. She had such fortitude – courage it's easy to forget. What we all especially remember is that she was such a happy person.

She used to visit me here, two or three times a year. We adored our days together down memory lane, but there was never enough time.' You can tell they'd have got on famously together... both dressing with style but little concerned with the fashion of the day, with a great sense of purpose, history... and the ridiculous, and conquering despair even over the loss of dear ones.

'The Queen Mother loved it here, as I'm sure she did at Balmoral and Mey. When it was time to return to London, she'd tell me: "It's like having to go back to school." We still feel she's with us,' a sentiment repeated at the other castles we're visiting. Lady Strathmore is among the friends who contributed a chapter to the BBC's book *The Queen Mother Remembered,* written before but purposefully not published till after her death aged 101 in 2002.

Soon three other visitors, academics, arrive and we set off for the castle. Little Car looking horribly insecure between Lady Strathmore's substantial vehicle and the academics' large black chauffer-driven limousine. As we see the Queen Mother's new Memorial Gates and sweep into the drive I recall Daniel Defoe saying: 'As you approach, it strikes you with awe and admiration, by the many turrets and gilded balustrades.' With the towering turrets jutting out high up from the tops of many walls, what a fairy-tale Castle it is. Because of its sheer size and exuberant style, my first impression is that it might be more at home in the Loire Valley than Scotland, but it is Scottish to the very core.

Indeed, as Mary leads her party of five, periodically briefly delaying others on their standard tours from proceeding to the next room but always thoughtful for them, all Scottish history seems to unfold. Eerily, at the bottom of the stone spiral staircase running the height of the main rooms, is the spot where Duncan was murdered and where Shakespeare got his inspiration for *Macbeth*. This (the room in which Princess Margaret was born) is where the Queen Mother slept, and here is her delightful private sitting room, part of a trio of rooms developed for the King and the Queen after their marriage. Slightly rearranging the furniture, Lady Strathmore – 'Call me Mary' – poses for a photograph by the over-sized fireplace of the Castle's splendid drawing room with its many pictures including a portrait of the present Earl of Strathmore and Kinghorne with Lady Strathmore and their son Toby. Throughout there are pictures and artefacts brimming with interest. It is the same in the gardens: the tree planted by King Faisal of Iraq, the turret on the lawn in which the pig had been kept, the drive the Queen Mother drove wildly up and down as a child, the new Princess Margaret memorial, the recently-restored walled garden.

If they could speak, what stories the Castle's walls could tell of royal visits since 1372, when King Robert II gave it to Sir John Lyon who was marrying his daughter – and what ghosts are said to have haunted the place through the centuries. As well as a political statement and a defensive structure, from the start it has been a family home, though not always a comfortable one.

Numerous additions and changes have been made over the centuries, and the gardens have also dramatically altered with the times. At the end of the 18th century, outer defence walls with their own towers were swept away to improve the parkland in the mould of Capability Brown. That outraged Sir Walter Scott who always felt that things historical should be respected. He seems to have spent a not-so-comfortable night at the Castle: 'I must own that when I heard door after door shut, after my conductor had retired, I began to consider myself as too far from the living, and somewhat too near to the dead.'

Everywhere Lady Strathmore is greeted respectfully by staff, informally enthusiastic. For such a grand building, there's a happy, relaxed atmosphere – not that the numerous visitors lack interest or their questions go unanswered. We're very impressed, as are our academic colleagues who we follow through the lengthy vaults to a reserved table at the back of the restaurant. The food is way above what you usually find in tourist attractions.

During our visit every famous name from Bush to Putin (while attending the G8 summit at Gleneagles) seems to crop up. All the great people who visit Scotland include the Castle on their wish list, and Lady Strathmore is still personally involved in their entertainment. The academics at our table are here because Nobel Prize co-winner Edmond Fischer is tomorrow being given an honorary degree at Dundee University, one of a string of such honours – 'It's embarrassing how many'– for discovering how the cells of proteins are controlled. Sitting next to me at lunch, he adds modestly: 'Why us? In science, if you're first you have to realise it will not be long before someone catches up.' Possibly his real success has been how to age gracefully. 'Life is fun.'

It is not quite farewell to Mary, since she is coming to dinner. The hotel's proprietors are delighted to see her though, since everyone is counted a VIP, there's no occasion for special treatment. Mary is a true delight. Later we exchange letters. [Later still she tells me the Post Office has been saved. 'I know "Countess" and "Queen Mother" are useful publicity tools, but the people asked me to help and I did. It's bad luck for those losing the Post Offices that are still going to be closed. It won't make sense in the long run, as has been discovered about many of the Beeching railway closures.']

To Balmoral Castle

Next morning we set off in early sunshine for Balmoral, roughly 50 miles away. We skirt Alyth to join a very B road, the B951, through Dykends, passing the start of several narrowing glens, enjoying an almost total absence of traffic until, after descending a steep hill with views to die for, we reach the quiet A93. That climbs up through Glen Shee and the Spittal of Glenshee, and continues to climb, now stuck behind an overloaded lorry, to the entrance to the Glenshee ski area. After several almost snowless winters they've enjoyed a bumper season here. It is over now, though; nothing looks less impressive than a ski resort's empty car park, line of dangling chair lifts, and closed entrance.

Alongside a vigorous Clunie Water, we reach Braemar, always attractive though – apart from its famous Highland Games –never seeming to have much to offer beyond the standard local gift range. The Dee Valley accommodates the only through route between the southern and northern Grampians.

At Balmoral we abandon Little Car, walk across the bridge over the river in the nick of time to catch the 'bus' – a tractor-drawn affair reminiscent of Tresco's on the Island of Scilly – up the Castle's impressive drive to the entrance to its tourists facilities.

With their woods, occasional trees and shrubs, the grounds are splendid, but the gift shop and restaurant not up to the Glamis standard...

understandable when one remembers that Balmoral is an essential part of the Monarchy's support system. Visitors are only welcome when the Queen and her family are not in residence, which counts out the late summer.

Everyone making their way to the one room open to the public, the massive Ballroom, looks up at the lines of neatly closed windows of the large main building, more of a house than a traditional castle. Since Queen Victoria bought Balmoral, whose romantic setting she especially appreciated, the view from the windows must have revived many weary spirits in good and hard times.

The ballroom is a showplace with much on display including a repeating video about the Royal family, but I soon find myself talking to one of the guides. No, she's not employed when the Queen moves in: 'There are too many of us here when we're open to the public to be needed then. Only the lucky ones get to work for them.'

Eventually I mention I'm writing this book and particular chapter. 'Have you arranged to see someone about the Queen Mother?'

No. I explain that the Press office at Buckingham Palace said I couldn't meet anyone today – and nobody would talk to me even on the phone any time.

'Not about the Queen Mother? That's no secret.' She's more surprised than I am. The Press office is notoriously stuffy, and it is who you are rather than what you're interested in that seems to count. Anyway I may be on a black list – over a party proposed by the Duchy office for the launch of the D&C book on *The Royal Duchy*. Naturally I agreed it would be a good idea; no charge was mentioned. It was at a very late stage that I was told the cost would be several times the profit we might make on the title. 'His Royal Highness will be most upset by your change of mind.' I doubt he ever knew; even in small businesses subordinates are more threatening than bosses, but it's the subordinates whose co-operation you rely on.

Though our visit will not linger as warmly in the mind as will those to the other two castles, I'm glad to have been here. It satisfies natural curiosity and I have to admit that, apparently in common with three quarters of adult males, I once dreamt of having afternoon tea with the Queen. I've always loved the wooded Dee, which is as good as it gets at Balmoral. And others have let me into the 'secret' that the Queen Mother was especially appreciative of the privacy accorded the family here.

On their marriage, and until becoming King and Queen, the Duke and Duchess of York lived in Birkhall, a few miles from the castle but still on the estate. Because of the war, they made relatively little use of Balmoral before the King's death. After that, the Queen Mother slightly extended and improved Birkhall and developed the garden as she did elsewhere, always with a theme and scented flowers. She also loved the secluded woods. Given a further refresher, Birkhall is now used by Prince Charles. As we leave we reflect what an amazing proportion of Balmoral's royal history has been in the lifetimes of Queen Victoria and our present Queen.

The Cairngorms National Park

At Crathie we take a minor road as a short cut to the A939, possibly Britain's longest section of A-rated road almost continuously to toss you about as you climb, swerve, brake and swerve again at the bottom of another hill. When I'm not in a hurry, I love it. Occasional speeders are a great nuisance though, since they're anxious to 'get there' rapidly, *they* regard anyone taking in the mountain scenery, occasionally deep-cut river crossings, and the pretence of civilised development where there's little of it, as an unwarranted hazard. The trouble is that for some not using this 'short cut' would add many miles.

There's only one place of the least substance: Tomintoul, Scotland's highest village. It makes local newspaper copy by being cut off in snow and the undignified behaviour of some of its citizens. I've found no decent resting place; traders clearly struggle. Since the population is only between 500 and 600, that's not surprising. Though only a village, it pretends to be a town. The minute centre, is actually town-like, and it gives the main road two right-angle bends.

The descent, right down to Spey Bridge, is perhaps my favourite section. To me the mountain edges looking more attractive than their top ranges though, on a rare clear day, we enjoy these from the air. The Cairngorms are still the graveyard of light planes caught in extreme weather, and climbing accidents happen regularly. Britain's most extensive block of uninhabited mountains, the Cairngorms are our last real wilderness.

They were loved by the Queen Mother who, at the end of her long life, was delighted to hear they were to become Britain's largest National Park. The 1949 National Park Act only covered England and Wales, Scotland's separate piece of legislation being one of the first to go through the new Scottish Parliament. We break our journey in the Square in Grantown-on-Spey so I can talk to the Park's chief executive, Jane Hope.

As a Civil Servant, she was working in London for what was then the Environmental Group when Devolution came along. In 1999, she successfully applied for a change to the Scottish Office. She master-minded the Scottish National Parks Act and then, as temporary chief executive, successively set up each of the two National Parks (Loch Lomond and The Trossachs, and The Cairngorms). 'I was thrilled to get the permanent Cairngorm post. Cycling to work and travelling round the National Park is a lot better than being stuck in a London office.'

With a population density of 11.6 per square mile, compared to 'sparsely populated' North York Moors's 46.1, the Cairngorms National Park is in several different local government areas, some of which cannot be reached from another without driving around the central roadless mountain block. At least parts of the glens on the periphery are included, as is Grantown-on-Spey, and the A9 from Carrbridge to the Pass of Drumochter, as well as Ballater and upper Deeside with Balmoral.

'It's a huge area, and we hold Board meetings in different places around it. It's quite a big Board, of twenty five, of which five are directly elected in wards, ten-appointed council members, and ten appointed by Ministers from those who apply to serve. They have many backgrounds and skills. We meet fortnightly. When it comes to staff, we're only about fifty.

Mine is a co-ordinating role; we work with partners. About half of our £4.5million a year goes on staff and print, the rest on grants for specific projects. Planning applications go to the local councils, but we have twenty one days in which to pull them in and determine them – on average about seventy critical ones a year out of a total of 500.

Another difference from the English National Parks is that our remit includes promoting sustainable economic and social development. Many communities are very much on the edge and need help.' She then outlines the Park's characteristics:

'At the heart is Britain's highest, most massive mountain range, a piece of the Arctic transported 800 miles south. We have forty nine summits over 3,000 feet – the Munros – and a quarter of Britain's threatened species, while 39 per cent of the Park is designated as of special scientific significance. People die on the Cairngorms; it's wild, delicately-balanced with harsh elements and poor soils. Also included is a huge variety of environments, forests around the foothills including much of Britain's surviving native woodland, flourishing polecats and red squirrels, and also the open, rolling heather moors, and straths and glens. It's endlessly varied and, though we're big for Britain, it's much more compact than Canada, the only other country with such diversity. It's wonderfully challenging.'

She hands me the usual reports, plans, maps and tourist brochures one expects from a National Park, and I feel it's perhaps time to leave. 'No hurry,' she says. 'It's not often I have such an interesting conversation.'

We've compared notes on how other National Parks were run in their early days – Dartmoor especially – and I discover she belonged to my County Book Society. 'I was often too busy to reject the selected book, but many of those I didn't want at the time, I've been glad to have since.' That was the idea.

'I'm usually the shadowy person behind the scenes,' she says when I confirm I'll mention her here. She obviously has more potential to develop yet, ex-Civil Servant with humanity. When I do leave, everyone I pass smiles; it's a happy office.

Run by a private company, the Cairngorm Mountain Railway is another distinct feature. Though running year round, out of the ski season, after the twenty-minute ride you arrive at a strictly-confined summit, where – unless you're lucky to pick a rare clear day – the main attraction is Britain's highest restaurant. Book for a sunset dinner in summer, enjoyable whatever the sky. It's easy if expensive to reach, but you still feel an adventurer.

The Dava, Nairn and 'To the North'

Today's Dava, the moorland area between Grantown and Forres/Nairn, is pretty empty, and it now seems ridiculous that the abandoned railway climbing steeply alongside the road once supported a station called Dava. Closure of local schools and the railway feature strongly in *An Upland Place*, a collection of Elizabeth Macpherson's popular columns in Scottish newspapers. I've been reading the volume that covers the early 1960s, among other things featuring the closure of the original railway route to Inverness, and the dramatic changes in farming. The author and her husband were the first of the upland farmers to abandon arable crops, but soon the grant system was changed to force others into grass and stock. She said that farmers:

> Cannot believe that the crops they have grown from time immemorial are not going to be wanted anymore. In bewildered fashion they keep on drawing up balance-sheets to send to their MPs in the hope that somehow they will convince the powers-that-be of the immensity of their error. All is saddened confusion which is not alleviated by saying that we must move with the economic times.

So to our nest beside the Moray Firth, unseasonably rough with an easterly gale removing much of our sandy beach. The sand comes and goes, though it may now be too late for a westerly gale to bring it back for this summer. Bare rocks are exposed at low tide, though there are ample sandy areas of our blue-flag beach which are but a small ingredient in our view. We look out across the Moray Firth to the opposite shores with the entrance to the huge Cromarty Firth through which cruise liners, oil rigs and tankers regularly pass. It may not be one of Scotland's grandest views but, never quite the same five minutes running, is thoroughly companionable. Though socialising much less than I used to do, it is hard to be lonely with such an outlook – and the flat walk along the prom of the 'Brighton of the North' reached across our lawn and private steps. (Nairn features in *Journey*, and it is pleasant to record that the small bookshop still makes a contribution to a town of cultural diversity.)

Even more than Londoners visiting Newton Abbot thought they must be near the end of the line, our visitors believe that civilisation ends a few miles north of Nairn. In both cases, there are well over a hundred miles to the surprisingly similar mainland ends. 'To the North,' conveys something of the same magic as 'Go West'.

There's hard driving before we reach Caithness, the Cornwall of the North. From Alness we leave the congested A9 to climb over high ground till, descending, there's a glorious view of the deep, sinuous Dornoch Firth which we run alongside before crossing over the long flat bridge. Beyond Golspie, our first short stop is at what is undoubtedly our finest-sited castle, Dunrobin, Scotland's largest house, built for the Dukes of Sutherland. The Dukes became incredibly wealthy when many of their unwanted 'subjects' were ejected in the Clearances. It is still being hotly debated whether or not the Dukes were the worst of the lairds. Certainly their own riches knew no bounds; they invariably sought out the best furniture, everything; their train (the last private one allowed to run on our railways) was kept in a bay platform of the Castle's own station.

Beyond Helmsdale, there are places where the A9 is still quite hairy and lorries get stuck even at normal times. Snow gates prevent access to the steep hill above the cliffs when it becomes impassable. Improvements continue, but there's no danger of the overpowering grandeur of this part of the coast being spoilt.

It being years since I've called at Lybster, we pop down the broad single street, no longer a museum piece with many shops with old-fashioned frontages. Most of them have closed. The harbour between two great headlands, reached at the end down a steep hill, still has lobster fishing, but the great days of herring are passing out of human memory. When the stone harbour replaced a wooden pier in 1830, Lybster was home to Scotland's third largest herring fleet. There's still good refreshment to be had in Lybster, including for us a light lunch. Barbara is with us and peckish.

Through Ulbster and Thrumster, and we're temporarily delayed by Wick's traffic before rounding Sinclair Bay and, passing mini Nybster and, then slightly inland, to John O'Groats which, like Land's End, trades on its name. People are queuing to be photographed under the signpost: Land's End 874 miles. Prominent among them are parties who've cycled the length of the country to raise money for charity.

'It's only my second time,' says Matt Marsden of York; 'for the rest of our group it's the third – so far.'

'It's harder cycling into the weather going south west, but you get a bigger welcome at Land's End,' adds Steve Kelsey.

Keith Hagger and John Baker talk about the money raised for a hospice and children's charity. 'It's still a great challenge and you feel it's worthwhile, but heck you need a proper cooked breakfast to get going in the morning.'

They swap notes with five others who've just arrived from Land's End. It makes us feel softies, especially as we walk off to the hotel's tearoom.

There's still magic at the 'ends', though views of the islands beyond, (in the case of the Orkneys with a car ferry from John O'Groats's harbour) there's a reminder that there's still more of Britain left. However, as with Cape Cornwall, nearby Dunnet Head (to which we pay a brief visit) offers more memorable uncommercialised cliffs. It is also further north. Being built on a 300ft headland hasn't always prevented Dunnet Lighthouse from being damaged by the ferocious Pentland Firth. After the recent storm, today only wavelets reach the huge nearby sandy beach; and not a living soul is in sight.

Barbara, who only arrived in Scotland yesterday, is getting tired; it's time to return, by a quiet B road across the flat, green countryside to Wick to check into our comfortable hotel beside the estuary.

Castle of Mey

Wick and Thurso are different from other towns. The countryside, with its green plateau reminiscent of west Cornwall, is unique in Scotland. Caithness *feels* isolated yet, on a small scale, life abounds. A very non-Cornish feature is the number of large lochs, and often there's a boat with just one fisherman, usually standing up. Solitude is prized here. Isolation, climate and history have converged to produce a hardy, reticent yet friendly people, always appreciative of visitors enjoying their corner of the world.

It was the perfect mix for the widowed Queen. In common with many visiting royals, she soon found her privacy was respected. She was greeted enthusiastically, but Caithness folk don't gawk. When she saw what became her beloved Castle of Mey, small but well turreted and that, having been neglected for years, it was for sale, she quickly fell in love with it. Restoring, furnishing and staffing her very own home, not an official residence, and leaving it for prosperity was her great project.

Overlooking the Pentland Firth, with the Orkneys, across the water, appearing nearer or further according to the weather, the Castle was away from prying eyes but close to many people of the kind she loved to entertain during her residence a few weeks each summer. She already had friends there and stayed with them, so was familiar with the countryside on the doorstep. Wick airport, and Scrabster harbour where family from the royal yacht *Britannia* could land, were close by.

There were challenges inside and out, the fierce wind being the hardest to control. Yet with the protection of the solid house behind her, she loved sitting on a bench in the shell garden with its colourful shrubs and plants. Behind the Great Mey Wall, the kitchen garden provided abundant harvests for her summer kitchen when staying and visiting guests created considerable demand. Joining her at dinner was obviously a prized privilege; many who loved to be counted friends avoiding going away during her 'season'.

Though she only bought the property after the king's death, she owned it for nearly half her life. Even more astonishingly, until she was into her second century, and despite her hip operations, she managed the steep spiral stairs that challenge many only half her age. Earlier in the year of her final visit, her daughter was flatly contradicted when said she assumed she wouldn't be going north. The Queen Mother was indeed a remarkable woman. My own mother, also born in 1900, died in 1981; The Queen Mother twenty one years later.

The things which specially impress are that the staff never saw her yawn or become tired even after guests at the 9pm dinner finally left; that she remembered people and even objects from a quite different context many years before; that she was always concerned for those who worked for her, and their families even if it would be another eleven months before they met next; and that she never failed to consult her bible and mark the passages to be read at Sunday morning worship.

A prize-winning farmer in her own right, she naturally played a major part in Caithness agricultural and sporting events, again somewhat different from those further away. To remain informed, when she was in the south she had the local weekly mailed to her. Though she could only spend a fraction of her year there, Caithness was a home as real as any. She would be delighted to know that Prince Charles still stays in the Castle each year and takes an active interest in the local economy. Now run by a trust, the Castle is closed for his stay, but open for the rest of the season.

So, suitably impressed by first sight of the solid and turreted though quite narrow L-shaped castle, standing guard across the Pentland Firth, we park, walk round and gaze. Compared with Dunrobin, it is minute, but that is not a fair measure, for there is just as much character – and that goes back a long way.

Built in the second half of the 16th century, Barrogill Castle, as it was then known, was for many generations the seat of the Sinclairs of Mey. Successive lairds led a luxurious, occasionally riotous, lifestyle, consuming huge quantities of wines, though it seems looking down on whisky simply because it was local. Rare fruits, foods and fine teas were accompanied by the very best in clothing.

By the 18th century, there were about seventy families of gentry in Caithness, owing little allegiance to Scottish culture and supporting the Anglican tradition though it was compulsory to pay dues to the Presbyterian Church. They were equally spendthrift with their legal bills, constantly quarrelling with each other, yet inter-marrying and sharing the same trades and economic background... and usually happy to forget disputes once the latest legal verdict had been given. It was little England beyond Scotland; it took eight days to reach the Scottish capital. The rich earlier history of Barrogill Castle, before she renamed it Castle of Mey, must have added to the Queen Mother's desire to rescue it. (Those 18th century days are vividly brought to life in *The Mey Letters,* John E Donaldson's collection of correspondence between and within families. Many letters are about money or lack of it to cover debts incurred in families living beyond their means.)

When I telephoned to explain the reason for my visit, I was treated courteously, and it was arranged I'd meet Major James Perkins, referred to by staff as Jimmy. But when we report to reception, they remembered me phoning, but – oh dear – don't seem to have told the Major. He's on guide duty in the drawing room. We're invited to look round, but not wander too far, while they arrange a relief.

Soon the Major comes smiling, and we are on our way. In through an impressive though not vast front hall we face the bottom of a delightful staircase, and into the homely and comfortable drawing room. The Major greets his temporary relief, who naturally smiles and looks us over. Redesigned by the seventh Laird of Mey, Sir James Sinclair, in 1736, the room skilfully combines historic and contemporary charm. This is where the Queen Mother usually read and listened to music, where afternoon tea was served, no doubt in style, and guests enjoyed their pre-dinner drinks. Says the Major: 'When it's that time of year, I still can't get used to the idea she's not here, that the Corgis won't bark. When I am about to open the door, I still wait; I can't help myself. Her presence is still very strong.'

Everything, the collection of chairs, sofas and occasional tables, plain walls with only a few pictures, though a grand large, ornate mirror over the fireplace, and a Flemish wool tapestry, is just as the Queen Mother left it. The guides point out the personal treasures arranged here and there – mainly little gifts especially from her grandchildren when they were young. Wide double doors that can be folded back to lead to the Equerry's Room. Here her bible, hymn book and psalter, beside a small pile of Castle of Mey stationery, have too recently ceased to be used to feel 'historic' in the way that the books or music of writers and musicians who died longer ago than their entire life span make it hard not to feel they should be in a glass case even if they're lying faded on a desk.

As in all great houses of the famous, the bedroom floor holds special fascination. Sheila is wide-eyed in the Queen Mother's Clothes Room; we feel for her because Princess Margaret never slept in the bedroom prepared and named for her, though when visiting off the royal yacht she did once rest in it.

So, very cautiously, down the spiral staircase to the grandest room, the dining room in an 1819 extension, compact but full of royal interest, the table set for ten. Late dinners seem to have been a mixture of ritual and informality. Guests were so arranged that, with a change when the plates of the main course were lifted, everyone conversed with the person on either side of them, but black ties were never worn. For the Queen Mother and staying guests, lunches were always picnics, sometimes in a bothy or other shelter overlooking sea or loch. When Prince Charles and Princess Anne were children and came to lunch off the royal yacht, the Queen Mother persuaded them to join in singing 'Across the sea to Skye' to the seals. Such comments from the Major help build an intimate picture.

He tells me more over coffee in the light and beautifully-equipped kitchen. 'The castle is a magical, magical place. None of the family were interested in taking it on, so the Queen Mother put it in the care of a trust. Nothing's changed, but we enjoy Prince Charles's visits and keeping up traditions such as cooking a Christmas cake for the school children.'

He adds: 'I knew the Queen Mother for forty four years. My grandparents were great friends with the Duke and Duchess of York before they became King and Queen. The Queen Mother had a wonderful sense of humour, duty and fairness. You can't ask for more. She'd met all the great heads of state except Hitler and Stalin and was concerned with affairs at the highest level, yet her attention to detail was wonderful.

In her nineties, I told her that her sticks would make less noise if rubber ferrules were added to their bottom, but she thought that might draw attention to her age. After she'd fallen and broken her hip at the Guildhall in Westminster, she asked her Lady-in-Waiting to write to me to say that the sticks now had rubber ferrules. I take my hat off to that.

Now you could call me Jack of all Trades. I seem to get involved in all kinds of things here.' His personal knowledge and enthusiasm are treasured; there'll never be another like him. Nor like Mrs Nancy McCarthy who brings our cuppas. Her late husband had managed the Queen Mother's two farms, as her two sons jointly do today. It was the Queen Mother's wish to keep it in the family.

There's a steady trickle of visitors, totalling just over 30,000 a year, though numbers are slightly down this year; high fuel prices have discouraged people taking holidays so far north. 'But I've no fears for the future,' is Major Perkins's final comment.

When we visit the garden, the wind bloweth. The wall and internal hedges are clearly needed, but most flowering bushes, espalier fruit trees and much else thrives. However, with reduced demand for produce, most of the vegetable garden has been replanted and there's excessive die-back on many of the new roses. There must have been many a disappointment in getting the garden really established, though perhaps the Queen Mother's experienced patient touch is missing now.

Leaving the Castle means we have only a few hours left in Caithness, which I always find addictive. Even buying a joint for tomorrow is an enjoyable social event, so friendly and delighted are the locals to meet visitors. Those along the Pentland Firth would especially welcome incomers to support their fragile economy but, despite bargain housing, this is one of the few parts of Remote Britain that doesn't attract southerners opting out of the rat race.

Perhaps it is just too remote without the kudos of living on an island? Not many seem to consider it, and those who do look round tend to be put off by the wind. Much of the year it is pretty constant, all pervasive, even inland. A pity a few more incomers are not attracted, for many villages have distinct character... even planned Halkirk, which never really took off but was familiar to the Queen Mother because of its great agricultural shows.

Caithness folk from the gentry down, have proved themselves hardy in many ways, especially in agriculture and fishing. So far as fishing is concerned, it is hard to know what would have been the toughest task: catching herring on small open boats and bringing them into the dangerous landing place at Ulbster, or carrying heavy basketfuls of them up the 365 zig-zag steps cut into the cliff's edge and on to the market at Wick, eight miles away.

Let the final word be the Queen Mother's. On receiving the Freedom of the Royal Burgh of Wick in 1956, she wrote:

> It is a delight to me that I now have a home in Caithness, a county of such great beauty, combining as it does the peace and tranquillity of an open and uncrowded countryside with the rugged glory of a magnificent coastline – the remote detachment of country villages with the busy and independent life of your market towns.

· XXXIV ·

AROUND THE LAKE DISTRICT

Planning the Journey and into Hadrian's Wall Country

Our journeys involve planning, often elaborate. What might be most interesting to see for the first time or to revisit? What will be the main themes to make good copy? What is the logical order of places on the route? What will be the best overnight stops? What indeed might a chapter or series of chapters be called?

My first choice of title was Lake District Peripheral, which expresses what I gradually hit upon, once more enjoying something of the Lake District without repeating its best-known core covered in *Journey*. Around the Lake District sounds nicer and still allows a slightly eccentric choice of places at which to spend nights, several of the first ones not in our preferred order because some, notably Tan Hill, were fully booked months ahead for the August Bank Holiday weekend. Many of the areas surrounding or around the Lakes are in dramatic situations where isolation, geology and the incidence of mineral wealth, have dictated fortune and often rapid changes.

Weather wise, the August Bank Holiday period has always been risky for touring. True to form, our journey south was delayed by floods, this time in the Midlands, cutting the West Coast mainline in two. We had to wait an hour at Edinburgh for Virgin to send a special train, empty, to replace the scheduled one that couldn't get through. With seat reservations accurately transferred, a fast journey and free food packs, we're soon happily in Carlisle and, not much later, in a hire car and quickly on minor roads in hilly country to Castle Carrock on the elevated edge of the north Pennines.

The small village has obviously enjoyed more prosperous times, our base for tonight now being the only hostelry: an upmarket Restaurant with Rooms, The Weary at Castle Carrock, near Alston and still in Cumbria. Weary we are not, but exhilarated by this discovery of a corner of England new to us. With everything now bathed in between-rainshower sunshine, we check in (first welcomed by the cat, Smudge), and then drive on – north.

At the lively little market town of Brampton, we squeeze the car onto the triangular cobbled market place graced by the octagonal Moot Hall with external stairs and square turret. Originally open air, the poultry, butter and eggs market became enclosed at the end of the 19th century. It is now the tourist office. There's a lot of history here. For example there is a ring to which bulls used to be tied up remaining from the days of bull baiting. An earlier building was used by Cromwell to accommodate prisoners.

Opposite there's a marvellous greengrocer of the type seldom found north of the border, and nearby the pub with the greatest floral display imaginable. The café we choose for tea also shows that they know how to look after themselves in this rugged part of England, only a few miles from Hadrian's Wall. This western part was first built with turf because of a shortage of local stone. There's a quarry nearby, still with Roman inscriptions, that in later years supplemented the stone brought from further afield to make things stronger. However, despite figuring prominently in local publicity, this far west, as to the east in Newcastle, the wall was steadily stolen, its stones used as a free source of building material.

Walking up a steep path to one of the 'milecastles' on the wall striding across the escarpment overlooking bare, undulating countryside is one of the treats of Remote Britain, but you have to go east from Brampton and use an access points off the B6318. Some time ago, we greatly enjoyed doing that on a bright but blustery day with clear long-distance views. A surprising number of people of all kinds, from an excited school party to elderly American tourists 'doing' British history in ten days, panted their way up and gazed unbelievingly at the way the wall presses on taking scant notice of the contours. A few were actually walking the wall, and so well aware of its ups and downs. What did the soldiers think of the section allocated to their legion to build? Each legion adapted a slightly different style.

Clever people though the Romans were, it seems ridiculous that the milecastles were spaced exactly evenly, 1,620 yards apart (a Roman mile), with two smaller turrets between each, irrespective of the steep terrain. The much smaller number of full-sized forts were more sensibly sited. The soldiers in the one whose remains we examined wouldn't have led a comfortable life, and it would have been a boring one so far from home at this extremity of the empire. How they must have longed for their women – or, for that matter, any women. The school group is imaginatively asked to think what life must have been like up here on the edge. 'What were their Roman baths like, Miss?' asked a young lad. Not naturally heated by spring water, for sure.

It is not often remembered that no fewer than four defensive walls were built across the narrow neck of Britain. Hadrian's Wall was the third, and best known because so much more remains to be seen. Man began taking a serious interest in his forebears surprisingly late in history. Hadrian's Wall is a World Heritage Site and northern England's most popular tourist attraction, not because it was always respected but that there was little incentive to remove materials from its remote central section. It was well into the 19th century before there was consensus that the wall deserved protection. Some stone was removed by builders even into the 20th century.

Though we don't see it today, we feel the wall's proximity and recall our exploration as we buy sandwiches for tomorrow's lunch from one of Brampton's bakers, admire some of the old red sandstone buildings, remember that at the café we read that once there were forty five pubs for a population of 3,000, and briefly look at the fine stained glass windows of the surprisingly large St Martin's Parish Church, significant as the only one designed by the Pre-Raphaelite architect, Philip Webb.

We head back toward our hotel, first over a level-crossing with the Carlisle to Newcastle railway, which reminds me that a pre-railway age railway, a wooden tramway, began transporting coal here back in 1775. And that Brampton's first proper railway stationmaster was Thomas Edmonton, inventor of the machine that printed most train tickets until well after nationalisation. The traditional thick, small card Edmonton tickets are still used by heritage railways. They were entrepreneurial and quick off the mark hereabouts.

North Pennines Area of Outstanding Natural Beauty

Seeing a left hand turn signposted at Talkin Tarn, I make an impromptu decision to take it. I recall hearing of Talkin Tarn (Talkin being the name of the nearest village) but know nothing about it. In fact it highlights the area's extraordinary glacial legacy. In a hollow gouged out by ice 10,000 years ago in the last Ice Age, what is technically known as a kettle hole, lies a 65-acre lake.

There's a little car park, and a notice telling us about glaciation and the North Pennines Area of Outstanding Natural Beauty: 'This is one of England's most special places in a stunning landscape of open heather moors and peatlands, attractive dales and hay meadows, tumbling upland rivers, wonderful woods, welcoming communities, intriguing imprints of a mining and industrial past, distinctive birds, animals and plants and much, much more.' I comment that it is good copy; Sheila is impatient to get to the lake, down a rough path lined with trees.

The car park, the natural 1-mile path around the lake, an unobtrusive café and boating station, are done so much better than we've found at many lakes. There's more: a blazing fire in the tea room looking out over the lake, bikes for hire with details of routes, windsurfing, rowing and canoeing, advice on orienteering, fishing and even camping.

The sheer size of the lake, its irregular shape, and its natural, largely wooded setting, obviously help but, apart from making the unpaved path accessible for wheelchairs, for once man has not insisted on improving on nature. Even the ducks look more naturally at home than in parks. They're not adverse to being unsuitably fed, however, and are skilled at moving between human feeders scattered along the banks. 'We've got the most ducks,' shouts a little girl holding her mother with one hand and lurching toward the water throwing bread with the other. 'What a happy scene,' says Sheila, who dashes back to the car to find allegedly stale food to become a food thrower herself. By the way, the lake is fed by underground streams.

Though it covers parts of several counties, the Area of Outstanding Natural Beauty (also a UNESCO European and Global Geopark, while Talkin Tarn is a Country Park) has many natural ambitions. One I especially like is encouraging visitors to collect seed from surviving natural upland hay meadows (today probably Britain's finest collection) and take part in an organised 'seed sowing' of fields that have lost their native species. At first I'm surprised to find such progress, but recall that this is the North with a capital N, often overlooked if not derided by southerners – though once again we hear that those who move up love it and are quickly rooted for life. I just hope too many don't come in to swamp things. Happily, little sign of that yet.

Crossing the fast-flowing Gelt, tumbling down through famous woods and gorges, back at The Weary at Castle Carrock, we are again greeted by Smudge. Like many hotel cats, she assumes (correctly, I'd say) that the best form of demonstrating the warmth of the establishment's hospitality is to spreadeagle and be available for tummy tickling. Just why else would anyone come? While I'm on all fours noticing her unusual black-and-white markings, with uneven black spots on all four white paws, Ian Boyd, the owner, arrives and tells me she's 16-years old.

He then explains that The Weary was meant to be a five-year project, but he's already been there seven years. 'We've a lovely staff brought up in the country,' he says, adding that he turned restaurateur (with as few up-market letting rooms) when he escaped industry so that he could bring up their children more healthily.

The whole place buzzes with gentle enthusiasm. Our waitress, an Australian lass in her gap year, says she loves working with the others.

The large, and tonight nearly empty, restaurant overlooks an outside area where meals are served when it is warmer than today. They obviously host many conferences and parties: a side room can be shut off. And even tonight they are busy with bar meals.

It has been a long but happy day. Once again Sheila says she'd like to return. I comment that we should make the most of our luxury, for it will be more basic for our next two one-night stops.

To Garrigill Post Office

Next morning's drive is one to die for. After overnight rain, the Pennines sparkle in speckled sunlight, burns are bubbling over their banks, and almost everything from sheep to industrial remains seems to fit perfectly into the landscape. Only a few of the newer buildings of a few more prosperous farms need editing out in our joyful vision. Moreover we have the contour-crossing B4163 almost totally to ourselves.

Soon we abandon the B road to take lanes, through Renwick climbing zig-zag up to the busy A686, with difficulty actually joining it because there's so little visibility and we have to start off on a steep slope with fast cars dashing round its own hairpin close by. Eventually we make it in front of a slow moving lorry, climbing steeply over more than another 100 metres by the final hairpin at Hartside Cross, where we're sufficiently ahead to pause to absorb one of northern England's finest views.

There's virtually uninhabited moorland north and south, though south just beyond Gamblesby Fell are what the OS calls Gamblesby Allotments. What does that mean, I wonder. To the west is a grand panorama of the Pennines down to the Eden Valley with a glimpse of the Settle & Carlisle Railway climbing dangerously close to inhospitable mountains where many died in its construction. The Lake District, Solway Firth and Scottish hills are all visible in the background.

Keeping my eye half on the mirror I see that, amazingly, the first thing behind us is not motorised but a mountain bike pedalled by a lad whose lungs must be close to bursting. Then the lorry shows up, and we move on. Its driver, and probably most others, won't be as thrilled as we are, the stiff gradients and hairpins no doubt regarded as a hindrance to civilised progress. And, indeed, when we pull off the road a short distance on, there's a veritable train of lorries which have been crawling so close together that an accumulation of frustrated car drivers have probably been glancing at their watches.

I tease myself remembering that many islands are the tips of former great mountains, sunken or eroded in geological time. Suppose the seas round Britain rose 1,000ft, what would the remaining islands be like? There'd be many more in the north than south, but with climate change, even here isolated groups might be idyllic wine-growing remnants of civilisation or lush tropical resorts... only there'd be no lowlanders to patronise them.

We descend rapidly to familiar Alston, twenty miles from the next town. There's time for a quick glance at the North Tyneside Railway, the highest narrow-gauge heritage line, which has taken over a short end section of the route of the former branch from Haltwhistle which once carried heavy coal traffic but ran only a few near-empty diesel units when I took my only round trip along its curves, steep gradients and expensive engineering works commanding great views. Then through the main street over the cobbles past the Market Cross. This is England's highest market settlement, though most of the shops, and many of the houses stoutly constructed against Pennine storms, were built for occupants very different from today's: the families of lead miners on the nearby moor.

Invigorated by just being here, we stop for lunch and save our sandwiches (supplemented by a couple of delicious-looking pastries) for tonight, when getting dinner might be difficult. Once by train, many times by car, I've always liked Alston, and indeed all such isolated little places – Middleton-in-Teesdale is another example – where the bakers and cafés know that the keener air at high altitude makes it harder for customers to resist attractive delicacies. Fed and watered, we take the Middleton-in-Teesdale road, again the B6277, leaving it after a few miles for the lonely village of Garrigill, under Cross Fell in the deep valley of the South Tyne.

For a new experience we are staying at the Post Office, the guest house over the business premises. The setting overlooking the village green couldn't be more inviting but, instantly, I sense two disappointments. The first is that, though picturesque, Garrigill isn't the natural working village it once was or even the permanent home of incomers, but a place of lots of holiday homes. Many are empty since their owners are at their main homes or gone abroad for the holiday weekend, while a few have fancy cars parked outside.

The other problem is that, as at nearly all rural post offices, there's an aura of death. [This was written before the government suddenly saw the light and, making a U-turn, withdrew the Post Office's card scheme from competitive tender that would almost certainly have led to thousands more closures.] Says our landlady, Anne Bramwell, who runs the business with her husband Clifford:

'The Post Office is undoubtedly on the way out. The card scheme, still used by many pensioners and others who need cash to spend, is going out to tender and is bound to be lost as have TV licences. We even have to buy our own licence online. With so much essential business stripped away, this Post Office can't survive. It won't affect us too much. We're both sixty five, but if it happens to younger people it's serious. Anyway, without the Post Office's traffic, many village shops aren't strong enough to survive. It's not what the Post Office pays us but the people it attracts that matter. If you have to go elsewhere to post a parcel, naturally you do your shopping there.'

She takes us through a side door up to the bedrooms. 'We're on the Pennine Way and the more recent cycleway brings many visitors, mainly southerners. With the guest house and shop we're kept busy,' she says. Their day starts early, the small hours receiving and sorting newspapers for a more distant retailer and many home 'deliveries', though that usually means just shooting a paper out through the car window. Then there are elaborate cooked breakfasts to cook – 'Don't ask for poached eggs, they're our disaster area' – and manning the shop and Post Office. She adds:

'But we look after ourselves; we never miss going to Newcastle on a Tuesday. Our daughter stands in for us. Despite being isolated, we've never been cut off even for one half day. But the school bus that used to be full now collects only six for primary school... and there are only six pensioners left in the village. Apart from coming to us for their newspapers, we don't see much of the owners of the holiday homes. They usually bring most things with them for their occasional stays. Sad really. But then things are always changing. When we came it was still big blocks of butter, rolls of bacon and paraffin at nine old pence a gallon, and the pen and pencil we used for Post Office work never failed as do computers. And there were two pubs.'

Being told that the remaining one isn't too reliable for evening meals, we eat our sandwiches in the guests' lounge on the second floor full of games and reading for wet days, and then walk through the pretty village. There are latest-model cars everywhere yet through most of its history the village has been far livelier – especially when the Quaker-owned London Lead Company was active and built many of the cottages for the miners working on Alston Moors towering overhead. Things would have been tough in those days but far more companionable. We cross the South Tyne by a bridge not far from its source, and generally nosey about but don't meet a single person on foot.

Liberating Country to Brough and on through Buttertubs Pass

Next morning, we continue in bright sunshine on the now somewhat busier B6277 over the sparkling moors. This also is liberating country with long distances between favourite haunts such as the fierce High Force Waterfall, an unbroken 21 metres and England's highest. Today, however, what catches our attention is a fortieth birthday celebration of the Durham Mountain Rescue Service, with high-tech gear on display together with information boards... and a marquee offering light refreshments including welcome tea and homemade cake. Those dressed in uniform are keen to converse. Richard Graham, from Barnard Castle, says: 'We are one of thirty or forty affiliated groups. We prefer our voluntary status and being free from government politics. Because I've always liked hillwalking and climbing, I became involved five years ago. As you can see, there's a great spirit.'

At Middleton-in-Teesdale (see *Journey*), we turn right onto the B6276 passing two large reservoirs before climbing steeply onto Stainmore, which I last saw between the smoke and smuts of a struggling steam train. For my taste, a touch too wild to be attractive, certainly not a place to get stuck... as many used to in former times in what are now the straggling twin villages of Church Brough, on the Roman road (now the A66), with its ruined Norman castle on the site of a Roman camp, and the more northerly Market Brough on a medieval road. Brough once had seventeen inns and sixty four coaches a day, though the railway passed it by. *Bradshaw* indexed it as Brough-under-Stainmore, referring to Barras and Warcop, stations on either side of Kirkby Stephen on the Darlington – Barnard Castle – Penrith line.

'It's been a downhill story,' says Philip Jarvis, whose Post Office is under dire threat. 'For thousands of years, starting well before Roman days, when lead mining began, this has been a communication centre. Mail coaches needed extra horses and trains two or three engines to get them over Stainmore. The market was weekly, cattle fairs quarterly. Now there are only a few struggling businesses. I'll still live here, in this building, but it won't be a Post Office. It's a sad place really.'

To which I might add that the few remaining trading establishments dotted along a street of a width more suited to a city centre seem to have given up heart. There's nowhere we especially want to eat, though eventually find a good if over-pressed restaurant serving those journeying along the A66. Places that have lost their former glory, as they unsuccessfully try to stave off defeat, undoubtedly have a macabre fascination (many were former coaching centres bypassed by railways), but we're glad not to be staying in Brough.

We had to make many enquiries to find anywhere to stay for the Bank Holiday weekend. Settling on Aysgarth means that we still have the finest part of today's journey ahead of us, into the Yorkshire Dales, not one of which ever comes as a disappointment (see *Journey*). First Birkdale on the edge of the National Park, and into an even more vertical landscape of high fields with stout stone walls often stretching up to the horizon (I recall that in publishing days it was better to have upright rather than landscape photographs) to Thwaite, tantalisingly just touching Swaledale before climbing, climbing up to Buttertubs Pass. This is possibly Yorkshire's finest.

I've been enjoying *Heart and Soul of the Yorkshire Dales*, with picture and words by David Tarn. Not only is he an imaginative but patient photographer prepared to wait years for the perfect shot, but his extended captions are of a quality few attain. My enjoyment of passing through the pass, sometimes on a ledge along a precipice, the very edge of the world, is enhanced by already having read this:

> The Buttertubs Pass road that squeezes between Lovely Seat and Great Shunner Fell takes you from Thwaite in Swaledale to Hawes in Wensleydale. It is without question one of the most spectacular roads in the country, and a wonderful drive. As you head south from Thwaite there is a sheer drop on the left of the road down into a deep valley that just seems to spill out into Swaledale.
>
> Can you imagine the work that went into building this and all the drystone walls in the Dales? This was not done as a work of art; this has a very real and practical use. None the less it is also a thing of beauty that speaks to us over the ages of hard work, endurance and craft. This landscape is wild and natural even if the hand of man has touched the whole area. Stones left strewn around the valleys by retreating glaciers have been gathered to build walls. Though 'manmade' these walls are as natural as a beaver's dam. Man has embellished what nature has done, it was nature not man who dug out the valleys in the first place.
>
> At the southern end of the road looking into Wensleydale and beyond the whole of the Dales seem to be laid out with Ingleborough overseeing the scene. In this view it is perhaps easier to appreciate just how trivial man's additions and alterations to nature's design are.

The Joys of Aysgarth

That brings us to Hawes, another old favourite, from which it is only a short hop along an A road to Aysgarth, where we check in for two nights at the George & Dragon Inn. Booked late when we were pleased to find anywhere, our room isn't great, but the food is obviously so esteemed as to attract diners from far and wide. I'm not surprised to learn from Collette Wormwell, who keeps the inn with her husband John, that they are hoping the AA will reclassify then as a Restaurant with Rooms, an increasingly popular designation. 'We've only two stars, and because of restricted lounges will never get three, but we already have a rosette for food. We definitely do not want to be one of the new category, Country Inns, where instead of stars there are things that confusingly look like rosettes but aren't.'

Next day, Sunday, not needing another feast, for lunch we go to a small tea room we'd noticed on the main road: one of the nicest tea rooms we've yet found, efficient and friendly, tables cleared as soon as people leave to make way for a steady stream of walkers and cyclists. Earlier, at a Communion service at the village church, a retired priest asked who we felt Jesus was... what we thought individually, not necessarily what we'd been told, and to bring those thoughts to the altar. Great. How I hate being told exactly what I've a duty to believe... deviations from the official line including that the world is flat leading to early radical thinkers as well as scientists and geologists going to the stake. It's frightening that Darwin is still seen by many Christians especially in America as the Devil. If only more appreciated the difference between belief and faith.

This and forty winks rules out exploring around Aysgarth afresh, for example revisiting Aysgarth Falls National Park Centre in its converted railway cottages. With its daily weather forecasts, accommodation booking and keen staff, the Yorkshire Dales National Park has often been a trendsetter. And how often have I felt I'd like to spend a month in just one of the choice Dales. It's not just that the Dales themselves are naturally delightful, but that the stone-built villages, often around greens of various shapes and sizes, some with clumps or even avenues of trees, farms, drystone walls, industrial remains, even lead museums, ordinary and steam railways – all seem to fit harmoniously. Then I've often commented on how the woollen industry seemed to enhance Yorkshire while brick-built cotton mills made Lancashire, anyway less well endowed with natural beauty, uglier. Certainly things like Dale village and church newsletters are more vibrant than one generally finds elsewhere. Perhaps I'm in danger of becoming a convert of Geoffrey Smith, of TV garden fame, who in *Journey* I described as a Yorkshire Nationalist.

As it is, we've time for just one more thing before dinner: a walk to Aysgarth's famous Edwardian Rock Garden. We're the only ones there, marvelling at the complex artificially-created vegetation-clad cascading stone walls, some damp with splashes from a waterfall, the tunnels (or lintels) under 'cliffs' through which I double up and still knock my head, and the enormous range of creepers, such as asatina procunbens which the books say isn't very hardy but grows very freely here. There's a profusion of its creamy yellow flowers with antirrhinum-like shaped lobes. There's also a profusion of ferns and mini-trees.

Angela Jouneika who runs the garden (free admission but donations welcome) comes from her home, Heather Cottage, across the road, to show us more detail. She explains that Heather Cottage was once a large nursery. 'Rock gardens were fashionable and the owner created this. It took him eight years. One at a time, boulders were brought down from the moor. But after several later owners, in 1988 the garden's destruction was only saved by English Heritage giving it emergency Grade II listing.

We bought Heather Cottage ten years after that by which time self-seeded ash and sycamores threatened the whole thing. We realised we'd accidentally acquired a national treasure, but were powerless to do anything about it... except seek funding. That took three to four years, when the Heritage Lottery Fund came up trumps, which paved the way to raise the rest we needed. Restoration – though much of it was like starting from scratch – was completed for the official opening in July 2003. We've promised to maintain it for at least ten years, but as every gardener knows, you have to keep at it.' Pulling the odd weed as she speaks, she adds: 'If you're a gardener, you can't help yourself.'

She then gives us strict instructions exactly where to cross the dangerous bend with her to Heather Cottage, a marvellous unrestored Arts & Crafts house, now a four-star guest house. Had we known about it earlier, it would have been a great place for us to stay, using the George & Dragon for dinner. Even tiny Aysgarth holds many joys.

Leyburn and Tan Hill, England's Highest Pub

Continuing east next morning, we're quickly out of the National Park and on the edge of the Vale of York. But all is by no means lost. At our first village stop, Wensley, there's another of those fine village greens, which before the age of digital photography, encouraged lavish use of film, and a grand, old-fashioned church demanding attention.

Then, high up on the last outcrop, Leyburn, a marvellous small market town with a trio of open squares that fully come to life on market days, Fridays, but are busy enough with scarce parking even this Monday August Bank Holiday. If the banks are on holiday [this was just before the great bank crash and credit crunch], few shops are... and what wonderful shops they are. We especially enjoy an old-fashioned ironmonger, an up-market grocer and private department store. The architecture, the whole setting is delightful and, again, they certainly know how to look after themselves in Yorkshire. On an initial reconnoitre we were attracted to a couple of cafés but, now there are queues outside both of them, settle for the restaurant in the department store. It is a good choice. Like that at Austins, the pride of Newton Abbot where I long lived, people of all kinds are equally at home. There are few things so classless as department store restaurants. We share a window table looking down on an animated scene with a family whose young daughter is excitedly discovering new joys of eating out.

'I don't want to see Brough ever again, but we must come back here,' says an equally hungry and enthusiastic Sheila.

There's certainly no shortage of things to do around here. For decades I've wanted to revisit Jervaulx Abbey (where the Cistercian monks had a tendency to upstage the monks of neighbouring abbeys) and I'd like to take a ride on the heritage railway to Darlington, the first major one to go bust but which has reopened. Among an incredibly wide range of tourist attractions on offer this weekend is a wartime event on the railway. They're even serving the wartime food we put up with rather than enjoyed but which turned out to be so much healthier than what we eat today.

Now for a very different location: a night in Britain's highest pub. Sheila insisted it must be included in our travels. She's vivid memories of walking part of the Pennine Way years ago and thawing out while enjoying its hospitality. Keeping surprisingly parallel with the route down which we came via Brough. We start serious climbing through moorland villages agog with Bank Holiday activity, and come to the market centre of Reeth, another place pleasingly clustered around a central green. Then we manage to get lost: map, signposts and personal directions seem at odds.

'You're going quite wrong,' says Sheila. 'Stop.' With convoys of cars struggling to pass in the narrow lane, easier said than done. 'There's a gateway you could back into.' I do, with some difficulty. The moment I've switched off the engine to study our whereabouts, a smart car pulls up behind me. This is obviously a private drive. I dash to the driver to apologise and say I'll be off in a moment but could he give me directions and tell me whether he's turning left or right himself. I follow him down the hill. 'Told you,' says Sheila as we return the way we've just come. When we find a signpost shyly hiding itself, things become easy.

The problem is that we could go up Arkangarthdale or Swaledale. Two people we asked gave contradicting advice, and both ways are mentioned in Tan Hill's website. Swaledale itself has more to offer, but the driver of the car whose gateway I blocked says that in wild weather the Arkangarthdale route is definitely the better at the top end. The Dale itself is perhaps less changed during the last hundred years than any other. Wild it certainly is and, once over the thousand foot contour, seriously bleak with a strong gusty wind. Soon we're in fog and then visibility is reduced again by horizontal rain which, driven by fierce wind, sounds like hail beating on the car. The windscreen wipers scarcely cope.

Standing at the point where the road crosses the Pennine Way, it must be a most welcome sight for serious walkers. But at 1,732ft, today what little we can see of it, Tan Hill Inn doesn't exactly look welcoming. Others have occupied all the handy parking so, after careful planning, we grab our belongings, getting soaked as we charge to the door. If outside all is wildness, inside seems total confusion. With our spectacles steamed up, we can only fumble slowly. Then we push our way to the bar where a sizeable proportion of Yorkshire's male population is waiting for a drink. They are patience personified. Despite the crowd, once we can see where we are, the atmosphere is almost serene.

'It'll quieten down directly,' says a young lad assistant, who helps us to the residents' quarters and puts us into a small bedroom with a mini-bathroom and loo which makes toilets on trains seem positively spacious. It works; there's all we need, and by the time we've had a snooze most of the day visitors have set off in their cars, vans, cycles and motorbikes. There's room to breathe, feel the warmth of the open fire, discover a menu and order. The meal is A1, just too large, for they're used to feeding hungry walkers and bikers.

The inn was built to serve the nearby coal mines which once powered the lead mines lower down. Since those industrial days, it has had a variety of curious as well as famous owners (a Mrs Peacock of the 1960s is especially remembered) and appealed to an ever-changing clientele. Once drovers paused to refresh themselves and their animals. Later posh people came to show off their new Bentleys. Then it became a fashionable place to dance. Those and other days used to be celebrated with a display in Reeth Museum. Though that has gone, the inn's walls are lined with historic photographs.

The present owners, Mike and Tracy, are no ordinary couple. Though 'I don't like pubs and don't drink', publicity conscious, she clearly delights in the pub and is probably making a packet from it. He'd sell it tomorrow. 'It's a diversion,' he says, to which she adds: 'And what fun'. They have business interests in Taunton (where their cat is now with their daughter), though at least she seems to be here at weekends when most of the money is made. They join us in the bar along with two sheep, Izzy the favourite, whose droppings on the stone floor she shovels into the fire. 'Saves coal.'

Of today's clientele: 'Very mixed, from farmers' formal dinners and corporate events to nudists and barn dances, children from Belarus and charitable events, but the daily bread and butter is walkers – we're midway along the 266-mile Pennine Way – cyclists, bikers, and ordinary tourists coming by car for the experience. We put on a more friendly face than has always been the case, and I've collected a loyal staff. At busy times, it's 250 meals a day. We have to remember everyone comes because we're unique and make them feel it's worth it.'

There's certainly no inn to rival it in publicity terms. It warrants a special entry in guide books and tourist brochures, and isn't shy about its merits in its website. It succeeds in coping with heavy peak demands despite being connected by no pipe or cable to the outside world. It really is isolated, self-contained. Water is from a borehole, electricity by generator and telephone by microwave link. 'We have to be very organised,' says Tracy giving the impression of being the least organised woman in the world and trading on eccentricity while obviously being brilliant at making money... but also supporting good causes.

As one might expect from such a show person, at core she's shy. What she's happiest talking about are ghosts: that of the former Mrs Peacock – 'I saw her figure walk across the room to the bar and leave' – a screaming cook, and three smoking gentlemen who many claim to have seen. Separated from us by a small dog very possessive of his favourite chair, one of the few guests left in the bar after dinner puts in: 'I don't believe in ghosts but I've smelt them, those smoking gents.' Jack Noble from Ashstead in Surrey is perhaps a typical punter, not quite believing the reality of the pub but revelling in it. As do we. It shouts Remote Britain.

· XXXV ·

ACROSS AND NORTH AND WEST OF THE LAKES

Across the Lake District

It is bright, sunny with only occasional hanging morning mist, as we set off from Tan Hill. At first the country is still wild, though at least visible, but we soon descend steeply down to Barras to find ourselves at the gateway to Brough. 'How about stopping for an hour or two?' I ask Sheila teasingly, as we make our way just bypassing Appleby (there we're both seriously tempted to stop) to join the A66.

Today is largely being devoted to what could be called a positional drive, one that has to be done but is still exhilarating through a kaleidoscope of great landscapes. As we have rediscovered in the last week, time spent to the east of the Lake District with its rich variety of some of England's finest scenery is especially enjoyable. But what of the lands to the north and south of the Lakes, and coastal strip linking them, little of which is within the National Park?

Previous experience reminds that immediately to the east of Carlisle, along the southern shores of the furthest inland part of the Solway Firth, the landscape is scarcely more exciting than that going east along the North Wales coast as road and railway find themselves on the bank of the Dee and ready access to 'civilisation' has led to urban development. But the coastal north west strip as far as Silloth, is definitely worth including.

To get there keeping around the Lake District's periphery involves excessive mileage, along the M6 and close to, if not actually through, Carlisle. So we cheat, and go straight through the Lakes calling at some of our well-loved places including Keswick.

If one spends a substantial part of one's life travelling, inevitably news comes through of things good, bad and worse. The first telephone call to the office since we left home reveals a chapter of horrors including two deaths, one of a child in distressing circumstances. It was raining hard and, being unable to find anywhere in the town to park, I was outside the former railway station for a sandwich lunch in the conservatory of the large Keswick Hotel that once linked it to the platforms, and still does for guests staying in its extensions in the former station offices. As explained in *Journey*, having had an office for a time and begun and ended many journeys here, I've always had a sharp mind's eye picture of the station frontage, faced with dark Lakeland stone. Now I will first recall that phone call, which dominates thoughts for the rest of our journey, especially along Derwent Water into Borrowdale and up Honister Pass with constant stopping on steep gradients in a downpour to let other traffic through.

It rains even harder as we drive past a somewhat shadowy Buttermere to our Bridge Hotel just beyond it.

Magical Buttermere

I've just been asked to read *Daffodils* aloud to a group of four Spaniards. Though I cannot understand a word when Ganzale Garsia-Pelayo reads it back in Spanish, the cadences tell exactly where we are in Wordsworth's most famous poem. After a leisurely breakfast I asked the Spaniards what brought them here. 'To study the Lake poets.' The party, including son Ian, seem to typify the guests at the Bridge Hotel, for they actually defy analysis. The business is built on attracting an eclectic bunch, all very deliberately here, to rest, read, walk and explore. Just the kind of people who bought David & Charles books: over after-dinner coffee later in the day, indeed two separate parties own up to having books I published. Were I still in business, I'd probably have sold some more. If there is a common thread, it is a deep respect for the Lakes, liking to be away from the crowds, and a desire to know more about this small part of our wonderful world.

Magically situated by a stream, the car park on the opposite bank, the hotel knows its market. Apart from the bar – 'Please use the entrance from the car park' – and little dependent on passing trade, it is a quiet hotel setting high standards in a matter-of-fact kind of way. It may be an odd example to choose to demonstrate its style, but it is predictable that its notice about avoiding unnecessary washing of towels is the shortest and least gauche we've yet seen in any hotel bathroom. I wonder what the Spaniards made of it. They're a serious quartet, quiet but with their own sense of fun – driven by enormous enthusiasm.

Tranquility reigns at all times in the restaurant and lounge; only when a few day-trippers come for a bar lunch (and again please use separate entrance) could we not hear each other's whisperings. The whole establishment is consciously unconscious. The food is excellent but there's no rosette. No showing off in any way. It could only be in a delectable but accessible and well-known part of Remote Britain. The fact that Buttermere is actually in the Lakes doesn't lessen its remoteness. It is uncrowded and little commercialised and, when it does get busy, it is usually with walkers.

Our bedroom overlooks the road, with occasional buses during tourist hours, but at other times even few cars. Opposite is a steep moss-covered bank with an intriguing path starting up Buttermere Fell. The nearby church at the centre of the parish tells us it is a small parish with only thirty seven homes. 'But we are proud of our little church, "built upon the rock", and anxious to maintain it and hand it onto our children in good condition. Pause and remember Alfred Wainwright, hill walker, guide, book writer and illustrator who loved this valley. Lift your eyes to the Haystacks, his favourite place. 1907-1991.' Inside there's a very small organ but gorgeous hand-embroidered hassocks displaying local scenes. When we come out, we dutifully look up at the Haystacks rising above the ridge.

The road by the Honister Pass comes down a steep hill with a signpost pointing to another, narrower way by which we could have come from Keswick, as daily does our waitress who says it usually reduces the time by twenty minutes. And just below the junction, there is a turn into a more recent development including large car park (served by buses in both directions which stop and then turn), another hotel, toilets and tourist shop with café.

Back in the 11th century, our hotel site was occupied by an armoury, bakery and grain store. A waterwheel was built to feed refugees fleeing from Norman devastation in Lancashire and Yorkshire. The mill, store and other building, which had been of wood, were rebuilt with slate, and over the centuries the millworkers' cottages often needed replacing. Times changed and, about 1734, the last miller sold the main building to the parish. It was when the first curate found he had too much space that a beer licence was obtained and the tradition of hospitality was established, though there were breaks when it was a private house. Apparently, even when again in the hospitality business, at times it became seriously run down. Now it has been in the same private ownership since 1978, though it is managed by the friendly and obviously efficient John and Adrian McGuire. 'We try to be attentive but not interfering,' says John. 'The tranquil surroundings set the tone. 'Piped pop music would be totally out of place.'

[Though we knew that Buttermere was the wettest place in England, shortly before this book finally went to press we were shocked to hear of the devastation brought to some of the places we visited from there.

The heaviest recorded rainfall anywhere in our country, over a foot in 24 hours, especially hit Cockermouth, whose main street was devastated, and demolished bridges in Workington. Here the main one across the Derwent close to its mouth cut the town in two, involving a diversion of thirty miles and claimed the life of a young policeman preventing others from crossing it. Network Rail's bridge remained intact and a temporary station on the north side of the river was built quickly, providing a service linking the two parts of the town. As elsewhere, I describe things as I found them.

We especially loved the footbridge over the river from the car park into Cockermouth and its delightful main street, and were deeply upset to see pictures of the state of the bridge and many of the shops we visited including the bookshop. Happily the community atmosphere suggests that eventually there will be a complete recovery.]

Cockermouth and Whitehaven

We are at home here as anywhere we've visited, the one disappointment being that we cannot see Buttermere itself from the hotel, though every time we drive the other way to points north and west, we enjoy the long run alongside Crummock Water on either side of which the OS graphically depicts contours so close as almost to be on top of each other. Over several days we come to enjoy familiarity with the River Cocker that flows out of Crummock Water and over millions of years has carved a broad Lorton Vale through the softer rocks. Lorton itself has a splendid large house in the pretty village where dusk must come early when the winter sun disappears behind 416-metre Fellbarrow. Then to Cockermouth, well inland where the Cocker joins the greater fast-flowing Derwent which however slows down considerably as it wends its way to reach the sea at Workington.

Walking from the main car park, we cross the combined river by a long footbridge to Cockermouth's tree-lined High Street, distinctly up-market from when I recall it at the end of the little town's days of being heavily influenced by nearby mining and other industrial activity. In common with many other places on the Lake District's periphery, it has become a desirable while a reasonably affordable place to live, and it's friendly. Visitors are still welcome because they're not in such numbers as in popular places including nearby Keswick. The optician is more than happy to provide a screw to an arm of my spectacles for nothing and with a smile, while going to the chemist is as social an occasion as in Scotland. I'm naturally drawn to the nearby Museum of Printing whose window retains my attention for a long time. There's much inside, the products of historic printing presses as well as the machines themselves, collected from far and wide. Though there are supermarkets, most shops are still privately owned, with keen competition between many in the same line of business. Overlooking part of the street is the statue of Lord Mayo, local MP who became Viceroy of India and is best known because he was assassinated.

A happier note is struck by the smaller Wordsworth Memorial opposite the large Georgian house in which both William and Dorothy were born. The house is run by the National Trust but attracts only a fraction of the attention of their later house, Dove Cottage, deep in the Lakes. Past and present blend quietly happily in Cockermouth. Points of interest range from Roman times to Wordsworth's youth and a still active brewery offering tours. There's also a useful Mineral Museum. 'Lovely little place,' says Sheila. It's of the Lake District though not actually in it.

Through a land once criss-crossed by industrial railways, our next planned stop in Workington doesn't happen. Funny how one takes against some places and favours others; Workington I've never liked, not because it's been so industrial and has seen better days, but maybe because the sample of people I've met over the years have been reluctant to soften and smile. So we push straight on down the coast (we're going in the opposite direction to the train journey described in *Journey*) to Whitehaven, which still grabs me. Remote from other towns, it once seemed highly individualistic, its shop frontages archaic. It isn't so obviously different today, but still has real individuality and, it always seems to me, a kinder people. Its harbour area is good, too.

Next, down the A596 to Egremont, a former mining and market town, again a friendly, little-visited place and an ancient one with its own series of annual rituals (such as Crab Fair and 'Parade of the Apple Cart' whose contents are thrown at onlookers). Then to Cleator and Cleator Moor, feeling even less in the swing of national life, though they are very Cumbrian. The Whitehaven, Cleator & Egremont Railway took high-grade iron ore mined by the 'red men' of Cumberland (there were also iron works on Cleator Moor itself) down to Whitehaven. The line hung on even with a few passenger trains mainly for miners well into nationalisation. It is now a cycleway, but generally there's more decline than a switch to tourism in this unknown corner of Remote Britain. Old men are still delighted to talk about the colourful if scarcely good old days and, if you're really interested, you can see just what was mined here in Cockermouth's Mineral Museum. Now it's abandoned railways, mines, subsidence, quarries and other abandoned works and bargain housing.

We are a good way back toward Cockermouth before taking to narrow lanes along the tree-fringed road alongside Loweswater, prettily situated among part woodland among the lower fells. Well over a mile long, and half a mile wide, in recorded history it has always been among the smaller of the lakes, the only one draining inland, by a stream into Crummock Water. It is deeply enjoyed by a small fraternity who love its peace. The National Trust rents a few clinker-built rowing boats. However, thousands of years ago Buttermere, Crummock Water and Loweswater were once a single large lake, eventually being separated by an accumulation of silt. So, continuing by narrow lane to the tip of Crummock Water, and home to our hotel for a leisurely gossip over an old-fashioned afternoon tea in the comfortable residents' lounge. This is the life.

Solway Coast Contrasts

Next day our first stop is Maryport which in recent years I've only seen from the train. 'Improved' it might be from the dire times immediately after the collapse of its lifeline coal-exporting business but, if tourism has brought in new blood, it is not obvious in the town centre this morning. True, car parking is scarce, and when I'm forced to leave a place in the street where I said I'd wait for Sheila, we have difficulty in reconnecting. Eventually my wheels come to rest outside one of many closed shops. Our impression isn't helped by being served the worst toasted sandwich ever in what we had concluded was the best choice of café or pub: how can toasted cheese and ham be so limp and tasteless? 'What's the toilet like?' asks Sheila. 'Fine apart from narrow, steep steps and no lock or bolt on the door.'

I'm all for getting away from Maryport, but Sheila notices a sign to the harbour... and we find a totally different world – of smiling people. Maybe there's a hidden barrier which automatically switches moods from gloom to pleasure? Once covered in coal dust, the harbour now sparkles. It looks great. It welcomes yachts, though there aren't many of them. Slightly to the west, there's a gleaming brand new leisure centre offering a host of facilities of no interest to us today except for a large café with scarcely anyone in it. 'Wish we'd known you were here; we'd have had lunch,' I say to the cheerful waitress, who replies that 'Hardly anyone, even the locals, realise we're here. We've only been open a few weeks.' We have a coffee and tasty pastry in spacious comfort hoping that the establishment will soon find its feet and pay its way and be integrated into local life.

While the train journey hugging the coast between Workington and

Maryport is top class, the coast continuing east (only seen by road) is, in a word, disappointing. Parts of the coast with a gap in the middle are an Area of Outstanding Natural Beauty. There are empty expanses of sand between rocky sections of beach. A solitary hotel seems in good order, and a few holiday camps are quite busy, while lone caravans are parked in windy positions. However, the few villages have obviously unrealised ambitions. They seem to cling grimly on the edge, almost expecting further setbacks.

Silloth, our destination, has had its fair share of failures, too, but has survived as an interesting little place. Its wide streets have never been fully justified, but even with a population of just 3,000, there are things to do. There's obviously a strong community feeling supporting good health, sport and other facilities and many amateur groups.

The only other time I've been here was by train from Carlisle, arriving with a couple of hundred day trippers. Without thinking – it's nearly at the end of the road, close to the sea – I park at the old, well-preserved station. It is now an excellent, very helpful visitors' centre.

Silloth, or to give it its full name, Silloth-on-Solway, was a planned town based on what for a time was known as Port Carlisle. A railway was laid on the former canal bed to serve the port and bring in tourists. There was a bathing establishment and bathing machines and even a 1,000-ft pier – with a railway from the station running along it for people and goods – from which steamers left daily for Liverpool and twice weekly for Dublin. Partly because it easily silted, the harbour never really took off, and the railway, opened in 1856, went bankrupt in 1862. It was rescued by the North British, and hence later became one of few LNER lines to reach the west coast. Because the North British could now run mineral and freight trains from Edinburgh to Silloth bypassing Carlisle where the Caledonian Railway interfered with the traffic, the harbour's business was boosted for a period.

But sand remained a problem even when the harbour was converted to a tidal basin. Later development was almost wholly tourist orientated, thousands of day trippers arriving on peak days in the twenties and thirties. Many poor Carlisle kids were given a rare visit to the sea by Sister Lillie (Elizabeth Davis), one of several 'good works' such out-of-the-way places threw up. Only in the war did the harbour, thought to be safe from German attack, seriously come back to life for a few years. And it was during the war that Silloth was at its busiest, especially with servicemen, many based at the new extensive nearby airfield (now home to industrial units). All hotels and other accommodation were booked solid; shops were busier in winter than they had been in peak season. However, while out of use, the pier was washed away in a storm.

The weather has frequently been unkind. The golf course is built on sand that systematically blocked the harbour. The small port and nearby village of Skinburness, and the road along the coast to it, established by the monks of Holme Cultram, were washed away in a 13th century storm. The monks had used it to export substantial quantities of wool from their sheep; they also established a salt industry on the marshes to the east where the RSPB reserve near the end of Hadrian's Wall now attracts many of the areas visitors. Peace brought leaner times, though as at many other resorts, passenger trains were busiest in the years not long before its closure, just before the rapid increase in car and coach traffic.

'An interesting story, but in some ways a sad one,' says the woman behind the counter from whom I buy a guide book. 'But people do love it here, and it's a wonderful place to live. Be sure to see it all... especially walk onto the Green to look at the fine buildings of Criffel Street and the church with the tall spire.'

The Green and the long promenade offer 'the ultimate in solitude', to cite the website, which also lays claim to an equable climate – though it's jolly windy this afternoon – and Turneresque sunsets. With its broad tree-lined boulevards, open spaces and long promenade, Silloth indeed has much that more popular resorts lack. The fact that it is not included in most guide books tells its own story. Finding people to talk to on the prom isn't easy, but those who come clearly enjoy the difference. Nearly all of my sample mention the Firth's birdlife. 'Coming here is the exact opposite of lazing around the crowded pool of a Spanish hotel,' says someone from Manchester. 'See, we've got the whole prom to ourselves.'

We return to Cockermouth and to our hotel by a network of lanes through productive but little-visited countryside generating substantial agricultural traffic; villages, farmhouses and cars also tell of matter-of-fact prosperity, though I recall the area was badly hit by foot-and-mouth about a decade ago. Sad to think we'll probably never come this way again... and lack time even to see what is left of Skinburness and, across the bay beyond where there's another wartime airfield, to Bowness-on-Solway, starting point for the little-needed Solway Junction Railway across to Scotland by a viaduct that ultimately cost more to demolish than to build (see *Journey*).

Down the West Coast and Patrick of the Hills

Next morning, with heavy rain forecast and clouds darkening from the west, we take our final trip along Crummock Water and through Lorton Vale to the main road just shy of Cockermouth, and proceed west and south on our circling of the Lake District. By train and road, I've often followed the coast to Seascale and its Sellafield nuclear power station, something else costing more to close than it did to build. At Ravenglass, my usual interest has been in the 'little' railway, the Ravenglass & Eskdale, but now we're going to Muncaster Castle to meet someone who personifies Remote Britain: Patrick of the Hills.

'Thanks for coming, but you haven't brought a very nice day,' he says. By the time we meet, Flit, the small black cat, has latched onto us. We're instantly at ease with Patrick, too, though he's a complicated character who seems to have led many lives. His name isn't simple, either: Patrick Gordon-Duff-Pennington. Of that, more anon for, with the weather set to get worse, we head straight out into the garden. Indeed, before I can get to grips with his career, making it plain that life isn't altogether straightforward, he breaks into verse:

I know how animals in cages feel
For not so long ago I walked the mountain tops
And felt my legs swing free across the summer grass,
But now I'm here in Muncaster
Imprisoned in a gilded cage by circumstance.
I've lost my freedom,
Lost my hope,
And never more may know the sun
Upon my moving limbs
The music of the wind among the rocks
So now I understand
How lions feel in cages.

We go along a broad and lengthy grassy terrace opposite the castle with, to its left, an extended shrub border full of promise and problems. He pokes here and there trying to encourage order. 'In 1930 there used to be thirty two gardeners; now it's head gardener, three boys and me and I'm still told we'll have to cut down.' Such are the socio-economics of all great houses and gardens. But so far as the terrace is concerned, he's far from given in. As we wander along with occasional pauses, he points out dozens of special shrubs and trees, pulls off dead branches, says he'll return later to do this and that. His interest is still very much outdoors – and Flit isn't put off by the rain either. 'If only you could see the view when it's sunny,' says Patrick. Especially to Sheila: 'You'll come back, won't you?'

Now something emerges about himself. For over twenty years he farmed on the hills north of Dumfries. 'I've had a happy life, though there've always been problems. In agriculture, it's often been my job to solve them. [He represented Scottish landowners and then became chairman of the Cumbrian National Farmers Union, outspoken but fair.] But being married to this place is difficult.'

His wife, Phyllida, inherited the castle, and his name combines with her family's. They live at one end, while his daughter Iona, who happens to be married to the son of Nairn friends, lives at the other. The part of the castle open to the public is inbetween. A serious business if it is to survive, the castle clearly needs a strong leader, who Iona undoubtedly is. She has very definite ideas. Being second (or third) fiddle to a daughter is hard for any man who has led his own career and enjoyed a life of meeting and being respected by top people. Yet he's thrown himself heart and soul into both castle and garden.

When he takes us to lunch in the decent castle-run café, he makes instant contact with visitors and is genuinely interested in their comments. This from his *Those Blue Remembered Hills,* a somewhat restless though never dull autobiography, tells of how things were in desperate times at the end of the regime of his father-in-law:

> In those far off days of 1983 Muncaster's need for publicity was soon apparent. Joan Freshwater introduced me to Radio Cumbria. She interviewed me about my favourite music and didn't mind being asked if she had pigtails as a girl. I contributed often, calling each week with news to interest them. Thus, on becoming Chairman of Cumbria NFU in 1986, my name was already known. Muncaster needed to diversify its income streams quickly without spending capital we didn't have. Our assets were a house severely needing maintenance; 320 acres of derelict woodland; three rented farms, one in-hand; estate houses mostly rather dilapidated; a no-hope caravan site set up so that it was impossible to generate income and employ a manager. An indifferent café was unprofitably franchised. The house and garden-opening business, geared to insufficient day visitors producing insufficient income. My father-in-law, considering we knew nothing about publicity, insisted we employed a man from Tunbridge Wells, to help. Married to a bank manager in Orpington, he wrote on green writing paper, and sent large bills. We said thank you more politely than we felt, but remembered him when a granddaughter bought two Buff Orpingtons at a farm sale.

Though he told me he'd have happily given me a copy, like most authors, he's pleased I'd actually bought one, though he insists on giving me his collection of poetry, *Patrick of the Hills,* a mixed bag with wonderfully perceptive and restful rural verses as well as unsettling dissertations on aspects of life with which he is less satisfied.

He's ever been the rebel, for example seeing Sellafield and its visitors' centre as good for the local economy when most were strongly opposed.

He suggests that opportunities to help with local employment were lost when opposed by members of the National Park Committee who were not working people from within its area. He's happy when introducing us to his two grandsons also working for the Castle's benefit. He's a people person, who really cares... and is great fun to be with, especially for Sheila since, undoubtedly, he's a woman's man.

· XXXVI ·

THE LAKE DISTRICT'S WEST AND ISLANDS AND ULLSWATER

Down the Lake District's West Coast

Sheila exclaims: 'I can see the sea.' Momentarily taking my eye off the rain-sodden road, I just about catch the horizon, a vague line between shades of grey. Instantly it vanishes as horizontally-driven rain obscures all beyond a few yards. And, sure enough, not concentrating for a few seconds, I splash into a deep puddle. It certainly knows how to rain on this side of the Lake District. We left Patrick of the Hills earlier than we would have chosen since there was another of those extreme weather warnings that crop up with increased frequency.

Conditions improve marginally as we turn inland at Silecroft and head along the switchback toward Broughton-in-Furness, just off the main road. Though half an hour ago we wondered if we would be able to reach Barrow-in-Furness safely tonight, we're tempted to glimpse once more at the hillside village of happy memories. Broughton typifies those outposts of quality scattered across Britain often in the most unlikely of areas.

I suppose a few people build good houses, an exceptional shop opens, and over the years things take off. We see that Broughton still has fine pubs (we've memories of excellent lunches at one of them), a Post Office, baker and tea shop, and a super greengrocer and butcher... the kind of collection that does estate agents' work for them in selling local property, of which there is a fine array, a few homes being extended or renovated.

Back to the coast by Foxfield station, where I once spent hours waiting for a passenger train, my pass to travel down the Coniston branch, then only served by goods trains, being valid only thus far, and we press on – slowly – through the rain. That however suddenly stops, and soon we're safely at Dalton-in-Furness and, now delayed only by heavy traffic, Barrow-in-Furness.

Though it is a long way by poor road and railway from other

industrial places, Barrow is possibly too large to qualify as Remote. Or is it? Distinctive, its buildings are a curious mixture of the down-and-out and welcome Victorian survivals of great style, and nowhere is the contrast more evident than on the waterside: a long, busy route with fascinating glimpses of docks, warehouses and great admin blocks that seem to exude the history of the town's very soul. Once you get to know it, Barrow grows on you. Though undoubtedly with rough edges, it's an honest place with character largely based on its self-dependent isolation – and the sea.

Roa Island

Once out of the built-up area, we continue east until at Rampside we turn south to the tip of the Furness mainland and cross to Roa Island by a causeway. The B&B into which we check is an odd building with a high tower. Not even having heard of Roa Island until recently, I'm delighted that there's an informative brochure in our comfortable en suite room. The building, it says, was built for 'the Furness industrialist H W Schneider as a holiday residence'. Later it served as a fisheries investigation laboratory, and as army premises in World War Two. As a guest house, it is now owned by Eden Retreat Ltd, a small company whose aim is 'to create establishments which embrace peaceful environments and natural surroundings'.

Roa Island compresses much into its mere 30 acres. There's Trinity Terrace, a row of houses built for ten Trinity House pilots, a watch tower and a Custom & Excise House. It is home to a modern lifeboat station serving Morecambe Bay and the Irish Sea. And there's a large seaside café with popular prices. There are a few other houses – and even an occasional bus service. Apart from a couple outside their front door enjoying the evening sunshine after a very wet day, there's an absence of human activity, but plenty of movement along the Piel Channel. Piel Island, to which we plan to go to meet the 'King of Piel' – (Sheila hopes she might pay for a round of drinks at the inn, which is said to be the price of being 'knighted', on my 79th birthday tomorrow), stands out clearly. The large inn is shrouded in a large plastic wrap.

The deep channel is key to Barrow's success as port and shipbuilding town, though for the largest of today's ships it needs constant dredging. There's a dredger out there now, being passed by a cargo ship overtaking a yacht.

Once there were steamers actually calling at Roa, a genuine island until it was bought in 1840 by a London banker, who built the causeway and a pier... for a railway. A handful of daily trains reached the terminus misleadingly called Piel. One connected with steamers for Fleetwood. Occasional goods trains crossed until 1936, when the tracks were replaced by the road. We have to cross the causeway for our evening meal in a pub at Rampside, wondering how profitable the Furness Railway's 'Piel branch' might have been in say 1887 when even a first class ticket from Barrow cost only 10d – not that many would have offered that luxury. It could be done for 7d for second class or 4d (not much more than today's penny) for third class.

Piel Island and its 'King'

Next morning we're up bright and early, looking forward to our visit to Piel Island. At breakfast we meet a retired teacher who used to take her classes there, while her hobby fisherman husband invariably had good catches. 'It's a bit primitive without mains electricity or gas, but there's mains water and a flushing toilet. We love it... and you'll enjoy the pub... only the back bar is open during the massive refurbishment.' She adds that 'the Barrow Council leases it to the landlord, chosen carefully to make sure he'll be a good "King". But I don't think he's been crowned yet, so won't be able to create any "knights". There's a great ritual based on history. I found an old book about it in the school library. The tradition of the King goes back a long way. You'll find the ruins of the old castle interesting, too.'

As we wait by the pier for the ferry, we go over what we have so far discovered about Piel. In common with most small parcels of land in strategic positions, its story is a microcosm of British history. Its name suggests that in ancient times it might have been a safe grazing place for cattle and sheep. Certainly the Celts and Romans were there. Furness Abbey, whose ruins we will visit later, was heavily involved in its prosperity, using it as a trading post, farming the land and keeping food in safe storehouses. The Abbey's dissolution was one of the island's major turning points; it passed to the King. The last attempt to improve the castle, now a romantic ruin, was at the time of the Spanish Armada. In the Civil War it became a resting place for the Parliamentarian fleet. Smuggling, a persistent activity, especially reared its head later; a petition to the King to allow it to have its own Custom House was successful.

The tradition of the island having its own 'King' goes back to 1487 when Lambert Simnel, a trader's son under the guidance of the Earl of Lincoln, landed claiming he was Earl of Warwick and so the rightful English King. His march toward London ended with defeat at the Battle of Stoke.

Described as a tranquil little piece of Heaven, Piel Island is even smaller than Roa, just twenty acres, owned by the people of Barrow to whom it was given in 1920 as a war memorial by the then owner, the Duke of Buccleuch. The King manages the island from his Ship Inn. Today that is the only habitation permanently occupied, though there is a block of six cottages used as holiday homes. There's a toilet block with showers – cold water only – for the numerous seasonal campers.

A small knot of younger passengers has gathered. 'Because the tide is running so fast, he won't be wanting to start too soon,' says one of them of the ferryman. And when he eventually gets into the ferry, he has problems starting the engine – and then manoeuvring the vessel in the fast tide. To my horror, he comes to the pier bow first, and asks passengers to jump on. Five years ago I could have done it easily, and I try several times... but just can't make it.

As the more agile watch, my face feels red. 'Don't get embarrassed,' says my gentle wife. 'If you can't, it doesn't matter.' So I retreat. 'If you come back in a couple of hours, I'll be able to come alongside in the usual way and you'll be fine,' says the boatman. As he crosses with the pub's first customers of the day, we sit looking across to Piel Island and the Piel Channel which since 1840, when Vickers began, has been used by numerous prestigious and other ships setting out on their maiden voyage. Beyond Piel is the eastern tip of the Isle of Walney. 'Why don't we go to Walney today?' asks Sheila. And so we do.

Several weeks later, I called the King, Steve Chattaway, to explain why we never made it to his inn. He says: 'You should have let us know. I'd have come with tractor and trailer to take you across from Walney. That's the way we bring our supplies across. The Roa ferry is sometimes tricky.'

I ask him about his crowning. 'They like the flamboyant approach. The crown was ceremoniously brought over from the Council's safe. I was in full medieval dress and was crowned by a previous King with six knights present. For good measure, two bucketfuls of chilled beer were poured over my head. It's a real ritual, generating a lot of publicity.

It's quite an adventure for us, especially after being relief signalman and then traffic manager at Barrow. In fact I'm still working for the railways two or three days a week as possessions manager when lines are closed for engineering work. We used to run pubs and have come back to it after twenty five years of bringing up our kids. I'm sure it's going to be a lovely lifestyle here, busy for much of the year but closed in winter. You don't forget the seasons on an island.'

Isle of Walney

Threading back through Barrow's traffic, we cross what the map still calls Barrow Island, though it was joined to the mainland in the industrial revolution, and cross over the bridge to Vickerstown, on the Isle of Walney, which I have been curious about for half a century and am at last visiting. We had originally intended staying at Vickerstown, but a friend advised us to avoid it as vandalism is rife and we'd feel uncomfortable even driving through it. Run down it has to be, for we hear that, whereas there were once 15,000 on Vickers' payroll, now there are only 4-5,000. Started in 1899, Vickerstown was a company town. Though like a misplaced piece of Glasgow's most densely-populated area, it doesn't actually strike us as too bad, and on the outskirts, especially on the sea-facing side, there are pleasant estates. We decide first to explore the island's northern end, going through North Scale, a village surprisingly unchanged from before Vickers' submarine and ship building days.

Walney was inhabited and there were farms in Domesday time, but North Scale seems to have begun in the early 13th century as a grange of the all-powerful Furness Abbey. By the end of the century, land was broken up in a way followed in much of Furness. The grange was split into four farms or burgages, each with four tenants. The arable land made twenty one common fields, each sub-divided into forty eight narrow strips or dales. Each tenant had three strips on each field. Though there was also land for cattle and horses, sheep were only introduced late in the 15th century after several of the tenants surrendered their holdings during a depression. Always ready to adjust to preserve their income, the monks built a cottage for the 'Sheppard' on 'Idle Cote'. The rent was no bargain.

Thanks to Vickers' expansion, few fields survive today, and we're no sooner going along a country lane with a couple of field gates before there's a barrier blocking the way. This, it transpires, is Vickers' private airfield. I ask the guard if I can go in just to turn. 'If you guarantee to go no further, sir.' Vickers have left their mark everywhere in and around Barrow. Today's company is actually BAE Systems, but locally it is universally called by its old name.

There's a wildlife sanctuary beyond here with a quarter of Britain's rare natterjack toads among other treasures. There's much evidence of ancient man, too, and a more recent but abandoned Vickers' gravel works. With the airport in the way, we're not too sure how to reach the sanctuary, and anyway planned to spend most time in the south. So we head back through Vickerstown and along what is a very narrow strip of land with low-lying fields between drainage channels. A high seabank prevents waves breaking over. There are active and abandoned farms, a few fields (some with sheep) having clear boundary fences, and some riding stables. Beyond the small village of Biggar there's a large static caravan site, a good one with a shop. Soon we're on a very narrow track with speed bumps and rare passing places to a sophisticated parking area at the nature reserve at the southern end. Not easily missed is an honesty box for the parking fee; the reserve's offices are already closed. Leading off from here a network of paths are well marked. One leads to where the narrow land suddenly turns at almost right angles heading toward Piel Island. At low tide, with a guide you can sometimes walk between the islands and, as already mentioned, supplies are taken across by tractor and trailer. We can also see minute Sheep Island to the left and Foulney Island to the right of Piel Island, each no doubt with its own legends.

We're so close to a major industrial town yet so remote. Though we like the tamarisk and sea holly, some of the vegetation is strange to us. When we stop and listen, there's a constant buzz of birds, insects and little mammals moving around the undergrowth. The more still and silent we become, the better attuned we are to hearing and then seeing some of the little birds, mostly familiar but no less exciting for that. In the background there's a show of sea birds. This is a reserve and a half.

Back at the car park, we examine the office block and study the notice of the day's sightings. 200+ Manx shearwaters, 100+ Sandwich terns, 100 common scoters and 90 gannets, with a few Arctic skuas, great skuas, fulmars and a couple of shags. Migrants include whinchat, wheatear, willow warbler, white wagtail, robin and whimbrel. By the pools there have been greenshank, redshank, godwit and teal. Raptors are represented by little owl, merlin, peregrine and kestrel, and waders by grey plover, turnstone, knot, sanderling, little egret, common and green sandpiper. Nine garden birds have been noted, and honey buzzard is listed as a rarity. Not a bad daily score for August, in the low season.

The notice also tells us that the area is part of Morecambe Bay Site of Special Scientific Interest, which also includes Piel Island. With its unusual habitats it is famous for attracting a large number of both wintering and passage birds.

'Isn't this some place,' says a lady from San Francisco, displaying a Save the Redwoods badge. Her friend from Utah (there's a whole wedding party of them) says she would have to come back in winter. An Englishman points out that it was wonderful for ornithologists in the peak bird season till there were too many humans. 'It's become very popular, but it is well organised. You have to give them that.'

We spend longer talking with Barbara Hartley from Sedbergh, Cumbria, the English book town we had intended visiting while in Aysgarth (chapter XXXIV) but ran out of time. I've memories of it being a lovely little town with a super old-fashioned narrow, curving main street, but had not realised it had followed Wigtown's Scottish example of benefiting from specialising in the way that has put Welsh Hay-on-Wye on the booklovers map.

She adds: 'By the way, have you heard about the natterjack toads at the northern end? That's one of the things about Walney. It takes a bit of getting here, but with two reserves and so much wildlife you're spoilt for choice.'

Returning to Biggar, we go into the village to look round. Feeling we could murder a cup of tea, but with nowhere seeming to offer any refreshment, we're surprisingly in luck. I've accidentally driven into a private dead end serving a group of homes and explain my mistake to a stocky gent washing his car. This is an island, so he's time to spare and asks where I'm from. That starts us talking and I begin asking questions. Suddenly he tells me he's Thomas Kendall, a builder, and ushers us into his home which he's done much to improve. Soon we're comfortably in their sitting room being served a birthday tea by his wife Marjorie, who is anxious to show us round pointing out their lifetime's unusual collection of ornaments.

They're deliriously happy in their home in the 'posh' area of Biggar. 'There are just thirty four houses in the village; a nice number,' says Thomas. 'But it hasn't always been so good here. The plague killed half of the island's population of about 250 in 1631. Where we are now became a farm hundreds of years ago and must have been pretty primitive until the monks built the track down the island. And in the first part of the last century, things seem to have been rough in Vickerstown. Nothing to complain of today. This is a friendly place. We're away from the crowds, but Barrow's right on the doorstep.'

Biggar Bank once attracted a large number of day trippers from Barrow, short of its own open spaces. Farmers, disliking the influxes, once fenced the area off and charged a discouraging admission fee. After repeatedly breaking down the fences, the trippers won the day. Barrow Council then took out a lease, opening it as a public recreation ground on Good Friday 1883. Soon after a Pavilion was erected. Business increased dramatically after the Furness Railway started a chain ferry and, when tramcars started crossing the bridge, opened in 1908, one of the area's first car parks was provided.

Today's trippers prefer mainland beaches they can drive to, and on hot sunny days few now come to bathe from Walney. The danger for this island, eleven miles long and scarcely anywhere more than a mile wide, is that its character will be spoilt by too many townies wanting to build their own houses and bungalows. The seasonal campers make their own impact, but the rule that for six weeks a year the static caravan park must be empty has prevented much residential use.

A footnote: Walney's least-welcome visitor was George Fox, founder of the Quakers. When he first came in 1852, unable to speak to the curate of North Scale, he visited a James Lancaster and apparently made a convert. With this success, he returned to Walney but was attacked by Lancaster's wife and other villagers accusing him of bewitching the convert. Lancaster saved Fox from injury by the armed reception gang by pushing his boat off the shore so he could safely get away. He never returned, but Lancaster preached the Quaker cause and even once accompanied Fox across the Atlantic.

Furness Abbey

Avoiding built-up Barrow, we check in at the Abbey House Hotel, excellent and in lovely gardens. Before dinner there's time to explore the grounds and wander down to Furness Abbey, which I've frequently seen and found intriguing when going past by train but have never had the opportunity to visit. Though they wouldn't have foreseen the trains along a double-track railway, the monk's naturally chose a glorious setting, a flat enclave in a wooded valley.

We hold onto each other to avoid slipping on the rough steep path down. We pause to glance at a train (virtually all are now dull two-car diesel units, but many times I came this way in comfort, sometimes on a sleeper), but then gaze at a veritable village of ruins. What influence the monks must have had and what a shame their Abbey has become a ruin, albeit such a pretty red sandstone one as to inspire Wordsworth to describe it in The Prelude: 'A mouldering pile with fractured arch, belfry, and images, and living trees, a holy scene!'

Wordsworth made early use of the local station for his visit, but generally Furness Abbey has been somewhat ignored because of its remoteness. Yet it seems to us just as striking as the more popular great Yorkshire abbeys. At its height it was certainly powerful, with huge farming, trading and mining interests covering much of today's southern Cumbria and stretching to the Isle of Man and Ireland.

It was founded in 1123 by Stephen, later King of England, in the Order of Savigny, but around 1150 became Cistercian when the two orders merged. Such were its riches that inevitably it attracted raiders, including from Scotland, though Robert the Bruce extracted a handsome ransom from the abbot when agreeing not to plunder or burn it.

In the 16th century things went badly. Famine, plague and war had taken a steady toll, and in 1536 Henry VIII picked it as the first of the large monasteries to be dissolved. After four centuries of wielding vast though declining power, it was the second richest of the English Cistercian monasteries. In the end the last abbot, Robert Pyle, gave it to the King. He had been prominent among those opposing the King's grab, and was anxious to save his skin. Being involved in the Pilgrimage of Grace (the protest against suppression) was treasonable. The monks were pensioned off at £2 a head.

Along with the small museum, the visitors' centre has just closed for the day and, unlike most abbeys, it lacks maps and descriptive notices. Serious-minded visitors rent a portable recorder to guide them. We therefore have to absorb in general terms this treasure in what is known as the Valley of Deadly Nightshade. With the vast range of ruins to ourselves as the sun sinks behind the western trees, it is easy to marvel at the mix of worldliness and Godliness.

Passionate belief had to be behind such a lovely creation, yet we reflect that it was paid for by sheep on the Lake District fells, the digging of peat, making and selling of salt, leasing fishing rights, mining and smelting, growing crops... and innumerable other trading activities. So well must it all have been orchestrated that it makes much of modern business, and especially banking (whose follies are being revealed daily on our travels as we all see our investments shrink) seem utterly amateur.

Not that over the centuries the abbots would have lacked crises including no doubt individual transgressions. The difference was perhaps that the trading greed was corporate, at least ostensibly for the glory of God, certainly not for individual monks, though by the standards of the day they were spoilt in some ways even as they led an austere life. 'The chairman of the Royal Bank of Scotland might have been a touch more modest had he got up to say prayers in the wee hours,' is my caustic comment as we stop in our gentle walk around more or less in silence.

Before lead was stolen from its roof, windows smashed and the theft of stone aided natural decay, the Abbey must have been as magnificent as any. Naturally it was not all built at once, for the steadily-earned riches financed many extensions and decorations. We like the spacious grass areas between sections of the ruins, and even the informality of arrangements, unusual for English Heritage, including tables and chairs allowing refreshments to be served around parts of the ruins.

When one imagines what it would have been like when it was all-of-a-piece without grassland gaps, the sheer scale overwhelms. More than enough, including most of the nave and central tower, survives to impress, but then the Perpendicular western tower, a later addition survives at 60ft was once 160ft high. And the seven vaulted tabernacled canopies flanking the high altar, which would have been used by the priest and assistants for mass, hint at what other fine detail has gone, though some unusual survivals are in the museum.

There are ample thoughts to keep up our spirits as we tackle the stiff climb back to our hotel for my birthday dinner. It seems a long time since I found my card from Sheila on my pillow at the Roa Island guest house this morning. A day to remember.

Ulverston, Holker Gardens and Grange-over-Sands

Next morning, avoiding built-up Barrow, we cut across to the coast road a little north of Rampside and follow it along the beach at Adlingham and Baycliff (obviously popular among Barrow folk) until forced slightly inland to Ulverston. With its random mix of cobbled alleyways, old-fashioned shops and a monument that at first glance looks like a lighthouse at the town's top, Ulverston is a place I've always liked.

We explore on foot, window gazing and popping into a few shops, and have morning coffee at a large pub commanding a view of much of the town. This is how market towns used to be. It is where Stan Laurel belonged and so its attractions now include a huge collection of memorabilia in the Laurel & Hardy Museum.

On our way back down I can't resist popping into a small but surprisingly busy bookshop, nor can I avoid buying another of those books of highly local interest which give such vivid glimpses of our past.

Lost Children: Ulverston's Workhouse in the 19th century is scarcely a bestseller, but June Whitehead tells a moving tale of the days when Ulverston, serving a flourishing iron-ore business, cotton and tanning also important, was an affluent, bustling place with theatres, bookshops and assembly rooms. Barrow-in-Furness was still waking itself up from being a sleepy village. 'We have many things to be proud of in our history, but the Victorian workhouse system is not one of them,' she says in her Foreword. Being poor, not being able to support oneself even in dire circumstances, was seen as disgraceful, yet the system bred poverty.

It is now hard to believe that in a period of great industrial growth and prosperity for this country there was also such desperate poverty, especially in the cities, and that those in greatest need were treated with such little sensitivity. The workhouses were grim, dispassionate institutions, often overcrowded and badly run and the stigma associated with them persisted long after many of the buildings were taken over and used as hospitals. No amount of new paint could eliminate it from the minds of the older generations and many sad stories were told to those nursing in Ulverston Hospital during the years when its days as a workhouse were still in living memory. This sad time in our history now lives on... in tales handed down through the generations.

My spirits sinking, I immediately delve into some of the horrible case histories, almost unaware of more people crowding into the shop. I'm brought back to life by the bookshop's owner, Liz Drew, offering us a glass of wine. We've happened on her retirement party, and join in the happy buzz – happy partly because the Bookshop at the Tinners' Rabbit (with a doorway to a separate high-class gift shop) has a new owner.

'I've had a long stint, and its very tying. I'm hoping to do a bit more publishing myself,' says Liz.

'But we'll miss you,' replies a chorus of satisfied customers. Even my publisher knew her. You don't have to run a vast emporium to make your mark in the book trade.

My purchase is already signed by the author, and Liz Drew adds that it was bought at her retirement party. So when those sad children with piercing eyes gaze at me from the cover, I shall recall the sharp contrast of emotions.

The railway takes a short cut by bridge, but to continue east along the coast we have to follow the road all the way round the deep incursion of salt water to Haverthwaite. As the tide goes out this becomes Cartmel Sands across which people sometimes walk. The huge sandy area of Morecambe Bay where cocklers have been in the news will also rapidly be exposed. Then a diversion to visit another garden attached to a great estate: Holker's Gardens. Again we walk round in the rain, alternately light and heavy, admiring the juxtaposition of formal gardens grassland with species trees, notably the Great Holker Lime with a girth of almost eight metres.

We love the steps up to a fountain with water cascading down channels on either side and imagine the scarlet display around it when the rhododendrons are out in spring. But here is another abandoned walled garden – apart from a few trees still clinging to the decaying mortar. Is it because the crops grown in walled gardens were not showy enough for tourists that their resurrection has such low priority? Lord and Lady Cavendish, who also welcome visitors to part of their stately home, have already done so much to improve the other parts of the garden that might the sheltered, walled area soon gain their attention?

Before having to seek shelter, we pause to talk to one of the gardeners, better-dressed for the weather than we are. Kate Harbinson, from Carnforth, one of a complement of three full and three part-time gardeners, says it's a lovely place to work but points out scores of rain-damaged flowers. 'The sad thing is that there are very few honeybees this year.' But she rejoices in a lone bumblebee, struggling in its search for nectar.

When I tell her I've just read the new New Naturalist book on bumblebees, she says that they are also under threat and that I should support the bumblebee conservation trust: http://www.bumblebeeconservationtrust.co.uk/ 'Bumblebees are such faithful, hardworking things, out early and keeping at it late each season.' It transpires she did a special bumblebee project while at horticultural college. With such committed professionally-trained men and especially women we have found in many gardens, there's real hope for the future, and it's good to note the respect in which they are clearly held by their employers.

To complete our almost circling the Lake District, we make for our favourite Grange-over-Sands for a light lunch at a favourite café. Or at least that was the plan, but such is the rain, and it would be quite a walk, that instead we go to the Cumbria Grand Hotel, which for David & Charles's 21st birthday we totally took over for a Victorian Weekend. That included walking several hundred people across Morecambe Bay guided by its famous Royally-appointed sand pilot (see *Journey*).

Sheila isn't too enthusiastic about the hotel's run-down look. 'It's vast – beyond what they can afford to keep in trim these days.' It transpires that since those jollifications, it was closed for several years. Though the place is a bit of a morgue, lunch actually isn't bad. To make so large an hotel sparkle for today's visitors would cost several millions, far more than has been, or no doubt can be, afforded in the attempt to bring it back to life.

Some Holiday

Now we're going on real holiday. Bliss: nothing is planned for a whole week at the Lakeside Hotel, at the bottom of Lake Windermere. This is where the passenger fleet is moored for the night and ships connect with trains – on a heritage steam line which however only goes to Haverthwaite. I recall that after changing at Foxfield having come down from Coniston, I changed again at Ulverston, and at Lakeside walked across to a steamer for Bowness, where I was staying. But we rejoice that the large 'steamers' such as *Teal* and *Swan* still ply their graceful way offering a frequent and much-used summer service.

That's when there's a summer. It rained, and I mean rained, all our precious week. We had a lovely upgrade to a lodge and watched the nearly empty ships pass, but it was pointless catching one. For the most part we read (books and the good Lakeland and Cumbrian magazines), and enjoyed being at leisure in that rarity of a fine hotel in a fine location. Our daily highlight was being visited by a score or so of ducks whose leader waddled to the French window and pecked at it to announce: 'Feeding time.'

One day, when it was a tad brighter, we did venture again to Grange-over-Sands, parking at the station, still hoping for that walk along the sea wall. As we approached there was another downpour. Many leaves obscured nasty raised edges of the paving stones outside the station, and Sheila tripped and fell, front down, sliding along on her face. A real bloody mess. That meant a visit to Kendal Hospital, where doctors agreed nothing serious had been done. It was the hospital where her brother-in-law Bryan had been sent after a stroke shortly before his death, and where Frances Lincoln, founder of this book's publishing house now run by her widower, actually died.

Ullswater and At Last a Cruise

After seven days of near continuous rain, the sun comes out as we prepare to leave. It lights up the day's first boat as it sets off up Windermere; if only we'd been staying, we could at last have enjoyed being on her. Never mind; the better day helps us enjoy the drive through outstanding scenery, first alongside Windermere to the outskirts of Windermere town, and then up through Troutbeck and over the dramatic Kirkstone Pass, where we comment that the whole world and his wife seem to have come out to celebrate the reappearance of the sun.

We relish great views as we descend through Patterdale with a sparkling Ullswater below. It takes a surprising time, and we have to take care as there is a cycle race, but in due course we reach The Inn on the Lake at Glenridding, a noble pile in beautifully-kept grounds, three star and thoroughly recommendable.

At the end of a snack lunch we simultaneously comment that today we could actually take a cruise... and the timetable shows a round trip is still possible later in the afternoon. When we reach the landing stage, complete with shop and café, there's some surprise we want to travel.

'You may have noticed we've been having lots of rain. The pier at Howtown is flooded so we can't land there.'

But, yes, they'll honour their commitment by running a non-stop round trip just for us. We board, and are just about to set off when a young couple arrive, doubling the takings. As we progress up the lake, the assistant skipper brings us all a cup of tea, and points out where the high water level has special impact. A cruise at last... and I've always specially enjoyed Ullswater, a long lake with real waves and a pair of major bends adding to the feeling of remoteness. It's of the Lake District but a bit aloof, on the periphery. Empty hills rise sharply, especially to the east.

As it happens we were here not so long ago, on our way back from Wales and, before we turn, see the famous hotel at which we then stayed, Sharrow Bay Country House. Then we run alongside the lane where we walked after lunch on that occasion.

At that hotel, I recall talking to Dr Angela Herrick over a pre-dinner drink in the drawing room about changes in the medical and book businesses, both revolutionised in our day. She's a great reader and will always be faithful to the printed book, never seduced by electronic versions. You certainly meet keen readers in the lounges of top hotels. Then a splendid meal before returning to our room with a view up the lake from the balcony where we sit in the sun.

Back to today, another interesting thing about Ullswater is that the first steamers were not for tourists but were working boats. Ours, the *Lady of the Lake*, the oldest of enterprising Ullswater Navigation's fleet of four (a fifth on the way), is aged 131. Built as a supply vessel for a lead mine, it once sank but, refloated, needing only minor patching. The staff told us that her sister plies Lake Titicaca in the Andes: they both had to be assembled on their respective lakes from what today would be called kit form. My publisher questioned whether there really was a sister ship, and when we asked the company to check the answer came back that it must just have been a legend.

So back to a near-deserted pier at Glenridding, having to avoid the flood affecting part of the car park to reach our car. Nearby is a monument to Donald Campbell whose first water speed record of 202.15mph was on Ullswater. Having steadily beaten this and become the first person to beat both the water and land speed records in a single year, he was killed when *Bluebird K7* flipped and disintegrated at over 300mph on Coniston Water. We well remember the numerous radio reports of his successful and failed attempts including his last words: 'I'm going... oh...' Today such noisy events would not be welcomed on the Lakes. Then to The Inn on the Lake for dinner and a sound night's sleep.

The reason for two recent visits to Ullswater is that, apart from being a favourite, it is close to the M6, offering easy access to Carlisle station. So again we turn in our hire car and catch a train for Edinburgh on our way home to Nairn.

· XXXVII ·

REMOTER ESSEX AND ITS ISLANDS

Saffron Walden and Great Dunmow

Though most of it is flat, Essex is a county of contrasts as we discovered especially on a trip to its remote islands. First however Saffron Walden, one of those places I've spent longer thinking about than visiting. The only time I stayed there was for Christmas 1937, when I was eight.

It was our one and only family Christmas away from home, and the first time I had heard people talking about excessive drinking. We four had a table to ourselves. At times unaccustomedly rowdy, the other score or so of guests shared a long central table. The experience of a pre-war market town and its principal inn made a deep impression. Every detail was fascinating, though not always comfortable.

We had changed trains at Audley End, crossing a snow-covered bridge to join the branch train for the last 1 miles. Arrival at the station and checking into the hotel are lost in emotion overcoming memory, but the station, where trains lingered before continuing their journey to the junction at the other end of the line (really a pair of separate branches that linked here), is strongly recalled. Probably for the first time, I studied the services and doodled an 'improved' timetable.

The station was on slightly raised ground and commanded a fine view of the town and, standing above it, the large church which I was disappointed that Mum, staunchly Methodist, didn't want to take me to see. Another noticeable building was the hospital; I wondered how bad it would be for those having to spend Christmas trapped there. Then I was with Dad when he saw (and later wrote a poem about) an old lady standing at her gate anxiously waiting to see if the postman had brought anything, and trudging forlornly back up her path when he hadn't.

With Mum and my younger sister, after it had become dark on Christmas Eve, I watched the tactics and enjoyed the banter of the market stall holders trying to sell out of perishable stock. That, too, was sad, especially when Mum pointed out those she described as well-heeled people who could perfectly well have paid a fair price, bargaining hard and almost certainly causing the trader loss. This was also the first time

I took an interest in trade, preparing the way for dealings in Newton Abbot market years later: see *Journey*. But the most poignant memory of all is of Mum warning that our Rose & Crown was a fire trap and telling us what to do if we had to get out quickly. The thatched roof, through which our dormer windows protruded, seemed the very devil threatening to spoil Christmas Day itself.

Mum was right, though it was not until thirty two years and a day later, on Boxing Day 1969, that eleven of the guests lost their lives in a vicious fire that destroyed the building. It was one of two Trust Houses (the other being Exmouth's Imperial) at which we stayed within months, in which guests were killed in later fires. The very name Saffron Walden has often spoken to me of fear.

I have frequently planned to return but, like so much of rural Essex, it is off the beaten track, not even with convenient M11 junctions. It has to be a destination in its own right, which it is today. Six decades later, I'm back in the market, as lively as ever, though much less of the produce has been grown locally, and a good part of what is now on offer wasn't heard of when I was a boy.

'How long have you been in Saffron Walden?' I ask a stallholder.

'More years than you'd remember.'

'The only time I've been before was for Christmas 1937, at the Rose & Crown.'

'Blimey. You'll see some changes.' After talking about the famous fire, he says: 'Developers soon had their beady eyes on the site. People were very upset that they didn't rebuild the hotel but let it go for commercial development. It's now Boots. It wouldn't happen today, and we're all keenly watching moves now that Lloyds Bank has burnt down.

You say you came by train? Crikey. First the station was a garage and then it went for housing and a car park. Remote Britain? Wouldn't say we're remote, but off the map, yes, still rural Essex with lots of country people though some work in London and at Stansted Airport. The market goes on in its old ways. People love it; we don't do too badly.'

As I go to Boots, I recall the large plaster bunch of grapes that used to hang outside the Rose & Crown. A real period piece, the building has been a great loss, but ironically my old *Murray's Handbook* points out that many timber buildings survive [and still do], the town having been free of the fires that swept through so many ancient places.

Murray and his modern successors are kind to Saffron Walden, but Murray delves into its charm and antiquities in much greater depth: 'A narrow tongue of land shoots itself out like a promontory, encompassed with a valley in the form of a horseshoe, enclosed by distant and delightful hills... The church, 200ft long, stands above the town, and has a handsome tower, with pinnacles and open-work battlements, surmounted by a crocketed spire, 193ft high.'

We listen to the local gossip in a café, and explore the narrow streets around the market with their half-timbered overhanging buildings, antique and second-hand bookshops. I like the vibrant colours of some of the old buildings which work well when there is a co-operative effort to create contrast and harmony. Named after a bulb – it's claimed that saffron was introduced here long before the tulip bubble – Saffron Walden is still very much a country place. We take our last glimpse of the church above the town between the chalk hills from Station Road, the name retained as in so many towns and villages long without trains.

In six decades, actually much less has changed here than in the world as a whole, and we still drive through real country, south to Thaxted with more half-timbered buildings and another landmark spire, towering above the church where Gustav Holst was organist while composing much of *The Planets*. On through more well-cultivated rolling hills to Great Dunmow for a night in a 15th century Restaurant with Rooms: a delightful bedroom across a courtyard with an excellent dinner and afterwards a walk around the village. Though Sheila notices some high-class dress shops, the place has obviously had better or at least more communal days. Where the footpath runs alongside a pond, with water meadows beyond, I ask a passer-by if he lives here and could spare a moment. He's soon telling me:

'Tesco has torn the heart out of our lovely village. Private shops are suffering and we're bound to lose more.' When I comment that though we're on the doorstep of Stansted Airport, we don't hear planes, any more than we did at Saffron Walden, he explains that they always fly around and not overhead. But adds:

'You know they're talking about another runway and big expansion, which would bring it closer to us. The village is totally divided. Employment is everything to some people, but there are lots of us anxious to protect what survives of rural Essex.'

I'm never proud of being born and spending my first years in Essex, but then that was at Gidea Park, decidedly not remote. Essex is a county partly swallowed up by London, and the remainder under its pull, yet still with gems of villages and very individual people. A county, too, of few main, congested roads (little motorway) yet huge systems of quiet narrow lanes.

Over the years I visited many Essex authors, from the famous and controversial such as anti-porn campaigner Mary Whitehouse to specialists only respected in their narrow spheres. Nearly all lived in out-of-the-way villages (Coggeshall is a good example) where they enjoyed what seemed a perfect lifestyle. Until, that is, they spoke of visiting an office or going shopping or an evening out, when so often it wasn't to the nearest local centre or county town but to Town. But then they couldn't imagine being 'cut off' in Devon leave alone Nairn. I'll say this: if Devon and Scotland are full of traditions and superstitions, but they grow yet more naturally out of the woodwork in every Essex village where history is long and never finished with.

To Southend-on-Sea

The taxi driver at Paddington – we've arrived from Bath – smiles when I say we want to go to Fenchurch Street. 'It'll take almost as long as getting to Heathrow... longer, possibly.' So it proved, though the meter doesn't tick as furiously as on the M4. He happens to be the first and the most interesting of the cabbies I ask to suggest the most remote place in London: see next chapter.

The smallest of the London termini, Fenchurch Street is a busier and happier place than when it served what for a time was known as the 'Misery Line'. It is hard to fault today's service, intense with interesting stopping patterns at peak times, and generous at others. Sitting in the train's front, we have a carriage almost to ourselves and make the best of clear windows. Until running along the sea at the approaches to Southend, the scenery isn't great, but if one works hard it is possible to catch glimpses of many different Essexes, from Romford where I was born but have always found too close to London to be its own place, to patches of intensive agriculture (even between Dagenham and new-town Basildon), creeks and Canvey Island. But how I'd hate to be a daily commuter.

Many commute from Southend-on-Sea and its string of surburban stations, several of them on the coast, yet Southend has always struck me as very much its own place. With over 150,000 people, it certainly has scale to support a major shopping centre, with enough who don't commute to keep it busy every day. And while its seaside can still be overcrowded, especially over the year's first fine weekends when there's a pent-up demand, it has better hotels and in most ways is more up-together than say Weymouth, with which it shares early royal support to get going as a resort. The Prince Regent chose it for a healthy home for Princess Caroline at the *south end* at what was then called Prittlewell. The town was renamed.

I've arranged a taxi to take us to Foulness tomorrow and, there being no other waiting at the station, call the same firm. It comes in a jiff, and we explain our plans to the driver, including the fact I've booked a superior car (supplement a few pounds) for tomorrow and that I've been told that the driver will come armed with the necessary pass to get onto the island where the Ministry of Defence exercises tight control. 'It's known as the mystery island,' says our driver.

Meanwhile we ask for a quick tour of the town and especially the prom. That's extremely long, changing its character passing slot-machine palaces and delightful Georgian houses. The beach could absorb an army, though it is not exactly pretty and this afternoon we see why Southend has to pretend it is on the sea. The sand or is it silt is a pretty gloomy colour.

Naturally we home in on the town's trademark, the mighty pier, so long that a mini-train runs for those in a hurry to be over the waves at low tide. Then to our promenade hotel at Thorpe Bay, up with the best of those commanding a view of the sea – except that, taking the afternoon off, it has almost disappeared,. We do so too; having a nap.

When we have a cuppa outside, we feel the stiff breeze coming off the sea – just visible in the distance, still reluctant to make our acquaintance. The Roslin, at the time of our visit the highest-rated of Southend's four AA hotels, may lack a rosette but obviously has a reputation for good food. At dinner, the dining room is crowded; fish is ingeniously prepared and everything excellent. By the time we finish, the sea has come close enough to warrant our crossing the road to examine it – as though it were a great novelty we seldom see rather than live closely overlooking from our main rooms at home. That's how the sea – so different at every point along our marvellous coastlines – bewitches us.

Next morning, our taxi arrives late, isn't a premier vehicle, and the driver says he knows nothing about a pass to Foulness which he says we should have organised ourselves.

The radio link blares into life. 'Mr Thomas ordered a premier car, and we're sending one out to him. Would you please apologise to Mr Thomas.'

'He's OK.'

'Would you please apologise to him.'

Silence. He's not of the apologising type. Neither is he good at taking advice for, when the manager explains where we are to meet the replacement car, we sail straight by. 'No matter,' says our driver. Despite my suggesting that he arranges a definite rendezvous, he then passes the replacement vehicle at speed.

Eventually we pull up beside the waiting premier car pointing in the wrong direction, and start transferring our luggage. The first driver's own washing, which he'd forgotten to leave at the launderette this morning, is also transferred. Thinking it to be ours, the second driver says: 'Shall

I give it back to him so he can drop it for you to pick up later.' Helpful, except it isn't ours and anyway we're not coming back to Southend.

Then, just about to start the engine, he adds: 'Excuse me, is it my imagination but wasn't there a second passenger?' The delay has made Sheila thirsty and she's popped to a shop for a bottle of water.

'So have you got a pass for Foulness?' I ask the new driver as we start once more. No – and he knows nothing about it being promised us by his firm when I made the reservation.

Quickly we are at the control point by the bridge to Foulness. I explain what's happened to the duty official... and that we live in the North of Scotland and have travelled here specially for this book. While frequently letting through those with passes, he looks worried. He's certainly sympathetic... and relieved when a senior official arrives.

Pauline Burrell, MOD Range Representative of the Defence Test & Evaluation Group, is also sympathetic. Giving me her card, she asks if we might be able to return tomorrow by when a pass could be issued. I explain our tight schedule and that we're a day's travel from home. 'Could we phone the shop to explain who we are and arrange to visit it?'

'Yes, but I'm afraid not today. I'd like to help. But there's nothing I can do but suggest you organise it another time.'

So NOT to Foulness, the Mystery Island

'You're not having much luck this morning,' says our driver. 'If it's any compensation, there's not really much to see. It's nearly all out of bounds firing ranges these days; even the pub and church have closed and many homes have been demolished as people have left. We'll now have more time to see interesting places.' Indeed we do, but I'm still curious about the mystery island, much of which is said to be below high tide level. Our driver does however call his office and gets me the telephone number of the shop so at least I have a contact. Foulness isn't the first place we've tried to get to for this book which, ultimately, we've learnt almost more about than had we actually visited.

The shopkeeper isn't very helpful, abandoning the phone the moment a customer comes through the door though, when I call back, I do prise out the name of the chairman of the Parish Council.

After we've returned home, Mr G Bickford who lives in Churchend, one of two settlements, the other being Courtend, takes the prize for being the hardest person to get hold of. He works irregular shifts and, if he's not at work, sleeping during the day or out with his wife, he's paying a visit off the island. Eventually he calls me and tells me:

'We're down to about 150 people, going down and down, because there isn't much here now. The church closed and is falling down, the pub closed a couple of years ago when the landlord retired and nobody was prepared to take it on and put it back in better order. The shop, which still has a Post Office is only open from breakfast to lunch. The Parish Council has no assets, no village hall or public paths, but a representative from the Ministry of Defence comes to our meetings and usefully discuss things like access problems.

I love it here. We've no vandalism or unwanted callers, but it's a bit bleak and not for everyone. Apart from a little farming, people commute to work or else work like I do for the defence people.' He proves particularly useful in saying I should get in touch with the person behind the Heritage Centre which is open each 1st Sunday in the months between April and October between noon and four. 'You don't need a pass to get to it, but you can't look round elsewhere.'

Once a journalist, always one. Never give up when first rebuffed. The smallest leads can eventually prove highly rewarding. So thank you shop.

Peter Carr, chairman of the Heritage & Archaeological Association, not only tells me more but trusts me with three of his precious books which arrive in next morning's post. He's a farmer, with 1,500 acres of barley and rape. Once world champion for yields on what has always been highly fertile soil, he has to employ four so 'we can blitz it when we're allowed access. We can be on a knife-edge at harvest time. Yes. It's a funny old place, not everyone's choice – another family of five are leaving by the end of the month – and we've only twice really been in the news.

In the 1953 floods when the sea was so rough at high tide that, though the surrounding wall was supposed to be high enough, sufficient water crashed over it to destroy it from the inside, and there was a mini-Dunkirk when everyone had to be rescued in a hurry. Then there was the proposal to put London's third airport on Maplin Sands alongside us. Crazy idea really, difficult land, fog and bird risks... and we're 50 miles from London, though we clearly see what we nickname the towers of Southend. Yet we're Britain's fourth largest island, after the Isle of Wight, Hayling Island and Sheppey: 7,000 acres with a fourteen-mile coastline and high sea walls. In a way it's only our past that knits us together as a community and stops us being overwhelmed by the military. We enjoy archaeological walks: two of those next weekend.'

The first of the trio of books is *Foulness: A History of an Essex Island Parish*. The title is misleading in that until the mid-16th century, when the island's church was built, the island was carved up between several mainland parishes, a trio of which had separate ferry services, the main route being to Burnham-on-Crouch. Foulness folk were often disadvantaged. Tithes had to be paid to the old and the new parishes, says the author, J R Smith, Essex's assistant archivist.

In those days, Foulness was really a series of separate marshes separated by drainage channels, with tracks running on the top of some of their banks around the periphery. The channels could only be crossed by a plank. The sole 'land' access was a long Broomway (so named because it was marked by poles), submerged at low tide, on which many people lost their lives over the generations. It might have been of Roman origin; certainly the Romans were on Foulness. The first inhabitants would have been shepherds.

When the population peaked at 754 in 1874, apart from the obvious problems of isolation, cottages were overcrowded and health extremely poor, attributed to damp and shortage of fresh water.

The first travel book on Britain to be translated into English (D&C did a facsimile reprint, itself now a collector's item) was *Camden's Britannia* of 1695, which described how dairying was at the heart of the marshes economy.

> Plentifull in grasse, and rich in Cattaile, but Sheepe especially where all their doing is in making of Cheese; and there shall ye have men take the womens office in hand and milke Ewes: whence those huge thicke Cheeses are made that are vented and sould not onely into all parts of England, but into forraign nations also, for the rusticall people, labourers, and handicraftes men to fill their bellies, and feed upon.

In later times, the emphasis changed to cereals, the rich, silty soil also supporting abundant flora, and Foulness is famous for its bird life.

Fowlness: The Mystery Isle 1914-1939 (Fowlness and Foulness were once common alternatives) tells a more personal story, lively in social background. The church and its ministers (the island's effective leaders) and choirs, the church school built for 120 pupils, a pioneer trestle bridge with a petrol railcar on it, steam threshers and family occasions are brought to life in words and pictures. For most, it was certainly no easy life. Agriculture was tightly controlled by the lord of the manor – no 'unusual' crops such as rape to be grown – the military ultimately buying out the manorial rights and sometimes seeming to act as cruelly as their private predecessors; for example, at one time relatives were denied access to tend the graves of their loved ones.

The final volume, *The Islands of Essex* by Ian Yearsley, not only puts Foulness in perspective but covers populated Canvey Island (see chapter XVIII) and Mersea Island (of which more in a moment) and a host of fascinating little isles such as nature-reserve Northey Island in the River Blackwater... mainly treeless islands (though one, another nature reserve, near Southend, is called Two Tree Island) which 'can be immensely beautiful and times when they can be immensely depressing'.

To Burnham-on-Crouch

So, back to our journey, turned away from Foulness, we head for Burnham-on-Crouch. At one point the land beyond Burnham is less than a mile as the crow flies from the flat north of Foulness, where its main quay is situated. However, on journeys up and down the East Anglian coast, one is used to major detours around rivers.

We start across a flat, featureless country through a series of villages to Rochford, a sprawling area of suburbs served by the inland railway route from Southend to London, which does brisk peak-hour business here. Since we have to come this far to round the River Roach, we decide to continue north to meet its estuary first on its south side. Our immediate destination is Baltic Wharf, a mile or so further upstream than Burnham-on-Crouch. Actually on Wallasea Island, it's reached by a bridge, of which we a scarcely aware.

There's a huge timber yard, served by large ships from the Baltic. One unloaded yesterday; they are still sorting some of its timber. There seems enough to supply every British builder's yard for months. There's also a busy marina with accommodation and other facilities. It is the kind of place at the edge of civilisation I love. Beyond here, Wallasea is an almost uninhabited marsh with a couple of rough tracks crossing the frequent north-to-south drainage channels. The deep river on whose banks we walk has long been the highway for commercial shipping as well as pleasure boating. Except for the noise of an occasional car, the only sound is of sea birds chattering away, there's a gentle breeze, but it's warm... and the sun shines.

After taking it all in, we go by a complicated series of lanes to reach the Crouch estuary's head at Battlesbridge where, typically today, a handsome grain store is now an antique centre. The road nearest the estuary on its other side is scarcely a speedway, and I'm envious of those travelling on an electric train along the single-track branch line through Burnham-on-Crouch to Southminster. It runs perfectly straight for some miles and is closer to the river, commanding better views, especially of what remains of Bridgemarsh Island.

That has a fascinating tale of how persistent, maybe misguided, man has always been in putting every possible acre of land to work. After a bad flood in 1736, it was drained, piled and given a sea wall. Cattle and sheep were kept there, profit also coming from the wild duck and eels thriving in the dykes. Even a causeway was built. But some of the animals were drowned in the next big flood, in 1887. The sea wall was patched up, and next clay for bricks was dug out and taken by narrow-gauge tracks to a quay. Thames Barges then took it on to brickworks across the river. This didn't pay for long and, after the great flood of 1953, the island was abandoned – though ironically not before some of its clay was used to fill sandbags to protect other parts of the inundated coast.

Burnham-on-Crouch is one of those places one instantly falls for. The main street and promenade along the river, linked by short cross streets, contain many delightful old buildings including pubs many wooden and painted. There are also more modern outstanding buildings, notably a fine Grade-II* listed Royal Corinthian Yacht Club of 1931. The red-brick octagonal clock tower of 1877 is worthy of attention, too. The black-brick quoins and diapering are distinctly unusual, as is the fact that the building stands on the wide pavement but by no means blocks it since there is a broad archway through it. A nice touch is a plaque in memory of Sidney Harvey 'who served this town as clockwinder at the tower for forty four years until his retirement in 1983'.

We are so taken by the little town that, walking along the street and coming across our driver, to his delight, tell him we're going to stay longer than first arranged. He knows just the pub for his lunch.

Burnham is a confident little place, twenty miles from the next and larger town, Colchester. The population is only 7,500, yet it has a frequent train service patronised by commuters to London. It is decidedly not commuterland though, and its strength is based on it acting as service centre for much of the Dengie peninsula between the rivers Crouch and Blackwater. Visiting yachts and tourism add to its success, but it is no more a holiday resort than commuterland. It feels like a town with a purpose, or better a set of mixed purposes, the broad main street as characterful as any, and the river's promenade thoroughly welcoming.

We're spoilt for choice for lunch, but picking The Contented Sole is spot on. High class but not pretentious, with sensible prices and matter-of-fact service, it is the kind of fish restaurant of which coastal Scotland is desperately short. Our sole is deliciously but unfussily cooked.

Apparently Burnham-on-Crouch wasn't always as attractive or even as healthy as today. Among the many writers who have commented on it, Daniel Defoe concentrated on 'the strange decay of sex'. Dengie peninsula men used to the damp and fogs tended to choose wives from higher areas who quickly succumbed and needed replacing.

Mersea Island and its Winery

We had originally planned to cross the peninsula near to its north eastern point at Bradwell Waterside, where there is a long history of shipping and smuggling, every age since the Romans changing the emphasis on trade. 'Now it's just a marina and power station,' our driver says. The old quay, once regularly visited by Thames Barges, isn't used commercially any more.

So we opt to go straight to today's last island, Mersea Island, though that involves going round the long estuary of the Blackwater with its mini-Osea Island (Defoe says Londoners came for sport, often returning 'with an Essex ague on their backs, which they find a heavier load than the fowls they shot') and Northey Island. The latter, now a quiet National Trust refuge, is famous for the 991 Battle of Marldon, recorded in a locally-woven tapestry in the tradition of the Bayeaux Tapestry.

We pass close to tonight's hotel on the way to the causeway called The Strood to Mersea Island, after which the road immediately divides into those for East and West Mersea. First East Mersea, hoping to catch a glimpse of the River Colne. Each lane ends in a gate and it all seems privately exclusive. I console myself by whistling, realising I've subconsciously chosen Onward Christian Soldiers... I'd read that Sabine Baring-Gould, better known for his time in Devon, was once Rector here.

So we retrace our steps to the entrance we noticed to Mersea Island Vineyard, whose founder-owner, Roger Barber, tells us his career was in electrical engineering in the smoke. 'This is retirement,' he says, pointing to the vineyard and a tractor and trailer on which his son is busy transferring stock. 'We do dry and medium dry... and also sparkling.'

When I'm foolish enough to say I'd enjoyed Camel Valley Brut from the edges of Bodmin Moor (chapter XXVIII), he replies 'Ours is honestly far better'. Since we're going home by public transport, we cannot take a sample bottle, and they don't do mail order. 'This is mainly a tourist island and we only sell wholesale, most of it on the island.' He has also started a local brewery. Undoubtedly a good businessman, he's franchised out the café, to which we invite our increasingly-friendly driver, who says: 'I've never had a day quite like this; a very interesting change.'

The café's ambience is great, our waitress taking such an interest in what we're doing that she's asked to be given details of this title when it is published. Would that more businesses franchised out their catering, for orchestrating, preparing and serving good food is far better done by self-motivated individuals in their own right. Corporate delegation with style is elusive.

I comment to nobody in particular that some writers talk about an archipeligo of Essex islands but, while most are chunks of marsh that just happen to have been separated from the mainland, this is quite different: the most island-like yet, the most ordinary, a piece of delightful wooded countryside with hills making it hard to realise we're still in Essex.

'But we are very much an island,' says Roger Barber. 'We realise that at spring tides when The Strood is impassable for a couple of hours twice a day. And in many ways we're unique. We have 30 per cent less rainfall than Colchester only two miles away, and 12 April is the latest we've ever had frost. Camel Valley can't equate that.'

He adds: 'With just 6,500 people living on the island of seven square miles, we have a strong feeling of community. A lot happens here.'

West Mersea is the larger settlement, a prosperous, brightly-painted little place with cafés and restaurants, small hotels and large camp sites, a busy marina on which Mersea Week is based, a lifeboat station and a range of churches. Many retired people live here, but The Strood takes others who work in Colchester... and brings visitors year round. There's also British history in miniature, with early Christianity, Danish raids in the 9th century, many Roman remains and those of an abbey or priory.

Tolleshurst Knights and Tollesbury and its Light Railway

So, at the end of a fascinating trip, we reach our Five Lakes Hotel at Tolleshurst Knights: four stars, AA 77 per cent and two rosettes, a civilised oasis in a good hotel desert. I've been reflecting on the economy of rural Essex. Basically it has always been a backward or traditional, almost deprived, area... yet has a remarkable record of full employment and avoidance of the worst effects of recessions: fewer ups and downs than most of Britain.

Agriculture still dominates. Farms may be very different from the days when most people actually worked on the land, but the very fact that it still yields riches means that large industrial plants remain rare. Moreover, while it has its downside, the fact that so many workers commute to London has also reduced the need for large-scale diversification.

With the notable exception of Southend-on-Sea, far enough away from London and populous enough to be its own place, I don't care much for Essex towns, which (though Colchester less than Chelmsford, and much less than Romford) seem to lack provincial pride. The villages and smaller towns where age-old superstitions as well as traditions are still amazingly strong, absorbed more than killed by commuters (except where there's an overwhelming number of them), retain their individuality... and their pubs with low doorways where an increasing proportion of people – these days women as well as men – have to duck. Ye Olde is relished, while there's just not the demand for many luxury hotels.

Five Lakes is warmly acceptable. Walking around the outside of the building with its wings of several lengths, takes a surprising time introducing us to a golf course, other sporting facilities and gardens including a large pond. To be successful, the large hotel has to be all-things to all people: many come for the sporting facilities, useful in attracting vital conference business, while it is a lovely setting for weddings and an automatic choice of hotel connoisseurs such as ourselves.

The big brasserie is mobbed and noisy, and we are glad to have opted for the restaurant, where a mere handful of us enjoy a truly super meal. The rosettes no doubt only apply here, not to the brasserie.

Next morning we give another taxi driver an adventure. Tolleshurst Knights is quickly dismissed as being a pleasant sprawling parish with little village core, though it is home to a Russian Orthodox monastery, Patriarchal Stavropegic Monastery, of St John the Baptist. Tolleshurst Knights was also a station on the long-defunct Kelvedon, Tiptree & Tollesbury Light Railway, a line I was especially sorry not to be in time to use. My father, Gilbert Thomas, obviously enjoyed writing about it.

> Truly, one need not travel far to discover things strange and unexpected. Kelvedon is little more than an hour's run from London, yet the tract of country that lies eastward of it is hardly surpassed by elemental peace by the remotest parts of Cornwall or Cumberland. The Tollesbury line carriages, while of an unusual and tramcar design, are of standard gauge. Only the stations possess the outward picturesqueness of the toy railway. It is the functional rather than the organic eccentricities that cause one to doubt whether one is really living in the 20th century.
>
> With much ado, we were despatched at schedule time. But we had not gone many yards before we stopped, and backed into the sidings to pick up some trucks. Within a quarter of a mile, we came again to a standstill, with much grinding of brakes and reverberation of buffers, the driver descending from his footplate to open the gates of a level crossing. Returning leisurely to his engine, he pulled the train through, and we then suffered the pangs and groans of another stoppage while the guard jumped off to close the gates. At Tiptree we returned five or six times to the platform. Since tickets are issued by the guard *en route,* no booking-offices are needed. Nor are there any

> signals or signalboxes. The solitary engine, fantastic as are some of its tricks, has apparently not acquired the art of running into itself.
>
> The evening train leaves Tollesbury before seven o'clock. A float drove up, and two churns of milk were deposited upon the station, where there already lay some dozen baskets of fruit consigned to Stratford Market. Then sundry villagers began to arrive. Fear seized me that the train might be uncomfortably crowded! I had not yet realised that one of the prime functions of the station was to supply a rendezvous for local gossip. The string of arks and wagons came to a spluttering standstill. A clergyman and one other person alighted.

The condensed quote is from the original of 1928, reprinted in *Double Headed.* Father went on to say there had been a long lay-over at Tollesbury while the crew and the porter gossiped with onlookers on the platform.

Many years ago I bought a series of mini-paintings of quaint stations, the best, obviously inspired by Tollesbury, being of one on a pier. Opened under the Light Railway Act to encourage cheaply-built rural lines, the KT&T never fulfilled expectations, but a mile extension across the marshes to the long pier on the Blackwater, opened a couple of years after the rest of the line, was inspired by the totally unrealistic expectation that a Continental ferry would serve it and a marina quickly develop. By the time of my father's trip, few if any trains ventured to it, though the timetable still left time to do so.

At least my father saw the Light Railway in its natural state. After the war, most people preferring to travel by the far faster bus, the tram-like carriages nearly always ran empty or with a handful of enthusiasts coming specially to experience the anachronism. But jam continued to be carried until 1962 and, when I was a boy, father and I felt we were supporting the line by eating the Tiptree-made brand.

Many country railways were built with ridiculous optimism, but the extension to the pier has to take the cake, so I'm curious to explore what remains. We note Tollesbury's decorative village sign of an agricultural scene – very Essex – and make our way to the site of the station, somewhat removed from the pretty village square, called Church Street.

How now to trace the route down to the pier? A gate blocks our way; I jump out and open it, persuading a somewhat reluctant taxi driver to come forward. Following what seems to be the lane round a bend, in a farmyard, we come to a handsome house and, to the driver's amazement, I jump out and ring the front doorbell. Andrew St Joseph is an interesting, helpful gentleman. Apologising for having to rush off to a conference he's leading, and so being unable to take us in his Land Rover, he says that virtually nothing remains of the pier or the line down to it – they were indeed lightly built – but if we venture down the lane until we reach a lake, we'll at least be able to see where it was. 'Don't go beyond the lake though; that's difficult.'

He does, however, have a moment for a brief conversation about what each of us does. I never cease to be amazed by the combinations of jobs people living in out-of-the-way corners combine to make a worthwhile lifestyle. He's a serious farmer, coastal expert redesigning defence works to resist erosion, a marine biologist and professional ornithologist and, I gather from what he first said, leads at least the occasional conference. Whatever his activity, he'd clearly be an enthusiastic leader.

Back in the car, despite being assured we've been given permission, our driver is nervous we are trespassing and, as we bump along a very rutted track, wonders if he'll be able to turn to get back. His HQ calls to ask when he'll be free, to which he replies along the lines that when a wild goose chase is over.

We duly reach the lake, the fields on either side no doubt part of Andrew St Joseph's farm, and my ambition is fulfilled as far as is practical. We certainly can't leave the taxi here to walk the remaining distance, and can see there's little trace of manmade disturbance along the Blackwater's shore. Across the water, not for the first time on the trip, we note the power station with its tall chimney at Bradwell Waterside. Coal in bulk is unloaded at a jetty in the river... so much less romantic than the small harbours from which the locally-mined stuff was exported along the coast, for example around St David's in Wales.

I now feel sorry for our driver, who has to reverse a long way along the rutted lane. 'Just hope nobody comes and asks what we're up to,' he says, breathing with relief when we are back at Tollesbury. 'Never been asked to do anything like that before. Though I'm always around the village, didn't know any of it was there. Fascinating what you're doing.'

Then back to the hotel for a light meal in the brasserie and by another taxi to Colchester's oddly-laid-out station for the express to Liverpool Street. Until recently National Express ran a fine restaurant car service; in a recession-inspired economy, all the staff have been sacked along with most of the East Coast mainline's helpful restaurant-car crews. Our swan-song breakfast and dinner, both excellent, were on a recent trip from home to the Central belt. Train travel steadily becomes less appealing, and we keep our fingers crossed that we will not lose our invaluable Highland sleeper which takes us home tonight.

· XXXVIII ·

THE LAST CHAPTER

Crowded and Lonely v Remote and Companionable

The world over, higher proportions of people live in cities. Many are extremely lonely, enjoying little neighbourliness, isolated in concrete jungles with congested traffic, fumes and noise. Especially so are incomers from the country, who nostalgically record a happy childhood when the seasons really meant something.

Conversely, those who shock friends by 'getting out of the rat race' to 'cut themselves off' in what their friends perceive as a wilderness, are usually happy, very few regretting the decision.

With more glamorous shopping, sophisticated entertainment, and not least better career opportunities, one cannot deny the advantages of city living, nor that there can be some disadvantages of living in remote areas, but in my lifetime the whole equation has changed in favour of the deep countryside. There are several important reasons for this.

Speaking specifically of Britain, though it applies in many developed countries, possibly the most important is rural modernisation. Even immediately after World War Two, many rural areas were seriously deprived. There was still real poverty, much housing was primitive and vast territories were without electricity or piped water. The late 1940s and 1950s were times of massive upheaval as thousands of miles of roads and lanes were dug up for the new services, welcomed hesitatingly but soon seen as universally necessary. The luxuries of yesterday are ever the necessities of today.

The 1950s also saw the beginning of the pruning of the railway system, initially causing great and (because bus replacements were hopelessly inappropriate) largely unnecessary hardship. That did, however, accelerate the growth of car ownership, personal mobility being another essential element in the rural revolution. Television and a home telephone quickly followed, and soon refrigerators, deep freezers, washing machines were as ubiquitous in rural as well as urban and suburban areas.

As wage rates shot up, farms themselves had to merge and modernise, thousands of miles of hedgerows being destroyed. With increased car ownership, mechanisation caused little hardship, those now having to find work in nearby towns enjoying a shorter and usually much pleasanter journey than their commuting urban counterparts.

At the same time, for many, suburban life became less satisfying. With many incomers, some of different ethnic backgrounds, and a higher proportion of women as well as men commuting to work, friendships with neighbours became less supportive. For the first time, many were unable to find someone to sit in when the gas man said he would cometh. Family life was also breaking down, more children living further away, even overseas. As the cities sprawled, the newer houses on the outskirts meant people living further from work and central facilities.

Then came Maggie Thatcher, saying that greed was good. Money became the major motivator. The new ethic meant longer working hours. That added to extended travel periods resulting in it becoming increasingly impracticable for both parents to take an active daily role in child rearing. While some of these factors also apply to country dwellers, it was usually on a less-hurtful scale.

The disappearance of village Post Offices and shops, country services and bus stops, telephone kiosks and – in some places even ferries – provided fewer meeting spots, but village halls and shows remain as popular as ever with incomers often taking leading roles – perhaps replacing the once almost-royal status of those living in the village's great house. Equality is on a scale that not so long ago seemed impossible. It increasingly matters what you are rather than who you are or what wealth you possess.

A new breed of local newsletters, keeping people in touch with social events, are eagerly read by young and old, and people of all occupations. In a brief summary it is impossible to get the balance totally right; check for yourself how that chronicle compares with your own experience. In broad brush, thus it is that, after generations of decline, even islands such as Skye are seeing populations rebuild, raising the worry that ultimately many places once seen as too remote will become too developed.

There is one other major factor, the companionship of the landscape. Whatever my circumstances, the view across the Moray Firth, with bird life changing with the seasons and the ebb and flow of the tide, has invariably prevented me suffering the worst pains of loneliness. Only yesterday I told Sheila that I soak it in, storing it, partly to strengthen my memory lest I suffer the misfortune of spending my last days looking out on a wall.

The vital role of place was one of this book's first themes. That its importance cannot be over-emphasised is stressed by the number of times it is mentioned by country people, long-established or incoming. Views are broadly valued, people are far more conscious of animal and birdlife around them, the state of the sea or rivers, and the progress of farm crops. They spend longer out of doors, just sitting, or enjoying access to open land or cliffs for walks. Holidays to get away from it all are far less important than to urban dwellers. Rural life has a natural pattern, for example the milk lorry's passage revealing the time. Everywhere leads to somewhere specific.

As mentioned before, many who fell in love with places on holiday, subsequently moved to them. At the beginning of the era of holidays with pay, that usually meant to a largish resort, perhaps with unrealistic choice of new home on a sprawling hillside with no bus service or local shop. Many who did that regretted it, and returned to 'civilisation'. Later on, moves into the real countryside were seldom regretted, and hardly ever are today. Car ownership, and especially the increase in the proportion of women who drive, again comes into it.

Belonging To Be

Time and time again, the view that country living is 'more natural' is supported by what people say. There's that lovely Devon phrase 'you belong to be'. Belonging to be is vital for me. Though the wrench from the West Country was challenging, quickly roots developed in Nairn, the first put down by the landscape itself.

Aiding the putting down of roots are the local media. It is not surprising that, as mentioned in chapter I, both the morning newspapers and broadcast news programmes serving the West Country and the North of Scotland enjoy a unusually high degree of loyalty. In a homogenous region, so much of the news is of common interest. And what a lot of real local news there is, from archaeological finds to fishing feats and problems, cliff accidents and rescues, the need for better communications, fairer prices for milk and the retention of cottage hospitals. Nor is it surprising that social links between the West Country and the North of Scotland are strong, or that there is equal interest in affordable housing for the locals on the Isles of Scilly and Scottish islands – or for that matter Holy Island off the Northumberland coast where fresh initiatives promise homes that locals will be able to afford. Even political behaviour is similar, currently all MPs in the Highlands and Cornwall being Liberal.

In a book such as this, researched and written over several years, it is impossible to keep things up to date. Rather than make a half-hearted attempt, ultimately I decided to ditch the heap of cuttings collected about developments in places visited. It is indeed astonishing how many changes have happened – or plans repeatedly discussed and amended – in many of the same places. My aim is always to present snapshots of Remote Britain as I found it. Many of the changes in the same places have indeed themselves become familiar friends: the continual ups and downs of the Harris Tweed industry being a startling example. 'Wildlifing', the re-introduction of extinct species such as beavers, with the report that the first in the Highlands for hundreds of years have already built dams, is another hot topic. In Scotland golf courses also stir strong feelings, from sheer fascination that those playing in Westray might have to take a ferry or the world's shortest flight to play the ninth hole in mini Papa Westray to anger at the threat of compulsory purchase of homes to clear the way for a new Trump golf resort near Aberdeen

Both Highland and West Country people are naturally more interested in such stories than those in more populated Scotland or England and, even today, new agricultural developments attract widespread interest across all rural areas. Few of us might have connections with the working of the land, but we're blind if we don't notice how harvesting methods have changed – and whether it is a good, or badly-delayed by the weather, harvest. Harvest Festivals still have real meaning in the countryside.

It is interesting, too, to make comparisons between humans and other living things. That remote living might be naturally beneficial as suggested by R J Berry, who analyses research, in his recent *Islands* in the New Naturalist Series. While there may be fewer species on islands, individuals within each species are different from those on the mainland, are more adaptable and have greater virility. Adaptability doesn't quite equate to happiness, but life on the edge clearly has advantages compared with that in densely-crowded, fully-developed regions where there is a greater commonality – in the same way that, with many fruits and plants, those which struggle somewhat with their soil or climate actually produce better quality crops than where they are intensively grown in an obviously suitable environment. No doubt further research will tell us more about the role of environment on humans as well as other species, yet amateur observation and gut research may not be far off the mark: remoteness drives individuality and common sense. Certainly in Britain's extremities we *care* about our environment, seeing ourselves as temporary caretakers. In the Highlands, you don't own a house, you 'have it' for your duration.

Remoteness in London?

Can you enjoy peace and quiet in the middle of cities? What is the most remote place in London itself?

London is not unique in having recent in-filling developments destroy oases of peace, often in run-down riverside areas. The renewed respect for the river in the city is something I particularly welcome, but it comes at the price of greater activity, if not uniform gentrification. It has gone along with a dramatic improvement of water quality of the rivers themselves. Isn't it marvellous that fish again swim under London Bridge?

Reinvigorated watersides are greatly enjoyed, in London, Glasgow, Bristol, Plymouth and Leeds to mention but a few. It is also hard to criticise the better use made of the thousands of acres of central areas abandoned by railways. Or, for that matter, the more intense use of stations as the number of trains has increased, taking more people off the roads.

But whereas one could find quiet, sometimes really lonely spots, if in neglected environments, by rivers or even on stations such as Euston and Paddington, that is now hard. So far as stations are concerned, an additional reason is that anyone going to the end of a platform is now seen as a security threat. The railway press has been full of stories of enthusiasts being harassed by over-zealous officials when innocently taking photographs in a perfectly legal way.

Among stations, Marylebone particularly stands out. Once there were so few trains on Sundays that, as legend had, it was a better place than a church for a quiet praying. British Rail indeed planned to close it... till a plan to use it to create a northern partner to Victoria coach station reached by private road through the approach tunnel led to a sudden change of mind. With extra platforms, Marylebone is busier than ever, Chiltern Trains pioneering welcome new services to Birmingham and beyond. If you want to get away from other pedestrians, try the bridge commanding views of the station and the line to the tunnel mouth. You won't however be free from traffic or its din.

Going back to watersides, noise pollution is strong even where environments have been greatly improved – along London's Thames Embankment and around the theatres and concert halls of the South Bank. The same is true of Little Venice, a canal rather than river oasis which has remarkably survived intact. It was a pleasant surprise that we could walk along one of Paddington station's platforms with clear directions all the way and without having to cross roads. Even if somewhat standardised, such improvements are most welcome. It's delightful, too, seeing knots of people waiting to join the water bus, a new service here as in many other places.

Little Venice has age-old charm, its bird life and island with truly weeping willows, branches touching the water, where the Regent and Grand Union Canals join. There's a delightful cast-iron bridge, waterside pub and a boat serving meals. We popped into British Waterways' exhibition boat, picking up a leaflet giving times of boats (every fifteen minutes at peak times) to London Zoo and Camden Lock together with those describing the Little Venice circular walk, walking in Docklands and the canals of the East End. A booklet entitled *There's a secret world on your doorstep* suggests that commuters who take 'the towpath to the office' cutting through the heart of the city will enjoy 'a quiet traffic-free route that will set you up for the day'.

Back to the downside, what oases there used to be from light pollution have also steadily been filled in. Even in London's great parks, in most ways a wondrous legacy, there is brighter lighting and a higher level of the background grind of traffic which indeed never dies completely even in 'quiet' Little Venice. Maybe it doesn't bother city people. A few visitors to Nairn indeed complain they cannot sleep because of our quietness and light summer nights. Deep in the country, many urban folk especially can't cope with the combination of silence broken by the early morning crowing of a repetitious cockerel, perhaps answered by a distant 'rival'.

Noise and light were not features mentioned by any of the London taxi drivers I asked to suggest what might be the most remote spot in London. Responses varied widely, one cabbie being unable to think of remoteness except in terms of picking up a fare to take them to somewhere more useful. When I suggested a few places, he tetchily replied: 'Never find a fare there.'

Most cabbies were more constructive. A common theme was the places they'd have suggested ten or fewer years ago but which have now been developed. Singled out as examples, were the large area of former railway land round King's Cross and St Pancras, and what at the time of writing is the vast construction site for the Olympics around Stratford. 'There used to be some really lonely nooks and crannies there', said Gerry Little, the driver who took us to Fenchurch Street (see previous chapter).

He added: 'It shows how things have changed, for years ago, when Cockney workers still stood out, I remember a lady passenger, seeing them in a queue with others waiting for a bus, asking "do they let the different classes on board these days?" But then ten years ago, though there were some rough areas close by, Gravesend didn't feel at all close to London, leave alone only five miles away. There are still a few quiet roads, even parallel to Regent Street that don't feel a bit like London, and there are a few quiet areas just off the Old Kent Road. But over the years, it is amazing how things have evened out and filled in.

Only the parks are really open areas now. I'll tell you what's the quietest cottage in London. It is where the head of the Royal Parks lives. I picked him up on his way home. In the park, at first I said I wasn't allowed to go down a road marked private, but he said it was OK. I left him at a tiny cottage surrounded by trees. London's quiet places are being steadily wiped out, but when the gates are locked at night the parks are still real oases of countryside.'

He added: 'And there's Hampstead Heath; that can still feel really cut off.' Hampstead Heath proved to be the place most mentioned by other cabbies. Other suggestions included the Secret Garden in Regents Park; Primrose Hill 'early in the morning with just a couple of walkers before it all gets going'; the 'big greenery' of Blackheath beyond Greenwich; Roehampton; Barnes by the Thames; Gordon Square ' a little oasis'; Kew Green; at weekends parts of East London such as Hackney Wick, 'a funny old world with waterways and stuff cut off by flyovers and railway land'; an unspoilt Thameside pub 'which I keep quiet about – don't want its character ruined by being publicised in a book'. Most said something on the lines of: 'If it's not very busy, it's being redeveloped.'

Pleasant Surprises and Disappointments

The book nearly finished, and starting to sort out things that have meanwhile been neglected, we're exhausted. Experience shows that even one night away from home can be wonderfully restorative so, on a lovely late spring morning, we're on our way along Loch Ness.

Sheila says she'll be pleased now that it will be possible to go on holiday where we choose, rather than where research necessitates. 'Not that I'd have missed anything we've done. Its been wonderful seeing so much. I'll especially remember the islands, the Western Isles so large, different from anything else and between themselves... getting the know the Scillies better... and Shetland. That was really great. Haven't we been lucky with the weather... heat wave in the Outer Hebrides one year, and next Shetland where they were irrigating while most of Britain soaked.'

I say that we've had no problems with rain or floods, and only twice fog, giving us a day holed up at Penzance heliport waiting to fly to the Scillies and, while on Shetland, not being able to fly to Fair Isle. That was an especial disappointment. To which Sheila replies we can still go there even if it's too late for the book, and then lists some of the places we've enjoyed on our journeys and can go back to 'just for ourselves'. I add a few of my own, to which she readily assents, though she cuts me short by complaining 'we never go back to the places we said we would'.

Marvellous that the list of 'great' ones is so extensive, but life isn't limitless. However, one night away doesn't disrupt things much – and though I was at my desk first thing, we're in time for a soup-and-sandwich lunch at our hotel, Fort Augustus's friendly Lovat Arms. Now under the wing of famous Inverlochy Castle, near Fort William, it has been splendidly restored and, though small, has an AA rating of 86 per cent as well as a red rosette.

'So you haven't brought a notebook,' says Sheila. Positively not, and our only thoughts about the book are thinking of the pleasant surprises we've enjoyed. The Yorkshire coast down to Spurn Point, places around the Lake District, notably Tan Hill, stand out as one-offs, though the delightful Lincolnshire Wolds, as much as the Yorkshire ones, were perhaps my most joyful surprise.

Giving thought to the folk facing coastal erosion, I then renew anxiety over suburban-like houses around the edges of some of the Fens. As more people discover great spots to take root in, building is taking place all over – even in remotest Skye and some pretty isolated places in the Outer Hebrides.

'Yes, but then we weren't expecting such unpopulated places on the Essex islands,' says Sheila. In truth I'd been ignorant of the very existence of Essex's islands until we planned to explore the coast. Most people I've spoken to since, including some from Essex itself, are just as ignorant. The cycle seems to have gone full circle: because so many of us dismiss Essex as commuterland, ironically some of its remoter areas are under much less pressure than better-known hideaways.

Peter Caton's self-published *Essex Coast Walks* chides me along with other travel writers for neglecting the best parts of his county. He sings its praises, emphasising the huge nature reserves and areas once so painstakingly won from the sea that have been given back to it, natural defences against erosion being more effective than manmade ones. Incidentally, one of his walks took him past Tollesbury Pier, substantially demolished in the war to prevent enemy landings. Wherever he walked, Peter was on his own: there's plenty of space for many more walkers, he says, hoping that future ones might not be so lonely. He ends with this tribute:

> Most of all, the Essex coast is remarkably beautiful. Even if the far view is lacking, a look downwards will so often provide beauty – a butterfly, a bird, marsh flowers or just the grasses. Small things that are so easy to miss when looking at a 'view'. Essex doesn't have the

stunning splendour of great cliffs, hills or bays, but its beauty is more gentle. Sometimes you have to look, but it's always there and what's more it's on my doorstep. My first thought on completing the walk was that I wanted to turn round and do it all again.

While we're finishing lunch, I record another disappointment, again through ignorance. While we were around Colchester, I didn't realise how close we were to Constable's Country. When, too late, I read that the National Trust arranges three tours of Flatford Mill daily in summer, booking essential, my first thought had been that my love of Constable might actually have been better served by not seeing it.

But that's churlish because, though intensely under the microscope, much of the small area that served Constable so well, is well-preserved. From across the water, Flatford Mill is just as he would have seen it. No artist was more attached to one small area but, never succumbing to formula painting, he rejoiced: 'The world is wide, no two days are alike, nor even two hours, neither were there ever two leaves of a tree alike since the creation of the world; and the genuine production of art, like those of nature, are all distinct from each other.' Perfection alas didn't yield much income, more pictures being sold in France than in his own country. Incidentally, Constable was one of the first to romanticise trade and industry.

So Constable's Country also has to be put on our agenda... and I'm sure Britain holds further secrets. Remoter Essex may be underestimated, yet how many people really appreciate how utterly complex Britain is, geographically, in climate, natural life, history, its villages and architecture? We're small, yet no other country has a greater, if as many, varied landscape riches. Having travelled this way and that across it for over sixty years, published dozens of books about it and written two travel books myself totalling over half a million words, I'm still nowhere near being able to claim I know anything like all of it. Possibly nobody ever has.

Fort Augustus

There is so much to see and know even in the small village at the western tip of 23-mile long Loch Ness. It came into existence as 'the most centrical point of the habitable part of the Highlands', a fortified strategic place roughly half way through the Great Glen, which almost makes the land to the north an island. Two hundred years ago the Caledonian Canal was opened from Inverness to the sea north of Fort William: the masterpiece of William Telford, many of whose other fine structures are scattered across the Highlands. It is at Fort Augustus that, having passed under a swing road bridge, boats are lifted by a staircase of lochs to one of the longer pieces of actual canal.

The village still has a touch of the outback, and has long been a staging post for travellers, but it has its own rich social life and certainly pride. The canal was opened too late to serve its intended purpose of saving ships and lives having to go round the stormy north of Scotland. Most naval and commercial vessels were already too big to fit. A few fishing vessels still use it; otherwise it is the familiar story: tourism. This started early, after young Queen Victoria had popularised the Highlands with her famous relating of 'our travels'. For many years paddle steamers ran the length of the canal daily, allowing passengers ample time to explore and refresh themselves while their boats were raised or lowered through the locks.

Then they opened a railway from Spean Bridge to the south of the canal and its associated lochs. It couldn't possibly pay. A route through the entire Great Glen to Inverness would be a boon, but there was never money enough for that. So generations of travellers have discovered that the only way to travel by train from Fort William to Inverness is via Glasgow. I've long advocated the running of a once or twice-daily bus (with a trailer for heavy luggage and bicycles) as part of the railway system, but the fact there's long been a demand doesn't mean it will happen. An extension of the Fort Augustus line to a second station at a pier on Loch Ness lasted only a few years, and vies with that to Tollesbury Pier as one of the greatest-ever railway follies.

Our walk starts by taking us along Station Road (the Lovat Arms began as the Station Hotel) and we see the remains of the substantial railway bridge. Fort Augustus said farewell to its last passenger trains in 1933, only a weekly coal train lingering on into post-war days. Other things have gone too, notably the Benedictine Monastery where we used to have lunch in its café. First the school closed and then the number of monks shrank below a viable level. Where soldiers once were based, and then monks prayed and taught, there are now luxury flats, the old building being gracefully preserved.

They don't forget things here; there's deep respect for history, with an especially lively Fort Augustus Preservation Trust. A super Heritage Trail is backed by a leaflet included a list of interesting dates. These start with the Abbot of Iona establishing a church in the 6th century and takes us through many disturbances such as in 1746 when the Jacobites blew up the fort's gunpowder store before the Battle of Culloden and the cruel 'racial cleansing' that followed, to the purchase of the Fort by Lord Lovat and his 1876 leasing the buildings to the Benedictines.

There's much to see, and inevitably I start collecting leaflets and making notes on scraps of paper. There's the smallest lighthouse in Britain guiding craft to the canal's beginning, the swing road bridge, a canal visitors' centre, the last of the original street lights powered by the monk's pioneer power station when most cities would remain gas lit for years, and old pubs, notably the King's Inn with many stories to tell of different and less peaceful eras. There are interesting shops and eateries, including an enterprising local supermarket and café: MacVeans.

Next morning, on another walk round the fascinating village, again visiting MacVeans, we may look vague or lost for, suddenly, we're offered help by a smallish, neatly-dressed lady with shiny, tidy hair. She should really be a television reporter, for in a few minutes she has prised out our reason for being here... not to mention our life history. I succumb and buy a new notebook: old habits are hard to kill, though this may well be the last time in my life I use one.

The staff tell us about the woman, Barbara Oliver, well-known for helping anyone she can. In fact she's been doing a disabled person's shopping for them. 'She does it for many others... quite a character.'

We've settled down to a quiet cup of coffee when she reappears, saying her husband Iain is lonely. Can we possibly come home with her for another cup of something? We planned on an early lunch before starting for home, but she is not to be turned down. 'You'll find my husband most interesting, and he you' she says. 'He used to be Lord Lovat's personal gamekeeper.' She gives us directions and says she'll keep an eye out for us. Sheila asks if she takes her husband out much? 'Not likely, we'd quarrel the whole time. He's at home and needs visitors like you.'

As soon as she's gone, the member of staff comes back, elaborating the directions. 'See what I mean about her being a character. We all love her; though she's not from here, she fits perfectly into the village. Mind you, she's not the only character we have. It's a very friendly place.'

A few miles on the road to Fort William, she's waving as we approach. With a pent up demand for company, her husband, rushes his sentences and questions, not knowing what to deal with first. They live in the old school house, whose walls he repaired and built up, making a new roof. When Barbara takes Sheila to the old school room, he becomes more focused, telling me about shooting contests and the different way of stalking in the Highlands. 'Lord Lovat was an accurate marksman, saying he couldn't allow foreigners to come here and beat us. I've always loved being outdoors; used to be belted for missing school. But I was a dirty old plumber for thirty years.' He produces various books, a couple on Welsh railways (she's originally from Swansea), more of local interest, and insists I take a duplicate copy of a local one to add to my collection.

Then all four of us meet for a cuppa. 'People think we're cut off, but it's a twelve month season here. Hogmanay brings coach loads, there are always walkers, hunters and fishermen.' It is late when we leave, promising to keep in touch. [A few weeks later we hear Iain has died.]

So we hurry to Drumnadrochit for lunch. Not a great one in what has never been a favourite place. But then it's built on the myth of the Loch Ness Monster, while Fort Augustus, though tiny, is a real place with more solid purpose.

Now, where to on our next trip?

BOOKS QUOTED AND MENTIONED

Acknowledgments with thanks are given to authors and/or publishers of the following titles from which there are brief indented quotations.

Bernay Arms Remembered. Sheila Hutchinson. 2003. Gorleston.

Calum's Road. Roger Hutchinson. 2006. Edinburgh.

Camden's Britannia (reprint of first edition in English of 1695). Newton Abbot.

Christian Theology of Place, A. John Inge. 2003. Aldershot.

Cotswolds, The: A New Study. Charles and Alice Mary Hadfield. 1973. Newton Abbot.

County Books, The: Kent. Richard Church. 1948. Bristol.

Divine Landscapes: A pilgrimage through Britain's sacred places. Ronald Blythe. 1998. Norwich.

Dinosaur Coast, The: Yorkshire Rocks, Reptiles and Landscape. Roger Osborne & Alistair Bowden. 2001. York.

Double-Headed: Two generations of railway enthusiasm. Gilbert Thomas and David St John Thomas. 1963. Newton Abbot.

Emperor Smith: The Man Who Built Scilly. Sam Llewellyn. 2005. Wimborne.

English Landscape, The. Contribution on Bodmin Moor by Robin Hanbury-Tenison. 2000.

Essex Coast Walk. Peter Caton. 2009. Leicester.

Everyman's Poetry. Dylan Thomas. Selected and edited by Walford Davies. 1997.

Facility of Locomotion, The: The Kington Railways. J B Sinclair & Dr R W D Fenn. 1991. Kington.

For Love Alone. Mother Mary Agnes. 2003.

Geology Explained in Dorset. John W Perkins. 1977. Newton Abbot.

Glamis: A Village History. 2000. Dundee.

Harris in History and Legend. Bill Lawson. 2002. Edinburgh.

Harris and Lewis. Francis Thompson. 1968. Newton Abbot.

Harris Way of Life, A. Gisela Vogler. 2002. Stornoway.

Heart and Soul of the Yorkshire Dales. David Tarn. 2007.

Herefordshire Village Book, The. Herefordshire Federation of Women's Institutes. 1989. Newbury.

Historical Atlas of East Yorkshire, An. 1996. Hull.

History of St Brewards, A: The Life of a Moorland Village. St Breward History Group.1988. St Brewards.

Islands, New Naturalist series. R J Berry. 2009.

Lost Children: Ulverston Workhouse in the 19th century. June Whitehead. 2006. Ulverston.

Murray's Handbook for Eastern Counties. 1892.

Murray's Handbook for Scotland. John Murray. 1894. Edinburgh.

Need for Roots, The. Simon Weil. 2002.

North York Moors, The: Landscape Heritage.1989. Newton Abbot.

Patrick of the Hills. Poems by Patrick Gordon-Duff-Pennington. 1998. Wasdale.

Queen Mother and Family at Home in Caithness, The. 1990. Wick.

Red Squirrels on the Isle of Wight. Helen Butler. 2004. Newport.

Riding for Life: A Journey across the North of England. Ann Bowes. 2003. Whitby.

Rosa's Island. Valerie Wood. 2001.

Sailing the Rails: A New History of Spurn and its Military Railway. Howard M Frost. 2001. Hull.

Shetland. James R Nicolson. 1972. Newton Abbot.
The Natural History of Shetland, New Naturalist series. R J Berry & J L Johnston. 1980.
Sixareen and her Racing Descendants, The. Charles Sandison. 2005. Lerwick.
Soay of our Forefathers, The. Laurance Reed. 1986. Edinburgh.
St Davids Peninsula. Jacki Sime. 1999. St Davids.
Stitch in Time, A: Unst's fine lace knitting. Unst.
Stories from the Fens and Wolds. John Large. 2001. Spilsby.
Story of Gower, The. Wendy Hughes. 1992. Llanrwst.
Those Blue Remembered Hills. Patrick Gordon-Duff-Pennington. 2004. Weardale.
Torridon, the Nature of the Place. Chris Lowe. 2000. Strathcarron.
Uists and Barra, The. Francis Thompson. 1974. Newton Abbot.
Upland Place, An. Elizabeth Macpherson. 2007. Kinloss.
Voyage to St Kilda. Monica Weller. 1998. Perthshire.
Wesleys, The. John Large. Spilsby.
Wye Valley, New Naturalist series. George Peterken. 2008.

The following titles are also mentioned. Authors are cited where mentioned by name.

AA Hotel Guide.
Biographical Dictionary of Eminent Welshmen, The.
Breakfast Book. David St John Thomas.
Bridge over Lyonesse: over 70 years of the Isles of Scilly Steamship Company.
Buddhism for Sheep.
Character of the English Countryside, The. Robin Hanbury-Tenison.
Chase the Wind. E V Thompson.
Concise Oxford Dictionary, The.
Dictionary of Eminent Welshmen, The.
Deserted Village, The. Goldsmith.
Discovering Bodmin Moor. E V Thompson.
Eating out: Places to eat in the Western Isles.
Ecology of the New Forest, The. Colin Tubbs.
England's Best Thousand Churches. Simon Jenkins.
Falklands. Ian J Strange.
For the Love of a Cat: A Publisher's Story. David St John Thomas.
Foulness: A History of an Essex Island Parish. J R Smith.
Fowlness: The Mystery Isle 1914-1939. John S Dobson.
Good Old Days. J W Irvine.
Gone to Pot: The life and work of John Clappison. Pauline Coyle.
Gower, New Naturalist series. Jonathan Mullard.
Gower Images. Harold E Grenfell.
Gower in Focus. Harold E Grenfell.
Grimsby: The story of the world's greatest fishing port. Peter Chapman.
Harpoon at a Venture. Gavin Maxwell.
Hell Bay: The classic novel of the Isles of Scilly. Sam Llewellyn.
Herring Girls in Stornoway, The: A lifestyle gone but not forgotten.
Islands of Essex, The. Ian Yearsley.
Isle of Taransay, The.
Isles of Scilly, The. Crispin Gill.
Isles of Scilly and Beyond, The.
Isle of Wight, The: Gem of the Solent. June Elford & Steve Gascoigne.

Jamaica Inn. Daphne du Maurier.
Johansen's Hotel Guide.
Journey Through Britain: Landscape, People and Books. David St John Thomas.
Kington Railway, The.
Land and Leisure. Allan Patmore.
Landscapes of the Wye Tour. Susan Peterken.
Landscape on Loan.
Lincolnshire. Pevser's Buildings of England series.
Light in the Wilderness, A. David Hird.
Living with the Heath.
Looking in the Distance: The human search for meaning. Richard Holloway.
Most Haunted Island. Gay Baldwin.
Mey Letters, The. John E Donaldson.
Murray's Handbook. Various.
Need for Roots. Simon Weil.
New Botallack 1835. Nicholas Power.
New Island. Ian J Strange.
North Uist in History and Legend. Bill Lawson.
North York Moors, The.
OAG Executive Flight Guide.
Observations on the River Wye... relative chiefly to Picturesque Beauty; made in the summer of the Year 1770. Rev William Gilpin.
Oxford Dictionary of Quotations.
Pilgrim's Progress, The. Ronald Blythe.
Queen Mother Remembered, The.
Railway Women. Helena Wojtczak.
Ring of Bright Water. Gavin Maxwell.
Royal Duchy, The.
Rough Guide.
Scilly Islands, The. Crispin Gill.
Scottish Islands, The: A Comprehensive Guide to Every Scottish Island. Hamish Haswell-Smith.
Severn Traders, The: West Country Trows and Trowmen. Colin Green.
Shipwrecks of the Isles of Scilly, The.
St Kilda. Colin Baxter.
Tennyson Family and Their Villages, The. John Large.
Tess of the D'Urbervilles. Thomas Hardy.
Tintern Abbey.
Treasure Island. Robert Louis Stevenson.
Tresco Abbey Garden: A Personal and Pictorial History. Mike Nelhams.
Under Milk Wood. Dylan Thomas.
Unknown Cornwall. C E Vulliamy.
Water Powered Industries of the Lower Wye Valley, The. S D Coates.
Well Beloved. Thomas Hardy.
West Country, The.
Whisky Galore. Compton Mackenzie.
Woodhall Spa Guide, The. Edward Mayor.
Wye Valley and its Associates, The: a Picturesque Ramble. Leith Ritchie.
Wye Valley, The. George and Susan Peterken.

INDEX

Readers are also invited to make use of the Table of Contents and the list of books quoted from or mentioned. Figures in **bold** relate to plate numbers.